PUBLIC HEALTH COMMUNICATION
EVIDENCE FOR BEHAVIOR CHANGE

LEA'S COMMUNICATION SERIES
Jennings Bryant/Dolf Zillmann, General Editors

Selected titles in Applied Communications
(Teresa L. Thompson, Advisory Editor) include:

Braithwaite/Thompson • Handbook of Communication and People
With Disabilities

Hummert/Nussbaum • Aging, Communication and Health: Linking
Research and Practice for Successful Aging

Nussbaum/Pecchioni/Robinson/Thompson • Communication
and Aging, Second Edition

Ray • Communication and Disenfranchisement: Social Health
Issues and Implications

Socha/Diggs • Communication, Race, and Family: Exploring
Communication in Black, White, and Biracial Families

Street/Gold/Manning • Health Promotion and Interactive Technology:
Theoretical Applications and Future Directions

Whaley • Explaining Illness: Research, Theory, and Strategy

Williams/Nussbaum • Intergenerational Communication Across
the Life Span

For a complete list of titles in LEA's Communication Series, please contact
Lawrence Erlbaum Associates, Publishers at www.erlbaum.com

PUBLIC HEALTH COMMUNICATION
EVIDENCE FOR BEHAVIOR CHANGE

Edited by

Robert C. Hornik
University of Pennsylvania

LEA LAWRENCE ERLBAUM ASSOCIATES, PUBLISHERS
2002 Mahwah, New Jersey   London

Lawrence Erlbaum Associates, Inc., Publishers
10 Industrial Avenue
Mahwah, NJ 07430

Cover design by Kathryn Houghtaling Lacey

Library of Congress Cataloging-in-Publication Data

Public health communication : evidence for behavior change / edited by Robert Hornik.
   p. cm.
Includes bibliographical references and index.
ISBN 0-8058-3176-2 (cloth) — ISBN 0-8058-3177-0 (pbk.)
   1. Mass media in health education. 2. Health promotion. 3. Health in mass media.
I. Hornik, Robert C.

RA440.5 .P83 2001
613—dc21
                                                 2001033784
                                                   CIP

Books published by Lawrence Erlbaum Associates are printed on acid-free paper,
and their bindings are chosen for strength and durability.

Printed in the United States of America
10 9 8 7 6 5 4 3 2 1

CONTENTS

Preface   xi

Introduction

Public Health Communication: Making Sense
of Contradictory Evidence   1
Robert C. Hornik

Part I: Deliberate Trials

1   Using Mass Media to Prevent Cigarette Smoking   23
    John K. Worden and Brian S. Flynn

2   Television Campaigns and Sensation Seeking Targeting
    of Adolescent Marijuana Use: A Controlled
    Time Series Approach   35
    Philip Palmgreen, Lewis Donohew, Elizabeth Pugzles Lorch,
    Rick H. Hoyle, and Michael T. Stephenson

3   Long-Term Effectiveness of the Early Mass Media
    Led Antismoking Campaigns in Australia   57
    John P. Pierce, Petra Macaskill, and David Hill

v

Part II: Evaluations of Full-Scale Interventions

4   The Contributions of Public Health Education Toward
    the Reduction of Cardiovascular Disease Mortality:
    Experiences From the National High Blood Pressure
    Education Program   73
    Edward J. Roccella

5   Increasing Seat Belt Use in North Carolina   85
    Allan F. Williams, JoAnn K. Wells, and Donald W. Reinfurt

6   The California Tobacco Control Program:
    A Long-Term Health Communication Project   97
    John P. Pierce, Sherry Emery, and Elizabeth Gilpin

7   The Impact of Antismoking Media Campaigns
    on Progression to Established Smoking: Results
    of a Longitudinal Youth Study in Massachusetts   115
    Michael Siegel and Lois Biener

8   Evaluating AIDS Public Education in Europe:
    A Cross-National Comparison   131
    Kaye Wellings

9   Effects of a Mass Media Campaign to Prevent AIDS
    Among Young People in Ghana   147
    Susan McCombie, Robert C. Hornik, and John K. Anarfi

10 Changes in Sun-Related Attitudes and Behaviors,
    and Reduced Sunburn Prevalence in a Population
    at High Risk of Melanoma   163
    David Hill, Victoria White, Robin Marks, and Ron Borland

11 Impact of a Mass Media Vasectomy Promotion
    Campaign in Brazil   179
    *D. Lawrence Kincaid, Alice Payne Merritt, Liza Nickerson,
    Sandra de Castro Buffington, Marcos Paulo P. de Castro,
    and Bernadete Martin de Castro*

12   Improving Vaccination Coverage in Urban Areas
     Through a Health Communication Campaign:
     The 1990 Philippines Experience   197
     Susan Zimicki, Robert C. Hornik, Cecelia C. Verzosa,
     José R. Hernandez, Eleanora de Guzman, Manolet Dayrit,
     Adora Fausto, and Mary Bessie Lee

13   Communication in Support of Child Survival:
     Evidence and Explanations From Eight Countries   219
     Robert C. Hornik, Judith McDivitt, Susan Zimicki,
     P. Stanley Yoder, Eduardo Contreras-Budge,
     Jeffrey McDowell, and Mark Rasmuson

Part III: Media Coverage and Health Behavior

14   Impact of Persuasive Information on Secular Trends
     in Health-Related Behaviors   251
     David P. Fan

15   The Effects of Professional and Media Warnings
     About the Association Between Aspirin Use
     in Children and Reye's Syndrome   265
     Stephen B. Soumerai, Dennis Ross-Degnan, and
     Jessica Spira Kahn

16   Reflections on Community Health Campaigns: Secular
     Trends and the Capacity to Effect Change   289
     Kasisomayajula Viswanath and John R. Finnegan, Jr.

Part IV: Cross-Case Overviews

17   "Behavioral Journalism" Accelerates Diffusion of Healthy
     Innovations   315
     Alfred L. McAlister and Maria Fernandez

18   From Prevention *Vaccines* to Community *Care*:
     New Ways to Look at Program Success   327
     William Smith

19 A Meta-Analysis of U.S. Health Campaign Effects
    on Behavior: Emphasize Enforcement, Exposure,
    and New Information, and Beware the Secular Trend   357
    Leslie B. Snyder and Mark A. Hamilton

Epilogue

Evaluation Design for Public Health Communication Programs   385
Robert C. Hornik

Author Index   407

Subject Index   421

To my late parents,
Florence and Simon Hornik,
who always did what was needed
when it mattered.

PREFACE

Robert C. Hornik
University of Pennsylvania

There is good evidence that public health communication has affected health behavior. This book brings together case studies from a variety of substantive health areas, prepared by the authors who have done the original research. These chapters show important effects and illustrate the central conditions for success. Also included are complementary analytic chapters, which sort through the evidence presented in both the case study chapters within and other studies published elsewhere.

Over the past few years, there have been notable trends in the areas of public health communication/education and health behavior. First, several major controlled evaluations of programs have shown either ambiguous or no evidence of effects (e.g., the Stanford Five City Program: Farquhar et al., 1990; the Minnesota Heart Health Program: Luepker et al., 1994; and the COMMIT program: COMMIT, 1995). Nonetheless, there is a large amount of health behavior change occurring in many important areas (e.g., smoking, blood pressure control, cholesterol consumption, condom use). Also, there is evidence that these behavior changes occurred in the context of major public communication/education efforts or in the context of changes in the public communication environment (e.g., the National High Blood Pressure Education Program, the California and Massachusetts antismoking campaigns, Sudden Infant Death Syndrome education, the Swiss and Dutch AIDS communication programs, the Philippines national immunization program, and the North Carolina highway safety program, as discussed in chap. 1 of this vol.). In addition, despite the ambiguous evidence from controlled trials, many public agencies assume that public health communication is a powerful tool for behavior change. As this is written, the Office of National Drug Control Policy is in the middle of a 5-year, nearly $1 billion National Anti-Drug Media Campaign to reduce adolescent drug use. The American Legacy Foundation has launched an antismoking campaign, including heavy use of mass media projected at a similar dollar cost.

According to one view, the controlled trial evidence is the relevant data, and there is little justification for the continued efforts at using public health communication for behavior change. Another view—and the view explicitly taken here—argues that there is good justification for considering this approach to intervention, if it can be done well. The first task is to understand why the large-scale community trials do not adequately test the hypothesis that public health communication matters for behavior change. The second is to show that there is credible positive evidence for the hypothesis. This book aims to demonstrate that there is good evidence. The evidence does not always conform to cookbook evaluation criteria and, viewed in isolation, may not be persuasive. The evidence is found in scattered and sometimes obscure sources. But, if the evidence can be viewed as a set of studies, and their common themes can be presented, then the persuasiveness is greater. The primary role of this book is to bring the successful cases together so that they can be understood as a set of studies.

The book begins with an overview outlining the contradictions: why the major community trials have produced ambiguous results and what the important cases are that support an inference of success. It introduces the major themes of the book: the alternative individual, social, and institutional models though which communication may have an effect; the central role of achieving a high level of exposure to messages; and the need for evaluation approaches that respect the way communication programs may have their effects.

Sixteen case studies from three literatures make up the next section of the book. These cases are not a representative sample of all public health communication programs. There is no claim here that these cases are typical of the field. Rather, they are deliberately selected because they provide support for a hypothesis; they are evidence that public health communication can affect health behavior. The first group presents the results of deliberate trials. The second group is evaluations done on "real" interventions, which were not designed to accommodate the evaluations. The third set includes studies of the effects of normal media coverage on health behavior.

The criteria for selection of cases included (a) strong evidence of change in a specific health behavior at the population level (the book does not include cases that only show evidence about knowledge or attitudes or intentions; evidence about behavior was required), (b) major exposure in the population to public health communication messages concerning that behavior, and (c) coherent evidence and a sensible narrative that attributes the behavior change, at least in part, to the communication exposure. All of the cases involve some substantial use of the mass media, although often as a complement to other interventions. The cases are drawn from experience in the United States, Europe, and in developing countries. They include programs addressing a great variety of behaviors.

The first group of three studies reports on interventions that were mounted as deliberate trials with a specific intention to study their effects; in all cases, these programs were able to incorporate a simultaneous formal comparison group or groups from the outset of the study. Worden and Flynn present the results of their 4-year intervention with younger adolescents, showing that antismoking advertising, supplementing ordinary in-school programs, produced a sharp decline in the initiation of smoking. Palmgreen and his colleagues present the results of their two-city antismoking advertising campaign, and, using a time series design, show that there were declines in marijuana use among high sensation seekers with each wave of their campaign. Next, there is a reprint of the Pierce, Macaskill, and Hill study of a two-city antismoking campaign in Australia, where first Sydney with Melbourne as the control city, and then Melbourne, getting a delayed treatment, show reduced smoking levels after a media campaign.

The second and largest set of case studies examines full-scale programs mounted to affect behavior, where interventions were done without accommodation to the needs of evaluation. These studies use time series analysis and other approaches to support claims of effects. Roccella, who has been involved with the National High Blood Pressure Education Program for many years, summarizes some of the important aspects of the communication program and the evidence for its success. The evaluation by Williams and his colleagues of the Click it or Ticket program, which increased seat belt use and reduced highway fatalities and serious injuries, is reprinted. Pierce and his colleagues next provide analysis of the effects of the California Tobacco Control Program and its large media component. They argue that it was successful, but its success was compromised when it lost some of the funding in a context where the tobacco industry was aggressively counterattacking. Siegel and Biener, in a reprinted article, present evidence that level of exposure to the Massachusetts antismoking campaign among young adolescents predicted their progression to smoking over the subsequent 4 years.

The remaining studies in this second section focus on sites outside of the United States. Wellings summarizes her evaluation of many of the AIDS public education programs in Europe during the early years of the epidemic. She finds that most had some success, with some associated with large change in sexual risk behavior. McCombie and her colleagues also present a study of HIV/AIDS education using mass media. The study, in Ghana, points to evidence consistent with both an increase in condom use and a small delay in sexual initiation. Hill and his colleagues describe the results of a successful campaign in Australia to limit sun exposure behaviors that put people at risk of melanoma. They show change in behavior and in incidence of sunburn. Kincaid and his colleagues present some time series data about demand for vasectomies in Brazil; the data show substantial effects of the mass media campaign, although those effects are diminished with time. In a study from the Philippines, Zimicki and her colleagues present evidence from a mass media-based childhood vaccination campaign. They show substantial increases in vaccination, and detail the specific types of knowledge that produced the observed effects. Finally, in a study summarizing 16 evaluations in 9 countries, Hornik and his colleagues provide evidence about the effects of public health communication projects on child survival-related behaviors. They found that about one half of the evaluated projects were successful, and complement the presentation of the evidence for success with evidence about why some were and some were not successful.

The third set of case studies documents the relation between media coverage of certain health issues and changes in related behaviors in the population. Conventionally, these are not thought about as public health communication interventions. Nonetheless, they belong in this book because the stimulation of media coverage of health issues is, indeed, an important strategy for agencies that want to promote change. Evidence that health behavior is responsive to shifts in media coverage is a central support for such work. Fan presents his original methodology (the ideodynamic model) examining the effects of media content (or information from any persuasive source) on any outcome measured over time. He includes four applications of his methodology relevant to health behavior: consumption of cocaine by teens, recidivism to smoking by quitters, HIV infection in gay men, as well as calls to the CDC National AIDS hotline. Soumerai and his colleagues tell the story of the decline in Reye's syndrome in the context of professional and popular press coverage of the dangers of aspirin. Finally, Viswanath and Finnegan, who were closely involved with the Minnesota Heart Health Trial, note how the effects of the program were overwhelmed by the ongoing favorable secular trends in heart risky behaviors. Then they argue and present evidence indicating that the favorable secular trends were themselves a reflection, in part, of the news coverage of heart disease, including coverage of the community trials.

The final section of the book includes four chapters, each of which presents a somewhat different overview or understanding of public health communication and its evaluation. The first chapter in this section, by McAlister and Fernandez, presents a review of a set of interventions all of which have used the technique of *behavioral journalism*, an intriguing way of mixing a deliberate intervention and natural news coverage. William Smith, one of the leading practitioners of public health communication and the closely related field of social marketing, argues that people misunderstand how to do health communication well if they think about it as a vaccine, or as a fixed (and easily evaluated) intervention easily transferred from one place to another. He applies a different metaphor, that of clinical practice, with its constant monitoring and adjustment of the specifics of treatment, as a model for constructing programs. Snyder and Hamilton summarize the literature in a different way; they report the results of their meta-analysis of 48 different health communication projects reporting behavioral outcomes. They conclude that, on average, the programs for which published evidence is available do show positive behavioral effects.

The final chapter is a literal and figurative bookend to the introductory chapter. Whereas the introductory chapter presents the broad themes to be illustrated by the many case studies in the book, the final chapter provides a different overview of the case studies. Rethinking each of the cases presented, it considers the issue of what research designs permit both reasonably confident inferences about effects, but are respectful about the way public health communication projects do their work. It provides an epilogue to the book, drawing together the case studies and the analytic chapters. The primary theme of the book is that there is good evidence for the effects of public health communication. This claim depends on accepting evidence from evaluation designs that are responsive to the nature of large-scale public health communication programs.

ACKNOWLEDGMENTS

Public Health Communication: Evidence for Behavior Change grows out of a conference in Washington, DC, in June 1997, organized by the Annenberg Public Policy Center of the Annenberg School for Communication at the University of Pennsylvania. I am grateful to the Public Policy Center, and its director, Kathleen Hall Jamieson, for support of that conference and for the preparation of this book. Antonia Sunderland managed the conference and much of the preparation of this book. Without her excellent work both would have foundered. The editors working on this project for Lawrence Erlbaum Associates, Linda Bathgate and Debra Ruel, have been consistently helpful and professional.

INTRODUCTION
PUBLIC HEALTH COMMUNICATION: MAKING SENSE OF CONTRADICTORY EVIDENCE

Robert Hornik
University of Pennsylvania

There is a contradiction in the emerging evidence about the effects of public health education and communication on health outcomes. Several large community trials have shown either minimal or no overall effects (COMMIT, 1995; Farquhar et al., 1990; Luepker, 1994; Winkleby, Taylor, Jatulis, & Fortmann, 1996). At the same time, there is substantial evidence coming from observational studies showing that there is major change in health behavior, and also that this behavior change is credibly associated with public health communication, including both deliberate communication programs and normal media coverage of health issues (as described in the other chapters of this volume). This chapter addresses that contradiction, focusing on both evidence and conceptual explanations for the effects. It concludes that the evidence from controlled trials is not adequate, largely because the trials do not produce much difference in exposure. Two possible explanations for the apparent success of some programs are that they achieve a high level of exposure, and they activate a complex process of change in social norms rather than working only to transfer knowledge. A focus on the favorable secular trend of many health behaviors, and on the changes in the public communication environment that have produced and might accelerate those trends, may be an appropriate focus for research and serve as the basis for the design of subsequent interventions.

This chapter begins by summarizing evidence from the community trials and from the observational studies that have shown contradictory results.

It then considers explanations for the contradiction. A final section suggests the implications of the analysis for the construction of public health communication and education programs, for approaches to doing evaluation of such programs, and for productive strategies for research to serve as the basis for future programs.

RESULTS: COMMUNITY TRIALS

A series of formal and expensive community trials have compared one or more intervention communities that received a program of public health education, along with complementary forms of health promotion, with matched control communities. Each of the trials showed either minimal or no overall differences between the intervention and control communities in health outcomes (usually smoking or other cardiovascular disease-related behaviors).

The Stanford Five City Project provided 5 years of cardiovascular risk reduction education through mass media and community-based activities to two small cities in northern California. These "treatment" cities were compared with two roughly similar control cities on their rates of change on relevant risk factors. The educational efforts have been serious, based on behavior change theory, and incorporate careful development and implementation of educational programs, including television and radio spots, printed materials, classes, contests, and correspondence courses. The project estimates each adult in the treatment cities would have been exposed to around 5 hours of education each year. That exposure would have been divided among the major behavioral objectives: weight loss, cigarette smoking, diet changes to restrict fat and cholesterol consumption, physical exercise, and blood pressure control (Flora, Maccoby, & Farquhar, 1991).

The evaluation, done with great care, is still a messy affair with the treatment and control cities not equivalent beforehand, and different methods of analysis giving quite different results. However, a reader disposed to take a skeptical view would conclude that the effects of the program were either small or not established. Almost all of the trends favored the treatment cities, but they were of a magnitude that did not rule out chance differences. Between the first and last measurement waves, and comparing independent samples rather than the cohort, only two of six risk factors showed a significantly larger effect ($p < .05$) for the treatment cities than for the control cities. The cumulative rates of change for estimated all-cause mortality risk, or coronary heart disease risk, were not different for the treatment and control cities either. Other ways of framing the data can give a more optimistic view, and not-yet-reported follow-up data gathered in each community 4 years after the end of the formal educational activity, and estimates of changes in morbidity and mortality may give a different picture. For the moment, the evaluation suggests no effects or an uncertain and small treatment city advantage (Farquhar et al., 1990; Winkleby et al., 1996).

The Minnesota Heart Health Program and the Pawtucket Heart Health Program were both descendants of the work done originally by Stanford and by a similar program in North Karelia, Finland. The Minnesota program compares three treatment cities with three control cities after a 6-year intervention; the Pawtucket evaluation compares one treatment and one control city after 7 years of intervention. The Minnesota program retrained a large number of health professionals, provided systematic risk factor screening, and used the mass media along with a variety of organized classes and contests to reach its audience. The Pawtucket program restricted itself to working through community organizations and a variety of volunteer outreach systems. Like the Stanford study, each program shows some evidence of effect on at least one outcome: Pawtucket shows some advantage to the treatment city in body mass index postintervention, and Minnesota shows some advantage among women whose smoking declined. However, both groups of researchers are very cautious and neither makes a claim for overall effect. Neither program shows a consistent pattern of pro-treatment city effects, or a beyond chance overall effect on cardiovascular risk (see Viswanath and Finnegan, chap. 16 in this volume, for a discussion of the Minnesota program).

The Community Intervention Trial for Smoking Cessation (COMMIT) was a 4-year program to accelerate the rate of quitting among heavy smokers. The program took place in 11 pairs of matched communities with random assignment of communities to treatment or control status. Each treatment community was given a little less than $900,000 over 4 years to employ its staff and undertake interventions that included "four primary channels: public education through the mass media and community wide events; health care providers; worksites and other organizations; and cessation resources" (COMMIT, 1995, p. 184). They specified 58 activities that each city was to undertake, and claimed the cities carried out more than 90% of them, although cities varied in the ways they carried out each activity. There were no overall differences in prevalence of smoking, nor in the quit rates of heavy smokers, which was the primary target. However, light and moderate smokers who were in the cohort followed for 4 years quit in the treatment cities at a significantly faster rate than in the control cities.

In all four of these community trials, there was a substantial downward secular trend in risk behavior, but it was similar between treatment and control communities. Three earlier trials, which have claimed stronger effects, are worth brief description here. The Stanford Three Community Study preceded the five community study, and is probably the program most referenced by community health communication programs around the world. It contrasted a control and two treatment communities and showed some differences between them in rates of decline in cardiovascular risk factors (Farquhar et al., 1977), including dietary behavior (Fortmann, Williams, Hulley, Haskell, & Farquhar, 1981). In its early years, the North Karelia (Finland) study, which has now reported 20 years of results, showed somewhat more rapid declines in coronary risk factors (including total cholesterol and blood pressure and smoking) in the demonstration county than in the comparison county (Puska et al., 1989).[1] The Australian North Coast *Quit for Life* program focused on cigarette smoking and has reported much more rapid quit rates for treatment communities than for one comparison community. None of these three efforts were evaluated with the sophistication of the COMMIT trial or the later Stanford or Minnesota programs, and their claims of effects might be challenged if the current standards for reporting effects were applied.

Overall, there was substantial success reported for the early programs and there was little statistically significant overall success for the later programs; however, each one of the later programs reported some advantage to the treatment communities in at least one subobjective or for one major subpopulation. Table I.1 summarizes these results, providing estimates of overall success for all programs, and one example of a success with a subobjective or subpopulation for the more recent trials.

There is also more recent evidence from other community trials, although perhaps on a smaller scale than the Stanford, Minnesota, and COMMIT trials. Worden and Flynn (chap. 1, this vol.) show that a 2-year media campaign produced a 35% decline in initiation of smoking among adolescents, which was still apparent 2 years after the end of the campaign. Palmgreen et al. (chap. 2, this vol.) use an interrupted time series design to show the decline in marijuana use after antidrug media advertising in Lexington and Louisville. Pierce, Macaskill, and Hill (1990; chap. 4, this vol.) show evidence for the success of an Australian campaign, comparing declines in smoking rates in Sydney, which received an earlier intensive antitobacco media campaign, and Melbourne, which received a delayed campaign. They show that Sydney's rate of smoking declined after the start of their campaign, whereas Melbourne showed a parallel decline only after its campaign was initiated.

Thus, although the *star* community trials have shown ambiguous results, there is some evidence from other trials and from subanalyses within

---

[1]One aspect of the North Karelia program is discussed in more detail by McAlister (chap. 17, this vol.).

TABLE I.1
Results of Community Trials

Study and Period of Intervention	Outcome Measure and Group Compared	Intervention Status (N of Communities)	% Relative Change from Baseline	Significance of Treatment-Control Difference
Stanford Three Community Study, 1972–1975	Overall CHD risk score after 2 years	treatment (2)	−18.0%	$p < .05$
		control (1)	+8%	
North Karelia Project, 1972–1982	CHD mortality, men, age standardized, 1974–1979	treatment (1)	−22.0%	$p < .01$
		control (1)	−12.0%	
Australia North Coast, 1978–1980	Decline in smoking prevalence	treatment (2)	−31.0%	$p < .05$
		control (1)	−13.0%	
Stanford Five Community Study, 1980–1986	Estimated CHD risk, independent samples	treatment (2)	−18.0%	n.s.
		control (2)	−18.0%	
	Body mass index kg/m2, independent samples	treatment (2)	+2%	$p < .02$
		control (2)	+5%	
Minnesota Heart Health, 1980–1986	CHD risk, independent samples	treatment (3)	−4.3%	n.s.
		control (3)	−7.1%	
	Smoking among women, independent samples	treatment (3)	−8.4%	$p < .01$
		control (3)	.0%	
Pawtucket Heart Health Program, 1983–1991	Projected CVD risk	treatment (1)	−16.3%	$p = .56$
		control (1)	−8.4%	
	Body mass index kg/m2	treatment (1)	+8%	$p < .04$
		control (1)	+3.4%	
COMMIT, 1989–1992	Quit rate of heavy smokers, cohort	treatment (11)	18.0%	$p = .68$
		control (11)	18.7%	
	Quit rate of light to moderate smokers	treatment (11)	30.6%	$p = .004$
		control (11)	27.5%	

the well-known trials that there have been worthwhile effects. An inference about the power of community trials would have been stronger had it been found for the overall results in Stanford, in Minnesota, and for the heavy smokers in the COMMIT program.

RESULTS: UNCONTROLLED PROGRAMS

If the results from the controlled trials are inconsistent, then they contrast sharply with some evidence from evaluations done on major programs without control communities. These are evaluations that were not able to manipulate the treatments available to people, but were able to examine naturally operating programs.

First consider the innovative National High Blood Pressure Education Program (NHBPEP). If the community trials were carefully constructed, carefully evaluated programs associated with small effects, then the NHBPEP has been a kitchen sink sort of program associated with massive effects. The NHBPEP involved many activities: institutional consensus building, education of health professionals, some public education through community organizations, and major efforts in mass media education. These media efforts included distribution of public service announcements for broadcast on radio and television, and stimulation of coverage of hypertension by various media outlets.[2]

The initiation of the NHBPEP in 1972 was closely associated with a large decline in rates of stroke in the United States. Between 1960 and 1972, before the initiation of the NHBPEP, the age-adjusted stroke mortality rate had declined at 1.6% per year for all U.S. Whites; from 1972 to 1984 the rate was 5.9% per year (McGovern et al., 1992). The decline in stroke mortality has been an "extraordinary public health achievement" (McGovern et al., 1992). The coincidence of timing is impressive, but attribution of the decline to the influence of the NHBPEP has to be considered controversial.

Nonetheless, there is strong evidence from controlled trials that control of hypertension is related to stroke mortality, and there is strong evidence that the NHBPEP was associated with a major increase in control of hypertension. The major alternative explanations for the decline in stroke mortality, improved treatment of stroke victims, or introduction of new medications do not fully account for the observed decline (Casper, Wing, Strogatz, Davis, & Tyroler, 1992; Jacobs, McGovern, & Blackburn, 1992; Kannel & Wolf, 1992; McGovern et al., 1992). There was considerable change in attention to and treatment of hypertension after the launch of

---

[2]See Roccella (chap. 4, this vol.) for a detailed presentation of this case.

the NHBPEP. In 1973–1974, 18% of 25- to 59-year-old male hypertensives in the Minnesota Heart Survey were under treatment, but 41% were under treatment in 1980–1982. For women, comparable numbers were 36% and 56%, respectively (McGovern, 1992). Evidence from other sources about the United States as a whole is consistent (Casper et al., 1992).

The notable behavior change patterns associated with the NHBPEP are found for other uncontrolled campaigns as well. Warner (1981) made a case for a substantial effect of the original televised smoking counteradvertising campaign between 1967 and 1970. The networks were required by the "Fairness Doctrine" then in force to match cigarette manufacturers' commercials with antismoking commercials. The period of broadcast of frequent antismoking commercials was associated with a reduction of 10% in per capita consumption of cigarettes. Attribution of this change to the counteradvertising effort is strengthened by the finding that when the counteradvertising effort was eliminated, per capita consumption increased 5%, returning to a trend present before the counteradvertising began (Erickson, McKenna, & Romano, 1990; Warner, 1981).

Several researchers have suggested that the antismoking campaign in California has produced large effects on cigarette consumption. Pierce (chap. 6, this vol.) presents the overall case for the effectiveness of the campaign and argues that it lost its power when its advertising budget was cut. Hu, Sung, and Keeler (1995) examined the relative roles of the tax increase and the mass media campaign and made some estimates of cost-effectiveness. They suggested that a $20 million media campaign produced a decline of about 232 million packs of cigarettes smoked over a 2-year period, or about $1 per 11 packs not smoked. If it is assumed that the effects of the campaign continue after the 2 years because people who reduced their smoking continue to smoke less, then the cost effectiveness ratio gets much better. Indeed, they estimate that the effect of the media campaign was such that each 10% increase in media time purchased (or about $2 million) would produce an additional decline of .5% in cigarette sales.

Siegel and Biener (2000; chap. 8, this vol.) provide comparable evidence from the Massachusetts antismoking campaign. A cohort of young adolescents was half as likely to progress to established smoking in the subsequent 4 years if they had higher exposure to antitobacco ads. Evidence from the Florida antismoking campaign suggests that it is having substantial success (MMWR, 1999).

The Swiss *Stop AIDS* campaign and the Netherlands AIDS program used mass media heavily to reach audiences believed to be at risk for infection with HIV. There were two sides to the mass media activity: Government authorities carefully developed television and radio advertisements, billboards, and newspaper inserts whose content was quite explicit in encouraging the use of condoms for protection. At the same time, as in much of the rest of the world, mass media provided full of coverage of AIDS. In both countries, the operation of the programs was associated with a period of substantial change in condom use. Among young people, self-reported use of condoms with all "casual" partners in the previous 6 months increased from 8% to over 60% in Switzerland, and from 9% to over 40% in the Netherlands, between early 1987 and late 1989. These are self-reported behaviors with the risks of such indirect measurement. However, the growth in usage rates was supported in a general way by evidence about parallel increases in condom sales (deVroome et al., 1990; DuBois-Arber, Jeannin, Konings, & Paccavo, 1997). Wellings (chap. 8, this vol.) discusses the Swiss and Dutch campaigns in the context of other European campaigns. McCombie et al. (chap. 9, this vol.) present data about a condom promotion and sexual delay campaign in Ghana, which suggests that it influenced both some delay in the onset of sexual initiation and increases in condom use.

The formal U.S. public communication effort to prevent AIDS is often described as weaker than the effort made in other countries, in particular because it was less explicit about the recommendations for condom use. But the U.S. data, although not as favorable as the Swiss or Netherlands data, still suggest a very large effect of the AIDS epidemic, and public communication around that epidemic, on condom use and on the incidence of sexually transmitted diseases. Reported condom use during last intercourse increased from 25% to over 50% among young people (Sonenstein, Pleck, & Ku, 1989), and gonorrhea rates declined from 1 million cases per year in 1975 (over 450 cases per 100,000 population) to around 350,000 in 1998 (around 130 cases per 100,000) (MMWR, 2000).

Public education campaigns, national press, and media advocacy have been used successfully to improve children's health. Large declines in death from Sudden Infant Death Syndrome (SIDS) in the Netherlands, New Zealand, Norway, and elsewhere are associated with public education campaigns. In the Netherlands, for example, there was a 1-year shift from 55% to around 27% of parents putting their children in the prone sleeping position, and there was a corresponding decline in SIDS rates (Engelberts, de Jonge, & Kostense, 1991). The U.S. data, in the context of the Back to Sleep campaign, shows favorable results as well. From 1992 to 1998, there was a decline from 70% to 17% in the proportion of infants placed prone (Willinger, Ko, Hoffman, Kessler, & Corwin, 2000). Zimicki et al. (chap. 2, this vol.) demonstrate that increases in timely immunization coverage from 35% to 55% in the Philippines were associated with a 1-year major public education effort. Parallel evidence of success from a variety of other communication programs in developing countries are summarized in Hornik et al. (chap. 13, this vol.). Soumerai and his colleagues (1992;

chap. 15, this vol.) show that the virtual disappearance of Reye's syndrome in the United States was associated with pulses in news coverage and professional media coverage of the aspirin controversy occurring before warnings appeared on aspirin bottles.

Changes in the frequency of other health-related behaviors have been associated with communication campaigns as well. Williams, Reinfurt, and Wells (1996; chap. 5, this vol.) reported the success of the North Carolina Click It or Ticket pro-seat belt campaign, which produced an increase from 64% to 80% in seat belt use, a 9% decline in highway fatalities, and a 7% decline in serious injuries. Hill et al., 1993; chap. 10, this vol.) presented evidence about the effectiveness of an antisunburn campaign in Australia, whereas Kincaid et al. (1996; chap. 11, this vol.) uses time series data to show some influence of a campaign to encourage vasectomy on the number of men who sought the operation.

In addition, one subsequent result may help put the analyses of the Stanford trial in the context of the uncontrolled studies. Among other health risks, the Stanford Five Community study presented evidence about cholesterol decline. The treatment cities were declining at the rate of .016 mmol/L per year in cholesterol level, which was slightly quicker than the decline in the control cities during the period of intervention. However, in the 4-year period after the immediate postsurvey reported from 1986 to 1990, Frank, Winkleby, Fortmann, Rockhill, & Farquhar (1992) reported that the two control cities declined at the rate of about .05 mmol/L per year, three times the rate during the treatment period for the treatment cities. In that period, cholesterol increased its presence on the national media agenda, recalling that in 1985 the National Cholesterol Education Program was launched.[3]

DISCUSSION

How is the sharp difference between the relatively unsuccessful controlled trials and the apparent success of the NHBPEP and the other, messier evaluations to be explained? Apparently, the better designed the evaluation of public health communication, the worse the evidence for important effects. It is tempting then to claim that apparent effects in less well-designed studies are artifactual, the result of inadequate research design. This chapter argues, on the contrary, that the lack of success shown by the programs with the best designed evaluations is the direct result of the constraints im-

---

[3]See Viswanath and Finnegan (chap. 16, this vol.) for a discussion of the chronology of such campaigns.

posed by the research design, and far more may be learned about how to intervene from the programs that do not have such powerful designs.

It may be that these trials were not appropriate approaches to testing the effects of public communication; they were not able to provide very much increase in exposure to treatment when the treatment and control communities were compared. The image of pristine treatment and control communities associated with the concept of the controlled trial is a false image. There was a great deal of background communication going on in these communities and the treatments may have provided only a very small increment in the levels of exposure to messages about these issues. Baumann, Suchindran, and Murray (1999), in a reanalysis of the COMMIT data, showed that indeed the extent of background noise was a crucial factor in the apparent lack of the program's success. They found more success in the treatment communities relative to their matched control communities when there was relatively little background change in the control communities. When change was already present in the control communities, the treatment communities were hard pressed to surpass them.

This concern about differences in exposure begins with the COMMIT trial. The program did not buy media time; they had available approximately $225,000 per community per year, which included the salaries of four staff people. In each city, the COMMIT program tried to reach its audience through five channels: smoking cessation kits, health care institutions, work sites, mass media, and religious organizations. The evaluation reports the exposure to messages through each of these channels. In only one of the five was there any statistically significant advantage in the level of audience-reported exposure to the so-called treatment communities. On a crude summed scale of all these activities, which varied from 0–45, the treatment communities had a summed mean of 15.2 and the control communities had a summed mean of 14.9. The treatment communities received very little more treatment than the control communities, for the very large amount of money spent. A supplemental analysis provided by the COMMIT authors showed some evidence of change in behavior among moderate smokers. Of particular relevance to this argument about exposure, they showed that the largest relative changes in moderate smoking for treatment versus matched control cities were in those places where the treatment city had relatively more total exposure to the campaign (COMMIT, 1995).

Stanford claimed that it provided an average of 25 hours of exposure to heart disease messages over the 5 years of its treatment. In the absence of other information, an estimate of annual exposure to messages about any one behavior would come from dividing 25 hours by 5 years and by the five different behaviors that were being recommended. Thus, each behavior was the subject, even under this optimistic claim, of 1 hour of messages per year. One hour of exposure per behavior per year may not be a very large amount of exposure. It is no surprise, then, that the treatment cities' growth in knowledge of cardiovascular disease risk factors was only a little more than the control cities'. Knowledge gain in the treatment cities was 1.6 on a 17-point knowledge scale. In the control cities it was 1.0 (Farquhar et al., 1990).

The Minnesota Heart Health program reported exposure to their interventions on a 0–10 scale averaging across four surveys undertaken during the 6 years of intervention. The mean exposure in the education communities was 2.5, and in the control communities it was 1.9. There was a significant difference, but it was small and in neither place was exposure very high compared to the maximum. Viswanath and Finnegan present these data with additional detail later in chapter 16.

The Pawtucket Heart Health program depended entirely on community outreach and organization-based education. It claims to have produced an average of about 0.4 contacts per person per year over a 7-year period in its treatment city, or a total of less than three contacts—not a very large amount of exposure.

This is a constant pattern across these studies and some other, similar ones. A great deal of funding is provided to do the evaluations. The comparisons of health effects are made with analyses done with great skill and interpreted with great caution. But despite the best intentions, these trials sometimes produced very good answers to an uninteresting question: If you do not do very much in the way of treatment, then can you have much effect? Indeed, the fact that each of these programs produced effects on some subobjectives is the remarkable outcome, not that they failed to reduce overall coronary heart disease risk.

Thus, it might be argued that these controlled trials do not provide very good evidence about the public health communication hypothesis. They do not respect the model of influence that comes from a social communication point of view; what then is the model of change that is expected to operate when public communication programs are created? One ought not to expect some sort of stimulus–response model to operate: for example, the clinician says that blood pressure is a concern and the patient responds by dietary changes and compliance with medication. Rather, a much more complex and social model of change is needed:

How might the NHBPEP have worked? One can imagine how the process of change occurs: a person sees some public service announcements and a local TV health reporter's feature telling her about the symptomless disease of hypertension. She checks her blood pressure in a newly accessible shopping mall machine and those results suggest a problem; she tells her spouse (who has also seen the ads) and he encourages her to have it checked. She goes to a physician, who confirms the presence of hypertension, encourages her to change her diet and then return for monitoring. Meanwhile, the physician has become more sensitive to the issue of hypertension because of a recent *JAMA* article, and some recommendations from a specialist society, and a conversation with a drug detailer, as well as informal conversations with colleagues and exposure to television discussions of the issue. The patient talks with friends at work or family members about her experience; they also increase their concern and go to have their own pressure checked. She returns for another checkup and her pressure is still elevated although she has reduced her use of salt; the physician decides to treat her with medication. The patient is ready to comply because all the sources around her—personal, professional and mediated—are telling her that she should. (Hornik, 1997, pp. 49–50)

The program is effective in this explanation not because of a public service announcement or a specific program of physician education. It is successful because the NHBPEP has changed the professional and public environment as a whole around the issue of hypertension. It has changed the physician's specialist organization and its support for aggressive hypertension treatment. It has changed the mall owners, who see making a blood pressure measurement machine available as a way to draw shoppers. It has changed the level of discussion in the press and in other channels so that people hear the message multiple times and from multiple sources. The NHBPEP has been a multicomponent program, and its scale may well have been what made it effective; it is beyond any evaluation to sort out just which elements of the program were effective. More important, it is likely to be misleading to attribute to a particular, focused set of actions what may well have been the product of complex mobilization: an impressive norm change within a society. This was not just an individually focused communication program, but a broader social marketing program designed to change all of the environment around a behavioral decision.

The controlled clinical trial may make sense when the thing to be studied is a discrete thing (a pill) that can be delivered or not delivered. With public communication, the treatment is much messier—it likely works, if it works, because of the effects of the specific messages that are created and delivered, but also because of messy diffusion through the social system: deliberate communication messages, and the conversations that ensue, and the coverage by other media outlets, and the demands put on institutions that then respond; health institutions that offer different advice and different treatments, commercial institutions that make condoms in flavors and foods in low fat versions; political institutions that disallow smoking in public places.

When any of these clinical trials tries to give a communication treatment to one place and not to a neighboring place, they are doing communication as if it were a pill and not a social process. Extraordinarily, they are trying to control for the national media machine, which is surely central to the changes in social norms that have been reflected in the remarkable secular trends in some healthy behaviors. Often, the public health communication intervention is a different sort of intervention, and evaluations of its effects need first respect how it is that the intervention is meant to work. Smith (chap. 18, this vol.) begins the process of explaining how such a broad-based intervention might be constructed. He contrasts the idea of the fixed intervention with the intervention as a constantly evolving set of actions chosen to be responsive to the observed changes in the target communities.

CONCLUSIONS

The substantial efforts in public health communication are founded in a recognition that much of health status reflects human behavior rather than medical treatment, prevention and not cure. That understanding led to efforts to provide direct messages to affect that behavior (e.g., "get a mammogram," "get screened for TB"), but soon such prescriptive messages were recognized as problematic. They did not seem to fit with the way people saw problems, and people did not respond.

This led to much attention being focused on understanding why it is that people do or do not do particular behaviors, and the development of models of health behavior choice. Efforts to construct health education programs centered on those understandings of human behavior—trying to influence the knowledge base, or the beliefs, or the social norms underpinning the behaviors rather than just recommending new behaviors. The Health Belief Model (Rosenstock, 1974), the Theory of Reasoned Action (Fishbein & Ajzen, 1975), Social Cognitive Theory and its concept of self-efficacy (Bandura, 1986), and Stages of Change (DiClemente et al., 1991) are all central models reflecting this logic. Most of the innovative work in public health communication has focused on the problem of developing high quality messages reflecting particular evidence about the underpinnings of health behavior. This has been a good thing.

At the same time, there has been less attention to the problem of exposure to those messages and how to make sure that a large part of the target audience is exposed to program messages, repeatedly. Solutions to the exposure problem have gotten second place on the agenda to the quality of messages. And that may be a crucial failing.

A basic principle of advertising is that all else being equal, the more people who are reached with a message and the more frequently they hear it, the more likely they are to respond. Health programs that intend to influence behavior, but then choose to rely on unpaid public service announcements that are broadcast rarely and in late night hours, should not be surprised at failure. The Defense Department has spent upward of $250 million in a year to locate recruits (DeLeon, 2000). The Department of Health and Human Services and most other agencies intending to influence health behavior have been expected to make do with time contributed by broadcasters, largely. Only recently has this reliance on donated time for campaigns to affect health behavior been reduced. The Office of National Drug Control Policy launched its National Anti-Drug Media Campaign in 1999, with a projected budget of around $200 million per year. The American Legacy Foundation, with its resources from the Attorneys' General settlement with the tobacco industry, has launched its own multichannel campaign in 2000 with a budget of $185 million for its first year. Other state antitobacco campaigns (including California, Massachusetts, and Arizona) have had tax revenues to spend on their advertising and public education efforts. Florida and Mississippi, early settlers in the tobacco wars, launched campaigns funded by settlement funds.

Clearly, having resources available to pay for educational and advertising costs makes the problem of achieving exposure simpler. However, the lack of such budgets does not eliminate the problem. Even without those budgets, the level of exposure achieved has to complement quality of messages as a central concern. Some public and private health agencies have become adept at gaining media attention through the provision of press releases and video materials and the creation of media events and other encouragement for media coverage of their concerns. Making use of multiple communication channels, using them over time, encouraging natural social diffusion of messages, and always counting the level of exposure achieved are basic principles of program design.

The demands for attention to careful message construction and to assuring adequate exposure to messages are themselves tied to a broader framework. Choice of messages and exposure strategies will reflect an underlying model, a theory, about how communication is to influence behavior.

There are three complementary models of behavior change implicit in many public health communication campaigns. The individual effects model focuses on individuals as they improve their knowledge and attitudes and assumes that individual exposure to messages affects individual behavior. The social diffusion model focuses on the process of change in public norms, which leads to behavior change among social groups. The institutional diffusion model focuses on the change in elite opinion, which is translated into institutional behavior, including policy changes, which in turn affect individual behavior. The models contrast the direct effects of seeing mass media materials (one sees a public service announcement, PSA, about the role of condoms in safe sex; one decides to follow the advice) with the indirect effects of the social diffusion model, discussion within a social network is stimulated by PSAs or media coverage of an issue; that discussion may produce changed social norms about appropriate behavior, and affect the likelihood that each member of the social network will adopt the new behavior. In the institutional diffusion model, media coverage of an issue may operate through either one or both of two mechanisms. Media coverage may affect public norms that affect institutional behavior or policymaker actions, or media coverage may lead policymakers to think that an issue is important and requires action, regardless of whether public norms have actually changed. If a social or institutional diffusion process dominates behavior change, then individuals' detailed knowledge about the benefits of a new health behavior may be less important than their belief that it is an expected behavior. In that case, substantial attention in the public environment, with multiple channels supporting the same change in behavior as in the NHBPEP, may be central to success.

There are some health behaviors (e.g., change in sleeping position to avoid SIDS or avoiding aspirin in the treatment of children's fevers) that may be highly responsive to simple information about the relative benefits of a new behavior. The new behavior is easy and low cost, and the consequence of the behavior is highly valued. Other behaviors may be more tightly woven into the social fabric for many people (sexual behavior, smoking), and will change only when social norms change. Still others may require supportive institutional change before it is feasible for individuals to change their behavior (the use of child car seats is made much easier when car seat and car manufacturers simplify installation).

Much of the history of research in health education and communication, and in the chapters in this volume, is the story of implementing and evaluating interventions. The discussion begins with an intervention and asks whether it has been successful in changing a behavior. However, there may be an alternative start point for health communication work. The process might start with trying to understand the extraordinary secular trends in some health behaviors that are already in place. There have been some extraordinary changes in smoking and other cardiovascular risk behaviors, in sexual risk behaviors, and in others. Rather than starting with an intervention and its evaluation, health communication research might sometimes start with the effects, the substantial secular change in behavior, and try to explain it.

In particular, health communication might focus on knowing what the role of public communication has been in affecting those trends, including both the deliberate communication interventions and public communication more generally. From that sort of review, starting with evidence about what has worked on a large scale, may come new ideas about how to use public health communication systematically to influence those behaviors.

Fan (chap. 14, this vol.) proposes one approach and discusses some examples for associating media coverage with changes in health behavior. Soumerai et al. (1992; chap. 15, this vol.) take a different approach to documenting the place of popular and professional media coverage in the change in treatments for Reye's syndrome. Viswanath and Finnegan (chap. 16, this vol.) argue for and show some evidence about the importance of the public media coverage of heart disease for the profound decline in morbidity and mortality.

Finally, accept that evaluations of public health communication programs will rarely produce the unequivocal evidence promised in randomized controlled trials of pills. Sometimes this is feasible for smaller scale trials, where enough resources can by mustered to produce a substantial additional dose of exposure (cf. Worden & Flynn, chap. 1, or Palmgreen et al., chap. 2, this vol.), but most often this is not the case. If evaluations are to respect the way that public communication programs work, then they will likely depend on alternative approaches: natural experiments, correlated time series, and other such nonexperimental and quasi-experimental approaches. They are less definitive methodologically than controlled trials, but they respond to the nature of the intervention at issue. A moderately good answer to the right question is better than a very good answer to the wrong question. The effects of communication interventions must be evaluated with a methodology that respects their character and the way they work, but is still credible enough to influence policy discussion. The final chapter of this volume returns to the issue of research design and considers which research designs have some promise of netting such moderately good answers.

In summary, consider the following statements:

- The evidence from controlled trials is probably not adequate to make any judgment about the effects of public health communication when the trials do not produce much difference in exposure. This is particularly true in a context where there is already a good deal of background exposure to messages.
- Some programs may work because they activate a complex process of change in social norms rather than because they transfer knowledge that produces behavior change. Level of exposure to messages is probably a central issue in constructing public education programs; one may need to get a lot of it before expecting effects.
- There is policy relevant evidence (if not from unchallengeable randomized controlled trials) that there is substantial secular change in important behaviors and in some cases that programs of public health communication may have important effects on those secular trends.

- Rather than using the evidence from controlled trials to reject the public health communication hypothesis, there is good reason to call for serious efforts to focus attention on the favorable secular trend, on communication approaches that have produced and might accelerate those trends, and on evaluation approaches that respect the underlying character of the way communication programs are meant to work.

REFERENCES

Bandura, A. (1986). *Social foundations of thought and action: A social cognitive theory.* Englewood Cliffs, NJ: Prentice-Hall.

Bauman, K. E., Suchindran, C. M., & Murray, D. M. (1999). The paucity of effects in community trials: Is secular trend the culprit? *Preventive Medicine, 28,* 426–429.

Casper, M., Wing, S., Strogatz, D., Davis, C. E., & Tyroler, H. A. (1992). Antihypertensive treatment and US trends in stroke mortality, 1962 to 1980 [see comments]. *American Journal of Public Health, 82*(12), 1600–1606.

Community Intervention Trial for Smoking Cessation (COMMIT) (1995). I. Cohort Results from a four year intervention. *American Journal of Public Health, 85,* 183–192.

DeLeon, R. (2000, March 8). "Statement of Honorable Rudy deLeon before the Military Personnel Subcommittee, House Committee on Armed Services on Sustaining the All-Volunteer Force." Accessed via Internet, July 27, 2000. www.house.gov/hasc/testimony/106thCongress/00-03-08DELEON.PDF

deVroome, E. M., Paalman, M. E., Sandfort, T. G., Sleutjes, M., de Vries, K. J., & Tielman, R. A. (1990). AIDS in The Netherlands: The effects of several years of campaigning. *International Journal of STD and AIDS, 1*(4), 268–275.

DiClemente, C. C., Prochaska, J. O., Fairhurst, S. K., Velicer, W. F., Velasquez, M. M., & Rossi, J. S. (1991). The process of smoking cessation: an analysis of precontemplation, contemplation and preparation stages of change. *Journal of Consulting and Clinical Psychology, 59*(2), 295–304.

Dubois-Arber, F., Jeannin, A., Konings, E., & Paccaud, F. (1997). Increased condom use without other major changes in sexual behavior among the general population in Switzerland. *American Journal of Public Health, 87*(4), 558–566.

Engelberts, A. C., de Jonge, G. A., & Kostense, P. J. (1991). An analysis of trends in the incidence of sudden infant death in The Netherlands 1969–1989. *Journal of Pediatrics and Child Health, 27*(6), 329–333.

Erickson, A. C., McKenna, J. W., & Romano, R. M. (1990). Past lessons and new uses of the mass media in reducing tobacco consumption. *Public Health Reports, 105*(3), 239–244.

Farquhar, J. W., Fortmann, S. P., Flora, J. A., Taylor, C. B., Haskell, W. L., Williams, P. T., Maccoby, N., & Wood, P. D. (1990). Effects of communitywide education on cardiovascular disease risk factors. The Stanford Five-City Project. *Journal of the American Medical Association, 264*(3), 359–365.

Farquhar, J. W., Maccoby, N., Wood, P. D., Alexander, J. K., Breitrose, H., Brown, B. W., Jr., Haskell, W. L., McAlister, A. L., Meyer, A. J., Nash, J. D., & Stern, M. P. (1977). Community education for cardiovascular health. *Lancet, 1*(8023), 1192–1195.

Fishbein, M., & Ajzen, I. (1975). *Belief, attitude, intention, and behavior: An introduction to theory and research.* Reading, MA: Addison-Wesley.

Flora, J., Maccoby, N., & Farquhar, J. (1991). Communication campaigns to prevent cardio-vascular disease. In R. Rice & C. Atkin (Eds.), *Public communication campaigns* (pp. 233–252). Thousand Oaks, CA: Sage.

Fortmann, S. P., Williams, P. T., Hulley, S. B., Haskell, W. L., & Farquhar, J. W. (1981). Effect of health education on dietary behavior: The Stanford Three Community Study. *American Journal of Clinical Nutrition, 34*(10), 2030–2038.

Frank, E., Winkleby, M. A., Fortmann, S. P., Rockhill, B., & Farquhar, J. W. (1992). Improved cholesterol-related knowledge and behavior and plasma cholesterol levels in adults during the 1980s. *Journal of the American Medical Association, 268*(12), 1566–1572.

Hill, D., White, V., Marks, R., & Borland, R. (1993). Changes in sun-related attitudes and be-haviours, and reduced prevalence in a population at high risk of melanoma. *European Journal of Cancer Prevention, 2,* 447–456.

Hornik, R. (1997). "Public Health Education and Communication as Policy Instruments for Bringing about Changes in Behavior." In M. E. Goldberg, M. Fishbein, & S. E. Middlestadt (Eds.), *Social marketing: Theoretical and practical perspectives* (pp. 45–60). Mahwah, NJ: Lawrence Erlbaum Associates.

Hu, T. W., Sung, H. Y., & Keeler, T. E. (1995). Reducing cigarette consumption in California: Tobacco taxes vs an anti-smoking media campaign. *American Journal of Public Health, 85*(9), 1218–1222.

Jacobs, D. R., Jr., McGovern, P. G., & Blackburn, H. (1992). The US decline in stroke mortal-ity: What does ecological analysis tell us? *American Journal of Public Health, 82*(12), 1596–1599.

Kannel, W. B., & Wolf, P. A. (1992). Inferences from secular trend analysis of hypertension control. *American Journal of Public Health, 82*(12), 1593–1595.

Kincaid, D. L., Merritt, A. P., Nickerson, L., de Castro Buffington, S., de Castro, M. P. P., & Martin de Castro, B. (1996). Impact of a mass-media vasectomy promotion campaign in Brazil. *International Family Planning Perspectives, 22*(4), 169–175.

Luepker, R. V., Murray, D. M., Jacobs, D. R., Mittelmark, M. B., Bracht, N., Carlaw, R., Crow, R., Elmer, P., Finnegan, J., & Folsom, A. R. (1994). Community education for car-diovascular disease prevention: Risk factor changes in the Minnesota Heart Health Pro-gram. *American Journal of Public Health, 84*(9), 1383–1393.

McGovern, P. G., Burke, G. L., Sprafka, J. M., Xue, S., Folsom, A. R., & Blackburn, H. (1992). Trends in mortality, morbidity, and risk factor levels for stroke from 1960 through 1990. The Minnesota Heart Survey. *Journal of the American Medical Association, 268*(6), 753–759.

MMWR (1989, March 10). Trends in screening mammograms for women 50 years of age and older—Behavioral Risk Factor Surveillance System, 1987. *Morbidity and Mortality Weekly Report, 38*(9), 137–140.

MMWR (1999, April 2). Tobacco use among middle and high school students—Florida, 1998. *Morbidity and Mortality Weekly Report, 48*(12), 248.

MMWR (2000, June 23). Gonorrhea—United States, 1998. *Morbidity and Mortality Weekly Report, 49*(24), 538–542.

Pierce, J. P., Macaskill, P., & Hill, D. (1990). Long term effectiveness of mass media led anti-smoking campaigns in Australia. *American Journal of Public Health, 80*(5), 565–569.

Puska, P., Tuomilehto, J., Nissinen, A., Salonen, J. T., Vartiainen, E., Pietinen, P., Koskela, K., & Korhonen, H. J. (1989). The North Karelia project: 15 years of community-based pre-vention of coronary heart disease. *Annals of Medicine, 21*(3), 169–173.

Rosenstock, I. M. (1974). Historical origins of the health belief model. *Health Education Monographs, 2,* 328–335.

Siegel, M., & Biener, L. (2000). The impact of an antismoking media campaign on progression to established smoking: Results of a longitudinal youth study. *American Journal of Public Health, 90*(3), 380–386.

Sonenstein, F. L., Pleck, J. H., & Ku, L. C. (1989). Sexual activity, condom use and AIDS awareness among adolescent males. *Family Planning Perspectives, 21*(4), 152–158.

Soumerai, S. B., Ross-Degnan, D., & Kahn, J. S. (1992). Effects of professional and media warnings about the association between aspirin use in children and Reye's syndrome. *Milbank Q, 70*(1), 155–182.

Warner, K. E. (1981). Cigarette smoking in the 1970's: The impact of the antismoking campaign on consumption. *Science, 211*(4483), 729–731.

Williams, A., Reinfurt, D., & Wells, J. K. (1996). North Carolina Governor's Highway Safety Initiative. *Journal of Safety Research, 27*(1), 33–41.

Willinger, M., Ko, C. W., Hoffman, H. J., Kessler, R. C., & Corwin, M. J. (2000). Factors associated with caregivers' choice of infant sleep position, 1994–1998: The National Infant Sleep Position Study. *Journal of the American Medical Association, 283*(16), 2135–2142.

Winkleby, M. A., Taylor, C. B., Jatulis, D., & Fortmann, S. P. (1996). The long-term effects of a cardiovascular disease prevention trial: The Stanford Five-City Project. *American Journal of Public Health, 86*(12), 1773–1779.

DELIBERATE TRIALS

1

USING MASS MEDIA
TO PREVENT CIGARETTE SMOKING

John K. Worden
Brian S. Flynn
University of Vermont

When cigarette smoking prevention programs are offered to students in grades 6 to 8, there is consistent evidence of reductions in smoking initiation that persist into the early high school grades (G. J. Botvin, Baker, Dusenbury, & E. M. Botvin, 1990; Elder et al., 1993; Glynn, 1989). These effects, however, are usually eroded by the end of high school (Ellickson, Bell, & McGuigan, 1993; Flay, 1985; Flay et al., 1989; Murray et al., 1988). More promising long-term results have been obtained when school smoking prevention programs were combined with other channels of influence on young people (Perry, Kelder, Murray, & Klepp, 1992; Vartiainen, Fallonen, McAlister, & Puska, 1990). This study combined school-based smoking prevention with mass media messages created through an intensive program development process (Worden et al., 1988), which targeted subgroups by developmental level, gender, and risk for smoking adoption in both program design and implementation.

METHODS

The study design included two treatment groups: Students received either a mass media intervention combined with a school program or a school program only over a 4-year period. Each treatment condition was implemented in two small metropolitan areas. Two matched pairs of Standard

Metropolitan Statistical Areas (SMSAs) were selected using U.S. census data; one pair was located in the Northeastern United States, and one pair was in Montana. Within each matched pair, one community received the media–school intervention and the other received the school-only intervention. Community selection was based on demographic and media market characteristics. Study samples were matched further with selection of specific school districts and feeder school units within these four SMSAs having lower adult educational attainment. An initial cohort of 5,458 students from the four SMSAs was established in Grades 4, 5, and 6 in spring 1985.

Annual classroom surveys of students in the study cohort were conducted over a 5-year period in each community to assess changes in smoking behavior and mediating variables, exposure to the interventions, and mass media use preferences; an additional school survey was conducted 2 years after the program was completed to assess long-term impact on smoking behavior (Flynn et al., 1994).

Mass Media and School Program Design

Both the school and mass media programs were based on common educational objectives derived from social learning theory and related behavior change theories (Akers, Krohn, Lanza-Kaduce, Radosevich, 1979; Bandura, 1977; Fishbein & Ajzen, 1972; Flay, DiTecco, & Schlegel, 1980; Green & Kreuter, 1991; R. Jessor, 1982; R. Jessor & S. Jessor, 1977). Four primary educational objectives were established that encouraged young people to have a positive view of nonsmoking, a negative view of smoking, skills for refusing cigarettes, and the perception that most people their own age do not smoke. Additional objectives concerned with cessation skills and awareness of tobacco marketing to youth were added later.

The mass media program consisted of television and radio messages, or "spots," produced for the study; each spot was either 30 or 60 seconds in length. These spots were designed to address the educational objectives and to appeal to the interests of the target audience as determined by diagnostic and formative research conducted with students in the study communities (Worden et al., 1988). The spots were placed as local paid advertising in the broadcast television programs, cable TV channels, and radio stations used most often by the target population. To ensure variety in production style, six different media producers were commissioned over 4 years to create 36 television spots and 17 radio spots in formats appealing to the target groups: situation comedy, rock video, cartoon, testimonial, and drama. The mix of spots was changed over time to keep pace with the maturing tastes of the target groups. An average of 190 broadcast TV, 350 cable TV, and 350 radio exposures were purchased in each of the four program years in each of the two targeted media markets, which were supplemented by time donated by media outlets, increasing the total number of spot broadcasts by about 50% in each market.

The school smoking prevention program for all four communities covered grades 5 through 10 and included grade-specific curricular materials, annual teacher training, and monitoring of program implementation. This curriculum was delivered by regular classroom teachers and required either three or four class periods per year over 4 years (Glynn, 1989). The three-grade study cohort was exposed to either the school program only or the combined mass media and school programs in Grades 5 through 8, Grades 6 through 9, or Grades 7 through 10.

Although the school program and media intervention shared common educational objectives, they were otherwise independent. This strategy assumed that the interventions would be more effective if presented to the adolescent audiences as coming from multiple, independent sources conveying similar ideas about smoking.

Measurement and Data Analysis

Smoking behavior was assessed by determining the number of cigarettes the respondent reported smoking in the past week. Those who had smoked one or more cigarettes in the past week were classified as "weekly smokers." Saliva samples were collected at the time that self-reports of cigarette smoking were provided, a technique that has been shown to increase the accuracy of self-reports among adolescents when the ability to detect cigarette use through analysis of saliva samples is explained to the survey participants (Murray & Perry, 1987). Saliva samples were collected using these procedures from students in all six classroom surveys conducted for this study to enhance the accuracy of cigarette smoking self-reports.

As shown in Fig. 1.1, the educational objectives for this project were used to structure the design of both the program elements and the selection of mediating variables used in evaluation. Most of the major mediating constructs defined by the educational objectives were measured with multiple item scales with good internal consistency reliability. These mediators included: "advantages of smoking" (seven items, range of scores 0–7, α =.75); "attitude toward smoking" (three items, range 0–3, α = .84); "perceived peer smoking" (three items, range 3–15, α = .70); and a single-item measure of smoking intention. All scales were coded so that higher values were associated with higher risk for cigarette smoking.

Comparisons between treatment groups on mediating and outcome measures were performed using analyses of variance, which considered communities, not individual students, as the units of allocation to treatment. F tests were used to test whether the two treatment groups showed parallel changes over time. For these tests, community within treatment by

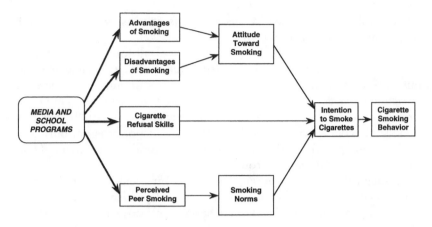

FIG. 1.1. Hypothesized relationships of mass media and school program effects, mediating variables, and behavioral outcomes.

time was used as the error term (Koepsell et al., 1991). The sums of
squares corresponding to the overall time by treatment interaction was further partitioned using orthogonal polynomials into its quantitative components (i.e., linear, quadratic, cubic). The F test presented for each dependent measure corresponds to the contrast representing the linear component
of this change, as it specifically tests whether the rate of increase is equal
for the two treatment groups.

RESULTS

The original cohort consisted of 5,458 students from grades 4 through 6.
Forty-seven percent (2,540) participated in the first five surveys. Thirty-
eight percent (2,086) participated in all six surveys. Among those from the
original cohort not included in these study samples, 82% left these communities or transferred to private schools, 15% were missing one or more
intermediate surveys, and 3% were refusals, nearly all from one district
that changed consent procedures midway through the study. To assess potential differences in survey participation, characteristics of those completing all six surveys were compared to those of all other cohort members.
The former were younger (10.7 vs. 10.9 years; $p < .01$) and less likely to
report sibling smoking (8.0% vs. 13.4%; $p < .01$), parental smoking
(51.0% vs. 64.9%; $p < .01$), or own smoking (1.3% vs. 5.1%; $p < .01$) at
baseline. Logistic regression models examining factors associated with follow-up confirmed that these variables contributed independently to follow-up success but did not interact with treatment group.

To assess the initial equivalence of treatment groups, baseline characteristics of students from the media–school and school-only communities were compared within the study sample. The media-school group included more females (51.8% vs. 47.0%, $p = .02$), were slightly younger (10.7 vs. 10.8 years, $p < .01$), and were more likely to have an older sibling who smoked (15.8% vs. 11.3%, $p = .06$). There were no other significant differences between treatment groups for other reports of family smoking, for seven measures of psychosocial risk factors for smoking, for own smoking, or for other substance use behaviors (Flynn et al., 1992).

Effects on Mediating Variables

The impact of the combined interventions on psychosocial mediators of smoking initiation, which had been targeted for change (see Fig. 1.1), is shown in Table 1.1. The pattern was similar for each measure. The groups were equivalent at Grades 4 through 6, then showed a significant difference in Grades 5 through 7, which persisted through Grades 8 through 10 (Flynn et al., 1992). Two mediators of smoking initiation that were not targeted for change by the interventions also were assessed. A psychosocial

TABLE 1.1
Comparison of Scores by Treatment Group at Grades 4–6
and Grades 8–10 for Mediating Variables

		Media-School Group		School-Only Group	
		Mean Score	*95% Confidence Interval*	*Mean Score*	*95% Confidence Interval*
Targeted psychosocial mediators of cigarette smoking					
Advantages	grades 4–6	.44	(.39, .49)	.42	(.36, .47)
	grades 8–10	.58	(.52, .49)	.81*	(.73, .90)
Disadvantages	grades 4–6	.71	(.67, .76)	.75	(.70, .80)
	grades 8–10	.69	(.64, .73)	.79*	(.74, .84)
Attitude	grades 4–6	.07	(.05, .09)	.09	(.06, .11)
	grades 8–10	.25	(.21, .29)	.37*	(.31, .42)
Peer smoking	grades 4–6	5.08	(4.97, 5.18)	5.32*	(5.19, 5.45)
	grades 8–10	8.01	(7.89, 8.13)	9.02*	(8.90, 9.15)
Smoking norms	grades 4–6	3.64	(3.57, 3.70)	3.77	(3.69, 3.85)
	grades 8–10	4.94	(4.82, 5.05)	5.56*	(5.43, 5.68)
Non-targeted psychosocial mediators of cigarette smoking					
Adult smoking	grades 4–6	3.53	(3.48, 3.58)	3.57	(3.51, 3.63)
	grades 8–10	3.21	(3.17, 3.25)	3.26	(3.22, 3.31)
Life stress	grades 4–6	.34	(.30, .38)	.34	(.30, .38)
	grades 8–10	.40	(.36, .44)	.38	(.34, .43)

*95% confidence intervals do not overlap for the two treatment groups at this grade level.

stress scale did not differ between treatment groups over 5 years and a measure of perceived adult smoking differed only at one of these surveys.

Effects on Cigarette Smoking Behaviors

Among those participating in all six surveys, weekly smoking for the media–school group increased from 1.0% in Grades 4 through 6, to 10.0% in Grades 8 through 10, and to 16.5% in Grades 10 through 12. For the school-only group, weekly smoking increased from 1.6% in Grades 4 through 6, to 15.7% in Grades 8 through 10, and to 24.0% in Grades 10 through 12 (Fig. 1.2). The relative reduction in smoking prevalence for the media–school group was 31% at Grades 10 through 12. When weekly smoking in Grades 10 through 12 was regressed on potential explanatory variables, five predictors met the criteria for inclusion in the model. The odds ratio for being a smoker in the media–school group was .62 (95% confidence interval: .49, .78), indicating reduced risk of smoking. Baseline smoking status was the strongest predictor (odds ratio = 3.38); girls (odds ratio = 1.49) and those having a smoking parent (odds ratio = 1.39) or sibling (odds ratio = 1.50) at baseline also were more likely to be smokers in grades 10 through 12. Similar results were found for alternate measures of cigarette smoking (Flynn et al., 1994). Analysis of variance based on community as the unit of assignment to treatment supported these results, showing significant differences between treatment groups without adjusting for covariates ($F1, 2 = 24.6$; $p = .04$), and after adjusting for age, gender, sibling smoking, parental smoking, own baseline smoking, and geographical region ($F1, 2 = 92.0$; $p = .01$). Further analyses by gender

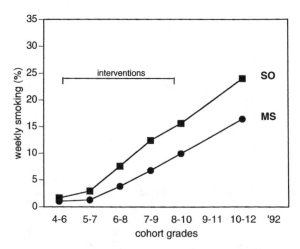

FIG. 1.2. Weekly smoking among students responding to all six surveys in the media–school (MS) and school-only (SO) treatment groups ($n = 2,086$).

indicated that the impact of the combined interventions was somewhat stronger for girls than it was for boys (Flynn et al., 1994).

Effects on Other Behaviors

The study also measured use of two substances that were not targeted for change by the interventions in all surveys. Reports of smokeless tobacco use in the past week and drinking beer more than once did not differ significantly by treatment group at baseline or in most subsequent school surveys (Flynn et al., 1992). Logistic regression analyses at Grades 10 through 12 showed no significant differences between the treatment groups for risk of drinking beer. Similar analyses for smokeless tobacco, however, showed an increased risk of use in the media–school group.

DISCUSSION

This study has demonstrated one way that mass media may be used for prevention by achieving 35% lower smoking among adolescents exposed to a smoking prevention campaign combined with school-based smoking prevention programs, as compared to the school-based programs alone. Although these results have not yet been replicated elsewhere, there is strong evidence that they are valid and generalizable.

The evaluation found consistent patterns of effect favoring the media–school group for both smoking behaviors and the mediators of these behaviors that were targeted by the interventions. Behavioral and mediating variables not targeted by the interventions generally failed to show any trend for higher levels of risk in the school-only group; these results confirmed that the effects reported here were due to the interventions and not due to a general tendency toward higher substance use in the school-only group. Further evidence for the consistency of these results can be seen by comparing the temporal ordering of the appearance of differences among the various targeted variables. As expected, differences between treatment groups generally appeared sooner in mediating variables and later in smoking behavior variables.

The two treatment groups had reasonably equivalent baseline characteristics, but tended to show the media–school group to be at higher risk for smoking. Baseline data indicated that the media–school group had more females; beginning at about grade 8 in these samples, girls were more likely to report smoking. Census tracts from which the media–school group was drawn showed higher population risks for smoking, as indicated by lower adult educational attainment and household income. Reductions in adolescent smoking in a context of relatively high smoking risks provide further evidence for the effectiveness of these interventions.

Despite some limitations of the study sample, the main results should be generalizable. The present analysis focused on the subset of students who participated in all surveys. More than half of the original cohort transferred out of these school systems during the 7-year study. These students tend to be at higher risk for smoking and should be considered as important targets for smoking prevention efforts (Pirie, Murray, & Luepker, 1988). Because the initial site had a low non-White population and other sites were matched to its characteristics, the study population included only 3.5% non-Whites. Demographic data showed that the study samples represented a lower income sector of the U.S. adolescent population. High levels of student cohort recruitment and retention provided good evidence for long-term intervention effects within this group. The effective strategies tested here should be applied in more diverse population groups in future studies.

A major feature of the design of the smoking prevention campaign evaluated in this study was adherence to a set of strategic principles derived from previous mass media research. From an earlier study (Worden et al., 1988), it was clear that youth preferred variety, with multiple messages coming from very different sources. To achieve this, it was decided to disperse the production of messages, or spots, among six different production companies. Every effort was made to avoid exhortations like "don't smoke!" Instead, the principles of social learning theory were followed, showing successful models (kids like the target group who are a little older and pretty "cool") saying things like "I don't smoke and I'm doing fine!" Demonstrating the use of tobacco was avoided, because even models that appear most negative to adults producing the messages could seem positive to some higher risk kids in the target group. Formats that appealed to the target group were used, especially situation comedy and cartoons, but also rock video and straightforward testimonials. Logos, slogans, or music that would tie the spots together were not used, because they would undermine the principle of variety.

A second major feature was the application of diagnostic and formative research in campaign development. Diagnostic surveys and focus groups were used to determine target group interests and perceptions. In order to learn as much as possible about the quickly changing tastes of the youthful target group, surveys were used to gather individual data on leisure interests, wishes, favorite TV shows and personalities, music performers, and perceptions of tobacco use; also included were questions used to classify students into high and low risk groups. Using data from the surveys, focus groups were then conducted with youth grouped according to risk to record their perceptions of these interests and preferences; these were then transcribed and placed along with the descriptive survey data for each gender, age, and risk group in a Writer's Notebook.

To begin the formative research and production process, producers were given the Writer's Notebook, strategic principles, and the educational objectives, and were asked to create a large number of spots in preliminary form for pretesting with the target group. Pretest spots were shown to youth in the target groups, who first rated them individually on appeal, followed by focus group discussions suggesting improvements that could be made prior to production. Youth also indicated which of the educational objectives were addressed by each spot. Spots that were successful in pretest were then produced in final form with the assurance that they appealed to the target group and conveyed the intended content.

Finally, to identify the most effective media channels and achieve high visibility, data gathered in school surveys were most valuable in linking gender, age, and risk of smoking adoption to specific TV shows, cable TV services (MTV was popular with higher risk youth), and radio stations. Each year, data were gathered from about 1,500 young people in each community receiving the campaign, allowing good precision for interpreting media use. Program preferences were identified according to gender, age, and risk group, and spots were placed that appealed to the subgroups in the pretests.

To interpret why this campaign had such a strong impact, it may be necessary to consider the fascination of American youth with a media-generated "youth culture" that pervades society, and to imagine how this campaign may have been embedded in that culture. In early focus groups for this study, target group members said they were not interested in having spots produced in their own hometowns. As project staff were conducting surveys and focus groups with the target group in the schools, it was apparent that students never associated these activities with the spots on the air. Several times they would ask "have you seen the spot about . . . ?" when asking about a spot from the campaign. It became evident that the spots on the air achieved high credibility and impact because they were not associated with hum-drum local activities, but were perceived as an integral part of a youth culture generated and facilitated by the mass media. By using varied production formats and avoiding the use of logos or slogans referring to local organizations or schools, and by accessing varied sources of production, this campaign may have merged into a powerful media stream that establishes norms for youth in society and impacts their behavior.

As important purveyors of youth culture, mass media have a unique capacity to restructure the attitudes, expectations, and perceived social environments of young people. Media are particularly appropriate for reaching young people in prevention campaigns because children spend more time watching television than attending school, and those at increased risk of becoming cigarette smokers or adopting other harmful behaviors are often the heaviest media users. With the substantial impact of the mass media campaign developed in this study on the prevention of adolescent cigarette smoking, it appears this may be one way to tap the power of media to impact youth for a positive purpose.

REFERENCES

Akers, R., Krohn, M., Lanza-Kaduce, L., & Radosevich, M. (1979). Social learning and deviant behavior: A specific test of a general theory. *American Sociological Review, 44,* 636–655.

Bandura, A. (1977). Self-efficacy: Toward a unifying theory of behavior change. *Psychological Review, 84,* 191–215.

Botvin, G. J., Baker, E., Dusenbury, L., Tortu, S., & Botvin, E. M. (1990). Preventing adolescent drug abuse through a multimodal cognitive-behavioral approach: Results of a 3-year study. *Journal of Consulting and Clinical Psychology, 58*(4), 437–446.

Elder, J. P., Wildey, M., deMoor, C., Sallis, J. F., Eckhardt, L., Edwards, C., Erickson, A., Golbeck, A., Hovell, M., Johnson, D., Levitz, M. D., Molgaard, C., Young, R., Vito, D., & Woodruff, S. I. (1993). The long-term prevention of tobacco use among junior high school students: Classroom and telephone interventions. *American Journal of Public Health, 83,* 1239–1244.

Ellickson, P. L., Bell, R. M., & McGuigan, K. (1993). Preventing adolescent drug use: Long-term results of a junior high program. *American Journal of Public Health, 83*(6), 856–861.

Fishbein, M., & Ajzen, I. (1972). *Belief, attitude, intention, and behavior: An introduction to theory and research.* Reading MA: Addison-Wesley.

Flay, B. R. (1985). Psychosocial approaches to smoking prevention: A review of findings. *Health Psychology, 4,* 449–488.

Flay, B. R., DiTecco, & Schlegel, R. (1980). Mass media in health promotion: An analysis using an extended information-processing model. *Health Education Quarterly, 7,* 127–147.

Flay, B. R., Koepke, D., Thomson, S. J., Santi, S., Best, J. A., & Brown, K. S. (1989). Six-year follow-up of the first Waterloo School Smoking Prevention Trial. *American Journal of Public Health, 79,* 1371–1376.

Flynn, B. S., Worden, J. K., Secker-Walker, R. H., Badger, G. J., Geller, B. M., & Costanza, M. C. (1992). Prevention of cigarette smoking through mass media and school programs. *American Journal of Public Health, 82,* 827–834.

Flynn, B. S., Worden, J. K., Secker-Walker, R. H., Pirie, P. L., Badger, G. J., Carpenter, J. H., & Geller, B. M. (1994). Mass media and school interventions for cigarette smoking prevention: Effects 2 years after completion. *American Journal of Public Health, 84,* 1148–1150.

Glynn, T. J. (1989). Essential elements of school-based smoking prevention programs. *Journal of School Health, 59,* 181–188.

Green, L. W., & Kreuter, M. W. (1991). *Health promotion planning: An educational and environment approach.* Mountain View, CA: Mayfield.

Jessor, R. (1982). Problem behavior and developmental transition in adolescence. *Journal of School Health, 52,* 295–300.

Jessor, R., & Jessor, S. (1977). *Problem behavior and psychosocial development: A longitudinal study of youth.* New York: Academic Press.

Koepsell, T. D., Martin, D. C., Diehr, P. H., Psaty, B. M., Wagner, E. H., Perrin, E. B., & Cheadle, A. (1991). Data analysis and sample size issues in evaluations of community-based health promotion and disease prevention programs: A mixed-model analysis of variance approach. *Journal of Clinical Epidemiology, 44,* 701–713.

Murray, D. M., Davis-Hearn, M., Goldman, A. I., Pirie, P., & Luepker, R. V. (1988). Four- and five-year follow-up results from four seventh-grade smoking prevention strategies. *Journal of Behavioral Medicine, 11,* 395–405.

Murray, D. M., & Perry, C. (1987). The measurement of substance use among adolescents—when is the bogus pipeline method needed? *Addictive Behavior, 12,* 225–233.

Perry, C. L., Kelder, S. H., Murray, D. M., & Klepp, K. I. (1992). Communitywide smoking prevention: Long-term outcomes of the Minnesota Heart Health Program and the Class of 1989 Study. *American Journal of Public Health, 82*(9), 1210–1216.

Pirie, P. L., Murray, D. M., & Luepker, R. V. (1988). Smoking prevalence in a cohort of adolescents, including absentees, dropouts, and transfers. *American Journal of Public Health, 78,* 176–178.

Vartiainen, E., Fallonen, U., McAlister, A. L., & Puska, P. (1990). Eight-year follow-up results of an adolescent smoking prevention program: The North Karelia Youth Project. *American Journal of Public Health, 80*(1), 78–79.

Worden, J. K., Flynn, B. S., Geller, B. M., Chen, M., Shelton, L. G., Secker-Walker, R. H., Solomon, L. J., Couchey, S., & Costanza, M. C. (1988). Development of a smoking prevention mass media program using diagnostic and formative research. *Preventive Medicine, 17,* 531–558.

Television Campaigns and Sensation Seeking Targeting of Adolescent Marijuana Use: A Controlled Time Series Approach

Philip Palmgreen
Lewis Donohew
Elizabeth Pugzles Lorch
Rick H. Hoyle
University of Kentucky

Michael T. Stephenson
University of Missouri

Campaigns directed at the prevention of drug abuse and other unhealthy behaviors often have relied on the mass media as the primary vehicle for disseminating prevention messages (Flay & Sobel, 1983; Rogers & Storey, 1987; Schilling & McAllister, 1990; Wallack, 1989). A current example is the largest drug abuse prevention effort in history, the Office of National Drug Control Policy's (ONDCP) 5-year, $2 billion National Youth Anti-Drug Media Campaign. The campaign is a multimedia effort that also seeks to stimulate community-based programs, but its central component is the targeted dissemination of televised antidrug ads and public service announcements (PSAs).

Although television is the most widely used prevention medium, attempts to isolate its effects often have suffered from shortcomings in campaign execution or evaluation. Television prevention campaigns frequently have failed to ensure widespread, frequent, and prolonged exposure to messages and have neglected audience segmentation or targeting (Flay & Sobel, 1983). The evaluations of such campaigns typically rely on post-campaign surveys or on longitudinal or panel designs that fail to account

sufficiently for pre- and postcampaign trends. With some notable excep-
tions (COMMIT, 1995; Farquhar et al., 1990; Flynn, Worden, Secker-
Walker, Badger, & Geller, 1995; Goldman & Glantz, 1998; Hu, Sung, &
Keeler, 1995; Murry, Stam, & Lastovicka, 1993; Pierce et al., 1998;
Pierce, Macaskill, & Hill, 1990), most trends have been subjected to visual
inspection or tests of means and proportions rather than procedures like
time series analysis. The use of control communities also is largely lacking.
It thus remains an open question as to whether televised PSA campaigns
can go beyond established effects on knowledge to produce behavior
change. This chapter presents evidence pertaining to this question from a
controlled study of the effects of three televised antimarijuana campaigns
targeted at adolescents.

THE SENTAR APPROACH

The intervention approach tested here revolves around a potent drug risk
factor, sensation seeking. Sensation seeking is a personality trait associated
with the need for novel, complex, ambiguous, and emotionally intense
stimuli and the willingness to take risks to obtain such stimulation (Zuckerman, 1979, 1994). The trait has a high heritability factor and a number
of biochemical correlates (Fulker, Eysenck, & Zuckerman, 1980; Netter,
Henning, & Roed, 1996; Zuckerman, 1979, 1990, 1994, 1996). It is a
moderate to strong predictor of use of a variety of drugs and earlier onset
of use, with high sensation seekers much more at-risk than low sensation
seekers (Kilpatrick, Sutker, & Smith, 1976; Pedersen, 1991; Segal, Huba,
& Singer, 1980; Zuckerman, 1979, 1994). These relations have been documented repeatedly among adolescents (Barnea, Teichman, & Rahar,
1992; Clayton, Cattarello, & Walden, 1991; Donohew, 1990). The construct is characterized by a relatively high degree of temporal stability and
is an important predictor of use across long developmental time spans
(Caspi et al., 1997; Masse & Tremblay, 1997).

High sensation seekers also have distinct preferences for particular message characteristics based on their needs for the novel, the unusual, and the
intense (Donohew, Lorch, & Palmgreen, 1991; Zuckerman, 1994). High
sensation seekers strongly prefer high sensation value messages, which
elicit strong sensory, affective, and arousal responses (Palmgreen et al.,
1991). Such messages tend to be novel, dramatic, emotionally powerful or
physically arousing, graphic or explicit, somewhat ambiguous, unconven-
tional, fast-paced, or suspenseful. Low sensation seekers prefer lower levels
of these message characteristics. Messages high in sensation value have
proven more effective with high sensation seeking teens and young adults
than low sensation value messages in producing intent to call a prevention

hotline, message recall, more negative drug attitudes, and lower behavioral intentions to use drugs (Donohew et al., 1991; Everett & Palmgreen, 1995; Palmgreen et al., 1991; Stephenson, 1999). Antidrug PSAs placed in high sensation value television programming also elicit significantly greater attention from high sensation seekers than they do when placed in low sensation value programs (Lorch et al., 1994).

This research has led to the development of a prevention approach called SENTAR (sensation seeking targeting). The approach can be summarized by four principles: (a) Employ sensation seeking as a major audience segmentation variable. (b) Conduct formative research with high sensation seeking members of the target audience. (c) Design prevention messages high in sensation value. (d) Place campaign messages in high sensation value contexts (e.g., TV programs).

These principles were employed in a campaign study demonstrating that high sensation value PSAs placed in TV programming watched by high sensation seeking older teens and young adults were effective in persuading this audience to call a drug hotline (Palmgreen et al., 1995). The study reported here also is SENTAR-based and sought to determine whether televised PSA campaigns could lead to changes in 30-day marijuana use by at-risk adolescents.

METHODS

Study Design

The study involved a 32-month controlled interrupted time series with switching replications (Cook & Campbell, 1979). Televised antimarijuana PSAs developed for adolescent high sensation seekers were shown January 1997 through April 1997 in Fayette County (Lexington), Kentucky. Similar campaigns were conducted January 1998 through April 1998 in Fayette County and in Knox County (Knoxville), Tennessee (see Table 2.1). Beginning 8 months prior to the first Fayette campaign and ending 8 months after the 1998 campaigns, personal interviews were conducted

TABLE 2.1
Controlled Interrupted Time Series Design With Switching Replications

Fayette County	baseline $O_1 \ldots O_8$	campaign 1 $O_9 \ldots O_{12}$	post-campaign $O_{13} \ldots O_{20}$	campaign 2 $O_{21} \ldots O_{24}$	post-campaign $O_{25} \ldots O_{32}$
Knox County	baseline $O_1 \ldots O_8$	baseline $O_9 \ldots O_{12}$	baseline $O_{13} \ldots O_{20}$	campaign 1 $O_{21} \ldots O_{24}$	post-campaign $O_{25} \ldots O_{32}$

Note. O_i corresponds to the *i*th observation.

with 100 randomly selected public school students each month in each county (Fayette: n = 3,174; Knox: n = 3,197). The population cohorts followed were in Grades 7 through 10 initially.

The design controlled for trends in marijuana use prior to the campaigns and allowed estimation of postcampaign trajectories (Cook & Campbell, 1979; Lewis-Beck, professional consultation, 1999). It also partially controlled for history (Campbell & Stanley, 1966; Cook & Campbell, 1979), because any national events affecting drug use should have affected both counties. In addition, contacts with school drug prevention staff and daily monitoring of the major newspapers in each county revealed no local or regional events or prevention efforts threatening comparability.

Because the cohorts in each county aged as the study progressed, marijuana use tended to increase due to sociodevelopmental or maturational factors. However, because teens in both counties reflected this secular trend, each county served as an appropriate control for the other. Because each monthly sample was independent, sensitization, testing, and attrition were minimized. External validity was enhanced by campaign replication at different sites and times, and the design allowed both within- and between-county evaluations of campaign impact.

The Study Communities

The design required two communities that were similar on a range of key characteristics. Although the population of Knox County, Tennessee (335,000), is about 50% greater than that of Fayette County, Kentucky (225,000), the populations were comparable on race, age, education, and income. Culturally, both counties share a significant southern heritage. Both counties also contain the major state universities and are served by the four major TV networks, independent stations, and multichannel cable systems (with no market overlap). Finally, university-housed survey research centers provided professional survey research capability in each county.

PSA Development

Eight focus groups of 8th through 12th graders scoring above the median on a sensation seeking scale for adolescents (and grouped by age and ethnicity—Black or White) expressed opinions on existing antidrug PSAs varying in sensation value and discussed risks associated with marijuana use. Only risks and consequences that were supported by research and considered salient by the focus groups were incorporated into PSA concepts with high sensation value characteristics such as novelty, drama, surprise, and strong emotional appeal. Each ad depicted four to five consequences of marijuana use, including aspirational consequences (effects on school, jobs, sports), social effects (on friendships, romantic interests, family), psychological/emotional effects (loss of motivation, impaired judgment, depression), and physical consequences (loss of coordination, "lung damage"—possible death from such damage was not mentioned due to adolescents' common feelings of near immortality). All actors in the ads were teens in the target age group, or slightly older. Care was taken to avoid stereotyping marijuana users as deviant "druggies." Storyboards of the ads were then evaluated by additional high sensation seeking teen focus groups. Revisions were made on the basis of these evaluations, and five concepts were produced professionally as 30-second TV spots and employed in all three campaigns (see Table 2.2 for ad descriptions). In addition, a few PSAs provided by the Partnership for a Drug-Free America (PDFA) were judged high in sensation value and included in the campaigns.

The Television Campaigns

A professional media buyer purchased ad time from local TV stations and cable companies, who also donated substantial PSA time (often exceeding a one unpaid ad to one paid ad ratio). Both the paid and donated spots were placed in programs that surveys indicated were watched by high sensation seeking (HSS) adolescents. The donated time was secured through the media buyer and a media breakfast held in each city at which the investigators explained the community benefits of the campaign(s) to key TV station and cable company personnel. This resulted in an average of 777 paid spots and 1,160 unpaid spots aired per campaign (there was little variation by campaign except for somewhat fewer unpaid spots in Knoxville). According to gross rating point (GRP) data (a measure of audience exposure), this high ad frequency resulted in at least 70% of the targeted age group being exposed to a minimum of three campaign ads per week. Ad recall data were also gathered from the monthly surveys by providing respondents in both counties with three to four sentence descriptions of each ad aired, beginning with the start of the first Fayette campaign and adding PSAs to the list (for the duration of interviewing) as they were introduced. Respondents were asked how certain they were (4-point scale) that they had seen each ad. Figure 2.1 shows profiles of the total percentages of HSS and low sensation seekers (LSS) in Fayette County who were "very certain" they had seen one or more of the five ads developed specifically for the campaign (PDFA ads were not included because they ran infrequently only in donated time, and because they had been on the air prior to the campaigns). As Fig. 2.1 shows (with some monthly variation due to sampling error), the five ads quickly achieved high levels of reach or audience penetration in the first Fayette campaign, with some drop in recall due to forgetting over the 8 months between campaigns.

TABLE 2.2
Description of Antimarijuana TV Ads Developed
for the Fayette and Knox Campaigns

"Michael"

A true story about Michael, a Black teenager who is shown playing Russian roulette with friends while smoking marijuana. Michael, who says, "I thought marijuana was no big deal," was paralyzed on one side when the gun went off. At the end of the ad, Michael is in a wheelchair by a window, says he takes medication everyday to stop convulsions, and says, "On weed you can't think straight: I only smoked for a few months, but now I'm on drugs for life."

"Dealer"

A White, teen, male drug dealer walks up to the camera with an "in your face attitude," and asks "Do you wanna get depressed or anxious? Get a little clumsy? Do something stupid?" and so on. The scenes that follow each of the dealer's questions include a girl crying in her room, a guy missing an easy dunk, and a guy arrested for having marijuana in his school locker. A message board asks, "Marijuana: how much do you want to pay?"

"Downer"

A teenager is sitting on a fence smoking marijuana with two friends when he suddenly loses his balance and falls backward and tumbles down a hill. During the teen's tumble, with his dog chasing him, the narrator talks about how weed can make you "lose your grip" on friends, family, jobs, etc. and "can really bust your lungs" (as the teen lands hard on his back at the bottom of the hill). A message on the screen reads, "Marijuana can take you down. And leave you there."

"Relationships"

A teenage girl and her boyfriend are in his messy (typical for a teenage boy) bedroom. She complains that since he started smoking marijuana he just lays around and is forgetting things (she says last night he forgot to give her a ride home from practice). He is looking through a pile of CDs and ignores her. She complains he avoids her like he avoids all his other "problems," and she walks out, slamming the door. A message board reads, "Marijuana: it's messed up a lot of relationships."

"True Lies"

A man on TV preaches about the evils of marijuana, while a group of teenage girls relaxes together. One of the girls acts disgusted with the TV message and starts to roll a joint. The other girls talk to her about ways people can get messed up on marijuana. The first girl stops rolling the joint, says she can see she's in the wrong place, and leaves. After she leaves, one of her friends is heard saying, "she's headed for a whole lot of trouble."

The second Fayette campaign (consisting of the same ads as Campaign 1 due to budget constraints, except for a few new Partnership ads), within 3 months, restored recall levels to their previous highs. As expected, because of both message and program targeting, HSS respondents generally manifested slightly higher recall of ads than LSS. Figure 2.2 shows very similar recall patterns for the Knox County campaign, although reach lev-

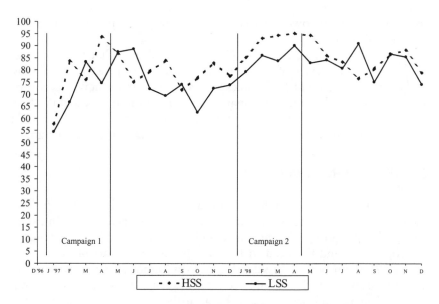

FIG. 2.1. Fayette County antimarijuana campaigns: Monthly reach percentages for low and high sensation seekers.

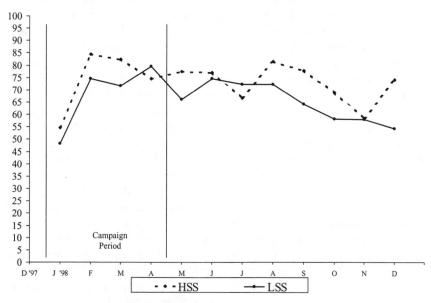

FIG. 2.2. Knox County antimarijuana campaign: Monthly reach percentages for low and high sensation seekers.

els were somewhat lower, perhaps due to the lower number of unpaid spots in this campaign.

It is clear, therefore, from the GRP and recall data that the campaign ads achieved high levels of exposure both in terms of penetration of most of the target audience of HSS adolescents as well as frequency of exposure. The exposure levels, in fact, compare favorably to those expected (90% of target audience reached an average of four times per week) by the ONDCP's well-financed National Youth Anti-Drug Media Campaign.

Sampling and Recruitment

Two standard survey sampling methods used to study adolescent substance use were not employed because of design considerations. Multistage area probability sampling was not feasible due to the narrow age range of the population and the need to follow a particular cohort of adolescents over a 32-month period. In-school surveys were not an option due to the need to interview 100 randomly selected students per month across four grades from various schools, and because the time series required interviews during summer and other periods when school was not in session.

Systematic random sampling with geographic and grade stratification was thus employed in each county to draw 32 monthly pools of potential respondents from enrollment lists of 7th through 10th graders attending public schools in spring 1996. Because all 32 monthly pools were drawn prior to when data gathering began in May 1996, any students who subsequently dropped out of school were included in each month's recruitment of respondents. Because neither public school system would allow telephone recruiters to ask for students by name, parents/guardians were contacted by telephone and asked if there was a child in their household in the specified grade range (e.g., Grades 8–11). If so, then the interview was described (including measurement of drug use) and oral permission was sought to interview the student in the home, followed by permission from the student (also after a description of the interview). Active parental consent and student assent were obtained at the time of the interview.

Interviews were private and anonymous, with self-administration of drug and alcohol items via laptop computer. Prevalence rates ordinarily are determined more accurately through self-administration (particularly via computer) as opposed to interviewer administration or telephone interviews (Aquilino, 1994; Johnson, Houghland, & Clayton, 1989; Turner et al., 1998; Wright, Aquilino, & Supple, 1998). Sampling, recruiting, and interviewing were conducted in Fayette County by the University of Kentucky Survey Research Center, and in Knox County by the Social Science Research Institute at the University of Tennessee. As an incentive, respondents received gift certificates worth $10.

Response Rates

Three response rates reflecting varying assumptions were estimated for Fayette County. These rates could not be estimated for Knox County because they required separating total refusals into three categories (parent refusals, child refusals, and hangups) not available from Knox. However, the recruiting and interviewing procedures were identical in Knox County, and the total numbers of completions, refusals, and households with no eligible children in Knox were very similar to Fayette figures. It is assumed, therefore, that the response rates for Fayette should also apply to Knox.

The minimal response rate (RR1) involved dividing the number of completions by the total number of students either known or estimated to be eligible. RR1 for Fayette County was 35.4%. Subtracting the estimated number of eligibles from the denominator for RR1 yielded an RR2 of 50.8%, or the response rate among those adolescents known to be eligible via screening. Finally, because nonresponse resulting from a child's direct refusal to be interviewed was most likely to introduce bias in estimates of substance use, RR3 was calculated by dividing the number of completions by the sum of completions and child refusals. RR3 for Fayette was 63.8%.

In the Fayette and Knox samples, demographics paralleled both census and school population figures (see later). Levels of marijuana use by 8th, 10th, and 12th graders in the samples were consistent with national norms reported by the University of Michigan's annual Monitoring the Future Survey (MTF, 1999). For example, 30-day marijuana prevalence among Fayette and Knox 12th graders was 25.5% and 20.3%, respectively, compared to 1997 and 1998 Monitoring the Future 12th-grade estimates of 23.7% and 22.8%. Use estimates for other substances also were consistent with national norms. Underrepresentation of drug users in the samples, therefore, was no more likely than for MTF, a widely referenced benchmark.

Sample Demographics and Other Characteristics

The Fayette and Knox samples matched closely on demographic variables, except where census or school population data led to expected differences (see Table 2.3). The two samples also did not differ significantly on sensation seeking, but the Fayette sample was significantly higher ($p < .001$) on most other drug risk factors (e.g, perceived peer and family drug use, delinquency), and significantly lower ($p < .001$) on most protective factors (e.g., religiosity, perceived sanctions for marijuana use, perceived future opportunities). These differences were reflected in significantly higher levels of use by Fayette County students of marijuana, tobacco, alcohol, and hallucinogens, whereas the Knox sample showed significantly greater use of inhalants and was equivalent on cocaine/crack use. Finally, the samples

TABLE 2.3
Demographic Characteristics of Fayette County
and Knox County Samples

	Fayette (n = 3,174)	Knox (n = 3,197
Mean age	15.6 years	15.5 years
Percent female	54%	54%
Father's Educ. (mean)	14.5 years	14.6 years
Mother's Educ. (mean)	14.4 years	14.1 years
Household income[a] (median category)	$50,000–$74,000	$50,000–$74,000
Ethnicity		
White	81.40%	90.50%
African American	15.20%	7.30%
Other	3.40%	2.20%

[a]Nearly identical Fayette and Knox income distributions across 9 categories.

did not differ on television viewing levels, and program choices were consistent with Arbitron data.

Thus, the samples were quite comparable in many ways, but there appeared to be a somewhat stronger pro-drug "culture" in Fayette County. Because identical sampling procedures were employed in both counties, any selection bias present should have been uniform. In any case, the generally small differences (although sometimes statistically significant due to large Ns) between the samples on the previous variables did not affect the ability to relate changes in substance use trends in each county to the effects of the campaigns.

Measures

Sensation seeking was measured with an 8-item Likert-type scale partially adapted from Huba, Newcomb, and Bentler (1981). The scale displayed good reliability (α = .78) and consistent ability to predict drug use, drug attitudes, and a variety of drug risk and protective factors. The dependent variable was the percent of each monthly sample reporting marijuana use in the last 30 days. Use of alcohol, tobacco, and other substances was also measured along with several risk and protective factors evaluated extensively in other studies (e.g., deviance, depression, religiosity, law abidance, family cohesiveness) (Newcomb & Felix-Ortiz, 1992).

Data Analysis

Missing data were infrequent (1.7% of observations). The expectation-maximization algorithm was used to impute values on these cases except for marijuana use (Shafer, 1997).

Each monthly sample was divided into high and low sensation seekers, based on medians for 12 Age × Gender × Ethnicity subgroups in the total sample ($n = 6,371$). Subgroup medians were employed to reduce the effects of possible age, gender, or ethnic bias of scale items (although analyses with total sample medians differed little from the subgroup median analyses). To reduce sampling error, the monthly estimates of high and low sensation seekers' 30-day marijuana use were adjusted for levels of 12 risk and protective factors that displayed the strongest zero-order correlations with individual 30-day use. For each of four subgroups (Fayette high and low sensation seekers, Knox high and low sensation seekers), analysis of variance (ANCOVA) was employed at the individual level with month of interview as a 32-level factor and 30-day marijuana use as the dependent variable. Covariates were deviance, religiosity, law abidance, GPA, depression, self-acceptance, perceived community use/approval of marijuana, perceived family use/approval of marijuana, perceived police/legal sanctions, perceived parental sanctions against marijuana, family cohesiveness, and perceived life opportunities. The 32 adjusted monthly means for each subgroup exhibited 25.9% less variance on average than the unadjusted means, yielded more accurate slope estimates, and reduced negative autocorrelation. These were employed in a regression-based time series procedure developed by Lewis-Beck (1986) involving the use of dummy variables to indicate intercepts and slopes, and intercept and slope changes due to interventions. This procedure is amenable to short time series containing less than 50 data points, which ordinarily cannot be analyzed via conventional transfer function methods.

Analyses involving low sensation seekers (not targeted in the campaign), as expected, revealed low levels of 30-day marijuana use, no developmental trends, and no campaign effects in either county. Therefore, this discussion concentrates on the targeted group—the high sensation seekers. Initial regression analysis of the Fayette County series for high sensation seekers revealed two outliers with z scores greater than 3.3 residual standard deviations. Following standard guidelines (J. Cohen & P. Cohen, 1983; Tabachnick & Fidell, 1996), these outliers were removed because the probability that they came from the same population as the other 30 points was extremely low ($p < .001$) and because outliers can increase negative autocorrelation and seriously distort estimates of slopes, intercepts, and proportion of variance explained. The Knox County series for high sensation seekers had only one outlier. Other procedures for reducing the impact of these outliers without removal (e.g., taking the natural log of the dependent variable: Lewis-Beck, 1986; Tabachnick & Fidell, 1996; Winsorizing: Tufte, 1974) also were employed and produced similar results.

RESULTS

Knox County Time Series

Regression plots for Knox County are shown in Fig. 2.3. As noted, low sensation seekers exhibited low levels of use, no developmental trend, and no indication of campaign effects. High sensation seekers, however, displayed a strong upward linear trend for the 20 months prior to the campaign, followed by a decline that began immediately after the start of the campaign and continued to the completion of data gathering. The time series regression results for high sensation seekers for a full model containing terms for all slope and intercept changes are displayed in Table 2.4. The regression model was significant ($F_{3, 27}$ = 8.94, p < .001; adjusted R^2 = .442), with very low autocorrelation (ρ = .032; Durbin-Watson statistic = 1.91).

The precampaign slope (b = .89; b = .84, when adjusted for the missing September 1996 outlier) was positive and significant (t = 4.89; p < .001). This indicates an upward trend in 30-day marijuana use by high sensation seekers of .84% per month over the 20-month precampaign period, for a total estimated absolute precampaign increase of 16.4% (from 16.6% to 33.0%). This doubling of use may be ascribed to normal sociodevelopmental changes as the cohort aged. The downward pre–post change in slope (δ = -1.38) was also significant (t = -3.41, p = .001). Overall, the model predicted an estimated 8.8% absolute drop in marijuana use over

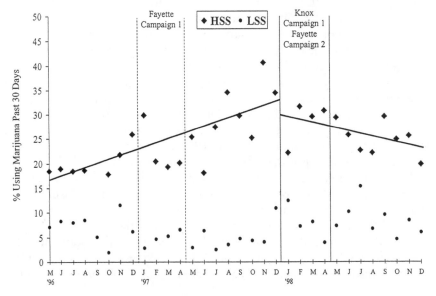

FIG. 2.3. Knox County 30-day marijuana use time series regression plots for high and low sensation seeking adolescents.

TABLE 2.4
Time Series Regression Results for Knox County

ANOVA					
Source	SS	df	MS	F	p value
Regression	503.8	3	167.9	8.94	< .001
Residual	507.4	27	18.8		
Total	1011.2	30			

Model Summary					
R	R Sq.	Adj. R Sq.	Std. Error of Estimate	Durbin-Watson	Rho
.706	.498	.442	4.34	1.91	.032

Regression Coefficients (Unstandardized) and Statistics				
	b	Std. Error	t	p value (1-tail)[a]
Constant	15.68	2.07	7.58	< .001
Precampaign Slope	.89	.18	4.89	< .001
Pre–Post Intercept Change	−3.11	3.28	−.95	.176
Pre–Post Slope Change	−1.38	.41	−3.41	.001

[a]Directional hypotheses based on assumptions of upward developmental trends and downward campaign effects on intercepts and slopes.

12 months, to a final level of 24.2%. The estimated drop in the relative proportion of high sensation seekers using marijuana was 26.7%.

Respecifying the regression equation without the nonsignificant term for intercept change (Lewis-Beck, 1986, professional consultation, 1999) resulted in a considerably larger F value for the variance due to regression ($F_{2, 28} = 13.01$ vs. $F_{3, 27} = 8.94$), slightly higher adjusted R^2 (.445), and a 25% increase in the t value associated with the pre–post campaign slope change ($t = -4.20$, $p < .001$). The regression plot for this analysis was very similar to Fig. 2.3 and therefore is not shown here.

Fayette County Time Series

Again, low sensation seekers exhibited low levels of use, no developmental trend, and no indication of campaign effects. For high sensation seekers, a series of regression analyses was required to clarify a more complex pattern of results than Knox County's due to the presence of two campaigns and an apparent wearing off of the effects of the first campaign. The first regression model containing all slope and intercept change terms was sig-

TABLE 2.5
Time Series Regression Results for Fayette County

ANOVA

Source	SS	df	MS	F	p value
Regression	429.5	5	85.9	4.14	.007
Residual	497.9	24	20.7		
Total	927.4	29			

Model Summary

R	R Sq.	Adj. R Sq.	Std. Error of Estimate	Durbin-Watson	Rho
.681	.463	.351	4.55	2.42	−.243

Regression Coefficients (Unstandardized) and Statistics

	b	Std. Error	t	p value (1-tail)[a]
Constant	17.46	3.85	4.54	< .001
Precampaign 1 Slope	2.70	.86	3.14	.002
Pre1–Post1 Intercept Change	−3.69	4.18	−.88	.190
Pre1–Post1 Slope Change	−3.04	.94	−3.23	.002
Pre2–Post2 Intercept Change	10.37	3.85	2.69	.013[b]
Pre2–Post2 Slope Change	−.65	.58	−1.13	.135

[a]Directional hypotheses based on assumptions of upward developmental trends and downward campaign effects on intercepts and slopes.
[b]Two-tailed test due to positive intercept change.

nificant ($F_{5, 24}$ = 4.14, $p < .007$), adjusted R^2 = .351 (see Table 2.5). The autocorrelation (ρ) of −.243 (Durbin-Watson = 2.42) was within the interval (+.30 to −.30) judged to be acceptable (Lewis-Beck, 1986; Rao & Griliches, 1969).

The downward change in slope at the start of Campaign 1 (δ = −3.04) was significant (t = −3.23, p = .002). However, a regression plot for this model (not shown) indicated that the effects of the first Fayette campaign appeared to wear off approximately 6 months after the campaign, leading to the significant change in intercept of +10.37% (t = 2.69, p = .013) in Table 2.5. It is surprising, in fact, that the Knoxville campaign did not display similar wearoff, because such trends are the norm in product advertising campaigns. The initial plot indicated, however, that the wearoff increase was reversed a few months into Campaign 2, followed by a downward trend similar to the trend observed for Campaign 1. The shape of the wearoff trend suggested that this portion of the time series would be more appropriately modeled as a linear regression line rather than an intercept change. A model incorporating this change was statistically significant ($F_{7,\ 22}$ = 3.45, p = .012) and displayed a slightly higher adjusted R^2 (.371 vs. .351) and lower negative autocorrelation (Durbin-Watson = 2.27; ρ = −.16) than the original model. The change in slope from the downward post-Campaign 1 trend to the upward wearoff trend was significant δ = 5.56, t = 2.69, p = .007), as was the negative slope change from the wearoff trend to the post-Campaign 2 period (δ = −5.91, t = −2.83, p = .005).

Because neither intercept change was significant in the aforementioned model, the model was respecified without the nonsignificant intercept change terms (Lewis-Beck, 1986). The final model yielded an improved fit ($F_{4,\ 25}$ = 5.52, p = .003, adjusted R^2 = .384) with lower autocorrelation (Durbin-Watson = 2.21; ρ = −0.14). The three slope changes in the model also increased in significance (p = .001, .003, .002 for δ_1, δ_2, δ_3, respectively). The final regression plot is depicted in Fig. 2.4, which illustrates how each campaign reversed upward trends in marijuana use. Note that the impact of Campaign 2 did not appear to begin until after the third month of the campaign, whereas the effects of the Knox County and first Fayette campaign appeared to begin almost immediately. Little was known entering the study about the length of campaign effect lags. This, as Lewis-Beck (1986) pointed out, is a common problem in interrupted time series analysis and primarily is an empirical issue if theory or prior research do not aid in specifying the lag. Following Lewis-Beck's (1986, professional

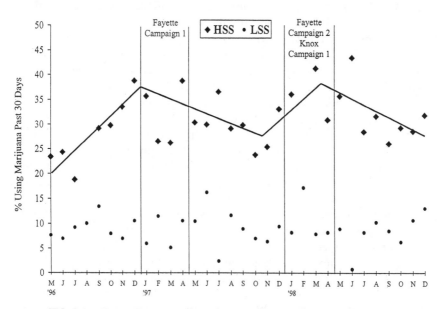

FIG. 2.4. Fayette County 30-day marijuana use time series regression with wear off trend for HSS and without nonsignificant intercept changes.

consultation, 1999) recommendations, several campaign effect start points were specified for each campaign in different regression models. Statistical significance of slope change parameters indicated immediate effects for Fayette Campaign 1 and the Knox campaign. The models for Fayette Campaign 2 indicated a 3-month lagged effect. This delay may have been due to the fact that budget constraints dictated the use of the same PSAs in both Fayette campaigns. This lack of novelty may have delayed the impact of Campaign 2 on HSS adolescents, who certainly would have preferred new spots. Also note that the start of the effects of this campaign are consistent with the within-campaign ad recall peak observed for this campaign (see Fig. 2.1). Perhaps cumulative, widespread exposure was needed to elicit a positive impact of this largely recycled "booster" campaign on a cohort that was now 1 year older (Grades 9–12).

DISCUSSION

The Knox County findings demonstrate significant campaign effects on high sensation seeking adolescents' marijuana use that were still evident several months after the campaign. The estimated 8.8% absolute drop (or 26.7% relative decrease) in marijuana use in Knox County probably understates the campaign's impact. Because marijuana prevalence does not peak until post-high school, and given that the cohort was only in Grades 9 through 12 at the campaign's start, a continued increase in marijuana use over the final 12 months without a campaign (although perhaps at a somewhat slower rate, according to recent cohort trends in Monitoring the Future Study data, 1999) would be expected. Assuming a rate of increase for the last 12 months of the time series half that for the first 20 months yields an estimated 30-day prevalence rate of 37.8% in December 1998. When compared to the model estimate of 24.2%, the result is an estimated 13.6% decline in prevalence, or a 36.0% decline in the relative proportion of high sensation seeking users. These are substantial reductions, even if they are halved by including the low sensation seeker sample (which as expected experienced no reduction) to obtain total adolescent population estimates.

The two interventions in Fayette resulted in rather short pre–post 1–post 2 series of 7, 12, and 11 points, respectively, and thus comparatively high standard errors for the regression coefficients. Precise estimates of reductions in marijuana prevalence are not possible, therefore. Overall, however, the Fayette findings provide additional evidence that televised PSA campaigns targeted at high sensation seeking adolescents can lead to significant reductions in marijuana use. This conclusion is strengthened by additional regression analyses (not included for space reasons) indicating that high sensation seekers' 30-day use of two other gateway substances— tobacco and alcohol—showed only the expected developmental increases in both counties, with no indications of any changes associated with the marijuana interventions. Inhalants, cocaine/crack, and hallucinogens also displayed no campaign effects, providing further evidence that the changes in marijuana use were not part of overall substance use trends.

Although research generally has shown that media campaigns coupled with other kinds of interventions are the most successful (COMMIT, 1995; Farquhar et al., 1990; Flora, Maccoby, Farquhar, 1989; Flora, Maibach, & Maccoby, 1989; Rogers & Storey, 1987), this study's results are consistent with a growing body of evidence, supplemented by many of the findings reported in this book, that media campaigns alone can have significant impacts on behaviors (Beck et al., 1990; Flay, 1987; Flynn et al., 1995; McDivitt, Zimick, & Hornik, 1997; Zastoway, Adams, Black, Lawton, & Wilder, 1993). The success of the three Fayette–Knox campaigns can be traced to four important principles from the public health campaign literature: (a) interventions based on well-tested social and behavorial theories are more likely to be successful (Donohew, Lorch, & Palmgreen, 1998; Flay, 1987; Maibach & Parrot, 1995; McAlister, Ramirez, Galavotti, & Gallion, 1989; Rogers, 1995; Rosenstock, 1990; Schilling & McAllister, 1990; Zimmerman & Vernberg, 1994); (b) widespread, frequent, and prolonged exposure to campaign messages is vital to campaign success (Flay, 1987); (c) audience segmentation is required to target messages to at-risk audiences (Backer, Rogers, & Sopory, 1992; Slater, 1996); (d) formative research should be employed throughout the audience segmentation, message design, and channel selection phases (Atkin & Freimuth, 1989).

Regarding audience targeting, the most successful schemes employ variables linked both to the behavior of interest and to the communication channels and message styles most preferred by the target audience (Slater, 1996). Most drug risk and protective factors do not relate to channel selection and message preferences. Research points to the need to target high sensation seekers in prevention campaigns because they are far more likely to use various substances, and because theory- and research-based strategies are available to guide the design of effective messages. In this study, antidrug messages from a variety of sources (e.g., school, parents, friends, PSAs) were probably sufficient to reinforce the strong antidrug stance of low sensation seekers and prevent an increase in marijuana prevalence during the high school years.

Applications

The results of this study augur well for the ONDCP antidrug campaign, which is similar in many important ways to those studied here. As in the Fayette and Knox campaigns, the antidrug messages for ONDCP are being developed, targeted, and disseminated according to principles derived from social and behavioral science, prevention research, and the SENTAR approach in order to reach the primary target audience of high sensation seeking adolescents (Office of National Drug Control Policy, 1997).

The SENTAR approach is not restricted to illicit drug abuse prevention, however. Sensation seeking, for example, is related to alcohol use (Clayton et al., 1991; Donohew et al., 1999; Newcomb & McGee, 1989; Zuckerman, 1994) and tobacco use (Clayton et al., 1991; Zuckerman, 1994), risky sex (Donohew et al., 2000; Horvath & Zuckerman, 1993; Zuckerman, 1994), crime (Horvath & Zuckerman, 1993; Zuckerman, 1994), deviance (Newcomb & McGee, 1991), drinking and driving (Zuckerman, 1994), and speeding (Zuckerman, 1994). Thus, a wide range of risk-related behaviors might be addressed more successfully through campaigns employing SENTAR principles.

Finally, what are the implications of this study's findings for the impact of televised PSAs in drug abuse prevention? Although the results of the time series analyses are compelling, it should not be broadly concluded that "televised anti-drug PSAs produce behavior change," or that "PSAs alone are sufficient for prevention purposes." The data do indicate that PSAs can affect drug behavior, but only in the context of carefully targeted campaigns that achieve high levels of reach and frequency, and with messages designed specifically for the target audience on the basis of social scientific theory and formative research. With these caveats, PSAs can play an important role in future prevention efforts.

ACKNOWLEDGMENTS

This research was supported by Grant DA06892 from the National Institute on Drug Abuse. We wish to express our gratitude to Dr. Ronald Langley, director, University of Kentucky Survey Research Center, and Sueanne McDonnell, project director, University of Tennessee Social Science Research Institute, for their professionalism and diligence in directing the personal interviews for this project. We especially thank Dr. Langley for sharing his expertise in questionnaire design, sampling, telephone recruiting, and interviewing procedures. IRB approval for this project was given on October 25, 1994.

REFERENCES

Aquilino, W. S. (1994). Interview mode effects in surveys of drug and alcohol use. *Public Opinion Quarterly, 58*, 210–240.

Atkin, C. K., & Freimuth, V. (1989). Formative evaluation research in campaign design. In R. E. Rice & C. K. Atkin (Eds.), *Public communication campaigns* (2nd ed., pp. 131–150). Newbury Park, CA: Sage.

Backer, T. E., Rogers, E. M., & Sopory, P. (1992). *Designing health communication campaigns: What works?* Newbury Park, CA: Sage.

Barnea, Z., Teichman, M., & Rahar, G. (1992). Personality, cognitive and interpersonal factors in adolescent substance use: A longitudinal test of an integrative model. *Journal of Youth and Adolescence, 21*, 187–201.

Beck, E. J., Donegan, C., Kenny, C., Cohen, C. S., Moss, V., Terry, P., Underhill, G. S., Jeffries, D. J., Pinching, A. J., Miller, D. L., Harris, J. R. W., & Cunningham, D. G. (1990). Update on HIV-testing at a London sexually transmitted disease clinic: Long-term impact of the AIDS media campaigns. *Genitourinary Medicine, 66*, 142–147.

Campbell, D. T., & Stanley, J. C. (1966). *Experimental and quasi-experimental designs for research*. Chicago, IL: Rand McNally.

Caspi, A., Dickson, D., Dickson, N., Harrington, H., Langley, J., Moffitt, T. E., & Silva, P. A. (1997). Personality differences predict health-risk behaviors in young adulthood: evidence from a longitudinal study. *Journal of Personality and Social Psychology, 73*, 1052–1063.

Clayton, R. R., Cattarello, A., & Walden, K. P. (1991). Sensation seeking as a potential mediating variable for school-based prevention intervention: A two-year follow-up of DARE. *Health Communication, 3*, 229–239.

Cohen, J., & Cohen, P. (1983). *Applied multiple regression/correlation analysis for the behavioral sciences*. Hillsdale, NJ: Lawrence Erlbaum Associates.

The COMMIT Research Group. (1995). Community Intervention Trial for Smoking Cessation (COMMIT): I. Cohort results from a four-year community intervention. *American Journal of Public Health, 85*, 183–192.

Cook, T. D., & Campbell, D. T. (1979). *Quasi-experimentation: Design and analysis for field settings*. Boston: Houghton Mifflin.

Donohew, L. (1990). Public health campaigns: Individual message strategies and a model. In E. B. Ray & L. Donohew (Eds.), *Communication and health: Systems and applications* (pp. 136–152). Hillsdale, NJ: Lawrence Erlbaum Associates.

Donohew, L., Hoyle, R. H., Clayton, R. R., Skinner, W. F., Colon, S. E., & Rice, R. E. (1999). Sensation seeking and drug use by adolescents and their friends: Models for marijuana and alcohol. *Journal of Studies on Alcohol, 60*, 622–631.

Donohew, L., Lorch, E. P., & Palmgreen, P. (1991). Sensation seeking and targeting of televised anti-drug PSAs. In L. Donohew, H. E. Sypher, & W. J. Bukoski (Eds.), *Persuasive communication and drug abuse prevention* (pp. 209–226). Hillsdale, NJ: Lawrence Erlbaum Associates.

Donohew, L., Lorch, E. P., & Palmgreen, P. (1998). Applications of a theoretic model of information exposure to health interventions. *Human Communication Research, 24*, 454–468.

Donohew, L., Zimmerman, R., Cupp, P. S., Novak, S., Colon, S. E., & Abell, R. (2000). Sensation seeking, impulsive decision-making, and risky sex: Implications for risk-taking and design of interventions. *Personality and Individual Differences, 28*, 1079–1091.

Everett, M., & Palmgreen, P. (1995). Influence of sensation seeking, message sensation value, and program context on the effectiveness of anti-cocaine PSAs. *Health Communication, 7*, 225–248.

Farquhar, J. W., Fortmann, S. P., Flora, J. A., Taylor, C. B., Haskell, W. L., Williams, P. T., Maccoby, N., & Wood, P. D. (1990). The Stanford Five-City Project: Effects of community-wide education on cardiovascular disease risk factors. *Journal of the American Medical Association, 264*, 359–365.

Flay, B. R. (1987). Mass media and smoking cessation: A critical review. *American Journal of Public Health, 77*, 153–160.

Flay, B. R., & Sobel, J. L. (1983). The role of mass media in preventing adolescent substance abuse. NIDA Research Monograph 47. In T. J. Glynn, C. G. Leukefeld, & J. P. Ludford (Eds.), *Preventing adolescent drug abuse: Intervention strategies* (pp. 5–35). Rockville, MD: National Institute on Drug Abuse.

Flora, J. A., Maccoby, N., & Farquhar, J. W. (1989). Communication campaigns to prevent cardiovascular disease: The Stanford community studies. In R. E. Rice & C. K. Atkin (Eds.), *Public communication campaigns* (2nd ed., pp. 233–252). Newbury Park, CA: Sage.

Flora, J. A., Maibach, E. W., & Maccoby, N. (1989). The role of media across four levels of health promotion intervention. *Annual Review of Public Health, 10,* 181–201.

Flynn, B. S., Worden, J. K., Secker-Walker, R. H., Badger, G. J., & Geller, B. M. (1995). Cigarette smoking prevention effects of mass media and school interventions targeted to gender and age groups. *Journal of Health Education, 26*(Suppl.), 45–51.

Fulker, D. W., Eysenck, H. J., & Zuckerman, M. (1980). A genetic and environmental analysis of sensation seeking. *Journal of Research in Personality, 14,* 261–281.

Goldman, L. K., & Glantz, S. A. (1998). Evaluation of anti-smoking advertising campaigns. *Journal of the American Medical Association, 279,* 772–777.

Horvath, P., & Zuckerman, M. (1993). Sensation seeking, risky appraisal, and risky behavior. *Personality and Individual Differences, 14,* 41–52.

Hu, T.-W., Sung, H.-Y., & Keeler, T. E. (1995). Reducing cigarette consumption in California: Tobacco taxes vs an anti-smoking media campaign. *American Journal of Public Health, 85,* 1218–1223.

Huba, G. J., Newcomb, M. D., & Bentler, P. M. (1981). Comparison of canonical correlation and interbattery factor analysis on sensation seeking and drug use domains. *Applied Psychological Measurement, 5,* 291–306.

Johnson, T. P., Houghland, J., & Clayton, R. (1989). Obtaining reports of sensitive behavior: A comparison of telephone and face-to-face interviews. *Social Science Quarterly, 70,* 174–183.

Kilpatrick, D. G., Sutker, P. B., Smith, A. D. (1976). Deviant drug and alcohol use: The role of anxiety, sensation seeking, and other personality variables. In M. Zuckerman & C. D. Spielberger (Eds.), *Emotions and anxiety: New concepts, methods, and applications* (pp. 247–278). Hillsdale, NJ: Lawrence Erlbaum Associates.

Lewis-Beck, M. S. (1986). Interrupted time series. In W. D. Berry & M. S. Lewis-Beck (Eds.), *New tools for social scientists: Advances and application in research methods* (pp. 209–240). Beverly Hills, CA: Sage.

Lorch, E. P., Palmgreen, P., Donohew, L., Helm, D., Baer, S. A., & Dsilva, M. U. (1994). Program context, sensation seeking, and attention to televised anti-drug public service announcements. *Human Communication Research, 20,* 390–412.

Maibach, E., & Parrott, R. L. (1995). *Designing health messages: Approaches from communication theory and public health practice.* Thousand Oaks, CA: Sage.

Masse, L. C., & Tremblay, R. E. (1997). Behavior of boys in kindergarten and the onset of substance abuse during adolescence. *Archives of General Psychiatry, 54,* 62–68.

McAlister, A., Ramirez, A. G., Galavotti, C., & Gallion, K. J. (1989). Anti-smoking campaigns: Progress in the application of social learning theory. In R. E. Rice & C. K. Atkin (Eds.), *Public communication campaigns* (2nd ed., pp. 291–307). Newbury Park, CA: Sage.

McDivitt, J. A., Zimick, S., & Hornik, R. C. (1997). Explaining the impact of a communication campaign to change vaccination knowledge and coverage in the Philippines. *Health Communication, 9,* 95–118.

The Monitoring the Future Study. Institute for Social Research, University of Michigan home page. Available at: http://www.isr.umich.edu/src/mtf/pr98t1ba.html. Accessed April 8, 1999.

Murry, J. P., Jr., Stam, A., & Lastovicka, J. L. (1993). Evaluating an anti-drinking and driving advertising campaign with a sample survey and time series intervention analysis. *Journal of the American Statistical Association, 88,* 50–56.

Netter, P., Hennig, J., & Roed, I. S. (1996). Serotonin and dopamine as mediators of sensation seeking behavior. *Neuropsychobiology, 34,* 155–165.

Newcomb, M. D., & Felix-Ortiz, M. (1992). Multiple protective and risk factors for drug use and abuse: Cross-sectional and prospective findings. *Journal of Personality and Social Psychology, 63,* 280–296.

Newcomb, M. D., & McGee, L. (1989). Adolescent alcohol use and other delinquent behaviors. *Criminal Justice and Behavior, 16,* 345–369.

Newcomb, M. D., & McGee, L. (1991). Influence of sensation seeking on general deviance and specific problem behaviors from adolescence to young adulthood. *Journal of Personality and Social Psychology, 61,* 614–628.

Office of National Drug Control Policy. (1997). *The National Youth Anti-drug Media Campaign communication strategy statement.* Washington, DC: Office of National Drug Control Policy.

Palmgreen, P., Donohew, L., Lorch, E. P., Rogus, M., Helm, D., & Grant, N. (1991). Sensation seeking, message sensation value, and drug use as mediators of PSA effectiveness. *Health Communication, 3,* 217–227.

Palmgreen, P., Lorch, E. P., Donohew, L., Harrington, N. G., Dsilva, M., & Helm, D. (1995). Reaching at-risk populations in a mass media drug abuse prevention campaign: Sensation seeking as a targeting variable. *Drugs and Society, 8,* 29–45.

Pedersen, W. (1991). Mental health, sensation seeking and drug use patterns: A longitudinal study. *British Journal of Addiction, 86,* 195–204.

Pierce, J. P., Gilpin, E. A., Emery, S. L., White, M. M., Rosbrook, B., & Berry, C. C. (1998). Has the California tobacco control program reduced smoking? *Journal of the American Medical Association, 280,* 893–899.

Pierce, J. P., Macaskill, P., & Hill, D. (1990). Long-term effectiveness of mass media led antismoking campaigns in Australia. *American Journal of Public Health, 80,* 565–570.

Rao, P., & Griliches, Z. (1969). Small-sample properties of several two-stage regression methods in the context of auto-correlated errors. *Journal of the American Statistical Association, 64,* 253–272.

Rogers, E. M. (1995). *Diffusion of innovations.* New York: The Free Press.

Rogers, E. M., & Storey, J. D. (1987). Communication campaigns. In C. R. Berger & S. H. Chaffee (Eds.), *Handbook of communication science* (pp. 817–846). Newbury Park, CA: Sage.

Rosenstock, I. M. (1990). The health belief model: Explaining health behavior through expectancies. In K. Glanz, F. M. Lewis, & B. K. Rimer (Eds.), *Health behavior and health education: Theory, research, and practice* (pp. 39–62). San Francisco, CA: Jossey-Bass.

Schilling, R. F., & McAllister, A. L. (1990). Preventing drug use in adolescents through media interventions. *Journal of Consulting and Clinical Psychology, 58,* 415–424.

Segal, B., Huba, G. J., & Singer, J. L. (1980). *Drugs, daydreaming, and personality: A study of college youth.* Hillsdale, NJ: Lawrence Erlbaum Associates.

Shafer, J. L. (1997). *Analysis of incomplete multivariate data.* London: Chapman and Hall.

Slater, M. D. (1996). Theory and method in health audience segmentation. *Journal of Health Communication, 1,* 267–283.

Stephenson, M. T. (1999). *Message sensation value and sensation seeking as determinants of message processing.* Unpublished doctoral dissertation, University of Kentucky, Lexington, KY.

Tabachnick, B. G., & Fidell, L. S. (1996). *Using multivariate statistics* (3rd ed). New York: HarperCollins.

Tufte, E. (1974). *Data analysis for politics and policy.* New York: Prentice-Hall.

Turner, C. E., Ku, L., Rogers, S. M., Lindberg, L. D., Pleck, J. H., & Sonenstein, F. L. (1998). Adolescent sexual behavior, drug use, and violence: Increased reporting with computer survey technology. *Science, 280,* 867–874.

Wallack, L. (1989). Mass communication and health promotion: A critical perspective. In R. E. Rice & C. K. Atkin (Eds.), *Public communication campaigns* (pp. 353–367). Newbury Park, CA: Sage.

Wright, D. L., Aquilino, W. S., & Supple, A. J. (1998). A comparison of computer-assisted and paper-and-pencil self-administered questionnaires in a survey on smoking, alcohol, and drug use. *Public Opinion Quarterly, 62,* 331–353.

Zastowny, T. R., Adams, E. H., Black, G. S., Lawton, K. B., & Wilder, A. L. (1993). Sociodemographic and attitudinal correlates of alcohol and other drug use among children and adolescents: Analysis of a large-scale attitude tracking study. *Journal of Psychoactive Drugs, 25,* 224–237.

Zimmerman, R. S., & Vernberg, D. (1994). Models of preventive health behavior: Comparison, critique, and meta-analysis. *Advances in Medical Sociology, 4,* 45–67.

Zuckerman, M. (1979). *Sensation seeking: Beyond the optimal level of arousal.* Hillsdale, NJ: Lawrence Erlbaum Associates.

Zuckerman, M. (1990). The psychobiology of sensation seeking. *Journal of Personality, 58,* 313–345.

Zuckerman, M. (1994). *Behavioral expression and biosocial bases of sensation seeking.* New York: Cambridge University Press.

Zuckerman, M. (1996). The psychobiological model for impulsive unsocialized sensation seeking: A comparative approach. *Neuropsychobiology, 34,* 125–129.

3

Long-Term Effectiveness of the Early Mass Media Led Antismoking Campaigns in Australia

John P. Pierce
University of California Cancer Center

Petra Macaskill
University of Sydney

David Hill
Centre for Behavioral Research in Cancer
Melbourne, Australia

Smoking prevalence in Australia did not decline much from 1974 to 1983 according to age-standardized comparisons (Hill, White, & Gray, 1980; Pierce, Aldrich, Hanratty, Dwyer, & Hill, 1987), in contrast to the pattern seen in other Western developed countries (Pierce, 1989). For this reason, a number of individual states in Australia introduced a coordinated campaign approach to promoting change in health behavior, as pioneered in cardiovascular disease by the Stanford Three Community Project (Farquhar et al., 1977) and the North Karelia Project (Salonen, Puska, Kottke, & Tuomilehto, 1981).

In 1983 in Sydney and in 1984 in Melbourne, the State Health Departments established antismoking steering committees composed of personnel from the health departments, the major voluntary organizations, health professional societies, and university public health departments. Television commercials were developed to motivate smokers to quit smoking and to set the agenda for professionals whom the campaign team hoped to involve in promoting nonsmoking, given the evidence of the effectiveness of medical advice (Kottke et al., 1988; Russell et al., 1979; Wilson et al.,

1988). The effectiveness of school education programs (Connell, Turner, & Mason, 1985) also made establishing such programs a high priority within the community. Although the campaign committees in both cities shared campaign materials and ideas, the actual activities undertaken within each city were dictated by the perceived local needs and opportunities.

A detailed evaluation was undertaken of the first year of the campaign in Sydney using Melbourne, which did not have a campaign that year, as a reference community (Dwyer, Pierce, Hannam, & Burke, 1986; Pierce et al., 1986). More than 80% of the population of Sydney remembered the television commercials. After these commercials were aired, use of services such as a telephone quit line and enrollment in cessation classes increased. The campaign was also associated with higher levels of intention to quit in Sydney, a variable that had previously been shown to be associated with actual quitting (Pierce, Dwyer, Chamberlain, Aldrich, & Shelley, 1987). Changes in smoking prevalence during the first campaign year were assessed by self-reported smoking behavior (after validation with salivary cotinine; Pierce et al., 1987) from both cross-sectional and longitudinal surveys. No decrease was seen in the reference city, Melbourne. The pooled estimate of the difference in smoking prevalence attributable to the campaign was 2.8% (95% confidence interval = .5, 5.1) (Dwyer et al., 1986).

Since 1984, the campaigns have continued in both Melbourne and Sydney, spearheaded each year by commercials shown on prime time television for 6 to 8 weeks during the winter months. This chapter assesses the long-term effect of this approach to reducing the prevalence of smoking. Data from both cities was used to determine whether the following key intermediate goals were achieved:

- High public awareness of the campaign during each campaign year.
- A strengthening of the stand of health professionals, particularly physicians, against smoking.
- An increased proportion of the smoking population who both believed that smoking was harming their own health and also was being influenced by their social network to quit smoking.

The effectiveness of the campaign was assessed by using self-reported smoking data from 1981 to 1987 for each city.

METHODS

General Design

This project has a before and after design in each of two intervention cities with a temporal lag of 12 months between the onset of the intervention in the second city. Prevalence data were obtained for several years before the onset of the intervention, as well as for the duration of the campaign. In 1983 and 1986, more detailed questions about health beliefs, intentions, and social influences were asked in each city. Small random surveys were undertaken approximately 2 months after the completion of each component of the television campaign to assess recall of commercials.

Mass Media Used in Campaigns

Television. In both Sydney and Melbourne, television advertising made up about two thirds of the media budget for the campaigns. Typically, commercial spots were purchased during prime or fringe time for approximately 4 of 8 weeks at the start of the campaign year. Approximately 40 spots per week were shown during a schedule designed to ensure at least 50% market penetration in the Sydney and Melbourne metropolitan areas during each year of the campaign.

Production of commercials followed research on messages that were likely to be effective among the target audience. These commercials were designed to use strong visual images of the health consequences of smoking. Further, they sought an emotive response among the audience to ensure attention and to maximize the likelihood that viewers would reassess the hazards of smoking and then possibly quit in the near future (for description, see Table 3.1) (Cook & Campbell, 1979; McGuire, 1981; Pierce, Dwyer, Chamberlain, et al., 1987; Pierce, Dwyer, DiGiusto, et al., 1987). All of the commercials ended with a "Quit line" telephone number that people could call 24 hours a day to hear a recorded informative and encouraging message about quitting smoking.

Other Mass Media. A concerted effort was made to coordinate all mass media advertising around a central theme that was dictated by the message in the major television commercial being run at the time. For billboard advertising, a simple message from the television commercial was displayed at numerous sites, especially those near mass transit locations. Advertising in newspapers included the normal large advertisement and, in Sydney, a section was purchased for journalistic coverage of smoking-related events and issues. Antismoking skits by major personalities complemented the normal quit smoking commercials on the radio. In addition, the campaign generated many news releases and events that resulted in substantial news coverage in all the mass media.

Physicians' Offices

In both cities, there was active collaboration with the Australian Medical Association to develop and distribute printed resources that physicians could use to encourage and help their patients quit smoking. In Mel-

TABLE 3.1
TV Commercials by City and Year

Commercial	Year			
	1983	1984	1985	1986
"Sponge"[a]	S	S, M	M	
"I've had enough"[b]	S	S, M	M	
"Mrs. Holden"[c]		S		
"Yul Brynner"[d]				S, M
"Heartbeat"[e]			M	M
"Stairs"[f]				M
"Mirrors"[g]			S	
"Tough guy"[h]			S	
"Mates"[i]			S	

Note. S = Sydney; M = Melbourne.
[a]an analogy between a sponge and a lung soaking up air
[b]smoking histories of three people outlining reason for quitting included ashtray on a girl's face and modeling of calling the Quitline
[c]a laryngectomy patient (with subtitles) outlining her smoking-related problems with communications
[d]a posthumous exhortation, "Whatever you do, don't smoke."
[e]cardiograph used to outline smoking effects on circulation
[f]mirror distortion to reduce fears of weight gain and stress with quitting
[g]linked smoking to shortening a young girl's life
[h]teens, visiting cancer patient, review smoking-related disease
[i]outlined social problems teens might face if they smoke

bourne, a special training videotape about smoking was produced and shown widely to family physicians. In Sydney, a special training program was available to family physicians to enable them more effectively to counsel their patients to stop smoking (Richmond & Webster, 1986).

Schools

In Sydney, two school programs were developed: a comprehensive kindergarten through 12th-grade curriculum and a grade-specific peer- or teacher-led curriculum. By 1986, 80% of all schools in Sydney had at least one person who was trained by the campaign team in conducting the program of choice for that school. Of the schools, 64% (88% of the 73% who responded) reported using these materials during the 1986 academic year. Further, the campaign team sponsored theater performances, rock concerts, and sports activities with antismoking themes.

In Melbourne, kindergarten through 12th-grade curriculum resources on smoking were made available to all schools, and project workers encouraged and helped teachers to use these resources. By 1986, in sample surveys of schoolchildren in both Sydney and Melbourne, more than 70% of 12- to 15-year-olds reported receiving at least minimal health education about smoking during the year (Salonen, Kottke, Jacobs, & Hannan, 1986).

Other Community Activities

Each year, the campaigns either organized smoking cessation clinics or informed the population in each city about the availability of clinics. Training programs were available for health educators who might be appointed to local government or other affiliated positions. In addition, quit smoking display stands were regularly erected and staffed in shopping malls and at public fairs.

Assessing Smoking Prevalence

Between 1981 and 1987, 68,136 males and 70,634 females age 16 and over from the suburbs of metropolitan Sydney and Melbourne were interviewed in their homes as part of an ongoing weekly survey. Sampling procedures, reported in detail elsewhere (Dwyer et al., 1986), involved selecting a household starting point at random from the electoral roll (in Australia, it is compulsory for citizens over age 17 to be registered on the electoral roll). Field interviewers proceeded to move from house to house in a clockwise direction until they obtained a cluster of 10 interviews from separate households. Within the household, the youngest person age 16 and over of a selected sex was interviewed. The resulting sample has been shown to be representative of the population on major sociodemographic variables (Dwyer et al., 1986).

Smokers were defined as those who responded positively to questions on whether they smoked factory-made cigarettes, roll-your-own cigarettes, cigars, or a pipe. In two separate subsamples, self-reported smoking was validated with biochemical analysis of saliva for the presence of cotinine (Pierce, Dwyer, DiGiusto, et al., 1987).

Measuring Campaign Exposure

For each year of the campaign, recall of the television commercials was assessed on separate random samples of the population of at least 1,000 persons in the 3 months following the completion of the television phase of the campaign. Shortly after the completion of each annual television campaign, a subsample of persons in Sydney was shown a set of six still photographs taken from the commercials. They were first asked whether they had seen the commercial and, if they responded yes, what the message was (care was taken that no "giveaway" words or cigarettes appeared in the photographs). In Melbourne, the respondents were asked whether they had seen any television commercials against smoking recently. The interviewer then probed all positive responses and recorded details of the message recalled.

Assessing Predictors of Quitting

In 1983 and 1986, additional random samples of the population of Sydney and Melbourne were surveyed. The Sydney survey included 271 smokers in 1983 and 557 smokers in 1986. The Melbourne sample included 217 smokers in 1983 and 550 smokers in 1986. Smoking respondents were asked to agree or disagree with a set of statements previously shown to be scales representing health beliefs and social influences (Pierce, Dwyer, Chamberlain, et al., 1987). The items in the health belief scale were: "Smoking cigarettes doesn't greatly affect my health," "The problems with smoking only affect heavy smokers," and "I'd rather enjoy life as a smoker than live a little longer without cigarettes."

The items in the social influence scale were: "I find that my smoking annoys people around me who don't smoke," "What I dislike about smoking is the smell that it leaves on clothes," "All the physicians that I know are strongly against smoking," "My close friends would prefer that I didn't smoke," and "I find that people are talking a lot more about smoking and the problems of giving up." Internal consistency reliability (Cronbach's alpha) on these scales has been previously reported at .57 on the health benefit scale and .56 on the social influence scale (Pierce, Dwyer, Chamberlain, et al., 1987).

Statistical Analysis of Prevalence

For the purpose of analysis, data were grouped into intervals of 6 months for each city and were adjusted for age and sex to the estimated population of Sydney in 1986 using direct standardization. Salonen et al. (1986) suggested using multiple linear regression models to evaluate the effectiveness of community-based intervention programs by testing for interaction effects between the type of community (intervention or reference) and the timing of the onset of the intervention effect. In this study, which lacked a nonintervention community, the following simplified form of the suggested model was fitted to each of the data sets.

$$P = \beta_0 + \beta_1\, C + \beta_2\, T + \beta_3\, CT + \beta_4\, S + \text{error}$$

where P represents the prevalence of smoking;

C is a binary indicator variable representing whether the data are from the precampaign ($C = 0$) or the postcampaign ($C = 1$) period;

T is the trend variable for time;

S is a binary indicator of season with a value of 1 for the first 6 months and −1 for the second 6 months of each year.

Using this model, β_0 is an estimate of the expected prevalence at the start of the campaign ($T = 0$) given the underlying trend in the precampaign period. β_1 is an estimate of the immediate effect of the intervention (as such an effect was demonstrated in McGuire, 1981). β_2 estimates the underlying trend in prevalence over the whole time period, and β_3 estimates the change in this underlying trend associated with the commencement of the campaigns. The coefficient β_4 provides an estimate of the effect of seasonal variation on the data. For each analysis, a model that included all the explanatory variables already described (full model) was fitted. A parsimonious model (adjusted for seasonal effect) was then developed by using backward elimination to remove variables other than S, with the chosen level of significance set at .05. This reduced model identifies the pattern of change in prevalence in relation to the timing of the campaigns. A series of curvilinear (polynomial) models were also fitted to the data. Quadratic and cubic models were compared with the linear parsimonious models described earlier to assess whether the more complex models fit the data better.

RESULTS

Population Knowledge of the Campaign

Awareness about the antismoking campaign was assessed by asking people in each city what they recalled about the most public aspect of the campaign, the television commercials (Table 3.2). For all the major commercials in these campaigns, there was little difference between the recall of the commercial and identification of an appropriate antismoking message. In both cities, more than two thirds of the community knew that an antismoking campaign existed in the years that such campaigns were conducted.

Action by Physicians

During the campaign, physicians' roles were assessed by asking respondents how strongly their physicians were against smoking; these data were them divided by age and sex for each city in 1983 and 1986 (Fig. 3.1). Be-

TABLE 3.2
Percentage of Males and Females Who Recalled
Television Advertising in Sydney and Melbourne

Year	% Males	% Females	N
Sydney (aided by picture prompt)			
1983	84	84	2,970
1984	72	80	1,046
1985*	79	76	996
1986	92	94	457
Melbourne (unaided)			
1984	70	67	886
1985	73	68	1,818
1986	68	67	1,830

*Only 14- to 19-year olds.

EFFECTIVENESS OF COMMUNITY ANTISMOKING CAMPAIGNS

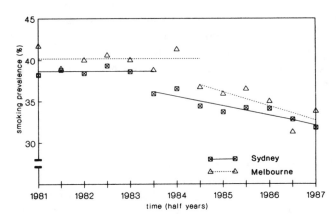

FIG. 3.1. Age-standardized smoking prevalence for males in Sydney and
Melbourne, 1981–1987.

fore the campaign, only 15% of males and females over age 40 in Sydney
thought their physicians were strongly against smoking. By 1986, this had
increased dramatically to 47% for males and 50% for females. In those
under age 40 in Sydney, this proportion increased from 36% to 48% in
males and from 28% to 46% in females. In Melbourne males, this proportion increased from 35% to 41% in those under age 40 and from 28% to
35% in those over age 40. In Melbourne females, this proportion increased from 27% to 47% in those under age 40 and from 33% to 37% in
those over age 40.

The Health Benefit/Social Influence Variable

A previous study (Pierce, Dwyer, Chamberlain, et al., 1987) demonstrated that only a combination of personal beliefs about smoking and the environmental influences to quit was associated with an increased likelihood to quit. This proportion reporting both social influence and health beliefs was low in those over age 40 in Sydney in 1983 (males, 10%; females, 12%). By 1986, this proportion had increased to 29% in males and 27% in females. In those under age 40 in Sydney, males increased from 34% to 53% and females increased from 30% to 44%. In those over age 40 in Melbourne, males increased from 21% to 29% and females increased from 22% to 32%. In those under age 40 in Melbourne, males increased from 30% to 43% and females increased from 31% to 41%.

Smoking Prevalence

The full and parsimonious statistical models fitted to the age-standardized data for men and women were considered separately for each city. For men, these models fit the data very well, explaining 96% of the variation in Sydney and 91% in Melbourne. For females, the best models did not fit quite so well, explaining 72% of the variation in the Sydney sample and 79% in the Melbourne sample. However, the most parsimonious model for the Melbourne women sample was not consistent with the other models. A consistent model fitted almost as well and explained 68% of the variation.

Figures 3.1 and 3.2 are graphical representations of the trends identified in the parsimonious models in conjunction with the observed data. For this presentation, the consistent model was chosen for Melbourne women.

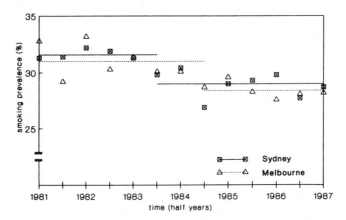

FIG. 3.2. Age-standardized smoking prevalence for females in Sydney and Melbourne, 1981–1987.

TABLE 3.3
Statistical Models for Smoking Among Males and Females in Sydney

Sydney		Full Model Estimate (SE)		Parsimonious Model Estimate (SE)	
Males	β_0	39.06	(.67)	38.67	(.28)
	β_1	−2.91	(.79)	−2.52	(.49)
	β_2	.13	(.20)		
	β_3	−.69	(.22)	−.58	(.10)
	β_4	−.04	(.18)	−.04	(.17)
		(R^2 = .96, 8df)		(R^2 = .96, 9df)	
Females	β_0	31.69	(1.02)	31.56	(.42)
	β_1	−2.11	(1.20)	−2.61	(.54)
	β_2	.05	(.31)		
	β_3	−.23	(.34)		
	β_4	.38	(.27)	.32	(.25)
		(R^2 = .77, 8df)		(R^2 = .72, 10df)	

Thus, the best estimate of smoking prevalence among Sydney men (Table 3.3) indicated that prevalence did not change in the 3 years before the campaign (June 1983) and was 38.7% (β_0 in the parsimonious model). From 1981 to 1987, there was no significant underlying trend in smoking prevalence other than that associated with the campaign. The introduction of the campaign coincided with an estimated immediate drop in smoking prevalence of 2.5 percentage points in that 6-month period. Continuation of the campaign was associated with a further drop of 1.12 percentage points per year ($2 - \beta_3$). These estimates are consistent with those provided by the full model.

For women, smoking prevalence had again been constant during the years before the campaign and was 31.6% in Sydney and 29.8% in Melbourne. In Sydney, there was an immediate drop of 2.6 percentage points associated with the introduction of the campaign, but smoking prevalence did not significantly decline in the later years of the campaign. Again, this estimate is consistent with that from the saturated model.

Men in Melbourne responded similarly to those in Sydney. As Table 3.4 shows, the expected prevalence of smoking at the beginning of the campaign (June 1984) was 40.1% (β_0). Again, there was no underlying trend. With the start of the campaign, there was an immediate drop of 2.9 percentage points. A further decline of 1.9 percentage points per year occurred in conjunction with the continued campaign. Once again, these estimates are consistent with those from the full model.

In Melbourne, two models fitted the data and, as indicated earlier, Model 2 is the preferred one. Smoking prevalence prior to the campaign was 30.9%. The immediate effect of the campaign was a 2.5 percentage

TABLE 3.4
Statistical Models for Smoking Among Males and Females in Melbourne

Melbourne		Full Model Estimate (SE)			Parsimonious Model Estimate (SE)	
Males	$\hat{\beta}_0$	39.89	(1.00)		40.12	(.42)
	$\hat{\beta}_1$	−2.64	(1.33)		−2.87	(.93)
	$\hat{\beta}_2$	−.06	(.22)			
	$\hat{\beta}_3$	−.89	(.36)		−.95	(.27)
	$\hat{\beta}_4$	.58	(.34)		.57	(.32)
		(R^2 = .91, 8df)			(R^2 = .91, 9df)	
				Model 1	*Model 2*	
Females	$\hat{\beta}_0$	29.77	(.83)	29.40 (.26)	30.93	(.41)
	$\hat{\beta}_1$	−.53	(1.10)		−2.52	(.61)
	$\hat{\beta}_2$	−.29	(.19)	−.37 (.07)		
	$\hat{\beta}_3$	−.04	(.30)			
	$\hat{\beta}_4$	.64	(.28)	.65 (.25)	.56	(.30)
		(R^2 = .80, 8df)		(R^2 = .79, 10df)	(R^2 = .68)	

point drop in smoking prevalence, again with no subsequent decline associated with the continued campaign. However, in this instance, the estimate from the full model is very different, highlighting the uncertainty that exists as to the true underlying model.

Comparison with Other Models

The goodness of fit of these parsimonious linear models was compared with quadratic and cubic models. In each case, the best-fit linear model was a superior fit to either of the alternative models, except for Melbourne women, again emphasizing the problems in interpreting this set of data.

DISCUSSION

This study suggests that smoking prevalence in the two major Australian capital cities did not decline prior to the campaign, as previously observed for the period from 1974 to 1980 for Australia as a whole (Hill et al., 1980; Pierce, 1989; Pierce, Aldrich, et al., 1987). The mass media-led antismoking campaigns coincided with a marked drop in smoking prevalence during the 6-month period immediately following the start of the campaign for all persons in Sydney and for men in Melbourne (the effect on Melbourne women is less clear). The estimated size of this immediate effect was 2.6 percentage points in Sydney. A larger 2.9% effect of the antismoking campaign was seen among Melbourne men 12 months later. If the model is accepted that suggests women in Sydney and Melbourne reacted similarly to the antismoking campaign, then the campaign immediately reduced smoking prevalence in Melbourne by 2.5%, an amount similar to the estimates of the effect obtained in both men and women for Sydney one year earlier. In the alternative model, women in Melbourne were the only group who recorded a decreasing prevalence of smoking during the precampaign period. Given that there was no downward trend in smoking prevalence throughout the 1970s (Hill et al., 1980; Pierce, 1989; Pierce, Aldrich, et al., 1987), this model must be considered less plausible.

For men in both cities, continued antismoking campaigns were associated with an average continued decrease in smoking prevalence of approximately 1.5% per year. The situation for women is less clear, but suggests that the continued campaigns in Sydney and Melbourne were not associated with any further decrease in smoking prevalence among women.

This analysis of changes in community smoking prevalence does not consider the effect that such campaigns may have on uptake of smoking. In any given year, the influence of new smokers between age 16 and 20 (the teen years included in this data set) on the overall prevalence will be small. Before any conclusions concerning the effectiveness of these campaigns can be made, changes in the uptake of smoking among teenagers need to be explored. However, even with the effect on uptake of smoking being unresolved, this study supports conducting coordinated mass media antismoking campaigns (using purchased television time) as an effective way to reduce smoking prevalence in the community. Whether conducting campaigns for up to 4 consecutive years is cost-effective will be the topic of another discussion.

ACKNOWLEDGMENTS

The Quit For Life project in Sydney was managed by the following Steering Committee: Dr. A. Cripps (Chair), J. Carson, G. Frape, B. Higham, T. Carroll, S. Chapman, T. Slevin, D. Waddell, J. Phillips (all New South Wales Department of Health), T. Dwyer and J. Pierce (School of Public Health, University of Sydney), J. Shaw, S. Walker (National Heart Foundation), E. Henry, G. Sarfaty, P. Goldsmith (New South Wales Cancer Council), D. Gadiel (Hospital Contributions Fund), B. Herriot (American Medical Association), I. Mullins Pharmacy Guild), A. Colvin, P. Murray (New South Wales Department of Education), and C. Ewan (University of Wollongong).

The Quit project and its evaluation in Melbourne were managed by the following committee members: N. Gray (Chair), D. Hill, D. Jolley, J. Houston, R. Borland (Anti Cancer Council of Victoria), K. McAllister, D. Reading (Victorian Smoking and Health Project), J. Maddox, J. Stephens, M. Petitt (Health Department of Victoria), D. Hunt (National Heart Foundation), and R. Robinson (Social Biology Resources Center).

We would like to thank Geoffrey Berry, Les Irwig, and Judy Simpson, Epidemiology and Biostatistics Section, Department of Public Health, University of Sydney; and Sing Kai Lo, a former member of the same department, for their helpful comments relating to this manuscript. Funding for this study was provided by the following sources: New South Wales Department of Health, the Victorian Department of Health, the Commonwealth Department of Health, the Anti-Cancer Council of Victoria, and the New South Wales Cancer Council.

REFERENCES

Connell, D. B., Turner, R. R., & Mason, F. F. (1985). Summary of the findings of the School Health Education Evaluation: Health promotion effectiveness, implementation and costs. *Journal of School Health, 55*, 316–321.

Cook, T. D., & Campbell, D. T. (1979). *Quasi-experimentation: Design and analysis issues for field settings.* Boston: Houghton Mifflin.

Dwyer, T., Pierce, J. P., Hannam, C. D., & Burke, N. (1986). Evaluation of the Sydney "Quit for life antismoking campaign: Part 2. Changes in smoking prevalence. *Medical Journal of Australia, 144*, 344–347.

Farquhar, J. W., Maccoby, N., Wood, P. D., Alexander, J. K., Breitrose, H., Brown, B. W., Jr., Haskell, W. J., McAlister, A. J., Meyer, A. J., Nash, J. D., et al. (1977). Community education for cardiovascular health. *Lancet, 1*, 1192–1195.

Hill, D. J., White, V. M., & Gray, N. J. (1980). Measures of tobacco smoking in Australia 1974–1986 by means of a standard method. *Medical Journal of Australia, 149*, 10–12.

Kottke, T. E., Battista, R. N., DeFriese, G. H., & Brekke, M. L. (1988). Attributes of successful smoking cessation interventions in medical practice: Meta analysis of 39 controlled trials. *Journal of the American Medical Association, 259*, 2883–2889.

McGuire, W. J. (1985). Attitudes and attitude change. In G. Lindzey & E. Aronson (Eds.), *Handbook of social psychology* (3rd ed.). New York: Random House.

Pierce, J. P. (1989). International comparisons of trends in cigarette smoking prevalence. *American Journal of Public Health, 79*, 1–6.

Pierce, J. P., Aldrich, R. N., Hanratty, S., Dwyer, T., & Hill, D. (1987). Uptake and quitting smoking trends in Australia 1974–1984. *Preventive Medicine, 16*, 252–260.

Pierce, J. P., Dwyer, T., Chamberlain, A., Aldrich, R. N., & Shelley, J. M. (1987). Targeting the smoker in an anti-smoking campaign. *Preventive Medicine, 16*, 816–824.

Pierce, J. P., Dwyer, T., DiGiusto, F., Carpenter, T., Hannam, C., Amin, A., Yong, C., Sarfaty, G., Shaw, J., & Burke, N. (1987). Cotinine validation of self-reported smoking in commercially run community surveys. *Journal of Chronic Disease, 40,* 689–695.

Pierce, J. P., Dwyer, T., Frape, G., Chapman, S., Chamberlain, A., & Burke, N. (1986). Evaluation of the Sydney "Quit for life" antismoking campaign: Part 1. Achievement of intermediate goals. *Medical Journal of Australia, 144,* 341–347.

Richmond, R., & Webster, I. (1986). Three year evaluation a programme by general practitioners to help patients to stop smoking. *British Medical Journal, 292,* 803–806.

Russell, M. A. H., Wilson, C., Taylor, C., & Baker, C. D. (1979). Effect of general practitioner's advice against smoking. *British Medical Journal, 2,* 231–235.

Salonen, J. T., Kottke, T. E., Jacobs, D. J., & Hannan, P. R. (1986). Analysis of community-based cardiovascular disease prevention studies—evaluation issues in the North Karelia project and the Minnesota Heart Health Program. *International Journal of Epidemiology, 15,* 176182.

Salonen, J. T., Puska, P., Kottke, T. E., & Tuomilehto, J. (1981). Changes in smoking serum cholesterol and blood pressure levels during a community-based cardiovascular disease prevention program—The North Karelia Project. *American Journal of Epidemiology, 114,* 81–94.

Wilson, D. M., Taylor, W., Gilbert, R., Best, J. A., Lindsay, E. A., Willms, D. G., & Singer, J. A. (1988). A randomized trial of a family physician intervention for smoking cessation. *Journal of the American Medical Association, 260,* 1570–1574.

EVALUATIONS OF
FULL-SCALE INTERVENTIONS

The Contributions of Public Health Education Toward the Reduction of Cardiovascular Disease Mortality: Experiences from the National High Blood Pressure Education Program

Edward J. Roccella
National Heart, Lung and Blood Institute

Public Law 92-423, the National Heart, Blood Vessel, Lung and Blood Act of September 1972, stated that "the (National Heart, Lung and Blood) Institute . . . shall conduct a program to provide the public and health professionals with health information . . . special emphasis shall be placed upon . . . diet, exercise . . . hypertension, weight control, and other factors affecting the prevention of arteriosclerosis and other cardiovascular diseases." In 1997, the National High Blood Pressure Education Program (NHBPEP) celebrated its 25th anniversary. This chapter describes how the NHBPEP has addressed this mandate for the last quarter century and reviews selected functional characteristics of the public health education campaign.

The NHBPEP is a natural extension of the biomedical research spectrum (Fig. 4.1). As an integral component of the spectrum, the primary function of the program is to translate research results into usable knowledge for clinicians and public health programs. The NHBPEP is grounded in a strong scientific base. Science drives the entire program and shapes the program's activities, including the public communications component. The NHBPEP is oftentimes one of the first points of contact between research study results and the public, thus it is highly visible. Therefore, the NHBPEP communications component in particular never advances beyond the available scientific information. In this manner, the program enjoys the

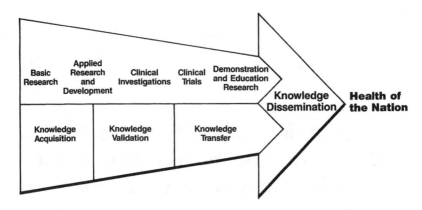

FIG. 4.1. National Heart, Lung and Blood Institute biomedical research
programs.

reputation of being a reliable and credible source of information. The
NHBPEP has a history of constantly reviewing data and information in order to reaffirm its educational messages, determine the effectiveness of program interventions, and plan future activities. Unlike rigorous scientific
studies, the NHBPEP does not have a fixed protocol and does not test pre-
determined hypotheses. Rather, it develops a series of plans as guides or
road maps used to reach the program's objectives. The plans are adjusted
or altered, or paradigm shifts and midcourse corrections are made that re-
set the direction it will take, the activity it will pursue, or the educational
message it must convey in order to reach the NHBPEP objectives.

SEGMENTING THE AUDIENCE

One educational message has never been used simultaneously to reach the
many different types of hypertensive patients and the heterogeneous mix of
the general public. The program partitions the target audience in several
ways. People having high blood pressure are divided into two groups,
those aware that they have hypertension and those not yet aware. The
aware group is further categorized into (a) people already in treatment
with controlled hypertension, so reinforcement advice can be offered that
attempts to keep them there; (b) those who have dropped out of care and
who must be convinced to resume treatment; (c) those being treated but
still unsuccessful in controlling their hypertension; and (d) those who never
began therapy and must be persuaded to do so.

The public without hypertension consists of multiple target groups.
Some are relatives and friends of a hypertensive patient. They can reinforce

appropriate action. Some will later develop high blood pressure and must be prepared to deal with it. Still others are candidates to take action to avoid developing hypertension altogether, and should be taught how to do this.

The general public and the hypertensive population have been segmented by age, gender, ethnic group, socioeconomic, and other demographic factors. For all these groups, hypertension has a different meaning and represents a different challenge. The educational messages for each group, the actions required, the skills needed to be learned, and the communications channels used by each may be different. Two examples are provided. Figure 4.2 shows a print message designed to reach middle-aged women whose preoccupation with other aspects of life may cause them to neglect getting their blood pressure checked. Figure 4.3 shows a print message that attempts to reach younger African American males who are less likely to visit a physician than the general population.

OUTREACH

With so many target audiences, a variety of dissemination channels must be employed to publicize the agreed on recommendations and to persuade a variety of program partners to promote the agreed on recommendations. Messages and material addressed to all components of mass media (i.e., television, radio, print ads, posters, billboards, booklets, and pamphlets) have been produced and distributed directly. Some program partners have developed and distributed their own program material. For example, Citizens for the Treatment of High Blood Pressure, the International Society of Hypertension in Blacks, the American Medical Association, and most state health departments have developed their own print educational material and public service announcements. An innovative mass media venture was the development of a semi-preproduced television program on hypertension that has been marketed successfully to a burgeoning number of local television magazine and talk shows. This project, packaged as a kit, contained a film clip to give a national flavor, a script to be followed either verbatim or as a general guide to the local television program's host, and a set of carefully prepared questions and answers to permit open dialog between the show host and a professional guest, usually a doctor or nurse. The clinician could tailor the script to the local audience.

Another visible device to raise public and patient awareness and to sustain interest has been National High Blood Pressure Month held every May. In 1990, 100,000 High Blood Pressure Month Kits were distributed to many professional organizations, state health departments, and community agencies. Each kit contains suggested newspaper articles, press releases, camera-ready artwork, and activities for the agencies to feature dur-

FIG. 4.2.   Print message designed to reach middle-aged women.

ing May, as well suggestions for posters and print ads. The organizations are encouraged to develop their media stories from the material and information, customize it to their target audiences and put their own name on it. In this way, local organizations increase their own visibility and work harder to disseminate materials and deliver the message.

FIG. 4.3.   Print message designed to reach younger African-American males.

PROGRAM IMPACT

During the last quarter century, the nation has experienced some remarkable results in preventing and controlling high blood pressure and reducing the consequences from this condition. Without a control group, any major national health education program cannot assess the exact magnitude of the program's impact. However, there have been significant changes in the hypertension control process in the United States associated with the activities of the NHBPEP that cannot be ignored.

Trends in Public Knowledge Regarding Hypertension

Data from national surveys of the public's knowledge, attitudes, and reported health behavior indicate that the proportion of respondents knowing that "hypertension" means "high blood pressure" increased from 24% in 1973 to 55% in 1985 (Roccella, 1985). This was an important concept for the program because early on it was determined that many individuals felt hypertension meant "nervous" tension, and because they considered themselves calm and not nervous, they could not have hypertension. In addition, some hypertensive patients only took their antihypertensive medication when they were tense or nervous. It was important for the program to dispel these myths and appropriate education efforts were developed. There is additional evidence that the public's knowledge about hypertension has increased. In 1972, 24% of the public knew the relation of high blood pressure to stroke, and 24% knew of the relation between high blood pressure and heart disease (Roccella, 1985). The program's public education campaigns worked to inform the population about the relation between high blood pressure and these diseases. In 1985, 77% and 92% of the public, respectively, knew of the relations between high blood pressure, stroke, and heart disease (National Heart, Lung, and Blood Institute, 1981; U.S. Department of Health and Human Services, 1986).

Trends in Physician Visits

Statistics on annual patient visits to private practice physicians are collected by IMS America and reported in the *National Disease and Therapeutic Index* (Fig. 4.4). Figure 4.4 indicates patient visits for hypertensive disease (hypertension and hypertensive heart disease) increased during the 1970s until 1976, when it began to decline following the national trend for decreasing all visits to physicians. Then, in 1979, visits to physicians for hypertension increased in a virtually linear fashion. At that time, the National Heart, Lung and Blood Institute released the results of the Hypertension Detection and Follow Up Program. This clinical trial demon-

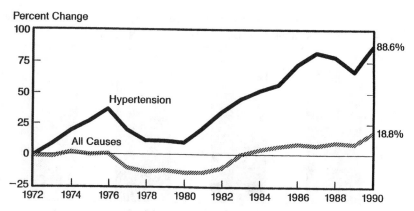

FIG. 4.4. Patient visits to doctors, all causes and for hypertension. Data from National Disease and Therapeutic Index, IMS America.

strated that treating mild hypertension reduced morbidity and mortality. The program exerted a special effort to persuade the public to have their blood pressure checked, and they responded. In 1990, Americans made about 89 million visits to physicians for high blood pressure, a 96% increase within the previous two decades, whereas visits to physicians for all causes remained relatively stable. The increased number of visits to physicians for hypertension is another indicator that the public has heard the educational messages to visit their physicians for high blood pressure.

Trends in Awareness, Treatment, and Control of Hypertension

In addition to data regarding the public's knowledge about hypertension, trend data regarding awareness, treatment, and control of high blood pressure has also been of interest in measuring the program effectiveness. Figure 4.5 describes blood pressure levels at 160/95 mm Hg level for four time period estimates. The data are derived from the National Health and Nutrition Examination Surveys (NHANES) conducted by the National Center for Health Statistics, part of the Centers for Disease Control and Prevention. In the NHANES survey conducted during 1971–1972, 51% of the hypertensive population was aware of its condition. In 1974–1975, this figure increased to 64%. During the NHANES 2 survey conducted from 1976 to 1980, 73% of the hypertensive population was aware of its condition. Provisional data from the Third National Health and Nutrition Examination Surveys (NHANES 3) conducted from 1988 to 1991 showed 84% of the hypertensive population was aware of its condition. Similarly, treatment rates (i.e., treating hypertensive patients with drugs) increased from 36% of the hypertensive population in 1971–1972 to 73% during

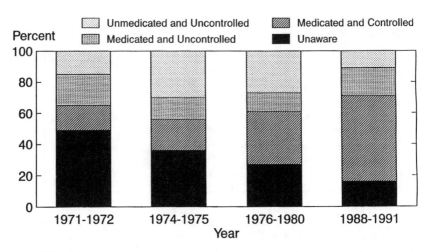

FIG. 4.5. Awareness, treatment, and control among hypertensives in the U.S. from the National Health and Nutrition Examination Surveys (NHANES).

the 1988–1991 NHANES survey. Control rates (i.e., lowering high blood pressure to less than 160/95 mm Hg) have also increased in a remarkable fashion from 16% of the hypertensive population controlling its condition reported in the NHANES 1971–1972 survey to 55% controlling its condition in the NHANES 1988–1991 survey.

Reductions in Mean Arterial Blood Pressure

Mean (average) blood pressures among the entire population compared in four national health surveys conducted between 1960 and 1991 (Fig. 4.6) suggest a reduction of 10 mm Hg systolic and 5 mm Hg diastolic pressure during this time period (Burt et al., 1995). This is additional evidence that the population has heard and acted on NHBPEP messages. These shifts in the population's distribution of blood pressure suggest that some hypertension is now being prevented. It has been estimated that reductions of mean arterial pressure of 3 mm Hg in the population would reduce 8% of strokes, 5% of coronary, and 4% of all deaths (Stamler, 1991).

Trends in Mortality Rates

A critical criterion in evaluating the national effort to control hypertension is the reduction in mortality rates. Since the NHBPEP was initiated, there has been a remarkable decline in age-adjusted death rates for stroke and coronary heart disease (Fig. 4.7). Although death rates for cardiovascular disease in general have been on a downward trend since the 1950s, coro-

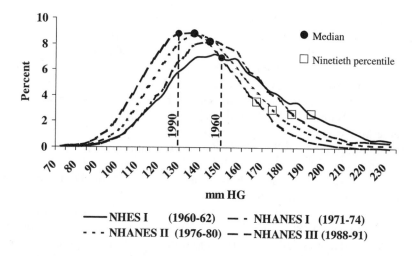

FIG. 4.6.   Smoothed weighted frequency distribution, median and 90th percentile of systolic blood pressure (SBP) in the United States, 1960–1991. Data from CDC and NCHS.

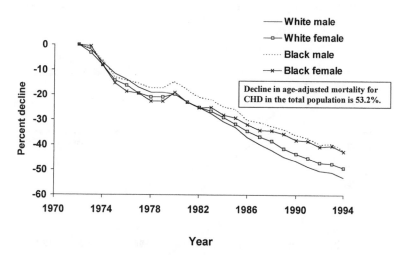

FIG. 4.7.   Percent decline in age-adjusted mortality rates for CHD by sex and race in the United States, 1972–1994. Prepared by the NHLBI using data from *Vital Statistics of the United States*, National Statistics. Age-adjusted to the 1940 U.S. census population.

nary heart disease mortality did not sharply decline until the 1970s, when it fell 27% between 1972 and 1982 (the first decade of the program). A more precipitous drop (44%) in death rate from stroke occurred during the same time period. Since the inception of the program, age-adjusted coronary heart disease mortality has declined by 53% and stroke mortality by 60%. The declines are real and are seen in both genders in African Americans and in Whites (Fig. 4.8) (Fifth Report, 1993). Because coronary heart disease and stoke account for almost one half of all deaths in the United States annually, this decline has had a substantial impact on the life expectancy and is one of the most gratifying of recent American health trends.

When a regression line of best fit is computed from the age-adjusted mortality rates during 1960–1972 and then cast forward to 1990, expected rates for age-adjusted stroke mortality can be determined (Fig. 4.9). In the year 1990 alone, 77, 500 Americans were alive that were expected to die from a stroke. This is in addition to those who did not have the event because their blood pressure was controlled (116,000 people), plus beneficial effects hypertension control had on the prevention of or reduction of heart failure, myocardial infarction, end stage kidney disease, retinopathy, and peripheral vascular disease. If only half of these projected stroke deaths alone were averted from just this one year because of better blood pressure control, then the effort in this public health education program has been well worth the investment (Roccella & Lenfant, 1992).

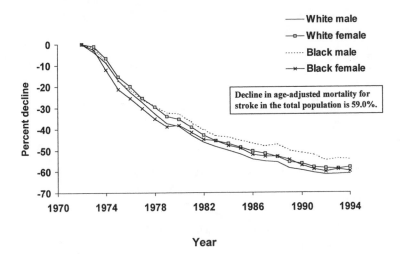

FIG. 4.8. Percent decline in age-adjusted mortality rates for stroke by sex and race, United States, 1972–1994. Prepared by the NHLBI using data from *Vital Statistics of the United States*, National Center for Health Statistics. Age-adjusted to the 1940 U.S. census population.

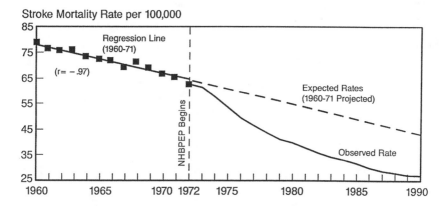

FIG. 4.9. Age-adjusted stroke mortality rates: Expected rates from a 1960–1971 regression line of best fit projected to 1990, and observed rates 1972–1990.

REFERENCES

Burt, V., Citler, J. A., Higgins, M. A., Horan, M. J., Labarthe, D., Whelton, P., Brown, C., & Roccella, E. J. (1995). Trends in the prevalence, awareness, treatment and control of hypertension in the adult U.S. population. *Hypertension, 26,* 60–69.

The fifth report of the joint national committee on the detection, evaluation and treatment of high blood pressure (1993). *Archives of Internal Medicine, 153*(2), 154–183.

The national disease and therapeutic index [Data reported annually]. Ambler, PA: IMS America.

National Heart, Lung, and Blood Institute (1981). *The public and high blood pressure: A second look, six year follow up survey of public knowledge and reported behavior* (DHEW Publication No. 81-2118). Washington, DC: National Heart, Lung and Blood Institute.

Roccella, E. J. (1985). Meeting the 1990 hypertension objectives for the national progress report. *Public Health Reports, 6,* 652–656.

Roccella, E. J., & Lenfant, C. (1992). Considerations regarding the cost and effectiveness of public and patient education programs. *Journal of Human Hypertension, 6,* 463–467.

Stamler, R. (1991). Implications of the intersalt study. *Hypertension, 1*(Suppl. 1), 16–20.

U.S. Department of Health and Human Services (1986). *Public perceptions of high blood pressure and sodium* (NIH Publication No. 86-2730). Washington, DC: U.S. Department of Health and Human Services, Public Health Service.

INCREASING SEAT BELT USE
IN NORTH CAROLINA

Allan F. Williams
Joann K. Wells
Insurance Institute for Highway Safety

Donald W. Reinfurt
University of North Carolina Highway Safety Research Center

Seat belt use in the United States is lower than in many other countries, even though all but two states now have laws requiring belt use. Overall use is estimated at 66%, but surveys indicate there is considerable variation in belt use among the states, with use rates ranging from 25% to 84% (National Highway Traffic Safety Administration, NHTSA, 1994). In contrast, reported use rates exceed 90% in Australia, Germany, and England (American Coalition for Traffic Safety and NHTSA, 1991; Hagenzeiker, 1991). Driver belt use in Canada averages 90%, and five provinces have belt use rates greater than 90% (Transport Canada, 1994).

Canada's successful seat belt laws provide a model for increasing belt use to very high levels. However, passage of provincial belt use laws did not initially result in high use rates. For example, British Columbia, Ontario, and Quebec enacted belt use laws in the mid-1970s, but use rates in the first few years were in the 40% to 60% range. In the early 1980s, provincial officials launched enforcement and publicity programs that substantially increased belt use (Jonah, Dawson, & Smith, 1982; Jonah & Grant, 1985; Lamb, 1982; Manduca, 1983). These programs varied, but all shared increased publicity about the importance of wearing seat belts, greatly increased enforcement of the law, and publicity aimed at heightening visibility and awareness of the intensified enforcement. Combined publicity and enforcement programs have continued in Canada to solidify and extend the belt use gains created by the initial publicity and enforcement activities, and these programs are credited with increasing seat belt use to around 90% (Dussault, 1990; Landry, 1991). Combined publicity and enforcement programs to increase seat belt use have also been successfully applied in France, the Netherlands, and New Zealand (Hagenzeiker, 1991).

Canadian-style publicity and enforcement programs have been used successfully in the United States, but these have been short-term programs conducted primarily in small or medium cities, including Elmira, New York (Williams, Lund, Preusser, & Blomberg, 1987); Albany and Greece, New York (Rood, Kraichy, & Carman, 1987); Rock Falls/Sterling, Galesburg, and Danville, Illinois (Mortimer, Goldsteen, Armstrong, & Marcina, 1990); and Modesto, California (Lund, Stuster, & Fleming, 1989). During the 1990s, the NHTSA promoted activities that encouraged belt use, with an emphasis on enforcement, which resulted in an increase in enforcement and public information activity in many states. However, there has been only limited application of this type of combined intensive and highly publicized enforcement campaigns in Canada.

North Carolina is one of the nine states with a "primary" belt use law, that is, a law that can be enforced for belt law violations alone. In states that have "secondary" laws, citations can be issued for nonuse of belts only when another traffic infraction, such as speeding, has occurred. The law was passed in spring 1985 with a 15-month warning ticket period starting in October 1985. Enforcement of the $25 citation for not using a belt did not begin until January 1987. At that time, statewide driver belt use was 78%, but it declined and stabilized at from 60% to 65% in 1992 (Reinfurt, 1994).

Increasing seat belt use in North Carolina was the initial aim of the Governor's Highway Safety Initiative, a multiyear program with the goals of reducing motor vehicle-related injuries, controlling costs, and providing a blueprint that could be followed by other states. Alcohol and other traffic law enforcement will be added in later stages of the initiative. Governor James B. Hunt officially inaugurated the program in fall 1993. The safety initiative involves a public–private partnership consisting of five groups: the North Carolina Governor's Highway Safety Program, automobile insurers and the Insurance Institute for Highway Safety, the North Carolina Insurance Commissioner's Office, NHTSA, and the University of North Carolina Highway Safety Research Center (HSRC). Funding for the program and its evaluation are provided by the automobile insurers and NHTSA.

Pilot programs designed to investigate and evaluate techniques for increasing belt use were conducted in spring 1993 in each of three North Carolina regions: the eastern coastal region (Elizabeth City), the central piedmont region (High Point), and the western mountain region (Haywood County) (Williams, Hall, Tolbert, & Wells, 1994). Each program was successful in increasing belt use. Driver belt use increased from 71% to 80% in Elizabeth City, from 67% to 81% in High Point, and from 43% to 82% in Haywood County. Information gained in the pilot programs was used in planning the statewide program. The current report examines the first two phases of the program to increase seat belt use in North Carolina statewide.

METHODS

The first statewide program took place in fall 1993, initiated in Raleigh by a news conference featuring Governor Hunt. Two weeks of public information about the importance of seat belt use and the upcoming enforcement were followed by 3 weeks of enforcement, 2 weeks without, and then 1 week with enforcement. Paid media advertisements emphasizing enforcement activities ran throughout the program. In fall 1993, informational advertisements about the program were placed in 15 major daily newspapers, once a week for 4 weeks, and there were 1,406 television and 3,154 radio spots. The general population was targeted in most of the media spots, but some were addressed specifically to young males.

More than 300 local police departments worked with county sheriff's offices and the state highway patrol during the enforcement phase. Seat belt checkpoints were the centerpiece, because of their high visibility, but roving patrols dedicated to seat belt enforcement were also employed. The checkpoints were manned primarily by police on overtime paid for with federal funds.

The second statewide seat belt program, intended as a "booster shot," replicated the fall 1993 program, but it was shortened to 3 weeks, and less media advertising was purchased. This program took place in July 1994. During the week of July 20, advertising was placed in 15 major daily newspapers, and there were 984 television and 1,470 radio spots.

To measure program effects on seat belt use, observational data were collected in November 1993 subsequent to the fall program; in May 1994, 7 months after the fall 1993 program; and in August 1994 following the July program. The November 1993 and August 1994 surveys were conducted at the same 72 sites that have been surveyed periodically in North Carolina since 1984, using a seat belt observational protocol developed by HSRC (Reinfurt, Campbell, Stewart, & Stutts, 1990). The 72 sites are a probability-based sample, designed to represent North Carolina drivers on the road. The May 1994 survey was based on 24 of the 72 original sites selected to also cover the three geographic regions of the state as well as the rural/urban and road type (e.g., interstate vs. city street) distribution of North Carolina.

Changes in injury crashes associated with the fall 1993 program were estimated using structural time series models (STAMP) that account for seasonal variation, cycles, stochastic trends, and effects due to other exogenous or intervention variables (Harvey & Durbin, 1986). Monthly data on police-reported crashes from January 1987 through March 1994 were used in this analysis, with October 1993 as the intervention point. This analysis examined monthly trends for the January 1987 through September 1993 period and projected the number of fatal and serious injuries (coded as K or A injuries in police-reported injury data) that would have been expected after September 1993 by fitting time series models to the monthly data. The estimated injury frequencies were then compared with the observed injuries for October 1993 through March 1994. Separate analyses were run for occupants covered by the seat belt law, noncovered occupants, and nonoccupants. Injuries in the latter two groups should not be affected by the seat belt program and thus provide useful comparison groups for assessing the contribution of the program to injury reduction.

Medical care and emergency service costs per injured person by injury severity were estimated using the basic methods described in Miller (1993) with the methodological upgrades described in Miller, Demes, and Bovbjerg (1993). Medical care costs include hospital, physician, rehabilitation, and prescription costs, and emergency services include police, fire, ambulance, and helicopter transport costs.

In addition, following the fall 1993 and summer 1994 programs, statewide telephone surveys were undertaken by the ICR Survey Research Group to gauge public awareness of program activities and reaction to the program. Random digit dialing techniques were used to select 500 North Carolina residents age 16 or older for the fall 1993 survey and 200 for the summer 1994 survey. A third statewide survey of 500 residents in September 1994 focused on drinking and driving, but it also repeated some of the questions asked in the earlier surveys. Note that percentages based on 500 interviews have a margin of error no greater than 4 points, at the 95% confidence level. For the sample of 200, the maximum margin of error is ± 7 points.

RESULTS

Enforcement and Media Activity

Table 5.1 shows the amount of funds spent for advertising and announcements in the fall 1993 program ($446,097) and the summer 1994 booster program ($158,720), along with the amount of checkpoint enforcement activity. The summer 1994 program was shorter than the fall 1993 pro-

TABLE 5.1
Summary of North Carolina Publicity and Enforcement Activities

| | October/November 1993 | | July 1994 | |
	Total	Weekly Average	Total	Weekly Average
Weeks of enforcement	4	—	3	—
Advertising purchases	$446,097	$111,524	$158,720	$52,907
Checkpoints	3,426	857	2,938	979
Seat belt citations	36,873	9,218	22,010	7,337

gram, although the number of checkpoints per week was higher (979 vs. 857, respectively). The number of citations for nonuse of seat belts given to motorists at the checkpoints and by roving patrols was 36,873 in fall 1993 and 22,010 in summer 1994. Comparative information on numbers of seat belt citations prior to "Click It or Ticket" is not available, but discussions with police suggest that a very substantial increase in citations occurred during the programs.

Police at checkpoints and in patrols dedicated to seat belt enforcement encountered many other offenders. In the two programs combined, 56 fugitives were arrested, 46 stolen vehicles were recovered, and other arrests were made (e.g., 61 people for firearm violations, 61 for felony drug violations, 238 for miscellaneous drug violations, and 2,094 for driving while intoxicated—even though all checkpoints were held during daytime hours).

Seat Belt Use

Seat belt use increased markedly in response to the fall 1993 program, dropped some by the following spring, although it remained well above baseline, and rose again in the summer 1994 program (Fig. 5.1). Driver belt use was 64% prior to program activity, increased to 80%, dropped to 73% in May 1994 (7 months after the initial publicity/enforcement program ended), and then rose to 81% after the summer 1994 booster effort. Right-front passenger belt use, typically lower than driver belt use, increased from 52% to 73%, dropped to 64%, and increased to 74% after the summer 1994 program. Combining the two groups, front seat occupant belt use was 79% after both the first and second publicity and enforcement programs.

The 24-site subsample of the 72 sites, used in May 1994 observations, provides a good approximation of results that would have been obtained if all 72 sites had been included. For example, based on these 24 sites, driver belt use in November 1993 was the same (80%) as for the 72 sites and was nearly the same (82% vs. 81%) in August 1994.

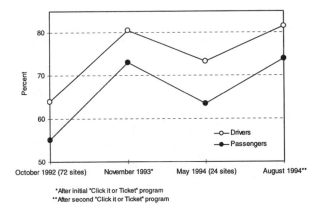

FIG. 5.1.   Percentage of front seat occupants using seat belts in North Carolina.

Table 5.2 displays driver belt use by location, time of day, and characteristics of the vehicles and drivers observed for the three observation periods. Use rates were higher in urban areas, and higher among car drivers, females, non-Whites, and older drivers. These differences in seat belt use typically have been found in prior surveys in North Carolina and elsewhere (Lund, 1986; Preusser, Williams, & Lund, 1991; Reinfurt et al., 1990; Wagenaar, Streff, Molnar, Businski, & Schultz, 1987). There were substantial increases in all categories in response to the fall 1993 program.

TABLE 5.2
Percentage of Drivers Using Seat Belts by Selected Characteristics

	October 1992 Pre-Program	November 1993 After Fall Program	August 1994 After Summer Program
Rural	54	74	73
Urban	68	84	85
Commuting hours	61	81	79
Noncommuting hours	59	78	77
Car	67	84	81
Cargo/large passenger van	36	65	68
Pickup	41	66	68
Male	53	73	74
Female	70	87	81
White	60	78	76
Non-White	65	84	85
Age < 25	56	75	76
Age 25–54	60	79	78
Age 55+	63	83	76

Most of these increases were retained in the August 1994 measurements that followed the summer 1994 program. There were significant decreases ($p < .001$, chi-square test), however, among women (87% to 81%) and among people age 65 and older (84% to 75%).

Analyses of seat belt use by region indicated divergent patterns (Table 5.3). There were substantial increases (14 to 25 percentage points) in all regions for both drivers and right-front passengers subsequent to the fall 1993 program. However, in the coastal and piedmont regions, seat belt use by front seat occupants increased even further after the summer 1994 program, with driver belt use reaching about 85%. In the mountain region, which had the largest percentage increase after the fall 1993 program, seat belt use by drivers and right-front passengers decreased between the fall 1993 and summer 1994 programs. These significant declines ($p < .001$, chi-square test) occurred primarily among women of all ages (81% to 73% decline for front seat female occupants) and among older occupants of both sexes (78% to 71% for those estimated to be age 45 or older). The statewide declines in belt use among women and older people, noted in Table 5.2, were confined to the mountain region.

Effects on Injuries and Costs

All of the injury projections were made by fitting structural time series models to monthly data series of the percentage of crash-involved occupants (or nonoccupants) who were killed or seriously injured during that month. These models, which contained stochastic levels, slopes, and seasonal factors, were used to make forecasts of the injury percentage for the 6-month period following the fall 1993 program (see Fig. 5.2). The actual

TABLE 5.3
Percentage of North Carolina Motorists Using Seat Belts, by Region

	October 1992 Pre-Program	November 1993 After Fall Program	August 1994 After Summer Program
Coastal			
Drivers	62	82	84
Right-front passengers	52	75	79
All front seat	59	80	83
Piedmont			
Drivers	68	82	86
Right-front passengers	58	74	78
All front seat	66	80	83
Mountain			
Drivers	51	76	72
Right-front passengers	44	69	65
All front seat	49	74	70

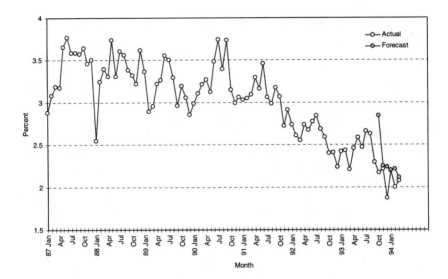

FIG. 5.2.   Percentage of front seat occupants with serious or fatal injury.

numbers of crash-involved occupants were then used to produce estimates
of expected number of serious and fatally injured occupants. Based on this
time series analysis for the period January 1, 1987, through September 30,
1993, 5,427 serious and fatal injuries to occupants covered by the law for
the 6-month period subsequent to the fall 1993 program were predicted
(see Table 5.4). There were 365 fewer such injuries than predicted, a
nearly 7% decrease.

For fatalities alone, there were 45 fewer than predicted (439 vs. 484), a
9% decrease. The inference that the declines following the fall 1993 program are attributable to the program is supported by the finding that for
occupants not covered by the law, as well as nonoccupants, serious and fatal injuries in the 6-month period were close to predicted values (i.e., there
was no evident shift).

TABLE 5.4
Results from STAMP Time Series Models

| | | Six-month Totals | | |
Group	Percentage Serious or Fatal Injury	Predicted	Percent Actual	Change
Covered occupants	Fatal	484	439	−9.3
	Fatal and serious injury	5,427	5062	−6.7
Noncovered occupants	Fatal and serious injury	449	431	−4.0
Nonoccupants	Fatal and serious injury	732	748	2.2

Thus, assuming that the 45 fewer deaths and 320 fewer serious injuries can be attributed to the seat belt program, the medical and emergency cost saving estimates are $14,593,240. (For details of the cost savings estimates, see Miller, 1993, and Miller et al., 1993.)

Public Opinion Surveys

The statewide telephone surveys revealed considerable knowledge about and support for the initiative. Key findings are summarized in Table 5.5. After the publicity and enforcement programs had ended, the great majority of respondents said they were aware of recent efforts to increase belt law enforcement (76%–85%) and thought the belt use law was being strictly enforced (74%–80%). Checkpoint awareness was very high. Among those who knew of recent efforts to increase belt use, from 88% to 92% knew about the checkpoints. After the fall 1993 program, 26% said they themselves had gone through a checkpoint; this figure was 33% after the summer 1994 program. About one third of all respondents surveyed knew the correct name of the program ("Click It or Ticket"). This was based on unaided recall (i.e., the respondents who said they were aware of recent efforts to increase enforcement were asked if they knew the name of the program and, if so, were asked to state the name). And nearly half of the respondents (46% and 44%, respectively) indicated that the program got them to increase their seat belt use.

Respondents were highly in favor of the program. The percentages in the table are combined from two alternative questions. Those who knew about the program (74%–85%) were asked if they were in favor of enforcement programs "like this" to encourage use of seat belts. Those saying they did not know about the program (15%–26%) were asked simply if

TABLE 5.5
Responses to Survey of North Carolina Drivers on the
Seat Belt Use Publicity and Enforcement Programs

	Percent		
	(N = 500) November 1993	(N = 200) August 1994	(N = 500) September 1994
Margin of error	±4	±7	±4
Think seat belt law strictly enforced	80	74	80
Aware of recent efforts to increase enforcement	85	76	82
Have gone through a checkpoint	26	33	—
Know correct name of program	38	33	29
Program increased belt use	46	44	—
In favor of programs like this	87	86	—

they were in favor of enforcement programs to encourage use of seat belts. In the November 1993 survey, 88% of those who knew about the program were in favor, and 78% of those who disclaimed knowledge of the program nevertheless favored such programs (for a combined total of 87%). The 86% figure for September 1994 is based on 87% in favor for those knowing about the program, and 80% in favor for those not knowing.

DISCUSSION

The results of the first two cycles of Canadian-style publicity and enforcement programs to encourage seat belt use in North Carolina indicate that substantial increases in belt use can be accomplished and the public supports such programs. The three pilot efforts and both of the statewide programs raised belt use to approximately 80% right after the end of each program. Belt use did not hold at 80%; 6 months after the fall 1993 statewide program it had dropped to around 75%. This pattern was also evident in Canada. Typically, belt use would peak at the end of a publicity and enforcement blitz, and then it would drop over the next few months, although not back to the baseline. Thus, the North Carolina experience mirrored the Canadian results.

Canadian programs were ratcheting up belt use with successive rounds of well-publicized enforcement. This happened in North Carolina, as belt use in two of the three regions reached more than 80% compliance. This did not occur in the mountain region, where belt use actually decreased compared with what it had been at the end of the first program, with the drop-offs occurring mainly among generally higher use groups: women and older people. Similar resources were applied in each region of the state, and the decline is not readily explainable. The mountain region has been the lowest use area in North Carolina since belt use began to be measured (i.e., 1985), and showed the greatest percentage increase of the three regions in the fall 1993 program. Presumably, decreases in belt use are most likely to come from new users, and the mountain region had a substantially higher proportion of people who were new users after the fall 1993 program than did the other regions.

Although injuries and medical care costs were reduced in North Carolina through achieving 80% belt use, it is important to increase belt use even further. The Canadian experience demonstrated that use rates in the upper 80%–90% range were not achieved in the short term, but required several years of effort and stronger sanctions, such as adding points on a driver's license. The Governor's Highway Safety Initiative was designed to be a multiyear program, with the expectation that higher use rates would become permanent in the later years of the program.

A few letters to editor in North Carolina newspapers had questioned the amount of police time given to seat belt enforcement, on the assumption that this was time taken away from attention to violent crime. In fact, the seat belt enforcement activity did result in arrests for criminal violations. Furthermore, North Carolina crime statistics, available by month through 1993, showed no unusual fluctuations in late 1993 compared to prior years (Easley, Coman, & Hawley, 1994).

The importance of achieving seat belt use higher than 80% is illustrated by a study done in North Carolina right after the fall 1993 program ended. The study was undertaken to determine the characteristics of the remaining minority (20%) of drivers observed who were still not using seat belts (Reinfurt, Williams, Wells, & Rodgman, 1996). Nonuse of seat belts was found to be associated with male gender; younger age; older vehicles; vehicles other than cars, especially pickups; and drivers with higher than average crashes and violations. This study and other similar ones (e.g., Preusser et al., 1991) indicate that the hard line group not using seat belts when required by laws are those people who most need the protection provided by belts. Converting these drivers to belt use would thus have a large payoff, but although the subgroups to target are known, this is obviously not an easy task. Follow-up telephone surveys of the observed nonusers in North Carolina indicated that many said they would respond to driver's license points, but not to higher fines. As in Canada, it may be necessary to increase the penalties to include driver's license points, at a minimum for repeat offenders, along with continued publicity and enforcement efforts, to achieve further gains in seat belt use in North Carolina.

ACKNOWLEDGMENTS

This work was supported by the Insurance Institute for Highway Safety. The chapter appeared as an article in *Journal of Safety Research, 27*(1), 33–41 (© 1996 by Elsevier Science) and is used here with permission.

REFERENCES

Dussault, C. (1990). Effectiveness of a selective traffic enforcement program combined with incentives for seat belt use in Quebec. *Health Education Research, 5*(2), 217–223.

Easley, M. F., Coman, J. J., & Hawley, R. P. (1994). *Crime in North Carolina: Uniform crime report 1993.* Raleigh: North Carolina Department of Justice, State Bureau of Investigation.

Hagenzeiker, M. P. (1991, September). *Strategies to increase the use of restraint system* [Summary]. Proceedings of a Workshop organized by SWOV and VTT at the VTI-TRB International Conference Traffic Safety on Two Continents, Gothenburg. SWOV Institute for Road Safety Research, The Netherlands.

Harvey, A. C., & Durbin, J. (1986). The effects of seat belt legislation on British road casualties: A case study in structural time series modeling. *Journal of the Royal Statistical Society Series A, 149,* 187–227.

Jonah, B. A., Dawson, N. E., & Smith, G. A. (1982). Effects of a selective traffic enforcement program on seat belt usage. *Journal of Applied Psychology, 67,* 89–96.

Jonah, B. A., & Grant, B. A. (1985). Long-term effectiveness of selective traffic enforcement programs for increasing seat belt use. *Journal of Applied Psychology, 70,* 257–263.

Lamb, A. (1982). *Seat belt awareness and enforcement pilot project.* Vancouver: Insurance Corporation of British Columbia.

Landry, P. R. (1991). SGI's five year occupant restraint initiative and selective traffic enforcement program. *Proceedings of the National Leadership Conference on Increasing Safety-Belt Use in the U.S.* (pp. 61–64). Washington, DC: National Highway Traffic Safety Administration.

Lund, A. K. (1986). Voluntary seat belt use among U.S. drivers: Geographic, socioeconomic and demographic variation. *Accident Analysis and Prevention, 18*(1), 43–50.

Lund, A. K., Stuster, J., & Fleming, A. (1989). Special publicity and enforcement of California's belt use law: Making a "secondary" law work. *Journal of Criminal Justice, 17,* 329–341.

Manduca, P. L. (1983). *Raising the seat belt wearing rate in the Province of British Columbia.* Vancouver: Insurance Corporation of British Columbia.

Miller, T. (1993). Costs and functional consequences of U.S. roadway crashes. *Accident Analysis and Prevention, 25*(5), 593–607.

Miller, T., Demes, J., & Bovbjerg, R. (1993). Child seats: How large are the benefits and who should pay? (SAE 933089). *Child occupant protection* (SP-986), pp. 81–89. Warrendale, PA: Society for Automotive Engineers.

Mortimer, R. G., Goldsteen, K., Armstrong, R. W., & Marcina, D. (1990). *Effects of enforcement on seat belt by drivers in selected cities in Illinois. Final report.* Champaign-Urbana, IL: Illinois Department of Transportation.

National Highway Traffic Safety Administration. (1991). *Proceedings of the National Leadership Conference on Increasing Safety-Belt Use in the U.S.* [Summary]. Washington, DC: Author.

National Highway Traffic Safety Administration. (1994). *Observed safety belt use rates reported by states as of December 1993.* Washington, DC: Author.

Preusser, D. F., Williams, A. F., & Lund, A. K. (1991). Characteristics of belted and unbelted drivers. *Accident Analysis and Prevention, 23,* 475–482.

Reinfurt, D. W. (1994). *Occupant restraint monitoring program. Final Report.* Chapel Hill, NC: University of North Carolina Highway Safety Research Center.

Reinfurt, D. W., Campbell, B. J., Stewart, J. R., & Stutts, J. C. (1990). Evaluating the North Carolina safety belt wearing law. *Accident Analysis & Prevention, 22*(3), 197–210.

Reinfurt, D., Williams, A. F., Wells, J., & Rodgman, E. (1996). Characteristics of drivers not using seat belts in a high belt use state. *Journal of Safety Research, 27*(4), 209–215.

Rood, D. H., Kraichy, P. P., & Carman, J. A. (1987). *Selective traffic enforcement program for occupant restraints. Final report* (DOT HS 807 120). Washington, DC: U.S. Dept. of Transportation.

Transport Canada. (1994). Results of June 1994 survey of seat belt use in Canada. *Traffic Safety Standards and Research, Transport Canada.* Ottawa, Ontario.

Wagenaar, A. C., Streff, F. M., Molnar, L. J., Businski, K. L., & Schultz, R. H. (1987). *Factors related to nonuse of seat belts in Michigan* (DOT HS 807 217). Washington, DC: U.S. Dept. of Transportation.

Williams, A. F., Hall, W. L., Tolbert, W. G., & Wells, J. K. (1994). Development and evaluation of pilot programs to increase seat belt use in North Carolina. *Journal of Safety Research, 25*(3), 167–175.

Williams, A. F., Lund, A. K., Preusser, D. F., & Blomberg, R. D. (1987). Results of a seat belt use law enforcement and publicity campaign in Elmira, New York. *Accident Analysis and Prevention, 19*(4), 243–249.

6

THE CALIFORNIA TOBACCO CONTROL PROGRAM: A LONG-TERM HEALTH COMMUNICATION PROJECT

John P. Pierce
Sherry Emery
Elizabeth Gilpin
University of California, San Diego

In November 1988, California voters passed Proposition 99, which established the Tobacco Tax and Health Protection Act and initiated the California Tobacco Control Program. Proposition 99 designated specifically how monies raised from the increased excise tax could be spent. These expenditure allocations can only be overruled by a four fifths majority of legislators and only if the changes fit within the general intent of Proposition 99. The resulting California Tobacco Control Program is widely perceived to be the largest and most comprehensive health promotion program ever undertaken to reduce the impact of tobacco on society. Following California's lead, a number of other states (Massachusetts, Arizona, Oregon) have increased the state excise tax on cigarettes and allocated part of the funds to support a statewide Tobacco Control Program. More recently, Florida has used monies available from their settlement of a lawsuit with the tobacco companies to support such a program. As of 1998, the California program is the only one that has had continuous funding for 6 years with representative data available for evaluation.

HEALTH PROMOTION VERSUS TOBACCO PROMOTION

The California initiative mandated that the money raised by the added tax be divided into six accounts with the following distribution: health education (20%), research on tobacco-related diseases (5%), hospital services

(35%), physician services (10%), and public resources (5%), with an unalloccated 25% to be distributed by the legislature across the other accounts as it sees fit. The California program is funded entirely from the health education account. The goals of the public health Tobacco Control Program are outlined by the Tobacco Education and Research Oversight Committee (TEROC), whose members are appointed by the governor, the legislature, and the superintendent of public instruction. In its 1997 report, this oversight committee noted that the program's strategy had been to create a social milieu and legal climate in which tobacco use is regarded as unacceptable (TEROC, 1997).

A central component of this program was an antismoking media campaign, funded at more than $90 million between 1989 and 1996. This campaign included paid advertisements that used a variety of communication channels (e.g., television, radio, outdoor advertising, and print). Although Proposition 99 was passed in November 1988 and the additional taxes went into effect on January 1, 1989, it took time for the enabling legislation to be enacted. The first two requests for proposals for the program released by the Department of Health Services occurred toward the end of 1989; they were for a media contractor and an evaluation contractor. The assessment process for these proposals was on the fast track and the first antitobacco advertisements were seen on television on April 10, 1990. Since its inception in 1990, the mass media antismoking campaign was designed to appeal to an adult audience, with approximately 60% of the messages targeted to a general audience and 25% targeted to specific minority communities (10% Hispanic, 10% Asian, and 5% African American). Only 15% of the messages were designed to appeal specifically to an adolescent audience.

But the public health community was not the only one trying to influence the smoking behavior of Californians over this time period. Traditionally, the tobacco industry has a very large marketing effort aimed at maintaining or increasing sales of tobacco products. Key elements of the tobacco industry's marketing strategy are the manipulation of product price to increase sales and communication and promotional campaigns to encourage product use. These campaigns include significant budgets for media advertising and multichannel promotional programs. The industry's marketing strategies in these areas conflict directly with the goals of the Tobacco Control Program. The tobacco industry also lobbies elected officials to promote favorable legislation to the industry. These lobbying efforts have included substantial campaign contributions to candidates for the legislature or state office (Balbach, Monardi, Fox, & Glantz, 1997). In addition, tobacco industry documents reveal that it pursued a well-developed, multipronged strategy designed to "eliminate" the Tobacco Control Program antismoking media campaign. This strategy included encouraging legislative intervention, organizing business-community opposition, convincing the Director of Health Services to withdraw or modify the campaign, and seeking intercession against the campaign by the Governor of California (Chilcote, 1990). Hence, in a very real way, the tobacco industry and the Tobacco Control Program are at war over the health of Californians. For the public health community, there is no acceptable or safe level of smoking, and for the tobacco industry, there is no apparent interest in getting out of the tobacco business.

CAMPAIGN MESSAGES

Setting a New Tone: Attacking the Image of Tobacco Companies

The first antismoking advertisement broadcast on television in California took an entirely new approach. The message of the advertisement did not focus on the health consequences of cigarette smoking, but rather on the predatory practices of the tobacco industry. Approximately 40% of the messages in the first 3 years of the campaign used this theme. The first advertisement, entitled "Board Room," showed a group of actors portraying tobacco industry executives sitting around a smoke-filled room. The chairperson of the meeting says:

> Gentlemen, gentlemen. The tobacco industry has a very serious multi-billion-dollar problem. We need more cigarette smokers. Pure and simple. Every day, 2,000 Americans stop smoking and another 1,178 also quit. Actually, technically, they die.
> That means that this business needs 3,000 fresh new volunteers every day. So forget all that cancer heart disease and stroke stuff.
> Gentlemen, we're not in this for our health.

The innovativeness of this approach ensured that this advertisement was shown nationally, as the news media were quick to focus on it and disseminate it widely. This advertisement was accompanied by full-page advertisements in all major newspapers in California entitled "First, the Smoke. Now, the Mirrors." It finished with the following:

> Today a surprising number of us can tell you that cigarettes are our #1 preventable cause of death and disability.
> So we seem to know about the smoke. But what about the really dangerous stuff—all those carefully polished, fatal illusions the tobacco industry has crafted to mess with our minds so they can mess with our lives.

The tobacco and advertising industries responded quickly to this new approach. One example of this is Bob Garfield's column in *Advertising Age*, which accused the campaign of feeding racial paranoia by trading on "a vile stereotype: the wealthy, white embodiment of evil" (Garfield, 1990). The "Board Room" advertisement became the "signature" advertisement for the California campaign and even in 1996, the majority of Californians could recall the advertisement (Glantz & Balbach, 2000). Approximately 40% of the media in the early years focused on the image of the tobacco industry.

However, the most controversial advertisement was made in 1994 when the campaign used actual footage from a congressional hearing, during which the chief executives of each of the major tobacco companies denied, under oath, that nicotine was addictive. The advertisement culminates with the question, "Do they think we're stupid?" The advertisement was first aired on September 29 of that year. A legal threat quickly followed from the tobacco industry, both to the Department of Health Services and to the major network television stations in California. Even though the advertising agency offered to indemnify the television stations, three refused to air the advertisement. The Department of Health Services publicly defended their right to make and use the advertisement; by early 1995, they had removed it from circulation (Glantz & Balbach, 2000).

After 1995, other advertisements were made on this theme. In a regressive set of decisions, the Department of Health Services refused to allow any advertisement to call into question the veracity of the tobacco industry. By 1996, the department had informed the advertising agency that no future advertisement would be approved if it used the words "tobacco industry," "nicotine addiction," "profit," or "lies." Further, every advertisement had to be cleared for each use, thus ensuring that advertisements using these terms, although previously approved and aired, would no longer be used in the campaign (Glantz & Balbach, 2000).

Building on Strength: Secondhand Smoke

California had been a leader in the push for clean indoor air laws starting in the 1970s and the Americans for Nonsmokers Rights (ANR) was headquartered in Berkeley. By the start of the Tobacco Control Program in 1990, 213 local communities had worked with ANR to pass local clean indoor air ordinances, and protecting nonsmokers from the hazards of secondhand smoke was quickly made a primary goal of the California Tobacco Control Program. Approximately 40% of all the media executions in the early years focused on a version of this message, which aimed at convincing people of the hazards of secondhand smoke to the nonsmoker, especially to children. In addition, the Tobacco Control Program provided both resources and technical assistance to local lead agencies (generally local government departments) and other groups to build on the media messages and promote local discussion and action relating to clean indoor air. One of the more effective campaign advertisements in this area was entitled "Victim's wife." In this commercial, an elderly smoker discusses how his wife always used to tell him that he should quit because "smoking kills." It finished with "I didn't know that the life that would be lost would be hers." In 1996, two thirds of adults and teenagers surveyed recalled this advertisement, giving it the highest recall rating for the year (Independent Evaluation Consortium, 1997).

Between 1990 and 1993, there was a significant increase in local activity related to clean indoor air ordinances so that more than 50 ordinances passed in that year (Glantz & Balbach, 2000). By 1994, a Sacramento ordinance had been in place for several years making all workplaces smoke free. Los Angeles and San Francisco had just passed such an ordinance; San Diego and San Jose were considering similar ordinances. In mid-1994, the California legislature passed a statewide law mandating that all workplaces in the state be smoke free.

Youth Access to Cigarettes

In 1991, the tobacco industry introduced its own "youth initiative" known as the "It's the Law" campaign. This program provided stickers that merchants could post to warn consumers that it was illegal to sell cigarettes to children. A 1991 tobacco industry document that surfaced as part of the tobacco industry litigation stated: "The ultimate means of determining the success of this ("It's the Law") program will be 1) a reduction in legislation introduced and passed restricting or banning our sales and marketing activities . . ." (J. J. Slavitt memo to Pat Tricorache re: Tobacco Industry Youth initiative, Feb. 12, 1991, Bates # 2500082629).

Youth access was a popular concept with merchants and appeared modeled after the supply strategy that had been popular in the antidrug campaign. In the early few years of the Tobacco Control campaign, this message was in approximately 10% of the campaign's media placements. However, by 1995–1996, the proportion of youth access messages had doubled. A widely used outdoor advertisement asked Californians to call a toll-free number if they ever saw a merchant selling cigarettes to kids. However, this message did not seem to resonate with Californians: Less than one third of adults and less than one quarter of 10th graders surveyed could remember it.

Promoting Cessation Services

One of the primary goals of the Tobacco Control Program was to reduce the prevalence of smoking in California, thus preventing tobacco-related diseases. The quickest way to reduce prevalence is to increase the proportion of the population who successfully quit. Accordingly, the California campaign focused approximately 10% of its media messages on promoting smokers to seek help to quit. These messages included a tagline with a toll-free number for the California Smoker's Helpline. This innovative and free telephone counseling cessation service provides assistance for smokers to quit and uses the media campaign to encourage smokers to use these services. The helpline quickly demonstrated that it could double the successful cessation rate (Zhu, Tedeschi, Anderson, & Pierce, 1996).

THE OFF-AGAIN ON-AGAIN MEDIA CAMPAIGN

The California media campaign has a checkered history. As already noted, it started with much fanfare and angered the tobacco industry. The first moves to curtail the program came from the legislative body in 1991. The media campaign was in the field in April 1990, but by April 1991, it had exhausted its 18-month budget. Rather than extend the contract, another request for proposals was released. The competition was won by the same advertising agency. However, on January 10, 1992, Governor Wilson vetoed the just-negotiated contract.

The administration's claims that the media program was ineffective were refuted a few days later when the preliminary report of the evaluation effort was released. In February 1992, the American Lung Association filed suit against the administration to have the program reinstated since Proposition 99 was a constitutional amendment, and mandated the conduct of a mass media campaign. The campaign was eventually reinstated in September 1992. Thus, between 1990 and the start of 1993, the mass media program had been "aired" for a total of only 15 months.

There was, however, a lot of news media coverage of smoking issues during this period. In December 1991, the *Journal of the American Medical Association* published three papers outlining the effectiveness of R.J. Reynolds' Joe Camel advertising program. One was based on the results of the first of the California Tobacco Surveys (CTS). These papers started a huge media story that continued for almost 6 months. Another major media story occurred with the release of the first results of the CTS in January 1992. The headline in the *San Francisco Chronicle* read "Anti-smoking program big hit—but Governor seeks to cut it." Similarly, the litigation against the administration relating to the media campaign received considerable media attention. In 1994, tobacco industry advertising was again a major news story with the release of the findings demonstrating that the Virginia Slims campaign was associated with a major increase in smoking only among young adolescent girls.

COMPARISON OF INTERVENTION EXPENDITURES

As indicated earlier, the California Tobacco Control Program is funded entirely from the Health Education Account Fund, which receives 20% of the revenues from the 25¢ per pack tax increase. Table 6.1 shows approximately one third of the overall Health Education Account budget as allocated to the Department of Education, with the majority of these funds supporting smoking prevention programs in local schools. The remainder of the budget is administered by the Department of Health Services. Initially, the Local Lead Agency Program accounted for approximately 42% of the total budget, although in fiscal year 1995–1996, this percentage was reduced to approximately 25%. Local Lead Agency funds are distributed at the local level and through special interest networks. The policy allows for considerable local discretion in the use of the money. The mass media campaign budget received a relatively constant amount of money, with the exception of a very low actual expenditure in 1995 to 1996. Innovative intervention projects in communities are supported under the competitive grants program.

In the first 7 years since the passage of Proposition 99, a total of $517 million has been spent on tobacco control interventions, an average of $74 million each year. From 1989 to mid-1993, there was an average annual expenditure of $85.5 million, with variation suggesting that funds from previous years were brought forward to the next, particularly in the category of competitive grants. California has a population of 25.5 million people age 12 and older. Thus, the average annual expenditure during this period was $3.35 per capita/year. However, beginning in mid-1993, there was a marked reduction in Tobacco Control Program expenditures: funds were diverted from the Health Education and Research accounts to indigent medical services. From mid-1993 to mid-1996, the average annual expenditure was only $53 million, $2.08 per capita/year. Of particular note is the substantial decline in expenditures in 1995–1996, when the media budget was decreased by one half, and the funding available at the local level was decreased by almost one third from the previous fiscal year. Thus, between these two periods, there was a reduction in the annual funding for tobacco control in California by a factor of 40%.

The estimated annual expenditures of the tobacco industry on advertising and promotion in California over the same time period are also presented in Table 6.1. These estimates—based on data from the Federal Trade Commission (FTC, 1997) report—take into account the relative size of the California population and assume that California was not differentially targeted by the tobacco industry. These calculations predict that the tobacco industry would spend about 10% of its total advertising and promotions budget to influence Californians directly. The tobacco industry is

TABLE 6.1
Expenditures Targeted at Tobacco Use in California ($Millions)

Tobacco Control Program[a]	Early Period				Later Period			Total
	1989–1990	1990–1991	1991–1992	1992–1993	1993–1994	1994–1995	1995–1996	1989–1996
Mass media	$14.3	$14.3	$16.0	$15.4	$12.9	$12.2	$6.6	$91.7
Local lead agency	$35.6	$35.4	$14.5	$17.8	$13.5	$16.4	$10.2	$143.4
Competitive grants	$3.3	$49.7	$1.1	$27.5	$15.1	$10.9	$9.7	$117.3
Local schools	$32.6	$32.6	$24.3	$23.3	$19.6	$16.8	$15.3	$164.5
Yearly Totals	$85.8	$132.1	$55.9	$84.0	$61.1	$56.3	$41.7	$516.9

Tobacco Industry[b]	Early Period				Later Period			Total
	1989	1990	1991	1992	1993	1994	1995	1989–1995
Advertising	$111	$114	$112	$99	$94	$89	$82	$795
Incentives to merchants	$100	$102	$116	$151	$156	$168	$187	$980
Promotional items	$122	$149	$207	$252	$332	$210	$201	$1473
Other	$28	$34	$31	$22	$22	$17	$19	$173
Yearly Totals	$362	$399	$465	$523	$603	$483	$489	$3,324

[a]Health Education budget reported in Balbach et al. (1997).
[b]10% of National Expenditures reported by Federal Trade Commission (1997).

required to supply the FTC with an accounting of the monies spent on advertising and promotion of manufactured cigarettes, but these figures do not include what it spends on promoting other tobacco products, such as cigars. Furthermore, these reports do not include industry expenditures for lobbying and political campaigns that may affect the conduct of the California Tobacco Control Program.

In 1989, traditional advertising approaches, such as print media and billboards, comprised approximately 30% of the total promotional expenditures of the industry; by 1995, this was reduced to 17%. Furthermore, by 1995, expenditures on traditional advertising amounted to only 41% of the amount the industry devoted to the category of promotional items. Promotional items, which are a combination of the FTC categories for coupons, retail value added, and specialty item distribution, comprised the largest proportion of the industry advertising and promotional expenditures in each year. The percentage for promotional items increased from a low of 34% of total expenditures in 1989 to a high of 55% in 1993.

The other major FTC category that the industry designates as promotional allowances covers expenditures to encourage wholesalers and retailers to stock and promote cigarettes. Table 6.1 labels this category "incentives to merchants" to better describe its purpose. Over a 7-year period, expenditures under this "incentives to merchants" category have risen steadily, from 27% to 38% of the total budget.

During the period from 1989 to 1992, the tobacco industry is estimated to have spent an average of $437 million/year or $17.14 per capita/year to persuade Californians to smoke. During the period from 1993 to 1995, the industry is estimated to have spent an average of $525 million/year or $20.59 per capita/year, for this purpose.

PROGRAM EVALUATION

The specific aims of the California Tobacco Control program included increasing the protection of nonsmokers, as well as reducing future tobacco-related diseases by encouraging a major decline in smoking prevalence and cigarette consumption (Pierce et al., 1994). The media campaign specifically targeted the secondhand smoke issue, and used several different themes to encourage cessation and reduce smoking prevalence.

Trends in the Protection of Nonsmokers

Figure 6.1 presents evidence about the protection of young children from secondhand tobacco smoke in the home. The graph displays the proportion of households with smokers and young children where in-home smok-

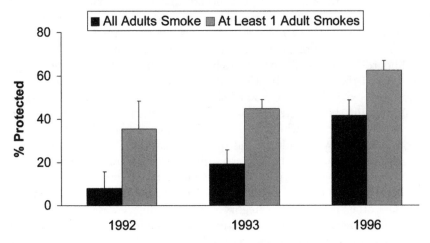

Protection of Young Children (0-5 years) in Households Where Adults Smoke

FIG. 6.1. Protection of young children (0–5 years) in households where adults smoke. Data from CTS (1992, 1993, 1996).

ing, according to adult survey respondents, is banned. In homes with children under age 6 where all adults smoke, the percentage with complete bans on smoking rose from 19% in 1993 to over 40% in 1996. In homes with young children where only some adults smoke, 42% were smoke free in 1993, and this figure jumped to over 65% by 1996. Approximately 89% of all children under age 6 were protected from secondhand tobacco smoke in the home in 1996, including households with and without adult smokers.

Nonsmoking workers were also protected from exposure to secondhand smoke. In 1990, 29% of nonsmoking indoor workers reported that someone had smoked in their work area within the previous 2 weeks. By 1993, the proportion of indoor workers who reported exposure to someone smoking by this measure had decreased by almost one fourth to 22%. By 1996, this proportion had almost halved again, to only 12%. Thus, between 1990 and 1996, the proportion of nonsmoking workers who were exposed to secondhand tobacco smoke declined significantly (see Fig. 6.2).

Trends in Per Capita Consumption in California and the Rest of the United States, 1983 to 1997

Figure 6.3 presents the trends from January 1983 through June 1997 in per capita cigarette consumption (packs/month) for persons age 18 and older for California and the remainder of the United States. Because these

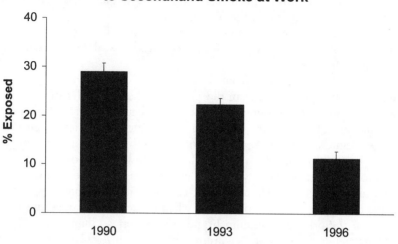

**Exposure of Nonsmoking Indoor Workers
to Secondhand Smoke at Work**

FIG. 6.2. Exposure of nonsmoking indoor workers to secondhand smoke at work. Data from CTS (1990, 1993, 1996).

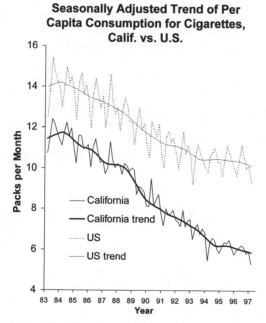

**Seasonally Adjusted Trend of Per
Capita Consumption for Cigarettes,
Calif. vs. U.S.**

FIG. 6.3. Seasonally adjusted trend of per capita cigarette consumption, California vs. United States. Data from Tobacco Institute and U.S. Census Bureau.

data are from wholesale warehouse removals, there is considerable variation; the level of removals in the last month of any quarter is strongly correlated with the removals in the first month of the next quarter. This variation has little to do with actual consumption and likely reflects business
practice. In order to remove this source of variability, data were combined
into 2-month intervals.

Over the entire period from 1983 to 1997, Californians consumed
fewer cigarettes per capita than did people in the remainder of the United
States. In California, around the time the Tobacco Control Program began, the rate of decline in per capita cigarette consumption appeared to
change. Beginning in 1994, the rate of decline in per capita consumption
slowed in California, which may reflect the lower level of resources devoted to the program, or the different messages used by the campaign after
1993. In the rest of the United States, consumption no longer appeared to
decline beginning around April 1993, when tobacco companies announced
a drop in the price of premium brands of cigarettes (Shapiro, 1993).

These trends in per capita cigarette consumption for California indicate
that there was a change in the rate of decline (slope) with the implementation of Proposition 99, and at least one change following the beginning of
the Tobacco Control Program. Additionally, because of the changes in
funding for the Tobacco Control Program, the period since the program
began is divided into two intervals: the early period, from January 1989
through June 1993 (fiscal year 1992–1993), and the later period, from July
1993 through March 1997.

Table 6.2 summarizes the changes in per capita cigarette consumption
in California and the rest of the United States. Before California's excise
tax increase in January 1989, monthly consumption had been declining at
an annual rate of .40 packs/person, so that in December 1988 Californians
consumed an average of 9.7 packs/person. After the start of the Tobacco
Control Program, the annual rate of decline in monthly consumption in-

TABLE 6.2
Summary of Decreases in Per Capita Cigarette Consumption

| Period | California | | Rest of U.S. | |
	Rate of Decline	Monthly Per Capita Consumption[a]	Rate of Decline	Monthly Per Capita Consumption[a]
Pre-1989 (Pre-Program)	−.40	9.7	−.36	12.4
1989–1993 (Early Period)	−.63	6.7	−.42	10.4
1993–1996 (Later Period)	−.27	6.0	−.08	10.3

Note. Data from Tobacco Institute and U.S. Bureau of Census.
[a]Packs/person: December 1988, June 1993, December 1996.

creased from .40 to .63 packs/person, so that in June 1993 Californians consumed an average of 6.7 packs/person. Thus, the early period in the Tobacco Control Program was associated with an increase by a factor of over 60% in California's annual rate of decline in per capita cigarette consumption. In the later period of the Tobacco Control Program, the annual rate of decline in monthly consumption decreased to .27 packs/person, only one third the rate of decline observed in the early period. Therefore, in December 1996, Californians were consuming 6.0 packs/person.

In December 1988, before the Tobacco Control Program began, residents in the rest of the United States consumed an average of 12.4 packs of cigarettes per person. Thus, the level of consumption was higher by a factor of 28% than that in California. In the period before the program began, monthly cigarette consumption had also been declining in the rest of the United States at an annual rate of .36 packs/person, roughly the same as in California. However, in contrast to California during the early period of the Tobacco Control Program (through fiscal year 1992–1993), where the rate of decline increased to .63, the rate of decline in the rest of the United States increased from .36 to .42 packs/person. At this time point, the level of consumption in the rest of the United States was higher than in California by a factor of 55%.

During the later period of the Tobacco Control Program, the annual rate of decline in monthly cigarette consumption in the rest of the United States was negligible (–.08). Although California's rate of decline had also slowed—to .27—this was still faster than in the rest of the United States. Thus, in December 1996, the level of per capita consumption in the rest of the United States was higher than it was in California by a factor of about 70%.

To summarize, during the early period of the Tobacco Control Program, per capita cigarette consumption decreased by a factor of 30% in California and by a factor of 16% in the rest of the United States. During the later period of the Tobacco Control Program, per capita consumption continued to decline in California, but only at one third of the rate of decline observed in the early period. In the rest of the United States, there was no further decline after 1993. Over the entire period from December 1988 to December 1996, tobacco consumption decreased in California by a factor of 38% compared to a factor of only 17% in the rest of the United States.

Trends in Smoking Prevalence

The previous evidence focused on per capita cigarette consumption from data about wholesale sales; this section presents parallel evidence for changes in smoking prevalence based on survey data. Before the California

Trends in Per Capita Consumption, California vs. U.S.

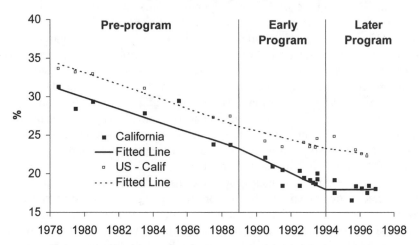

FIG. 6.4.   Trends in per capita cigarette consumption, California vs. United
States. Data from "Has the California Tobacco Control Program Reduced
Smoking" by J. P. Pierce et al., September 9, 1998, *JAMA, 28*(10), 893–899.

Tobacco Control Program began in 1989, smoking prevalence declined at
about the same rate in California (–.74%/year) as the rest of the United
States (–.77%/year) (see Fig. 6.4 and Table 6.3). The rates of decline were
not statistically different, but prevalence in California was below that for
the rest of the United States. The rate of decline increased (became more
negative) significantly in California after the program began ($p < .001$),
whereas in the rest of the United States it did not. As a result, the rate of decline from 1989 through 1993 was significantly greater ($p < .05$) by a factor
of nearly 90% in California (–1.06%/year) than in the rest of the United
States (–.57%/year). After 1993, neither the rate of decline in California nor

TABLE 6.3
Summary of Decreases in Smoking Prevalence

Period	California		Rest of U.S.	
	Rate of Decline	Smoking Prevalence[a]	Rate of Decline	Smoking Prevalence[a]
Pre-1989 (Pre-Program)	–.70	23.9	–.75	26.7
1989–1993 (Early Period)	–1.09	18.6	–.66	23.5
1993–1996 (Later Period)	–.16	18.1	–.27	22.7

Note.   Data from NHIS (1978, 1979, 1980, 1983, 1985, 1987, 1988, 1990, 1991, 1993,
1994), CTS (1990, 1992, 1993, 1996), BRFS/CATS (1991–1995), CPS (1992–1993).
[a]Prevalence in December 1988, June 1993, December 1996, January 2000.

in the rest of the United States was significantly different from zero and in both California and the rest of the United States, the change in the rate of decline was significantly less ($p < .001$) than in the preceding period.

Adolescent Smoking

Currently, appropriate national data for comparison of adolescent smoking are unavailable. However, Monitoring the Future data should soon be available, which will enable a comparison of adolescent data.

CONCLUSIONS

The California Tobacco Control Campaign had a large effect on adult smoking behavior in the first 3 years as assessed by representative surveys of smoking prevalence and trend analyses of sales data (per capita cigarette consumption). Between 1994 and 1996, there was no additional reduction in smoking behavior observed among adults. Per capita consumption showed a reduction in the rate of decline in California and in the rest of the United States during the late Tobacco Control Program period, which, in contrast to the prevalence results, suggested that California's rate of decline was still faster than that achieved elsewhere. Across the whole period there was a major, consistent trend for increasing protection of nonsmokers from secondhand smoke.

There is good reason to believe that the mass media component of the campaign was central to its success in the early period. A microanalysis of the per capita consumption data demonstrated that the initial effect of increased cigarette price had worn off by August 1989 and per capita consumption had started to rise again (Pierce et al., 1993). With the start of the media campaign, per capita consumption again started to decline, and this decline lasted as long as the first wave of the media campaign was being aired. A second reason supporting the media campaign's effectiveness was the ferocity with which the tobacco industry attacked it (on the principal that the industry only attacks what it thinks it is being effective against its interests).

The question is why the campaign lost its effectiveness against adult smoking prevalence. Certainly, there was a change in the ratio of expenditure on campaigns by the tobacco industry and the Tobacco Control Program. Clearly, these two campaigns dueled over the attention and behavior of the population. During the effective period of the Tobacco Control Program, the ratio of expenditure was 5:1 in favor of the tobacco industry. During the period when the Tobacco Control Program had lost its effect, the ratio was 10:1. Further, this decline in ratio was brought about mainly by a reduction in the expenditures of the Tobacco Control Program.

This decline in tobacco control expenditure was not caused by a loss of revenue from declining cigarette sales. Some insight into this issue can be gained by considering an internal memorandum of the Tobacco Institute in 1990, which was uncovered as part of a legal discovery for one of the state lawsuits against the tobacco companies. This memorandum outlines a strategic plan for combating the California Tobacco Control Program (Chilcote, 1990). It calls for the implementation of four strategies: lobbying the California legislature to take away the tobacco control budget, organizing minority groups to demand a change in the content of the program, convincing the director of health services to pull or modify the proposed media messages, and encouraging the governor to intercede against the program.

There is evidence that each of these strategies was successfully implemented in California. For example, Governor Wilson initially vetoed the budget in 1992, although he reconsidered in the aftermath of mounting public indignation. Along with the governor, the legislature made an outright attempt to divert the monies from the Tobacco Control Program. They were taken to court and told they did not have the right under the constitution to make such a diversion. However, monies were very clearly diverted from the campaign at a time when it was being most effective.

The Wilson administration was also very effective in changing the character of the media campaign. By 1995, the administration had eliminated the pointed advertising that focused on the image of the tobacco industry. Additionally, they had refocused the campaign to emphasize a message the tobacco industry had also been using as part of its campaign: It is against the law for kids to buy cigarettes. There are numerous psychological reasons to believe that such a message might build demand for cigarettes among rebellious adolescents.

Another possible reason may have been a change in the level of grassroots activity against smoking. During the effective first period, there was an enormous amount of activity focused on passing local ordinances. This local-level action was so successful that there was a new antismoking ordinance each week somewhere in California. The tobacco industry worked hard at the state legislative level to preempt future ordinances with a general law that applied across the state. They were successful in splintering the tobacco control advocates on the final law that passed banning smoking in all workplaces. Additionally, local advocates who received money from the Tobacco Control Program were told by the leader of the Senate at the time that they could not lobby the legislature for the program. Finally, the action call in the second period was very different from that of the first period. During the first period, the action call was to pass an ordinance to protect the health of the nonsmoker. During the second period, the people of California were told to pick up the phone and report anyone whom they saw selling cigarettes to kids. The call to action had gone from one of altruism to one of "ratting." There was a significant reduction in money available to local lead agencies and the effective activities of grass-roots efforts may have suffered as a result.

A third issue was the sudden and major drop in premium cigarette prices enacted by the tobacco industry in 1993. The newspapers reported that Wall Street's reaction to this price drop was one of considerable concern, because it was the first time the industry had demonstrated that it was vulnerable. It is possible that the marked drop in the prices of premium brands was sufficient to lead smokers who were about to quit (for various reasons, including price) to reconsider their decision. However, it is unlikely that any such price effect lasted more than a few months.

In conclusion, the California experience demonstrated that a tobacco control program fronted by a good media campaign can be very effective in changing smoking behavior. However, it is also clear that the message used in such a campaign matters. California has demonstrated very clearly that an effective campaign will provoke the ire of the tobacco industry. The California experience also showed that if the program is conducted within the government system, then the tobacco industry will use very effective lobbying strategies to change both the funding and the content of the program so as to reduce its effectiveness.

REFERENCES

Balbach, E. D., Monardi, F. M., Fox, B. J., & Glantz, S. A. (1997). *Holding government accountable: Tobacco policy making in California, 1995–1997.* San Francisco, CA: Institute for Health Policy Studies, School of Medicine, University of California, San Francisco.

Chilcote, S. D. (1990, April 18). *Memoranda to members of the executive committee of the tobacco institute.* Washington, DC: The Tobacco Institute.

Garfield, B. (1990, April 16). California's anti-smoking ad fans flames of racial paranoia. *Advertising Age,* p. 70.

Glantz, S. A., & Balbach, E. (2000). *Tobacco war: Inside the California battles.* Berkeley: University of California Press.

Independent Evaluation Consortium of the Gallup Organization, Stanford University, University of Southern California. (1997, October). *Final report independent evaluation of the California Tobacco Control Prevention and Education Program: Wave I data, 1996–1997.* Sacramento, CA.

Pierce, J. P., Evans, N., Farkas, A. J., Cavin, S. W., Berry, C., Kramer, M., Kealey, S., Rosbrook, B., Choi, W., & Kaplan, R. M. (1994). *Tobacco use in California: An evaluation of the Tobacco Control Program, 1989–1993.* La Jolla, CA: University of California, San Diego.

Pierce, J. P., Farkas, A., Evans, N., Berry, C., Choi, W., Rosbrook, B., Johnson, M., & Bal, D. (1993). *Tobacco use in California 1992: A focus on preventing uptake in adolescents.* Sacramento, CA: California Department of Health Services.

Shapiro, E. (1993, April 5). Cigarette burn: Philip Morris price cut on Marlboro jolts industry and upsets rosy profit assumptions. *Wall Street Journal*, pp. A1, A10.

Tobacco Education and Research Oversight Committee (TEROC). (1997). *Toward a tobacco-free California: Renewing the commitment*. Master Plan for the CA Tobacco Control Program.

U.S. Federal Trade Commission. (1997). *Federal Trade Commission Report to Congress*. Pursuant to the Federal Cigarettes Labeling and Advertising Act. Washington, DC: Federal Trade Commission.

Zhu, S.-H., Tedeschi, G. J., Anderson, C. M., & Pierce, J. P. (1996). Telephone counseling for smoking cessation: What's in a call? *Journal of Counseling and Development, 75*(6), 93–102.

The Impact of Antismoking Media Campaigns on Progression to Established Smoking: Results of a Longitudinal Youth Study in Massachusetts

Michael Siegel
Boston University School of Public Health

Lois Biener
University of Massachusetts, Boston

Preventing smoking is a public health priority (U.S. Department of Health and Human Services, 1994). Public health practitioners have begun to use counteradvertising to prevent smoking initiation (Alcalay, 1993; Blum, 1994; Burns, 1994; Dorfman & Wallack, 1993; Erickson, McKenna, & Romano, 1990; Goldman & Glantz, 1998; McKenna & Williams, 1993; Pechmann, 1997; Siegel, 1998; Wallack, 1981). Antitobacco media campaigns are being conducted in at least seven states, and with the recent settlement of state to-bacco lawsuits, money may soon be available for campaigns in other states (Pechmann, 1997; Siegel, 1998).

Despite the growing use of antismoking media campaigns, little is known about their effectiveness. Existing research has focused on their impact on adult smoking cessation or overall cigarette consumption (Dwyer, Pierce, Hannam, & Burke, 1986; Flay, 1987; Hamilton, 1972; Hu, Sung, & Keeler, 1995; Lewit, Coate, & Grossman, 1981; Pierce, Macaskill, & Hill, 1990; Popham et al., 1993; Schneider, Klein, & Murphy, 1981; Warner, 1977). The few studies of the impact of these campaigns on youth smoking had mixed results. Community- and school-based interventions highlighted by a mass media campaign reduced smoking initiation rates among adolescents in Vermont, New York, and Montana (Flynn et al.,

115

1992, 1994, 1997; Secker-Walker, Worden, Holland, Flynn, & Detsky, 1997; Worden et al., 1996), Minnesota (Perry, Kelder, Murray, & Klepp, 1992), North Karelia (Vartiainen, Paavola, McAlister, & Puska, 1998), and Norway (Hafsted et al., 1997), but failed to influence smoking behavior among youths in southern California (Flay et al., 1995) or the southeast United States (Bauman, LaPrelle, Brown, Koch, & Padgett, 1991).

Existing studies have evaluated the results of research demonstration projects; it is not clear whether similar results could be expected from government-funded statewide media campaigns, which tend to target more homogeneous populations, provide less control over individual exposure, and introduce political factors that influence program effectiveness.

Only two studies, both using repeated cross-sectional survey designs, have examined the impact of government-funded, statewide mass media antismoking campaigns on youth smoking. Murray et al. found no significant change in the prevalence of youth smoking associated with a statewide, mass media-based intervention in Minnesota (Murray et al., 1992; Murray, Prokhorov, & Harty, 1994). Popham et al. (1994) found a small but significant decrease in youth smoking prevalence in California; however, the absence of a control group makes it impossible to attribute this effect to the media campaign.

This study examines the relation between exposure to a statewide antitobacco media campaign and changes in smoking status among youths by using a cohort design. The results of a 4-year, longitudinal study of a cohort of Massachusetts youths are reported. To assess the independent effect of the statewide antismoking media campaign on youth smoking behavior, the rate of progression to established smoking among youths who recalled exposure to television, radio, and outdoor antismoking advertisements at baseline was compared to youths who did not recall such exposure, controlling for exposure to antismoking messages from sources not related to the media campaign.

METHODS

The Massachusetts Antismoking Media Campaign

In 1992, Massachusetts voters approved a ballot initiative that increased the cigarette excise tax and established a comprehensive antismoking intervention that includes a media campaign (Siegel & Biener, 1997). The tax increase went into effect on January 1, 1993, and the media campaign was initiated in October 1993. The media campaign was conducted primarily through advertisements on television, on the radio, in newspapers, and on billboards. However, the aspects of the media campaign aimed at youths were almost entirely restricted to television, radio, and outdoor advertisements.

Of the $735,000 spent on advertisements that targeted youth during the first 6 months of the media campaign (the time during which the baseline survey took place), 80% was allocated for television advertisements, 14% for radio spots, 5% for billboards, and only 1% for newspaper advertisements (Arnold Communications, 1999). It should be noted that the goal of the early part of the Massachusetts antismoking media campaign was to expose a broad cross-section of the population, rather than specifically to target high-risk youths.

Design Overview

A 4-year follow-up telephone survey was conducted of a cohort of Massachusetts youths, age 12 to 15 at the time of the initial survey in 1993, to examine the relation between baseline exposure to the statewide antismoking media campaign and subsequent rates of progression to established smoking. Exposure to the three major channels of the media campaign was measured by ascertaining whether a respondent recalled having seen an antismoking advertisement on television or on billboards, or having heard one on the radio.

Rates of progression to established smoking between groups were compared on the basis of their reported baseline exposure to television, radio, and outdoor antismoking advertisements using multiple logistic regression, and controlling for age; race; sex; baseline smoking status (baseline susceptibility to smoking); smoking by parents, friends, and siblings; hours of television viewing; and baseline exposure to antismoking messages not related to the media campaign.

Sample

The 1993 Massachusetts Tobacco Survey, conducted by the Center for Survey Research, University of Massachusetts, Boston, was based on a probability sample of Massachusetts households drawn using random-digit dialing (Biener, Fowler, & Roman, 1994). On the basis of initial interviews with adult household informants in 11,463 households, a representative sample of youths was selected. Between October 1993 and March 1994, extended interviews were completed with 75% of eligible youths, yielding a final baseline sample of 1,606 youths; of these, 1,069 were between age 12 and 15.

Between November 1997 and February 1998, attempts were made to contact these 1,069 youths for a follow-up interview. It was not possible to locate 328 (30.7%) and interviews were completed with 618 (57.8%).

The primary analyses in this study are based on the 592 youths in this cohort who were not established smokers (as defined later) at baseline.

Measures

Progression to Established Smoking. Following Pierce, Gilpin, Farkas, and Merritt (1996) progression to established smoking was defined based on the number of cigarettes respondents reported having smoked in their lifetime. Youths who had smoked 100 or more cigarettes were classified as established smokers. The theoretical rationale and validation of this measure of adolescent smoking have been established previously (Choi, Pierce, Gilpin, Farkas, & Berry, 1997; Pierce, Choi, Gilpin, & Merritt, 1996; Pierce, Farkas, Evans, & Gilpin, 1995). This measure avoids the problem of the irregularity of smoking during adolescence and the problem of unreliable adolescent recall of smoking behavior during the past 30 days by establishing a defined threshold of total lifetime cigarettes smoked to measure regular smoking behavior. Self-reports of smoking behavior could not be validated because the survey was conducted via telephone.

Exposure to Antismoking Media Campaign. Baseline exposure to the statewide antismoking media campaign was assessed by ascertaining whether respondents recalled exposure to any antismoking messages or advertisements on television, the radio, or billboards in the past 30 days.

The baseline exposure measures were validated by comparing them to respondents' recall (at follow-up) of nine specific antismoking television advertisements that had aired during the previous 4 years, and also to the frequency of their reported exposure (at follow-up) to television, radio, and outdoor antismoking advertisements.

Exposure to Antismoking Messages Not Related to the Media Campaign. At baseline, respondents were asked whether they recalled any antismoking messages during the past 30 days in posters or pamphlets, in newspapers or magazines, at sporting events, or at school. These sources most likely do not reflect exposure to the media campaign, because these channels were not major ones used in the youth component of the media campaign. These exposures were controlled by including a variable in the analysis reflecting whether a respondent reported exposure to antismoking messages in more than one of these four media.

Potential Confounding Variables. The effects of several potential confounding variables were examined: (a) age group (12–13 years vs. 14–15 years); (b) sex; (c) race (non-Hispanic White vs. other); (d) baseline smoking status; (e) average hours of television viewing per day (measured at follow-up only); (f) presence of at least one adult smoker (a parent or sibling) in the household (at baseline); and (g) presence of at least one close friend who smoked (at baseline).

Baseline smoking status was classified into three categories: nonsusceptible nonsmokers, susceptible nonsmokers, and experimenters. Nonsmokers were defined as respondents who had smoked no more than one cigarette in their lives. Experimenters were those who had smoked more than one cigarette (but fewer than 100). Nonsmokers were classified as nonsusceptible to smoking if they answered "no" to the question, "Do you think that you will try a cigarette soon?" and "definitely not" to the questions, "If one of your best friends were to offer you a cigarette, would you smoke it?" and "At any time during the next year do you think you will smoke a cigarette?" This measure of susceptibility to smoking has been shown reliably to predict progression to established smoking (Choi et al., 1997; Pierce et al., 1995, 1996, 1998).

Television viewing behavior at follow-up was assessed by asking respondents how many hours of television they usually watched on weekdays and on Saturdays. Respondent's answers to these two questions were averaged and the result was coded into categories of no television viewing, up to 2 hours, and more than 2 hours of television viewing per day.

Mediating Variables.   To identify differences in knowledge or attitudes that might mediate the effect of an antismoking media campaign, eight questions were asked in the follow-up survey that reflected specific knowledge or attitudes addressed by the statewide media campaign: (a) Does smoking low-tar and low-nicotine cigarettes reduce people's risk of illness? (b) Can inhaling someone else's cigarette smoke cause lung cancer? (c) Do cigarettes contain poisonous chemicals? (d) Do cigarettes cause permanent wrinkles? (e) Do tobacco companies purposely advertise to get young people to start smoking? (f) Do nonsmokers prefer to go out with smokers or nonsmokers? (g) Does smoking make it harder or easier to do well at sports? (h) What proportion of kids at your high school are smokers?

Data Analysis

Logistic regression analyses was performed using baseline exposure to antismoking messages on television, on the radio, and on billboards as three independent variables and progression to established smoking as the dependent variable. All of the potential confounding variables were entered simultaneously into the model. Ninety-five percent confidence intervals (CIs) for odds ratios (ORs) were calculated using standard errors estimated by the Wald test (Hosmer & Lemeshow, 1989). All analyses were conducted using the SAS statistical package (SAS Institute, 1994).

The possibility was explored of interactions between television, radio, and outdoor advertising exposure and three of the covariates (age group, sex, and race) by adding (each in a separate regression) each of the relevant interaction terms to the model. The likelihood ratio test (Hosmer & Lemeshow, 1989) was used to determine whether the addition of an interaction term improved the overall fit of the regression model. Following Hosmer and Lemeshow (1989), a likelihood ratio test significance level of .15 was used as the criterion for inclusion of interaction terms. Thus, interactions that were found to improve the overall model fit at this .15 level were included in the final regression model.

To investigate the effect of exposure to the antismoking media campaign on the mediating variables, a comparison was made of respondents' knowledge and attitudes at follow-up between respondents who were exposed and respondents who were not exposed to television, radio, and outdoor antismoking messages at baseline. Three sets of logistic regression analyses were conducted using exposure to television, radio, or outdoor antismoking messages as the independent variables and the eight specific knowledge and attitude variables as dependent variables. The study controlled for the effects of age; sex; race; baseline smoking status; baseline exposure to smoking by parents, siblings, and friends; television viewing; and exposure to antismoking messages unrelated to the media campaign.

The baseline survey data set included weights that reflected each respondent's initial probability of selection. Because the primary objective of this study was to draw conclusions about the impact of exposure to the antismoking media campaign on progression to established smoking among members of this specific cohort, rather than to generalize to the state as a whole, unweighted analyses were conducted. Estimated standard errors do not account for design effects in the original baseline survey.

RESULTS

Exposure to Antismoking Television Advertisements and Validation of Exposure Measure

Among the 592 youths in the sample, 422 (71.3%) reported baseline exposure to antismoking messages on television. At follow-up, the mean number of television advertisements recalled by youths who had reported baseline television exposure (5.5) was significantly higher than the mean number recalled by youths who had reported no baseline television exposure (4.6) ($p = .0001$). Youths with baseline exposure to the television advertisements were also significantly more likely to report a higher frequency of exposure at follow-up ($p = .027$).

In the cohort, 195 youths (32.9%) reported baseline exposure to antismoking messages on the radio and 339 (57.3%) reported baseline exposure to antismoking messages on billboards. Youths who reported baseline exposure to radio advertisements and outdoor advertisements were significantly more likely to report higher exposure to radio (p = .001) and outdoor (p = .002) antismoking advertisements at follow-up.

Characteristics of the Study Population

There were no significant differences in age, sex, race, or baseline smoking status between youths who were and those who were not exposed to antismoking messages in each of the three media. However, youths who reported exposure to antismoking messages in one medium were significantly more likely also to report exposure in the other media (Table 7.1).

Youths exposed to television antismoking messages at baseline were significantly less likely to have an adult smoker in the household, but there was no significant difference between the exposed and unexposed youths in having at least one close friend who smoked (Table 7.1). Youths exposed at baseline to radio and outdoor antismoking messages were significantly more likely to have a close friend who smoked, but there was no significant association between exposure to radio or outdoor antismoking advertisements and having an adult smoker in the household.

Examination of Interaction Effects

Only one interaction was found significantly to improve the overall fit of the regression model (using a .15 level of statistical significance): that between exposure to television antismoking advertisements and age group. Therefore, this interaction term was included in the final regression model. Because of the presence of this interaction effect, the relation between exposure to television antismoking advertisements and progression to established smoking is reported separately for the two age groups.

Predictors of Progression to Established Smoking

The overall rate of progression to established smoking among the 592 youths in the cohort was 25.3% (95% CI = 21.8%, 28.8%). Among youths age 12–13 at baseline, those who had reported exposure to antismoking television advertisements at baseline were significantly less likely to have progressed to established smoking than those who had not reported such exposure, after controlling for the simultaneous effects of ex-

TABLE 7.1
Baseline Characteristics of Massachusetts Youth Cohort
by Exposure to Antismoking Messages on Television

	Exposed to Antismoking Messages on Television at Baseline (%) (N = 422)	Not Exposed (%) (N = 170)	Full Cohort (%) (N = 592)
Age at baseline			
12–13 years	51.2	53.5	51.9
14–15 years	48.8	46.5	48.1
Sex			
Male	50	48.2	49.5
Female	50	51.8	50.5
Race/ethnicity			
White, non-Hispanic	69	64.1	67.6
Other	31	35.9	32.4
Baseline smoking status			
Nonsusceptible nonsmoker	56.2	60.2	57.3
Susceptible nonsmoker	35.1	28.9	33.3
Experimenter	8.8	10.8	9.4
Baseline exposure to antismoking messages on the radio*			
No	60	84.7	67.1
Yes	40	15.3	32.9
Baseline exposure to antismoking messages on billboards or big signs*			
No	39.1	51.8	42.7
Yes	60.9	48.2	57.3
Baseline exposure to antismoking messages in other media[a]			
None or one medium only	21.6	45.3	28.4
More than one medium	78.4	54.7	71.6
Average hours of television viewing per day[b]			
None	3.6	7.7	4.8
Up to 2 hours	56	46.2	53.1
More than 2 hours	40.5	46.2	42.1
At least one adult smoker in household*			
No	64.7	54.1	61.7
Yes	35.3	45.9	38.3
At least one close friend smokes			
No	36	38.2	36.7
Yes	64	61.8	63.3

Note. Cohort includes only youths who were not established smokers (had smoked fewer than 100 cigarettes in their life) at baseline.

[a]Exposure to antismoking messages: (1) in newspapers or magazines, (2) in posters or pamphlets, (3) at sporting events, and (4) at school.

[b]Television viewing was measured at follow-up only.

*$p < .05$ for overall chi-square test (tests for significance of differences in distribution of variable for youths exposed vs. unexposed to antismoking messages on television at baseline).

posure to antismoking radio and billboard advertisements, exposure to antismoking messages not related to the campaign, television viewing, age, sex, race, baseline smoking status, and baseline exposure to smoking by parents, siblings, and friends (OR = .49; 95% CI = .26, .93) (Table 7.2). However, among youths age 14–15 at baseline, there was no significant effect of exposure to television antismoking advertisements on progression to established smoking (OR = .94, 95% CI = .48, 1.83).

Baseline exposure to antismoking advertisements on the radio (OR = .86; 95% CI = .55, 1.37), on billboards (OR = .85; 95% CI = .55, 1.31) and in other media (OR = 1.37, 95% CI = .83, 2.27) was not significantly associated with subsequent progression to established smoking (Table 7.2).

Effects of Baseline Exposure to Antismoking Advertisements on Mediating Variables

Baseline exposure to antismoking advertisements on television was not associated with subsequent differences in seven of the eight specific smoking-related knowledge and attitude variables tested (Table 7.3). However, youths who were exposed to antismoking advertisements on television at baseline were more than twice as likely to report at follow-up that fewer than half of the students at their high school were smokers (OR = 2.34, 95% CI = 1.40, 3.91). The relation between exposure to television antismoking advertisements and this outcome—an accurate as opposed to an inflated perception of youth smoking prevalence—differed by age group. Among youths age 14–15 at baseline, 26.9% of exposed youths had an accurate perception of youth smoking prevalence at follow-up, compared with 18.2% of unexposed youths (p = .13). Among youths age 12–13 years at baseline, 30.8% of exposed youths had an accurate perception of youth smoking prevalence at follow-up, compared with 13.3% of unexposed youths (p = 0.001).

Baseline exposure to radio and outdoor antismoking advertisements was not associated with subsequent differences in any of the eight smoking-related knowledge and attitude variables (data not shown).

CONCLUSIONS

This is the first longitudinal study to examine the effect of a statewide antismoking advertising campaign on smoking initiation among youths. The study found a significant effect of exposure to television antismoking advertising on progression to established smoking during a 4-year period that was specific to younger adolescents. It found no significant effect of exposure to radio or outdoor advertisements. It also found that youths ex-

TABLE 7.2

Adjusted Odds Ratios for Progression to Established Smoking
Among Massachusetts Youth Cohort, 1993–1994 to 1997–1998

	Adjusted Odds Ratio	95% Confidence Interval
Baseline exposure to antismoking messages on television[a]		
No	1.00	
Yes	.49	.26, .93
Baseline exposure to antismoking messages on the radio		
No	1.00	
Yes	.86	.55, 1.37
Baseline exposure to antismoking messages on billboards or big signs		
No	1.00	
Yes	.85	.55, 1.31
Baseline exposure to antismoking messages in other media[b]		
None or one medium only	1.00	
More than one medium	1.37	.83, 2.27
Average hours of television viewing per day[c]		
None	1.00	
Up to 2 hours	1.38	.48, 3.98
More than 2 hours	.98	.34, 2.89
Age at baseline		
12–13 years	1.00	
14–15 years	.64	.30, 1.37
Sex		
Male	1.00	
Female	1.11	.73, 1.67
Race/ethnicity		
White, non-Hispanic	1.00	
Other	.69	.44, 1.09
Baseline smoking status		
Nonsusceptible nonsmoker	1.00	
Susceptible nonsmoker	1.87	1.19, 2.92
Experimenter	8.53	4.29, 16.96
At least one adult smoker in household		
No	1.00	
Yes	1.63	1.07, 2.49
At least one close friend smokes		
No	1.00	
Yes	2.70	1.58, 4.59
Exposed to television antismoking messages and in 14- to 15-year-old age group (interaction term)		
No	1.00	
Yes	1.92	.78, 4.75

Note. Odds ratios are adjusted for all other variables in the table. Cohort includes only youths who were not established smokers (had smoked fewer than 100 cigarettes in their life) at baseline (N = 592).

[a]Represents effect on youths age 12–13 years, because older youths are represented in the interaction term.

[b]Exposure to antismoking messages: (1) in newspapers or magazines, (2) in posters or pamphlets, (3) at sporting events, and (4) at school.

[c]Television viewing was measured at follow-up only.

TABLE 7.3
Adjusted Odds Ratios Associated with Baseline Exposure
to Antismoking Television Advertisements for Smoking-Related
Knowledge and Attitude Variables Among Massachusetts
Youths at Follow-up, 1993–1994 to 1997–1998

Outcome Variable[a]	Adjusted Odds Ratio	95% Confidence Interval
Smoking low-tar and low-nicotine cigarettes does not reduce people's risk of illness	.81	.49, 1.33
Inhaling someone else's cigarette smoke can cause lung cancer	.94	.35, 2.50
Cigarettes contain poisonous chemicals	.72	.30, 1.70
Cigarettes cause permanent wrinkles	1.01	.51, 1.99
Tobacco companies purposely advertise to get young people to start smoking	1.02	.55, 1.88
Nonsmokers prefer to go out with nonsmokers	1.03	.68, 1.57
Smoking makes it harder to do well at sports	.94	.40, 2.22
Less than half of kids at your high school are smokers	2.34	1.40, 3.91

Note. This table reports results for a model in which baseline exposure to antismoking advertisements on television is the predictor variable. Odds ratios are adjusted for age, sex, race, baseline smoking status, presence of at least one adult smoker in the household at baseline, presence of at least one close friend who smoked at baseline, television viewing (measured at follow-up only), and baseline exposure to antismoking messages on the radio, on billboards, or in other media (posters or pamphlets, newspapers or magazines, sporting events, school).
[a]Measured at the follow-up survey.

posed to antismoking television advertisements were more likely to have an accurate as opposed to an inflated perception of youth smoking prevalence; this effect was significant only for younger adolescents.

There are several reasons why this observed effect represents a true association between television antismoking advertising and smoking initiation, rather than an effect due to bias or confounding. First, the observed effect is not explained by differences in susceptibility to smoking between the exposed and unexposed youths. Second, the observed effect is not explained by baseline differences in peer, sibling, or parental smoking. Third, the results are not explained by baseline differences in educational status of the adult informant. After adding this variable to the model, the effect of television antismoking advertisements on progression to established smoking among young adolescents was unchanged (OR = .52, 95% CI = .27, .99). Fourth, it would be expected that the confounding effects of an unknown variable would have appeared after controlling for baseline susceptibility to smoking; peer, parental, and sibling smoking; and baseline educational status of the adult informant. The odds ratio for the association between television antismoking advertisements and progression to established smoking among young adolescents was virtually unchanged after adding all of the aforementioned covariates.

Fifth, the results of this study are not explained by differential loss to follow-up. The response rate for youths exposed to television antismoking advertisements at baseline (58.7%) was only slightly higher than for unexposed youths (55.6%). Moreover, the proportion of experimenters and susceptible nonsmokers among all exposed nonsmokers at baseline who were successfully followed was identical to that among the exposed nonsmokers who were not followed (43.8%). In other words, if the study had been able successfully to follow the entire cohort of exposed youths, then it would not have expected to find any different rate of initiation based on baseline susceptibility, the strongest predictor of smoking initiation in the model.

There are two potential explanations for why the study found an effect of exposure to television, but not radio or outdoor antismoking advertisements. First, it is possible that television is a more powerful medium for reaching adolescents. Second, it is possible that the exposure of Massachusetts youths to radio and outdoor antismoking advertising was not extensive enough to affect their smoking behavior.

The finding that the Massachusetts antismoking media campaign was only effective in reducing smoking initiation among younger adolescents may indicate that older adolescents are resistant to antismoking messages. It is also possible that the specific messages used in the Massachusetts media campaign were more salient among young adolescents. Others have noted that interventions targeted toward older adolescent experimenters must be carefully crafted to address their high risk of smoking initiation (Choi et al., 1997).

The findings suggest that the effect of the media campaign on smoking initiation may be mediated, in part, by its effects on perceived youth smoking prevalence. Youths with baseline exposure to antismoking television advertisements were more likely 4 years later to have an accurate (as opposed to inflated) perception of the prevalence of youth smoking. Perceived smoking prevalence is known to have a strong influence on youth smoking initiation (Chassin, Presson, & Sherman, 1990; Chassin, Presson, Sherman, Corty, & Olshavsky, 1984; Collins et al., 1987; Sussman et al., 1988; U.S. Department of Health and Human Services, 1994). The Massachusetts advertisements aimed to denormalize tobacco use by showing youths that smoking by their peers is not the norm. The first advertisement featured a crowd of youths mobilizing to "make smoking history in Massachusetts." Subsequent advertisements attempted to show adolescents that smoking among peers their age was not the norm in Massachusetts.

Although the baseline exposure measure indicates exposure that occurred between October 1993 and March 1994, the effect observed in this study is probably due to the cumulative impact of the media campaign over the entire study period. Baseline exposure to television antismoking advertisements correlated strongly with later recall and frequency of exposure to advertisements. Thus, the independent variable is actually high versus low exposure, rather than exposure versus no exposure.

There are several limitations to this study. First, the exposure measure used assesses recall, not actual exposure to advertisements. It is impossible to tell whether exposed and unexposed youths differed in terms of actual exposure or if the youths differed only in terms of their attentiveness to the advertisements. Attentiveness to advertisements and recall of exposure may reflect some underlying variable that relates to smoking initiation risk and could confound the study results. However, no such variable was identified.

Second, the baseline survey (October 1993–March 1994) ran concurrently with the opening of the media campaign (October 1993), and it is possible that some early respondents who said they were not exposed had little chance to be exposed. Such an effect (misclassification of exposure status among "unexposed" early responders) would have blurred the true differences between the exposed and unexposed groups, leading to a bias toward the null hypothesis.

Third, these results do not imply that any antismoking media campaign is likely to be effective. Massachusetts spent more than $50 million, or about $8 per capita, on its campaign during the first 4 years (Arnold Communications, 1999). This is a particularly high per capita expenditure on counteradvertising, even when compared to other states with similar campaigns (Pechmann, 1997). Less intense campaigns would not be expected to have the same effect.

Fourth, it should not necessarily be concluded that radio and outdoor antismoking advertisements are not effective. These were not the predominant media used in the Massachusetts campaign. Nor should it necessarily be concluded that media campaigns cannot be effective in reaching older adolescents. A substantial difference (in the right direction) was found in perceived youth smoking prevalence between exposed and unexposed youths. With a larger sample size, this difference might have been statistically significant.

Finally, it is always possible that some unknown confounder could explain the observed association between exposure to antismoking television advertisements and reduced rates of progression to established smoking.

Despite these limitations, this study provides evidence that antismoking media campaigns may reduce smoking initiation among youths, especially among younger adolescents. Future research should attempt to confirm these findings in other populations and, using study designs that specifically quantify media exposure, further explore the age-specific effects of media campaigns, identify possible mediating variables, and examine the relative effectiveness of different types of advertising messages. A study design using a comparison group that had no exposure to antismoking advertisements would be ideal; however, this may be increasingly difficult given the sharing of media across states and the upcoming national media campaign.

ACKNOWLEDGMENTS

This work was supported by grants from the Robert Wood Johnson Foundation, Substance Abuse Policy Research Program (grant 031587) and the Massachusetts Department of Public Health, Massachusetts Tobacco Control Program (Health Protection Fund). This chapter originally appeared as an article in the *American Journal of Public Health, 90*(3), 380–386, in March 2000. We thank the American Public Health Association for permission to use it here.

REFERENCES

Alcalay, R. (1983). The impact of mass communication campaigns in the health field. *Social Science and Medicine, 17,* 87–94.
Arnold Communications. (1999). *Overview of Massachusetts Tobacco Control Youth Media.* Boston: Arnold Communications.
Bauman, K. E., LaPrelle, J., Brown, J. D., Koch, G. G., & Padgett, C. A. (1991). The influence of three mass media campaigns on variables related to adolescent cigarette smoking: Results of a field experiment. *American Journal of Public Health, 81,* 597–604.
Biener, L., Fowler, F. J., Jr., & Roman, A. M. (1994). *Technical Report: 1993 Massachusetts Tobacco Survey.* Boston: Center for Survey Research, University of Massachusetts.
Blum, A. (1994). Paid counter-advertising: Proven strategy to combat tobacco use and promotion. *American Journal of Preventive Medicine, 10*(Suppl. 3), 8–10.
Burns, D. M. (1994). Use of media in tobacco control programs. *American Journal of Preventive Medicine, 10*(Suppl. 3), 3–7.
Chassin, L., Presson, C. C., & Sherman, S. J. (1990). Social psychological contributions to the understanding and prevention of adolescent cigarette smoking. *Personality and Social Psychology Bulletin, 16,* 133–151.
Chassin, L., Presson, C. C., Sherman, S. J., Corty, E., & Olshavsky, R. W. (1984). Predicting the onset of cigarette smoking in adolescents: A longitudinal study. *Journal of Applied Social Psychology, 14,* 224–243.
Choi, W. S., Pierce, J. P., Gilpin, E. A., Farkas, A. J., & Berry, C. C. (1997). Which adolescent experimenters progress to established smoking in the United States? *American Journal of Preventive Medicine, 13,* 385–391.
Collins, L. M., Sussman, S., & Mestel-Rauch, J. (1987). Psychosocial predictors of young adolescent cigarette smoking: A sixteen-month, three-wave longitudinal study. *Journal of Applied Social Psychology, 17,* 554–573.

Dorfman, L., & Wallack, L. (1993). Advertising health: The case for counter-ads. *Public Health Reports, 108,* 716–726.

Dwyer, T., Pierce, J. P., Hannam, C. D., & Burke, N. (1986). Evaluation of the Sydney "Quit for Life" anti-smoking campaign. Part 2: Changes in smoking prevalence. *Medical Journal of Australia, 144,* 344–347.

Erickson, A. C., McKenna, J. W., & Romano, R. M. (1990). Past lessons and new uses of the mass media in reducing tobacco consumption. *Public Health Reports, 105,* 239–244.

Flay, B. R. (1987). Mass media and smoking cessation: A critical review. *American Journal of Public Health, 77,* 153–160.

Flay, B. R., Miller, T. Q., Hedeker, D., Siddiqui, O., Britton, C. F., Brannon, B. R., Johnson, C. A., Hansen, W. B., Sussman, S., & Dent, C. (1995). The television, school, and family smoking prevention and cessation project. VIII. Student outcomes and mediating variables. *Preventive Medicine, 24,* 29–40.

Flynn, B. S., Worden, J. K., Secker-Walker, R. H., Badger, G. J., Geller, B. M., & Costanza, M. C. (1992). Prevention of cigarette smoking through mass media intervention and school programs. *American Journal of Public Health, 82,* 827–834.

Flynn, B. S., Worden, J. K., Secker-Walker, R. H., Pirie, P. L., Badger, G. J., & Carpenter, J. H. (1997). Long-term responses of higher and lower risk youths to smoking prevention interventions. *Preventive Medicine, 26,* 389–394.

Flynn, B. S., Worden, J. K., Secker-Walker, R. H., Pirie, P. L., Badger, G. J., Carpenter, J. H., & Geller, B. M. (1994). Mass media and school interventions for cigarette smoking prevention: Effects 2 years after completion. *American Journal of Public Health, 84,* 1148–1150.

Goldman, L. K., & Glantz, S. A. (1998). Evaluation of antismoking advertising campaigns. *JAMA, 279,* 772–777.

Hafstad, A., Aaro, L. E., Engeland, A., Andersen, A., Langmark, F., & Stray-Pedersen, B. (1997). Provocative appeals in anti-smoking mass media campaigns targeting adolescents— the accumulated effect of multiple exposures. *Health Education Research, 12,* 227–236.

Hamilton, J. L. (1972). The demand for cigarettes: Advertising, the health scare, and the cigarette advertising ban. *Review of Economics and Statistics, 54,* 401–411.

Hosmer, D. W., & Lemeshow, S. (1989). *Applied logistic regression.* New York: Wiley.

Hu, T., Sung, H. Y., & Keeler, T. E. (1995). Reducing cigarette consumption in California: Tobacco taxes vs an anti-smoking media campaign. *American Journal of Public Health, 85,* 1218–1222.

Lewit, E. M., Coate, D., & Grossman, M. (1981). The effects of government regulation on teenage smoking. *Journal of Law and Economics, 24,* 545–569.

McKenna, J. W., & Williams, K. N. (1993). Crafting effective tobacco counteradvertisements: Lessons from a failed campaign directed at teenagers. *Public Health Reports, 108*(Suppl. 1), 85–89.

Murray, D. M., Perry, C. L., Griffin, G., Harty, K. C., Jacobs, D. R., Jr., Schmid, L., Daly, K., & Pallonen, U. (1992). Results from a statewide approach to adolescent tobacco use prevention. *Preventive Medicine, 21,* 449–472.

Murray, D. M., Prokhorov, A. V., & Harty, K. C. (1994). Effects of a statewide antismoking campaign on mass media messages and smoking beliefs. *Preventive Medicine, 23,* 54–60.

Pechmann, C. (1997). Does antismoking advertising combat underage smoking? A review of past practices and research. In M. E. Goldberg, M. Fishbein, & S. E. Middlestadt (Eds.), *Social marketing: Theoretical and practical perspectives* (pp. 189–216). Hillsdale, NJ: Lawrence Erlbaum Associates.

Perry, C. L., Kelder, S. H., Murray, D. M., & Klepp, K. I. (1992). Communitywide smoking prevention: Long-term outcomes of the Minnesota Heart Health Program and the Class of 1989 Study. *American Journal of Public Health, 82,* 1210–1216.

Pierce, J. P., Choi, W. S., Gilpin, E. A., Farkas, A. J., & Berry, C. C. (1998). Tobacco industry promotion of cigarettes and adolescent smoking. *JAMA, 279,* 511–515.

130   SIEGEL AND BIENER

Pierce, J. P., Choi, W. S., Gilpin, E. A., Farkas, A. J., & Merritt, R. K. (1996). Validation of susceptibility as a predictor of which adolescents take up smoking in the United States. *Health Psychology, 15,* 355–361.

Pierce, J. P., Farkas, A. J., Evans, N., & Gilpin, E. (1995). An improved surveillance measure for adolescent smoking? *Tobacco Control,* 4(Suppl. 1), S47–S56.

Pierce, J. P., Macaskill, P., & Hill, D. (1990). Long-term effectiveness of mass media led antismoking campaigns in Australia. *American Journal of Public Health, 80,* 565–569.

Popham, W. J., Potter, L. D., Bal, D. G., Johnson, M. D., Duerr, J. M., & Quinn, V. (1993). Do anti-smoking media campaigns help smokers quit? *Public Health Reports, 108,* 510–513.

Popham, W. J., Potter, L. D., Hetrick, M. A., Muthen, L. K., Duerr, J. M., & Johnson, M. D. (1994). Effectiveness of the California 1990–1991 tobacco education media campaign. *American Journal of Preventive Medicine, 10,* 319–326.

SAS Institute Inc. (1994). *SAS/STAT Software: Changes and enhancements, Release 6.10.* Cary, NC: SAS Institute.

Schneider, L., Klein, B., & Murphy, K. M. (1981). Governmental regulation of cigarette health information. *Journal of Law and Economics, 24,* 575–612.

Secker-Walker, R. H., Worden, J. K., Holland, R. R., Flynn, B. S., & Detsky, A. S. (1997). A mass media programme to prevent smoking among adolescents: Costs and cost effectiveness. *Tobacco Control, 6,* 207–212.

Siegel, M. (1998). Mass media antismoking campaigns: A powerful tool for health promotion. *Annals of Internal Medicine, 129,* 128–132.

Siegel, M., & Biener, L. (1997). Evaluating the impact of statewide anti-tobacco campaigns: The Massachusetts and California tobacco control programs. *Journal of Social Issues, 53,* 147–168.

Sussman, S., Dent, C. W., Mestel-Rauch, J., Johnson, C. A., Hansen, W. B., & Flay, B. R. (1988). Adolescent nonsmokers, triers and regular smokers' estimates of cigarette smoking prevalence: when do overestimations occur and by whom? *Journal of Applied Social Psychology, 18,* 537–551.

U.S. Department of Health and Human Services. (1994). *Preventing tobacco use among young people: A report of the surgeon general.* Atlanta, GA: US Department of Health and Human Services, Public Health Service, Centers for Disease Control and Prevention, National Center for Chronic Disease Prevention and Health Promotion, Office on Smoking and Health.

Vartiainen, E., Paavola, M., McAlister, A., & Puska, P. (1998). Fifteen-year follow-up of smoking prevention effects in the North Karelia youth project. *American Journal of Public Health, 88,* 81–85.

Wallack, L. M. (1981). Mass media campaigns: The odds against finding behavior change. *Health Education Quarterly, 8,* 209–260.

Warner, K. E. (1977). The effects of the anti-smoking campaign on cigarette consumption. *American Journal of Public Health, 67,* 645–650.

Worden, J. K., Flynn, B. S., Solomon, L. J., Secker-Walker, R. H., Badger, G. J., & Carpenter, J. H. (1996). Using mass media to prevent cigarette smoking among adolescent girls. *Health Education Quarterly, 23,* 453–468.

8

EVALUATING AIDS PUBLIC EDUCATION IN EUROPE: A CROSS-NATIONAL COMPARISON

Kaye Wellings
London School of Hygiene and Tropical Medicine

Many European countries developed substantial public education programs, making heavy use of mass media to address the HIV/AIDS (human immunodeficiency virus/acquired immunodeficiency syndrome) epidemic during the 1980s and early 1990s. This chapter reports on an effort to evaluate those somewhat diverse programs cross-nationally. There is some credible evidence for effects of those programs and some evidence that the size of the programs was associated with those effects. Part of the story, however, is the difficulty of evaluating such programs in a single nation or across nations in the urgent context of implementing national programs.

ATTRIBUTING OUTCOME TO INTERVENTION

A major problem relating to evaluation of the efficacy of public health campaigns is that of attributing outcome to intervention—the necessity for which is often held to be a central canon of evaluation of public health interventions: "The attributability of indicators is a characteristic which must be kept in mind at all times during evaluation, so that it can be assured that the outcome which the indicator is measuring is actually the result of the intervention or programme being evaluated" (Heymann & Biritwum, 1990).

There is not universal agreement on the feasibility of this idea. The view is also widely held that a particular outcome can rarely be ascribed to a specific intervention because a really effective campaign will have an effect far beyond its original remit, creating media discussion and providing the impetus for local efforts. This is particularly relevant in the case of AIDS, where an explicit objective of many campaigns was to effect a favorable climate in which interventions could be received. The objective of changing the social environment made it particularly difficult to disentangle the effects of specific interventions designed to improve knowledge and change attitudes and behavior in individuals, from those aimed more broadly at facilitating a favorable climate in which AIDS public education could take place.

Nevertheless the policymaker, charged with the task of cost-effective utilization of public resources, understandably wants to know which of the interventions have greatest impact and effectiveness. The researcher's role is to devise methods of achieving this objective. The more rigorous quasi-experimental methods—using phased implementation, randomized field experiments, the application of media weight bias, or simple random assignment of individuals to one group or another by which one group exposed to the intervention is compared with a control group with no such exposure—were contra-indicated in the case of AIDS-preventive strategies. There were definite practical, political, ethical, and in some cases, economic obstacles to the implementation of these strategies.

The *dose-controlled approach* requires time to implement and so was contra-indicated by the precipitate nature of the epidemic and the urgency and haste with which politicians needed to be seen to be responding to it. The urgent need for the data made it morally indefensible to deny people interventions in the interests of scientific accuracy. Further, quasi-experimental designs are difficult to apply to mass media campaigns because, ideally and by definition, virtually everyone is exposed to them. Most important, the success of the experimental approach depends on being able to ensure that observed differences in outcomes between treatment and control group do not arise from any other factors than the intervention under investigation.

Hypothetically, the European situation can be seen as a natural experiment in this respect. In the absence of opportunities for experimental work, cross-national comparisons might be usefully seen as presenting alternative opportunities for the assessment of different intervention strategies. Where constraints of time and budget have prevented the kind of controlled implementation that would permit a thoroughgoing comparison of the relative effectiveness of different interventions within countries, the European context can be seen as a kind of laboratory in which efficacy evaluation can take place.

The ultimate aim of AIDS preventive interventions has been to further halt spread of HIV. However, because of the long incubation period of

HIV and imperfections in the surveillance system set up to monitor its transmission, outcome measures related to morbidity and mortality have not been appropriate to evaluation in the context of the epidemic. Attention has turned instead to the variables most relevant to reducing HIV transmission, the adoption and maintenance of behaviors that protect uninfected individuals against infection with HIV and protect those already infected against discrimination and isolation.

An investigation of public response to the AIDS epidemic as reflected in knowledge, attitudes, and behavior measured has the potential to provide insights into the differential effects of social contexts, public health strategies, and specific intervention strategies in relation to AIDS public education. These indicators have been chiefly measured by means of survey investigation. The stock-in-trade of evaluation of public education in relation to the general population, particularly interventions deploying the mass media, has been the knowledge, attitude, and behavior (KAB) survey. Typically, the KAB survey investigates exposure to, recall, and comprehension of campaign messages and self-reported behavior change.

In 1993, the Europe Against AIDS Programme of the European Community commissioned the Sexual Health Programme at the London School of Hygiene and Tropical Medicine (LSHTM) to carry out a study, the aim of which was to attempt a comparative analysis of AIDS-related KAB surveys across Europe. In all, 18 KAB surveys were identified from a total of 14 countries. Surveys that collected data at more than one time point were used for the purpose of comparing data. More than one-point prevalence is needed for the purpose of cross-national comparisons, because single time points will be far more likely to reflect variations in methodology. In practice, this meant the inclusion of tracking surveys and the exclusion of surveys done at one time at the stage of data analysis.

Each of the countries did some sort of public education, often using the mass media. However, the efforts varied quite sharply from country to country and over time with regard to the behavioral focus of messages, the tone of messages, and the sheer size of the efforts. Differences among sites are explored as the findings are presented.

THE FINDINGS

Perceived Seriousness of the Disease

Results from KAB surveys showed high levels of awareness of AIDS relative to other preventable diseases. In most countries, the advent of the AIDS epidemic in the early 1980s was accompanied by a great deal of publicity, media coverage, and public alarm. As a result, high levels of public awareness may have been more a consequence of prior sensitization to the issue than to the interventions themselves.

A belief in personal susceptibility was low in most European countries. Although the degree of personal susceptibility might be expected to reflect the numbers of people with AIDS in each country, this does not appear to have been the case. Personal susceptibility in the United Kingdom, for example, was high and incidence of AIDS was low when compared with other European countries. The United Kingdom was the country that produced the most fear-arousing campaigns in Europe. The "Don't Die of Ignorance" campaign, in 1986 and 1987, was criticized for excessively evoking anxiety in an attempt to motivate the public. Its message "Don't Die of Ignorance" was superimposed on apocalyptic images of icebergs, tombstones, and lilies. Sex was strongly associated with death and doom-laden messages were delivered against a background of dark and foreboding purples, blacks, and reds.

By contrast, in France, a belief in personal susceptibility was low, yet this was a country with higher than average AIDS prevalence, three times higher than that of the United Kingdom. In France, AIDS public education began late. In 1988, the Agency for Health Promotion mounted the first campaign, some 2 years later than in other European countries. It is difficult to escape the conclusion, then, that in the United Kingdom and in France, the level of campaigning rather than the size of the AIDS epidemic was the important determinant of levels of personal susceptibility.

Knowledge of Routes of Transmission

In general, surveys revealed high levels of knowledge on major transmission routes for HIV, higher than for other major diseases (Table 8.1). Yet, misinformation persisted and although attempts were made to reduce this, exchange of saliva, kissing, insect bites, and swimming pools continued to be perceived as routes of transmission. Knowledge of the ways HIV was not transmitted is important first in terms of minimizing social disruption (blood supplies) and second to prevent ostracizing those at risk or HIV carriers (Wellings, 1992).

The majority of respondents did not see shaking hands with a person with AIDS as a method of transmission. However, there was a large amount of ambiguity about saliva and insects as routes of transmission. Moatti (1992) attributed this to the media coverage and experts being contradictory and ambiguous in some of their transmission messages. This underlines the importance of presenting theoretical risks (e.g., the possibility of saliva being a route of transmission) in a clear and simple manner to the general population rather than creating doubts and fears.

Table 8.1 brings some of the findings on knowledge of routes of transmission together. No assumptions should or can be made about differences

TABLE 8.1
Knowledge of Transmission Routes in Selected European Countries

	FRA June 1987 (%)	GER February 1987 (%)	IRE February 1987 (%)	NOR January 1986 (%)	SPA July–September 1987 (%)	SWE March–April 1986 (%)	SWI April–May [c] 1986 (%)	UK February 1986 (%)
Sexual intercourse: m + f	93.5	96.0[b]	97.0	85.0	78.0	—	88.0	62.0
Sexual intercourse: two men	[a]	[a]	[a]	95.0	90.0	—	[a]	95.0
Sharing needles for drug use	75.4	83.0	96.0	93.0	90.0	—	—	63.0
Kissing	10.5	41.0	—	33.0	46.0	30.0	26.0	21.0
Being bitten	10.0	21.0	—	21.0	—	29.0	—	33.0
Shaking hands	0.5	1.0[b]	—	3.0	6.0	—	32.0	2.0
Sharing utensils	9.0	15.0	15.0	13.0	25.0	—	[a]	11.0
Public toilets	9.5	19.0	26.0	—	27.0	30.0	21.0[d]	7.0
Giving blood	37.3	—	73.0	32.0	—	—	—	44.0
Receiving blood	—	87.0	91.0	95.0	89.0	—	54.0	92.0

Note. FRA = France: AGORAMETRIE Research Institute (Moatti et al., 1990); GER = Germany: IfD commissioned by Zeitschrift "Ja" (Federal Centre for Health Information, 1994, commissioned by Central Office of Health Education); IRE = Ireland: Irish Marketing Surveys for Health Education Bureau; NOR = Norway: Markedsog Mediainstituttet for Health Direcorate (Kraft & Rise, 1988); SPA = Spain: Centro de Investigaciones Sociologicas (CIS); SWE = Sweden: Institute for Social Medicine, Uppsala University (Brorsson, 1989); SWI = Switzerland: IUMSP, Lausanne; UK = United Kingdom: British Market Research Bureau for Central Office of Information (DHSS and Welsh Office, 1987).

[a]Question mentioned only sexual intercourse and did not make distinction between sex with a man and sex between two men.
[b]Question first asked in November 1986.
[c]Spontaneous mention.

between levels of knowledge between countries on the basis of the data presented. The dates in Table 8.1 are chosen to mark the earliest time appropriate survey data were available, rather than for purposes of comparison. For the sake of clarity, data for only one date are presented, though the trends continue to show the same differences between countries.

The responses again, to some extent, reflect the epidemics. In the United Kingdom, for example, one of the few countries in which drug use has not been a major risk category, the proportion of survey respondents who believe this to be a major transmission route for HIV is lower than it is for other countries. But responses also appear to reflect the content of the public education campaigns. For example, Spain was the only country in Europe in which health promotion agencies suggested that the virus could be transmitted via a shared toothbrush, and this appears to have been reflected in the proportion of the Spanish public who believed HIV to be transmitted by casual contact, kissing, and sharing utensils. This proportion was higher in Spain than in any other country.

Knowledge of Risk Reduction Strategies

The two messages that predominated in public education campaigns were to use a condom and to restrict the number of sexual partners, preferably to one, mutually exclusive relationship. Subordinate messages—including being careful about the choice of partners, practicing safer sex techniques, and abstinence—were featured less commonly. Very few countries, Spain being a notable exception, attempted to introduce the message to avoid needle sharing into campaigns addressed to the general public. Selective emphasis on each of the main messages varied with political and cultural factors, as did the extent to which attempts were made to broaden the range of messages further. Against this background, it is interesting to note the degree to which the choice of messages officially transmitted might appear to have influenced public perception of risk reduction strategies—for example, whether the Swiss public was more or less likely than the British or Swedish to cite condom usage as the primary risk reduction strategy.

Knowledge of the protective effects of condoms was high. In the United Kingdom, 95% of the population agreed with the statement "using a condom reduces the risk of getting HIV" (DHSS, 1987). It is interesting to note the degree to which the choice of official risk reduction messages influenced public perception of risk reduction strategies. Condom use was by far the most common response, but in countries like Ireland and Italy, where the condom message was not as widespread, the response was lower than in Switzerland and France, where campaigns were heavily dependent on the condom message.

The synergy of the Swiss *STOP AIDS* campaign was achieved by the repeated use of the condom shape as the "O" of tonight, of OK and of STOP, as the sun over a holiday scene, and as the moon over Swiss capital cities such as Geneva and Zurich. In 1987, church groups protested against the heavy reliance on the condom, and urged an alternative strategy based on monogamy as the risk reduction message. The Swiss Federal Office of Public Health replaced the condom with a wedding ring, which was met with a howl of protest from the Swiss public, who complained that the government was meddling in their morals instead of their health. The offending advertisement was removed and the condom reinstated.

In France, two parallel and distinct messages were transmitted. The first, a solidarity message, "AIDS is everybody's business," was linked to HIV/AIDS, whereas the second, to use a condom, carried no reference to AIDS. In no other country was there such a strong focus on the condom message. In Germany, there were condom advertisements, but they were not so prominent. In the Netherlands, the focus was on safer sex. And in the United Kingdom, advertisements carried an amalgam of messages to take a sexual history, to reduce the number of sexual partners, and to use a condom, with no clearly dominant message.

The dominance and purity of the condom message in Switzerland and France seem to have brought results. The greatest gains in terms of increases in condom use were, in fact, seen in these two countries (Fig. 8.1). In these two countries, a steep upward trend is observed both in knowledge of condoms as a risk reduction strategy, and in condom use itself.

It may be that the controversy generated in certain countries by the message to use condoms brought it to the public notice as effectively as did deliberate attempts to promote them, for it was not the efficacy of condoms as prophylactics that was cast in doubt in discussions, but the moral seemliness of promoting them. In Ireland, a country perhaps most exceptional in Europe in the extent of the hold on public morals of the Catholic church, the proportions mentioning monogamy and condom use were more equally balanced. However, over the period of the most intensive campaigning efforts, the number of people spontaneously mentioning condom use as an effective preventive measure increased from less than one half to more than two thirds, whereas the proportions mentioning monogamy and avoidance of casual sex decreased slightly.

Reducing numbers of partners, avoiding casual sex, and promoting faithfulness have also been promoted as risk reduction strategies in some countries. None of these have reached the high level of knowledge achieved by condom use. Switzerland introduced faithfulness in their prevention campaigns, but knowledge of this reached a peak in 1989 and then started to decline. There seems to be an inverse relation in knowledge of condom use and other risk reduction strategies in countries that strongly

Condom use
respondents reporting casual partners

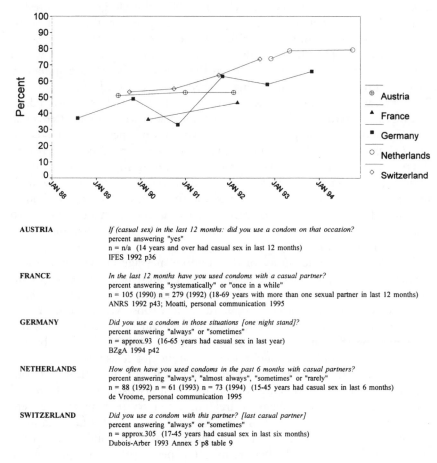

AUSTRIA   *If (casual sex) in the last 12 months: did you use a condom on that occasion?*
                   percent answering "yes"
                   n = n/a (14 years and over had casual sex in last 12 months)
                   IFES 1992 p36

FRANCE   *In the last 12 months have you used condoms with a casual partner?*
                   percent answering "systematically" or "once in a while"
                   n = 105 (1990) n = 279 (1992) (18-69 years with more than one sexual partner in last 12 months)
                   ANRS 1992 p43; Moatti, personal communication 1995

GERMANY   *Did you use a condom in those situations [one night stand]?*
                   percent answering "always" or "sometimes"
                   n = approx.93 (16-65 years had casual sex in last year)
                   BZgA 1994 p42

NETHERLANDS   *How often have you used condoms in the past 6 months with casual partners?*
                   percent answering "always", "almost always", "sometimes" or "rarely"
                   n = 88 (1992) n = 61 (1993) n = 73 (1994) (15-45 years had casual sex in last 6 months)
                   de Vroome, personal communication 1995

SWITZERLAND   *Did you use a condom with this partner? [last casual partner]*
                   percent answering "always" or "sometimes"
                   n = approx.305 (17-45 years had casual sex in last six months)
                   Dubois-Arber 1993 Annex 5 p8 table 9

FIG. 8.1.   Condom use by casual sex.

promoted condoms. For example, the Netherlands has high knowledge of condom use and very low responses to reduction in numbers of partners; the same is true for Switzerland. On the other hand, the United Kingdom, which was less bold in promoting condoms, had high responses for other risk reduction strategies as well.

Table 8.2 compares data from three countries with different selective emphases in terms of the "moral" message to practice monogamy or restrict numbers of partners, and the "pragmatic" messages to use a condom, at roughly the same point in time. Results show the selective empha-

TABLE 8.2
Knowledge of Risk Reduction Techniques

	Netherlands Oct 1988[a] What does the term safer sex mean to you? (%)	Switzerland Oct 1988[b] Methods of preventing AIDS infection (%)	UK Jul/Oct 1988[c] What does the term safer sex mean to you? (%)
Reducing no. partners	33	48	61
Using condoms	82	92	75
Careful choice of partner	n.a.	25	31

[a]Data from de Vroome, Paalman, and Sandfort (1990).
[b]Data from Wellings and McVey (1990).
[c]Data from IUMSP, Lausanne (unpublished report).

ses on different messages in different countries are to some extent reflected in the responses for each country. (These were spontaneous rather than prompted responses.) In all three countries, using a condom is the risk reduction strategy that most commonly comes to mind, but the proportion of respondents mentioning it is highest in Switzerland, where the condom message was dominant; slightly lower in the Netherlands, where a more diversified message was broadcast; and lowest in the United Kingdom, where considerable political ambivalence attended the condom message. Nevertheless, nearly half the Swiss respondents and one third of the Dutch respondents also mentioned restricting the numbers of partners, and one quarter mentioned careful choice of partner. Content of risk reduction messages in the campaigns seems not to be directly reflected in perceptions of the effectiveness of each.

Evidence of Behavior Change

Data on the behavior of the general population is sparser and less satisfactory than that on knowledge and attitudes in terms of comparability. In relation to questions on sexual behavior, comparability is limited further by the use of different bases. In some cases, agencies avoided possible offence to a general population by focusing on the sexually active, by filtering out those respondents who reported having had more than one partner in the last year and asking the most sensitive questions only of that subgroup. Methods varied from country to country so that in some countries the denominator included the whole population and in others only the population who were sexually active. In an attempt to achieve post hoc standardization, denominators were recalculated when necessary and wherever possible (where data were available with which to do so).

Numbers of Partners. More or less irrespective of the country, the figures relating to number of partners—whether expressed in terms of multiple partners or casual partners—fluctuate within fairly narrow bands (Figs. 8.1 and 8.2). The question wording varies from the candidly factual in the French question, *In the past 12 months how many different sexual*

Respondents reporting multiple partners
in recent time period

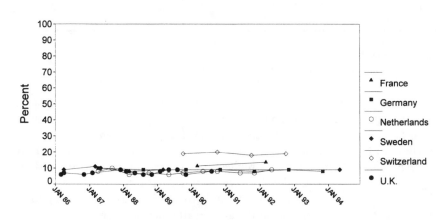

<table>
<tr><td>FRANCE</td><td>In the past 12 months, how many different sexual partners have you had?(write down the number)
percent writing down more than one partner in last 12 months
n = 916 (1990) n = 1927 (1992) (18-69 years)
Moatti, personal communication 1995</td></tr>
<tr><td>GERMANY</td><td>During the course of a year it is quite possible that one has more than one partner, and many people sometimes have a casual fling which then becomes intimate. In the last 12 months, have you had more than one partner with whom you were intimate, I mean, with whom you had sexual intercourse?
percent answering "yes"
n = approx.2295 (16-65 years)
Christiansen, personal communication 1995</td></tr>
<tr><td>NETHERLANDS</td><td>In the past six months, have you had sex with a steady partner only or also with other people?
percent answering "with steady partner and other(s)" or "casual partners only"
n = approx.1015 (15-45 years)
Dingelstad, de Vroom & Sandfort 1992 p5 table 4a</td></tr>
<tr><td>SWEDEN</td><td>Have you had more than one sexual partner during the last 6 months?
percent answering "yes"
n = approx.2369 (16-44 years)
Brorsson 1994 p16; Brorsson 1989 p30</td></tr>
<tr><td>SWITZERLAND</td><td>Have you changed steady partners once or met a new partner in the course of the year?
percent answering "yes"
n = approx.2602 (17-45 years)
Dubois-Arber 1993 p132, table 6.2.4</td></tr>
<tr><td>UK</td><td>In the last 12 months, how many men/women have you had sexual intercourse with? Please include every man/woman you have had sexual intercourse with in the last 12 months, even if only once.
percent reporting 2 or more partners of opposite sex in last year
n = approx.1963 per quarter (16 years and over)
HEA/BMRB 1987 p127 table 61; HEA/BMRB 1990 p32 table 30; HEA/BMRB 1992 p85 table 6b</td></tr>
</table>

FIG. 8.2.   Condom use by multiple partnerships.

partners have you had? (Write down the number), to the more enabling and permissive German question, *During the course of a year it is quite possible that one has more than one partner and many people sometimes have a casual fling which then becomes intimate. In the last 12 months have you . . . ?*

At the European level, it would seem that few changes in terms of number of sexual partners have occurred as a result of the AIDS epidemic. The proportions of people reporting more than one person in the last year remained remarkably static.

Condom Use.   The proportion of the population who claimed to have used condoms in the recent past was small at the aggregate level. Between one quarter and one third of people across Europe claimed to have used a condom in the recent past (Fig. 8.1). Interpretation of such results has led in some cases to a criticism of campaigns for not having achieved their objectives. Yet, as has been pointed out elsewhere (Wellings, 1988), although large-scale changes in behavior are often assumed to be necessary, the actual numbers of people who need to effect changes in their behavior in order to reduce the risk of HIV transmission is relatively small. The proportion of people who report having had more than one partner in the past year in the United Kingdom, for example, is around 10% (Fig. 8.1). If the 4% to 6% reporting homosexual relations, and the 1% who inject drugs is added, then the proportion actually at risk is relatively small (HEA/BMBR, 1992).

It is at the level of subgroup activity that the gains really become apparent. Fig. 8.1, the proportion of respondents with casual partners who reported condom use, shows marked upward trends for most countries but especially for Germany (one night stands), Switzerland (last casual partner), and France (multipartnered heterosexuals). The increase in reported condom use in young people was equally noticeable (Fig. 8.1). The marked increase in the United Kingdom data between 1990 and 1992 may in part be attributable to a change in the survey methodology. Major progress was made in Switzerland and, when the data for young people was further divided into those respondents who always use condoms, the results were even more impressive (Fig. 8.1). It is important to remember that the purpose of AIDS public education is not only to initiate protective behaviors, but also to maintain them.

Reports of behavior change in relation to condom use are more marked than those with respect to restrictions in numbers of partners. Figures for condom use show some remarkable achievements over the period of most intensive campaigning (e.g., 1986–1989). Furthermore, although it is clear (as far as indicated by the data) that higher rates of condom use seem to have been achieved in some countries than in others, this is not the case for reductions in numbers of partners, exclusivity in relationships, reductions in the prevalence of casual sex, and so on.

In terms of sexual behavior, on the whole, people seem to opt for two main preventive measures (i.e., monogamy and condom use). The practice of safe, nonpenetrative sexual techniques does not seem to have played an important role, even among those having sex with casual partners. Very few surveys even contain questions about nonpenetrative sex, which in itself is an indicator of the rarity of such activity and of its low priority as a risk reduction strategy. Even in the Netherlands, one of the few countries to actively promote safer sex practices other than condom use, the numbers reporting adoption of this protective measure are low.

DISCUSSION

Difficulties of International Comparisons

Clearly in practice, differences between countries make it impossible to hold constant all other variables save the intervention itself. Direct comparisons are also difficult because of methodological differences between surveys and measurement effects within each. The multiplicity of different social, cultural, political, and health factors operating in the different countries rules out any kind of controlled analysis. Just as the campaigns themselves are context specific, so too are the methods used to appraise them.

The practical frustrations of dealing with secondary data quickly become apparent in the context of European comparisons. Social and cultural factors play a major part in the selection of methods. Postal surveys among the socially obedient Swedes and Norwegians, for example, dependably produce response rates of 60% or more, whereas in Britain and Germany response rates of 30% are nearer the norm. Similarly, telephone surveys can be conducted in Switzerland and France safe in the knowledge that more than 95% of the population have a telephone, but the same assumption cannot be made for many other European countries. It may be possible to use sexual vernacular in the Netherlands or Denmark, where sexual terms do not double as terms of abuse, but the same words may offend in other countries and could risk reducing the response rate.

There have also been budgetary constraints on the capacity to conduct evaluative research. Mass media campaigns are expensive, and extensive evaluation was seen by some as an unnecessary luxury, or alternately as a means of cost cutting. Countries that were less energetic in terms of execution of campaigns were also, not surprisingly, less energetic in terms of evaluating them, so it tends to be difficult to evaluate public education in less active countries. In some countries (e.g., Belgium and Finland), little money has been made available for evaluation. In others (e.g., France, Spain, Norway), surveys have been more sporadic and smaller scale. In Great Britain and in Switzerland, by contrast, substantial sums of money have been spent on large-scale continuous KAB surveys. As a result, comparisons often have to be made between surveys with very different sample sizes, ranging from under 1,000 per survey (Ireland) to over 2,000 per survey (Germany, Sweden, and United Kingdom, per quarter).

Moreover, there has been no standardization of wording in the KAB surveys conducted in the context of HIV/AIDS prevention in the European countries. A WHO protocol for such a standard instrument, although valuable for developing countries and for Eastern Europe, was completed too late for use in most of the Western European countries. Differences in question wording are substantial. There was still no guarantee of comparability in the underlying constructs. This has important implications when we need to make clear the basis for confidence that between-country differences genuinely reflect between-country differences in response to public education around the AIDS epidemic, and not the manner in which the data was collected or the method by which comparison was achieved.

Thus, cross-national comparison of data is hampered by the lack of comparability. Even when there is a common research protocol and a shared language, when there is good access to the data available, and a good overall knowledge of the national cultures, the problems of a macrosociological comparison are seemingly formidable.

Social Desirability Effect

The main methodological problems of KAB surveys are those of validity and reliability. Those most likely to be willing to disclose details of their personal opinions and behavior cannot be taken to be representative of the population as a whole. Surveys of this kind are particularly susceptible to the influence of the social desirability response.

These difficulties were exacerbated in relation to the assessment of HIV/AIDS preventive strategies. The pace and precipitate nature of the AIDS epidemic made it difficult to set in place the necessary evaluative procedures and resulted in hasty preparation of evaluation work in most countries. The cautionary note of Fishbein and Middlestadt (1989) that "the AIDS epidemic is much too serious to allow interventions to be based on some communicator's untested and all too often incorrect intuitions about the factors that will influence the performance or non-performance in a given population" went largely unheeded at the start of the epidemic (p. 232).

Simple methodological principles, those relating to order effect in question formulation, for example, seemed to be overlooked. Part of a Norwegian survey had to be repeated because of failure to take account of the biasing effect of question order (Kraft & Rise, 1988). In the United Kingdom, an expensive piece of research had to be abandoned because insufficient time had been invested in its preparation, and in Sweden inadequate piloting failed to reveal difficulties of understanding certain questions (Brorsson, 1989). Hopefully, subsequent generations of programs will benefit from past mistakes.

Pre- and posttest surveys and tracking surveys (involving repeating the same set of questions at intervals of similarly selected samples) offers an improvement over cross-sectional data, but provide no assurance that what is being measured is the effect of a particular intervention and not a generalized response to the AIDS epidemic. In the case of the AIDS epidemic, the usual problem of interference was heightened. Public knowledge was accumulating, through media coverage, commercial advertising, and so on, at such a pace that even a short time lag could result in a change in measures with or without intervention. Not only has it been difficult to separate out the effects of national campaigns from the effects of national news coverage, but overspill between countries has made it difficult to separate out the effects of one national campaign from another. In Ireland, for example, 75% of households receive British TV. So the Irish public had been heavily exposed to British campaigns before the start of their own in 1987 (Harkin & Hurley, 1988).

Clearly, there have been real difficulties in prospectively controlling for intervening variables in the evaluation of AIDS preventive activities. Nevertheless, although experimental design was not feasible, imaginative analysis and interpretation of results have compensated in some cases. Attempts have been made in several countries to attribute outcome to intervention retrospectively. One method of effecting this has been to partially disaggregate the data at the analysis stage using outcome variables to discriminate between those who have and have not been exposed to campaigns. The evaluation of the Dutch "excuses" campaign designed to encourage condom use, for example (de Vries, 1989), compared responses of those who claimed to have recalled the campaign with those of others who had no recall. A statistically significant higher level of endorsement of the messages of the campaign among respondents who claimed to have seen the campaign, provides support for attributing the effects to the campaign. Alternatively, it has been possible to select and measure the retention of information attributable only to the campaign, for example, in the United Kingdom (Wellings & Orton, 1988).

Comparisons on the basis of existing data are difficult. Provided, however, that time trends are used in the analysis, trends in the data may be compared with greater confidence that the scale of change in different countries reflects real differences and not variations contingent on the measuring instrument.

What is most striking about these data is that, despite differences in question wording relating to different time periods, frequencies, and so forth, and despite all the differences in methods of data collection, sample selection, and so forth, the data show remarkable consistency across Europe. Despite the fragility of the data and the frustrations of dealing with data resulting from differently designed and conducted surveys, it is difficult to avoid the conclusion that those campaigns that set out single-mindedly to increase condom use, and in which those responsible for public education were most resolute in countering resistance, seem to have made greater progress in achieving their goals than have countries in which there was a greater degree of hesitancy over the condom message. It seems as if those countries where AIDS public education has maintained a constant presence and a continuous flow are characterized by an increase in condom use more than those where campaigns have been peaks and troughs of activity.

REFERENCES

Brorsson, B. (1989). *Allmanheten och HIV/AIDS; Kunskaper, attityder och beteende 1986–1989* [Public opinion and HIV/AIDS: Knowledge, attitudes and behaviour 1986–1989]. (Rep. No. 9). Uppsala University.

BZgA (1994). *AIDS in öltentlichen Bewustein der Bundesrepublik: Wiederholungsbefraging 1993* [AIDS in the public consciousness of the Federal Republic: Repetition inquiry, 1993]. Cologne: Federal Centre for Health Information (Author).

de Vries, K. (1989). STD Foundation, The Netherlands, personal communication.

de Vroome, E. M. M., Paalman, M. E. M., & Sandfort, T. G. M. (1990). AIDS in the Netherlands: The effects of several years of campaigning. *International Journal of STD & AIDS, 1,* 268–275.

DHSS and Welsh Office (1987). *AIDS: Monitoring response to the public education campaign, February 1986–February 1987.* London: Her Majesty's Stationery Office.

Fishbein, M., & Middlestadt, S. E. (1989). Using the theory of reasoned action as a framework for understanding and changing AIDS-related behaviours. In V. M. Mays, G. W. Albee, & S. F. Schneider (Eds.), *Primary prevention of AIDS* (pp. 322–348). Newbury Park, CA: Sage.

Harkin, A. M., & Hurley, M. (1988). National Survey on public knowledge of AIDS in Ireland. *Health Education Research, 3*(1), 25–29.

HEA/BMRB (1992). *AIDS testimonials advertising monitor; Evaluation of winter campaign 1991/2.* HEA Research Report, London.

Heymann, D. L., & Biritwum, R. (1990). *Evaluation of the effectiveness of National AIDS programmes.* Geneva: World Health Organization.

IUMSP. Unpublished report. Lausanne, Switzerland: Institute for Social and Preventative Medicine.

Kraft, P., & Rise, J. (1988). AIDS public knowledge in Norway 1986. *NIPH Annals, 11*(1), 19–28.

Moatti, J. P. (1992). Impact on the general public of media campaigns against AIDS: A French evaluation. *Health Policy, 21,* 233–247.

Moatti, J. P., Dab, W., Pollak, M., Quesnel, P., Anes, A., Beltzer, N., Ménard, C., & Serrand, C. (1990). Les attitudes et comportements des Français face an SIDA. *La Recherche, 223,* 888–895.

Wellings, K., & McVey, D. (1990). Evaluation of the HEA AIDS press campaign: December 1988 to March 1989. *Health Education Journal, 49*(3), 108–117.

Wellings, K., & Orton, S. (1988). Evaluation of the HEA public education campaign: February to June 1988. *HEA AIDS Programme Information Pack.* London: Health Education Authority.

Wellings, K. (1988). Do we need to change sexual behaviour, should we and can we? *Health Education Journal, 46,* 57–60.

Wellings, K. (1992). *Assessing AIDS prevention in the general population.* Report for the EC Concerted Action Assessment of AIDS/HIV Preventive Strategies, IUMSP, Lausanne, Switzerland.

9

EFFECTS OF A MASS MEDIA CAMPAIGN TO PREVENT AIDS AMONG YOUNG PEOPLE IN GHANA

Susan McCombie
Georgia State University

Robert C. Hornik
University of Pennsylvania

John K. Anarfi
University of Ghana

Ghana is located in West Africa and has an estimated population of 18 million, with about 47% under age 15 and 31% living in urban areas. The former British colony attained independence in 1957 and has an economy dominated by agriculture; cocoa, coffee, rice, and cassava are the major crops. The first AIDS cases were reported in the late 1980s, but like many countries in West Africa, the incidence of HIV was relatively low in the early 1990s.

In 1991, the Ministry of Health launched a multimedia campaign designed to increase awareness of AIDS and to promote AIDS prevention in Ghana. The campaign was designed by Apple Pie, a local advertising agency with assistance from AIDSCOM, a U.S. Agency for International Development (USAID) technical support project implemented by the Academy for Educational Development that assisted governments and organizations in the developing world in HIV prevention activities between 1988 and 1993.

In 1990, exploratory focus group work was conducted to identify key issues for the campaign. At that time, awareness of AIDS was high, but it was not seen as an important problem in the country. Many felt that AIDS was a problem only for prostitutes and people who traveled outside the country. The campaign was directed predominantly at young people, and

used a combination of television and radio advertisements designed to disseminate the following messages: (a) AIDS is not a foreign disease. (b) A
person can have the virus for 5 or more years and still look healthy. (c)
Personal behavior changes are necessary to prevent its spread. A number
of materials were produced to be distributed in conjunction with the campaign, including posters, comic books, badges, key rings, and T-shirts.

The core of the broadcast campaign consisted of three television spots.
The first was directed at the general population, and used a rainstorm
scene with narration emphasizing the dangers of AIDS and the need to prevent transmission. A subtle reference to condoms was implied in a discussion of "rainboots." A second spot showed young men discussing sexual
relationships, with one advising the other to stick to his regular partner to
avoid AIDS. The third showed a mature man advising two young men to
avoid chasing girls because of the risk of AIDS. Each advertisement contained some basic information about AIDS, with emphasis on the healthy
carrier state and length of the incubation period. All were followed by a
campaign tag phrase—"Don't be careless, get protection"—with advice to
visit a health center for more information.

The campaign began in August 1991 and continued until June 1992. By
December 1991, each region had also participated in a regional launch, at
which materials such as posters, comic books, badges, and condoms were
distributed. The launches involved traditional community meetings (dur-
bars) that often involved speakers from the Ministry of Health and local
officials.

A school outreach component was also included in which assemblies
were held at secondary schools around the country. A typical assembly
would include lecture/discussion by medical personnel, question and answer periods, showing a film about AIDS, and distribution of pamphlets,
comic books, and posters. A total of 58 schools were visited during the
campaign. An evaluation of the campaign was conducted to assess the impact of the broadcast media messages on knowledge, attitudes, and behavior among the target population.

The Annenberg School for Communication at the University of Pennsylvania was asked to oversee the evaluation of the project. The basic research questions for the evaluation included establishing whether a substantial portion of the population was exposed to the campaign, and
whether they changed their beliefs and their sexual behavior in response.
This chapter summarizes the results of the evaluation.

METHODS

Two surveys of knowledge, attitudes, and practices among 15- to 30-year-
olds were conducted. The first survey, done in July 1991, established base-

line data prior to the campaign launch. The second survey was conducted one year later in July 1992.

The surveys were conducted in two regions of Ghana: Central (Cape Coast) and Brong-Ahafo (Techiman). Both areas are predominantly Akan speaking, but with some cultural variation between the Fante in the Cape Coast area and the Brong of the Techiman area. Cape Coast is a coastal settlement noted for its large number of educational institutions. The traditional occupation is fishing, but the educational institutions offer employment to a sizable segment of the educated population. Techiman, on the other hand, is set in a transition zone between the forest to the south and the savannah to the north. Farming is the traditional occupation, but the town is better known for its commercial activities, including a large periodic market that attracts people from all over Northern Ghana.

In the first survey, 21 interviewers and 4 supervisors carried out the field interviews. All team members were students or staff of the Institute of Statistical, Social, and Economic Research, University of Ghana. The supervisors were all males, and there were 6 female and 15 male interviewers. In the second survey, all of the supervisors and 17 of the interviewers remained on the survey team. Seven new interviewers were added. Of the interviewers, 9 were females and 14 were males. The questionnaire was translated into Akan and translated back into English independently to check for clarity. Interviews were conducted in Akan or English, depending on the choice of the respondent.

Data from the 1984 census were used to select 50 clusters at random from lists of enumeration areas (EA). The selection was stratified to overrepresent urban areas. Fifteen urban and 10 rural clusters were selected from each region. Within each cluster, the first house was selected near the center of the EA or the place the EA was named for (i.e., Barclays' Bank). In each house, all households were listed and one was randomly selected. (In Ghana, a number of unrelated households may occupy a single large house.) The individual to be interviewed was selected randomly from a list of all persons from 15 to 30 years old who had slept in the selected household the preceding night. Interviewing continued by going to adjacent houses until 30 interviews per cluster were completed. This strategy oversampled households near the center of the EA, and thus risked being unrepresentative of the general population. However, because the approach was repeated at both interview waves, comparability over time, which was central to claims of campaign effects, was not threatened.

In order to keep the samples as comparable as possible, most of the originally selected clusters were retained in 1992. Seven of the 50 were replaced with adjacent areas. Interviewers were instructed to select new households and not interview the same individuals. To control for a possible interview effect (a change in the person's responses based on knowledge gained from the original interview), each person was asked if they had been interviewed the previous year, and this information was recorded on the questionnaire. In 1992, only 6% said they had been interviewed before.

The basic research design was a pre–post campaign comparison of similar samples. It was not feasible to incorporate a control group that was not exposed to the campaign given the pattern of widespread broadcast exposure. It was possible, then, that any observed pre–post differences had other causes than direct effects of the campaign. The 12-month period between surveys included not only the advertising campaign, but also other media coverage of AIDS, and an independent intervention designed to stimulate use of condoms for contraceptive purposes. Thus, a constant concern was differentiating the effects of the campaign from other sources of influence, where that was possible. Each analysis then features two elements. First, there is a simple presentation of the pre–post campaign data, searching for evidence that there was a statistically significant change in an outcome. Second, there is the report of additional analyses meant to differentiate the campaign effects from other influences.

Data entry was performed using SPSS/PC. Analysis was performed using SPSS/PC and SPSS 5.0 for Windows.

Characteristics of the Sample

The surveys were not designed to be nationally representative, and all of the findings here overrepresent urban areas, where educational level and income are higher. Table 9.1 shows the basic demographic characteristics of the respondents for the two surveys. There were two important differences. In the second survey, a larger proportion of women was interviewed. There was also a slightly lower educational level, with fewer having completed secondary school in 1992. The change in educational level partially reflected the shift in sex distribution, because women in Ghana are less likely to complete a secondary education.

Differences between the two samples need to be taken into account in making inferences about changes over time. Potential artifacts from changes in the sex distribution can be ruled out by stratifying the sample by sex for key comparisons, such as reports of sexual behavior.

One of the expected outcomes of the campaign is increased knowledge, which is associated with higher educational levels. A decrease in average educational level between the two samples will tend to underestimate, rather than overestimate, improvements (i.e., increases in knowledge) over time. The same applies to any increase in condom use, a behavior generally associated with higher educational levels. Thus, if there are increases in knowledge, despite a slightly lower educational level, one can be more certain that there were actual improvements than if the educational level had gone up in the second survey.

TABLE 9.1
Characteristics of the Sample

	1991	1992
Sample size	1,553	1,499
Male (%)	55.4	49.3*
Female (%)	44.6	50.7*
Mean age	22.0	22.0
Household wealth score	4.2	4.2
Educational level (%)		
None	11.0	12.8
Some elementary	21.9	22.6
Completed elementary	27.4	28.1
Some secondary/junior secondary	18.8	21.4*
Completed secondary/technical/commercial	18.3	13.0*
Postsecondary	2.6	2.0
Media Exposure (%)		
Radio in household	67.2	65.7
Listen to radio at least once per week	69.2	68.4
TV in household	30.1	34.5*
Watch TV at least once per week	71.2	70.6

*Significant difference by chi-square test, $p < .05$.

The wealth score, which was calculated based on possession of a number of household amenities, remained exactly the same. There was an increase in TV ownership, which may reflect sampling variation or actual changes in the population under study. Exposure to TV remained the same, and shows a much higher percentage than ownership due to the common practice of gathering at the homes of those who own a TV to watch.

Table 9.2 shows the percent of men and women who were married, had a regular partner or no partner, as well as the percent who had ever had

TABLE 9.2
Percent Married, with Partner and Children by Sex and Time of Survey

	Men		Women		Total	
	1991	1992	1991	1992	1991	1992
Married	17.2	20.0	32.5	34.7	24.0	27.5*
Regular partner	37.7	33.0	29.9	28.6	34.2	30.8*
No partner	45.1	47.0	37.7	36.7	41.8	41.8
Ever had children	22.8	26.3	48.3	48.6	34.2	37.6
N	860	739	693	760	1553	1499

*Significant difference by chi-square test, $p > .05$.

children. Note that women were more likely than men to report being married or in a steady partnership and having children. This reflects the fact that women enter partnerships and reproduce at earlier ages than men in this population.

In 1992, both sexes were slightly more likely to report being married as opposed to having a regular partner. The distinction between a marriage and a stable partnership is complex in this culture. Couples may live together for years and produce children, but have yet to complete all of the requirements to be technically "married." Reports of partnership status for those in this situation vary according to the individual and context in which the question is asked. Given this and the fact that the proportion who had no steady partner remained the same, the shift in marital status was not considered to be a cause for concern in comparing the two surveys.

RESULTS

Reach of the Campaign

The first question considered is the extent of exposure to the campaign. Was it successful in reaching the target population? Who was reached and by which media?

Based on results of the baseline survey, the potential reach of the campaign was expected to be high. The proportion who never watched TV or listened to radio was low. In the whole sample, 70% watched TV at least once a week and from 68% to 69% listened to radio at least once a week. In 1992, only 7% said they never watched TV or listened to radio (4% in urban, 12% in rural areas). Thus, more than 90% of the sample could potentially have heard the campaign messages. Differences in access to media were noted according to region, urban versus rural, and sex. Rural people and women were somewhat less likely to report access to television and radio. On the basis of these patterns, it was expected that women in rural areas would show the least exposure to the campaign.

Television.   Television exposure was considered in relation to the following question: "Have you heard anything about illness on television in the last two months?" If the respondents answered yes, then they were asked what illness it was about. There were significant increases in mentioning AIDS among both sexes and in urban and rural regions (Table 9.3). Overall, 58% mentioned hearing about AIDS on television in 1992, up from 38% in the baseline survey. As expected from the differences in exposure to information identified in the baseline survey, rural women were the least likely to be exposed to the messages on television. Still, there

TABLE 9.3
Exposure to Campaign by Sex and Urban Versus Rural

		Men		Women	
		1991	*1992*	*1991*	*1992*
Mentions hearing about AIDS on	Rural	48.3	65.3	32.6	46.7
radio in the last 2 months	Urban	50.8	67.2	42.4	61.1
Mentions seeing something about	Rural	28.8	53.0	19.8	37.3
AIDS on TV in the last 2 months	Urban	46.0	66.1	47.4	64.7
Completes phrase "Don't be careless:	Rural	NA	47.7	NA	26.5
Get *Protection*"	Urban	NA	56.4	NA	47.8

*All changes between 1991 and 1992 are significant by chi-square test, $p < .05$.

was an increase, and 37% of women in rural areas mentioned hearing about AIDS through this medium, up from 20% in 1991.

Radio. Similar results were obtained with respect to radio exposure. The question was: "Have you heard anything about illness on the radio in the last two months?" Again, if the respondents answered yes, then they were asked what illness it was about. Overall, 61% mentioned hearing about AIDS on radio in 1992, as compared to 45% in 1991. As with television, rural women were less likely to be exposed than rural men or people in urban areas. However, even among rural women, almost half (47%) mentioned hearing about AIDS in the last 2 months.

Completion of the Campaign Phrase

By itself, a significant increase in hearing about AIDS on TV or radio is not definitive evidence of exposure to the campaign. News broadcasts and other media attention might have also increased over the same time period.

To control for this, campaign exposure was also considered in relation to the ability to recognize the phrase that was repeated with each advertisement in the campaign. Respondents were prompted with "Don't be careless, get _____," and asked if they could complete the phrase. Responses of "protection" or its equivalent in Akan were considered correct. This provides a conservative measure of those who actually heard the broadcasts. It may be an underestimate because not all those who have heard the ads would be able to remember the exact wording.

Among the whole sample, correct completion of the phrase was high (46%). Of those who could complete the phrase correctly, 51% said they had heard it on television, and 46% said they had heard in on the radio. The pattern of correct answers matches potential exposure to the campaign, with rural women showing the lowest completion rate, and urban men the highest. One fifth (21%) of those who reported that they did not watch TV or listen to radio were able to complete the phrase, although correct completion was much higher among those with media exposure (51%). After radio and TV, posters, health workers, friends, and car stickers were the most frequently mentioned places for learning the phrase.

Changes in Knowledge and Attitudes

Both surveys showed that virtually everyone had heard of AIDS. Before any mention of AIDS in the interview, respondents were asked to name the most serious diseases for people their age in Ghana. In 1991, only 37% mentioned AIDS as one of the three most serious diseases. In 1992, this figure increased to 58%, with 51% mentioning AIDS before any other disease (Table 9.4). There was also a decrease in the proportion who agreed that young people in Ghana do not have to worry about AIDS (25% to 16%).

There were also changes in the response to "Who can get AIDS?" The proportion who said anyone could get AIDS increased from 29% to 39%. There was a corresponding decrease in mentioning people who travel outside Ghana (14% to 10%). There was also a decrease in the proportion who believed AIDS could be cured.

Measures of basic knowledge of transmission were already high in 1991, and showed few changes. Sexual transmission was the most commonly mentioned method (92%), and was the only one addressed by the

TABLE 9.4
Awareness and General Knowledge

	1991	1992
Heard of AIDS	98.8	99.9*
Mentions AIDS as most serious disease for young people in Ghana	28.0	50.5*
Who can get AIDS?		
Anyone	28.6	38.6*
Promiscuous people	53.9	50.9
Prostitutes	50.7	44.0*
People who travel outside Ghana	13.7	9.8*
Agrees with statement		
Most young people in Ghana don't have to worry about AIDS.	25.4	15.9*
AIDS can be cured.	45.6	21.1*
People with AIDS should be quarantined.	87.5	83.8*
I would be afraid of catching AIDS by working next to someone.	70.7	69.4
If my brother had AIDS, I would speak to him in public.	51.3	51.0
If my brother had AIDS, I would shake his hand.	31.9	33.8

*Significant difference by chi-square test, $p < .05$

campaign. One type of knowledge specifically addressed by the campaign showed a significant increase. This was knowledge of the incubation period. In 1991, less than 10% said that a person could have the virus for as long as 5 years without becoming ill. In 1992, more than one quarter said it could be over 5 years before an individual became ill.

The majority continued to express fear of catching AIDS by working next to someone, although there was a significant decrease in agreeing that people with AIDS should be quarantined. However, support for quarantine remained high at 84%. Responses indicating rejection of a hypothetical brother with AIDS remained high. Only one half said they would speak to him in public without hesitation, and only one third said they would shake his hand. The lack of improvement in these attitudes is not surprising, because these issues were not addressed by the campaign.

Knowledge and Attitudes about Condoms

Everyone was shown a condom and asked if they knew what it was. The proportion who recognized the condom increased from 84% to 87%. Those who did not recognize it were asked if they knew what condoms were. In 1992, 96% either recognized the condom or said they knew what condoms were, up from 94% in 1991. Condom recognition continued to be higher among men than women (91% vs. 83% in 1992). Because the campaign did not specifically mention condoms, these small increments could be attributed to secular change from other promotional efforts.[1]

With respect to the purpose of condoms, there was an increase in the proportion who mentioned AIDS and/or sexually transmitted diseases (STDs; 49% to 63%). More mentioned both prevention of pregnancy and prevention of diseases (22% to 29%) and fewer mentioned only pregnancy prevention as the purpose of condoms (35% to 21%).

Fewer agreed that condoms do not help to prevent AIDS (28% to 20%) and there was an increase in intentions to use condoms in the future (50% to 53%).

Interpersonal Communication about AIDS

One of the main campaign messages directed at the general population emphasized "Talk to your family." Although the overall percent who had talked to anyone about AIDS in the last 2 months increased from 20% to

---

[1]Another communication effort that was ongoing in Ghana that related to condoms was designed by SOMARC, another USAID project. Until 1992, this campaign emphasized the Panther condom's use in family planning. In June 1992, a campaign had just been launched to market the Protector condom, with the emphasis on general protection, but without reference to AIDS.

26%, reports of discussions with family members or partners did not increase and remained low at 4%. Most of the increase was seen in talking to friends (15% to 20%), the category that was the highest at baseline. The other campaign message about communication emphasized talking to health workers. Although it represented a significant increase, the proportion remained low at 2%.

Changes in Reported Sexual Behavior and Condom Use

Initiation of Sexual Activity. Over 80% of the respondents had begun sexual activity. Among the whole sample, there was no change between 1991 and 1992 in the proportion who had ever had sex. Because the majority had already had sex by the time of the campaign, substantial change was not expected in this age group after 1 year. However, there is evidence of a decline in initiation among the youngest individuals. In fact, among 15-year-olds, only 27% had ever had sex in 1992, as opposed to 44% in 1991. This is statistically significant ($\chi^2 = 4.2$, $p < .05$), even though the sample size for 15-year-olds is only 138.

Partner Number. Because not all of the individuals who have ever had sex are currently sexually active, a number of other measures were used to examine changes in reported sexual behavior. Just over half of the sample reported sexual activity in the preceding 3 months, and this proportion did not change over time (54% in 1991, 55% in 1992). Table 9.5 illustrates the mean number of partners for three time periods: last 3 months, last year, and lifetime. It includes all respondents, with those who were not sexually active given a score of zero.

The results show one significant change, a decrease from .93 to .79 as the mean number of partners in the last 3 months for men. The number of

TABLE 9.5
Mean Number of Partners Reported

	1991	*1992*
Men		
Last 3 months	.93	.79*
Last year	1.77	1.61
Lifetime	5.79	5.79
Women		
Last 3 months	.55	.61
Last year	.88	.84
Lifetime	2.08	1.96

*Significant at $p = .028$ based on two-tailed t test.

partners for women is significantly lower than men, and showed no changes. The low numbers reported by women may reflect more reluctance among women to reveal sexual activity. Among men, the decrease in reported number of partners in the last 3 months resulted partially from the reduction in sexual initiation among younger men. In addition, among men who were sexually active, fewer had more than one partner in 1992 (24% vs. 32% in 1991, $\chi^2 = 5.9$, $p < .05$).

Condom Use.   Condom use was examined among the subsample of persons who had at least one partner in the last 3 months ($n = 1,667$). Table 9.6 shows the proportion who reported condom use the last time they had sex. In both surveys, men reported approximately twice as much condom use as women. Overall, there was a significant increase in last-2-month condom use (12% to 16%).

The increase occurred predominantly among people who were unmarried or reported more than one partner. Among married individuals who reported sex only with their spouse, reported condom use actually decreased slightly. Thus, the increase was not due to any widespread increase in condom use for contraception. This finding provides support for the claim that response to the campaign messages (i.e., concern about disease) was responsible for the change.

The ability to show changes in knowledge and behavior over the same time period as the campaign is one piece of evidence that the campaign

TABLE 9.6
Percent Who Used a Condom the Last Time by Sex,
Partner Status, Time, and Media Exposure

	1991	1992	n
Men	17.1	21.2	860
Married, one partner	11.6	8.2	217
Low media exposure	11.5	4.7	69
High media exposure	11.6	10.1	148
Unmarried or multiple partners	18.5	27.4*	643
Low media exposure	14.0	20.8	225
High media exposure	20.8	30.6*	418
Women	6.5	11.7*	807
Married, one partner	7.1	7.8	426
Low media exposure	2.8	7.4	256
High media exposure	13.5	8.3	170
Unmarried or multiple partners	5.8	16.7*	381
Low media exposure	5.3	12.0	214
High media exposure	6.7	21.7*	167
Total	12.4	16.2*	1667

*Significant difference by chi-square test, $p < .05$.

worked. However, changes over time could be due to a number of other factors. Another piece of evidence would be to show that change was confined to people who were exposed to the campaign. Because the greatest exposure occurred through the broadcast media, the population was classified based on frequency of exposure. Each individual was given one point for each day per week they reported watching TV or listening to radio. Those with a score of 7 or higher were considered to have high exposure, and represented 52% of the population. Table 9.6 shows that the increase in condom use among those who were unmarried or had multiple partners was of greater magnitude and statistically significant in the high exposure group.

Because media exposure is associated with educational level, and baseline condom use tended to be higher in the high exposure group, a logistic regression analysis was performed to control for possible confounders. The sample was restricted to 1992 respondents who were unmarried or had multiple partners ($n = 461$). This analysis was designed to examine the strength of the association between media exposure and condom use after the campaign. After controlling for wealth, educational level, age, and sex, high media exposure continued to be significantly associated with condom use (odds ratio 1.7, 95% confidence interval 1.1–2.8).

The stable association between exposure and behavior in the 1992 data, even when controlled for background characteristics, is important. There is also a tendency for the magnitude of that association to be larger in 1992 than it was in 1991. For men who were unmarried or with multiple partners, there was a 6.8% difference in high-versus-low exposure gap in 1991 compared to a 9.8% difference in 1992. For women, the 1991 high-versus-low exposure gap of 1.4% grew to 9.7%. The only statistically significant changes for subgroups in Table 9.6 are for the high exposure groups of both sexes who are unmarried or with multiple partners. Further evidence of the effect of the campaign would be a significant interaction between media exposure and pre–post measurement. However, there was not a significant interaction in this case, and it is not possible to sort out whether this apparent differential growth is a chance difference, or whether the sample sizes did not provide sufficient power to find these differences significant.

STD Indicators.   Self-reported behavior in the area of sexuality and AIDS is often considered of low validity. This is evident in this study, where men's reports of number of partners show changes but women's do not, and there is considerable discrepancy between the percentages of men and women who report using condoms. A concern could be raised that the campaign influenced knowledge, attitudes, and reports about behavior, but that actual behavior did not change.

An attempt to generate an indirect measure of sexual behavior was made by asking about symptoms of STDs. If this measure changes in the expected direction, then it provides additional evidence of behavior change. The questions about STD symptoms followed a series of questions, all phrased as "When was the last time you had (a fever)?" The STD indicator questions were phrased in terms of symptoms, rather than disease names that may not be recognized or are associated with stigma. The questions preceded any mention of AIDS or sexual behavior to minimize reactivity. Men were asked when the last time they had burning on urination or discharge from their penis, and women were asked when the last time they had lower abdominal pain with a vaginal discharge unrelated to menstruation. These questions were meant to provide an indicator of urethritis or gonorrhea. Both sexes were asked the same question about the last time they had a sore in the genital area. It was assumed that reports from women would be of less use, because of the high frequency of asymptomatic disease and confusion with non-STD gynecological complaints.

Table 9.7 shows the results of these questions. Among men, there were significant decreases in reports of symptoms compatible with urethritis and with reports of a genital sore in the last year. Women's reports did not change significantly, which is not unexpected given the lack of specificity of symptom reports among women.

CONCLUSIONS

The broadcast campaign was successful in reaching a large percentage of the population in these regions. Spontaneous reports of hearing about AIDS on television or radio increased significantly, and almost one half of

TABLE 9.7
Percent Who Reported Symptoms of STD

	1991	1992
Men		
Urethritis—Last 6 months	14.6	10.7*
Urethritis—Last year	20.9	16.2*
Urethritis—Ever	33.0	26.8*
Genital sore—Last year	5.9	3.4*
Women		
Urethritis/PID—Last 6 months	16.9	14.9
Urethritis/PID—Last year	19.1	19.1
Urethritis/PID—Ever	20.6	22.5
Genital sore—Last year	5.9	5.8

*Significant difference by chi-square test, $p < .05$.

the sample population completed the campaign tag phrase correctly. As expected, exposure was highest in urban areas and lowest among rural women. Still, more than one quarter of rural women could complete the campaign phrase, indicating that the campaign had a substantial reach even among populations with less access to information and lower exposure to broadcast media.

The results show increased awareness of AIDS as a serious disease for young people in Ghana, with an improvement in understanding of the length of the incubation period and reduced belief in a cure. However, there was no evidence of response to messages that one should talk to their family about AIDS and stigma surrounding the disease remained high despite increased knowledge.[2] There were several significant changes in reported sexual behavior between 1991 and 1992. Fewer 15-year-olds were sexually active in 1992. In addition, there was a decrease in the number of partners reported by men who were sexually active.

Of those who were sexually active, more used a condom the last time they had sex. The increase in condom use was confined to those who were unmarried or had multiple partners, suggesting that it was not due to an overall increase in condom use for contraception. The association between condom use and media exposure among this group was significant after controlling for age, sex, educational level, and wealth. Additional support for the reported changes in sexual behavior comes from the reports of symptoms suggestive of STD. There were decreases in reports of symptoms of urethritis and of genital sores among men.

It is difficult to separate the effects of one campaign from other communication activities that use the same channels. Promotion of family planning and messages about the dangers of teenage pregnancies were ongoing in Ghana during the period that the AIDS campaign was launched. Typically, multiple efforts reinforce each other and it is difficult to quantify the amount of change due to one campaign. Nonetheless, there is a consistent pattern of evidence here supporting a reasonable claim that the campaign was successful. There was a clear pattern of credible reports of high exposure to the campaign and there is a pattern of belief and behavior change consistent with specific campaign messages. Furthermore, there is evidence that media exposure was associated with behavior after the campaign even when confounding variables were statistically controlled, and there was a nonsignificant tendency for that association to be stronger after the campaign than it was before the initiation of the campaign. Given this overall pattern of results, there is good reason to conclude that the campaign had a substantial impact on knowledge. There is also evidence that it had a smaller but measurable impact on sexual behavior.

---

[2]Since 1992, a number of other communication efforts have occurred in Ghana, and the findings in this study should not be considered current.

ACKNOWLEDGMENTS

This research was funded by the U.S. Agency for International Development through the AIDSCOM project, AIDS Technical Support, Contract No. DPE 5972-Z-00-7070-00. We would like to thank the staff of the Ministry of Health, Apple Pie, and the Academy for Educational Development for their involvement in the campaign and the evaluation.

10

CHANGES IN SUN-RELATED ATTITUDES AND BEHAVIORS, AND REDUCED SUNBURN PREVALENCE IN A POPULATION AT HIGH RISK OF MELANOMA

David Hill
Victoria White
Centre for Behavioural Research in Cancer
Melbourne, Australia

Robin Marks
University of Melbourne

Ron Borland
VicHealth Centre for Tobacco Control
Melbourne, Australia

Incidence and mortality rates of cutaneous melanoma have increased steeply in recent decades in most Western industrialized countries (Muir et al., 1987). With increasing concern about ozone depletion occurring throughout the world, fears have been expressed about increased risk of melanoma as a result of the increased ultraviolet radiation (UVR) (Jones, 1987). Australia has the highest rate of melanoma in the world. The incidence in Australia is related to latitude of residence, but even in the southernmost mainland state of Victoria, the age-standardized incidence rate in 1988 was 22.8/100,000 men and 21.3/100,000 women (Giles, Farrugia, Silver, & Staples, 1992). Not only has concern about melanoma prevention been expressed in Australian health policy documents (Health for All Australians Committee, 1988), but it has also been identified as a cancer prevention priority for Europe (MacKie et al., 1991).

Episodic exposure to sunlight sufficient to cause sunburn has been shown to be a major risk factor for cutaneous melanoma (Armstrong, 1988; MacKie & Aitchison, 1982; Osterlind et al., 1988). Sunburn is a person-specific sign of a biologically active dose of UVR recently received by the skin. Sunburn is a valuable measure in that it reflects individual differences both in exposure to sunlight and individual susceptibility to sunlight. On the basis of the known risk factors, interventions to reduce melanoma on a population basis should aim at reducing the type of sunlight exposure associated with sunburn.

The prevalence of sunburn has been related to the ambient levels of UVR on the days on which sunburn has occurred, at least for recreational periods in White urban populations (Hill et al., 1992). More importantly (from the point of view of personal protection and the public health opportunities to intervene), behavioral factors have been shown to contribute to the occurrence of sunburn, independently of prevailing UVR levels (Hill et al., 1992). In other words, people are able to exert some control over their degree of risk of developing melanoma.

Various intervention programs have been undertaken in several countries warning of the risks of UVR exposure in the causation of melanoma. However, the published literature on interventions is small, and restricted to subgroups such as university students (Cody & Lee, 1990), dermatology patients (Robinson, 1990), Caucasian neighborhoods (Putnam & Yangisako, 1982), outdoor workers (Borland, Hocking, Godkin, Gibbs, & Hill, 1991), and preschool children (Boldeman, Jansson, & Holm, 1991). Despite there having been several population-wide campaigns to influence sun protection behavior (Cameron & McGuire, 1990), no behavioral evaluations of comprehensive programs have been published yet.

The present study was carried out in a population that had been exposed already to a public education program conducted principally through school and by public service announcements in the mass media throughout summer, annually, for several years (Rassaby, Larcombe, Hill, & Wake, 1983). The theme of this campaign had been "SLIP! SLOP! SLAP!" (slip on a shirt, slop on a sunscreen, slap on a hat). Although conducted with a modest budget (approximately US $0.02 per head of population in its last year), it achieved high levels of public awareness (Borland, Hill, & Noy, 1990). This early program was expanded to a large-scale comprehensive program, which was launched as the SunSmart campaign late in 1988.

Substantial funding for the new campaign was made available by the Victorian Health Promotion Foundation, which in turn acquires its funds through a levy on tobacco constituted under the Victorian Tobacco Act 1987. The SunSmart campaign was conducted throughout the State of Victoria (population 4.3 million) from the end of spring (November 1988) to the end of the southern hemisphere summer (February 1989) and was repeated for a similar period in the following year. The total budget in the first year was AUS $994,000 (US $0.18 per capita) and in the second year AUS $1,140,000 (US $0.23 per capita). Full-time staff levels varied between three and four, and these were supplemented with part-time staff in periods of peak activity. The budget was expended in the following proportions: mass media, 34%; salaries, administration, and overheads, 28%; community, schools, and targeted programs, 24%; evaluation, 8%; and public relations, 6%. The major communication strategy was a mass media campaign to raise awareness, to model preventive behavior, and to present "SunSmart" behavior as fashionable, particularly for young people. The central image of the campaign contrasted two young women: one sunburned, the other "SunSmart" yet elegant and attractive. The theme was used in television, radio, and outdoor advertising. In schools, comprehensive teaching resources were distributed at all levels, and schools were encouraged to develop policies and practices to reduce student sun exposure. Structural change initiatives included work with labor unions and other organizations leading to guidelines for worker solar protection. In addition, downward pressure on the price of sunscreen was applied, and strategies were implemented to increase shade at recreational venues and to encourage fashion houses and magazines to promote protective hats and clothing. There were also sponsorships—for instance, the SunSmart sponsorship of surf lifesavers and a major ocean yacht race—and unplanned factors such as increased media coverage of stratospheric ozone depletion.

This chapter describes the changes in sun-related beliefs and behavior, and changes in the prevalence of sunburn over a 3-year period in an Australian population considered at risk for malignant melanoma against a change context of health promotion. In the first year there was the base level of health promotion typical of the preceding 8 years, and in the second and third years there was a greatly expanded SunSmart health promotion campaign designed to reduce sunlight exposure.

METHOD

The procedures and measures have been described in detail elsewhere (Hill et al., 1992). Briefly, residents of Melbourne (population 3 million) were sampled by telephone interview in the summers of 1988 ($n = 1,655$), 1989 ($n = 1,397$), and 1990 ($n = 1,376$). Interviewing was done by a well-known polling organization following careful training of its experienced staff in the use of the standard interview schedule. Respondents were informed that the survey was about people's attitudes toward being out in the sun, but they were not told that the research interest was skin cancer.

Interviews took place over the 13 weeks of the Australian summer, from the beginning of December to the end of February, with over 100 interviews conducted each week. Respondents, from age 14 to 69, were contacted on Monday evenings. And, if they were outside for longer than 15 minutes on the previous weekend during the 4 hours around solar midday, then they provided detailed reports of their activities, the amount of skin exposed, and any sunburn subsequently experienced. The amount of skin exposure was calculated from detailed reports from respondents about clothing worn (including sleeve and trouser or skirt length), type of headgear, and sun protection factor (SPF) of sunscreen used. In separate analyses of hat and sunscreen use, hat was taken to mean any headgear and sunscreen to mean only those for which the SPF was 12 or greater. Skin type was classified by respondents' self-report on how their unprotected skin typically reacted to 30 minutes exposure to strong sunshine at the beginning of summer. Highly sensitive subjects would "just burn and not tan afterwards"; moderately sensitive subjects would "burn first, and then tan"; and nonsensitive subjects would "not burn at all, just tan." Respondents also indicated their desired level of suntan and responded to a 15-item battery of Likert-scaled statements covering a range of sun-related beliefs. Most of these were worded favorably to sun exposure so as to minimize confounding of intended campaign effects with acquiescence or social desirability response sets.

For the observation days each year, atmospheric temperature at 3:00 p.m. was obtained from the Bureau of Meteorology. The Australian Radiation Laboratory provided UVR levels measured at 10-minute intervals between 11:00 a.m. and 3:00 p.m. (daylight saving time) for the Melbourne metropolitan region. These values were averaged to give a single value expressed in units of W/m². UVR levels were not available, due to technical problems, for one weekend (the first weekend in January 1988). Estimates based on other meteorological observations, including cloud cover and temperature, were substituted for these missing data. The mean 3:00 p.m. temperatures were as follows: 1988, 22°C (range: 15°C–36°C); 1989, 24.6°C (range: 17°C–37°C); 1990, 22.5°C (range: 17°C–34°C). Mean UVR levels were 1.7 W/m² (range: .9–2.8) in 1988, 1.6 W/m² (range: .7–2.7) in 1989, and 1.2 W/m² (range: .4–1.9) in 1990.

Analysis

The first year was treated as a baseline for comparison with the following 2 years. As sampling was stratified by sex, bivariate analyses were conducted on men and women separately. Logistic regression analyses using the statistical package GLIM (Payne, 1985) were conducted to determine whether agreement to the belief items had changed over the years. For these analyses, effects of age and sex were controlled. The relation between year and hat, sunscreen use, and sunburn were examined first by chi-squared tests. An index of clothing coverage (which indicated the proportion of total body surface area covered by clothing), head gear, and footwear during the period the respondent was outdoors was calculated for respondents surveyed in each year (Hill et al., 1992). Analysis of variance was used to compare means on this scale across years. Analyses were conducted for each age and skin type category separately. Where bivariate analyses revealed significant associations between year and the variables under investigation, data for men and women were pooled and multivariate analyses were conducted to examine the change across years after adjusting for potential confounders.

Analysis of covariance was used to compare mean scores on the clothing index across years after adjusting for effects of sex, age, and skin type. For the categorical variables, multiple logistic regression models were developed, again using the statistical package GLIM. This technique enables odds ratios (OR) and 95% confidence intervals (CI), which are adjusted for all variables, to be calculated from the regression coefficients in the logistic model. Odds ratios for the second and third survey years are relative to the first year. In models examining the use of hats and sunscreen, adjustments were made for effects of age, sex, and skin type. For models of sunburn, ORs were also adjusted for effects of 11:00 a.m. to 3:00 p.m. mean UVR and 3:00 p.m. ambient temperature. In addition, because there is a possibility of a seasonal effect on the chance of being sunburned (i.e., there is a greater chance of being burned early in summer than later, because the skin is likely to build up melanin during the summer), ORs were also adjusted for the month of the survey. In these analyses, both temperature and survey month were treated as categorical variables, whereas UVR remained a continuous variable as its association with sunburn was found to be linear. There was no significant interaction between UVR and year.

RESULTS

On the assumption that changes in dispositions (e.g., beliefs and attitudes) precede changes in behavior, the study first looked for evidence of such changes across time. Table 10.1 gives the percentage endorsing each of 16 survey items that might indicate the disposition to take (or not to take) sun protection measures for the base year and the following 2 years. After adjusting for sex and age, there was a significant effect of year for all but one item. The perceived severity of skin cancer was already very high and rose only very slightly over 3 years. There was a marked change in perceived susceptibility to skin cancer, with substantially fewer people denying their

TABLE 10.1
Trends in Dispositional Variables Among a Sample of Melbourne
Residents Before and During SunSmart Campaigns

Survey Item	% Endorsing			p^a
	1988 (n = 1,655)	1989 (n = 1,397)	1990 (n = 1,376)	
Perceived severity				
Skin cancer is a dangerous disease.	97	97	99	.002[b]
Perceived susceptibility				
There is little chance that I'll get skin cancer.	41	36	29	.001[b]
Pro-tan beliefs				
I feel more healthy with a suntan.	51	46	39	.001[b]
A suntanned person looks more healthy.	66	60	53	.001[b]
A suntanned person is more healthy.	17	13	9	.001[b]
It's worth a lot of effort to get a suntan.	30	23	19	.001[b]
Once you get a suntan it's easier to enjoy the summer.	62	54	43	.001[b]
A suntan protects you against skin cancer.	20	17	18	.112[b]
Pro-tan normative beliefs				
Most of my close family think that a suntan is a good thing.	50	37	29	.001[b]
Most of my friends think a suntan is a good thing.	69	63	52	.001[b]
Tan motivation				
I like to get a dark or very dark tan.	20	17	12	.001[b]
Protective tendencies				
I take great care to avoid getting sunburned.	71	75	76	.003[b]
Often in summer sunshine I don't bother putting on a hat.	63	57	55	.001[b]
In summer sunshine I usually take care to put on some sunscreen.	72	75	79	.001[b]
Perceived barriers				
I find it difficult to protect myself against the sun.	22	17	20	.003[c]
Nontargeted belief				
A lot of sun throughout life ages the skin.	88	88	93	.001[c]

[a]χ^2 test, 2 df
[b]Linear trend significant
[c]Linear trend not significant

risk of getting skin cancer. Except for the belief that a suntan protects against skin cancer, endorsements of the entire set of pro-tan beliefs that were assumed to cause resistance to health education messages declined significantly. Over the second and third years, respondents were less likely to believe suntanned people looked, felt, or actually were more healthy (than the untanned). They were also less likely to think the effort of getting a suntan was worthwhile or that they could enjoy the summer better once they had a suntan. There was a large reduction in the percentages believing their family or friends approved of a suntan. The aforementioned trends were reflected in changes in a key motivational index, desire for a tan, in which there was a substantial drop in the proportion saying they like to have a "dark" or "very dark" tan. Conversely (not shown in the table), there was an increase from 39% to 51% in those who did not desire any degree of suntan.

Table 10.1 also shows trends in "protective tendencies" (i.e., respondents' reports of the care usually taken to protect against the sun and typical hat and sunscreen use). These measures, which are regarded here as dispositional indicators rather than accurate measures of behavior, all showed changes across time. There was little change in the perceived difficulty of protecting oneself against the sun, nor in the widely held belief that a lot of sun throughout life ages the skin. For all but two beliefs, there was a significant linear trend across years (Armitage, 1955).

If respondents reported being outdoors between 11:00 a.m. and 3:00 p.m. (summer time) on the preceding Sunday, then they were asked what they were doing, how long they were outside, and the extent of their hat, clothing, and sunscreen use. Similar questions were asked for the preceding Saturday. The following behavioral data relates to Sunday for Melbourne residents outside on Sunday, and for Saturday if the person was outside on Saturday but not Sunday. There was a significant reduction in proportions of men and women reporting having spent more than 15 minutes outside between 11:00 a.m. and 3:00 p.m. For men, the proportion decreased from 85% in the baseline year to 76% in 1989 and 72% in 1990 (χ^2 = 35.8, df = 2, $p < .001$). For women, the proportions decreased from 69% in 1988 to 66% in 1989 to 54% in 1990 (χ^2 = 35.2, df = 2, $p < .001$). Although older people were relatively less likely to be outside (χ^2 = 7.3, df = 2, $p < .05$), the decrease in the proportions of different age groups spending time outside did not vary significantly across years.

Table 10.2 sets out for the 3 years of the study the levels of hat and sunscreen use and the proportion of total body surface covered by clothing for men and women by age group and skin type. Significant increases in hat use ($p < .001$) were seen for both sexes. By the third year, 32% of males and 26% of females who were outside between 11:00 a.m. and 3:00 p.m. for longer than 15 minutes on summer weekend days reported having worn a hat. A further breakdown (not shown in Table 10.2) showed that among hat wearers, relatively higher proportions wore wide-brimmed hats than less protective headgear in the second and third years than in the first (χ^2 = 5.0, df = 1, $p < .05$). The use of sunscreens also increased among both men ($p < .05$) and women ($p < .01$) so that, by 1990, 15% of men and 25% of women who were outside applied sunscreens. Whereas for men sunscreen use increased significantly only among those with highly

TABLE 10.2
Sun Protection Behavior of Melbourne Residents Out-of-Doors

	Men			Women		
	1988 (n = 676)	1989 (n = 532)	1990 (n = 497)	1988 (n = 586)	1989 (n = 459)	1990 (n = 374)
Percentage who wore a hat						
Total	23	29	32[b]	14	24	26[b]
Age (years) 14–29	19	21	26	9	19	24[b]
30–39	18	30	32[a]	16	24	26
40–69	33	41	41	19	33	31[a]
Skin type HS	31	46	39[a]	16	26	24
MS	23	26	34	13	23	29[b]
NS	17	22	22	11	22	21[a]
Percentage who used sunscreen						
Total	10	14	15[a]	16	22	28[b]
Age (years) 14–29	12	14	16	16	20	24
30–39	5	12	18[b]	15	23	39[b]
40–69	9	15	9	17	25	26
Skin type HS	10	21	24[b]	23	28	32
MS	12	16	12	16	21	30[b]
NS	6	6	11	5	18	17[b]
Mean proportion of body clothing-covered						
Total	.68	.65	.72[b]	.68	.63	.69[b]
Age (years) 14–29	.66	.62	.71[b]	.64	.58	.67[b]
30–39	.70	.65	.71[a]	.70	.65	.71
40–69	.70	.71	.73	.72	.70	.73
Skin type HS	.72	.71	.74	.72	.67	.72[a]
MS	.68	.64	.72[b]	.67	.62	.68[b]
NS	.64	.63	.69[a]	.67	.58	.69[a]

Note. HS = highly sensitive; MS = moderately sensitive; NS = not sensitive
[a] $p < .05$
[b] $p < .01$

170

sensitive skins, use of sunscreens increased for women with moderately sensitive and nonsensitive skins. The increase in use of sunscreens was due to both a shift from less to more effective sunscreens over the 3 years (χ^2 = 42.9, df = 2, p < .001) and to a reduction in the proportion using no sunscreen after the first year (χ^2 = 6.7, df = 1, p < .01). For both men and women, the proportion of body surface covered by clothing changed over the years, but for both groups the effect was mainly due to respondents in 1989 reporting less clothing coverage than in either the preceding or following year.

Multivariate analyses were conducted on the entire data set. The crude proportion of respondents wearing hats was 19% in 1988, 26% in 1989, and 29% in 1990. After adjusting for confounders, this increase was highly significant (χ^2 = 38.2, df = 2, p < .001). The adjusted OR for wearing a hat by the second year of the study was 1.64 (95% CI, range 1.33–2.01), whereas the OR for the third year was 1.82 (95% CI, 1.27–2.25). For sunscreen use, the overall proportion using sunscreen in 1988 was 12%, increasing in 1989 to 18% and in 1990 to 21%. Multivariate tests showed this increase to be significant (χ^2 = 29.5, df = 2, p < .001). For sunscreen use, the adjusted ORs were 1.56 (95% CI, 1.23–1.99) for the second year and 1.89 (95% CI, 1.48–2.41) for the third year. For hat use there was no interaction between year and age, indicating that similar increases in hat use were seen in all age groups across the survey years. At the beginning of the study, sunscreen use, although not common in any age group, was slightly greater among the younger people. By the third year of the study, sunscreen use was most common among the 30- to 39-year-old respondents. The interaction of age and year was significant (χ^2 = 13.3, df = 4, p < .01). Adjusted ORs indicated that, by the third year of the study, people from age 30 to 39 were far more likely to use sunscreen than they were in the first year (OR = 3.84, 95% CI, 2.35–6.26). As might be expected, persons with more sensitive skin had higher base levels of hat and sunscreen use. No significant interaction between year and skin type was found in the multivariate analyses for either sunscreen use or hat wearing, indicating that increases in use of hat and sunscreen were similar across skin types.

The mean proportion of body area covered in each of the 3 years was .69 in 1988, .64 in 1989, and .71 in 1990. After adjusting for effects of sex, age, and skin type on clothing coverage, a significant difference in mean clothing coverage was found across years ($F(1,2210)$ = 7.12, p = .005). There were no significant interactions indicating that this pattern was consistent across all groups.

Trends in sunburn were monitored for 3 years. Early in the interview, after having given their age, skin type, skin color, and preferred level of tan, respondents were told: "The next questions are about sunburn. By sunburn we mean any amount of reddening after being in the sun." They were then asked, "Did you get at all sunburned yesterday (Sunday)? What about Saturday?" Sunburned respondents were asked which parts of the body were burned (Hill et al., 1992), and whether the burn was "red without being tender," "red and tender," or "red, tender and blistered." Table 10.3 gives the percentages of sunburn for men and women over 3 years, with all sunburn (top of table) and tender sunburn (below) separated, broken down by groupings of sex, age, and skin type.

The base for the percentages in Table 10.3 is all the respondents who were in Melbourne on the Saturday or Sunday, regardless of whether they were outdoors between 11:00 a.m. and 3:00 p.m. Eleven percent of the respondents had traveled outside the metropolitan area of Melbourne and 1% of the respondents reported being sunburned, although they were not outside between 11:00 a.m. and 3:00 p.m. As the appropriate UVR data were not available for these cases, they were excluded from the following analyses. However, analysis conducted on the entire data set showed similar findings to those reported here. Results showed reductions in sunburn in all groups. These reductions were significant for women overall, women from age 30 to 39, and women with nonsensitive skin ($p < .05$ in each case). Tender sunburn occurred in a minority of those who were burned, and although the trends were similar to total sunburn, they failed to reach statistical significance in any group.

Multivariate analyses were conducted on the data for the entire data set. The proportion of respondents burned was 11% in 1988, 10% in 1989, and 7% by 1990. As these results might have been confounded by variations in UVR levels, temperature and seasonal differences across the survey years, differences between years were examined after adjusting for the effect of these variables. In addition, the study adjusted for the influence of sex, age, and skin type groups. After making these statistical adjustments, there was a significant reduction in the proportions of those sunburned over the 3 years ($\chi^2 = 11.5$, $df = 2$, $p < .01$). The adjusted OR for being sunburned in 1989 was .75 (95% CI, .57–.99) and for 1990 it was .59 (95% CI, .43–.81), indicating that the risk of being sunburned was lower in 1989 and 1990 than it was in 1988. Similar analyses performed on the proportion of respondents with tender sunburn showed no significant effect of year in any of the age, sex, and skin type groups.

CONCLUSIONS

This study suggests that a significant reduction in exposure to risk of melanoma can occur in an urban population over a relatively short period of time. Given that there was no interaction between survey year and UVR

TABLE 10.3

Trends in Weekend Sunburn Among a Sample of Residents Who Had Spent the Weekend in Melbourne

		Men			Women		
		1988 (n = 699)	1989 (n = 605)	1990 (n = 608)	1988 (n = 753)	1989 (n = 616)	1990 (n = 629)
Percentage with any degree of sunburn							
Total		14	12	10	9	8	5[b]
Age (years)	14–29	15	13	11	9	12	6
	30–39	11	14	9	13	7	5[a]
	40–69	13	9	7	6	4	3
Skin type	HS	17	14	12	9	9	6
	MS	17	15	11	10	11	6
	NS	8	6	5	7	3	1[a]
Percentage with tender sunburn							
Total		6	4	5	4	2	3
Age (years)	14–29	7	6	7	6	4	4
	30–39	6	4	2	5	2	2
	40–69	3	2	4	2	1	2
Skin type	HS	9	6	6	5	3	4
	MS	6	6	6	4	3	3
	NS	3	1	3	2	1	0

Note. HS = highly sensitive; MS = moderately sensitive; NS = not sensitive
[a] p < .05
[b] p < .01

on sunburn occurrence, which was taken as the chief index of risk, this is unlikely to be due to an artifact of reporting or of variations in weather over the years. It has been shown previously that sun protection behavior independently predicted sunburn in this population prior to the commencement of the SunSmart campaign (Hill et al., 1992), and the data suggest that the reductions in sunburn over the 2 years reported here were due to behavior change. The trends in self-reported behavior suggest that the effect was due to increased hat and sunscreen use rather than increased clothing coverage, and to fewer people going out into the sun during the period of greatest risk. This pattern is particularly interesting and may indicate a behavior-specific response to the SunSmart campaign, because advertising emphasized hat and sunscreen use rather than overall clothing coverage. The somewhat puzzling deficit in clothing coverage in 1989 compared to 1988 and 1990 could be explained by the hotter temperature that year; people may have shed clothing in the heat but compensated by greater use of other forms of protection.

The greatest amount of change over the 3 years of the study was found in dispositional variables such as health beliefs, motivations, perceptions of social norms, and beliefs favorable to suntanning. The SunSmart campaign was based on a stages-of-change model (Prochaska & DiClemente, 1983). That change should occur first and most extensively in dispositional variables is consistent with this model, which holds that attitudinal change is likely to precede behavior change, and changes in habitual behavior are preceded by extended periods of contemplation of the pros and cons, trial behaviors, and reversion to previous behavior patterns. The level of change in dispositional variables augurs well for further behavior change and sunburn reduction, provided sun protection behavior is rendered easy to carry out by environmental and other structural changes, and is encouraged by reinforcers such as social approval (Green, Kreuter, Deeds, & Partridge, 1980).

It is of interest in this respect that reductions in the perceived difficulty of achieving sun protection were modest over the 3 years of the study. Evidently, the behavior change reported was achieved during the same time that the levels of perceived difficulty remained similar. Although the aim should be to make sun protection even easier, it seems that the barriers to personal initiative can never be completely eliminated, so people should also be encouraged to believe sun protection is worth the trouble it takes. Another reason why the perception of difficulties may be resistant to change is that as people learn more about the subtleties of sun exposure and sun protection, they may see it as increasingly difficult to attain adequate protection.

The results suggest that sun protection practiced by men, judging by their prevalence of sunburn, was still inferior to that of women. Given that the case fatality rate of melanoma is higher in men than in women (Blois, Sagebiel, Abarbanel, Caldwell, & Tuttle, 1983), development of programs that will influence men at least as much as they do women is a priority for the future. Hat use by the third year was similar in both sexes, but men used sunscreens barely half as often as women; therefore, strategies to encourage men to understand, accept, and use sunscreens effectively may give the greatest payoff.

Other sociodemographic target groups highlighted by the study are adolescents and young people, who, despite levels of hat and sunscreen use comparable to older age groups, were burned more often throughout the period of the study and may have failed to reduce sunburn levels as much as older people. This could be partly due to less clothing coverage in the younger age group and the fact that they spend more time outdoors and engaged in activities (e.g., water sports) associated with high risk of sunburn (Hill et al., 1992).

The SunSmart health promotion campaign was imaginative, well funded, and comprehensive, and its introduction brought about reduced exposure to a presumed melanoma risk factor—sunburn. Stronger research designs are needed to establish causality, but there is converging evidence consistent with the conclusion that the campaign played a part in the changes reported. There were high levels of public awareness and self-reported behavior change in response to the campaign's first summer (Borland et al., 1990), and increased awareness of the campaign in its second year (Borland, 1992a). If the campaign were responsible for changes in behavior and sunburn levels, then attitudinal change would be expected to be consistent with the behavioral change, as was found. When specifically questioned, respondents in independent samples reported having made extra efforts to protect themselves as a result of the campaign (Borland, 1992a; Borland et al., 1990). However, increased public concern about ozone depletion, something not generated by the campaign, might also have played a part and serves as a reminder that fortuitous events should also be taken into account (Borland, 1992a, 1992b).

Although the public is undoubtedly concerned about cancer and has fears about the dangers of ozone depletion, translating such concerns into appropriate behavior change at a population level is neither straightforward nor easy. This is because there are deeply ingrained values and habits that are a barrier to personal behavior change. In addition to this study, others have shown how much value is placed on the suntan, at least among predominantly Anglo-Celtic populations (Broadstock, Borland, & Gason, 1992; Cockburn, Hennrikus, Scott, & Sanson-Fisher, 1989). Substantial and sustained change in sun-related behaviors of populations at risk for melanoma is therefore unlikely to occur unless comprehensive programs are mounted and extend over many years. Melanoma prevention should be approached at several levels and with varied strategies, including (where possible) a facilitating "umbrella" of persuasive mass media advertising, public relations, role modeling of SunSmart behaviors by opinion leaders for various population segments; health education programs for all school levels and for parents and others caring for children; and a wide range of policy development to make sun protection easy to practice at an individual level. Examples of these are ensuring that effective, inexpensive sunscreens are available widely, that shade is available in school grounds and other public places, that summer uniforms have broad-brimmed hats, and that work practices and equipment are conducive to sun protection. Health promotion programs also need to exploit favorable developments (e.g., publicity about ozone depletion or the fashion for hats) and counter unfavorable trends (e.g., the emblematic value of a winter suntan).

It has been shown in identical surveys over three successive summers that sun protection attitudes and behaviors changed favorably and sunburn levels were reduced in a large urban population exposed to an extensive health promotion campaign on solar UVR protection. The demonstration of appropriate changes in knowledge and attitudes accompanied by behavior change is good, although not conclusive, evidence that educative elements of the SunSmart campaign have contributed to the changes. By contrast, had the case been that the reduction in sunburn and the associated behavior changes occurred without concomitant or previous changes in knowledge and attitudes, then it would be fair to conclude that the educative components of the program were unlikely to have contributed to those changes. This study is the first to show significant reductions at a population level in one of the major risk factors for melanoma.

Moreover, these results support the continuation and extension of such programs to prevent the rising incidence of melanoma in fair-skinned populations and to help offset the potential threat to individuals of future stratospheric ozone depletion (MacKie & Rycroft, 1988).

ACKNOWLEDGMENTS

We thank Dr. Colin Roy and Dr. Peter Gies, Australian Radiation Laboratory, for supplying solar ultraviolet radiation data; Dr. Theresa Theobald for preparing the data set for analysis; Ms. Sue Noy for details of the SunSmart and earlier sun protection campaigns; Dr. John Hopper; Assoc. Professor Damien Jolley and Ms. Margaret Staples for statistical advice. The Anti-Cancer Council of Victoria, Victorian Health Promotion Foundation, and ESSO Australia funded this study.

REFERENCES

Armitage, P. (1955). Test for linear trends in proportions and frequencies. *Biometrics, 2,* 375–386.

Armstrong, B. K. (1988). Epidemiology of malignant melanoma: Intermittent or total accumulated exposure to the sun? *Journal of Dermatologic Surgery and Oncology, 14,* 835–849.

Blois, M. S., Sagebiel, R. W., Abarbanel, R. M., Caldwell, T. W., & Tuttle, M. S. (1983). Malignant melanoma of the skin: The association of tumor depth and type, and patient sex, age and site with survival. *Cancer, 52,* 1330–1341.

Boldeman, C., Jansson, B., & Holm, L. E. (1991). Primary prevention of malignant melanoma in Swedish urban pre-school sector. *Journal of Cancer Education, 6,* 247–253.

Borland, R. (1992a). Public awareness and reported effects of the 1989–90 SunSmart campaign. In *SunSmart Evaluation Studies No 2* (pp. 9–17). Melbourne: Anti-Cancer Council of Victoria.

Borland, R. (1992b). 1989 spring sun survey: Preliminary findings. In *SunSmart Evaluation Studies No 2* (pp. 93–96). Melbourne: Anti-Cancer Council of Victoria.

Borland, R., Hill, D., & Noy, S. (1990). Being SunSmart: Changes in community awareness and reported behavior following a primary prevention program for skin cancer control. *Behavior Change, 7,* 126–135.

Borland, R., Hocking, B., Godkin, G., Gibbs, A., & Hill, D. (1991). The impact of a skin cancer control educational package for outdoor workers. *Medical Journal of Australia, 154,* 686–688.

Broadstock, M., Borland, R., & Gason, R. (1992). Effects of suntan on judgments of healthiness and attractiveness by adolescents. *Journal of Applied Social Psychology, 22,* 157–172.

Cameron, I. H., & McGuire, C. (1990). "Are you dying to get a suntan?"—the pre- and post-campaign survey results. *Health Education Journal, 49,* 166–170.

Cockburn, J., Hennrikus, D., Scott, R., & Sanson-Fisher, R. (1989). Adolescent use of sun protection measures. *Medical Journal of Australia, 151,* 136–140.

Cody, R., & Lee, C. (1990). Behaviors, beliefs and intentions in skin cancer prevention. *Journal of Behavioral Medicine, 13,* 373.

Giles, G., Farrugia, H., Silver, B., & Staples, M. (1992). *Victorian Cancer Registry 1988 Statistical report.* Melbourne: Anti-Cancer Council of Victoria.

Green, L. W., Kreuter, M. W., Deeds, S. G., & Partridge, K. B. (1980). *Health education planning: A diagnostic approach.* Palo Alto, CA: Mayfield.

Health for all Australians Committee (1988). *Health for all Australians.* Canberra: Australian Government Publishing Service.

Hill, D., White, V., Borland, R., & Roy, C. (1992). Melanoma prevention: Behavioral and non-behavioral factors in sunburn among an Australian urban population. *Preventive Medicine, 21,* 654–669.

Jones, R. R. (1987). Ozone depletion and cancer risk. *Lancet, 2,* 443–446.

MacKie, R. M., & Aitchison, T. (1982). Severe sunburn and subsequent risk of primary cutaneous malignant melanoma in Scotland. *British Journal of Cancer, 46,* 955–960.

MacKie, R. M., Osterlind, A., Ruiter, D., et al. (1991). Report on consensus meeting of the EORTC Melanoma Group on educational needs for primary and secondary prevention of melanoma in Europe. Results of a workshop held under the auspices of the EEC Europe against Cancer program in Innsbruck, April 1991. *European Journal of Cancer, 27,* 13117–13123.

MacKie, R. M., & Rycroft, M. J. (1988). Health and the ozone layer: Skin cancers may increase dramatically. *British Medical Journal, 297,* 369–370.

Muir, C. S., Waterhouse, J., Mack, T., et al. (1987). Cancer incidence in five continents. *IARC Scientific Publications, 5*(88).

Osterlind, A., Tucker, M. A., Stone, B. J., et al. (1988). The Danish case-control study of cutaneous malignant melanoma 11. Importance of UV light exposure. *International Journal of Cancer, 42,* 319–324.

Payne, C. D. (Ed.). (1985). *The GLIM system manual.* Release 3.77. Oxford: Numerical Algorithms Group.

Prochaska, J. D., & DiClemente, C. C. (1983). Stages and processes of self-change in smoking: Towards an integrative model of change. *Journal of Consulting and Clinical Psychology, 51,* 390–395.

Putnam, G. L., & Yangisako, K. L. (1982). Skin cancer comic book: Evaluation of a public education vehicle. *Cancer Detection and Prevention, 5,* 349–356.

Rassaby, J., Larcombe, I., Hill, D., & Wake, F. R. (1983). Slip Slop Slap: Health education about skin cancer. *Cancer Forum, 7,* 63–69.

Robinson, J. K. (1990). Behavior modification obtained by sun protection education coupled with removal of a skin cancer. *Archives of Dermatology, 126,* 477–481.

CHAPTER

11

IMPACT OF A MASS MEDIA VASECTOMY
PROMOTION CAMPAIGN IN BRAZIL

D. Lawrence Kincaid
Alice Payne Merritt
Liza Nickerson
Sandra de Castro Buffington
Johns Hopkins University

Marcos Paulo P. de Castro
Bernadete Martin de Castro
Promoção da Paternidade Responsável
São Paulo, Brazil

Vasectomy has been available throughout much of the world for decades, and it has become a major family planning method in some countries. By 1991, vasectomy had been chosen by approximately 41.5 million couples worldwide (Liskin, Benoit, & Blackburn, 1992). About three fourths of vasectomy users are concentrated in China and India, where government programs have long supported the method. In China, for example, an estimated 30.4 million men underwent vasectomies between 1971 and 1981; this method accounted for 11% of all contraceptive use in 1981, a proportion exceeded only by the proportions of couples using the intrauterine device (IUD; 42%) or female sterilization (38%) (Xu, 1993).

Chinese vasectomy rates vary greatly, however, by province and region. Although some research has ascribed these important regional differences to socioeconomic, cultural, and service quality factors (Xu, 1993), other studies have attributed higher rates in China's Sichuan Province to vasectomy promotion to party members (Zhang, 1994) and to educational campaigns that provide specific information relevant to the needs of sterilization candidates (Involving Male Participation, 1995).

In Africa, where vasectomy is rarely used, a Kenyan nongovernmental organization implemented a mass media vasectomy promotion project in

1992–1994 (Kiragu, Kiriuki, Wilkinson, & Onoka, 1995). The intervention, conducted by Innovative Communication Systems, used a wide array of promotional techniques—on-site training for service providers, periodic television talk shows, newspaper advertisements with coupons directing men to family planning sites, newspaper articles, film clips, booklets, posters, leaflets and flyers, and motivational talks held at work sites. (One of the planned components of the campaign, radio and television promotional spots, had to be canceled, however, because of the Kenyan Broadcasting Corporation's fears of public and political backlash. The private Kenyan Television Network eventually broadcast the spots, but in the Nairobi area only.)

Twelve-month monitoring of service records in six sentinel vasectomy sites showed that even though the cancellation of the planned broadcast weakened the campaign considerably, the number of vasectomies performed had increased by 125% after 6 months of the Kenyan campaign. Clients who cited newspapers as their main source of referral were more likely to have made a vasectomy-related visit to a clinic than were those referred by other sources. By the end of the project, 835 individuals had requested vasectomy information using the newspaper coupons.

Several Latin American countries have also developed mass media communication approaches to increase vasectomy promotion. In Guatemala, for example, a project used radio spots and a male promoter to increase awareness and acceptability of vasectomy (Bertrand, Santiso, Linder, & Pineda, 1987). An evaluation of the project found that although knowledge and attitudes in the experimental groups did not significantly improve compared with those in the nontreatment group, the number of vasectomies performed increased significantly.

A similar project in Colombia used a clinic-oriented mass media approach (Vernon, Ojeda, & Vega, 1991) and tested three types of experimental clinics: a traditional clinic offering both male and female services simultaneously, a traditional clinic with specially designated hours for men only, and a male-only clinic. Outreach activities promoting the clinics included a 5-month mass media campaign with radio spots, newspaper advertisements, and leaflets distributed at workplaces. Experimental clinics performed nearly twice as many vasectomies as control clinics during the project.

THE BRAZILIAN CONTEXT

Brazil had a modern contraceptive prevalence rate of 55% in 1986, with the pill and female sterilization together accounting for nearly 95% of all modern method use (Arruda, Rutenberg, Morris, & Ferraz, 1987). The total rate of modern contraceptive use for São Paulo state in 1986 was 62%.

This state also had the highest rates of use of male methods (3.1% for the condom and 2.4% for vasectomy). These levels of use were due in part to the opening of the first male-oriented health and sexuality clinic by Promoção de Paternidade Responsável (PRO-PATER) in São Paulo in February 1981 (de Castro, Mastrorocco, de Castro, & Mumford, 1984).

PRO-PATER was founded to provide medical and educational services for male contraception and sexuality. In addition, it conducts biomedical and psychosocial research on fertility, infertility, and male sexuality. In May 1988, PRO-PATER inaugurated a second São Paulo clinic, which targeted men from lower socioeconomic groups.

Initially, PRO-PATER relied mostly on word-of-mouth communication from satisfied clients to promote its services. In 1983, however, a 3-minute broadcast about vasectomy and PRO-PATER on national television reached an estimated audience of 40 million people. Clinic attendance in the month after the broadcast was double that of the previous month, and the number of vasectomies performed in 1984 exceeded those done in the previous year by 50%. In 1985, after a 10-week newspaper and magazine promotion conducted with assistance from the Population Council, the mean daily number of new clients increased by 66%, and the mean number of vasectomies performed per day increased by 54% (Forfeit, de Castro, & Franco Duarte, 1989).

THE 1989 CAMPAIGN

In 1989, PRO-PATER collaborated with the Johns Hopkins University Population Communication Services project, with funding from the U.S. Agency for International Development, in a mass media communications project to promote vasectomy in three Brazilian cities: São Paulo, Salvador, and Fortaleza. These three are among the five largest cities in Brazil.[1] This chapter presents the results of an evaluation of the impact of this mass media campaign.

One clinic in the developed South (PRO-PATER in São Paulo) and three clinics in the less-developed Northeast participated in the project. The Northeast clinics were the Centro de Estudos, Pesquisa e Atendimento em Reprodução Humana (CEPARH) in Salvador, and two clinics affiliated with the Programa de Orientação e Planejamento Familiar (PRO-VAS) in Fortaleza. CEPARH was established in 1984 and offers contraceptive services to women as well as men; PRO-VAS was founded in 1987 solely to provide male contraceptive services.

---

[1] São Paulo is one of the largest cities in the world, with a 1994 population of roughly 16 million people. See United Nations Population Division (1995). *Urban agglomerations, 1994*. Wall chart. New York: United Nations.

The 1989–1990 project attempted to standardize the information provided to potential vasectomy clients and to eliminate some of the public's misconceptions about how the operation is performed, its effect on sexual functioning, and its long-term health effects. The specific communication objectives were to increase knowledge and awareness of vasectomy and to increase the number of vasectomies obtained by lower middle-class men from age 25 to 49. This chapter presents quantitative data from the evaluation of the second objective.

The 1989–1990 campaign was implemented in four distinct phases: precampaign public relations events were held; television spots were broadcast in May and June 1989, and were rebroadcast in September 1989; and a follow-up mini-campaign was conducted early in 1990. The slogan, "Vasectomy is an act of love," served as the main theme for the campaign. A 30-second television spot was developed and pretested by a local advertising agency (the Denison Agency) in four focus-group discussions with vasectomized and nonvasectomized ever-married men from age 25 to 49. Discussion group responses were used to revise the advertisement.

The television spot featured a pair of animated hearts—one male, one female—that depicted the purpose of vasectomy, its safety, and its noninterference with lovemaking. In the final version, the two animated hearts entered the screen to wedding music. Through animation and the sounds of excitement and kissing, the hearts united twice and produced babies— little dancing hearts.

On the male's third attempt to unite with his partner, the female scolded him and pushed him away. A vasectomy was depicted by two bars drawn across the male heart. A voiceover then said: "Vasectomy, the male operation, is a quick and painless way to avoid unwanted pregnancies." Once again, the two hearts united to the sounds of kissing and excitement. The campaign slogan closed the spot. This was followed by the tag line, "For further information, contact (clinic name and phone number)."[2]

A companion piece for radio featured a father explaining vasectomy to his son, followed by the same slogan and tag line. To maintain consistency and reinforce the television message, the pamphlets, billboard, and magazine ads all used the same image of two amorous hearts.

A precampaign public relations promotion to generate interest among the print and electronic press was also conducted in the three cities. Activities included issuing press releases that described the project and personally contacting key members of the Brazilian press.

---

[2]The "dancing hearts" advertisement was popular among diverse audiences and won various national media awards and three advertising industry awards—the gold medal at the Fourth London International Advertising Awards, the bronze medal at the 32nd International Festival of Publicity Films in New York, and the Bronze Lion medal at the 37th International Festival of Advertising Films in Cannes, France.

The main television campaign ran from May 18, 1989, to June 30, 1989; on the day before the campaign was launched, the advertising agency held a press conference at PRO-PATER for representatives of 10 broadcast and print news organizations. The head of the clinic also appeared on a variety of television talk shows.

The rebroadcast of the television spots from September 19 to 29 (on the same broadcast schedule of 2–5 times daily from 8:00 p.m. to midnight) ran unaccompanied by additional events. The follow-up minicampaign from January 2, 1990, to March 4, 1990, consisted of an ad in the mass circulation magazine *Veja*, an electronic billboard in downtown São Paulo with the "dancing hearts" motif, and a direct mailing of pamphlets to *Veja* subscribers.

Between March 1989 and June 1990, the campaign and the events surrounding it stimulated roughly 70 news stories on television, radio, daily newspapers, trade journals, weekly and monthly magazines, and television talk show discussions. The precampaign public relations efforts exposed editors and reporters to the campaign, so the spot itself (and the awards it earned) generated cost-free publicity in the form of news coverage. During the campaign, the press coverage extended spontaneously beyond the three clinic cities to at least seven others. In the total 15-month period, the combined public relations activities and press coverage reached an estimated four million people (United Nations Department of Public Information, 1990).

EVALUATION

The campaign was evaluated by examining clinic records and sources of referral. Although baseline and follow-up sample surveys of men in São Paulo and Salvador were also conducted, those results are reported elsewhere (Lordêlo & Morris, 1991; PRO-PATER, 1990; Sakamoto, Freire, & Morris, 1989). The data from clinic records and brief interviews conducted with callers, visitors to the clinics, and patients are presented here. The mean numbers of monthly visits and calls, and the mean monthly numbers of vasectomies—for PRO-VAS in Fortaleza, CEPARH in Salvador, and PRO-PATER in São Paulo—were available for the 7 months preceding (October 18, 1988–May 17, 1989) and the 5½ months immediately following (July 1, 1989–December 15, 1989) the 6-week campaign (May 18, 1989–June 30, 1989). Thus, any effects from the subsequent January–February 1990 minicampaign are not reflected in these data.

Calls and visits to the clinics increased markedly during the campaign: The average number of calls and visits per month at the PRO-VAS clinics in Fortaleza increased 133%, from 15 to 35 during the campaign. In the 6 months afterward, the monthly mean dropped to 12, a level even lower than that seen in the 6 months before the campaign (Involving Male Participation, 1995).[3] At the CEPARH clinic in Salvador, mean monthly calls and visits rose from 39 to 105, an increase of 169%, and thereafter fell to 85, or an increase of 118%.

The most dramatic change occurred at the PRO-PATER clinic, where mean monthly calls and visits first rose from 529 in the 6 months before the campaign to 1,911 during the campaign, an increase of 261%, then fell back to a level of 679 in the 6 months following the campaign, representing an increase of 28%. Thus, the television spots seem to have generated a substantial increase in the number of calls and visits to the clinics.

The monthly mean number of vasectomies performed at the PRO-VAS clinics increased from 12 in the 6 months preceding the campaign to 25 during the campaign, and then fell to 7 in the 6 months following completion of the campaign. These numbers reflect an initial increase of 108%, and a subsequent decrease of 42%. The mean monthly number of vasectomies performed at CEPARH increased from 32 to 51 during the campaign, and continued to increase to 59 in the 6 months following the campaign, for an intermediary increase of 59% and a later increase of 84%. Vasectomies performed at São Paulo's PRO-PATER clinic increased by 82%, from a mean of 303 a month in the 6 months before the campaign to 550 during it. The mean then dropped off slightly to 542, for an increase of 79% during the roughly 6-month follow-up period.

This pattern of an initial increase in demand followed by a drop to a plateau higher than the original level is common in mass media promotions. When postcampaign levels drop below the original level, researchers usually presume that preexisting demand "bunched up" during the promotion period, and no net increase in performance will occur over the long term.

The PRO-PATER Clinic

Because the PRO-PATER clinic had been in existence for longer than the other clinics and was more closely involved in the evaluation, this section analyzes in depth the impact of the campaign on the São Paulo clinic only. The analysis is based on detailed time series and source-of-referral data, which were unavailable for clinics in the Northeast.

---

[3]The PRO-VAS clinics that participated in the project in Fortaleza were a small freestanding one and a larger one at the Federal University in Ceará run in conjunction with the Sociedade de Assistência à Maternidade, Escola Assis Chateaubriand (SAMEAC) Institute. Because a public-sector strike during the campaign closed the university-based clinic for months, only one PRO-VAS clinic remained open during the whole campaign, and the postcampaign decline in performance is exaggerated as a result.

The São Paulo clinic data cover an extended 18-month postcampaign period from July 1989 through December 1990. The data are daily averages, a more precise measure than monthly averages because the clinic was not open for services for the same number of days each month. Table 11.1 presents the daily mean and the total number of telephone inquiries, clinic visits, and vasectomies performed for five distinct periods: the 7 months prior to the initiation of the campaign (October 18, 1988–May 17, 1989); the 6-week campaign (May 18, 1989–June 30, 1989); the 5½ months immediately following the campaign (July 1, 1989–December 15, 1989); the 2-month follow-up mini-campaign (January 2, 1990–March 4, 1990); and the 2½ months immediately following it (March 5, 1990–May 17, 1990).

The daily number of telephone calls jumped from 25 to 95 during the 6-week campaign, an increase of 276%; they then fell back to an average of 33 calls per day in the 5½ months immediately following, and gradually declined to 29 per day during the 2-month minicampaign and to 22 per day in the period after the minicampaign.

Mean daily visits to the clinic increased by 138% during the campaign, from 21 to 51. Over the year after the campaign, visits declined to 30 per day, and then fell to 24 during the final period studied; this last daily average represents a net increase of 13% from the baseline level. An analysis of the ages of men who visited the clinic before, during, and after the campaign showed no significant differences.

The number of vasectomies performed increased from an average of 15 per day before the campaign to a mean of 28 per day at the conclusion of the media campaign (an 81% increase); the daily average declined to 24 in the 5½ months immediately following the campaign and then to 22 and 19 per day, respectively, at the conclusion of the minicampaign and in the months following it. The final average was thus about 24% higher than that at baseline.

During the precampaign period, other persons were the dominant sources of referrals among clinic callers. In the 7 months prior to the campaign, 55% of callers said they were referred by friends and relatives, compared with 5% by television and 15% through the print media. These percentages had shifted dramatically by the conclusion of the 6-week campaign, when 58% of the sources of information cited were television spots, compared with 20% friends and relatives and 10% the print media. The proportion of radio referrals was only 5%.

In the first 5½ months immediately following the campaign, the proportions shifted again, with television representing 34% of referrals, friends and family 43%, articles or ads in the print media 6%, and radio broadcasts 2%. Following the minicampaign, the proportion of referrals that were from magazines and newspapers increased to 17%, a trend that continued into the final 2½ months, peaking at 20%. (This increase corresponds to the ad placed in *Veja* and the direct mailing to subscribers.)

TABLE 11.1
Indicators of Clinic Performance by Timing in Relation to Mass Media Campaign, PRO-PATER Clinic, São Paulo, Brazil, 1989–1990

Indicators	Precampaign	Campaign	Postcampaign	Minicampaign	Post-minicampaign
		Numbers			
Telephone inquiries					
Daily mean	25.4	95.4	32.8	28.9	22.1
Period total	3,278.0	2,861.0	3,741.0	1,070.0	1,171.0
Clinic visits					
Daily mean	21.4	51.0	30.3	30.7	24.1
Period total	2,758.0	1,529.0	3,449.0	1,137.0	1,276.0
Vasectomies					
Daily mean	15.2	27.5	23.5	22.4	18.8
Period total	1,960.0	825.0	2,981.0	827.0	997.0
		Percent Distribution			
Referrals					
Television	4.5	57.9	33.8	12.2	6.1
Radio	na	5.0	2.0	1.1	0.1
Magazines/newspapers	15.3	10.0	6.2	17.1	20.3
Friends/relatives	55.0	20.2	43.3	52.7	49.1
Electronic billboard	na	na	na	.8	.1
Mailing list	na	na	na	na	6.3
Other	25.2	6.8	14.7	16.2	18.0
Reason for call					
To schedule appointment	92.8	62.7	52.2	47.3	27.8
For information	7.2	37.3	47.8	52.7	72.2
Total	100.0	100.0	100.0	100.0	100.0

Note. na = not applicable

The electronic billboard in downtown São Paulo was a very minor referral source, accounting for fewer than 1% of referrals at any time. The proportion of television referrals ultimately declined to its baseline level of about 6% almost a year after the 1989 campaign. The proportion of referrals from other persons also returned to a level close to its initial one (approximately 50%).

Cost-Effectiveness Analysis

Table 11.2 shows that television broadcast time accounted for the greatest proportion of the total cost of the campaign—$78,615 of the $172,910 spent.[4] According to the clinic referral data, television also had the greatest impact on clinic calls and visits. Although costs were approximately the same for the radio broadcasts, magazine ads, and direct mailing, radio referrals to the clinic never exceeded 5% of referrals throughout. Thus, a combination of television and magazine or newspaper promotion appears to have produced the best results for vasectomy promotion in Brazil. But was the additional impact of television worth the higher costs?

To answer this question, a simple cost-effectiveness ratio was computed based on the total cost figure of $172,910 and the monthly data on mean numbers of calls, visits, and vasectomies performed. The differences between the precampaign and campaign periods and between the campaign and postcampaign periods, multiplied by their respective 6-week and 5½-month durations, yields a total net gain in clinic visits and calls of 3,264, and a total net gain in vasectomies of 1,854 for the period beginning May 18, 1989, and ending December 15, 1989. Dividing the total cost by each of these net increases yields cost-effectiveness ratios (which can be expressed as the cost of motivating each additional call, visit, or operation) of $53 per visit or call and $93 per vasectomy.[5]

Longitudinal Analysis

An interrupted time series analysis of monthly vasectomy data from PRO-PATER shows an immediate and substantial increase in vasectomies performed after the start of the mass media campaign. Figure 11.1 graphs the number of vasectomies performed each month, from January 1988 through December 1990, interrupted by the 1989 mass media campaign. As expected, vasectomy performance increased substantially immediately following the mass media campaign. (The 1-month lag after the campaign

---

[4]To make comparisons over time more stable, all costs reported in this article are in U.S. dollars rather than in Brazilian currency, which fluctuated greatly over the period. There was no correction for inflation in the U.S. dollar, however.

[5]The total cost used for these calculations included only the communication and promotion costs in Brazil; the cost of the vasectomy was excluded, as were any technical assistance costs.

TABLE 11.2

Total Costs (in U.S. $) of Mass Media Vasectomy Campaign in Three Brazilian Cities by Type of Cost

City	Total	Fixed Production	Television	Radio	Pamphlet	Magazine	Billboard	Direct Mail
Total	172,910	61,103[a]	78,615	6,740	9,273	6,777	4,223	6,179
São Paulo	120,162	31,833	62,085	5,924	3,091	6,777	4,223	6,179
Fortaleza	23,068	14,610	5,243	124	3,091	na[b]	na	na
Salvador	29,679	14,610	11,287	692	3,091	na	na	na

[a]The total fixed radio and television production costs ($43,830) were allocated equally among all three cities. The São Paulo production costs also include fixed costs of $17,273 for the magazine publicity, electronic billboard and direct mail.
[b]na = not applicable

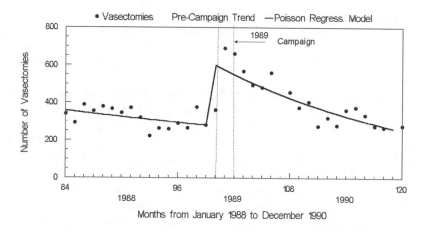

FIG. 11.1.   Effect of mass media campaign on number of vasectomies performed per month and Poisson regression, PRO-PATER Clinic, São Paulo, 1988–1990.

began resulted from the time required to visit or call the clinic and schedule the operation.)

The number of vasectomies peaked during the month immediately after the campaign, when 689 vasectomies were performed, compared with an average of 310 operations during the period before the campaign; the monthly average after the campaign was 401 vasectomies. One-way analysis of variance revealed that this difference was statistically significant at $p < .01$.

The analysis of the mean differences before and after the campaign does not take into account changes in the slope, however. After the dramatic increase in vasectomies, there was a gradual decline through 1990, when performance leveled off at precampaign levels. Poisson regression analysis, which takes each monthly time point into account, provides a more sensitive analysis of the data than does simple analysis of variance (McCullagh & Nelder, 1989). The precampaign versus postcampaign difference was treated as a dummy variable, and the time–campaign interaction was included in the regression. For the 3 years depicted in Fig. 11.1 (1988–1990), all three variables—time, campaign, and time–campaign interaction—were statistically significant at $p < .001$.[6]

The results of the regression analysis are indicated by the solid line in Fig. 11.1. During this 3-year period, the overall effect of time was negative, indicating a general downward trend in the number of vasectomies

---

[6]The overall regression model was also statistically significant at $p < .001$ ($\chi^2 = 644.1$, $df = 3$, $N = 37$), and it explained approximately 46% of the variance in clinic performance.

performed. The effect of the campaign was positive, increasing the number performed. The interaction between time and campaign was negative, however, indicating that the downward slope of vasectomy performance became significantly more negative after the communication campaign ended.

The greater negative slope after the campaign raises questions about the long-term trend in vasectomy performance at the PRO-PATER clinic. Specifically, did performance continue to decline after the 1989 mass media campaign? To answer this question, data was obtained from PRO-PATER on all vasectomies performed from the clinic's opening in February 1981 through the end of 1992. Figure 11.2 graphs these data relative to the timing of three mass media events undertaken over that extended period: a 3-minute report about vasectomy broadcast on national television in 1983, a print-only campaign in 1985, and the multimedia campaign of 1989.

The solid line in Fig. 11.2 shows the level of performance predicted from the Poisson regression of the number of vasectomies on the variable time using the three mass media events as dummy variables, and their interactions with time and the cost of the operation. After a steep increase in the number of vasectomies performed in the first 3 years, there was an abrupt jump after the 3-minute television report in 1983, followed by a gradual decline. The first mass media promotion in 1985 also produced a significant jump in clinic performance, followed by another gradual decline.

The results of this second regression analysis are presented in Table 11.3. All variables were statistically significant except for the interaction between time and the 1985 print campaign. The regression indicates that time had a statistically significant, positive effect over the entire 12-year

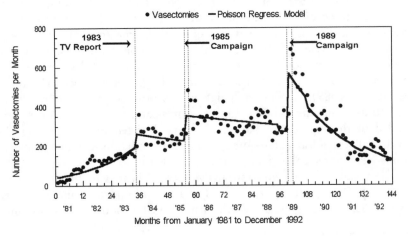

FIG. 11.2.   Effect of media events on number of vasectomies performed per month and Poisson regression, PRO-PATER clinic, São Paulo, 1981–1992.

TABLE 11.3
Poisson Regression Coefficient (and 95% Confidence Interval)
for Number of Vasectomies Performed per Month

Variable	Coefficient		t value	p
Time	.045	(.041, .048)	24.334	.001
TV (1983)	2.149	(1.922, 2.376)	18.587	.001
Time–TV interaction (1983)	−.052	(−.058, −.047)	−17.696	.001
1985 campaign	.244	(.010, .477)	2.046	.041
Time–campaign interaction (1985)	.004	(−.001, .009)	1.558	.119
1989 campaign	3.755	(3.557, 3.954)	37.022	.001
Time–campaign interaction (1989)	−.030	(−.032, −.028)	−30.198	.001
Cost	−.002	(−.003, −.002)	−6.700	.001
Constant	3.872	(3.730, 3.924)	77.303	.001

Note. No. of observations = 143 months; χ^2 (df = 8) at 8071.438; probability = .000; and pseudo R^2 = .7468.

period, even after controlling for the effects of the other variables in the model.[7] All three media events—1983, 1985, and 1989—had positive, statistically significant effects and, as expected, cost had a statistically significant negative effect.

The interaction between time and the initiation of the 1989 campaign was statistically significant and negative, indicating that after the multimedia campaign ended, the downward slope decreased further, to a significantly lower negative value. This change is readily apparent in Fig. 11.2. The solid line that fits the data between 1985 and 1989 slopes downward, but is much less steep than the slope occurring after the 1989 campaign.

The trend between the 1985 and 1989 media campaigns is also negative, but not significantly different from the slope before the 1985 print campaign. Although the 1985 campaign increased the number of procedures performed, the same downward trend continued until the multimedia campaign of 1989. After this last campaign, the downward trend in performance became even more pronounced.

Once the data are extended to the 3 years beyond the 1989 campaign, the negative slope in performance after the 1989 campaign is even more dramatic. By 1992, vasectomies had dropped to the level recorded 10 years earlier. The simple correlation between time and the number of vasectomies before the 1989 campaign was .81 and positive; after the campaign, the correlation (−.82) was exactly reversed. Thus, in a broader historical

---

[7]The overall model was statistically significant at $p < .001$ (χ^2 = 8071.4, df = 8, N = 143). The model explained 75% of the variance in clinic performance from its beginning in 1981 to December 1992.

context, the 1989 campaign appears to have only temporarily reversed a long-term downward trend in the number of vasectomies provided by the PRO-PATER clinic.

Several hypotheses may explain this long-term downward trend. The first is financial. As external funding declined and the cost of supplies increased, PRO-PATER had to charge clients more. This price factor was exacerbated by a general increase in the cost of living in Brazil after 1989, including a major devaluation in the nation's currency.

Another hypothesis concerns an increase in competition from new providers of vasectomy services. These probably included some of the 44 physicians in the Sao Paulo area who were trained by PRO-PATER. The organization's promotional efforts, especially the 1989 television campaign, most likely stimulated attendance at other São Paulo providers.

Although no provider data are available to test the alternative provider hypothesis, it was possible to investigate the cost increase hypothesis using price quotes from PRO-PATER for January 1987 through December 1992. From January 1987 through December 1988, a vasectomy cost $62 and in January 1989 it increased to $110; the price rose again in January 1990 to $155, then again in January 1991 to $165, and finally peaked in August 1991 at $181. In January 1992, the price dropped to approximately $117.

This cost factor was included in the Poisson regression analysis. The small downward shifts in the solid line representing the numbers of vasectomies predicted from the regression model (Fig. 11.2) occur whenever the cost of the operation changed. In fact, the increasing costs of vasectomy had a statistically significant negative (downward) effect on the number of vasectomies performed (Table 11.3).

CONCLUSIONS

The quasi-experimental research design used in this evaluation (comparing pretest and posttest measures among one sample of men) was insufficient to determine whether the mass media campaign caused the increase in calls and visits and in vasectomies; the only way to rule out the possibility that other factors caused the changes is to use a control group for comparison. However, the pattern of change in the predominant referral source from interpersonal sources to television, and then back again once the campaign ended, increases confidence in a causal inference. Causation is also supported by the timing of the effect, because it occurred immediately after the campaign began and no other known events or circumstances were observed.

The longitudinal analysis of PRO-PATER clinic data reveals that all three mass media events had a significant impact on the number of vasectomies performed, and the greatest impact resulted from the multimedia campaign of 1989, which used prime-time television and radio spots. Data on clinic referral sources indicate that television played an important role in motivating men to visit the clinics.

The effect of the television campaign, which received international awards for its creative merit, was clear in its impact on clinic inquiries, visits, and operations performed. Furthermore, evidence exists, especially for the São Paulo clinic, that the mass media campaign had a significant effect on clinic performance.

The long-term analysis, however, implies that some kind of ongoing promotion is necessary to maintain a given level of clinic activity or to raise activity to a new level. The PRO-PATER experience suggests that without periodic mass media promotions, clinic performance will gradually decline over the long term. A well-designed mass media campaign can increase clinic performance even during a period of relative decline, and even when costs to clients are rising.

The simple cost-effectiveness analysis reveals that the promotional cost of $93 per additional client is about the same as the cost of the vasectomy itself. Whereas the cost-effectiveness ratio may seem high at first, it should be considered within a historical and cultural context, because vasectomy has traditionally been a difficult method to promote in Latin cultures. The near doubling in price of the procedure in the first months of 1989 also affected the ratio. For example, in January 1989, the cost of a vasectomy at PRO-PATER increased from nearly $62 to about $110, where it remained during the campaign.

Taking the method's effectiveness into account further reduces the apparent size of the promotional costs. For example, because a vasectomy provides an average of 10 couple-years of protection against pregnancy (Bertrand, Mangnani, & Knowles, 1994), the promotion cost per couple-year of protection is $9.30. Moreover, given the relative difficulty of motivating Brazilian men to adopt vasectomy (e.g., compared with that of motivating Brazilian women to begin using the pill), the cost seems reasonable. Although it is often easier for potential acceptors to adopt temporary methods, such as the pill, it is also easier to discontinue use, and pill discontinuation rates can run as high as 50% within 1 year of use in developing countries (Larson, Islam, & Mitra, 1991; Perez & Tabije, 1996).

In most communication cost-effectiveness analyses, estimating long-term effects is difficult because of research costs and time constraints. In the research, where long-term vasectomy data were examined, the regression analysis confirms the significant, positive effect of three media interventions on clinic performance. Unfortunately, the long-term effects appear ultimately to have been offset by concomitant increases in costs and by the presence of alternative sources for the operation.

The effectiveness estimates also do not reflect the expected diffusion effect—that is, an increase in word-of-mouth promotion by the rising number of new vasectomy clients and future potential clients. Because the current number of vasectomized men is still low in Brazil, such men probably do not yet constitute the critical mass needed to accelerate the procedure's diffusion. Some type of future mass media promotion is thus still necessary; the long-term trend of PRO-PATER clinic performance suggests that such regular, periodic mass media promotions could maintain or increase the prevalence of vasectomy.

Mass media promotions and discussions of vasectomy should be continued at a level and a frequency sufficient to maintain public interest. One possibility is to inaugurate an annual "Vasectomy Week" promotion, followed by a weekend of inexpensive, prime-time promotional spots every 3 months. Perhaps then the growth in the number of vasectomy acceptors will produce the critical mass of satisfied users needed to multiply the effects of mass media promotional efforts by means of personal advocacy.

REFERENCES

Arruda, J. M., Rutenberg, N., Morris, L., & Ferraz, E. (1987). *Pesquisa Nacional Sobre Saúde Materno-infantil e Planejamento Familiar—1986* [National survey of maternal–child health and family planning—1986]. Rio de Janeiro: Sociedade Civil Bem-Estar no Brasil.

Bertrand, J. T., Mangnani, R. J., & Knowles, J. C. (1994). *Handbook of indicators for family planning program evaluation*. Chapel Hill, NC: Carolina Population Center, the Evaluation Project.

Bertrand, J. T., Santiso, R., Linder, S. H., & Pineda, M. A. (1987). Evaluation of a communications program to increase adoption of vasectomy in Guatemala. *Studies in Family Planning, 18*(6), 361–370.

de Castro, M. P. P., Mastrorocco, D. A., de Castro, B. M., & Mumford, S. D. (1984). An innovative vasectomy program in São Paulo, Brazil. *International Family Planning Perspectives, 10*(4), 125–130.

Foreit, K. G., de Castro, M. P. P., & Franco Duarte, E. F. (1989). The impact of mass media advertising on a voluntary sterilization program in Brazil. *Studies in Family Planning, 20*, 107–116.

Involving Male Participation. (1995). *People and Development Challenges, 2*(3), 7.

Kiragu, K., Kiriuki, J. W., Wilkinson, D. W., & Onoka, C. (1995). *The vasectomy promotion project (Kenya): Evaluation results* (Working paper). Baltimore, MD: Johns Hopkins University Population Communication Project.

Larson, A., Islam, S., & Mitra, S. N. (1991). Pill use in Bangladesh: Compliance, continuation and unintentional pregnancies. *Report of the 1990 Pill Use Study*. Dhaka, Bangladesh: Mitra and Associates.

Liskin, L., Benoit, E., & Blackburn, P. (1992). Vasectomy: New opportunities. *Population Reports*, Series D, No. 5. Baltimore, MD: Population Information Program, Johns Hopkins University.

Lordêlo, E. R., & Morris, L. (1991). *Conhecimentos e Atitudes em Relação à Vasectomia Entre Homens de Salvador—1989* [Knowledge and attitudes about vasectomy among men in Salvador—1989]. Salvador, Brazil: Fundação de Apoio à Pesquisa e Extensão.

McCullagh, P., & Nelder, J. A. (1989). *Generalized linear models.* New York: Chapman & Hall.

Perez, A. E., & Tabije, T. L. (1996). *Contraceptive discontinuation, failure, and switching behavior in the Philippines.* (DHS Working Paper No. 19). Calverton, MD: Macro International.

Promocão da Paternidade Responsável (PRO-PATER) (1990). *Vasectomia: Faça por Amor* [Vasectomy: An act of love]. Baltimore, MD: Johns Hopkins University Population Communication Services.

Sakamoto, C. P. M., Freire, H. S., & Morris, L. (1989). *0 Homem e a Vasectomia na Cidade de São Paulo: Um Estudo de Conhecimento, Atitudes, e Comportamento—Fase II, 1989* [Men and vasectomy in the city of São Paulo: A study of knowledge, attitudes, and behavior—1991]. São Paulo, Brazil: Centro Materno Infantil de Planejamento Familiar.

United Nations Department of Public Information. (1990). *World Media Handbook.* New York: United Nations.

Vernon, S. R., Ojeda, G., & Vega, A. (1991). Making vasectomy services more acceptable to men. *International Family Planning Perspectives, 17,* 55–60.

Xu, B. (1993). Male sterilization in China. *British Journal of Family Planning, 19,* 243–245.

Zhang, J. (1994). A good example: Sichuan province. *Integration, 39,* 19.

12

Improving Vaccination Coverage in Urban Areas Through a Health Communication Campaign: The 1990 Philippines Experience

Susan Zimicki
Robert C. Hornik
University of Pennsylvania

Cecelia C. Verzosa
Academy for Educational Development, Washington, DC

José R. Hernandez
Department of Health, San Lazaro Compound, Manila, Philippines

Eleanora de Guzman
HEALTHCOM, Dakar, Senegal

Manolet Dayrit
Adora Fausto
Department of Health, Manila, Philippines

Mary Bessie Lee
University of Pennsylvania

Since the WHO Expanded Program on Immunization (EPI) was instituted in 1974, there has been a considerable increase in worldwide vaccination. Programmatic factors identified as important in achieving and maintaining high coverage include an adequate supply of vaccine (Cutts, Soares, et al., 1990; Subramanyam, 1989), accessibility of vaccination sites and convenient hours for vaccination (Belcher, Nicholas, Ofosu-Amaah, & Wurapa,

1978; Cutts, Rodrigues, Colombo, & Bennett, 1989; Friede, Waternaux, Guyer, de Jesus, & Filipp, 1985), short waiting times (Cutts, Soares, et al., 1990a; Eng, Naimoli, Naimoli, Parker, & Lowenthal, 1991; Unger, 1991), and low rates of "missed opportunities" for vaccination (Cutts, Glik, et al., 1990; Cutts et al., 1989; Cutts, Soares, et al., 1990; Loevinsohn, 1989; Steinhoff, Cole, Cole, John, & Pereira, 1985).

However, even when vaccines are readily available and service delivery is good, coverage rates may still be low due to problems of knowledge, attitudes, and perceptions about vaccination (Cutts et al., 1989; Eng et al., 1991; Hanlon, Byass, Yamuah, Hayes, Bennett, & M'Boge, 1988; Streatfield & Singarimbun, 1988). These can include more general knowledge and attitudes about the utility of vaccination, such as a less scientific, more fatalistic notion of disease and a generally lower use of preventive services (Hanlon et al., 1988); lack of knowledge about what diseases vaccine prevents (Cutts et al., 1989; Hanlon et al., 1988; Streatfield & Singarimbun, 1988); a belief that EPI diseases are not serious (Streatfield & Singarimbun, 1988); as well as lack of "logistic knowledge" about the time and place vaccination is available (Belcher et al., 1978) or about the appropriate age or interval to bring the child for vaccination (Cutts et al., 1989; Eng et al., 1991; Cutts, Glik, et al., 1990; Streatfield & Singarimbun, 1988).

One response to identification of these deficiencies is to provide the necessary information through mass media. However, information provision is usually only one of many components of program improvement (and, frequently, is barely mentioned in descriptions of mass media campaigns; see, e.g., Unger, 1991; Risi, 1983; Balraj & John, 1986); thus, it has been difficult to evaluate its effect. The question is important, because mass media is not an inevitable element of immunization programs. Continued use of mass media does require evidence that it contributes to the success of programs.

The 1990 national communications campaign to support the Philippines immunization program provided an opportunity to assess the effectiveness of using a mass media component. The immunization program reported here was managed by the Philippines Department of Health's Maternal and Child Health Services in collaboration with the Public Information Health Education Service, with technical assistance from the Communication for Child Survival program (HEALTHCOM) in the development, implementation, and monitoring of the communication elements of the program.

Because the campaign focused on urban areas, physical access to health facilities was not an issue. Moreover, the Philippines has generally good levels of health service provision, which did not change greatly during the campaign. Thus, it provided an opportunity to examine the effect of mass media dissemination of information about vaccination, which could be analyzed independently from other major changes in health services. The analysis demonstrates that improvement in coverage can be linked to an increase in knowledge about vaccination, which in turn is related to exposure to the communication elements of the campaign.

MATERIALS AND METHODS

The Communication Campaign

The vaccination communication campaign in the Philippines was carried out in two major phases: a pilot phase in Metro Manila in 1988, which then led to a nationwide campaign in 1990. This chapter focuses on the nationwide campaign, which used the program strategies piloted in the successful Metro Manila measles immunization communication campaign.[1] Three essential elements of the strategy were focusing on measles as a "hook" to get mothers to bring their children to the health center; emphasizing logistic knowledge in the mass media messages, in particular popularizing a single day of the week as "vaccination day" and giving clear information about the age for measles vaccination; and focusing on urban areas, which had lower vaccination rates than rural areas.

The measles vaccination was selected for promotion because measles was the most common childhood communicable disease recognized by mothers and the third largest killer of infants and children in the country. Also, because the measles vaccination is the final one in the series, it could draw children who had not received earlier vaccinations, particularly DPT and OPV, and ensure they received these vaccinations as well. A single day of the week was selected as "vaccination day" because it gave mothers a time when they could be sure that vaccinations would be given at any health center. As part of the planning for the nationwide campaign, consultations with the regional immunization officers resulted in the selection of Wednesday as the vaccination day and a decision to focus on urban areas, which had lower vaccination rates than rural areas.

Because of the large number of cities to be covered by the campaign, it was necessary to conduct a number of precampaign activities with city and health personnel in different parts of the country. In July and August 1989, area planning conferences were held with regional immunization officers, provincial health officers, city health officers, municipal health offi-

---

[1]Details about the Metro Manila campaign can be found in Verzosa, C., Bernaje, M. G., de Guzman, E. M., Hernandez, J. F. S., Reodica, C. N., & and Taguiwalo, M. M. (1989, December). *Managing a communication program on immunization*, Academy for Educational Development.

cers, and city/municipal EPI coordinators to give them an overview of the campaign and their roles in the activities and to address their concerns. In September 1989, meetings were held with the mayors of the campaign cities (who control the city health centers) to obtain their support and cooperation in campaign activities.

Orientation of clinic personnel to the campaign began in February 1990. There were three master "sales conferences," one-day meetings with regional health staff who were informed about the campaign and encouraged to convene similar meetings in their own areas. These meetings were held to reinforce Department of Health (DOH) policies about vaccinations, prepare clinics for the increased demand and the focus on the Wednesday vaccination day, and gain clinic personnel involvement in the campaign.

The mass media element of the campaign was carried out between March 16, 1990, and September 22, 1990. Four television and four radio advertisements were broadcast, and advertisements were printed in newspapers reminding people that Wednesday was free vaccination day at the health centers. Other promotional materials included posters, bunting, and welcome streamers for health centers to display, as well as stickers for jeepneys (shared ride taxis) and tricycles, and T-shirts for health center staff.

The communication materials focused on the danger of measles and its complications, and recommended that children from age 9 to 12 months be taken to the health center for vaccination. They said that vaccinations were free and would be available on Wednesdays at health centers. The campaign slogan, included in all communication materials, was "*Iligtas si baby sa tigdas*" (Protect your baby from measles).

Evaluation

The evaluation presented here is based on data obtained from two sources: two surveys of caretakers of children less than 2 years old in Metro Manila, Luzon, Mindanao, and Visayas; and a pre–post study of 60 health centers in the same geographical areas.

Surveys.   The first survey was carried out in July and August 1989, before the campaign; the second, in August 1990, was taken near the end of the campaign. Using a structured questionnaire in the relevant local language, interviewers obtained information about the family's socioeconomic status, the child's vaccination status, use of the health care system, the experience the last time the child was taken to be vaccinated, knowledge about vaccination, exposure to media, and specific recall of any advertisements about vaccination. The same questionnaire was used for both surveys.

A woman was eligible to be a respondent if she was the mother or permanent caretaker of a child less than 2 years old. The sample of women interviewed was obtained using a multistage cluster sampling strategy, with a cluster size of 10 (sampling stages are summarized in Table 12.1). Weighted analyses were used to adjust for differences in some characteristics of respondents interviewed in the two surveys (Table 12.2) and for geographical representation. Unless otherwise noted, all estimates reported here are weighted. Further, all coverage estimates reported are based on mothers' reports as well as vaccination cards; as found elsewhere (Gareaballah & Loevinsohn), examination of the Philippines data indicated that, although the possibility of some overreporting (particularly for measles vaccination after the campaign) could not be ruled out, excluding claimed vaccinations would substantially underestimate vaccination coverage (data not shown).

It is important to note that the absolute level of coverage reported here cannot be compared directly to estimates based on other procedures. The sample of mothers surveyed was restricted to relatively less well-off people, those who were considered to be in the "D" and "E" categories of the five category "ABCDE" scale used by market researchers. Thus, it might differ from other estimates—for example, those based on distributed vaccines, on card-verified data only, or with different samples (i.e., rural as well as urban people, other social classes as well as "D" and "E," or with other provinces included). This evaluation seeks to establish the effects of the

TABLE 12.1
Sampling Procedure

Stage	
1	Allocation of interviews to: A. Manila (400 interviews) B. Cities outside Manila (800 interviews)
2	Probability proportionate to size sample of: 3 cities in Luzon 4 cities in Visayas 3 cities in Mindanao
3	Round 1: Random sample of voting districts with substantially D and E populations[a] Round 2: Next (previously unselected) voting district on geographically ordered list
4	Random selection of cluster start
5	Interviews with 10 mothers/caretakers of children < 2 living in adjacent or nearest houses in a randomly determined direction from the cluster start

[a]D and E are the lowest categories of the five-category ABCDE scale used by market researchers. Approximately 90% of the population in the Philippines belongs to categories D and E.

TABLE 12.2
Significant ($p < .01$) Differences Between Respondents Interviewed in
1989 and 1990 (Weighted to Account for Area Representation Only)

Characteristic	1989 Survey		1990 Survey	
	Measure	N	Measure	N
Born in a small city (%)	6.2	1,200	15.5	1,198
Speaks English with children (%)	20.7	1,200	6.2	1,200
Has electricity (%)	91.5	1,200	95.6	1,200
Has radio (%)	72.4	1,200	78.2	1,200
Last child born at home (%)	37.3	1,200	30.9	1,200
Average income category (1–10)	4.6	1,116	5.5	1,153
Average years of school—respondent	9.6	1,199	10.1	1,198
Average years of school—husband	10.1	1,155	10.4	1,167

campaign and the process through which it occurred. Given the cost constraints that limited the sample, it cannot be said to represent the absolute level of vaccination in the Philippines.

Health Center Study. A simultaneous health center study provided parallel evidence about what was happening at the facilities that were to meet the demand stimulated by the communication campaign. The health center study included three components: structured interviews with staff of 60 health centers, observations of 10 children who attended the health center on a day when vaccinations were given at a subset of 20 centers, and exit interviews with the adults accompanying the observed children as they left these 20 health centers. All health centers were visited in August 1989 through October 1989 and July 1990 through September 1990.

The structured interviews with health center staff concerned general information about the particular clinic and its customary practices with regard to vaccination, supplies, and record keeping. Observations centered on the interaction between the health center clients and the staff person giving vaccinations, and the interview with the client outside the health center, which took less than 5 minutes, included questions about clinic accessibility, waiting time, knowledge concerning vaccinations, and examination of the child's card to determine missed opportunities that day.

Most of the 60 health centers included in the study were selected because the majority of caretakers in an individual cluster (60 of the 120 clusters in the first survey) had named the center as (a) the center they attended, if they used the public health system; or (b) the health center nearest to where they lived, if they did not use the public health system. For a few clusters, either no health center was named by a majority of individuals or the one that was named was unavailable for the study; in these latter cases, another nearby health center was substituted.

RESULTS

Effect of the Campaign

Between 1989 and 1990 vaccination coverage improved substantially (Table 12.3). The proportion of fully vaccinated children from age 12 months to 23 months increased from 54% to 65%, and the average number of vaccinations for all children less than age 2 increased from 4.32 to 5.10. The most striking result, however, is that the main change during this period was an improvement in the timeliness of vaccination, particularly in the proportion of children finishing "on time," estimated as the proportion of children between age 9 months and their first birthday who had received all eight vaccinations (from 32% to 56%). This advantage holds up even if only card-verified data are included (an increase from 22% to 32%). The increase in timeliness is particularly apparent in comparing the age-specific proportions of fully vaccinated children in 1989 and 1990 (Fig. 12.1). In 1990, about 65% of children were fully vaccinated at age 12 months, a level that in 1989 was attained at about age 24 months. Figure 12.1 shows both a timeliness effect and some indication of a cohort effect, with children who were less than age 1 year at the start of the cam-

TABLE 12.3
Improvement in Vaccination Coverage Between 1989
and 1990 Surveys According to Different Measures

Estimator *(Claimed and Verified Information)*	*Percent*		*Rate* *Diff.*	*Rate* *ratio*	*Signif.*[b]
	1989	*1990*			
12–23 month coverage: Proportion of children 12–23 months of age who had all 8 vaccinations	53.6 (446)[a]	64.5 (461)	10.90	1.20	$p < .01$
Starting on time: Proportion of children < 4 months of age who had at least one vaccination	43.3 (255)	55.6 (196)	12.30	1.28	$p < .01$
Finishing on time: Proportion of children 9–11 months old who had all 8 vaccinations	32.2 (184)	56.2 (193)	24.00	1.75	$p < .01$
Appropriate measles: Proportion of children 9–23 months of age who had measles vaccination	53.3 (630)	68.2 (653)	14.90	1.28	$p < .01$
Appropriate early vaccinations: Proportion of children 2–8 months of age with at least 4 vaccinations	47.7 (441)	56.2 (442)	8.50	1.18	$p < .01$
Mean number of vaccinations	4.32 (1,200)	5.10 (1,195)	.78	1.18	$p < .01$

[a]Figures in parentheses are denominators
[b]χ^2 or t test, as appropriate

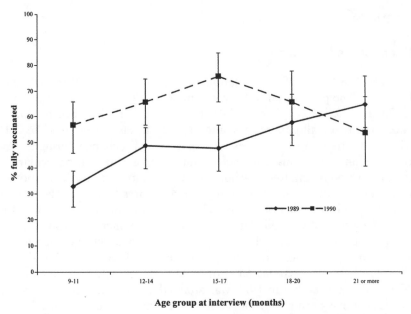

FIG. 12.1. Age-specific proportions of children who were fully vaccinated (all eight vaccinations) at the time of the surveys completed in 1989 (before the mass media campaign) and in August 1990 (5 months after the start of the campaign). The 95% confidence limits (bars) are corrected for the design effect associated with the cluster sampling procedure.

paign attaining a higher level of coverage than older children. There was an ongoing upward trend in vaccination levels already in place in the Philippines when this program was initiated in 1989. However, it was too gradual a slope to explain the extent of the change achieved in 1 year during this program.[2]

Mechanism of Effect

There is substantial evidence that the program worked by increasing knowledge about vaccination among the caretakers of young children. There were large increases in knowledge about vaccination between 1989 and 1990, and the increases, which were associated with the improvement in vaccination practice, were also related to exposure to the mass media campaign. There is no evidence of any programmatic change that could account for the increase in vaccination, such as increases in vaccine supplies,

---

[2]The secular trend was estimated from the time plot of measles vaccination by age 12 months among 12- to 23-month-old children demonstrated in 51 city and provincial level EPI surveys undertaken by the Philippines Department of Health with assistance from the Resources for Child Health (REACH) project between February 1988 and March 1990.

increased outreach efforts, or reorganization of clinic services to reduce waiting time. Moreover, the available findings concerning the interaction between health workers and those coming for vaccination suggests that increased health education efforts at health centers cannot account for the change in knowledge.

Knowledge About Vaccinations Changed. The surveys conducted in 1989 and 1990 included measurements of 22 items of knowledge about vaccination: 8 measurements specifically about measles vaccination, because the campaign focused on measles, and 14 measurements concerning other vaccinations and vaccination in general.

People knew more about measles vaccination after the campaign than before. On every question there was a statistically significant improvement between 1989 and 1990 (Table 12.4). When baseline correct knowledge was over 80%, the improvements were small, but when baseline knowledge was lower, the improvements were often over 20 percentage points.

Knowledge about other vaccinations also improved between the two surveys, although not so sharply (Table 12.5). The increase in average proportion correct for these questions (4.8%) was only about one third the increase for the eight questions about measles (15%). Such an overall comparison of the changes in knowledge about measles and about the other vaccinations can only be tentative, because not all the questions are identical. However, comparison of similar questions shows that in every case, a greater improvement occurred with respect to knowledge about measles vaccination than about other vaccinations.[3] Moreover, the lack of change in knowledge about specifics of other vaccinations (Questions 7–9 in Table 12.5), particularly about the number of doses of OPV necessary, suggests that the experience of actually getting the vaccinations is not the chief means of acquiring knowledge about them. The greater change in knowledge about measles suggests the importance of the communication efforts, given the emphasis on that antigen during the media campaign.

Vaccination Coverage Is Related to Knowledge. A series of regression analyses using survey year and knowledge variables to predict number of vaccinations indicated that a subset of 4 of these 22 knowledge items are particularly important in explaining the influence of the campaign on vaccination practice. These four knowledge items were chosen because they were the only items that had independent effects on the relation between survey year and vaccination performance. They include three questions about measles (Questions 2, 7, and 8 in Table 12.4) and one

---

[3]Question 2 in Table 12.4 with Questions 1–3 in Table 12.5; Question 3 in Table 12.4 with Questions 4–6 in Table 12.5; and Question 7 in Table 12.4 with Question 13 in Table 12.5.

TABLE 12.4
Changes in Knowledge About Measles Vaccination
Between 1989 and 1990 Surveys

	Percent correct			
Measles Knowledge Question	1989 (1,200)	1990 (1,195)	Change	Signif. (χ^2)
1. (Open ended:) "Some children get measles and others do not. Is there any way to protect a child from getting measles?" If says yes, "What can one do to protect a child from getting measles?" (mentions vaccination)	53.2	73.2	20.0	< .01
2. "Here is a list of diseases: please tell me against which of these diseases a child can be protected by vaccination?" (mentions measles)	87.8	94.5	6.8	< .01
3. "When (child name) has all the vaccinations he/she needs will he/she still be likely to become sick from measles?" (says no)	48.0	65.4	17.4	< .01
4. "Would you say that measles is a serious or not so serious disease?" (says it is serious)	81.1	86.6	5.5	< .01
5. "Would you say that measles can lead to complications or not?" (says it can lead to complications)	81.0	95.6	14.6	< .01
6. "Mothers should never take measles for granted" (agrees)	80.7	91.2	10.5	< .01
7. "As far as you know, at what age should a child get vaccination for measles?" (gives answer between 38–52 weeks)	45.1	66.1	21.0	< .01
8. "The best age for a child to get measles vaccination is 3–5 months old." (disagrees)	32.6	57.9	25.3	< .01
Average proportion correct	64.8	78.8	15.1	

about all vaccinations (Question 13 in Table 12.5); three of the four are about the timing of vaccinations.

Evidence that the campaign worked through knowledge may be seen clearly in Fig. 12.2, which shows for both surveys the relation between practice and a knowledge score (range 0–4) created by summing responses to the four critical knowledge items, with respondents receiving one point for each correct answer. Strikingly, the lines are almost identical, indicating that the relation between knowledge and practice is about the same in both years. However, respondents scored higher on knowledge in 1990, averaging 2.97 correct responses, than in 1989, when the average score was 2.3.

In 1989, before the campaign, surveyed children had an average of 4.32 vaccinations; in 1990, they had 5.10 vaccinations, an increase of almost

TABLE 12.5
Changes in Knowledge of Other Vaccinations
Between 1989 and 1990 Surveys

Vaccination Knowledge Question	Percent Correct			
	1989 (1,200)	1990 (1,195)	Diff.	Signif. (χ^2)
1. "Here is a list of diseases: please tell me against which of these diseases a child can be protected by vaccination?				
whooping cough *(mentions)*	63.7	69.4	5.7	< .01
2. tuberculosis *(mentions)*	77.0	81.9	4.9	< .01
3. polio *(mentions)*	90.3	91.6	1.3	ns
4. "When (child name) has all the vaccinations he/she needs will he/she still be likely to become sick from:				
whooping cough?" *(says no)*	39.4	48.1	8.7	< .01
5. tuberculosis?" *(says no)*	61.0	70.9	9.9	< .01
6. polio?" *(says no)*	64.2	74.3	10.1	< .01
7. "There is no vaccination to protect a newborn baby from tetanus." *(disagrees)*	66.2	62.5	−3.7	ns
8. "For a child to be fully protected against polio, only one dose of vaccine is necessary." *(disagrees)*	62.9	61.4	−1.5	ns
9. "BCG vaccination protects children from getting whooping cough." *(disagrees)*	18.4	18.7	.3	ns
10. "Polio Vaccination is given by drops in the mouth."*(agrees)*	80.8	85.8	5.0	< .01
11. "Even if a child has a cold and a low fever a child should still be given vaccination." *(agrees)*	18.2	25.1	6.9	< .01
12. "As far as you know, by what age should a child begin getting vaccination?" *(answer is 4 weeks or less)*	50.7	58.8	8.1	< .01
13. "As far as you know, by what age should a child have all the vaccinations he/she needs?" *(answer is between 38 and 52 weeks)*	65.0	78.1	13.1	< .01
14. "It's best for a child to finish getting all vaccinations by his first birthday." *(agrees)*	91.9	90.6	−1.3	ns
Average proportion correct	60.7	65.5	4.8	

20%. If that difference is largely explained by the effects of the campaign on knowledge, then if one "controls" for knowledge there should be little effect left. Results of a series of multiple regression analyses, summarized in Table 12.6, demonstrate the expected pattern. The original gap in vaccination levels between the 1989 and 1990 samples is essentially explained by knowledge differences between the two samples. Once knowledge is

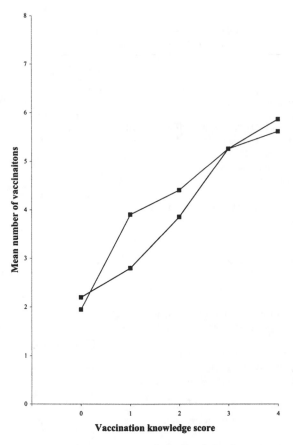

FIG. 12.2.   Mean number of vaccinations for all children age 0–23 months,
by vaccination knowledge scores in 1989 and 1990.

controlled for, no significant difference in vaccination practice between the
2 years remains.

Knowledge Is Related to Campaign Exposure.

There is good evi-
dence that the changes in knowledge were related to exposure to the mass
media campaign. The public communication campaign was well remembered by the survey respondents (Table 12.7), including a particularly high
proportion who could complete the campaign slogan "Iligtas si baby *sa
tigdas.*" The low number of correct responses given to the same questions
in the 1989 survey indicates that these were not random correct guesses.
There were some 1989 respondents whose responses suggested they had
been exposed to mass media information about measles. Most of these respondents were in Manila and had been exposed to the roughly similar pi-

TABLE 12.6
Effect of Knowledge on 1989–1990 Vaccination Differences

	Absolute Difference	Percentage Explained	Signif. of Diff.
1989–1990 difference in vaccination	.77[a]		$p < .01$
Amount of that difference accounted for by 4 knowledge items	.54	70%	
Remaining difference not explained by knowledge	.23[a]	30%	ns

[a]This analysis summarizes the results of a multiple regression analysis. These are the unstandardized coefficients for a variable representing the time a survey was completed estimated with and without the knowledge items in the equation. Expressed in alternate statistical language, the simple bivariate correlation between survey year and vaccination level is .122 ($p < .0001$); the partial correlation, controlling for the knowledge variables is .04, a nonsignificant coefficient ($p = .07$).

TABLE 12.7
Exposure to Media Materials

Variable	1989 Survey (N = 1200)	1990 Survey (N = 1195)	Signif. (χ^2)
Heard or saw an ad	31%	84%	$p < .01$
Could complete last word of campaign rhyme	13%	72%	$p < .01$
Of those who recalled the ad:	(N = 372)	(N = 1003)	
Agreed that ad said that vaccinations were free	68%	94%	$p < .01$
Mentioned that ad said that Wednesday was vaccination day	6%	74%	$p < .01$
Average score on 4-point campaign recall scale constructed from these items	.71	3.03	

lot campaign mounted in 1988. This permitted them to recall the catch phrase of the campaign and know that the advertisements emphasized that vaccines were available without cost. However, the 1988 campaign featured Friday as the "vaccination day," explaining why virtually no one answered that question correctly in 1989.

A second type of supporting evidence for the effects of mass media on knowledge was the response to the general question, "Can you tell me where/from whom you learned about vaccination? Anyone/any place else?" The broad tendency was for responses to this question to focus on health system components: clinic staff or private physicians. That did not change between 1989 and 1990. However, there was a striking increase in mentions of mass media between the two surveys. In 1989, about 11% and, in 1990, 35% of the respondents mentioned radio or television as among their sources for such knowledge. Although this is not evidence about the source of any specific knowledge, it does indicate that, in gen-

eral, people were seeing mass media as a more significant source for information about vaccination than they had before the campaign.

The third type of evidence is the most direct. A measure of recall of
campaign messages was created from respondent's replies concerning the
items listed in Table 12.7. A caretaker could receive from 0 to 4 points depending on how many of the items were answered in a way consistent with
exposure to the media campaign (α = .85). Comparison of the campaign
message recall score with the level of knowledge both before and after the
campaign shows the importance of such exposure in the achievement of
higher vaccination knowledge (Fig. 12.3). The exposure measure was unrelated to knowledge in 1989, as expected, but exposure was strongly related to knowledge in 1990.

The most convincing evidence that exposure to the mass media campaign was an important influence on knowledge comes from an analysis to
explain the gap in knowledge (Table 12.8). The difference between the
knowledge scores of respondents in 1989 (2.3) and 1990 (2.97) is .67, of
which almost two thirds can be explained by the effects of the campaign
exposure variables. Once they are controlled, the remaining gap is .24, less
than one third of the original. The remaining difference was not explained
by any of the other variables measured, including area of the country,

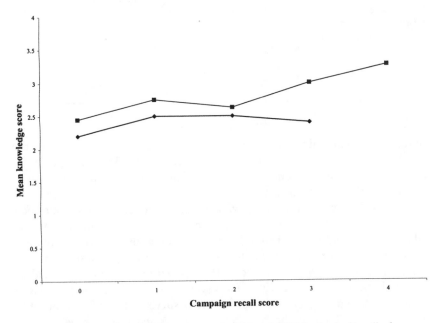

FIG. 12.3. Mean knowledge scores in 1989 and 1990 by level of recall of
the mass media campaign. Each point displayed represents at least 50 respondents.

TABLE 12.8
Effect of Campaign Exposure on 1989–1990
Knowledge Differences (n = 2,395)

	Absolute Difference	Percentage Explained	Signif. of Difference
1989–1990 difference in vaccination knowledge	.67		$p < .01$
Amount of that difference accounted for by 4 campaign recall items	.43	64%	
Remaining difference not explained by campaign recall items	.24	36%	$p < .01$

caretakers' education or wealth, recency of exposure to the health center, or number of vaccinations the child had received. Overall, whereas exposure does not account for all of the gain in knowledge, it is a substantial influence.

The Increase in the Average Level and Timeliness of Vaccination Cannot Be Explained by Improvements in Other Program Components. Available evidence indicates that most programmatic factors were relatively stable.

Missed Opportunities. One of the most important aspects of health worker practice that affects vaccination coverage is the level of missed opportunities—whether children receive fewer than all the vaccinations for which they are eligible at the time of each contact with the health system. Information from both the health center study and the surveys indicates that missed opportunities did not decline significantly in conjunction with the campaign. During each of the 20 health center visits, cards of 10 children were examined to determine whether or not they had received all the vaccinations for which they were eligible that day. Across four antigens (with little difference among antigens), approximately 16% of the children were not given all the appropriate vaccines in 1989. In 1990, there was a small but not statistically significant increase to 21%.

Although the presence of observers at the health centers may have decreased the likelihood of missed opportunities, these results are corroborated by analysis of vaccination data recorded during the surveys. From these data, a "lower limit" estimate of missed opportunities can be calculated, because no information was recorded about visits to health centers when no vaccinations were received. Children did not receive appropriate vaccinations at 24.6% of sessions during the campaign, a rate no different from that during sessions in 1988 and 1989 (22.4%). Analysis by individual antigen indicates that, compared with 1988 and 1989, rates of missed opportunities during the campaign were slightly higher for BCG (21.0% in 1988 and 1989; 27.0% during the campaign) and DPT (7.2% vs. 10.2%), remained unchanged for OPV (9.0% vs. 10.3%), and decreased slightly, although not significantly, for measles (27.5% in 1988 and 1989 vs. 25.4% during the campaign).

Vaccine Supply. Vaccination coverage can be inhibited by shortage of vaccine and vaccination supplies, and planning for the campaign included provision for an increase in supplies. Interviews with providers during the health center study indicated that needles, syringes, and measles vaccine were all in shorter supply in 1990 than in 1989, both on the day of the provider interviews and in the previous 3 months. Other vaccines were all adequately supplied. Vaccination cards were in short supply on both measurement waves, with only a slight tendency for current supplies to be worse in 1990 than in 1989. These shortages suggest that demand for vaccination was greater than anticipated. However, evidence from the caretakers' surveys suggests that supplies very nearly met the increased demand. In the 1989 survey, 2% of caretakers who visited the clinics in the previous year claimed ever to have been turned away because of shortages; that proportion was only slightly greater, at 4%, in 1990. Overall, these data suggest that the improvement in vaccination coverage occurred despite some shortfall in vaccination supplies.

Accessibility. Few people claimed to have visited health centers and found them closed in either year. Waiting times for vaccination at clinics were generally short, and they seem to have declined slightly according to the caretakers' surveys. Nonetheless, the absolute differences between 1989 and 1990 in waiting times was small.

Increases in Knowledge Cannot Be Attributed to Improvements in Health Center Practice. One possible explanation for the observed improvements in knowledge is that caretakers learned about vaccination during visits to health centers. However, evidence that health clinic personnel changed their way of interacting with their clients is less convincing than evidence for the media exposure effects. Data come from two sources: the caretaker surveys and the exit interview portion of the health center study. In both cases, there was little change in the reported character of the interaction or in the level of accurate knowledge that caretakers took away from their health center visit.

The interviews with caretakers in their homes indicate very little change in what happened at health centers. About 39% of respondents both years said that someone at the clinic knew them by name, and about 75% said someone had told them about side effects of vaccination at the last visit.

There were small, but significant, increases in the proportion who reported being told against which diseases the vaccine protected (50.5% in 1989 and 54.5% in 1990), and in the proportion who said that someone had reminded them about vaccination in the past 3 months (15.9% in 1989; 20.4% in 1990). These small differences do not explain the observed improvements in vaccination levels.

Caretakers interviewed as they left the health centers reported roughly similar experiences in 1989 and 1990. The time they spent with the clinic personnel was about 10 minutes both years, and almost all (85% in 1989 and 89% in 1990) were told when to bring the child back or that the child had received all needed vaccinations. In both years 38% said that someone had told them about possible side effects of the vaccination, and in both years about the same proportion could tell the interviewer accurately what vaccination their child had received (63% in 1989; 72% in 1990, difference not significant). One exception to this pattern of little change was a sharply increased proportion of exit interviewees saying that "someone explained about vaccinations": 18.4% in 1989, but 75.5% in 1990. However, this result is quite difficult to interpret, as no parallel change was seen in responses to more specific questions that were asked about the interaction, whether of exit interviewees or of caretakers.

If some essentially unobserved change in health center practice affected knowledge, frequency of contact with the health center would likely be associated with better knowledge. However, in 1990 the average knowledge scores of caretakers who report 0, 1–3, and 4 or more visits to the health center in the past year are almost exactly identical (averaging 2.97, 2.97 and 2.92 respectively). In summary, there is little evidence that changes at the clinic in the way that vaccination sessions were conducted produced the increased knowledge that explains most of the increased vaccination levels.

DISCUSSION

The evidence suggests that the mass media information campaign was largely responsible for the improvement in vaccination coverage. Health center practice was essentially the same during the campaign as in previous years. The rate of missed opportunities for vaccinating children was very slightly worse, as were vaccine supply shortages, and only small changes in health worker interaction with vaccination clients were noted. In contrast, changes in knowledge about measles vaccination, and in particular about the appropriate age for vaccination were substantial.

There were three essential elements of campaign strategy: the concentration on urban areas, the focus on measles, and the emphasis on knowledge of details of time and place and age. The decision to focus on urban areas was prompted by their lower vaccination rates. While the urban areas are at an undoubted disadvantage because of higher rates of disease transmission, this is somewhat offset by easier access to services. In contrast to rural areas, physical access of the urban population to health facilities and of health center staff to supply sites is not a constraint; moreover, dissemination of information is likely to be greater.

In this program, the focus on measles and logistical knowledge—the age for vaccination and the times and places vaccinations would be available—translated directly into the messages disseminated in the television and radio advertisements and incorporated in posters. The designation of a particular day for vaccination could help keep cost down, since concentrating clients on a day reduces wastage and improves efficiency (Phonboon, Shepard, Ramaboot, Kunasol, & Preuksaraj, 1989). The change in knowledge about the appropriate age for vaccination relates directly to the major effect of the campaign on timeliness of vaccination. This effect can be important, as the Philippines moves into a later stage of measles control (Cutts, Henderson, Clements, Chen, & Patriarca, 1991), in view of the evidence that one-dose vaccination of young children may be more effective than a two-dose vaccination strategy that achieves the same coverage (McLean & Anderson, 1988).

The effect of the campaign was not limited to measles vaccination. This "spillover" is most likely to be due to a heightening of awareness about vaccination generally, rather than the concurrent administration of other needed vaccinations when children came for measles. Improvements in vaccinations levels increased well before the 8.5-month age at which they become eligible for measles (Table 12.3). If the spillover was only the result of other vaccinations given when children came for measles, the vaccination improvement would have been restricted to children eligible for measles.

It is important to point out that the Philippines campaign differed from classical "mass campaigns" (Robinson, 1982; Unger, 1991) in a number of important respects. Most importantly, it was a communications campaign in support of routine vaccination services. There was a long planning period, so that vaccine supplies were reasonably adequate for the demand created; health service staff were alerted through the "sales conferences" and their local meetings; the campaign was centralized, in terms of a unique policy and a universal provision of vaccination on Wednesdays, usually in addition to other days selected by local staff. Quality of services provided did not appear to suffer; there was no increase in waiting times or decrease in the proportion of clients told when to come back, a situation that contrasts markedly with that reported for some mass campaigns (Unger, 1991).

A number of factors contributed to the success of the campaign. First, the urban sample represents a media-using population. More than 60%

claimed to own televisions and 73% claimed to own radios, with more than 50% owning both. In the 1990 survey, most of the non-owners also claimed to be listeners and watchers, with only 2% describing themselves as neither watchers nor listeners. In this context of very heavy media access and use, the intensive mass media-based promotion campaign clearly found the channels to reach its audience. Second, the high level of public access to mass media was reflected in the expertise available to the Department of Health to develop and produce high-quality radio and television spots. Finally, and most important, the campaign supported a routine system that was ready to serve the increased demand associated with the media campaign.

Even with the successful media campaign, on-time coverage in these cities did not exceed 65%, and 18-month coverage was just below 80%. If measles is to be controlled and transmission interrupted in the urban situation, coverage of 95% or more may be needed (J. Clements, personal communication). Achieving a high level of control will depend on using all available tools and strategies, of which mass media-based information campaigns should certainly be one.

ACKNOWLEDGMENTS

HEALTHCOM was a 14-year program providing technical assistance to developing countries to promote and refine the use of communication and social marketing methods to influence health practices as an element of an effective child survival strategy. It was sponsored by the Office of Health, Bureau for Research and Development of the U.S. Agency for International Development and was administered by the Academy for Educational Development (contract # DPE-5984-Z-00-9018-00). Subcontractor Porter/ Novelli provided assistance in social marketing strategies; the Center for International, Health, and Development Communication (CIHDC) at the Annenberg School for Communication, University of Pennsylvania was responsible for evaluating the impact of HEALTHCOM activities.

The surveys reported in this chapter were carried out by TRENDS, Inc., and the health center studies by Kabalikat ng Pamilyang Pilipino, with technical advice by the CIHDC. We would like to thank the Department of Health, specifically Undersecretary Mario Taguiwalo, Ms. Mayette Bernaje of the Public Information Health Education Service, and the EPI staff; Dr. Mercedes Abad and the staff of TRENDS; Dr. Maria Teresa Bagasao, Ms. Maricel Pabalan, and the staff of Kabalikat ng Pamilyang Pilipino; and the HEALTHCOM staff, both in Washington and the Philippines.

Helpful comments on previous drafts were provided by John Clements, Alan Andreason, and Michael Favin, Susan McCombie and Susan Wat-

kins. We are grateful to David Boyd and to REACH for providing information about results of the EPI surveys carried out in 1988 through early 1990.
This chapter was reprinted (with slight alterations) from the *Bulletin of the World Health Organization, 72*(3), 409–422. Copyright 1994 by the World Health Organization. We gratefully acknowledge their permission.

REFERENCES

Balraj, V., & John, T. J. (1986). Evaluation of a poliomyelitis immunization campaign in Madras city. *Bulletin of the World Health Organization, 64*(6), 861–865.

Belcher, D. W., Nicholas, D. D., Ofosu-Amaah, S., & Wurapa, F. K. (1978). A mass immunization campaign in rural Ghana: Factors affecting participation. *Public Health Reports, 93*(2), 170–176.

Cutts, F. T., Glik, D. C., Gordon, A., Parker, K., Diallo, S., Haba, F., & Stone, R. (1990). Application of multiple methods to study the immunization programme in an urban area of Guinea. *Bulletin of the World Health Organization, 68*(6), 769–776.

Cutts, F. T., Henderson, R. H., Clements, C. J., Chen, R. T., & Patriarca, P. A. (1991). Principles of measles control. *Bulletin of the World Health Organization, 69*(1), 1–7.

Cutts, F. T., Rodrigues, L. C., Colombo, S., & Bennett, S. (1989). Evaluation of factors influencing vaccine uptake in Mozambique. *International Journal of Epidemiology, 18*(2), 427–433.

Cutts, F. T., Soares, A., Jecque, A. V., Cliff, J., Kortbeek, S., & Colombo, S. (1990). The use of evaluation to improve the Expanded Program on Immunization in Mozambique. *Bulletin of the World Health Organization, 68*(2), 199–208.

Eng, E., Naimoli, J., Naimoli, G., Parker, K. A., & Lowenthal, N. (1991). The acceptability of childhood immunization to Togolese mothers: A sociobehavioral perspective. *Health Education Quarterly, 18*(1), 97–110.

Friede, A. M., Waternaux, C., Guyer, B., de Jesus, A., & Filipp, L. C. (1985). An epidemiological assessment of immunization programme participation in the Philippines. *International Journal of Epidemiology, 14*(1), 135–141.

Gareaballah, E. T., & Loevinsohn, B. P. (1989). The accuracy of mother's reports about their children's vaccination status. *Bulletin of the World Health Organization, 67*(6), 669–674.

Hanlon, P., Byass, P., Yamuah, M., Hayes, R., Bennett, S., & M'Boge, B. H. (1988). Factors influencing vaccination compliance in peri-urban Gambian children. *Journal of Tropical Medicine and Hygiene, 91*(1), 29–33.

Loevinsohn, B. P. (1989). Missed opportunities of immunization during visits for curative care: Practical reasons for their occurrence. *American Journal of Tropical Medicine and Hygiene, 41*(3), 255–258.

McLean, A. R., & Anderson, R. M. (1988). Measles in developing countries: Part II. The predicted impact of mass vaccination. *Epidemiology and Infection, 100*(3), 419–442.

Phonboon, K., Shepard, D. S., Ramaboot, S., Kunasol, P., & Preuksaraj, S. (1989). The Thai expanded programme on immunization: Role of immunization sessions and their cost-effectiveness. *Bulletin of the World Health Organization, 67*(2), 181–188.

Risi, J. B., Jr. (1983). Control of measles in Brazil. *Reviews of Infectious Disease, 5*(3), 583–587.

Robinson, D. A. (1982). Polio vaccination—a review of strategies. *Transactions of the Royal Society of Tropical Medicine and Hygiene, 76*(5), 575–581.

Steinhoff, M. C., Cole, P., Cole, A., John, T. J., & Pereira, S. M. (1985). Evaluation of the opportunities for and contraindications to immunization in a tropical paediatric clinic. *Bulletin of the World Health Organization, 63*(5), 915–918.

Streatfield, K., & Singarimbun, M. (1988). Social factors affecting use of immunization in Indonesia. *Social Science and Medicine, 27*(11), 1237–1245.

Subramanyam, K. (1989). Vaccine distribution: An operations research study. *Reviews of Infectious Disease, 11*(Suppl. 3), S623–S628.

Unger, J. P. (1991). Can intensive campaigns dynamize front line health services? The evaluation of an immunization campaign in Thies health district, Senegal. *Social Science and Medicine, 32*(3), 249–259.

CHAPTER

13

Communication in Support of Child Survival: Evidence and Explanations from Eight Countries

Robert C. Hornik
Judith McDivitt
Susan Zimicki
P. Stanley Yoder
Eduardo Contreras-Budge
Jeffrey McDowell
University of Pennsylvania

Mark Rasmuson
Academy for Educational Development, Washington, DC

The HealthCom project sheds light on the potential for large-scale health communication in developing countries to reach target populations and achieve substantial behavior change. Sixteen interventions supported by HealthCom addressed vaccination, diarrheal disease treatment, and other child survival-related practices. Evaluations of 10 national or regional public health communication programs in 8 developing countries asked whether such programs, carried out on a large scale, influenced health practices. Evidence from paired before and after surveys, supplemented in some sites by time series or control area data, demonstrated substantial success in 9 of the 16 evaluated outcomes, with absolute increases of from 12% to 26% of the population adopting recommended behaviors. Evidence points to the inference that observed changes were the result of the communication interventions. Both cross-site evidence and results from individual programs suggest explanations for why some programs did or did not work. They include the match between intervention goals and structural opportunities for behavior change; the use of communication channels that reach much of the audience; and the choice of specific messages that address, from the audience's perspective, the barriers to and the benefits of the target behavior.

INTRODUCTION

An emphasis on prevention as a complement to curative health services promises both improved health outcomes and reduced costs (U.S. Department of Health and Human Services, 1991). Developing countries have an acute need for prevention, with health systems that are often underfunded and sometimes inaccessible to parts of the population (World Development Report, 1993). Approaches for prevention include environmental changes (e.g., building safer highways), legal restrictions (e.g., raising the drinking age), fiscal barriers (e.g., higher taxes on cigarettes), and specific health system interventions like screening and health communication. This chapter focuses on public health communication to promote specific health practices, reporting the evaluation results of 10 large-scale communication programs meant to influence child survival.

Public health communication is one strategy proposed to reduce child morbidity and mortality in developing countries (U.S. Agency for International Development, 1991; United Nations Children's Fund, 1991). The most widespread use of public health communication in developing countries has been for the promotion of family planning (Coleman & Meyer, 1990; Elkamel, 1993; Hindin et al., 1994; Lettenmaier, Krenn, Morgan, Kols, & Piotrow, 1993; Nariman, 1993; Piotrow et al., 1992; Piotrow et al., 1990; Valente, Kim, Lettenmaier, & Glass, 1994). Additionally, programs have addressed behavior related to nutritional status (Hornik, 1985), breastfeeding (Habicht et al., 1986; Parlato, 1990), diarrheal disease treatment (Claeson & Merson, 1990; El-Rafie et al., 1990), immunization (UNICEF, 1985), and human immunodeficiency virus (HIV) transmission (Convisser, 1990). Advocates see this strategy as a reasonable cost complement to investments in service delivery (Goldman & Pebley, 1994; Hornik, 1988, 1989; Kotler, 1982; Ling et al., 1992; Manoff, 1984; McDivitt et al., 1993; Novelli, 1990), but questions remain about its feasibility and effectiveness on a large scale in developing country environments. Much of the evidence of success and particularly failures of public health communication remains unpublished, available only in the "gray" literature of technical reports to funding agencies.

During the 1980s, the U.S. Agency for International Development's (USAID) Communication for Child Survival project with the Academy for Educational Development, known as the HealthCom project,[1] worked

---

[1]HealthCom was sponsored by the Office of Health, Bureau for Research and Development of the U.S. Agency for International Development and was administered by the Academy for Educational Development (Contract No. DPE-5984-Z-00-9018-00).

with national and local governments in 17 countries to transfer expertise in using research-based public health communication methodology. The goal of these programs was to change health behavior related to child survival, specifically treatment of diarrhea through the use of oral rehydration therapy (ORT), immunization against childhood diseases, timely initiation of breast-feeding, adoption of modern contraceptive methods for birth spacing, or consumption of vitamin A capsules to reduce night blindness and other risks to child survival. Communication programs usually complemented enhanced resources, such as vaccines or packets for use in ORT.

The HealthCom project provided an opportunity to evaluate the broad policy of using public health communication to improve health status in developing countries. The results reported here address whether those programs influenced health behavior, enabling assessment of both the effectiveness and feasibility of this policy. This chapter summarizes elements of published and technical reports of evaluations of 10 HealthCom programs in 8 countries: Ecuador, Indonesia (Central Java and West Java), Jordan, Lesotho, Peru, the Philippines (Manila and national), Swaziland, and Zaire (see Table 13.1). Results from major evaluations of HealthCom-sponsored diarrheal disease programs in Honduras and the Gambia have been reported elsewhere (Baume, 1990; McDowell & McDivitt, 1990).[2] Full reports of results from all other sites are available from the first author as technical reports.

The projects presented here were developed at a particular time in the history of health communication. They were idea and experience driven, but did not, particularly in the earlier years, fit easily under any health communication/behavior change theoretical framework. There were some central ideas that dominated the work: the projects were to be client driven, based in evidence concerning how the audience thought about the behavior and the health problem at issue. Message strategies reflected the translation by project leaders of what audiences said in focus groups and/or in surveys about the advantages and disadvantages of a behavior. Because some of the field staff were drawn from marketing and advertising, this was often phrased in terms of the benefits and barriers associated with a behavior. These characteristics were not explicitly derived from a formal health behavior theory, but closely parallel the costs and benefits of the Health Belief Model or the positive and negative consequences of the Theory of Reasoned Action.

---

[2]Those results, although complementary to those reported here, are based on a somewhat different methodology. Also, the results presented here are confined to countries in which *HealthCom* operated, but for which adequate evaluative data are unavailable, were Papua New Guinea, Paraguay, Guatemala, Nigeria, and Malawi.

TABLE 13.1
Descriptions of Ten HealthCom Projects

Country & Topic	Interventions	Evaluation Methods
Ecuador Immunization Diarrhea	Six vaccination days with mass mobilization component between October 1985 and August 1987. Radio and television campaigns. Training of health workers. Posters, comic strips, pamphlets, ORS mixing bags, promotional objects.	Three surveys of 1,474, 2,702, & 1,453 caretakers of children under age 5 in December 1985, July 1986, and April 1987.
Indonesia (West Java) Diarrhea	Two campaigns in July–September 1989 and February–March 1990, using radio, mobile film, ads and billboards. Training of health workers and volunteers. Special print materials for health workers.	Before/after surveys of 1,000 mothers of children under age 5 in March 1988 and 1990.
Indonesia (Central Java) Vitamin A capsules Diarrhea	For Vitamin A: 6-week radio campaigns twice a year from July 1988 to October 1989. Banners and health volunteer manuals. Training of health volunteers in 1988 and 1989. Vitamin A capsule distribution every February and August starting in August 1988. For Diarrhea: Two 2-month radio campaigns on dehydration and fluids in 1989. Campaign on giving foods from September to December 1989.	Two surveys of 800 mothers of children under age 5 in October 1988 and 1989 in intervention and control areas.
Jordan Breast-feeding & supplementation	Radio and television broadcasts in May–July, 1989 and March–April, 1990. Seminar on breast-feeding practices for professionals.	Before/after surveys of 950 caretakers of children under age 2 in 1988 and 1990.

	Intervention	Evaluation
Lesotho Immunization Diarrhea	Training of health workers. Radio spots broadcasting in 1988. Pamphlets, flyers, and flip charts in 1988. Teaching modules for primary schools in 1989.	Before/after surveys of 1,200 caretakers of children under age 5 in November 1987 and March 1990.
Peru Birth spacing Immunization	For birth spacing: Television and radio campaign (September 1984–July 1985), posters, and booklets. For immunization: Immunization week in October 1984. Three television and radio campaigns between October 1984 and August 1985. Posters.	For birth spacing: Ministry of Health monthly records of new contraceptive acceptors between January 1983 and June 1985. For immunization: Clinic records on number of vaccinations given from January 1983–March 1985. Data from multiwave National Nutrition and Health Survey of 20,000 households from April–November 1984.
Philippines (Metro Manila) Immunization	Six-week campaign February–March 1988 using television, radio, newspaper ads, posters, and T-shirts. Every Friday established as vaccination day. Training of health workers in sales conferences in January 1988.	Before/after surveys of mothers of children under age 2 in September 1987 (320), January 1988 (600), and April 1988 (600).
Philippines (National Urban) Immunization	Master sales conferences in February 1990. Six-month campaign using television, radio, newspaper ads, posters, bunting, and T-shirts. Every Wednesday established as vaccination day.	Before/after surveys of urban mothers of children under age 2 in July 1989 and August/September 1990.
Swaziland Diarrhea	Radio campaign from September 1985 to April 1986. SSS mixing flyers and posters. Training of health workers and local yellow flag volunteers.	Before/after surveys of 450 rural mothers of children under age 5.
Zaire (Lubumbashi) Diarrhea Immunization	Training of health workers in April and June 1990. Development of print materials. Brief radio vaccination campaign July 1990.	Before/after surveys of 1,150 mothers of children under age 3 in October 1989 and 1990 in city of Lubumbashi.

The most explicitly influential theorists were behaviorists, coming out of the Skinnerian tradition, with their emphasis on reward and punishment as determinants of behavior change. However, their influence was mostly in the discipline they imposed on the formative research process. They insisted that planning research should include close observation of the details of the doing of the recommended behavior—what was entailed in taking a child for a vaccination or in mixing oral rehydration solution at home. They argued that in choosing a specific behavior to recommend, program planners needed to understand what all the steps were to accomplish the behavior. If a child were to be taken for vaccination, then this would be influenced by the perceived value of the vaccination, but also by the specific pains and pleasures of obtaining the vaccination: the walk to the clinic, the care of the siblings left behind, the time in the waiting room, the interaction with the health center's staff, the child's response to the vaccination both at the clinic and after returning home.

It is important to note that this set of evaluations focuses on changes in health practices; it does not address the impact of changes in those practices on morbidity and mortality. In focusing on health practices, it was assumed that the epidemiological evidence for the positive effects of these practices on health outcomes was well-accepted (Clemens et al., 1988; Hornik, 1988; Kotler, 1982; Salariya et al., 1978; Snyder et al., 1982; Victora et al., 1990) and preceded the decision to invest in a program with an objective of behavior change. Because the cost of obtaining outcome data on morbidity and mortality would have been prohibitive, the study relied on prior evidence for the link between these health practices and worthwhile health outcomes, rather than looking for such health outcome evidence directly.

The evaluations examined effects on 16 different outcomes across the 10 programs. Nine of those 16 outcomes (4 of 6 immunization projects, 3 of 6 ORT projects, and 2 of 4 projects addressing other outcomes) were substantially favorable, with absolute increases in recommended practices from 10% to 26%, and relative increases from 20% to 400%. These results provide evidence for the effectiveness of the programs.

Noting the variation in success, explanations for relative success, effectiveness, and feasibility are considered. What must happen for a program to be successful? Many such explanations will be idiosyncratic to a particular program: for example, the dynamism of its leadership or the tensions in a local political context. However, there are some explanations that apply across countries. These findings provide illustrative evidence about three core hypotheses explaining variation in success of health communication programs: (a) The success of a communication program is limited by opportunities for behavior change. (b) Success will reflect the ability of communication channels to reach audiences. (c) Success will vary according to how responsive message strategies and messages are to the audiences' perspectives.

MATERIALS AND METHODS

Communication Programs

This discussion first outlines the common communication strategy, and then presents the major results from evaluations of HealthCom programs. The programs evaluated here were carried out in eight countries. Although more than one program may have occurred in each country, program sites were distinct; nonetheless, all programs share some common characteristics that make up the HealthCom methodology.

In general, full-time technical assistance staff worked with national health communication offices for at least 2 years. Initially, project staff and their counterparts chose one or more focus behaviors, determined by national health priorities. They then began extensive research with members of the general population to define the potential audience's perceptions of the health problem, current treatment practices, how decisions about treatment alternatives were made, and sources of treatment and information that were available. The next phase was to develop a formal communication plan that defined the strategy in terms of specific audiences, behavioral objectives, messages, mix of mass and print media and interpersonal channels, required coordination with service delivery activities, and timing each phase of the program. Implementation of the plan included pretesting materials and monitoring progress toward objectives, with some readjustment of activities as problems arose. Table 13.1 summarizes the programs included in this report.

All of the programs focused on mothers or others who cared for young children (henceforth "caretakers"), on the basis that caretakers' health practices on behalf of their children were central to children's health status. The focus behaviors—diarrheal disease treatment (6 programs), vaccination (6 programs), consumption of vitamin A capsules (1 program), adoption of modern contraceptive methods (1 program), and timing of breast-feeding initiation (1 program) and supplementation (1 program)—varied across HealthCom sites, but they shared the requirement that caretakers take action.

Clearly, these target behaviors are quite different from one another in their openness to influence from a communication campaign. Diarrheal disease treatment calls on diagnostic skills, demands the introduction of some behaviors (encouraging drinking and eating) that may be inconsistent with prior practice, requires slow administration of liquids to a possibly recalcitrant child, and may require frequent repetition. But diarrhea is often recognized as dangerous, and parents are anxious to address the problem. Vaccination requires parents to bring children to a clinic on a specific schedule, but does not address an urgent problem or demand extensive skill building for the parent. Adoption of modern contraception is quite a different behavior than either diarrheal disease treatment or vaccination because it affects adults directly and impinges on fundamental values. It is possible that some of the explanation for differences in effects among the projects evaluated reflect variation in the nature of the behavior itself.

Programs used a mix of mass media, print materials (including posters and flyers) and, usually, interpersonal channels that involved health personnel and sometimes volunteer outreach workers. Many programs complemented mass media outreach with the retraining of health staff (8 of 10 sites) and of volunteers (5 of 10 sites) in technical skills and outreach strategies. Sites with such training components varied sharply in the proportion of health staff actually retrained, the extent of retraining and its effect on their practices, and the proportion of the audience they reached. Often communication components complemented modifications in primary health care service delivery, including increased availability of vaccines or oral rehydration salts packets.

Sampling and Data Collection

Most of the findings reported here compare baseline surveys and one or more surveys conducted after implementation of the communication programs. Exceptions are noted in the tables.

The evaluations surveyed large, representative samples of caretakers of children in the age range appropriate to the intervention (in most cases, children under age 5), drawn through multistage cluster procedures. In three or four stage samples, districts or other large geographic units were chosen in target areas randomly, with probability proportional to population size; smaller geographic units and caretakers within these units were then chosen randomly or on a systematic basis (e.g., every fifth house) after a random start. Two-stage samples involved only random selection of census areas and then systematic random sampling of caretakers within census areas. In all cases, existing census area sampling frames developed by national census offices or by commercial research organizations were used.

Even when weaknesses in the sampling frame or imperfect sample selection procedures risked some biases, the procedures were consistent over time. Thus, although the representativeness of the sample with respect to the population as a whole may be challenged, the comparisons over time are likely to be trustworthy. Additional details of sampling procedures are available from the authors.

In African sites, one of the authors trained and supervised interviewers. Elsewhere, local professional research organizations collected and coded the data under the supervision of one of the authors. Because the authors prepared almost all questionnaires in collaboration with ministries of health or other national counterparts, the questions asked across sites about each relevant behavior were comparable.

Measures of Effect

Vaccination Levels in Ecuador, Lesotho, Peru, Philippines (Manila and National), and Zaire. Children's vaccination levels were measured in two ways: by examining the child's health card, if it was available, or by asking the child's caretaker if the child had received each vaccination. Using card measures alone substantially underestimates coverage rates, particularly for older children whose cards are often unavailable (Zimicki et al., 1994). The coverage levels reported here are based on both health cards and caretakers' reports. (The only exception to this is the case of Ecuador, where estimates of preprogram coverage were based on dated evidence from health cards examined during subsequent waves of data collection; thus, only card-based estimates were available for assessing this project's success.) The study reports the proportion of children from 12 to 23 months old who had all vaccinations recommended by the World Health Organization (WHO) to prevent tuberculosis (BCG), diphtheria, pertussis and tetanus (DPT), polio (OPV), and measles. In addition, supplemental measures that assess timely completion, such as the proportion of children completing the vaccination series before their first birthday, are also reported.

Diarrheal Disease Treatment in Ecuador, Indonesia (Central Java, West Java), Lesotho, Swaziland, and Zaire. Use of oral rehydration therapy (ORT), either as a packet-based oral rehydration solution (ORS) or as a home-mixed water–sugar–salt solution (SSS), was measured by asking caretakers open-ended questions about the most recent episode of diarrhea among any of their young children. Caretakers were asked whether they had used any treatment at all, whether the episode had been treated at home and what was given, and whether the child had been taken anywhere for treatment and what was given. If caretakers mentioned giving the particular form(s) of ORT recommended in the communication campaign in response to any of these questions, then they were counted as having used ORT for the last case of diarrhea. ORT use is reported only for recent cases (in the last 2 or 4 weeks, depending on the site).

Vitamin A Capsule Coverage in Central Java. Use of vitamin A was determined by asking caretakers if each of their children younger than age 5 had ever received a vitamin A capsule and, if so, when. A child who

had received a capsule during the month of the most recent capsule distribution was categorized as having been covered during the campaign.

Birth Spacing in Peru. The success of the birth spacing campaign
was measured by the number of new family planning acceptors who came
to government health clinics based on reports from Ministry of Health archives. The numbers reported per area per month after the campaign were
compared to the number of acceptors expected without a campaign. The
estimate of the expected number took into account both overall demand
for services other than family planning at clinics in each month, and the
precampaign trends in visits of new acceptors.

Breast- and Supplemental Feeding Practices in Jordan. Delay in
breast-feeding initiation was determined by asking each caretaker whether
she breast-fed, whether she started breast-feeding during the first day the
child was born and, if so, how many hours after delivery she started
breast-feeding. Supplementation of breast-feeding was measured by asking
if the child had been weaned and, if not, whether the caretaker was regularly giving the child any other food besides breast milk, such as powdered
milk, cereals, or cooked rice. The proportions of children 1 to 3 months
old who were not receiving supplementation at the time of the interview
were compared at each interview wave.

RESULTS

Nine of the 16 program results reported here provide evidence for positive
effects of the HealthCom-supported interventions. Because interventions
were implemented as part of national or regional programs, it was not
possible to incorporate control areas in most of these studies. Nonetheless,
a substantial basis exists that HealthCom programs led to the observed
changes. Although the logic of such claims overlaps across interventions,
exposition will be clearest if each health practice is examined separately.
The discussion begins with a brief review of each set of results, including
cases where no substantial effect occurred. It then discusses the basis for
inferring that a case was successful based on reviewing evidence that the
observed change was not due to secular trend, and the communication activity, per se, was responsible for the change rather than only changes in
the functioning of the health service.

Vaccination

In four of the six sites, there were significant increases in full vaccination
coverage of children from 12 to 23 months old (Table 13.2). In these four
sites, the absolute increases ranged from 10% to 24%, with relative in-

TABLE 13.2
Immunization Results for Six Projects

Project Site (Time period of activities)	Before Level (n)	After Level (n)	Change in Timely Completion
Peru	25%	37%	10–11 month complete improved from
1 month	(1,600)	(251)	18% to 27%
Zaire (Lubumbashi)	77%	82%	No overall change
3 months	(418)	(427)	
Philippines (Manila)	35%	55%	9–11 months complete improved from
4 months	(198)	(220)	29% to 38%
Philippines (National)	**54%**	**64%**	9–11 months complete improved from
6 months	(446)	(461)	32% to 56%
Ecuador	28%	52%	By 12 months complete improved from
18 months	(510)	(369)	20% to 43%
Lesotho	74%	76%	No overall change
36 months	(288)	(289)	

Note. Results in bold are statistically different at least at $p < .01$.

creases ranging from 25% to more than 85%. Evidence about timely completion of vaccinations is shown in the final column of Table 13.2. In all sites, the gains in timely completion (all vaccinations received before a child's first birthday) were about equal to or better than the coverage results among children from 12 to 23 months old. In the Philippines national campaign, in particular, the improvement in timely completion was substantially larger than the improvement in coverage of children from 12 to 23 months old. In two sites, Zaire and Lesotho, virtually no change occurred. In both of those sites, the baseline vaccination rates were much higher than in the other cases, suggesting that a reasonably effective vaccination system already existed. The mass media component of these programs was also quite weak, with relatively few caretakers reporting exposure to media messages.

The Basis of Inference for Successful Cases

Peru. A 1-month campaign was associated with a change from 25% to 37% of children fully vaccinated. Two types of evidence support a claim that this was due to the campaign and not to any preexisting secular trend. The "before" 25% coverage level is an average from five comparably sampled waves of a National Nutrition and Health Survey conducted over the 6 months prior to the vaccination campaign. Those five waves showed a flat trend in vaccination rates. The "after" coverage level of 37% came from a similarly sampled sixth wave conducted in the month after the vaccination campaign. Thus, the observed increase of 12% in 1 month is quite unlikely to be the result of spontaneous change. Further, the number of vaccinations reported by clinics to the Ministry of Health was consistent with this pattern, with the campaign month producing double the number of vaccinations that would be expected from the slowly increasing trend of the previous 22 months. Available evidence does not permit separation of the effects of the mass media campaign, per se, from local mobilization efforts that were linked to it (Hornik et al., 1987).

Philippines, Manila. Surveys just before and after a 4-month campaign found that the percentage of children fully vaccinated increased from 35% to 55%. Change of this size in such a short period of time is striking. Given international experience in vaccination programs, there is no credible threat that a change of this magnitude was merely the result of a secular trend.

More difficult is the challenge of sorting out the effects of the communication component of the campaign from complementary changes that took place in health facilities, possibly as the result of retraining health personnel and changes in policy. For example, some decline occurred in clinic failures to vaccinate eligible children (missed opportunities). However, the survey results indicated sharp increases in caretakers' knowledge of children's need for a measles vaccination, as well as knowledge of when to bring children in for vaccination. Also, a large increase in the number and timeliness of visits to obtain vaccination was closely associated in time with the launch of the communication campaign. These types of evidence make it likely that the success of this campaign was due both to the demand stimulated by the mass media program, and the improved quality of clinic services once caretakers arrived.

Philippines, National. A 6-month campaign was associated with an increase from 54% to 64% in full coverage for children from 12 to 23 months old, and an improvement from 32% to 56% between annual surveys in timely completion of vaccination for children from 9 to 11 months old. Changes were associated with evidence that exposure to campaign media was very high, knowledge of the timing for vaccination increased substantially, and those caretakers most exposed to the campaign were the ones who learned the timing knowledge and whose children, in turn, most sharply increased in their vaccination levels. Finally, for the national campaign, in contrast to the earlier Manila campaign, no evidence existed for the most likely alternative explanation for change, namely simultaneous improvement in vaccination-supportive practices by medical clinics. Availability of vaccine, missed opportunities, and treatment of patients remained constant between measurement waves. This case is presented in detail in chapter 12 of this volume (Zimicki et al., 1994).

Ecuador. Evidence from vaccination cards indicated that coverage for children from 12 to 23 months old increased from 28% to 52% during an 18-month campaign. Examination of the time series of "on-time coverage" of successive birth cohorts (percent complete at exact age 1) supports the inference that this change reflected the campaign. A substantially flat trend for all cohorts reaching age 1 in the 2 years before the campaign gave way to a rapid increase in trend. Survey results indicate that individuals who reported higher exposure to the media campaign were more likely to have vaccination knowledge and were more likely to have children with higher vaccination rates, even after controlling for preexisting differences in socioeconomic status (Hornik et al., 1991).

Use of Oral Rehydration Therapy (ORT) for Treatment of Diarrhea

Four of the six sites evaluated showed significant increases in the use of ORT (Table 13.3). In two sites these increases were quite likely due to HealthCom efforts (Swaziland and Ecuador), in one site possibly due to those efforts (Lesotho) and in one site probably unrelated to those efforts (Central Java). The last two showed no overall changes (West Java and Zaire).

A major issue, even for programs that appeared to achieve increases in use, is whether the absolute levels achieved were satisfactory. From a biomedical view, few cases (perhaps 5% or less) risk moderate or severe dehydration if untreated (Victora et al., 1990). However, in practice, no programs limited themselves to a target audience of this at-risk 5%. All programs promoted preventive use of ORT before any signs of dehydration appeared. None were willing to promote home treatments after signs of dehydration had appeared, recommending instead that children with such signs be brought to the clinic.

Two programs showed no gain. In Zaire, the ORT promotion program was limited to some retraining efforts with clinic staff, which may explain the overall low level of ORT use and lack of behavior change. Special outreach efforts were limited to only one zone of the city. In that zone, ORT use increased relative to its baseline level, although the samples were not large enough to be confident of the results. In West Java, the program included training of health workers and village volunteers and some mass media efforts; a minority of caretakers recalled exposure to the mass media campaign (see Table 13.7).

In a third case, Central Java, messages focused on encouraging fluid intake during episodes of diarrhea, rather than use of ORT. A significant gain in the volume of fluids given in the intervention area of Central Java seemed only to be part of a secular trend because it was matched by gains

TABLE 13.3

Diarrheal Disease Treatment Results for Six Projects

Project Site (Time Period of Activities)	Criterion Measure	Before Level	After Level	Other Noteworthy Findings
Swaziland 7 months	Use of SSS (4 weeks)	**36%** (164)	**48%** (132)	Using and knowing correct formula increased from 4% to 17%.
Indonesia (Central Java) 12 months	Use of more fluids (last case)	39% (370)	55% (401)	Control area gained from 45% to 59%.
Ecuador 18 months	Use of ORS (2 weeks)	**5%** (archival)	**20%** (515)	Before estimate from MOH archive and after estimate from survey and archive.
Zaire (Lubumbashi) 18 months	Use of ORT (4 weeks)	17% (444)	19% (536)	In focus zone increase from 9% to 21%.
Indonesia (Central Java) 24 months	Use of ORS (2 weeks)	23% (112)	24% (113)	
Lesotho 36 months	Use of SSS or ORS (4 weeks)	**42%** (261)	**60%** (288)	Cases treated at all increased from 58% to 75%.

Note. Results in bold are statistically different at least at $p < .01$.

in a control area. This is not claimed as a successful case. This program was preceded and complemented by other training of health staff, and those efforts should be credited with the observed effects.

The Basis of Inference for Successful Cases

Swaziland. Surveys indicated that the use of water–sugar–salt solution (SSS) for a recent case of diarrhea increased from 36% to 48% in about 7 months. The proportion using both the solution and knowing the correct mixing formula quadrupled from 4% to 17%. Information from registries kept at a sample of clinics demonstrated that the proportion of caretakers who reported treating children's diarrhea at home with SSS before coming to the clinic increased from about 40% at the initiation of the campaign to 60% within 2 months, where it remained for the next 6 months. Evidence that the communication activity was specifically influential comes from the positive association between exposure to campaign messages and the amount and quality of SSS use. More than 60% of the population reported exposure to the radio programs on which campaign messages were aired. An analysis controlling for differences in educational level indicated that those with high exposure were significantly more likely to use SSS with good knowledge of the mixing formula (Hornik, 1989; Hornik et al., 1987).

Ecuador. An analysis combining information from a Ministry of Health archive about ORS packet distribution and survey data showed that caretaker's use of ORS for a recent case of diarrhea increased from 5% or less to about 20%. The timing of this increase provides evidence that it was due to the national child survival program, which included promoting ORS packet use and increased access to packets through clinics and distribution to caretakers on national vaccination days. The change occurred within the first 2 to 3 months of the campaign, and was steadily maintained over the succeeding 16 months. Although it is difficult to separate the effects of increased access to packets from the specific effects of the communication efforts, exposure to the public promotion campaign was associated with caretakers' trying ORS and knowledge of correct mixing procedures (Hornik et al., 1991).

Lesotho. Caretakers' last treatment of diarrhea with ORS or SSS increased from 39% to 61% in the 3 years between surveys. The gain in use of ORT in Lesotho was almost entirely due to caretakers' increasing tendency to treat cases at all, which changed from 58% to 75%. In this case, an argument that the increase was due to a secular trend rather than the specific intervention is viable. Prior to the HealthCom intervention, a substantial amount of SSS/ORS was already in use. In addition, the project continued training health workers to reinforce ORT use. Mass media promoted the message that mothers should not leave diarrhea untreated, but it was a weaker part of this intervention. A minority of caretakers was exposed to mass media messages. Thus, whereas a good deal of positive change in practice came about during the HealthCom intervention, it is attributed to the program only tentatively (Yoder & Zheng, 1991).

Other Health Behaviors

The HealthCom program in Central Java aimed to increase twice-yearly consumption of megadose vitamin A capsules by children from 1 to 5 years old. Recent capsule coverage increased from 24% after the first campaign to 40% after the third campaign, but only among children who lived in a precinct with a health post where most capsules were distributed (Table 13.4).

In Jordan, program objectives were to encourage caretakers to initiate breast-feeding within 6 hours after birth and to avoid introducing weaning foods in addition to breast-milk until a child was at least 4 months old. Some increase in early initiation of breast-feeding took place, largely restricted to mothers who gave birth at home or in public hospitals (Table 13.4). The percentage of infants given no supplemental foods before 4 months showed no change.

The Peru birth spacing program encouraged women to seek information about modern contraceptive methods at their local health clinic. The number of women coming each month for such advice increased about 57% during the period after the campaign was launched. That upward trend, however, seemed to reflect two existing secular trends: More people were using the clinics in general, and more women were coming in for family planning advice before the campaign was launched. Based on those secular trends, the predicted number seeking advice was essentially the same as the observed number (Table 13.4).

The Basis of Inference for Successful Cases

Central Java: Vitamin A Coverage. Restricting the analysis to precincts with health posts, this study compared intervention and control areas that both started with children's vitamin A consumption at about 24%. The intervention area showed an increase in consumption to 40%, with the control area remaining at 25%. The effects of the communication-specific elements of this program cannot be isolated from complementary local promotional efforts to distribute capsules. Given low levels of reported exposure to mass media materials (about 20% of survey respon-

TABLE 13.4
Other Health Behavior Outcomes for Four Projects

Project Site (Time Period of Activities)	Criterion Measure	Before Level	After Level	Comments
Indonesia (Central Java) 2 months	Vitamin A consumption during program month	24% (223)	40% (203)	In precincts with health posts (control region increased 24% to 25% only)
Jordan 12 months	Initiation of breast-feeding within 6 hours after birth	38% (500)	56% (525)	Among women giving birth *not* in private hospitals, incrased from 42% to 68%
Jordan 12 months	No supplementation among children 1 to 3 months old	41% (140)	45% (119)	
Peru 8 months	New contraceptive acceptors per hospital area per month	182 (Predicted if no effects)	178 (Observed)	Census of all hospital areas

235

dents reported hearing radio messages), it is likely that the local promotion efforts were more important (McDivitt & McDowell, 1991).

Jordan: Early Initiation of Breast-Feeding. A time series analysis by birth cohort established that prior to the campaign, the proportion of mothers initiating breast-feeding within 6 hours after birth was stable at around 40%. The intervention coincided with an upturn in the trend, which, within 1 year, plateaued at just under 60%. Regression analysis demonstrated that the increase was independently related to both main components of the intervention: retraining health personnel and exposure to media materials (McDivitt et al., 1993). Improved initiation of breast-feeding was equally prevalent among women giving birth in public hospitals and at home, providing evidence of direct media influence.

DISCUSSION

Earlier research suggests that under the appropriate circumstances, large-scale public health communication can substantially influence health practices related to child survival in developing countries. This summary of health communication work over a 10-year period in eight countries provides a stronger base for this inference, demonstrating the effects of large-scale campaigns on several health behaviors in diverse regions of the world.

In addition, these evaluations show that programs do not always achieve measurable impact. The purpose of this chapter has been to present the full range of results, which immediately raises the question: What makes some programs more successful than others? On the one hand, site-specific idiosyncrasies partly explain the differences. On the other, cross-national explanations from the HealthCom project may address the question. This discussion presents three possible explanations: limitations associated with the structural context of the project, variation in exposure to project messages, and the extent to which project messages were well adapted to the audience. Evidence from cross-site comparisons and from examples in single sites is used to address each question.

The Need for Opportunities to Change Behavior

Communication programs attempt to persuade people to adopt new practices, and often those new practices are difficult to adopt. Even if they are convinced of the utility of immunization, parents cannot vaccinate their children themselves. If the local clinic is short of vaccine, rejects children who have slight fevers, or vaccinates only during restricted hours or days of the week, then a communication program promoting vaccination cannot have much effect. Most often, the programs evaluated here took the steps necessary to identify and meet potential demand. In some cases, however, restriction on the opportunity to engage in the recommended behavior was reflected in the results. Three telling examples follow.

Vitamin A Promotion in Central Java. The communication program in Central Java encouraged families to bring in children from age 1 to 5 to obtain a vitamin A capsule, but limited access to capsules restricted the opportunity to take this action. Capsules were mostly available at local health posts, which were open one morning per month, but they were offered only one morning every 6 months. Because the health post days varied from precinct to precinct, the mass media messages could identify the site and the month, but not the specific day to obtain the capsules. Knowing what day to come depended on local mobilization efforts. The health posts operated in only some precincts because posts were still being established. In areas where no health posts existed, families could obtain capsules at a neighboring precinct's post if they knew when it operated. All these factors limited the opportunity for taking the recommended action. Evaluation results clearly show the effects of this restricted opportunity.

Overall, target communities that received the intensified vitamin A promotion showed only a slight advantage over the control communities (Table 13.5). Prior to the campaign, capsule distribution in both had reached about one fourth of the population, a reflection of previous efforts at promotion and distribution. Afterward, intervention communities improved slightly, and the control communities did not change. When the analysis is restricted to precincts where the opportunity to obtain capsules was easier because a health post operated during the campaign, however, the intervention advantage is larger. Precampaign rates in the control communities remained unchanged during the campaign, even though they had operating health posts. The communities where the health posts and the intervention were present improved sharply, with a relative increase of 67%.

This result speaks to opportunities for communication to change behavior in two ways. On one side, improvements in practice occurred where the possibility of taking the recommended action existed. On the other, even in precincts with health posts, the influence of the promotion activity on behavior was limited, possibly because the window for action was only one morning every 6 months.

Oral Rehydration Therapy in Ecuador. The Ecuador Child Survival program promoted oral rehydration solution (ORS) in packet form, recommending how to mix and use it during every episode of diarrhea. Packets were to be available from health clinics and through special distribution during vaccination campaigns. The program included intense promotion through mass media and other channels of communication. Within the first few months, the incidence of ORS use increased from 5% to nearly 20% of all cases. For the following 15 months, no additional improvement occurred. This ceiling on use appears to reflect the lack of opportunities to obtain ORS packets.

Clinics did not dependably focus their treatments on ORS. Caretakers brought nearly one third of all children treated for diarrhea to the clinic, some of whom were also treated at home. Even after they got to the clinic, however, only one third ended up using ORS; all of the rest (as well as some who used ORS) used other medicines, mostly antidiarrheals or antibiotics.

Parents treated 74% of the children at home, including 6% who were also treated at the clinic, and about 25% used ORS. Because ORS was largely unavailable in local pharmacies or stores, parents had obtained most of the packets used at home from previous visits to clinics, or mass distribution of packets during vaccination campaigns. Because mass distributions of ORS packets had ended, clinic distribution was critical to home use of ORS. Given the inconsistency of clinics' ORS use, that supply was not assured. Parents did not bring most children with diarrhea to the clinic; without access to packets outside clinics, promoting ORS use for every case had no likelihood of success. Thus, the promotion of ORS hit a ceiling reflecting two limitations on opportunities to perform the recommended behavior: clinics' failure to treat consistently with ORS or provide ORS packets, and lack of an ongoing extra-clinic source of supply.

Early Initiation of Breast-Feeding in Jordan.   Among other objectives, the Jordan program encouraged women to initiate breast-feeding within 6 hours of their babies' births. Mass media promotion complemented parallel training efforts among staff in public hospitals. On average, the program achieved some success: In a representative sample, about

TABLE 13.5
Administration of Vitamin A (Central Java)

	1988 Level (n)	1989 Level (n)	Change (Significance)
All precincts			
Intervention	25%	32%	7.0%
	(454)	(438)	($p < .05$)
Control	24.4%	24.6%	0.2%
	(280)	(295)	($p = .975$)
Precincts with health posts			
Intervention	24%	40%	16.0%
	(223)	(203)	($p < .001$)
Conrol	24%	25%	1.0%
	(267)	(283)	($p = .88$)

TABLE 13.6
Correct Initiation of Breast-Feeding (Jordan)

	1988 Level (n)	1989 Level (n)	Change (Significance)
All locations	37% (492)	56% (514)	19% ($p < .001$)
Private hospitals	17% (107)	24% (139)	7% ($p = .25$)
Public hospitals	43% (300)	69% (291)	26% ($p < .001$)
At home	41% (86)	67% (84)	26% ($p < .001$)

one fifth more mothers than before reported initiating breast-feeding within 6 hours after the program (Table 13.6). The most interesting result, however, is that women giving birth in public hospitals and women giving birth at home both reported marked changes. Because both groups of women showed the same pattern, it could be inferred that effects were due to communication efforts as well as to any training of hospital staff.

The most striking comparison, however, is with women who gave birth in private hospitals. They initiated breast-feeding within 6 hours only slightly more after the program than before; the difference was not significant. This finding suggests that women in private hospitals either did not want to adopt this practice or the hospitals discouraged them from doing so, regardless of the women's exposure to the health communication. It may be that the relatively elite women giving birth in private hospitals are themselves uninterested in adopting the practice. Some evidence exists that private hospitals' operating procedures mitigate against adopting this behavior; for example, private hospitals were much less likely to provide shared rooms for mothers and newborns. Thus, the health promotion effort may have foundered in private hospitals due to the lack of opportunity to take the recommended action.

In each of these examples, the program activity had a noticeable effect. Nonetheless, for particular populations, the lack of opportunity to engage in the recommended practice limited success. Programs that promote new behaviors must work within existing constraints to behavior or remove structural barriers to performing the desired behaviors.

Using Communication Channels That Reach the Audience

Arguments about channels are central to both theory and practice in the field of communication (Hornik, 1989; Rogers, 1983). Much of the argument concerns the relative roles and effects of mass media and interpersonal channels in campaigns, with the frequently repeated theme that mass media are good for awareness but only interpersonal channels influence behavior. Much of the framework of that argument focuses on the influence of each channel, given equal exposure. Equal exposure is rarely achieved, however. In practice, comparisons between channels must pay attention both to their relative reach—what audience exposure they achieve—and to their relative effects once audiences have been exposed. This section examines the differences among communication programs in reaching their target audiences and the association of reach and effect.

Differences in Exposure to Channels. A critical question to ask about any large-scale public health communication program is whether the program reached the majority of the target audience. Many educational programs with excellent content achieve limited effects precisely because they never reach the largest portion of the target audience.

The major channels used in the projects were radio, television, and paid and volunteer health workers, with some distribution of print and other promotional materials. Specific measures of exposure to the mass media component varied depending on the site and the details of the campaign. In all but one site, survey results provided evidence about exposure to mass media campaign messages. Measures included self-reported regular television watching or radio listening during the times that messages were broadcast, recall of specific messages broadcast, and recognition of print materials. In Peru, television and radio rating information provided media exposure estimates.

In 9 of these 16 programs, classified as "high exposure" sites, 60% or more of the population reported exposure to campaign messages on radio or television. In one program, Indonesia-West Java, there was moderate exposure, around 40%. In the other six sites, mass media exposure was lower, between 20% and 30%. In Lesotho and Zaire, regular health programs with limited audience attention incorporated HealthCom radio materials, possibly explaining low exposure in those sites. In Central Java, low ownership of radios may explain low exposure. Only 48% of mothers lived in a household with a radio, the lowest for any of the sites.

As Table 13.7 shows, exposure to program messages predicts level of program success. Of the six programs operating in low exposure environments, only two (28%) were successful. In contrast, seven (82%) of the nine high exposure programs produced substantial change in behavior. This is an association and not an experimental result; programs with strong mass media components were likely to be successful in other components. Nonetheless, evaluation of a health communication program requires some assessment of success in reaching the audience. Clearly, programs that communicate with a large audience are more successful than those that do not.

TABLE 13.7
Mass Media Message Exposure Level and Program Success

Success of Program	Exposure Level: Low (< 30%)	Medium (30%–60%)	High (> 60%)
Little or no change	Central Java ORS Lesotho vaccination Zaire ORT Zaire vaccination	West Java ORS	Jordan supplementation Peru contraceptive use
Substantial change	Central Java Vitamin A Lesotho ORT		Ecuador ORS Ecuador vaccination Jordan breast-feeding initiation Philippines (Manila) vaccination Peru vaccination Philippines National vaccination Swaziland SSS

Measures of exposure to mass media channels were independent of measures of the outcome variables; the degree of program exposure for both individuals and sites could be classified independently of their health practices. This permitted analysis of the influence of exposure on behaviors (as in Table 13.7). In contrast, for measures of exposure to one type of interpersonal channel—health workers at clinics—such independence between the measure of exposure and the measure of effect is lacking. Exposure to clinic-based interpersonal sources are tautologically related to measures of behavior that takes place in the clinic (like vaccination and clinic-based use of ORS); anyone who performed those behaviors had face-to-face contact with the clinic staff. Measures of educational contact with clinic staff were not independent of measures of behaviors requiring clinic contact. Thus, evaluation results offer no meaningful way to calculate the association between interpersonal contact in clinics and most program outcomes as was done for mass media exposure.

It is possible to examine the effects of contact with health workers for behavior done at home. Programs in Lesotho and Swaziland focused on home treatment of diarrhea, in the form of sugar–salt solution. Clinic workers were charged with promoting the home use of this solution; their role was essentially educational because the majority of diarrheal cases required no other treatment. In Lesotho, respondents reported contact with health workers substantially more often than they did exposure to diarrheal messages on mass media channels. About 40% of caretakers reported contact with a clinic-based health worker about diarrhea during the campaign period. This high level of interpersonal contact may explain the relative success of the Lesotho program, despite the low level of mass media exposure there (see Table 13.7).

Swaziland provides a particularly instructive set of results about channel exposure and its effects (Hornik, 1989). The study suggested that, indeed, interpersonal contact with either a health worker or an outreach worker was more highly associated with correct ORT behavior than was substantial exposure to the radio messages (Table 13.8). The effect of exposure to each channel was estimated from a regression equation predicting the use of SSS for the last case of diarrhea from the level of exposure to each channel.

Those who had contact with either type of interpersonal source were about 20% more likely to use SSS appropriately, whereas those with high exposure to the radio messages were about 14% more likely to use SSS appropriately, in each case, compared to those with low exposure on the channel.

However, even though radio was less effective per contact, it achieved more in aggregate. The audience reach of radio was nearly three times the reach of interpersonal other channels. It reached nearly 60% of the population, whereas health workers reached about 20% and outreach workers even fewer. By one calculation, 8% more of the entire population (13% effect multiplied by 60% reach) used SSS appropriately as the result of exposure to radio, and less than 4% (20% effect multiplied by 20% reach) used SSS appropriately as the result of contact with either interpersonal source.

These results point to two general conclusions. First, the effective reach of mass media or interpersonal channels differs from one project to another. This suggests caution in lumping all communication projects into a single category. Part of the difference in success among communication projects (for the HealthCom projects and others) may be that some projects reach many more members of their target audience than do others.

Second, care should be taken in drawing conclusions concerning the relative effects of different channels. Per contact, an organized interpersonal channel may be more persuasive than a mass media channel; nonetheless, one cannot conclude at an aggregate level that interpersonal channels are more effective than mass media channels. It has proved difficult to reach much of the population with organized interpersonal channels on a regular

TABLE 13.8
Channel Effects on SSS Use in Swaziland ($N = 431$)

Channel	Percent Exposed (a)	Effect of Exposure (b) (Unstandardized Regression Coefficient)	Channel Effect (a × b)
Clinic	22%	18%	4%
Outreach	16%	20%	3%
Radio	60%	14%	8%

basis. The advantage in numbers reached by mass media channels may more than overcome any disadvantage in effectiveness per person reached.

The Choice of Appropriate Messages

Good communication programs do not define their messages merely to be medically correct. A program's objectives (e.g., increasing timely completion of vaccination) are not the same as the messages most likely to achieve those objectives. Good programs try to create messages that solve problems that audiences recognize. Messages must fit into frameworks that audiences use to understand and define their actions concerning a problem. Much of the formative research that precedes the development of a communication plan involves research about understanding what actions different segments of an audience are already taking about a behavior, what leads them to take particular actions, and what keeps them from acting in the recommended way. The following cases illustrate the importance of understanding how the audience sees a problem.

Zaire ORT Promotion. An objective of the Zaire program was to promote use of ORT for treatment of diarrhea. An ethnomedical study combined with results from the baseline survey made it clear, before program initiation, that respondents did not classify all diseases for which loose stools were a symptom as the same thing. Indeed, they gave six different disease names for illness involving loose stools, and used quite different treatments for each (Table 13.9). For example, they described a disease called (in Swahili) *kuhara*, which, given its symptoms, was ordinary diarrhea. More than half of the respondents in the survey said they used some form of ORT as a home treatment for *kuhara*. In contrast, for two other diseases, *lukunga* (involving loose stools and other symptoms suggesting dehydration) and *kilonde ntumbo* (possibly including dysentery), traditional medicine was often used, and fewer than one sixth of the respondents reported using ORT at home. This sharp contrast led program planners away from an intention to talk about ORT as a treatment for diarrhea only, and instead to recommend the use of ORT for each of these diseases separately (Yoder, 1995).

TABLE 13.9
Diarrhea Treatment by Disease Name (Zaire)

Disease Name	% Used ORS	(N)
Kuhara	52%	98
Kilonde Ntumbo	9%	121
Lukunga	13%	44

Ecuador ORS Use. Most countries are unlikely to be able to afford the no-cost provision of ORS packets for use in every case of diarrhea. In such a situation, a communication program might seek to teach caretakers to initiate treatment with ORS when they observed particular characteristics of a case, such as the presence of particular symptoms (frequent stools, a great deal of thirst, listlessness, or appearing dehydrated) or the number of days the child had been ill. Either symptoms or length of illness might then serve as cues for treatment choice. Assuming both cues were medically acceptable, it might be preferable to emphasize the cue that the mother was already using to make her judgments, rather than trying to encourage her to make use of a cue she did not customarily use.

In Ecuador, the number of symptoms a mother recognized was not important in increasing her use of ORS: 16% who reported few symptoms in the last episode used ORS; only 22% who reported many symptoms used ORS. In contrast, the number of days the child was ill did predict use of ORS. Parents gave ORS to about one seventh of the children who had been ill 1 or 2 days; they gave ORS to 2.1 times as many of those who had been ill for 4 or more days (Table 13.10). In this context, if message designers had to choose between these cues, they should consider number of days ill as a framework for their messages. Such messages might build directly on that existing perception: "Each day of diarrhea weakens your child: ORS will keep him strong." Or they might argue with current practice: "Don't wait for 3 days: A child with diarrhea should be treated with ORS by the second day." In either case, and depending on what public health authorities believed was appropriate policy, the messages would be constructed to respond to a conceptual framework that was already operating.

This particular result might not hold in another country (and it did not hold in Ecuador for other behaviors, like decisions to bring a child to a

TABLE 13.10
Diarrhea Treatment Choices by Symptoms
and Number of Days Ill (Ecuador; N = 519)

	% Used ORS	(N)
Number of symptoms		
0–3	16%	32
4–6	21%	43
7–9	21%	61
> 9	23%	30
Number of days ill		
1	15%	86
2	14%	143
3	23%	128
> 3	30%	162

Note. χ^2 = 14.1, *df* = 3, *p* < .01.

clinic), but the analysis suggests that messages would be more and less effective depending on how they fit with the conceptual frameworks of the audience. Across sites, caretakers consistently used perceived severity of the diarrheal episode as their criterion for treatment choice, but were much less consistent in their response to other perceived symptoms (Yoder & Hornik, 1994).

Philippines Immunization. Direct evidence about the significance of choosing one message rather than another comes from the results of the Philippines national immunization program. That program was mildly successful in increasing coverage for children from 12 to 23 months old (54% vs. 64% covered), but was much more successful in increasing timeliness of completing vaccinations (32% vs. 56% covered by the first birthday). The communication program focused on measles immunization. It included messages about the benefits of immunization, as well the logistics of obtaining the vaccine, particularly the age at which the child should be vaccinated. Of the two types of messages, benefits and logistics, the results clearly show that the messages about logistics—and particularly about the need to have the child vaccinated before 12 months—were more critical. Large increases occurred in the proportion of mothers who learned they were to complete their children's vaccination series before the child's first birthday. Mothers' increasing knowledge about the timing of the vaccination series largely explained the change in vaccination practice achieved during the campaign (Zimicki et al., chap. 12, this vol.).

Health communication programs vary in their use of channels that reach the population of interest. Similarly, they vary in their use of messages that might influence the audience to change behavior. Programs increase their likelihood of success if their messages fit clients' language and conceptual framework, and address factors that predict clients' practices.

CONCLUSIONS

Under appropriate circumstances, large-scale health communication can substantially influence health practices related to child survival in developing countries. Evidence from the HealthCom project substantially supports this inference, demonstrating effects across regions of the world and across several health behaviors. Some explanations have been offered to explain why some programs are more successful than others, including opportunities for behavior change, the reach of communication channels, and the fit of messages with audience's worldview.

Others have given this advice before (Backer, Rogers, & Sopory, 1992; Rice & Atkin, 1989; Salmon, 1989). New and specific evidence for the power of each principle justifies repetition, however. Too often, planners and implementers of health communication programs have followed the advice only irregularly. Of course, neglect of these principles is not invariably a sign of technical deficiency. Sometimes when health communication programs are unsuccessful, an apparent technical shortfall hides a basic political failure. For example, a program may not do the research to clarify the conceptual framework used by an audience. This can result from lack of skill in doing such audience research; it may also result from budget shortfalls for vehicles or field expenses, reflecting political priorities. Nonetheless, technical flaws are common enough, whether in the choice of target behaviors, communication channels, or messages. Overcoming such technical weaknesses, although they may not guarantee success given political limits, promises worthwhile health practice changes.

Nine of the evaluations summarized here (and in the source documents) make some case for success. However, there are some limitations on those conclusions. Some research designs permitted stronger inferences than others. In particular, there is some possibility that historically simultaneous interventions might have been partial causes of the observed changes in some sites. Nonetheless, there is generally substantial evidence favoring attribution of success to the HealthCom project for each program, much more of which is to be found in the full evaluations.

Perhaps the greater risk is not that those programs purported to be successful were not, but that the circumstances of success are not easily replicable. These evaluations were undertaken with an explicit policy purpose: to understand whether public health communication was a worthwhile strategy to address child survival-related behaviors in developing countries. The evidence presented here is evidence that such programs can affect those behaviors, when the programs are heavily funded by an outside agency that also supports skilled technical assistance. That is the essential question for this book with its focus on evidence for effects of communication programs. Whether these programs were an effective practical mechanism, absent the special circumstances of their support here, was not the question addressed in this summary of the evaluations. That issue, associated with the institutionalization of health communication skills and institutions, is addressed directly (and only sometimes optimistically) in the source documents.

REFERENCES

Backer, T., Rogers, E., & Sopory, P. (1992). *Designing health communication campaigns: What works?* Newbury Park, CA: Sage.
Baume, C. (1990). *The HealthCom resurvey of oral rehydration therapy practices in Honduras.* Menlo Park, CA: Applied Communication Technology.

Claeson, M., & Merson, M. H. (1990). Global progress in the control of diarrheal diseases. *Infectious Disease Journal, 9*(5), 345–355.

Clemens, J. D., Stanton, B. F., Chakraborty, J., Chowdhury, S., Rao, M. R., Ali, M., Zimicki, S., & Wojtyniak, B. (1988). Measles vaccination and childhood mortality in rural Bangladesh. *American Journal of Epidemiology, 128*(6), 1330–1339.

Coleman, P. L., & Meyer, R. C. (1990). *Proceedings from the Enter-Educate Conference: Entertainment for social change.* Baltimore: Center for Communication Programs.

Convisser, J. (1990). *The Zaire mass media project (PSI Special Reports, Report No. 1).* Washington, DC: Population Services International.

Elkamel, F. (1995). The use of television series in health education. *Health Education Research, 10*(2), 225–232.

El-Rafie, M., Hassouna, W. A., Hirschhorn, N., Loza, S., Miller, P., Nagaty, A., Nasser, S., & Riyad, S. (1990). Effect of diarrheal disease control on infant and childhood mortality in Egypt. *Lancet, 335,* 334–338.

Goldman, N., & Pebley, A. (1994). Health cards, maternal reports and the measurement of immunization coverage: The example of Guatemala. *Social Science and Medicine, 38*(8), 1075–1089.

Habicht, J.-P., DaVanzo, J., & Butz, W. P. (1986). Does breastfeeding really save lives, or are apparent benefits due to biases? *American Journal of Epidemiology, 123*(2), 279–290.

Hindin, M. J., Kincaid, D. L., Kumah, O. M., Morgan, W., Kim, Y. M., & Ofori, J. K. (1994). Gender differences in media exposure and action during a family planning campaign in Ghana. *Health Communication, 6*(2), 117–135.

Hornik, R. (1985). *Nutrition education: A state-of-the-art review.* ACC/SSCN State-of-the-Art Series Nutrition Policy Paper No. 1. Rome: UN Administrative Committee on Coordination-Subcommittee on Nutrition.

Hornik, R. (1988). *Development communication: Information, agriculture and nutrition in the third world.* New York: Longman.

Hornik, R. (1989). Channel effectiveness in development communication programs. In R. Rice & C. Atkins (Eds.), *Public communication campaigns* (2nd ed., pp. 309–331). Beverly Hills, CA: Sage.

Hornik, R., Contreras, E., Ferencic, N., Koepke, C., Morris, N., Torres, M., Pareja, R., & Smith, W. (1991). *Results from the evaluation of the Premi/HealthCom project in Ecuador.* Philadelphia: CIHDC Working Paper Series No. 1003.

Hornik, R., McDowell, J., Romero, J., & Pareja, R. (1987). *Communication and health literacy: Evaluation of the Peru program 1984–1985.* Philadelphia: CIHDC Working Paper Series No. 113.

Hornik, R., Sankar, P., Huntington, D., Matsebula, G., Mndzebele, A., & Bongani, B. (1987). *Communication for diarrheal disease control: Swaziland program evaluation 1984–1985.* Philadelphia: CIHDC Working Paper Series No. 114.

Kotler, P. (1982). *Marketing for nonprofit organizations.* Englewood Cliffs, NJ: Prentice-Hall.

Lettenmaier, C., Krenn, S., Morgan, W., Kols, A., & Piotrow, P. (1993). Africa: Using radio sopa operas to promote family planning. *Hygie, 12*(1), 5–10.

Ling, J., Franklin, B. A., Lindsteadt, J. F., & Gearon, S. A. (1988). Social marketing: Its place in public health. *Annual Review of Public Health, 13,* 341–362.

Manoff, R. K. (1985). *Social marketing: New imperative for public health.* New York: Praeger.

McDivitt, J., & McDowell, J. (1991). *Results from the evaluation of the HealthCom project in Central Java.* Philadelphia: CIHDC Working Paper Series No. 1002.

McDivitt, J., Zimicki, S., Hornik, R., & Abulaban, A. (1993). The impact of the HealthCom mass media campaign on timely initiation of breastfeeding in Jordan. *Studies in Family Planning, 24*(5), 295–309.

McDowell, J., & McDivitt, J. (1990). *The HealthCom resurvey of oral rehydration therapy practices in The Gambia.* Menlo Park, CA: Applied Communication Technology.

Nariman, H. N. (1993). *Soap operas for social change.* Westport, CT: Praeger.

Novelli, W. (1990). Applying social marketing to health promotion and disease prevention. In K. Glanz, F. Lewis, & B. Rimer (Eds.), *Health behavior and health education: Theory research and practice* (pp. 342–368). San Francisco: Jossey-Bass.

Parlato, M. B. (1990). The use of mass media to promote breastfeeding. *International Journal of Gynaecology & Obstetrics, 31*(Suppl. 1), 105–113.

Piotrow, P. T., Kincaid, D. L., Hindin, M. J., Lettenmaier, C. L., Kuseka, I., Silverman, T., Zinanga, A., Chikara, F., Adamchak, D. J., Mbizvo, M. T., Lynn, W., Kumah, O. M., & Kim, Y. M. (1992). Changing men's attitudes and behavior: The Zimbabwe Male Motivation Project. *Studies in Family Planning, 23*(6), 365–375.

Piotrow, P. T., Rimon, J. G. II, Winnard, K., Kincaid, D. L., Huntingtion, D., & Convisser, J. (1990). Mass media family planning promotion in three Nigerian cities. *Studies in Family Planning, 21*(5), 265–273.

Rice, R., & Atkin, C. (Eds.). (1989). *Public communication campaigns.* Newbury Park, CA: Sage.

Rogers, E. (1983). *Diffusion of innovations.* New York: The Free Press.

Salariya, E. M., Easton, P. M., & Cater, J. I. (1978). Duration of breast-feeding after early initiation and frequent feeding. *Lancet, 2,* 1141–1143.

Salmon, C. (Ed.). (1989). *Information campaigns: Balancing social values and social change.* Newbury Park, CA: Sage.

Snyder, J. D., Yunus, M., Wahed, M. A., & Chakraborty, J. (1982). Home-administered oral therapy for diarrhea: A laboratory study of safety and efficacy. *Transactions of the Royal Society of Tropical Medicine and Hygiene, 76*(3), 329–333.

United Nations Children's Fund. (1985). *Assignment children: Universal immunization by 1990.* New York: UNICEF.

United Nations Children's Fund. (1991). *The state of the world's children 1991.* New York: Oxford University Press.

U.S. Agency for International Development. (1991). *Child survival 1985–1990: A sixth report to Congress on the USAID program.* Washington, DC: USAID.

U.S. Department of Health and Human Services. (1991). *Healthy people 2000: National health promotion and disease prevention objectives* (DHHS Publication No. PHS 91-50213). Washington, DC: U.S. Department of Health and Human Services.

Valente, T. W., Kim, Y. K., Lettenmaier, C., & Glass, W. (1994). Radio promotion of family planning in the Gambia. *International Family Planning Perspectives, 20*(3), 96–104.

Victora, C., Kirkwood, B. R., Fuchs, S. C., Lombardi, C., & Barros, F. C. (1990). Is it possible to predict which diarrheal episodes will lead to life-threatening dehydration? *International Journal of Epidemiology, 19,* 3.

World development report 1993. (1993). New York: Oxford University Press.

Yoder, P. S. (1995). Examining ethnomedical diagnoses and treatment choices for diarrheal disorders in Lubumbashi Swahili. *Medical Anthropology, 16*(3), 211–247.

Yoder, P. S., & Hornik, R. (1994). Perceptions of the severity of diarrhea and treatment choice: A comparative study of HealthCom sites. *Journal of Tropical Medicine and Hygiene, 97,* 1–12.

Yoder, P. S., & Zheng, Z. (1991). *HealthCom in Lesotho: Final evaluation report.* Philadelphia: CIHDC Working Paper Series No. 1005.

Zimicki, S., Hornik, R., Verzosa, C. C., Hernandez, J. R., de Guzman, E., Dayrit, M., Fausto, A., Lee, M. B., & Abad, M. (1994). Improving vaccination coverage in urban areas through a health communication campaign: The 1990 Philippines experience. *Bulletin of the World Health Organization, 72*(3), 409–422.

MEDIA COVERAGE AND HEALTH BEHAVIOR

14

IMPACT OF PERSUASIVE INFORMATION ON SECULAR TRENDS IN HEALTH-RELATED BEHAVIORS

David P. Fan
University of Minnesota

For some researchers, controlled experiments constitute the gold standard for assessing the effectiveness of health communication. This perspective might be appropriate for clinical trials in which medical interventions are well under the control of the investigator, as would be true for comparisons of the relative effectiveness of lumpectomies or radical mastectomies for breast cancer.

However, the controlled experiment approach is problematic for evaluating communication effects because the population is constantly under bombardment by health information from a wide variety of sources, including the mass media. As noted elsewhere (Viswanath & Finnegan, chap. 16, this vol.), a frequent impetus for health campaigns is press reports of pivotal events like the surgeon general's report on smoking in 1964 (Public Health Service, 1964). Such events mobilize scientists, public health advocates, and government agencies to take actions that are further reported in the press and add to the information climate both before and during any deliberate intervention efforts. This mass media communication then affects the secular trends in behavior. As a result, intervention efforts often begin after secular trends show the population already moving in the desired direction under mass media influences (Viswanath & Finnegan, chap. 16, this vol.).

The mere existence of secular trends suggests that the public is responding to significant influences not controlled by health intervenors. However, these influences can include intervention efforts because a major source for health information can be press reports of interventions. Indeed, the possibility should at least be contemplated that a major effect of an intervention effort is not the intervention itself but news about that intervention. Obviously, controlled experiments and quasi-experiments are unable to evaluate the effects of such interventions that move from the experimental group to the control population in unintended ways.

RATIONALE FOR TIME TREND ANALYSES

Fortunately, time series methods can be used to assess the influences on secular trends that cannot be controlled. The data for time trend studies can come from uncontrolled experiments or even from observations of systems in which there is no experimental manipulation at all. Astronomy is the prototypical science in which conclusions are based on observation alone. The key to time series analyses is that the system should change over time and there should be enough time points to distinguish hypotheses leading to different expected relationships.

Sufficient time dependent observations can test theories as robustly as controlled experiments. For example, among the most solidly grounded theories in physics are those involving gravity. Those theories were established entirely from observational data, including those in the time dimension, because gravity is always present and cannot be eliminated for controlled studies. Similarly, in health communication at the population level, the mass media effects can only be assessed by observational data using time trend analyses because this communication channel is also outside the control of the researcher.

IDEODYNAMIC TIME TREND THEORY

This chapter uses the ideodynamic theory designed to predict both opinion (Fan, 1985a) and behavior (Fan, 1985b) time trends from persuasive information available to the public. The focus is on behavior, so the theoretical discussion refers to behavior with the understanding that arguments apply equally to opinion and knowledge.

Ideodynamics is a macrotheory that predicts the fractions or percentages of large populations exhibiting mutually exclusive behaviors over time. It does not attempt to predict individual behavior. Consider, for example, the population of high school seniors in the United States divided into two groups $y_{U,t}$ and $y_{N,t}$ reporting that they had either used or not used cocaine within the past month (Johnston, O'Malley, & Bachman, 1992). The subscripts are U for Used, N for Not used, and t for time.

The ideodynamic time series equation is

$$y_{U,t} - y_{U,t-1} = k_U \, F_{U,t} \, y_{N,t-1} - k_N \, F_{N,t} \, y_{U,t-1}. \tag{1}$$

In this equation, the difference between y_U at $t - 1$ and t on the lefthand side gives the change in percent y_U using cocaine between two time points. The equation indicates that this change would be an increase if there is both persuasive information in the form of a persuasive force function $F_{U,t}$ in favor of use at time t and if there are nonusers $y_{N,t-1}$ who were available for recruitment at time $t - 1$ because conversion is from time $t - 1$. The multiplication gives the appropriate result that there should be no gain if there is either no persuasive information $F_{U,t}$ in favor of use or if there is no one left to persuade in which case $y_{N,t-1} = 0$. Persuasibility constant k_U gives the fraction of the remaining nonusers $y_{N,t-1}$ changed for a given amount of persuasive information $F_{U,t}$ in favor of use. The product term to the right of the minus sign in Equation 1 gives the reverse transition of users to nonuse.

For example, if it is assumed that

a) The effect of one unit of pro-cocaine use information (e.g., one paragraph in a newspaper) is .004 ($k_U = .4$).

b) The effect of one unit of anticocaine use information is .002 ($k_N = .002$).

c) There were 10% recent users, and 90% recent nonusers (U,$t - 1$) = .10; (N,$t - 1 = .90$).

d) There were 20 anti-articles and 3 pro-articles in the time period between t and $t + 1$ (e.g., over a one-day period).

then the predicted level of use for the current day t is .004 × 3 × .90 − .002 * 20 * .10 + .10, which is equivalent to .107, thus the formula would suggest that use would increase from time t to time $t + 1$ of about .7%.

This minimal equation can be expanded to replace the single persuasive force function times its persuasibility constant by the sum of a variety of forces, each with a different constant reflecting different powers of persuasion. The structure of the F functions is general with the only requirements being that each F function only favors one idea, that it be positive in sign, and that it be a function of time. Most commonly, the F functions have been constructed from mass media stories scored by computer to favor different ideas. Each story is given its full value on its date, followed by an exponential decay with the half life of one day being a consensus value for a variety of news stories (Fan, 1988).

The multiplication of the F and y terms in Equation 1 means that both the F values and their errors are damped by multiplication by y values all between zero and one. In consequence, this equation can be implemented using computed values of y_t as the y_{t-1} for the next time interval. In this iterative method, the prediction error at any time includes errors in F from all earlier times. However, the damping means that the variance is stable with only recent errors making important contributions.

The same recursive method cannot be used for linear autoregressive time series models because their errors do not damp so the prediction becomes progressively more uncertain with time. To prevent this increase in the error, the standard method is to use *measured* values of y_{t-1} as a predictor of y_t. This use of measured y_{t-1} has two important disadvantages. One is that a large portion of the variance at time t is explained by measured behavior at $t - 1$, thereby decreasing the sensitivity of the model to variables that lead to behavior change. The other difficulty is that the time series data must include measured behavior values at all times $t - 1$, a requirement making the model difficult to apply when behavior data are sporadic and/or sparse.

The removal of these restrictions in ideodynamics by using the iterative computation means that:

- It is possible to see significant persuasive information effects with just 10 or so behavior time trend values in contrast to the 50 or so needed using first order, autoregressive methods (Fan, 1997).
- Behavior predictions can be made at the 24-hour intervals: before the first available behavior measurement, between behavior measurements, and after the last behavior measurement so long as suitable persuasive information is available for the computation. Computations at such small time intervals give a more detailed picture of expected population behavior over time than is possible with standard autoregressive models and can even predict survey values into the future if assumptions are made about the nature of future persuasive information.
- Behavior trends analyzed need not have uniformly spaced or frequently measured time points.

These advantages permitted the application of ideodynamics to demonstrate the effects of health communication for time series that would otherwise have been difficult to explore. The InfoTrend method for the computer content analysis of news media text (Fan, 1990, 1994) further facilitated the exploration of the effects of the press on health behaviors.

DEMONSTRATIONS OF THE IMPACT OF HEALTH COMMUNICATION

The ideodynamic method was substantially successful when applied to 63 time series in which persuasive information was used to predict knowledge, opinions, and behaviors for a variety of topics—including those in the health arena (Fan, 1997). Although arguments can be made for alternative theories for any one time series, consistent predictions for 63 time trends suggests the theory is indeed sound with unexpected results coming not from inadequacy in the ideodynamic theory, but rather from omission of some important persuasive information acting on the population. The robustness of the theory permits it to be used as a method for determining the relative importance of different types of persuasive information.

In other words, if the prediction is inaccurate, the implication is that some important persuasive information is missing from the analysis. If the prediction is good and if there are enough dependent variable data points for critical tests, then the input persuasive information can be subdivided into different types with each one given its own weight through a separate persuasibility constant as used in Equation 1. The relative values of the estimated constants will then show the respective impacts of different types of information.

Two fundamental tenets of the theory are that changes in knowledge, attitudes, and behavior are only the result of exposure to persuasive information, and the effect of a unit of persuasive information is constant over a period of time. The first assumption is less irksome than it may seem because persuasive information can include internally generated information (self-persuasion), although in practice the approach is particularly focused on the effects of externally generated information, particularly mass media content.

Because health communication is mainly designed to affect behavior, some examples of successful applications to behavior are considered, along with implications about the most efficient types of persuasive information for the behavior examined.

Cocaine Use by High School Seniors

One example for which ideodynamics was able to demonstrate the effectiveness of health communication was in the domain of cocaine usage by high school seniors in the United States within the last month (Fan & Holway, 1994).

One type of persuasive information included in the analysis was press discussion divided into these six types: (a) the use of cocaine causing harm to other members in the family of a cocaine user; (b) denial of cocaine use by prominent persons and other individuals that could send the message that cocaine use was undesirable; (c) punishment of users, both legally and in other forms like job loss; (d) medical harm from use, including death from an overdose; (e) other reasons to avoid use; and (f) all reasons to use cocaine combined, including the pleasures due to highs and rushes.

Another type of information included was that favorable use due to the introduction of crack cocaine which had become important enough by 1983 so that, according to a survey, 2.4% of the cocaine users were smoking crack. By 1986, this number had increased to 6.7%. This introduction was not accompanied by press coverage favorable to crack while its use was rising, but the persuasive force in favor of crack use due to this nonmedia input was assigned to be a mathematical straight line from 2.4% to 6.7% between the average mid-April survey times in these two years. This line was extended to July 15, 1986, when the press started to cover crack as being responsible for the death of basketball star Len Bias.

The persuasive force discouraging use in the ideodynamic analysis was the combination of press information of types a–e listed previously. The persuasive force favoring use during the analysis time period from 1979 to 1991 was given by the very small amount of pro-cocaine media information (type f) added to the mathematical function described for crack introduction. These press and crack persuasive forces were able to predict self-reported cocaine use (Fig. 14.1) with an R^2 of .99 showing that essentially all of the relevant persuasive information was included in the analysis.

This study indicates that press coverage of the dangers of cocaine could account for all of the decline in the use of this drug. However, the press contained almost none of the information favorable to use. That information was present during the introduction of crack beginning in 1983 and also in the time period from 1977 to 1979 when powdered cocaine use was rising. Given the absence of knowledge about pro cocaine information in the earlier time period, use was not modeled from 1977 to 1979. During this time, there was almost no press coverage of cocaine.

The press coverage pattern is as expected. The press covers an issue only after it becomes prominent. Also, once a health problem is identified, the press does not usually speak about the advantages of an unhealthy lifestyle.

Recidivism to Smoking by Quitters of Tobacco Smoking

The Multiple Risk Factor Intervention Trial data (MRFIT; Hughes, Hymowitz, Ockene, Simon, & Vogt, 1981) were used for studies of recidivism to tobacco smoking by recent quitters. These data included data on the time

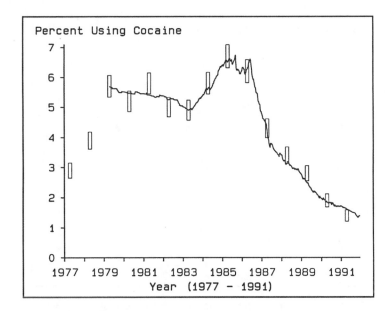

FIG. 14.1.   Percent of high school seniors reporting cocaine use in the last 30 days. The line is the ideodynamic prediction. The symbols are self-reports of use with the widths being the beginning and ending dates of the survey and the height being the 95% confidence based on sample size.

at which recent quitters from smoking restarted, as well as secondary cessation by these recidivists.

The first step was to predict the chances that a quitter would restart. Because the pressures for such resumption were likely to arise internally from psychological and physiological factors, mathematical functions were proposed to describe these factors. It was postulated that a successful quitter would be subject to two internal forces: an exponentially declining "euphoria" that would lead to resistance to restarting, and a simultaneous exponentially decreasing "nostalgia" or "craving" for tobacco that would encourage resumption. The total persuasive force for recidivism would be the product of the two exponential functions, thus combining euphoria at having quit with craving for more tobacco. These were assumed to be the only forces acting on the recent quitters because smoking begins in the teens for most people, so there should be no other forces acting on the sample of men from age 35 to 57 to make them start smoking.

A fit to the MRFIT data gave a very short euphoria half-life of 1.1 days and a long craving half-life of 8.5 months. Therefore, the craving to resume was much longer lasting than the very transient resistance to smok-

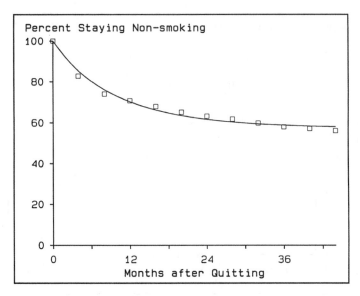

FIG. 14.2.   Percent of quitters of tobacco smoking who stay nonsmoking.
The line is the ideodynamic prediction and the symbols are survey data.

ing due to euphoria at having quit. With these constants, the predicted recidivism matched the observed data with an R^2 of .99 (Fig. 14.2).

A second set of predictions was made in which the recidivists were
assumed to be subject to a constant pressure both from the MRFIT program
and from the mass media and other sources to quit once more. This secondary cessation was also predicted successfully. The total number of nonsmokers at 44 months, including those who had quit and those who had resumed
and/or quit again was 76%, quite close to the observed value of 80%.

The estimated euphoria, craving, and intervention constants could then
be used in simulation computations to predict the likely result of different
strategies. In general, sustained intervention over longer time periods at
lower levels should give better success than more intense efforts for shorter
periods of time.

HIV Infection in Gay Men

The dependent variable for HIV infection was not a survey of the population, but was a back calculation (Brookmeyer, 1991) of earlier infections
in gay/bisexual men based on knowledge of the incidence of AIDS and the
latent time period between infection and development of the symptoms.

The theory for HIV infection (Fan, 1993) assumed that gay/bisexual
males could be divided behaviorally at any time into two groups, those behaving safely and those behaving unsafely with respect to HIV transmis-

sion. A person could sometimes act safely and sometimes take risks. It was not necessary that the same person stay in either group.

There was assumed to be a spontaneous and constant persuasive force in the direction of risky sexual behavior. A large component of this force could be internally derived, as in the case of smoking recidivism. This force would act on those acting safely.

Simultaneously, there was also an inherent and constant persuasive force toward either no sex or safe sex, which acted together with mass media to change their behavior to a safe mode. For the computation, safe sexual behavior was equivalent to abstinence.

For a first approximation, it was further assumed that infected and noninfected men behaved in the same manner. With these considerations, a prediction was made for the percent of population acting in a risky fashion. The parameters of the prediction equation were set to give a reasonable fit to the three survey points for risky sexual behavior by gay men in San Francisco (Fig. 14.3, top frame). This curve showed no change until the end of 1982, at which time the Centers for Disease Control announced that AIDS was a sexually transmitted disease. After this time, there was a dramatic drop in high-risk behavior, from about 75% to 20%–30%.

Even though they were not enough for statistical significance, the three points were able to fix parameters that could then be used in the HIV infection prediction. This prediction made the assumption that infection required risky behavior by both an infected and an uninfected individual. Therefore, the infection rate was predicted by the product of the percentages for infected and uninfected gay/bisexual men acting riskily. In addition to the behavioral conditions just discussed, actuarial tables were used to account for the more rapid death from AIDS of the infected men. Two predictions were made using the upper and lower limits of 1.5% ($R^2 = .99$) or 3.5% ($R^2 = .98$) for all men having had same-sex contact within the past year (Fig. 14.3, bottom frame). These percentages were based on surveys (Rogers & Turner, 1991), which are in the range found consistently in recent times.

The only nonconstant feature of the analysis was news coverage showing that HIV infection was both dangerous and transmitted sexually. This information depressed risk behavior to a level about one third of that before news about the sexual nature of AIDS. Fortunately, HIV infection requires two partners for transmission so the infection rate is the result of the product of the percent who took risks, with one infected and the other not. Therefore, the drop in infection is the square of one third, or about 10%. With this drop, the prediction was for a stabilization in the percent of infected gay/bisexual men by the mid-1980s after the rise in the early 1980s, which preceded the permeation of the population with news about the dangers of infection (Fig. 14.3, bottom frame).

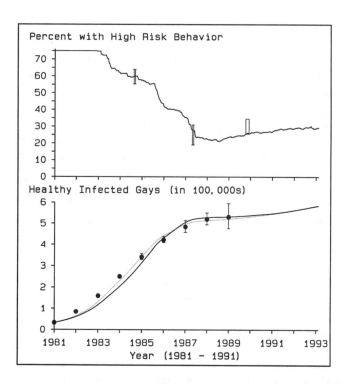

FIG. 14.3. Time trends in risky sexual behavior and HIV infection in gay/bisexual men. Top frame: Percent of gay/bisexual men, both infected and not infected with HIV, reporting high risk sexual behavior plotted as in Fig. 14.1. Bottom frame: Number of gay/bisexual men infected with HIV but not yet showing the symptoms of AIDS. The ideodynamic predictions are the lines and the symbols are back calculation inferences. The dotted line assumes that men who have sex with men constitute 1.5% of all males; the comparable number for the solid line is 3.5%.

Calls to the CDC National AIDS Hotline

The case of calls to the Centers for Disease Control (CDC) National AIDS Hotline was informative because comparisons could be made between the relative effects of the news and advertising in the form of public service announcements (PSAs) sponsored by the CDC and by others. The agency monitored both these types of advertisements as well as attempts to call the hotline (Fan, 1996).

In addition to the advertisement volume, news media items were scored for discussion of AIDS and HIV. The following four types of persuasive in-

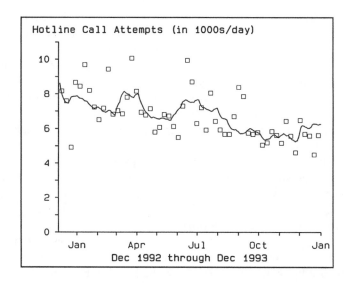

FIG. 14.4. Number of attempts to call the CDC National AIDS Hotline. Actual volume of call attempts is the symbols, and the line is the ideodynamic prediction.

formation were then used to predict the volume of hotline calls: CDC PSAs, PSAs by others, news stories in newspapers, and television news transcripts. Counteracting this desire to call was a constant pressure to forget or be distracted. Each type of information was given its own persuasibility constant and it was found that the predicted time trend matched the actual volume of attempts to call the hotline with an R^2 of .7 (Fig. 14.4).

Perhaps the most interesting outcome of this study was that only the CDC PSAs contributed in a statistically significant manner. This was to be expected because only these PSAs consistently included the hotline telephone number.

CONCLUSIONS

The studies in this chapter show that it is possible to use the ideodynamic theory both to predict likely effect of persuasive information and to assess those types of information with the most impact on behaviors. Because the theory can predict behavior without including actual behavior measurements, it was possible to say that weak but sustained antismoking intervention was likely to be more effective than strong but short-term efforts. The iterative nature of the ideodynamic computation means that it is also possible to predict what behavior in the population is likely to be based on persuasive information alone, without actually measuring the population, once the parameters of the system have been estimated.

In the studies examined, a variety of types of health information were evaluated, ranging from survey-based inferences about the desirability of using crack cocaine, through computer-analyzed print and electronic media news stories, to internally derived craving for tobacco after quitting and spontaneous urges for risky sex among gay/bisexual men. These various types of persuasive information were evaluated for their ability to change health behaviors in the form of cocaine consumption, recidivism to smoking by recent quitters, HIV infection in gay/bisexual men, and calls to the CDC National AIDS Hotline.

In all cases, the expected result was obtained. The news media did not contain information favorable to cocaine use, but it could explain the drop in cocaine use by high school seniors in the last month from 6% to 7% in 1985 to around 1% in 1991 (Fan & Holway, 1994). Exponential declines for euphoria and craving with quite different time constants could predict recidivism to smoking by recent quitters. News media reports on the dangers of AIDS and its transmission by sexual means could depress risky sexual behavior among gay/bisexual men from about 75% to 20%–30%, and this reduction could account quantitatively for the drop in HIV infection in the mid-1980s. The gradual decline in calls to the CDC National AIDS Hotline could be predicted from the diminution in CDC PSAs, which carried the hotline phone number. Other PSAs or news media coverage did not consistently have this number.

No health communication interventions (except for the CDC PSAs) were included among the persuasive information in making these four sets of predictions, because the population under consideration was that in the nation as a whole. Therefore, microeffects due to interventions in localized subpopulations, the essence of controlled quasi-experiments, should not have made major contributions. However, as already noted, interventions receiving national media attention would have been included in the analysis. This generalized diffusion of information about the intervention could have led to major effects of the intervention effort in a way that would not have been found in the quasi-experiments because the outcome would have been a shift in the secular trend in all communities.

Mass media news reports real-world events like interventions, thus it would not have been able to distinguish mass media coverage from anything else that moved with the same time course as the mass media. However, it was unlikely that there would have been many other factors moving in parallel with the media for all 63 of the time trends studied (Fan, 1997).

Besides predicting behavior, the ideodynamic analysis also gives a means for assessing the direct effects of specific health information interventions on the public nationwide. After ideodynamic time series studies confirmed that the press contained the bulk of the relevant persuasive information, text discussing specific interventions can be identified to see the extent to which those interventions contributed to the total information affecting the population. However, this strategy could not account for indirect effects in which, for example, the success or failure of an intervention would affect the efforts of other health professionals.

Overall, the results included herein make two strong recommendations: First, it is necessary to include all persuasive information in analyses of population behavior. It is insufficient to focus on just those messages provided in health campaigns. The effects of the campaign can be obscured by other information available to the public, especially from the mass media. Also, health campaigns should make reasonably frequent measurements of attitudes, behaviors, and information provided both by the campaign and by other sources, including the mass media. These data will permit ideodynamic time trend analyses of the variety of forces moving secular trends. Ideodynamic studies will complement those on experimental and control populations. These controlled studies cannot, by themselves, explain secular trends.

REFERENCES

Brookmeyer, R. (1991). Reconstruction and future trends of the AIDS epidemic in the United States. *Science, 253,* 37–42.

Fan, D. P. (1985a). Ideodynamics: The kinetics of the evolution of ideas. *Journal of Mathematical Sociology, 11,* 1–24.

Fan, D. P. (1985b). Ideodynamic predictions of the evolution of habits. *Journal of Mathematical Sociology, 11,* 265–281.

Fan, D. P. (1988). *Predictions of public opinion from the mass media: Computer content analysis and mathematical modeling.* Westport, CT: Greenwood Press.

Fan, D. P. (1990). *Information processing expert system for text analysis and predicting public opinion based on information available to the public.* U.S. Patent 4,930,077.

Fan, D. P. (1993). Quantitative estimates for the effects of AIDS public education on HIV infections. *International Journal of Bio-Medical Computing, 33,* 157–177.

Fan, D. P. (1994). *Information processing analysis system for sorting and scoring text.* U.S. Patent 5,371,673.

Fan, D. P. (1996). Impact of the mass media on calls to the CDC National AIDS Hotline. *International Journal of Bio-Medical Computing, 41,* 207–216.

Fan, D. P. (1997, November). *Sixty-three time trend explorations of the impact of the media and other persuasive information on public opinion.* Paper presented at the annual conference of the Speech Communication Association, Chicago.

Fan, D. P., & Holway, W. B. (1994). Media coverage of cocaine and its impact on usage patterns. *International Journal of Public Opinion Research, 6,* 139–162.

Hughes, F. H., Hymowitz, N., Ockene, J. K., Simon, N., & Vogt, T. N. (1981). The Multiple Risk Factor Intervention Trial (MRFIT): V. Intervention on smoking. *Preventive Medicine, 10*(4), 476–500.

Johnston, L., O'Malley, P., & Bachman, G. (1992). *Smoking, drinking, and illicit drug use among American high school seniors, college students and young adults: Volume 1. High school seniors.* Rockville, MD: National Institute on Drug Abuse.

Rogers, S., & Turner, C. (1991). Male-male sexual contact in the USA: Findings from five sample surveys. *Journal of Sex Research, 28*, 491–519.

Public Health Service. (1964). *Smoking and health.* Report of the Advisory Committee to the Surgeon General of the Public Health Service (PHS Publication No. 1103). Washington, DC: U.S. Department of Health, Education and Welfare, Public Health Service, Center for Disease Control.

15

THE EFFECTS OF PROFESSIONAL AND MEDIA WARNINGS ABOUT THE ASSOCIATION BETWEEN ASPIRIN USE IN CHILDREN AND REYE'S SYNDROME

Stephen B. Soumerai
Dennis Ross-Degnan
Jessica Spira Kahn
Harvard Medical School and Harvard Pilgrim Health Care

In many industrialized nations, the proliferation of health technologies has coincided with increased numbers of epidemiological studies on the risk of injury resulting from medical products and services (Nelkin, 1989). Every few months, a previously unknown hazard associated with a commonly used product is reported in the scientific literature or at scientific meetings. Such reports are often followed by waves of media attention on the dangers in question, accompanied by public and scientific debate about the "correct" interpretation of these risks. As Feinstein and others (Feinstein, 1988) pointed out, all too often faulty studies purporting to show cause-and-effect relations between common products and severe adverse outcomes gain widespread media attention, further scaring an already suspicious American public. Media reports tend to concentrate on rare but dramatic hazards, and often fail to report more common but serious risks, such as motor vehicle accidents (Singer & Endreny, 1987). Some have suggested that this cycle has created a public "epidemic of apprehension"—even about health technology.

On the positive side, the mass media may be a major channel in alerting the public to important and well-documented dangers, such as the carcinogenic potential of asbestos in workplaces, schools, and homes, particularly if the scientific and medical literature diffuses more slowly to appropriate decision makers. In these situations, governments and professional health associations are faced with a dilemma: At what point does sufficient evidence exist to justify public warnings about the potential dangers of specific products that also impart significant health benefits?

Beyond this issue lies another fundamental question: Under what circumstances can the lay and medical press influence professional and consumer behavior? Technology-related hazards often appear suddenly and under conditions of uncertainty, and such situations do not lend themselves practically or ethically to the methodological demands of experiments. A fair number of studies exist on the modest effects of mass media campaigns targeting well-established risk behaviors, such as smoking (Flay, 1987) and seat belt use (Robertson et al., 1974). However, few explorations of media-related changes in health product use appear in the literature. One study used time series analysis to observe increases in rates of discontinuation of intrauterine devices (IUDs) and birth control pills following increased news coverage about their adverse effects (Jones, Beniger, & Westoff, 1980). Similarly, the Kellogg Company's national television advertising campaign on the role of fiber in preventing cancer was associated with an increase in the market share of Kellogg's and other bran cereals (Warner, 1987).

Changes in personal habits are of a different character than changes in purchase decisions following warnings about newly discovered hazards of commonly used products. The desired behavior change represents not the establishment or cessation of a habit, but simply substitution of one product for another closely related product. Marginal changes in behavior are likely to be somewhat easier to achieve than the elimination of a strongly established routine, or adoption of a completely new one (Warner, 1987).

This chapter addresses the question of how the media can change consumer behavior vis-à-vis popular health-related products by focusing on the diffusion of risk information about the relation between use of aspirin and Reye's syndrome, a rare but potentially fatal or severely debilitating illness usually occurring in young children with flu, varicella, or other viruses. First, the epidemiological evidence supporting the aspirin–Reye's syndrome association is reviewed. Second, the actions of several public and private organizations and the key events that played important roles in promoting or impeding public awareness are described. Third, there is discussion of the relations between the quantity and timing of medical and lay media attention to this issue, other public education activities, and decreases in the use of aspirin for children, and reductions in disease incidence. Finally, based on previous research in health education, risk perception, and changing professional behavior, some specific characteristics of risk communication (exemplified by the Reye's syndrome case), which may facilitate changes in health behaviors in response to mass communications, are proposed.

EPIDEMIOLOGICAL STUDIES

Reye's syndrome (RS) is a disease of acute encephalopathy, characterized as a viral illness progressing to delirium, fever, convulsions, vomiting, disturbed respiratory patterns, stupor, seizures, or coma (Trauner, 1982, 1984). The syndrome occurs most often in children between age 5 and 15, and its effects are independent of race, ethnicity, and gender (Trauner, 1982). Epidemics are often correlated with influenza and varicella outbreaks, as well as other viral conditions. The syndrome was first described by R.D.K. Reye in the early 1960s (Reye, Morgan, & Baral, 1963), and possible associations between ingestion of salicylates and subsequent development of RS was first suggested as early as 1962 (Trauner, 1984). National surveillance for RS was begun by the Centers for Disease Control (CDC) during the 1973–1974 nationwide outbreak of influenza B. In late 1976, CDC and state health departments intensified surveillance of the syndrome and have continuously maintained surveillance since that time. During the first several years of monitoring, from 250 to 550 cases of RS were reported each year to the CDC, with the largest number of cases occurring during years of influenza A activity. Fatality rates reached 40%, but have declined to 20%–30% more recently (Hurwitz, 1988).

Between 1980 and 1982, three case-control studies were published that represented the first major investigations in the United States on the link between ingestion of aspirin and subsequent development of Reye's syndrome. A Michigan study indicated that children with RS were more likely to have received aspirin during a viral illness preceding the onset of RS than controls (Waldman et al., 1982). The authors were among the first to conclude that "aspirin taken during viral illness may contribute to the development of RS." Studies in Ohio and Arizona similarly observed an association between aspirin use and Reye's syndrome (Barrett et al., 1986; Halpin et al., 1982; Starko et al., 1980).

Although no extensive warning campaigns were begun prior to the case control findings, the CDC did publish a recommendation in *Morbidity and Mortality Weekly Report* (MMWR) that "parents should be advised to use caution when administering salicylates to treat children with viral illnesses, particularly chicken pox and influenza-like illnesses" (MMWR, 1980, p. 539). In 1982, the chairman of the CDC Committee on Infectious Disease, Vincent Fulginiti, concluded that the three studies in Michigan, Ohio, and Arizona showed a strong association between aspirin use and RS, stating that "it is the consensus of the committee that there is high probability that the administration of aspirin contributes to the causation of RS" and recommending that aspirin not be prescribed for children with chicken pox or influenza (Fulginiti, 1982, pp. 811–812).

Publication of the study findings was accompanied by substantial controversy over their scientific validity, resulting in the formation of a U.S. Public Health Service (PHS) task force to investigate the possible link. The PHS conducted a pilot study in 1984 supporting the findings of the earlier studies (Hurwitz et al., 1985), and a main study from January 1985 to May 1986, which involved 50 pediatric care centers in the United States. The main study included 27 RS cases and 140 controls, and found a strong association between salicylate ingestion during an antecedent illness and the onset of RS (odds ratio, 40; lower 95% confidence limit, 5.8; Hurwitz et al., 1987). The authors concluded that the risk of RS is related to both exposure and quantity of salicylates ingested, and suggested that over 90% of RS cases are associated with salicylates. More recent evidence indicates that there may be a dose–response relation, further validating the previous attributions of a causal relation (Pinsky, Hurwitz, Schonberger, & Gunn, 1988).

The publication of these epidemiological studies initiated many years of active controversy about the hypothesized association, as well as further research on the clinical, pharmacological, and epidemiological bases of the relation. Many government and private organizations contributed to the public debate about risks, sometimes in opposite directions.

Although a complete picture of the 10-year history of these controversies is impractical, it is useful to examine the major events and organizations involved in public, professional, and media communication campaigns. To accomplish this goal, a comprehensive review was conducted of medical and lay media reports identified from computerized searches, published documents from the CDC, weekly pharmaceutical reports (e.g., *Weekly Pharmacy Report*/"The Green Sheet"), and files maintained by one of the most active private organizations involved in the controversy, Public Citizen's Health Research Group (HRG).

MEDICAL AND PHARMACY REPORTS

Following publication of the first epidemiological findings, articles began to appear in medical journals reporting on the studies, analyzing their methods, and concluding with tentative advice about prescribing aspirin to children with fever and chicken pox or influenza. The medical news section of *JAMA*, for example, published an article in March 1982 recommending acetaminophen as a safe and effective alternative to salicylates for these children (Anonymous, 1982). Because of the proven benefits of aspirin for arthritis and other conditions in children, there were also vigorous debates on the issue of whether labels should be placed on salicylate-containing drugs. For example, in a November 1982 issue of the *American*

Journal of Diseases of Children, a proponent for warnings argued that "even the fragmentary evidence available does provide some biologic plausibility for the association of aspirin to the development of RS" (Glezen, 1982, p. 972). Other physicians disagreed strongly with the concept of an aspirin warning label, calling it "premature and alarmist," and commenting that the informed pediatric community had not reached a consensus about the possible hazards of aspirin use (Brown, Fikrig, & Finberg, 1983). Letters to the editors argued that the studies were flawed, and parents may stop giving aspirin completely if the child has an uncertain diagnosis.

Two years later, articles about RS began to appear in pharmacy journals. For example, in March 1984, *American Pharmacy* published an article describing the PHS pilot study and advising that "the public health would be served if an error is to be made by making it on the side of caution" (Murphy, 1984, p. 45). After the pilot study was completed in 1986, the same journal concluded there was a high probability that aspirin contributes to the development of RS, and urged pharmacists to educate parents about the association and to suggest alternatives for treatment of fever (Bess, Helms, & Carter, 1986). In late 1984, the American Pharmacy Association, a professional organization registering the community of professional pharmacists, launched a voluntary educational campaign about RS. The campaign included distribution of warning posters to 50,000 members through a weekly newsletter.

GOVERNMENT ACTIVITIES

Publication of the first three studies linking aspirin and RS resulted in public sector activities to assess the evidence and plan future positions. The Food and Drug Administration (FDA) and the CDC, both within the U.S. Public Health Service, were the primary actors in the federal government (see Table 15.1). The CDC and its staff carried out the most rigorous epidemiological studies, and also communicated and interpreted study findings for the media and public. The FDA was responsible for insuring that any important information on risks of aspirin would be communicated both to consumers and health professionals through public statements, information campaigns, and aspirin warning labels. However, the agency faced two competing pressures: one from the Reagan administration and its Office of Management and Budget, which was attempting to reduce regulatory oversight of private industry; and the other, from Congress and citizen groups, which were demanding government-required warnings about suspected risks as expeditiously as possible.

The aspirin–RS link was not unknown to the FDA at the time when the three state studies were published. As early as 1976, the FDA reported in-

TABLE 15.1
Timeline of Major Events and Educational Activities

Year	Government Agencies	Warning Labels	Industry	Health Research Group
1980	CDC recommends in MMWR that caution be used when administering salicylates to treat viral illnesses in children	—	—	—
1981	—	—	—	
1982	CDC committee finds "high probability" that aspirin contributes to causation of RS; recommends that aspirin not be prescribed for children with chicken pox or influenza Surgeon general column on association to 8,000 newspapers; Q&A brochures distributed to pharmacies and primary care physicians	—	Schering-Plough sends letters to pediatricians stating that recent reports and news stories on relation between aspirin and RS are "misleading and unjustified"	HRG sues FDA to require warnings on aspirin products
1983	FDA sends TV PSAs to 800 TV stations;* newspaper column to 1,500 newspapers	—	CCC press release to news outlets: "Doctors Counter FDA Campaign—Equal Time Request Threatened"	HRG news release: "Government Undercuts Efforts to Warn Parents about RS . . ."

Year				
1984	—	—	CCC television and radio PSA stating that "No medication has been proven to cause Reye's ..." American Pharmacy Association warning poster sent to 50,000 members	Letter from HRS to news assignment editors of 1,000 TV stations urging them not to broadcast industry (CCC) PSA
1985	DHHS secretary sends letters on CDC pilot study to pediatricians, family physicians, newspapers, and broadcast outlets	DHHS secretary calls for voluntary labeling by aspirin manufacturers	Aspirin Foundation of America starts voluntary "RS precautionary program," including PSAs, store posters, and signs distributed by sales reps	—
1986	—	Warning labels required on all aspirin products	—	—
1987	—	—	—	—
1988	—	RS warning made permanent, and new requirement that manufacturers place an "attention-getting" statement on the "principal display panel" of packaging to refer to the new warning		

*PSAs revised and sent again in subsequent years.

dications of a possible association (FDA, 1976). It was not until 1982, however, that the agency took an active role in the controversy. In early 1982, an FDA working group conducted a direct audit of the raw data of several state health department studies, and co-sponsored a workshop to discuss the issue with the CDC and the National Institute of Allergy and Infectious Diseases. At the completion of the meeting, a majority of the scientists concluded that the evidence suggesting an association was sufficiently strong to warrant warning health professionals and parents. The pressure on the FDA began to mount in many quarters.

By late March 1982, the U.S. House of Representatives Subcommittee on Oversight and Investigations had conducted a preliminary investigation of FDA actions. John Dingell, chairman of the subcommittee, was particularly critical of the FDA's failure to comply with CDC recommendations. Richard Schweiker, Secretary of the Department of Health and Human Services (DHHS), announced in June 1982, a directive to the FDA to undertake an educational campaign aimed at health professionals and parents, and a requirement that aspirin labeling be changed to advise against its use in children with influenza or chicken pox. The August *FDA Drug Bulletin* included this information, and served as a further warning to health professionals (FDA, 1982). The FDA plan also included broadcasting a series of radio public service announcements (PSAs) and sending brochures to 150,000 pharmacists and 100,000 physicians. However, Secretary Schweiker stopped the proposed rule making concerning aspirin labeling in fall 1982. Several factors probably accounted for this decision. First, on November 9, the American Academy of Pediatrics advised DHHS that labeling of aspirin should be delayed until there was more conclusive evidence of the association. Second, based on notes obtained during congressional hearings, the chairman of the House Committee on Natural Resources, Agriculture Research and the Environment also implied that DHHS was acting too quickly. So, on November 18, DHHS announced that new studies were necessary to solve the dispute, and formed a task force to examine the evidence further (Green Sheet, 1982b).

The public information campaign, however, did get under way in late 1982, when the Surgeon General issued a newspaper column on the association to 8,000 news outlets. In addition, 673,000 copies of an FDA question and answer brochure were distributed to pharmacies and primary care physicians. The Assistant Secretary for Health also sent letters to physicians enclosing a brochure on RS (U.S. Dept. of Health & Human Services, 1982; Green Sheet, 1982a).

Other potentially more powerful components of the education campaign did not have a smooth beginning. In fall 1983, for example, about half a million FDA-produced pamphlets were to have been distributed to 4,200 supermarkets warning parents of the association, but distribution was banned by the Secretary of DHHS and the pamphlets remained in a warehouse, due in large part to strong lobbying and threatened lawsuits by an aspirin industry-financed organization of pediatricians, the Committee on the Care of Children (CCC), which was created to counteract the warning campaign. An October 1983 letter from the CCC's attorney outlined the industry's charge that the supermarket pamphlet was misleading in implicating aspirin and salicylates as causes of RS, and specifically called for a halt to the publicity campaign and recalls of distributed materials (Chayet, 1983). Distribution of a 30-second radio announcement to 5,000 radio stations was also canceled. Television PSAs, however, had already been sent to approximately 800 commercial television stations in fall 1983. During this time, a newspaper column prepared by the FDA was distributed to approximately 1,500 newspapers, as well as a new 60-second PSA to 200 television stations. The information in the approved materials was not fundamentally different from previous FDA messages and thus was not affected by the CCC's actions.

The publication of the 1984 PHS pilot study prompted additional waves of FDA and DHHS activity. The Institute of Medicine had already reviewed the data and concluded that they revealed a strong association between RS and the use of aspirin (Institute of Medicine, 1983). New DHHS Secretary Heckler stated that the study was "not completely conclusive—but its findings do show an association between the use of aspirin and the onset of RS in children and teenagers" with flu and chicken pox (Kronholm, 1985). Subsequently, Secretary Heckler arranged for letters on the pilot study to be sent to pediatricians, family physicians, newspapers, and broadcast outlets. In addition, in early 1985, she called for voluntary labeling of aspirin products by the Aspirin Foundation of America. She requested that manufacturers remove any labels recommending aspirin for flu or chicken pox in children, and that all aspirin labels contain information on the possible association between aspirin and RS, and a recommendation that aspirin not be used in these circumstances without consulting a physician.

The extent of voluntary compliance by the aspirin industry was controversial. In November 1985, due in part to the pressure from public interest organizations and several U.S. senators, and a realization that the voluntary program was not sufficient, a regulation was approved by Secretary Heckler requiring all salicylate-containing over-the-counter (OTC) medications to be labeled beginning in June 1986. The warning label required the following statement: "Warning: Children and teenagers should not use this medication for chicken pox or flu symptoms before a doctor is consulted about Reye's syndrome, a rare but serious illness" (Green Sheet, 1985). This warning was required to precede any additional warning that may appear. The FDA public information campaign continued, with a focus on parents of older children and teenagers who were likely to be self-medicating (FDA, 1985). The campaign included posters for physician's offices, store posters, PSAs for radio and TV, and new brochures and letters for the public and health professionals.

In June 1988, the FDA requirement for RS warning was made permanent, and a rule was passed requiring that manufacturers place "attention-getting statements on the principal display panel" of packaging to notify consumers about the new warning (Green Sheet, 1988).

CONSUMER ADVOCACY ORGANIZATIONS

Several private organizations with an active interest in pharmaceutical regulation quickly became embroiled in the 10-year debate and evolution of policies. One of the most active and litigious organizations was the Health Research Group (HRG), led by Sidney Wolfe. In early 1982, the organization, which has frequently intervened in congressional and agency rule making concerning safety and efficacy of pharmaceuticals, petitioned the FDA to require warning labels on aspirin products.[1] They also publicized the FDA's delay of a major public health campaign about RS, charging that the aspirin industry attempted to stop the government from issuing warnings. In addition, the organization asked the House Committee on Energy and Commerce to investigate FDA delays.

In May 1982, the HRG and the American Public Health Association sued the FDA in Federal District Court in Washington, DC, asking for a requirement that manufacturers place warnings on aspirin products. However, the suit was dismissed in March 1983, when the court ruled that the FDA had not unreasonably delayed rule making on this issue, and that although it was considering such regulations, it had begun an educational campaign to warn the public about potential risks. The court observed, however, that plaintiffs made a strong case that the proposed labeling should be expedited, and left open the possibility for re-filing the case if they disagreed with the agency's final decision. In late 1983, HRG sent out a number of news releases charging that the government continued to undercut efforts to warn parents about the aspirin–RS link. It also decried the administration's banning of educational materials (PC/HRG, 1983).

In late 1984, the HRG sent a letter to over 1,000 television stations and several hundred radio stations concerning a PSA by the CCC. In it, they quoted the Assistant Secretary for Health's conclusion: "The CCC's mes-

---

[1]Wolfe, S. (1982). Details of these events were obtained with the kind permission of Dr. Sidney Wolfe from the files of the Health Research Group, 2000 P St. NW, Washington, DC 20036. See Public Citizen documents No. 817, 821, 836, 917, 922.

sages are misleading . . . and fly in the face of scientific evidence." The letter further urged the broadcasters to report the government's message as often as possible, and not to broadcast the message from the drug industry group (PC/HRG, 1984).

On January 9, 1985, the HRG asked FDA Commissioner Frank Young to promulgate a regulation requiring all aspirin products to carry a prominent warning label explicitly stating that aspirin should not be used to treat chicken pox or flu symptoms in anyone age 19 or younger (PC/HRG, 1985a). Later that month, the HRG petitioned the Federal Trade Commission to require aspirin manufacturers to warn patients about the strong aspirin–RS association (PC/HRG, 1985b). In March 1985, the group testified before the House Committee on a bill requiring warning labels, advertisements, and store signs concerning aspirin and RS. Wolfe stated that the voluntary labeling program was a "cruel disaster" based on phone surveys of 53 drug stores in 31 states, and gave examples of aspirin products found in drug stores with labels recommending their use for treatment of flu. They found that none of the surveyed stores had aspirin products with warning labels. In addition, only 17 of the 53 stores had posters, many of which were produced by the American Pharmaceutical Association (PC/HRG, 1985c).

ASPIRIN INDUSTRY CAMPAIGNS

Pharmaceutical companies with large shares of the aspirin market played a major role in helping to shape the public debate about the aspirin–RS controversy. Aspirin industry representatives met many times with the FDA, and submitted several analyses to federal officials involved in the labeling and dissemination process. Their earliest efforts were to critically evaluate the case control studies, and to publish reports questioning their conclusiveness. In March 1982, Plough, Inc. sent letters to pediatricians questioning the validity of recent reports and news stories linking aspirin to RS and recommended continuing to prescribe aspirin for the reduction of fever in children (PC/HRG, 1982). Other industry-sponsored reports were published as articles or letters in medical journals. For example, the June 1982 issue of *Pediatrics* contained an industry-sponsored report suggesting that prodromal illness severity was a confounding cause of increased aspirin use in children with RS (Wilson & Brown, 1982).

In November 1982, the CCC filed suit in Federal District Court in Boston seeking a temporary restraining order to prevent the FDA from implementing its public information campaign. Later that month, the District Court in Boston denied the petition for a restraining order, and in March 1983, the CCC withdrew its lawsuit. Later that year, the CCC submitted a citizens' petition to the FDA requesting it to issue regulations governing publicity, and asserting that the public education campaign on RS and aspirin was inappropriate. A representative of the CCC met with Assistant Secretary Edward Brandt in an attempt to stave off the publicity campaign. In a letter soon after the meeting, he stated:

> We believe that the massive Government publicity campaign is based on nothing more than sheer speculation and the inability to admit previous error. We believe that the publicity has caused and will continue to cause needless panic, loss of confidence of patients in their physicians, delayed diagnosis of RS, and additional fatal overdose problems related to other medications.
>
> We ask that the present publicity campaign be halted and that materials which have already been distributed be recalled because of the hazard to the public. Instead, we believe that a public service announcement which calls attention to the need for early diagnosis of Reye Syndrome together with the caution relative to the use of all antipyretic medication would be most appropriate. (Chayet, 1983, p. 4)

In October 1983, the CCC sent letters to all commercial television stations, claiming that equal time and the fairness doctrines would apply if PHS RS ads were run. The organization also sent letters to supermarkets who were to receive the new question and answer brochures, advising them that displaying the brochure would be a violation of FDA labeling requirements. The organization also sent a press release entitled "Doctors Counter FDA Campaign—Equal Time Request Threatened," which claimed that most scientific experts agreed that early studies were seriously flawed, and according to their legal counsel, the FDA was providing misleading and deceptive information. Other industry representatives claimed that the public education program would contain information on the aspirin–RS association, and would thus bias the case-control study designed by the PHS.

Finally, in October 1984, the CCC released a public service announcement to television and radio stations outlining its alternative position in the controversy: "Stay tuned for a medical bulletin on RS . . . We do know that no medication has been proven to cause Reye's . . . if you would like further information, contact the CCC." The announcement was made by a physician, who stated that he was a member of a group of 1,200 pediatricians from across the country. This was the same PSA that was denounced by the Health Research Group and the DHHS.

Industry representatives also attempted to obtain pre-publication raw data from the CDC pilot study for the stated purposes of determining the validity of study conclusions and defending itself against lawsuits brought by parents of alleged RS victims (Kolata, 1986a). After the pilot data (corroborating the early findings of an aspirin–RS link) were submitted to the prestigious *New England Journal of Medicine* for possible publication, the Plough, Inc. director of clinical affairs wrote *NEJM*'s editor, Dr. Arnold Relman, calling for a more complete and objective "review of all scientific data underlying this Pilot Study which we believe may be serious[ly] flawed" (Vastagh, 1985, p. 1). The letter described a number of potential biases in the study and requested they be considered "so that a balanced presentation of this subject matter is available through the *New England Journal of Medicine*" (p. 4). Eventually, in 1986, Plough, Inc. obtained a subpoena allowing its scientists to examine raw data from the government-sponsored study provided that the identities of study participants be excluded (Kolata, 1986b).

In January 1985, after Secretary Heckler's call for voluntary labeling of aspirin-containing products, the policy of the aspirin industry began to change gradually. The first to respond was Schering-Plough, Inc. Members of the Aspirin Foundation followed (Sterling, Bristol-Meyers, Miles, Burroughs-Wellcome, Merrill-Dow, and Procter & Gamble). The factors responsible for these changes in industry policy are not fully understood. The credibility bestowed on the claims of warning proponents resulting from the publication of the pilot study probably accounted for some of the softening in the industry's position. A *Boston Globe* interview with Dr. Joseph White, the president of the Aspirin Foundation, reported his statement that although the government had not yet proven an association between aspirin and RS, the foundation was agreeing to voluntary labeling "to protect those at risk, create some peace and quiet and get some people off the backs of the industry" (Robinson, 1985). The programs, negotiated in meetings with the FDA, included television public service announcements, store campaigns with posters and signs distributed by manufacturers' representatives, and label changes. Some large retailers also planned their own public education activities, including posters and signs in the nonprescription drug sections of pharmacies and food stores.

In 1985, more than 800,000 warning posters were distributed, and radio and TV PSAs were prepared under the auspices of the Aspirin Foundation. In October, the FDA announced that the voluntary relabeling and educational effort was working well, and that 68% of children's aspirin on store shelves by the first week of November had the new labeling (Green Sheet, 1985). Drug store marketing services also contained information on the warning poster and a letter from the FDA commissioner urging cooperation with the voluntary program. Although not all manufacturers were equally active in promoting the educational messages, clearly there had been a softening of the aspirin industry's position following the pilot study. This shift in attitude continued and was reinforced by the publication of the final CDC study in 1987 (Hurwitz et al., 1987).

CHANGES IN THE INCIDENCE OF REYE'S SYNDROME

By 1987, the incidence of Reye's syndrome had declined to its lowest level since monitoring began in the mid-1970s. The FDA reported in the October 1987 *FDA Drug Bulletin*: "It appears that the rate of RS has decreased markedly in the U.S., probably as a result of PHS and voluntary industry publicity and educational efforts, and that parents are heeding warnings— including those from health professionals and that on the aspirin product labeling—to avoid giving aspirin to children and teenagers with symptoms of chicken pox or flu" (p. 29).

Because of the large number of organizations involved, it is difficult to know with certainty what elements or groups were most effective in changing public and professional behavior to reduce the incidence of RS. A quantitative analysis of the timing and intensity of communications from government, the lay and medical press, industry, and other organizations is crucial to an understanding of the changes that occurred. Although cause-and-effect relations cannot be shown by such analyses, it is informative to isolate the "turning point" in RS incidence and compare it to periods of increased intensity in specific types of public communications.

The treatment of influenza and chicken pox frequently involves advice from a family physician or pharmacist, as well as independent treatment decisions by parents. If the campaign was successful, then it would have raised the awareness of both health professionals and parents concerning the aspirin–RS link. Several studies have documented a congruence between the government and public health messages and physician knowledge and behavior. For example, G. L. Rahwan and R. G. Rahwan (1986) reported that 91% of pediatricians and 98% of pharmacists no longer recommended aspirin for children with fever or pain, and an almost identical proportion instead recommended acetaminophen. Similarly, an FDA research group used pharmaceutical marketing data to demonstrate that physician prescribing of aspirin to children declined significantly from 1980 to 1985, while acetaminophen prescriptions rose (Arrowsmith, Kennedy, Kuritsky, & Faich, 1987). This effect was not significant for adults, suggesting a selective effect of the publicity and warnings on aspirin use in children.

Other studies suggest that parents became aware of the aspirin–RS association during the 1980s. For example, in 1985, Morris and Klimberg (1986) conducted a national telephone survey of 1,155 parents of children under 20 to determine medication use during episodes of influenza or chicken pox. Fifty-three percent of parents surveyed were aware of the contraindications against aspirin use, 40% could spontaneously recall the name RS, and 84% had heard of RS based on a recognition test. Among the group of children who had chicken pox, about 58% of their parents said they gave their child a medication; of these medicines, 54% were nonaspirin products, and only 6% were aspirin. Similar figures were also found for children with influenza.

Although the aforementioned studies suggest that consumer and professional knowledge and behavior had improved by 1985, it is not clear which public and professional communications were the catalysts for these changes. Because many of the aspirin labeling requirements and federally sponsored education programs were delayed, it was hypothesized that the lay and professional media were the primary mechanisms for educating physicians and parents in the early years of this controversy (1981–1983). In order to better understand these temporal relations, time series measures of Reye's syndrome incidence and the quantity of lay and medical press reports on this topic were constructed, as well as indicators of the timing of major government and private actions or educational programs that might have affected parental and professional behavior directly or indirectly by stimulating media coverage.

Sources of Data on RS Incidence and Media Coverage

Data on the estimated yearly incidence of RS per 100,000 population less than age 18 from 1977 (when expanded reporting was initiated) to 1989 were obtained from the CDC RS surveillance system (MMWR, 1989). One threat to validity of these data is that increased media attention may itself have resulted in increased case detection over time. Fortunately for this analysis, however, such an effect would result in positive trends in RS incidence. This effect would, if anything, mask a true association between the quantity of media reports and the incidence of RS.

The MEDLINE system, a biomedical/health care database covering well over 3,000 journals, was used as an index of physician and health professional exposure to original articles, reports, or commentaries on the relation between aspirin and Reye's syndrome between 1974 and 1989. Two computerized indices were used to examine the quantity of exposure to this topic given by the lay press: the National Newspaper Index[2] and the Magazine Index.[3] Reviews were confined to four continuously reporting major national newspapers: the *Los Angeles Times*, the *New York Times*, the *Wall Street Journal*, and the *Washington Post*.

---

[2]National Newspaper Index™, produced by Information Access Company, Foster City, California, indexes the *Christian Science Monitor* (1/1/79–present), *Los Angeles Times* (11/1/82–present), *New York Times* (1/1/79–present), *Wall Street Journal* (1.1.79–present), and *Washington Post* (9/25/82–present). This index was searched via DIALOG Information Retrieval Service.

[3]Magazine Index™ is also produced by Information Access Company, and indexes more than 435 popular American and Canadian magazines, covering the years 1959–1970 and 1973–present. This index was searched via DIALOG Information Retrieval Service.

Any article that included "aspirin" or "salicylates" and "Reye's Syndrome" in the headlines, text, or descriptors was counted as one "warning" on aspirin and RS. Inspection of a large sample of medical and lay reports confirmed that virtually all mentioned the possible role of aspirin in causing some cases of RS. The previous indicators were not meant to represent all media, because radio and television were also powerful influences on attitudes and beliefs concerning the aspirin–RS link. However, previous studies have indicated that television coverage usually closely parallels newspaper coverage (Winsten, 1985).

ASSOCIATION OF MEDIA REPORTS AND RS INCIDENCE

Figure 15.1 indicates the trends in the number of medical citations, newspaper, and magazine reports and the incidence of RS from 1974 to 1989. Until 1980, very little medical reporting on this relation was observed, except for a small increase in the number of medical reports in 1976 coinciding with the initial FDA bulletin suggesting the possibility of a relation between aspirin use and Reye's syndrome. The number of medical citations increased suddenly from 4 in 1980, to 8 in 1981, to between 20 and 30 per

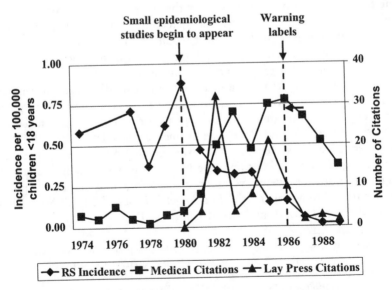

FIG. 15.1. Trend in number of medical and lay press citations on aspirin and Reye's syndrome, and in incidence of Reye's syndrome among children. Newspaper index limited to four continuously reporting national newspapers described in text.

year from 1982 to 1988. Interestingly, the trends in newspaper and magazine citations were similarly flat at close to zero during the years 1979–1980 and, like the medical reports, first peaked in 1982 at over 30 citations.

Although no formal content analyses of newspaper and magazine reports were conducted, a review of a sample of these stories conveyed several general messages that tended to recur in each time period. During 1982, the first major spike in lay media coverage, the stories covered government, industry, and consumer responses to the initial state studies, labeling delays, and pressures on FDA to take stronger actions. Other reports covered proposals for warning labels on aspirin containers, industry opposition to these proposals, and government announcements of the need for new federally sponsored studies. For example, under the headline "Warning Issued on Giving Aspirin to Children," a *New York Times* article gave a clear warning at the same time that it reported early government plans to deal with the issue: "The Government announced plans today to advise doctors and parents against using aspirin to treat children's chicken pox or flu-like symptoms because studies have linked aspirin to Reye's Syndrome, a rare but often fatal children's disease" (Hinds, 1982b, p. 29).

In a more vivid, personal, and compelling story told on the "CBS Evening News" (CBS, 1982), Dan Rather introduced the issue to millions of Americans:

Another childhood killer is called the Reye's Syndrome, which attacks the brain and liver. When children run high fevers, most parents reach for the aspirin bottle right away. But now there's some concern that when the fever is brought on by the flu or the chicken pox, aspirin can actually produce the Reye's Syndrome. This disease is not always fatal, but Meredith Vieira has the story of one little girl who did not survive and of the role aspirin might or might not have played.

In 1983, the media continued to cover the battles between the consumer groups and the aspirin industry, as well as to provide investigative reports on the reasons for halting labeling requirements. On November 30, 1983, the *New York Times* ran an article with the following headline: "U.S. Puts Off Aspirin Warnings." On the same day, the *Washington Post* ran its article on the decision of the Reagan administration to halt the distribution of 500,000 warning pamphlets in supermarkets (Atkinson, 1983). Although these reports often focused on controversies and accusations, they also continued to alert the public and professionals to the strong possibility that aspirin could cause Reye's syndrome in children.

The coverage during the second "pulse" of news reporting (winter/spring 1984–1985) focused on the results of the CDC pilot study linking aspirin with RS. Other articles covered Secretary Heckler's call for voluntary labeling of aspirin products, and charges that the aspirin industry attempted to slow the spread of warning information. One example is an article in the December 15, 1984, issue of the *New York Times*:

> WASHINGTON, DECEMBER 14—Some time in early spring, a federal regulation is expected to go into effect that will require all packages of aspirin or medicines containing aspirin to carry a warning about a childhood disease. . . . Dr. Sidney M. Wolfe, head of the Health Research Group . . . said his group had petitioned for it 3 1/2 years ago. . . . If mandatory warnings had been in place on all aspirin products several years ago, the toll of death and brain damage would have been much lower. (p. 21)

When the pilot study was completed, a January 9, 1985, *Los Angeles Times* story led with the following:

> WASHINGTON—A new federal study has found such a strong association between the use of aspirin in children and the often-fatal Reye's Syndrome that scientists are expected to call for an immediate warning against the drug's use on ill youngsters. (Cimons, 1985, p. 1)

A front-page report published by the *Boston Globe* on January 17, 1985, implied that the aspirin industry-financed organizations (e.g., the CCC) slowed the government's response to the aspirin–Reye's link:

> In 1981, federal health officials . . . concluded that there was a link between aspirin and Reye's syndrome.
>   But it was not until last week that the Secretary of Health and Human Services, Margaret M. Heckler, asked that aspirin products be labeled to warn against the danger to children. . . .
>   In the intervening three years, . . . the aspirin industry has repeatedly frustrated attempts by health officials to warn the public of the dangers, insisting—with some support in the medical community—that the studies were flawed. . . .
>   According to Globe interviews with medical and government officials involved in the controversy, the industry has used its access in the deregulation-minded political corridors of the Reagan Administration to help block mandated labeling of its product . . . (Robinson, 1985, pp. 1, 8)

Finally, at the end of this year, a series of articles discussed the required labeling to go into effect in 1986.

It is interesting to note that the initial cautionary statements made by the FDA in 1976, and the CDC in 1980, were not clearly associated with any changes in disease incidence (see Fig. 15.1). However, the broad media coverage stimulated by the publication of the three state studies, the CDC's committee report in 1982, and government and private statements on the issue, coincides with a sudden and consistent downward trend in Reye's syndrome incidence.

Before 1981, the yearly incidence of Reye's syndrome ranged between .3 and .9 cases per 100,000 population less than age 18. These swings in incidence rates have been found to correspond with high or low incidence rates for influenza A and varicella in the United States (Barrett et al., 1986). Coincident with the sudden increase in medical and lay press reports in 1982, the incidence rates of Reye's syndrome fell to their lowest level and remained stable for three consecutive years. The second peak in lay press reports in 1985 began a period of further decline, at the end of which incidence of RS had declined to only 25 cases per year (a rounded incidence rate of zero per 100,000).

CONCLUSIONS

Our analysis suggests that the professional and lay media were important communication channels in alerting health professionals and parents about the relation between aspirin and Reye's syndrome, particularly during the early years of the controversy (1981–1983). The nationwide decline in disease incidence coincided with declines in the use of aspirin for childhood fevers, and provides further evidence of the validity of the epidemiology studies reporting the aspirin–RS link.

Interestingly, in view of the fact that warning labels were the subject of the most controversy, by the time aspirin product labeling was required in 1986, a large part of the decline in RS incidence had already occurred. At the same time, it is likely that the continuing education and labeling changes have probably served to maintain and reinforce the new behaviors after the lay press discontinued its reporting of this topic in recent years.

How can the success of this largely media-based health communications campaign be explained, given the inconsistency of previous mass media campaigns in changing human behaviors? For example, the Stanford Three Communities Study (TCS) found that mass media alone was relatively unsuccessful in achieving long-term changes in cardiovascular risk behavior until it was supplemented with face-to-face counseling (Farquhar et al., 1977). Similarly, mixed results of media-only interventions have been reported for smoking behavior (Flay, 1987).

Part of the explanation of the success of the RS risk communications is the simplicity of the problem and desired behaviors in comparison to more complex habit-driven behaviors like smoking and exercise, which are resistant to change by information alone. Previous analyses have correlated increased pill and IUD discontinuation rates for 5 to 6 months following unfavorable news stories about these birth control methods, partly due to the availability of alternative techniques (Jones et al., 1980). In the present analysis, parents (or their physicians and pharmacists) simply switched from aspirin to acetaminophen (e.g., Tylenol) when treating symptoms of flu or chicken pox; the latter medication is equally available and inexpensive, so no barrier other than habit existed to its use. Given the nature and severity of the illness, simple information provision could induce change without the need for changing underlying motivations.

The aspirin–RS link was especially newsworthy given the combination of a rare, uncontrollable but serious disease affecting a highly valued, vulnerable population, linked to a common, over-the-counter product. The maneuverings of the aspirin industry, medical profession, government health agencies, and community watchdogs kept the issue alive for a number of years. This resulted in widespread and *repeated* exposure by television, radio, and print media, as well as in professional journals over a short period of time.

Another key ingredient was the comprehensiveness of the communications (Pasick & Wallack, 1988–1989), involving multiple communication channels to reach various target audiences (including parents, physicians, pharmacists, and other health professionals). These multiple levels of reinforcement increased the probability that a given parent, consulting with these professionals, would obtain advice to give acetaminophen instead of aspirin to children with flu or chicken pox. For example, Morris and Klimberg (1986) suggested that over half of 1,155 parents would only give medications recommended by their physician for treating these conditions.

This case study also focused on one potential obstacle to effective risk communication—counteradvertising by an industry-based health organization, the Committee for the Care of Children. In situations when conflicting health messages are communicated to the public, there is less likelihood of achieving desired behavioral objectives. In this case, however, the conflicting messages may not have affected public attitudes toward the credibility of government warning messages due to the energetic work of the HRG and others in strongly discouraging networks from airing industry-based PSAs.

Another important issue was the inability of government agencies to state warning messages conclusively and understandably at a time when there was still uncertainty about the scientific validity of the epidemiological studies. Combined with the pressures of legal suits from the aspirin industry, these factors led to some overly scientific and circumspect public communications. For example, the 1985 government radio and TV PSAs carried the following language: "A rare but serious childhood disease called Reye's Syndrome may develop in children who have chicken pox or flu. Although the cause of RS is not known, some studies suggest a possible association with medicines containing salicylate or aspirin. So it is prudent to consult a doctor before giving these medicines to children and teen-agers with chicken pox or flu."

Legal requirements to use words like "association" and "salicylate" may have reduced the comprehensibility of key messages and the resulting impact of the FDA messages. The lay press, on the other hand, were more flexible in publishing warning messages in less ambiguous terms. For example, one headline appearing in the *Washington Post* on February 11, 1982, stated, "Children With Chicken Pox, Flu Shouldn't Use Aspirin, U.S. Says." Similarly, on April 28, 1982, the *New York Times* headlined an article, "Aspirin Linked to a Children's Disease" (Hinds, 1982a).

Although the number of Reye's syndrome cases has declined dramatically, one issue has not been addressed adequately in the existing literature: To what extent did aspirin use decline in individuals who benefited substantially from this medication (e.g., juvenile rheumatoid arthritis, adults with angina, etc.) and who are not at risk for Reye's syndrome? In other words, did the media campaign selectively affect the target population (children and adolescents with chicken pox and flu), or did these effects spill over into other nontargeted conditions and groups? This must have represented a key concern of industry when responding to the pressure for warning campaigns and labeling changes. Potential public overreaction to a concern about the risks of aspirin use threatened sales of a product that was not only profitable, but of great clinical value. The evolving stance of the aspirin industry indicated both their acceptance of the validity of repeated epidemiologic findings, and also their confidence that aspirin use for other indications would not decline precipitously.

Is it possible to generalize from this experience to other types of public health warning campaigns? In situations when a common product could be causing a rare but devastating illness, where the behavior change message is simple and clear, and where safer and inexpensive alternative products are equally available and acceptable, it appears that a media-based educational campaign directed at both consumers and providers through multiple channels can facilitate substantial changes in behavior, even in the absence of product warnings or active industry acceptance. The sharp decline in U.S. sales of apples and apple juice following widespread publicity about the dangers of the chemical Alar (Shabecoff, 1989) provides a similar example of the power of the lay press in shaping consumer behavior. Consumer groups can and should play an important role in hastening public action and in keeping well-validated health product risks media-worthy.

In the absence of future controversies about the link between aspirin use and RS, which might precipitate more media coverage, it will be interesting to observe whether the new behaviors will continue, fostered only by professional and public memory of the issue and the continued presence of product warnings.

ACKNOWLEDGMENTS

This work was supported in part by grant HS-05554 from the Agency for Health Research and Quality, Rockville, Maryland; and subgrant CRTA-11 from the Pew Charitable Trusts/Management Sciences for Health, Boston. Reprinted with permission from *The Milbank Quarterly* (1992) 70(1), 155–182.

REFERENCES

Anonymous. (1982). Reye's syndrome–aspirin link: A bit stronger. *Journal of the American Medical Association, 247*(11), 1534–1539.

Arrowsmith, J. B., Kennedy, D. L., Kuritsky, J. N., & Faich, G. A. (1987). National patterns of aspirin use and Reye syndrome reporting, United States, 1980 to 1985. *Pediatrics, 79*(6), 858–863.

Atkinson, R. (1983, November 30). Pamphlets warning of aspirin risk temporarily reposing in warehouse. *Washington Post, 106*, p. A3.

Barrett, M. J., Hurwitz, E. S., Schonberger, L. B., & Rogers, M. F. (1986). Changing epidemiology of Reye syndrome in the United States. *Pediatrics, 77*, 598–602.

Bess, D. T., Helms, R. A., & Carter, C. A. (1986). Reye's syndrome and salicylates: Update for pharmacists. *American Pharmacy, NS26*(2), 16–17, 20–22.

Brown, A. K., Fikrig, S., & Finberg, L. (1983). Aspirin and Reye's syndrome. *Journal of Pediatrics, 102*(1), 157–158.

CBS [Columbia Broadcasting System]. (1982). Transcript of April 30 broadcast of interview by Dan Rather on subject of Reye's Syndrome.

Chayet, N. (1983, October 14). Letter to Edward Brandt from the files of Public Citizen/Health Research Group, p. 4.

Cimons, M. (1985, January 9). New study strongly links aspirin, Reye's syndrome. *Los Angeles Times*, pp. 1, 6.

Farquhar, J. W., Maccoby, N., Wood, P. D., Alexander, J. K., Breitrose, H., Brown, B. W., Jr., Haskell, W. L., McAlister, A. L., Meyer, A. J., Nash, J. D., & Stern, M. P. (1977). Community education for cardiovascular health. *Lancet, 1*, 1192–1195.

FDA. (1976, November). Reye's syndrome—Avoid antiemetics in children. *FDA Drug Bulletin, 6*(5).

FDA. (1982, August). Salicylate labeling may change because of Reye syndrome. *FDA Drug Bulletin, 12*(2), 9–10.

FDA. (1985, December). Reye syndrome update. *FDA Drug Bulletin, 15*, p. 40.

FDA. (1987, October). Study verifies association of aspirin with Reye syndrome. *FDA Drug Bulletin, 17*(3), 29.

Feinstein, A. R. (1988, December 2). Scientific standards in epidemiologic research for the menace of daily life. *Science, 242*(4883), 1257–1263.

Flay, B. R. (1987). Mass-media and smoking cessation: A critical review. *American Journal of Public Health, 77*, 153–160.

Fulginiti, V. (1982). Aspirin and Reye's syndrome. *Pediatrics, 69*(6), 810–812.

Glezen, W. P. (1982). Aspirin and Reye's syndrome [letter]. *American Journal of Diseases of Children, 136*, 971–972.

Green Sheet. (1982a, September 27). Reye's Syndrome education campaign mounted by HHS. *Weekly Pharmacy Reports*/"The Green Sheet," *31*(39), 2.

Green Sheet. (1982b, November 29). HHS' publicity campaign on Reye's syndrome/aspirin will continue. *Weekly Pharmacy Reports*/"The Green Sheet," *31*(48), 4.

Green Sheet. (1985, December 23). Aspirin/Reye's syndrome standard label warning. *Weekly Pharmacy Reports*/"The Green Sheet," *34*(51/52), 2–3.

Green Sheet. (1988, June 27). Reye syndrome final rule revises OTC aspirin label warning and makes it permanent. *Weekly Pharmacy Reports*/"The Green Sheet," *37*(26).

Halpin, T. J., Holtzbauer, F. J., Campbell, R. J., Hall, L. J., Correa-Villasenor, A., Lanese, R., Rice, J., & Hurwitz, E. S. (1982). Reye's syndrome and medication usage. *Journal of the American Medical Association, 248*, 687–691.

Hinds, M. D. (1982a, April 28). Aspirin linked to a children's disease. *New York Times, 131*, p. 20.

Hinds, M. D. (1982b, June 5). Warning issued on giving aspirin to children. *New York Times, 131*, p. 20.

Hurwitz, E. S. (1988). The changing epidemiology of RS in the U.S.: Further evidence for a public health success [editorial]. *Journal of the American Medical Association, 260*(1), 3178–3180.

Hurwitz, E. S., Barrett, M. J., Bregman, D., Gunn, W. J., Schonberger, L. B., Fairweather, W. R., Drage, J. S., LaMontagne, J. R., Kaslow, R. A., & Burlington, D. B. (1985). Public health service study on Reye's syndrome and medications: Report of the pilot phase. *New England Journal of Medicine, 313*(14), 849–857.

Hurwitz, E. S., Barrett, M. J., Bregman, D., Gunn, W. J., Pinsky, P., Schonberger, L. B., Drage, J. S., Kaslow, R. A., Burlington, B., Quinnan, G. V., LaMontagne, J. R., Fairweather, W. R., Dayton, D., & Dowdle, W. R. (1987). Public Health Service Study of Reye's Syndrome and Medications: Report of the Main Study. *Journal of the American Medical Association, 257*(14), 1905–1911.

Institute of Medicine, Division of Health Promotion and Disease Prevention. (1983, September). *The PHS study of the Reye syndrome: An initial evaluation.* Review of a protocol by the Committee on the Reye Syndrome and Medications. Washington, DC: National Academy Press.

Jones, E. F., Beniger, J. R., & Westoff, C. F. (1980). Pill and IUD discontinuation in the United States, 1970–1975: The influence of the media. *Family Planning Perspectives, 12*(6), 293–300.

Kolata, G. (1986a, October 18). Dispute over access to Reye's study data. *Science, 230*(4723), 297–298.

Kolata, G. (1986b, January 10). Reye's data to be turned over to company. *Science, 231*(4734), 112.

Kronholm, W. (1985, January 9). Health and Human Services Secretary Margaret Heckler urged the aspirin industry on Wednesday to voluntarily warn its customers of a possible link between aspirin and the sometimes-fatal children's disease known as Reye's syndrome. *Associated Press*, Washington, DC.

MMWR. (1980, November 7). Reye syndrome—Ohio, Michigan. *Morbidity and Mortality Weekly Reports, 29*(44), 532–539.

MMWR. (1989, May 12). Reye syndrome surveillance—United States, 1987 and 1988. *Morbidity and Mortality Weekly Reports, 38*(18), 325–327.

Morris, L. A., & Klimberg, R. (1986). A survey of aspirin use and Reye's syndrome among parents. *American Journal of Public Health, 76*(12), 1422–1424.

Murphy, D. H. (1984). Public health service initiates new study on aspirin–Reye link—But is it really necessary? *American Pharmacy, NS24*(3), 41–45.

Nelkin, D. (1989). Communicating technological risk: The social construction of risk perception. *Annual Review of Public Health, 10*, 95–113.

Pasick, R. J., & Wallack, L. (1988–1989). Mass media in health promotion: A compilation of expert opinion. *International Quarterly of Community Health Education, 9*(2), 89–110.

Pinsky, P. F., Hurwitz, E. S., Schonberger, L. B., & Gunn, W. J. (1988). Reye's syndrome and aspirin. *Journal of the American Medical Association, 260*(5), 657–681.

Public Citizen Health Research Group. (1982, March 12). Letter from HRG files.

Public Citizen/Health Research Group. (1983, November 29). News release No. 922.

Public Citizen/Health Research Group. (1984, November 5). Letters addressed to Frank Young, FDA commissioner and to news assignment editors. Document No. 982.

Public Citizen/Health Research Group. (1985a, January 9). Letter to Frank Young, FDA commissioner. Document No. 996.

Public Citizen/Health Research Group. (1985b, January 16). Letter to James C. Miller III, FTC chairman. Document No. 997.

Public Citizen/Health Research Group. (1985c, March 15). Testimony of Sidney M. Wolfe, M.D., before the House Health Subcommittee Hearings on HR1381 requiring warning labels, advertisements, and store signs concerning aspirin and Reye's Syndrome. Document No. 1005.

Rahwan, G. L., & Rahwan, R. G. (1986). Aspirin and Reye's syndrome: The change in prescribing habits of health professionals. *Drug Intelligence and Clinical Pharmacy, 20*(2), 143–145.

Reye, R. D. K., Morgan, G., & Baral, J. (1963, October 12). Encephalopathy and fatty degeneration of the viscera—A disease entity in childhood. *Lancet*, pp. 749–752.

Robertson, L. S., Kelley, A. B., O'Neill, B., Wixom, C. W., Eiswirth, R. S., & Haddon, W., Jr. (1974). A controlled study of the effect of television messages on safety belt use. *American Journal of Public Health, 64*, 1071–1080.

Robinson, W. V. (1985, January 17). Aspirin industry slowed US on Reye's peril, officials say. *Boston Globe*, pp. 1 and 8.

Shabecoff, P. (1989, May 16). Apple industry says it will end use of chemical: Consumers' reaction to risks of alar is cited. *New York Times, 138*, pp. 1, 19.

Singer, E., & Endreny, P. (1987). Reporting hazards: Their benefits and costs. *Journal of Communication, 37*(3), 10–26.

Starko, K. M., Ray, C. G., Dominguez, L. B., Stromberg, W. L., & Woodall, D. F. (1980). Reye's syndrome and salicylate use. *Pediatrics, 66*, 859–864.

Trauner, D. A. (1982). Reye's syndrome. *Current Problems in Pediatrics, 12*(7), 8–9.

Trauner, D. A. (1984). Reye's syndrome. *Western Journal of Medicine, 141*, 206–209.

U.S. Department of Health and Human Services. (1982, September 20 & November 18). HHS news [press release].

U.S. Puts Off Aspirin Warnings. (1983, November 30). *New York Times, 133*, p. 11.

Vastagh, G. F. (1985, August 27). Letter from Plough, Inc. director of clinical affairs to Arnold Relman, p. 1

Waldman, R. J., Hall, W. N., McGee, H., & Van Amburg, G. (1982). Aspirin as a risk factor in Reye's syndrome. *Journal of the American Medical Association, 247*, 3089–3094.

Warner, K. E. (1987). Television and health education: Stay tuned [editorial]. *American Journal of Public Health, 77*(2), 140–142.

Wilson, J. T., & Brown, R. D. (1982). Reye syndrome and aspirin use: The role of prodromal illness severity in the assessment of relative risk. *Pediatrics, 69*(6), 822–825.

Winsten, J. A. (1985). Science and the media: The boundaries of truth. *Health Affairs, 4*(1), 5–22.

16

REFLECTIONS ON COMMUNITY HEALTH CAMPAIGNS: SECULAR TRENDS AND THE CAPACITY TO EFFECT CHANGE

Kasisomayajula Viswanath
National Cancer Institute

John R. Finnegan, Jr.
University of Minnesota

Summarizing the history of public campaigns a decade ago, Rogers and Storey (1987) proposed that researchers' experience could be described in three developmental periods. The first was the minimal effects era (1940s–1950s) distinguished by some spectacular campaign failures and recognition of the limited and often indirect role of mass media in generating campaign effects. This era nevertheless pointed toward a more sophisticated understanding of campaign effects and how to achieve them strategically and tactically (Cartwright, 1949, 1954; Hyman & Sheatsley, 1947; Starr & Hughes, 1950).[1]

The second period, the 1960s and 1970s, was characterized as the "campaigns CAN succeed" era. Here, some of the lessons of the previous era were applied successfully, especially in health campaign settings. For example, the North Karelia (Finland) Study's and the Stanford Three-City Project's achievement of significant cardiovascular behavior and risk factor

---

[1]The Rogers and Storey description of campaign effects parallels how "media effects" have been conceived over time. The so-called limited effects era of media research was subsequently followed in the 1960s by an emphasis on cognitive outcomes and recognition that media can have powerful effects on such outcomes. However, some critics have argued that the proponents of limited effects have understated the media effects and that later scholars may have overinterpreted the qualified and careful conclusions of research in 1940s and 1950s. For a discussion, see Becker, McCombs, and McLeod (1975); Chaffee and Hocheimer (1985); and Gitlin (1978).

change as part of quasi-experimental community designs suggested a bright future for campaigns that employed multiple intervention strategies during an extended period of time (Maccoby, Farquhar, Wood, & Alexander, 1977; Puska, Tuomilehto, Nissinen, & Vartainen, 1995; Stern, Farquhar, Maccoby, & Russell, 1976).

Rogers and Storey described the third era, the 1980s, as one of "moderate effects." During this period, health campaigns especially flourished, continuing to grow more sophisticated in their application of theory and planning frameworks, and in their use of multiple-strategy, community-based campaigns. Although the period was notable for some major campaign failures, there were notable successes as well, both in the United States and internationally.

Since the Rogers and Storey analysis first appeared, has a fourth era begun? If so, should the period since 1987 be characterized as one of reflection on the capacity to affect change through health campaigns? This has been driven by the publication of the results of the nation's three largest heart disease prevention community trials at Stanford, Minnesota, and Pawtucket; some later generation studies; and by the experience of HIV/AIDS prevention. This period has been characterized by deep reflection on the capacity of campaigns to achieve population behavior change. This period has been moving toward reconsideration of traditional campaign models driven by reassessments of the following factors:

- "secular" trends in population health behavior change and related community variables
- expansion of the communication system, especially since the 1980s
- expectations by public health campaign planners of achievable population behavior change
- the limits of traditional campaign evaluation models to measure and detect effects differences
- the failure of low socioeconomic status (SES) groups to benefit equally from secular change in heart disease patterns compared to higher SES groups
- public health efforts to explore intervention models where outcomes are not individual behavior change per se, but change in public policy with the potential to affect population behavior; and widespread dissemination of effective behavior change strategies and programs

SECULAR TRENDS AND HEART DISEASE CAMPAIGNS

The first generation of major American community trials was funded by the National Heart, Lung and Blood Institute (NHLBI) beginning in the late 1970s to test the hypothesis that community-based, multiple strategy public health campaigns could reduce cardiovascular disease risk in whole communities (Blackburn, 1981; Maccoby & Farquhar, 1975). These studies followed on the initial successes of the North Karelia (Finland), Stanford (California) Three-City, and North Coast (Australia) projects, which demonstrated that population-based community campaigns could be effective in reducing heart disease risk and mortality (Egger, Fitzgerald, & Frape, 1983; Maccoby et al., 1977; Salonen, Puska, & Kottke, 1981).

Design characteristics of the first generation of American trials including the Minnesota Heart Health Program (MHHP), the Stanford Five-City Project, and the Pawtucket (Rhode Island) Heart Health Program are displayed in Table 16.1. The studies were similar in their quasi-experimental controlled designs that made use of baseline surveys and multiple follow-up cohort (panel) and cross-sectional surveys. Intervention strategies were also similar. Each utilized multiple approaches, including a wide range of community organization, interpersonal, group, mass media, and small media strategies, during an intervention period of between 5 and 7 years (Farquhar, Fortmann, Maccoby, et al., 1985; Jacobs et al., 1986; Mittelmark et al., 1986).

Results of these studies on heart disease risk factors were reported between 1990 and 1995. Although each study showed some significant but modest risk factor-specific effects (Table 16.1), these were attenuated by strong secular changes in reference communities (Carleton et al., 1995; Farquhar et al., 1990; Luepker et al., 1994). That is, the studies were frequently able to observe significant change in intervention communities for a time in selected risk factors, but secular trends in reference communities

TABLE 16.1
Study Design Characteristics of Early American
Community Trials in Heart Disease Prevention

Characteristics	Stanford	Minnesota	Pawtucket
Funding period	1978–1996	1980–1993	1980–1996
Locale	CA	MN, ND, SD	RI, MA
Communities	5	6	2
Treatment	2	3	1
Baseline surveys	1	2–4	1
Follow-up cross-sectional surveys	3	4–5	4
Follow-up cohort surveys (panels)	3	3	4
Intervention period	1980–1986	1981–1989	1984–1991
Years of intervention in treatment communities	5	5–6	7
Significant risk factor changes (p < .05)	Body Mass Index Diastolic BP (women)	Smoking prevalence (women in treatment cohort)	Body Mass Index
Risk factor results published	1990	1994	1995

often closed the gaps by campaigns' end (Luepker et al., 1994). A joint analysis by Winkleby, Feldman, and D. M. Murray (1997) pooled risk factor data from the three trials and confirmed the same phenomenon—modest risk factor changes attenuated by unexpectedly strong secular trends that frequently eliminated significant differences by the studies' close.

Paradoxically, many strategy-specific, experimental substudies nested within the larger community trials demonstrated strong effects in changing heart disease risk behaviors and factors (Fortmann et al., 1995; Luepker et al., 1994; Mittelmark, Hunt, Heath, & Schmid, 1993). In Minnesota, for example, several controlled substudies showed significant effects on cardiovascular disease (CVD) related behavior and risk factors. Murray and colleagues (Murray, Luepker, Pirie, & Grimm, 1986), in a controlled study of the effects of a risk factor screening center, demonstrated significant change in blood cholesterol, diastolic blood pressure, resting heart rate, and the use of blood pressure medication. They later demonstrated the effectiveness of direct mail at two levels of exposure compared to a control group in encouraging blood pressure follow-up with a physician, and in several other related behaviors.

Perry, Kelder, D. M. Murray, and Klepp (1992) demonstrated the effectiveness of school-based programs combined with a community campaign on the smoking, nutrition, and physical activity behavior of adolescents. Among the most impressive findings were that high school seniors (tracked from sixth grade) were 40% less likely to be smoking in the intervention community compared to their counterparts in the reference community (the effect was even greater for young women). There were also significant changes in physical activity and eating patterns.

How does one account for the results of these community trials and what insights may be gained into the capacity of campaigns to effect change?

The principal argument has several parts as follows:

1. Significant secular change in heart disease mortality and risk factors has been occurring in the United States since the early 1960s and accelerated sharply during the period of the large community trials due to improvements in clinical diagnoses and treatment of people with existing heart disease, and increasing adoption of preventive behaviors by the public.

2. This accelerated change was propelled in part by a dramatic increase in heart disease news coverage by the mass media, but also because of changes in the U.S. communication system, expanding the number of television and other information channels through which news disseminates.

3. Increases in heart disease treatment and prevention news coverage were stimulated by the influential role of federal and state government agencies, private health groups, public health advocates, and scientists in placing

heart disease high on the media's, and therefore the public's, agenda of important health issues. This occurred through the funding, conduct, and reporting of heart disease research, the creation of scientific consensus conference documents, treatment guidelines, and other policies.

4. The traditional campaign evaluation models of the large American community trials were framed in expectation of relatively little change in reference communities. That is, the power to detect difference hinged in part on relatively stable reference community trends. In a highly dynamic secular trend, the models lacked power to detect difference as a function of the limited number of assigned units (communities); and the limited number of measurement points over time (community-by-year means).

5. The campaign intervention models of the large American community trials were framed also in the expectation of relatively little change in reference communities, especially in exposure to heart disease prevention information and programs. They did not anticipate either major changes in community media systems or the increased dissemination of heart disease prevention news, information, and programming, and in any case were unable to sustain a significant difference in exposure over time.

SECULAR TRENDS IN CVD MORTALITY AND RISK FACTORS

Evidence of secular change in heart disease mortality and risk factor levels is provided in Figs. 16.1 and 16.2. Figure 16.1 displays ischemic heart disease mortality in the United States as consecutive, 5-year adjusted rates among men and women from 1955 through 1989. The data show that heart disease peaked in the United States in the early 1960s and has been declining since that time. For example, analyses performed by the NHLBI have shown that heart attack mortality alone reached a peak in 1963. And, by 1992, it had declined by 57%, a reduction of some 2% to 3% annually (NHLBI, 1994).

A number of studies have sought to locate the causes of this remarkable decline. For example, investigators have hypothesized regarding heart attack mortality that there may be both lower incidence of new events and improved survival due to changes in medical and emergency treatment of heart attacks. Studies to date suggest a combined effect is responsible (NHLBI, 1994). Regarding declines in heart disease more generally, investigators have hypothesized that they may be due to improved clinical diagnoses and treatment, but also to population changes in preventive behavior. Figure 16.2, for example, shows trends in U.S. population prevalence from 1962 to 1993 in three key risk factors directly linked to atherosclerotic processes: hypertension, high blood cholesterol, and cigarette

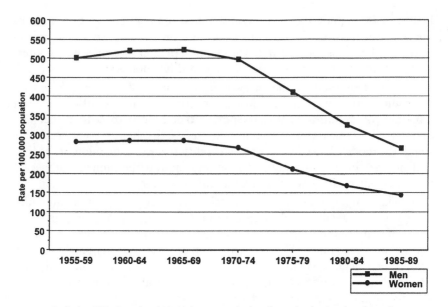

Includes ICD-9 codes 410-414; rates calculated on the basis of at least 2 year's data for each 5-year period. From *International Mortality Chartbook*, 1955–1991. National Center For Health Statistics, Centers For Disease Control, Atlanta, GA.

FIG. 16.1. Age-adjusted 5-year mortality rates for ischemic heart disease in the United States, 1955–1989.

smoking. The general trend is a decline in population prevalence of the three risk factors over the past 30 years. Between 1965 and 1994, smoking among U.S. adults age 18 and older declined from about 43% to about 25%. Similarly, from 1962 through 1991, persons with high blood cholesterol declined from about 32% to 21%. Hypertension, however, showed a slightly different pattern. In 1962, U.S. population prevalence of hypertension was about 37%. This actually rose slightly through 1980 to about 40% before a steep decline set in to reach less than 25% in 1991.

Hunink and colleagues (1997) reviewed U.S. data from 1980 to 1990 to estimate the contribution to declining heart disease mortality of improved risk factor levels as well as improvements in medical treatment. The study developed a computer simulation to model the U.S. population between age 35 and 84 to forecast mortality and risk factor trends. They found in part that actual coronary mortality in 1990 was about 34% lower than would be predicted if coronary risk factor levels, case fatality, and event rates had remained the same as in 1980 (among those with and without diagnosed heart disease). When secular changes in these factors were included in the model, coronary mortality in 1990 was predicted to within

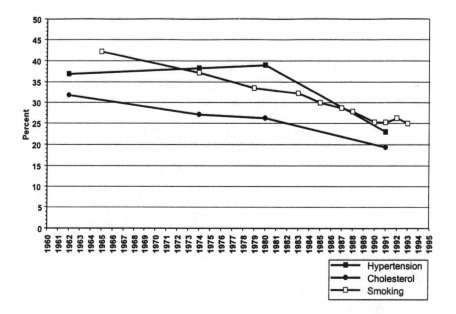

*Hypertension ≥ 140/90 mmHg (20–74 years old; age adjusted), High cholesterol ≥ 200 mg/dl (20–74 years old; age adjusted), Smoking = current smokers (≥ 18 years old; age adjusted). From National Center for Health Statistics (CDC).

FIG. 16.2. Trends in U.S. population prevalence of hypertension, high blood cholesterol, and cigarette smoking, 1962–1993.

3% of the observed mortality. The study also concluded that about 50% of the decline in heart disease mortality between 1980 and 1990 could be explained by primary and secondary risk factor reduction. More than 70% of the decline in mortality occurred among people with diagnosed heart disease, suggesting the effects of risk factor and behavior change, and improved clinical treatment and management. About 25% of the decline was explained by primary prevention, that is, risk factor behavior change among persons without diagnosed heart disease.

PUBLIC OPINION AND MEDIA PUBLICITY ABOUT HEART DISEASE

Has media publicity about heart disease played a role in propelling these secular trends in the United States generally and in affecting the results of the community trials in particular? Several theoretical points about the role of the mass media and several observations about population exposure to heart disease information suggest that it has had an effect.

From a theoretical perspective, investigators have noted that the mass media play a significant role in establishing the public agenda of important issues (Hilgartner & Bosk, 1988; McCombs & Shaw, 1977). Strong media attention to an issue tends to increase or at least reinforce the salience of an issue as perceived by the public. The media's role in public discourse extends beyond attention to, and amplification of, a particular issue, to also defining how to think about an issue and why an issue is a "social problem" (Blumer, 1971; Entman, 1993; Faupel, Bailey, & Griffin, 1991; Mauss, 1975). The cumulative effect of long-term media attention to an issue may eventually affect changes in public knowledge and perceptions as some dimensions of an issue become nearly universally accepted (Viswanath, Finnegan, Hannan, & Luepker, 1991). For example, Donohue, Olien, and Tichenor (1990) examined U.S. public opinion about the health effects of smoking from 1954 through 1981. In a national Gallup Poll conducted in 1954, about 41% of American adults believed that smoking was a cause of lung cancer. By 1981, this had increased to about 83% (Table 16.2) and by 1987 to about 89%. Similarly, polls have found that between 1964 and 1987, the belief among U.S. adults that smoking causes heart disease increased from 40% to 77%.

Public opinion and knowledge of other aspects of heart disease risk have also changed. Table 16.3, for example, presents results of U.S. public opinion surveys on several heart disease-related issues. From 1983 to 1995, adults reporting they had ever heard of high blood cholesterol rose from 77% to 93%. Knowledge of the ideal cholesterol level rose from about 16% in 1986 to about 69% in 1995. In 1983, about 35% of adults reported having their blood cholesterol checked. This increased to 75% by 1995. Polls from 1985 through 1992 show that a fairly steady 85% of the adult population reported having had their blood pressure checked at least once per year, with about 56% reporting more than one blood pressure check per year during the same period.

What is the evidence for media attention to the issue of heart disease? Figure 16.3 shows media news coverage of heart disease for the period from 1980 to 1992 in eight major market U.S. daily newspapers and three major television networks. The period was selected because it coincided with the period of most intense intervention in the three American community trials. The newspapers were selected based on the availability of indexes during the entire period and also to include major newspapers from across the country. The data showed that whereas heart disease is a "repertoire" health story for the news media (i.e., a story that receives more or less constant attention at some average level of coverage), there were large spikes in news coverage that occurred from about the third quarter of 1982 through the first quarter of 1988, a period of about 5 years. A major factor in this news coverage was the reporting of results from major trials

TABLE 16.2
Public Opinion About Smoking and Disease, 1954–1987

Question	Survey, Year	All Adults "Yes" (%)	Low Education "Yes" (%)	Medium Education "Yes" (%)	High Education "Yes" (%)
Smoking causes lung cancer	Gallup, 1954	41%	39.9%	40.2%	48.9%
	Gallup, 1957	50%	45.1%	45.8%	60.4%
	AUTS, 1964	66%	—	—	—
	AUTS, 1966	66%	—	—	—
	Gallup, 1969	71%	64.3%	69.7%	79.8%
	Gallup, 1971	71%	—	—	—
	Gallup, 1977	81%	71.9%	79.8%	91.0%
	Gallup, 1981	83%	72.7%	84.1%	91.7%
	AUTS, 1986	92%	—	—	—
	Gallup, 1987	87%	—	—	—
	NHIS, 1987	89%	—	—	—

(Continued)

TABLE 16.2
(Continued)

Question	Survey, Year	All Adults "Yes" (%)	Low Education "Yes" (%)	Medium Education "Yes" (%)	High Education "Yes" (%)
Smoking causes heart disease	AUTS, 1964	40%	—	—	—
	AUTS, 1966	42%	—	—	—
	Gallup, 1969	54%	56.5%	56.5%	68.5%
	Gallup, 1977	68%	61.1%	67.7%	73.6%
	Gallup, 1978	68%	—	—	—
	Gallup, 1981	74%	64.2%	73.6%	86.6%
	NHIS, 1985	90%	—	—	—
	AUTS, 1986	78%	—	—	—
	NHIS, 1987	77%	—	—	—
Smoking causes cancer and heart disease	Harris, 1966	36%	—	—	—
	Harris, 1969	50%	—	—	—
	Harris, 1974	74%	—	—	—
	Harris, 1975	74%	—	—	—
	Harris, 1986	88%	—	—	—

Note. Data from U.S. Surgeon General (1989). Reducing the health consequences of smoking: 25 years of progress; G. A. Donohue, C. N. Olien, and P. J. Tichenor (1990, May 19). *Knowledge gaps and smoking behavior.* Paper presented to the annual conference of the American Association for Public Opinion Research, Lancaster, PA; and Harris Poll collection, Institute For Research in Social Science (IRSS), University of North Carolina at Chapel Hill.

TABLE 16.3
Public Opinion and Self-Reported Behavior
About Blood Pressure and Blood Cholesterol

Question	Survey, Year	All Adults "Yes" (%)
Ever heard of high blood cho-	NCEP, 1983	77%
lesterol?	NCEP, 1986	81%
	NCEP, 1990	95%
	NCEP, 1995	93%
Know that cholesterol below	NCEP, 1983	—
200 mg/dl is desirable?	NCEP, 1986	16%
	NCEP, 1990	65%
	NCEP, 1995	69%
Had cholesterol checked?	NCEP, 1983	35%
	NCEP, 1986	46%
	NCEP, 1990	65%
	NCEP, 1995	75%
Have blood pressure checked	Harris, 1985	86%
at least once per year?	Harris, 1986	84%
	Harris, 1987	84%
	Harris, 1988	82%
	Harris, 1989	84%
	Harris, 1991	84%
	Harris, 1992	85%
Have blood pressure checked	Harris, 1985	57%
more than once per year?	Harris, 1986	55%
	Harris, 1987	57%
	Harris, 1988	54%
	Harris, 1989	54%
	Harris, 1991	56%
	Harris, 1992	56%

Note. Data from National Cholesterol Education Program (NCEP), National Institutes of Health (1995); Harris Poll collection, Institute For Research in Social Science (IRSS), University of North Carolina at Chapel Hill.

and research studies, including the Multiple Risk Factor Intervention Trial (MRFIT), the Hypertension Prevention Trial (HPT), the Lipid Research Trial (LRT), the Framingham Study, the Coronary Primary Prevention Trial (CPPT), and many other group and clinical studies and consensus conference results that appeared in medical journals or were reported at major national meetings. The major spikes in news coverage of heart disease (sometimes representing many-fold increases in coverage over usual levels) occurred during the period of most intense intervention in the three American trials that themselves generated both local and national news coverage. Along these lines, Finnegan, Viswanath, Kahn, and Hannan (1993) reported that surveys of the MHHP reference communities showed significant increases from 1980 through 1990 in the public's reporting of

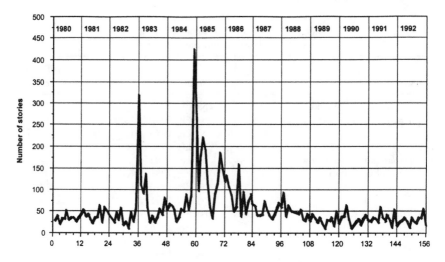

FIG. 16.3.   Heart disease news coverage in 8 major-market newspapers and
3 TV networks, 1980–1992. Data from *New York Times, Washington Post,
Detroit Free Press, Chicago Tribune, New Orleans Times-Picayune, St. Louis
Post-Dispatch, LA Times, San Franciso Chronicle,* ABC, CBS, NBC.

the number of sources from which they could recall receiving heart disease
information.

CHANGES IN MEDIA INFRASTRUCTURE

At the same time that news coverage of heart disease showed temporal
spikes, profound changes in the nation's communication infrastructure
were also occurring (and continue to occur). The availability of consumer
satellite television receivers, consumer videocassette recorders (VCRs), and
cable television systems increased dramatically during the period after
1980. For example, cable television increased exponentially from about
4,000 systems in 1980 to about 12,000 systems nationwide in 1992
(*Broadcasting & Cable Yearbook*, 1994). Whereas cable systems originated in the 1950s to rebroadcast local television signals to hard-to-reach
areas, in the 1980s they expanded across the country to carry dozens of
channels to more than 6 of 10 U.S. households. The expansion of this capacity coincided with the development of national news and entertainment
channels now estimated to reach some 63% of American households by
cable alone (*Broadcasting & Cable Yearbook*, 1996). Finnegan et al.
(1993) reported that the communities of the MHHP entered the study in
1980 with small cable television systems (12 local channels or fewer) or

none at all. By the close of the intervention almost 10 years later, each of the six communities possessed cable systems of 30 or more channels, including most of the available national news and entertainment channels. The effect of this growth in communication infrastructure was that even relatively small communities received the same cable programming as large metropolitan communities. Finnegan and colleagues (1993) also discussed the effect of this change on the public's reporting of media sources of heart disease information in the MHHP reference communities. They found that irrespective of community size (small town, regional city, metropolitan area suburb), there was a significant increase over time in reporting television as a source of heart disease information. Thus, not only was there an increase in heart disease news coverage during the period, there was also an increase in the number of media channels with the potential to disseminate such information.

SETTING THE MEDIA'S AGENDA

Media message production research notes that although the mass media may act independently at times in the generation of news, routine news gathering and production processes endow news sources with a central role in influencing the media's agenda of important issues in the first place (Finnegan & Viswanath, 1997; Gandy, 1982; Sigal, 1973). News sources typically include representatives of important, established social institutions, organizations, and groups seeking to mobilize media and therefore public attention to issues they regard as important (Hilgartner & Bosk, 1988). Studies have demonstrated that much—if not most—news content can be traced to the organized activity of various interests seeking to increase the importance of an issue on the public agenda as part of their efforts to guide social change (Shoemaker & Reese, 1991). Research in this vein also notes that news sources not only help to define important issues for the media, but also help to define the "framework" of meaning in which the issue is reported (Entman, 1993).

Increased news coverage of heart disease was likely propelled by the influential role of medical and public health institutions, including government agencies, the network of scientist-researchers, and public health advocacy groups seeking to identify heart disease as a national problem, and, through their influence, to channel public attention, resources, and power to reduce its impact. Some sense of this considerable, guided social change activity can be gleaned from Fig. 16.4. Although by no means comprehensive, it charts population prevalence changes in three key heart disease risk factors (smoking, hypertension, and high blood cholesterol) contrasted

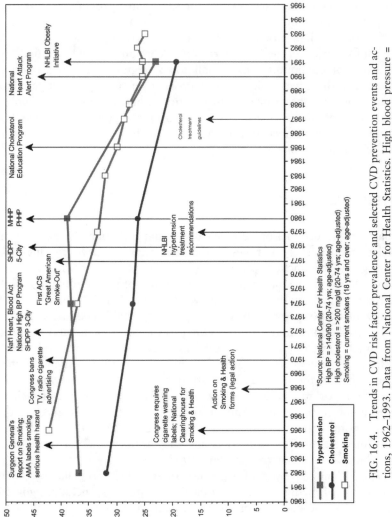

FIG. 16.4. Trends in CVD risk factor prevalence and selected CVD prevention events and actions, 1962–1993. Data from National Center for Health Statistics. High blood pressure = >140/90 (20–74 years, age adjusted). High cholesterol = >200 mg/dl (20–74 years, age adjusted). Smoking = current smokers (18 years and older, age adjusted).

with the occurrence of important public policy events and activities aimed at reducing the impact of heart disease.

Take the issue of smoking, for example. Researchers began to note a link between smoking and its damaging effects to health prior to World War II, and the American Medical Association (AMA) itself publicized the growing body of scientific evidence against smoking in 1954. However, it was not until 1964, with the publication of the U.S. surgeon general's first report on smoking and health that the issue began to climb in importance on the national agenda of health issues. The surgeon general's report was a benchmark of growing consensus among government agencies, researchers, and health advocacy and professional groups, including the AMA, the American Heart Association (AHA), the American Lung Association (ALA) and the American Cancer Society (ACS), that smoking was a menace to the nation's health that needed to be reduced. As Fig. 16.4 indicates, this report was shortly followed by public policy requiring warning labels on cigarette packages and advertising; the establishment of a National Clearinghouse for Smoking and Health, an organization emphasizing legal action against smoking; and the banning of cigarette advertising on radio and television. National education efforts, such as the ACS's Great American Smokeout, soon followed and have continued as part of this guided social change effort ever since.

Similarly, growing scientific and policy consensus about the importance of reducing high blood pressure resulted in congressional passage of the National Heart, Blood, Vessel, Lung and Blood Act in 1972. This united government and public and private health agencies in expanding the authority of the National Heart, Lung and Blood Institute (NHLBI, part of the National Institutes of Health). It established the National High Blood Pressure Education Program (NHBPEP) and poured millions of federal dollars into hypertension research and public and professional education (NHBPEP, 1992). State coalitions also developed and were funded for local hypertension detection and treatment efforts. Many studies and trials in the 1970s demonstrated the benefits of reducing blood pressure, often through the use of newly developed drugs. In 1979, these led to the development of consensus conference recommendations designed to accelerate adoption of more effective hypertension treatment and prevention protocols in the medical community. These activities coincided with a steady decrease in hypertension since 1980 (Fig. 16.4).

Scientists since before World War II have studied the role of blood lipids and diet in the development of heart disease. However, consensus about its contribution did not coalesce into clear policy directions until the mid-1980s following dramatic results of large cholesterol-lowering drug trials such as the Coronary Primary Prevention Trial (CPPT) and others. Based on this research, the National Cholesterol Education Program was established by the NHLBI in 1985, and was followed in 1987 by consensus conference guidelines on treatment and prevention to accelerate uptake of new diagnosis and treatment protocols in the medical community.

Thus, policy advocacy activity by the network of government agencies, scientists, and public health advocates not only generated substantial media attention, it also led to the expansion of guided social change capacity for the prevention of heart disease, an important lesson for health communication campaigns (Viswanath & Finnegan, 1998). This can be seen in policy advocacy activities that expanded the NHLBI to focus on hypertension and other heart disease risk factors through increased research and many subsequent national public and professional education programs. Private organizations, such as the American Heart Association (AHA), expanded their research and public and professional education enterprises as well.

There is also evidence that the media themselves responded to increased health policy and research activity (and reader interest) by expanding their capacity to report health news. An increasing number of newspapers, for example, reported establishing special health, medicine, and science news sections during the 1980s and also hired specialist reporters (Locke, 1984).

EFFECT ON THE COMMUNITY TRIALS: DESIGN AND EFFECTS EXPECTATIONS

The American community trials occurred in this context of an increasingly influential scientific and public health enterprise that generated widespread dissemination of heart disease information propelled in part by expansion of the media system itself. The American community trials were a natural incremental outgrowth of heart disease prevention research strategies increasingly focusing on population health. They were also themselves part of the larger secular trend.

However, the designs of American community trials in heart disease prevention did not anticipate dynamic secular trends in information dissemination into reference communities, let alone major secular changes in risk factor behavior and mortality. This had two effects. First, intervention efforts were unable to sustain significant exposure over time to exceed exposure trends in reference communities. Second, the studies' evaluation designs were less able to detect intervention-reference differences in the face of dynamic secular trends.

For example, Fig. 16.5 shows patterns of exposure to heart disease prevention information and programs in the MHHP communities drawn from cross-sectional surveys in each MHHP community. Data were based on questions framed so that respondents in both intervention and reference communities could indicate to what heart disease prevention programs and information they had been exposed at each time point. The data show an

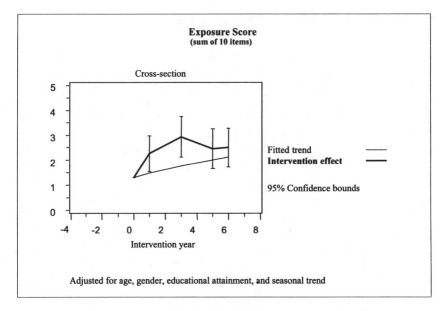

FIG. 16.5.   Exposure to heart disease prevention messages and programs in
the Minnesota Heart Health Program, 1980–1989.

increasing secular trend in such exposure over the 5 years of active intervention in the MHHP. Intervention communities were able to exceed the
trend in the reference communities at a statistically significant level only
through year 3 of the intervention. By years 5 and 6, the difference in exposure between intervention and reference communities was not statistically significant.

Luepker and his colleagues (1994) and D. M. Murray (1997) suggested
that in the face of dynamic secular trends, the MHHP and other American
trials faced limits in their evaluation to detect differences in outcomes. D.
M. Murray (1997) suggested that the American trials' designs were likely
underpowered to detect anything less than a medium to large effect difference between intervention and reference communities.

Along these same lines, Fishbein (1996) noted that public health campaigns using controlled designs are usually powered to detect medium to
large effect differences in outcomes (on the order of a half to a full standard deviation, or a 20%–60% change in a proportion). In comparison to
effect sizes commonly achievable and regarded as successful in the commercial realm (e.g., a 1%–2% increase in market share), he argued that
public health expectations of achievable behavior change are unrealistic
and unwarranted. Designs that will detect only medium to large effect sizes
distort any sense of "substantively meaningful" and realistically achievable
changes in health outcomes of 5% to 10%.

DIFFERENTIAL IMPACT OF SECULAR TRENDS

Secular trends in heart disease prevention from 1980 to 1992 included large amounts of media-generated news and information that might have contributed to the modest outcomes detected by the American community trials. Yet, it is important to point out that the impact of secular trends is differential across population subgroups, as has been identified repeatedly by several scholars (Viswanath & Finnegan, 1996). In particular, the primary beneficiaries of such changes, in general, are members of higher socioeconomic status compared to the members of lower socioeconomic status. Such differential impact in the realm of public health was documented on several risk factors, including smoking (Donohue, Olien, & Tichenor, 1990; Millar, 1996), number and variety of sources of CVD information (Finnegan et al., 1993), campaign effects (Davis, Winkleby, & Farquhar, 1995), and improvement in heart disease outcomes (Anderson, Sorlie, Backlund, Johnson, & Kaplan, 1997; Iribarren, Luepker, McGovern, Arnett, & Blackburn, 1997; McDonough, Duncan, Williams, & House, 1997; Sorlie, Backlund, & Keller, 1995; Smith, Wentworth, Neaton, R. Stamler, & J. Stamler, 1996; Williams & Collins, 1995; Winkleby, 1997; Winkleby, Jatulis, Frank, & Fortmann, 1992). Data from various studies suggest that the benefits of changes in the environment facilitating healthy behavior accrue differentially among population subgroups with those from higher social class usually benefiting the most.

SUMMARY

In summary, although the discrete data provided in support of the propositions herein do not make direct causal linkages, they do suggest that it is necessary to account for the totality of the environment and its influences on health behavior. In conceptualizing campaign effects, therefore, effects must be thought of in terms of the larger social context in which they may occur. Within such an environment, campaigns are thought to be one factor contributing to changes in risk behavior. Media coverage may influence public knowledge; efforts of social groups and scientists may influence public policy and media coverage; and media coverage may also influence public policy and vice versa, all of which may influence public knowledge leading to changes in health behavior. Data have been provided that suggest that each of these elements co-occurred and acted on public behavior in the MHHP. For example, Fig. 16.3 showed that media coverage of risk factors had been a steady repertoire for journalists and even increased during 1981–1986, which corresponds with a decrease in hypertension and cholesterol (Figs. 16.2, 16.4), and an increase in the percentage of people who were aware of high cholesterol and people who had their cholesterol checked (Table 16.3). Similarly, increased activity in public and policy arenas coincided with decreases in risk factors such as smoking (Fig. 16.4). The surgeon general's report on smoking, followed by other activities such as warning labels and a ban on cigarette advertising on electronic media, correlated with the declining proportion of smokers in the population (Fig. 16.2). At the same time, public knowledge about the harmful effects of smoking increased steadily (Table 16.2). The co-occurrence of these factors fostered an atmosphere that encouraged changes in risk behavior, which led to the results that were found.

CONCLUSIONS

The outcomes of the American community trials in heart disease prevention have theoretical and methodological ramifications. On a theoretical level, campaign planners, evaluators, and other stakeholders should consider expanding their definition of campaign effects; take into consideration the social and secular context of campaigns; and include variables that potentially impede campaign effects among all social groups. Methodologically, campaign designs should have the power to detect smaller or even subtle shifts in the dependent variables.

Secular trends in heart disease prevention and health promotion may be interpreted as a dynamic process of open social systems. Community-based campaigns are conducted in field settings that allow little or no control over the secular environment. In such open systems, secular trends are composed and generated by two interrelated forces: the mobilization of social institutions and social elites, and the subsequent mobilization of the mass media to focus on a particular issue (Viswanath & Demers, 1999). In the case of heart disease, characteristics of this process included: ongoing identification, definition, and redefinition of heart disease as a public health problem by scientists and researchers; development of strategies for ameliorating and preventing modifiable aspects of risk; mobilization for its amelioration and prevention by the network of scientists, government agencies, and public and private advocacy groups; allocation of resources and expansion of social system capacity for prevention and health promotion; and channeling of media and public attention.

Remember that this process occurred over a long period of time (since at least the end of World War II) and in the larger context of an increasing national preference for planned social change (Tichenor, Donohue, & Olien, 1980). Organization and mobilization on campaign topics by public and policy institutions, social movement organizations (SMOs), and scientific communities have played a crucial role in identifying and defining heart disease as a social problem warranting action by community members. The role of scientific reports in peer-reviewed journals, workshops, and conferences organized by such groups serve as instructive examples of how information sources can initiate and generate secular trends. Their efforts, in turn, engage media attention.

Extensive media coverage of scientific issues and the ubiquitous nature of contemporary media systems means that information on subjects of campaign interest spread quickly and widely, leading to "contamination" of experimental settings. Dynamic secular trends could be speedily generated with the right degree of mobilization by organized and powerful forces in the system. Looking beyond campaign settings, an advantage of such secular trends is that synergy could be generated among social groups and institutions to mobilize the communities on public health issues. Perhaps such synergy may be necessary to counter the multibillion dollar advertising and promotional efforts of the forces encouraging unhealthy behaviors among the public.

The mass media's role in this setting is to provide crucial links among the various elements of the social system. As mobilization (for heart disease prevention) waxes among social institutions and elites, so too does media attention to the issue. Media attention links mobilized institutions and elites to the public by increasing the salience of an issue by means of news and information dissemination that also influence public knowledge. However, the media also link mobilized social institutions and elites to those not yet mobilized on an issue. For example, media reporting of mobilization activity by some institutions and elites may influence other institutions to join the movement, or even to allocate resources to help solve a problem (Zald & McCarthy, 1979). In the case of heart disease prevention, mobilization of scientists and the public and private health community ultimately influenced Congress to allocate greater resources that expanded national capacity to address the problem. It is important to point out that in an open systems framework, this is a process that repeats so long as powerful groups remain mobilized. It is also important to point out that expanded system capacity to deal with a specific problem (heart disease) likely bears some generalizability to at least other health problems, and perhaps to other social problems more broadly. Thus, the collective general capacity of the social system to strategize and solve problems is supported and refined by specific problem-solving experience in more limited issue areas.

Finally, the history of public health campaigns also documents that when attention to prevention wanes, risk and mortality tend to increase. Also, there is good reason to be concerned that lower socioeconomic groups may be left behind when public attention to prevention wanes. Without sufficient attention to the factors of social systems that impede benefits to the lowest socioeconomic status (SES) groups, it can be expected that worsening health and mortality will affect the lowest SES groups first and foremost, just as the highest SES groups may have benefited first and most from mobilization efforts thusfar. Although this chapter focused on making an argument for the general process through which media may have influenced cardiovascular risk behavior, there remains the substantial issue of differential effects among social groups, which must be examined.

REFERENCES

Anderson, R. T., Sorlie, P., Backlund, E., Johnson, N., & Kaplan, G. A. (1997). Mortality effects of community socioeconomic status. *Epidemiology, 8,* 42–47.

Becker, L. B., McCombs, M. E., & McLeod, J. M. (1975). The development of political cognitions. In S. H. Chaffee (Ed.), *Political communication* (pp. 21–63). Beverly Hills, CA: Sage.

Blackburn, H. B. (1981). Primary prevention of coronary heart disease. In J. A. Spittel (Ed.), *Clinical medicine* (Vol. 6, pp. 1–23). Philadelphia: Harper & Row.

Blumer, H. (1971). Social problems as collective behavior. *Social Problems, 18*(3), 298–306.

Broadcasting and Cable Yearbook (1994; 1996).

Carleton, R. A., Lasater, T. M., Assaf, A. R., Feldman, H. A., MacKinlay, S. et al. (1995). The Pawtucket Heart Health Program: community changes in cardiovascular risk factors and projected disease risk. *AJPH, 85*(6), 777–785.

Cartwright, D. (1949). Some principles of mass persuasion: Selected findings of research on the sale of United States War Bonds. *Human Relations, 2,* 253–267.

Cartwright, D. (1954). Achieving change in people: Some applications of group dynamics theory. *Human Relations, 4,* 381–392.

Chaffee, S. H., & Hocheimer, J. (1985). The beginnings of political communication research in the United States: Origins of the Limited Effects Model. In E. M. Rogers & F. Balle (Eds.), *The media revolution in America and Western Europe* (pp.). Norwood, NJ: Ablex.

Davis, S. K., Winkleby, M. A., & Farquhar, J. W. (1995). Increasing disparity in knowledge of cardiovascular disease risk factors and risk-reduction strategies by socioeconomic status: Implications for policymakers. *American Journal of Preventive Medicine, 11*(5), 318–325.

Donohue, G. A., Olien, C. N., & Tichenor, P. J. (1990, May). *Knowledge gaps and smoking behavior.* Paper presented to the annual conference of the American Association for Public Opinion Research (AAPOR), Lancaster, PA.

Egger, G., Fitzgerald, W., & Frape, G. (1983). Results of large-scale media antismoking campaign in Australia: North Coast Quit for Life program. *British Medical Journal, 287,* 1125–1128.

Entman, R. M. (1993). Framing: Toward clarification of a fractured paradigm. *Journal of Communication, 43*(4), 51–58.

Farquhar, J. W., Fortmann, S. P., Flora, J. A., Taylor, B., Haskell, W. L., Williams, P. T., Maccoby, N., & Wood, P. (1990). Effects of community wide education on cardiovascular disease risk factors: The Stanford Five-City Project. *JAMA, 264*(3), 359–365.

Farquhar, J. W., Fortmann, S. P., Maccoby, N., and others (1985). The Stanford Five-City Project: Design and methods. *American Journal of Epidemiology, 122,* 323–334.

Faupel, C. E., Bailey, C., & Griffin, G. (1991). Local media roles in defining hazardous waste as a social problem: The case of Sumter County, Alabama. *Sociological Spectrum, 11,* 293–319.

Finnegan, J. R., & Viswanath, K. (1997). Communication theory and health behavior change. In K. Glanz, F. M. Lewis, & B. K. Rimer (Eds.), *Health behavior and health education: Theory, research and practice* (2nd ed., pp. 313–341). San Francisco, CA: Jossey-Bass.

Finnegan, J. R., Viswanath, K., Kahn, E., & Hannan, P. (1993). Exposure to sources of heart disease prevention information: Community type and social group differences. *Journalism Quarterly, 70*(3), 569–584.

Fishbein, M. (1996). Editorial: Great expectations, or do we ask too much from community-level interventions? *AJPH, 86*(8), 1075–1976.

Fortmann, S. P., Flora, J. A., Winkleby, M. A., Schooler, C., Taylor, C. B., & Farquhar, J. W. (1995). Community intervention trials: Reflections on the Stanford Five-City Project Experience. *American Journal of Epidemiology, 142*(6), 576–586.

Gandy, O. (1982). *Beyond agenda-setting. Information subsidies and public policy.* Norwood, NJ: Ablex.

Gitlin, T. (1978). Media sociology: The dominant paradigm. *Theory and Society, 6,* 205–253.

Hilgartner, S., & Bosk, C. L. (1988). The rise and fall of social problems: A public arenas model. *American Journal of Sociology, 94*(1), 53–78.

Hunink, M. G., Goldman, L., Tosteson, A. N., Mittleman, M. A., Goldman, P. A., Williams, L. W., Tsevat, J., & Weinstein, M. C. (1997). The recent decline in mortality from coronary heart disease, 1980–1990: The effect of secular trends in risk factors and treatment. *JAMA, 277,* 535–542.

Hyman, H. H., & Sheatsley, P. B. (1947). Some reasons why information campaigns fail. *Public Opinion Quarterly, 11,* 412–423.

Iribarren, C., Luepker, R. V., McGovern, P. G., Arnett, D. K., & Blackburn, H. (1997). Twelve-year trends in cardiovascular disease risk factors in the Minnesota Heart Survey: Are socioeconomic differences widening? *Archives of Internal Medicine, 157,* 873–881.

Jacobs, D. R., Luepker, R. V., Mittelmark, M. B., Folsom, A. R., Pirie, P., Mascioli, S., Hannan, P. J., Pechacek, T., Bracht, N., Carlaw, R., Kline, F. G., & Blackburn, H. B. (1986). Community-wide prevention strategies: Evaluation design of the Minnesota Heart health Program. *Journal of Chronic Disease, 39*(2), 775–788.

Locke, R. (1984). Health, science and technology: what newspapers are doing to meet growing reader interest. *ASNE Bulletin* 670(September): 3–10.

Luepker, R. V., Murray, D. M., Jacobs, D. R., Mittelmark, M. B., Bracht, N., Carlaw, R., Crow, R., Elmer, P., Finnegan, J., Folsom, A. R., Grimm, R., Hannan, P. J., Jeffrey, R., Lando, H., McGovern, P., Mullis, R., Perry, C. L., Pechacek, T., Pirie, P., Sprafka, J. M., Weisbrod, R., & Blackburn, H. (1994). Community education for cardiovascular disease prevention: Risk factor changes in the Minnesota Heart Health Program. *AJPH, 84*(9), 1383–1393.

Maccoby, N., & Farquhar, J. W. (1975). Communication for health: Unselling heart disease. *Journal of Communication, 25*(3), 115–126.

Maccoby, N., Farquhar, J. W., Wood, P., & Alexander, J. (1977). Reducing the risk of cardiovascular disease: Effects of a community-based campaign on knowledge and behavior. *Journal of Community Health, 3*(2), 100–114.

Mauss, A. L. (1975). *Social problems as social movements.* Philadelphia: Lippincott.

McCombs, M. E., & Shaw, D. L. (1977). The agenda-setting function of the press. In M. E. McCombs & D. L. Shaw (Eds.), *The emergence of American political issues: The agenda-setting function of the press* (pp. 1–8). St. Paul: West Publishing.

McCombs, M. E., & Shaw, D. L. (1993). The evolution of agenda-setting research: 25 years in the marketplace of ideas. *Journal of Communication, 43*(2), 58–67.

McDonough, P., Duncan, G., Williams, D., & House, J. (1997). Income dynamics and adult mortality in the United States, 1972 through 1989. *AJPH, 87*(9), 1476–1483.

Millar, W. J. (1996). Reaching smokers with lower educational attainment. *Health Reports, 8*(2), 11–19.

Mittelmark, M. B., Hunt, M. K., Heath, G. W., & Schmid, T. L. (1993). Realistic outcomes: Lessons from community-based research and demonstration programs for the prevention of cardiovascular diseases [Review]. *Journal of Public Health Policy, 14*(4), 437–462.

Mittelmark, M. B., Luepker, R. V., Jacobs, D. R., Bracht, N. F., Carlaw, R., Crow, R. S., Finnegan, J. R., Grimm, R. H., Jeffery, R. W., Kline, F. G., Mullis, R. M., Murray, D. M., Pechacek, T. F., Perry, C. L., Pirie, P. P., & Blackburn, H. (1986). Community-wide prevention of cardiovascular disease: Education strategies of the Minnesota Heart Health Program. *Preventive Medicine, 15*, 1–17.

Murray, D. M., Luepker, R. V., Pirie, P., & Grimm, R. H. (1986). Systematic risk factor screening and education: A community-wide approach to prevention of coronary heart disease. *Preventive Medicine, 15*, 661–672.

Murray, D. M. (1997). Design and analysis of group-randomized trials: A review of recent developments. *Annals of Epidemiology, 7*(S7), S69–S77.

NHBPEP (1992). *National high blood pressure education program: 20 years of achievement.* Bethesda, MD: National Heart, Lung & Blood Institute.

National Heart, Lung and Blood Institute (1994). *Morbidity and mortality chartbook on cardiovascular, lung, and blood diseases.* Bethesda, MD: National Institutes of Health.

Perry, C. L., Kelder, S. H., Murray, D. M., & Klepp, K. I. (1992). Communitywide smoking prevention: Long-term outcomes of the Minnesota Heart Health Program and the Class of 1989 Study. *AJPH, 82*, 1210–1216.

Puska, P., Tuomilehto, J., Nissinen, A., & Vartainen, E. (1995). *The North Karelia Project: 20 years results and experiences.* Helsinki, Finland: National Public Health Institute.

Rogers, E. M., & Storey, J. D. (1987). Communication campaigns. In C. R. Berger & S. H. Chaffee (Eds.), *Handbook of communication science* (pp. 817–884). Newbury Park, CA: Sage.

Salonen, J., Puska, P., & Kottke, T. (1981). Smoking, blood pressure and serum cholesterol as risk factors of acute myocardial infarction and death among men in eastern Finland. *European Heart Journal, 2*, 365–373.

Shoemaker, P. J., & Reese, S. D. (1991). *Mediating the message: Theories of influences on mass media content.* New York: Longman.

Sigal, L. V. (1973). *Reporters and officials.* Lexington, MA: Heath.

Smith, G. D., Wentworth, D., Neaton, J. D., Stamler, R., & Stamler, J. (1996). Socioeconomic differentials in mortality risk among men screened for the multiple risk factor intervention trial: II. Black men. *AJPH, 86*, 497–504.

Sorlie, P. D., Backlund, E., & Keller, J. B. (1995). US mortality by economic, demographic, and social characteristics: The National Longitudinal Mortality Study. *AJPH, 85*(7), 949–956.

Starr, S. A., & Hughes, H. M. (1950). Report on an educational campaign: The Cincinnati Plan for the United Nations. *American Journal of Sociology, 55*, 389–400.

Stern, M. P., Farquhar, J. W., Maccoby, N., & Russell, S. H. (1976). Results of a two-year health education campaign on dietary behavior: The Stanford Three-Community Study. *Circulation, 54*(5), 826–833.

Tichenor, P. J., Donohue, G. A., & Olien, C. N. (1980). *Community conflict and the press.* Beverly Hills, CA: Sage.

Viswanath, K., & Demers, D. (1999). Mass Media from a macrosocial perspective. In D. Demers & K. Viswanath (Eds.), *Mass media, social control and social change: A macrosocial perspective* (pp. 3–28). Ames, IA: Iowa State University Press.

Viswanath, K., & Finnegan, J. R. (1996). The knowledge gap hypothesis: Twenty-five years later. In B. Burleson (Ed.), *Communication Year Book 19* (pp.). Menlo Park: Sage.

Viswanath, K., & Finnegan, J. R. (1998, April). *Agitating for social change: Media, social movements and the promotion of healthy lifestyles.* Presented to the ninth annual University of Kentucky Health Communication Conference, Lexington, Kentucky.

Viswanath, K., Finnegan, J. R., Hannan, P. J., & Luepker, R. V. (1991). Health and knowledge gaps: Some lessons from the Minnesota Heart Health Program. *American Behavioral Scientist, 34,* 712–726.

Williams, D. R., & Collins, C. (1995). US socioeconomic and racial differences in health: Patterns and explanations. *Annual Review of Sociology, 21.*

Winkleby, M. A. (1997). Accelerating cardiovascular risk factor change in ethnic minority and low socioeconomic groups. *Annals of Epidemiology, 7*(S7), S96–S103.

Winkleby, M. A., Jatulis, D. E., Frank, E., & Fortmann, S. P. (1992). Socioeconomic status and health—how education, income, and occupation contribute to risk factors for cardiovascular disease. *AJPH, 82*(6), 816–820.

Winkleby, M., Feldman, H. A., & Murray, D. M. (1997). Joint analysis of three US community intervention trials for reduction of cardiovascular disease risk. *Journal of Clinical Epidemiology, 50*(6), 645–658.

Zald, M. N., & McCarthy, J. D. (1979). *The dynamics of social movements: Resource mobilization, social control, and tactics.* Cambridge, MA: Winthrop Publishers.

CROSS-CASE OVERVIEWS

17

"Behavioral Journalism" Accelerates Diffusion of Healthy Innovations

Alfred L. McAlister
Maria Fernandez
*University of Texas Health Science Center at Houston,
School of Public Health*

"Behavioral journalism" is a communication technique based on the investigations and reporting of real cases of behavior change (McAlister, 1995; McAlister, Ama, Barroso, Peters, & Kelder, 2000; McAlister, Johnson, et al., 2000). It has been developed mainly for use in public health "community studies" in which researchers attempt to produce significant change in geographically defined populations. The communicator using this technique may follow a marketing model to identify audiences and the channels for reaching them, but the message construction process is ultimately that of the journalist: telling authentic stories about people's actions. Unlike traditional journalists, the behavioral journalist uses methods based on behavioral science theory and research methods. Interviewing, editing, and presenting of stories are based on theoretical concepts about how attitude change, skill acquisition, and improved self-efficacy expectations (Bandura, 1986) influence the behavior change process (Prochaska & DiClemente, 1983). Formats for behavioral journalism may include documentary and talk shows on television, all types of news and feature stories, dramatic narratives, and testimonials or any other technique that conveys information about why and how people change their behavior.

This chapter outlines the theoretical basis and working methods of behavioral journalism. Case studies are presented with some evaluative evidence. A final discussion presents implications for the practice of journalism and the design of social change campaigns.

The basic concept behind behavioral journalism is social modeling, which is the observational or imitative learning process in which words,

315

emotional response, and other behaviors of models are reproduced or approximated by observers (Bandura, 1977). Numerous studies have examined the attributes of message sources (social models) that are effective in influencing change in attitudes, beliefs, decision making, and the acquisition of new patterns of behavior in other people (McGuire, 1989). Popular models in television or other mass media are particularly influential in all stages of learning. Factors such as attractiveness, perceived social competence, and perceived expertise and trustworthiness contribute to the power of specific models. Powerful influences on beliefs and decisions occur when observers perceive similarities between models and themselves, as when they report that they "identify" with public figures or dramatic characters in the mass media. But many social change objectives involve more than just a decision to change and may require a person to learn challenging new skills of self-control and lifestyle management.

In their Stages of Change, or Transtheoretical Model, Prochaska and DiClemente (1983) identified distinct stages in the behavior change process, noting that transition between stages depends both on information, attitude change, and the development of new personal abilities. Skill acquisition, which is facilitated by the demonstration of complex sequences in a gradual, step-by-step process, is accomplished through modeling when different parts of an action sequence are explicitly identified and repeated by a model (Bandura, 1986). Learning is also facilitated when models show realistic standards for self-reinforcement. This is particularly important in the trial-and-error learning of the type associated with difficult tasks.

Modeling is a concept with obvious applications for journalism and its use in the construction of mass communication campaigns. People are naturally interested in details of relevant experiences of other people and this explains the support for our vast industries of communication. Much dramatic entertainment, from children's cartoons to cinema, performs explicit modeling functions, as do myths and parables. News and various real or simulated documentary information provides the most relevant information about real experiences. This is shown by the vast audiences for television news and the growing popularity of talk shows revealing intimate personal information about habits and standards of behavior. A major determinant of whether particular individuals adopt a new behavior is whether they are exposed to members of their peer group who are also adopting that behavior. That suggests that the diffusion of an innovation can be accelerated by using mass communication to increase exposure to peer modeling of innovations that help people reach individual or collective goals for improved well-being.

In any given population, depending on the threats to health that are most evident, varying numbers of individuals can be found who are coping with that threat with more or less success. Finding such people and using the mass media to increase peer exposure to their modeling information is the central process in behavioral journalism. This insures credible messages that reflect real circumstances. At the same time, it allows for the use of modeling techniques to improve learning (e.g., selective focus on critical attitudes or skill components of a behavior or enhanced display of cues or contingencies). With planned peer modeling by early adopters of behavior change, the audience becomes the message.

Although the use of fictional role models in popular entertainment formats is the most commonly advocated form of planned modeling outside of the advertising model (Bandura, 1986), directive stories about fictional characters may be patronizing and miss the real issues that concern the audience. The journalistic tradition emphasizes sources with credibility and attempts to accurately reflect histories and situations.

Three distinct formats provide such models for behavior change. The first, illustrated by the approach of the North Karelia, Finland, project described next, essentially televises group counseling sessions in which individuals describe their efforts to change an unhealthy behavior. The second method is documentary journalism in which reporters present the stories of individuals who report on their struggles to change behavior. This is exemplified by the South Texas program. Finally, there is the incorporation of role model stories into printed materials that are distributed to members of the target audience, individually. This approach was used in the CDC's Community Demonstration Projects.

NORTH KARELIA, FINLAND

The North Karelia Project in Finland illustrates an effective co-production arrangement in which behavioral scientists originated and shaped the content of a behavioral journalism television series as part of a cardiovascular disease prevention campaign (McAlister, Puska, Koskela, Pallonen, & Maccoby, 1980; Puska et al., 1987). To promote population behavior change (especially smoking cessation), Finnish public television produced documentary broadcasts entitled "Keys to Health," which have been aired eight times in varying forms since 1978.

In the Finnish television series, a group was selected from volunteers seeking to stop smoking and, in some programs, to lose weight, reduce blood pressure and cholesterol, or to increase exercise and improve stress coping. The group members were chosen from the volunteers who were most prepared to change and had personal attributes that might increase attractiveness and perceived similarity to the different population segments that were to be reached in North Karelia. In a typical program, behavioral instruction from professional health educators and nutritionists was combined with directed group discussion in the studio and taped segments illustrating how instructions were put into action at home, work, or the leisure place. The number of broadcasts ranged from 8 to 15 over a 6- to 12-month period, with each broadcast segment lasting 30 to 45 minutes. The group discussion topics and the selection of material for broadcasting was determined by theoretical concepts of how people can stop smoking, including a strong emphasis on problem-solving skills for relapse prevention. The content and sequence followed the studio group through the stages and processes of change: first risk awareness, then preparations leading to a quit date and, finally, specific skills and attitude changes for maintenance of nonsmoking.

There is evidence that the programs were attractive to audiences, particularly if there was substantial local promotion of viewing. For example, a 1984–1985 series, which addressed a variety of heart disease relevant behaviors, reached from 35% to 55% of the nation and a higher proportion in North Karelia where local volunteers promoted viewing. Between 10% and 15% of the entire nation watched five or more broadcasts, and an even higher percentage of the North Karelia population, about 25%, watched that many broadcasts. In addition, many viewers reported attempting to quit smoking and adopting other recommended behaviors. Those who reported viewing more programs were also more likely to report behavior change. For example, 20% of the smokers who watched five or more programs attempted to quit, whereas only 4% of all smokers did so. This, by itself, is open to challenge as evidence for the effects of the program (it may have been that those more ready to change also watched more of the programs), however, the differences between North Karelia and the rest of Finland lend some confidence. The rates of change were higher in North Karelia than in the rest of Finland, in proportion to the different levels of viewing achieved in each place. If it is assumed that the levels of readiness to change were equal in both places, then the difference in rate of change associated with differences in level of viewing the program is consistent with a claim of influence (Puska et al., 1987).

SOUTH TEXAS

Behavioral journalism in a different format has been used in tandem with community organization to promote smoking cessation and cancer screening in community studies in south central Texas (Amezcua, McAlister, Ramirez, & Espinoza, 1990; McAlister et al., 1992; Ramirez & McAlister, 1988).

The first campaigns began with a local press conference and news release providing data on local mortality attributable to smoking and other major behavioral risk factors for disease and injury. At the press conference, appeal was made to the community to become involved in fighting these "killers" (risk factors). Appearances by local officials, such as the mayor and county judges, with project staff increased the perceived newsworthiness of these press conferences. Because numerous contacts were made with reporters and editors prior to the event, it was extensively covered by the local press.

Following the press conferences, individuals to serve as models for the selected health behaviors (e.g., smoking cessation) were recruited and featured in radio and television news and talk shows, and in newspaper feature stories in the "behavioral journalism" format (McAlister, 1995). The negotiations, during which individual media outlets agreed to participate on a regularly scheduled basis, were completed in advance of the press conference. Under these agreements, project staff were responsible for finding and pre-interviewing the social models, assisting in scheduling of taping (broadcast) and photography (print), and providing background material for relevant health or behavioral issues. This type of publicity-based strategy brought a level of programming that would not be possible through production and purchase of airtime. Some media outlets agreed to participate with incentive, whereas others asked for modest reimbursement through purchase of advertising space or for staff time for taping of broadcast segments.

The development of stories was explicitly guided by research and theorization concerning the process of smoking cessation. Concepts from the Stages of Change model (Prochaska & DiClemente, 1983) and other sources were used to determine message objectives and the actual interview questions used by journalists. Topics covered all stages of change. For example, stories to prepare for action told about the ways children or other family members influenced quit attempts. Stories about maintenance covered topics such as "counter-conditioning" (what people learn to do instead of smoking). This led to stories about prayer, new relaxation techniques or leisure activities, and so on.

Project control of content varied across sites and media. In one town, newspaper role model stories were written by project staff and run without editing. Generally, however, a reporter assumed creative control of the feature. In one example, a role model was found who had used the techniques of making a list of reasons to stop smoking and of asking for social support from significant others. Project staff arranged an interview between this person and newspaper reporter, provided a short biosketch and list of questions to elicit the role model's story. They specifically requested that attention be paid to the role model's technique of reason listing. The resulting story included a large photograph of the role model reading from his list, which modeled an important skill in urge management. The story also described the social support he received from his friends and family.

In the community in which the most intensive media activity occurred, two cable television stations, two radio stations, and two newspapers featured distinct Spanish-language role model stories each week. In addition, regional media offered weekly role model stories in one English and one Spanish television station, and in one English-language newspaper. The result was that over a 4-year period, 94 English- and 258 Spanish-language modeling displays were featured in television news, a total of 379 news stories were printed about role models, and more than 1,000 radio messages provided similar information (McAlister et al., 1992). After 4 years, exposure recall was above 80% and recognition was above 95% for participants in the panel study. This level of media involvement over time was facilitated by a careful cultivation of media contacts, and by a rotating schedule of topics (tobacco, AIDS, nutrition, cancer screening, alcohol and drug abuse, safety). It was also helpful to offer exclusive rights to campaign features within a given medium, feature cross-promotions between media, and mobilize community participation in promoting the media campaign.

A network for interpersonal communication was organized as in the North Karelia Project. Community organization led to the recruitment of a network of more than 400 peer networkers who reached almost every household in the community by distributing from 8,000 to 10,000 calendars and newsletters each month. The major role of these networkers was to increase attention to the behavioral journalism campaign. They were also trained to encourage individual efforts to stop smoking and a survey of the volunteers found that most did so at least occasionally.

Five years of follow-up in panels of heavy smokers from study and comparison communities yielded evidence of increased cessation in the campaign community (McAlister et al., 1992). The community-wide campaign was delivered to the entire population (20,000–25,000 adults) at a relatively low cost ($30,000–50,000 per year) (McAlister et al., 1992).

Following success in small cities in south Texas, the behavioral journalism method was brought to Houston, where two major publicity campaigns were conducted with extensive coverage by television and newspapers. The television broadcasts included talk show formats with smokers learning about how to quit and documentary material depicting their behavior (e.g., increased physical activity or new relaxation techniques). During the week in which the smokers attempted to quit, daily morning news broadcasts followed their progress. Newspaper stories also related their progress with specific details about new attitudes and skills. The material focused explicitly on messages linked to stages and processes of change in the transtheoretical model (Prochaska & DiClemente, 1983) and the talk show sessions were partly led by Professor Carlo DiClemente. The program gained a high degree of publicity and a follow-up survey found that viewership was above one third of all cigarette smokers in the Houston area. Although there was no comparison group, a survey yielded an estimate that approximately 45,000 people tried to stop smoking with the program and 10,000, approximately 1% of all smokers, may have stopped permanently. Whereas the percentage effect of behavioral journalism in this case may have been small, its practical significance is great in a large population.

AIDS COMMUNITY DEMONSTRATION STUDIES

Beginning in 1988, the Centers for Disease Control (CDC) and Prevention began to seek scientifically based approaches for promoting HIV-avoiding behavior in populations outside of public health clinics in which most education and research is conducted (McAlister, Johnson, et al., 2000). Although considerable risk reduction was seen to be taking place among some groups (gay men) and in some settings (drug treatment programs), whole communities at risk were not being reached. To investigate population approaches to AIDS education, the CDC organized a set of community demonstration studies in which behavioral journalism was the primary communication method (McAlister, Ama, et al., 2000). This approach has some useful features for handling the topic of sexuality in cross-cultural communication between public health agencies and the subcultures they seek to influence. Behavioral journalism puts the communicator in the role of an investigative reporter who uses theories of behavior change to interview community members about their personal processes and struggles in behavior change (e.g., using condoms with a reluctant partner). Without learning from community members themselves, there is no way for a communicator to know how people can realistically accomplish what they seek to promote. The community members know what language to use to describe the behaviors. They also know about the actual attitudes and barriers that must be overcome. These concerns are especially important when relaying prevention information to cultural and ethnic minority groups. The usefulness of AIDS prevention information for racial and ethnic minorities depends on the development of culturally and linguistically appropriate messages that are deemed trustworthy by the intended audience (Amaro, 1988).

The AIDS Community Demonstration Projects (ACDP) used peer-delivered behavioral journalism newsletters to promote condom and bleach use in five cities among presumably hard-to-reach urban groups at increased risk of HIV infection. The study groups were injecting drug users not seeking treatment (Denver and Long Beach), the female sex partners of male injecting drug users (Long Beach and New York), sex traders or prostitutes (Long Beach and Seattle), men who have sex with men but do not identify themselves as gay (Seattle), youth living away from parents (Seattle), and sexually active residents of inner-city communities with high rates of syphilis (Dallas).

Campaigns combining peer modeling through behavioral journalism and peer outreach were organized to influence change in attitudes, perceived norms, and self-efficacy expectations, which in turn were to produce movements across stages toward more consistent practice of risk-reduction behaviors (condom use and injection hygiene). Communication activities were implemented in seven separate campaigns in five cities, beginning in July 1991 and ending in June 1994. The participating agencies produced print media in newsletter formats that presented "role model" stories about members of the local populations who were achieving HIV risk reduction (Corby, Enguidanos, & Kay, 1996). Potential role models who were performing, or who intended to perform, the target behaviors were interviewed with questions that corresponded to theoretical concepts about behavior change, particularly emphasizing evaluative attitudes, perceived norms, and perceived behavioral control. For example, to identify skills that help people behave consistently, respondents already consistently using condoms were asked to give details about how they were able to perform the behavior in different situations (e.g., when intoxicated or when a partner resists). Based on the interviews, stories were prepared with accompanying photographs or figures, headlines, and captions to emphasize the attitude change and/or skill acquisition message.

In the behavioral journalism newsletters, most text was brief and low in literacy requirements. Action photographs and cartoon figures were used to portray actual behaviors. For example, a set of illustrations developed by the Dallas project presented the real experiences that accompanied attitude change and increased self-efficacy expectations. The text read: Woman: "Here, Ruben. Before you put it in, put this on!" Man: "No Baby! By the time I fuss with that I won't be hard anymore!" Woman: "Oh? Well I guess I'll just have to be creative and show you how fun this can be!" Woman: "There! You don't feel soft to me!" Man: "Ooooohh!" Caption: "Have fun! Let your partner put it on for you!"

In each site, local review groups approved the sexually explicit messages for distribution to high risk groups. Between 28 and 36 newsletters were produced for each site and audience, usually in monthly issues containing two or three stories each. More detailed accounts of program implementation are published elsewhere (Centers for Disease Control and Prevention, 1996; *Public Health Reports*, 1996).

The newsletters were distributed by networks of peer volunteers, and to a lesser extent by outreach workers who used the role model stories to encourage individuals to adopt risk-reduction behaviors. Positive responses to the message are praised, especially any hint that the behavior in the story might be imitated. Negative misperceptions were corrected. Condoms and, where appropriate, bleach kits were distributed along with the newsletters at all sites. A smaller number of materials were also available at various local stores and other sites.

In each city, treatment and comparison areas were formed from census tracts or other geographic sectors that ranged in size from a single housing development in New York (4,798 residents) to the whole Seattle area in the case of men who have sex with men but do not gay-identify. In selected sites or areas in each location, brief "street-intercept" interviews were conducted in a semi-randomized fashion to measure self-reported behavior and cognitions in the study populations. During a 41-month period (February 1991–June 1994), 10 waves of interviewing (each lasting from 2 to 5 months) were carried out in each area, allowing investigators to measure change in the study and comparison areas. The primary variables measured in these surveys were behavioral self-reports and intentions for condom use and for injecting drug users' needle hygiene (use of bleach to clean injection devices). Condom use was staged separately for main and other partners.

Other questions asked respondents whether they recalled receiving information about HIV and, if so, they were asked to describe what they received. Subjects naming or describing the newsletters were coded as "exposed" to the intervention and, in the later waves, were asked how many times they had received or seen that material.

Results from quasi-experimental studies provide evidence of behavioral journalism communication effects on condom use (McAlister, Johnson, et al., 2000). As of early implementation, consistent condom use with non-main partners increased from 23% to 33% among campaign-area respondents while it decreased slightly among comparison-area respondents. Also, among intervention-area respondents, a much higher proportion of exposed respondents (41.3%) than of nonexposed respondents (27.1%) reported consistent condom use (McAlister, Johnson, et al., 2000).

Because the media and interpersonal communications were designed to work together, the independent effect of the newsletters cannot be disentangled from the effects of interpersonal distribution and provision of free condoms. Those with the highest exposure to messages are also the most likely to report interpersonal contacts associated with distribution of the materials.

CONCLUSIONS

Behavioral journalism is currently being studied in applications to other public health and social problems. Behavioral journalism campaigns to modify cultural norms related to violence and intergroup hostility have been conducted in Finland and in Houston, where university and high school "Students for Peace" use newsletters and TV news publicity to display peer models for nonviolence and positive group relations. Early results from these studies have shown short-term effects on attitudes and behavior in the school-based projects employing students' behavioral journalism (e.g., Liebkind & McAlister, 1999; McAlister, Ama, et al., 2000). As in the previous community studies, these projects are combining behavioral journalism with organized interpersonal communications from community and student volunteers.

As noted earlier, community organization may add to the influence of a behavioral journalism campaign in different ways. Community organization increases exposure and attention to the media communication and provides direct social reinforcement for efforts toward behavior change, as shown in all of the case studies. Organized interpersonal communication can magnify the impact of behavioral journalism. But similar effects occur with the unprompted exposure and natural expressions of social reinforcements that occur when people watch news stories and talk about their reactions. Naturally occurring interpersonal influence processes govern the behavioral effects of all forms of communication and these are undoubtedly related to the television viewing effects seen in national audiences in Finland and in the demonstration projects in Houston, where community participation was not organized. Although effects are smaller without community organization, data from the case studies suggests that behavioral journalism alone can influence at least some significant change in large populations.

Although the label is new, the essential concept of behavioral journalism is not original. Many communication campaigns have been based on publicity about "early adopters." For someone oriented toward the marketing approach, this technique may simply be categorized as a special form of testimonial advertising, which poses as news and uses theory to select content. For those oriented toward journalism and publicity as a way of influencing public opinion on health and social issues, the "behavioral" technique provides a guideline for using theory to maximize the impact of their stories and news coverage. Major news reports with significant and widespread implications for individual behavior change or public policy are frequently accompanied by reactions on the street or by illustrative stories about how people are responding to the new information. Reporters or publicists often select these stories to promote specific behavioral responses in their audience. Such efforts can be enhanced by the use of theory to determine story content and presentation.

The combined talk show and documentary format that was used in the Finnish campaigns is similar to that of most contemporary talk shows in the United States. It is safe to assume that when Oprah Winfrey hosts a program featuring people discussing a book, it will influence both purchases and actual reading behavior. When they give explicit information about how people handle sensitive personal problems that most people are reluctant to discuss, even the most sensational talk shows may be providing useful learning opportunities that would not be available otherwise. The rapid growth of the talk and reality-based programming formats on television shows that audiences are eager for news about the ways other people handle problems and challenges. By using the techniques of behavioral journalism, popular communicators can satisfy that interest in ways that promote healthy adaptation in their audiences. Many talk show hosts and producers explicitly use their programs to present models for behavior change, often including experts who identify elements of behavior change with reference to theories and self-help concepts. Unfortunately, too many programs concentrate (to get an audience) on the most arousing or sensational aspects of the behavior they seek to change (e.g., bad personal or social effects). This leaves little time to examine issues related to the entire process of behavior change. Thus, fear-arousing programs often fail to teach the skills that people need to avoid the threat. Theoretical concepts in behavioral journalism provide a way for popular "infotainment" producers to pursue social objectives more effectively.

The case studies reviewed here provide some evidence for independent effects of behavioral journalism, but further research is needed. Future studies need to create "media-only" groups to isolate effects of mass communication.

REFERENCES

Amaro, H. (1988). Considerations for prevention of HIV infection among Hispanic women. *Psychology of Women Quarterly, 12*, 429–443.

Amezcua, C., McAlister, A., Ramirez, A., & Espinoza, R. (1990). Health promotion in the Mexican American community: A su salud. In N. Bracht (Ed.), *Organizing for community health promotion: A handbook* (pp. 257–277). Newbury Park, CA: Sage.

Bandura, A. (1977). *Social learning theory.* Englewood Cliffs, NJ: Prentice-Hall.

Bandura, A. (1986). *Social foundations of thought and action.* Englewood Cliffs, NJ: Prentice-Hall.

Centers for Disease Control and Prevention. (1996, May 10). Community level prevention of human immunodeficiency virus infection among high-risk populations: The AIDS Community Demonstration Projects. *MMWR Recommendations and Reports, 45*, RR-6.

Corby, N. H., Enguidanos, S. M., & Kay, L. S. (1996). Development and use of role model stories in a community-level HIV risk reduction intervention. *Public Health Reports, 3* Suppl. 1, 54–58.

Fishbein, M., Guenther-Grey, C., Johnson, W. D., Wolitski, R. J., McAlister, A., Reitmeijer, C. A., O'Reilly, K., & The AIDS Community Demonstration Projects. (1996). Using a theory-based community intervention to reduce AIDS risk behaviors: The CDC's AIDS community demonstration projects. In S. Oskamp & S. Thompson (Eds.), *Safer sex and drug use: Understanding and preventing HIV risk behavior.* Thousand Oaks, CA: Sage.

Jemmott, J. B., III, & Jemmott, L. S. (1994). Interventions for adolescents in community settings. In R. J. DiClemente & J. L. Peterson (Eds.), *Preventing AIDS: Theories and methods of behavioral interventions.* New York: Plenum.

Liebkind, K., & McAlister, A. (1999). Extended contact through peer modeling to promote tolerance in Finland. *European Journal of Social Psychology, 29,* 765–780.

Mays, V. M. (1989). AIDS prevention in Black populations: Methods of a safer kind. In V. M. Mays, G. W. Albee, & S. F. Schneider (Eds.), *Primary prevention of AIDS: Psychological approaches* (pp.). Newbury Park, CA: Sage.

McAlister, A. (1995). Behavioral journalism: Beyond the marketing model for health communication. *American Journal of Health Promotion, 9*(6), 417–420.

McAlister, A., Ama, E., Barroso, C., Peters, R., & Kelder, S. (2000). Promoting tolerance and moral engagement through students' behavioral journalism. *Cultural Diversity and Minority Psychology, 6*(4), 363–373.

McAlister, A., Johnson, W., Guenther-Grey, C., Higgins, D., O'Reilly, K., Fishbein, M. (2000). Behavioral journalism for HIV prevention: Community newsletters influence risk-related attitudes and behavior. *Journalism and Mass Communication Quarterly, 77*(1), 143–159.

McAlister, A., Puska, P., Koskela, K., Pallonen, U., & Maccoby, N. (1980). Mass communication and community organization for public health education. *American Psychologist, 35*(4), 375–379.

McAlister, A., Ramirez, A., Amezcua, C., Pulley, L., Stern, M., & Mercado, S. (1992). Smoking cessation in Texas–Mexico border communities: A quasi-experimental panel study. *American Journal of Health Promotion, 6*(4), 274–279.

McGuire, W. J. (1989). Theoretical foundations of campaigns. In R. Rice & C. Atkins (Eds.), *Public communication campaigns* (2nd ed., pp. 43–66). Newbury Park, CA: Sage.

Prochaska, J. O., & DiClemente, C. C. (1983). *The transtheoretical approach.* Homewood, IL: Dow Jones-Irving.

Public Health Reports (1996). Special Issue. *3*(Suppl. 1).

Puska, P., McAlister, A., Niemensivu, H., Piha, T., Wiio, J., & Koskela, K. (1987). A television format for national health promotion: Finland's "Keys to Health." *Public Health Reports, 102*(3), 263–269.

Ramirez, A., & McAlister, A. (1988). A su salud. *Preventive Medicine, 17,* 608–621.

18

FROM PREVENTION VACCINES TO COMMUNITY CARE: NEW WAYS TO LOOK AT PROGRAM SUCCESS

William Smith

Academy for Educational Development, Washington, DC

Does public communication change health behavior? What evidence of such change is convincing? And how can inconsistencies of effects across studies be explained?

This book focuses on communication effects. Communication is a vast concept that runs the gamut from any exchange between two or more people to the study of mass media effects on large-scale populations. This chapter restricts communication to any organized deliberate attempt to influence human behavior through large-scale message strategies—that is, by exposing large-scale populations to messages about behavior. It includes all channels of communications—interpersonal, paid media, earned media, and digital media. It refers, henceforth, to this subset of the broader communication concept as "public communication." This definition excludes what is called "secular" communication events, such as Magic Johnson's announcement of his HIV status, the death of Princess Di, or news coverage of the cigarette deal. This distinction is tricky. Take the news coverage of the proposed 1997 cigarette deal. If that coverage could be shown to have been orchestrated deliberately by a specific intervention program (e.g., media advocacy), then it would be included as part of the definition of public communication. This chapter is interested in intention as well as effect in this somewhat narrow and arbitrary definition of public communication. If there is a deliberate attempt to influence news coverage of an issue, then such an intervention qualifies as public communication under the definition herein.

A dilemma is that the discussion here is more concerned with behavior than communication. Therefore, it also refers to "programs of behavior change," which may or may not have public communication components as defined previously. Take, for example, a law banning smoking on airplanes, or a tax on cigarettes. It may indeed take a media advocacy approach to enact such a law or tax, and a media campaign to publicize them, but once enacted and acknowledged, they function as independent, noncommunication determinants or influences on behavior. The comments throughout this chapter are interested in the orchestration of these noncommunication effects on human behavior with communication itself. Reference is made to these interactions from time to time, as "behavior change interventions," "prevention programs," or perhaps "programs of behavioral influence." These noncommunication interventions may include communication elements, but they are always broader in some way than messages about behavior.

First, the chapter considers the ways to measure success and the importance given to the concepts of efficacy, replicability, and sustainability. It then turns attention to the differences among target behaviors as an important explanation for the inconsistencies of effects among programs. It reviews a variety of ways that have been used to distinguish between behaviors, including private sector marketing models and popular behavioral theories.

Finally, the chapter argues that asking so often "what works" inadvertently establishes a vaccine model of evidence in the minds of many policymakers and practitioners. The "vaccine" metaphor brings with it a number of assumptions about communities and behavior change. This chapter proposes a different metaphor. It proposes thinking of communities as though they were biological entities, similar in complexity to the human body—highly organized systems and subsystems that interact to produce change in individual and community behavior. Communities differ from each other just as people's biological makeup differs; and communities are also similar, just as one person's biology shares some similarities with that of others.

I stumbled on this insight after many years of reading the *Journal of the American Medical Association* (*JAMA*) and discovering only recently the "Clinical Crossroads" section of the journal. Previously I had given all my attention to case control studies of interventions and clinical trials. Lynn (1997) noted four critical conditions for successful management of terminal illness:

Understand the patient's story,	*understand the audience*
Understand the body,	*understand the health behavior*
Understand the care system,	*understand the delivery systems for care and messages*

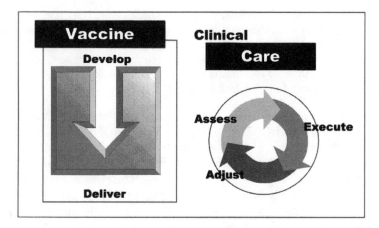

FIG. 18.1.   Two metaphors for intervention development.

Understand yourself,   *understand your organization's re-sources*

This seemed so parallel to what makes a successful behavioral intervention (as suggested in italics) that I was intrigued. Lynn continued: "The most important single guidepost to good care is for the professional to listen to and come to understand the patient and the family" (p. 1638). I believe this simple principle also underlines all successful prevention.

Admittedly, people in the business of behavior change do not like to think of behavior as a disease, or communities as a biological body. I don't either. I accept the limitations of the analogy. Suspend for a moment the literalness of the analogy and try to look at the critical distinction I am trying to make between a *vaccine* model of disease prevention, which is largely characterized by a *develop and deliver* mentality, and a *clinical care* model of disease prevention, characterized by an *assess, intervene, and adjust* mentality. I believe within the distinction between the vaccine and care metaphors lies a more realistic approach to develop and evaluate interventions. See Fig. 18.1 as a way to contrast vaccine and care metaphors.

WHY FAILURES MATTER: BECAUSE THE PUNDITS HAVE POWER

In an otherwise excellent review of primary prevention of alcohol problems, Moskowitz (1989) concluded in discussing policy implications:

> There is currently little evidence to support the efficacy of primary prevention programs. Although such programs may influence knowledge, beliefs or atti-

tudes, they generally do not affect behaviors or problems. Thus, it may be useful to employ them as adjuncts to effective prevention policies. Administrators may adopt them to help them feel that they are doing something positive to address a community problem. In sum, the effects of mass media campaigns appear similar to those of educational programs. Knowledge is most likely to be influenced and behavior least likely. (p. 57)

In a current national debate on the effectiveness of HIV prevention programs, headlines such as "Why AIDS Prevention Failed?," and recent books, such as Patton's *Fatal Advice: How Safe Sex Education Went Wrong* (1996) have led many professionals and practitioners in the field to question the effectiveness of AIDS prevention. The most common evidence cited for these beliefs is that the infection rate among gay men in San Francisco remains at about 2%, coupled with a rise in the number of young gay men becoming infected with HIV despite many years of AIDS education (Green, 1996). Similarly, critics of drug treatment programs regularly point out that close to half of all recovering addicts fail to maintain complete abstinence during the first year following treatment (Patton, 1996). At the U.S. Agency for International Development (USAID), which has been one of the pioneers in applying communication systematically to problems of maternal child health, family planning, and HIV/AIDS prevention, several key professionals are questioning whether the cost of communication approaches makes these approaches unsustainable by developing countries. This concern is provoking intense interest in community-based approaches, which avoid the use of mass communication as a "top down" intervention in favor of interpersonal networks that develop from the grassroots. Community-based approaches are seen, without hard evidence to substantiate effectiveness, to be more affordable to overextended national governments. Interestingly, in almost all of these debates, important differences among behaviors are glossed over. At a number of recent meetings on communication, communication and marketing strategies have been lumped together as outmoded or as failures, and grand arguments have been made for the "ineffectiveness" of campaigns, mass media, social marketing, and other poorly used definitions for deliberative purposeful programs to influence individual behavior on a large scale. The failure of a campaign to change eating behavior is used as an argument to disregard communication campaigns altogether and search for some other magic bullet.

These concerns can be summarized by three common questions that increasingly emerge from political debates concerning most modern programs of behavioral influence:

Did it work?	Efficacy
Will it work for other problems?	Replicability
Will it work forever?	Sustainability

The "it" refers to a specific purposeful intervention to influence human behavior—a peer outreach program, a program of policy change, a new tax incentive, a media advocacy effort, a communication campaign. These three questions are also reflected in the criticisms already cited. Moskowitz (1989) asked, for example, "Does communication work?" and concluded the answer is no, it does not work to change behavior. The critics of marketing AIDS prevention concluded that it has failed because marketing has not changed the behavior of everyone (2% continuing infection rate). They further argued that if marketing failed to solve AIDS in Africa, it is damaged goods and can no longer be trusted among the pantheon of proved strategies. Finally, critics at USAID question programs whose success cannot be sustained after resources to support the success are withdrawn. Efficacy, replicability, and sustainability have become the acid tests of success for modern behavioral interventions. These tests are critical because they are the tools used by policymakers to set funding priorities. To address the growing cynicism about effects and the dreadful confusion over replicability and sustainability, it is critical to be clearer about what works, about the conditions under which interventions can work, and about the effective means to measure what works.

There are many things to say about program efficacy, replicability, and sustainability. The intention here is not to review knowledge about each broad class of interests, but rather to use them as an organizing principle for three specific points. The section on Efficacy discusses the need to establish "Best Practices" in order to ensure that what is labeled as "health communication" has some chance of succeeding. The section on Replicability focuses on the ways in which differences in behaviors make it difficult to replicate even successful programs. And, finally, the section on Sustainability discusses how a vaccine model of program development and implementation creates false expectations for the sustainability of programs and should be replaced by a clinical care metaphor. Best practices, behavioral differences, and a vaccine metaphor interact to influence judgment of efficacy, replicability, and sustainability. This chapter focuses on these specific aspects of the three areas.

EFFICACY: DOES COMMUNICATION WORK TO CHANGE BEHAVIOR?

The answer is much the same as the answer to the question, "Does surgery save lives?" Yes, but not all lives or all surgery. The comparison of communication and surgery, although it may seem somewhat farfetched, offers an interesting perspective on an understanding of effects. Surgery may be essential to remove a tumor or stop internal bleeding of a vital organ, but surgery is not indicated in the treatment of respiratory infections, AIDS-related dementia, diabetes, or numerous other life-threatening conditions. And surgery, even if it is indicated, but performed by a licensed plumber or electrician, is not anticipated to have the same results as surgery performed by an experienced surgeon. Furthermore, heart surgeons are rightly reluctant to perform cornea transplants, recognizing, as they do, that specialization among surgeons is not an affectation but a necessity.

Just as surgery improves health, communication changes behavior—but not all behavior and not all communication. Communication is also subject to a set of basic conditions that must be in place in order to anticipate success. There are a number of reasons why a communication program might appear to fail. See Table 18.1 for a brief discussion of the four types of failures common to communication interventions.

As Table 18.1 suggests, communication works, but not if it attempts to substitute for needed structural changes (strategy failure). Communication works, but not if it addresses the wrong determinant of behavior (executional failure). Communication works, but not when well-designed programs do not get the exposure necessary to produce success (another executional failure). Communication works, but not when instruments are insensitive to a long-term strategy (measurement failure). And communication works when it is not expected to change deeply held behaviors through one-time, flashy national media campaigns (expectation failure).

Communication, like surgery, must meet certain "best practices" if it is to be expected to make a predictable contribution. One of those practices is to work in combination with services and policy to influence complex behavior. Although it is true that communication has demonstrated an independent effect in some cases, it is far more common to see communication acting with other interventions (structural changes, policy advocacy, and regulation) to produce large-scale effect.

The surgery analogy also demonstrates the danger of continuing to ignore the need for best practices. Imagine for a moment that large numbers of untrained and poorly equipped people were allowed to perform surgical

TABLE 18.1
Four Types of Failures Common to Communication Interventions

---

1. STRATEGY Failure: Communication is really not the problem. People need better services, and messages are inadequate in themselves to affect change.
2. EXECUTION Failure: Messages are badly needed, but they are poorly constructed, lack adequate exposure, and/or are addressed at the wrong audience.
3. MEASUREMENT Failure. Communication was the right answer; it was well delivered, but poorly evaluated. Either the instruments measured the wrong change or time was inadequate to permit the change to become detectable.
4. EXPECTATION Failure. The problem is that real change occurred, but did not meet the expectations of planners or funders. A success was declared to be a failure.

---

interventions at will. Imagine that the advice of the few highly trained and experienced surgeons practicing surgery was regularly disregarded by hospital administrators who insisted that these surgeons had to operate on cases of diabetes and food poisoning, often without electricity, in street corner operating rooms, using kitchen knives instead of scalpels. Imagine that the success rate of surgery began dropping dramatically with thousands of these pseudo-surgery failures being widely reported and analyzed. Would it be good public policy to discredit the entire practice of surgery because these amateurish efforts were described as "surgery failures"? Clearly, in the practice of prevention, communication, and behavior change, skilled practitioners, adequate resources, and appropriate techniques are necessary in order to succeed.

Yet, this is precisely the state of too many health communication and prevention programs today. There are far more slogans and pamphlets than there are programs to deliver them effectively. There is far too great a reliance on focus groups, and there are far too many evaluations that ignore theory and fail to track incremental change over time. Many well-meaning but inexperienced individuals working with totally unrealistic and inadequate resources are addressing problems where there is no reasonable expectation for quick success. I have been privileged to speak at national and international conferences for years now. In the course of my responsibilities as a reviewer for both the *Journal of International Health Communications* and the *Journal of Social Marketing*, I continually make contact with people and programs with pathetically small budgets ($10,000–$30,000) that intend to "change public attitudes," or even to "change behavior" about some complex social issues—domestic violence, excessive consumption of products, Americans' love affair with the automobile, food safety, and so on. A typical discussion often goes like this:

> If Americans understood how important XXXXXXX was, they would act to protect themselves. . . . Here are the facts Americans do not have, but I don't know how to reach them. . . . Could you organize a series of focus groups for us to assess how to get through to Americans best? . . . We need a slogan. . . . You, communication people, are so good at this . . . and what about advocacy? I hear that getting your message in the media can be powerful. . . . Oh, and we don't have very much money, I think I can scrape $10,000 out of this year's budget and if we can produce some results then I can make a case for more resources next year . . .

Consider a set of useful, best practices. These are described as behaviors rather than principles—behaviors that are a useful starting point in establishing some shared sense of what makes good programs of behavior change for social benefit.

Best Practices: An Initial List

Set Measurable Social Goals. Define the social goal of the program in measurable terms (e.g., reduction in mortality/morbidity, incidence of violence, school dropouts, improvements in air/water quality, or other hard measures).

Identify Objectives in Terms of Behaviors that Influence the Goal.
Define *program objectives* as targeted behaviors that will positively influence the achievement of the social goal. Describe the ways that behavior is expected to influence the goal. Clarify whether the objective is to change an existing negative behavior or to stabilize and positively reinforce an existing positive behavior.

Define Behavior as a Combination of Action, Audience, and Circumstance. Define *targeted behavior* as action, by a segment of a population under specific circumstances, designed to accomplish the social goal. "Using a condom to prevent the transmission of HIV/AIDS," for example, appears to be a socially beneficial behavior. But, in fact, for a teenage female to use a condom for the first time with a boyfriend is significantly different than a teenage female using a condom for the 100th time in her professional work as a female sex worker. The definition of behavior as action, segment, and condition implies a significant amount of information about various populations and their actions in order to refine the behavioral target. It represents one of the earliest and most important best practices. This practice encompasses the selection of both audience and behavior and is sometimes referred to as "segmentation." The focus should be on behavior, not attitudes, knowledge, beliefs, or any other intermediate variable such as communication products, channel exposure, or public support. Although these intermediate variables can be indispensable as a means to influence the behavior, they should not be the focus for measuring success.

Use Research to Define Intervention Opportunities. Make decisions based on multifaceted and multidisciplinary research that triangulates direct observation of the target behavior, qualitative exploration of the determinants of the behavior, and representative sampling of the target population through surveys. The implications for the further development of best practices are vast here. The kinds of research, the sequence of research development, and the quality of research execution and interpretation are open to much discussion and debate. It is clear, however, that effective behavior change interventions are best driven by research on the behavior (action, segment, and conditions) and its possible determinants.

Identify Theory-Based Determinants of Behavior.   Define the proposed "determinants" of the target behavior/audience using a clearly defined theoretical base. In selecting a theoretical base, reflect on both external structural determinants and internal attitudes and beliefs. *Determinants* are defined as those factors influencing adoption or maintenance of a specific target behavior (action, segment, conditions). The implication here is that as any one characteristic (action, segment, or condition) of the behavior changes, the determinant may also change. This too is a rich area for further development of best practices. The number and usefulness of theoretical bases—the optimal way to define and monitor determinants—are absolutely critical to improving the ability to define best practices.

Describe How Interventions Are Intended to Influence Determinants.   Describe the proposed intervention in terms of how it will influence specific determinants and therefore the behavior itself. An *intervention* is defined here as any organized, deliberate set of activities designed to influence the specific determinants of behavior. Interventions can be discrete, time-limited events like campaigns, or continuous activities like the provision of regular immunization services.

Achieve Sufficient Scope/Exposure to Accomplish the Objectives.   Define the scope of the intervention necessary to achieve sufficient coverage in order to achieve the behavioral objective. Effective interventions must be experienced by the target audience in order to be effective. Despite the seeming simplicity of this notion, one of the greatest flaws to date in interventions has been their inability to achieve sufficient exposure, or scope, to have the intended impact. Scope and exposure are strongly tied to the availability of resources and the complexity of the behavior.

Ensure Fidelity of Intervention Delivery.   Conduct the intervention with sufficient quality to ensure that the exposure is to the intended message. Here again, is a large realm for additional best practices. Interventions vary considerably in scope: from single television PSAs to vast cadres of peer leaders dispersed over time through multiple organizations. There are numerous lessons learned about different interventions that have been codified in manuals and guides.

Monitor the Intervention.   Define and execute monitoring procedures that track exposure to the intervention, indicate the audience's response to the selected determinants and their influence on the behavior, and identify unanticipated results and side effects.

Adapt the Intervention to Meet the Changing Needs of the Audience. Adjust and refine all programmatic decisions—including the selection of targeted behaviors, the definition of determinants, as well as the nature and execution of the intervention itself—in light of monitoring information in order to achieve the established social goal.

It is refreshing that the programs reviewed in this book represent complex interventions that meet most of the practices identified here. The National High Blood Pressure Program (Roccella, chap. 4, this vol.), the North Carolina "Click It or Ticket" Program (Williams et al., chap. 5, this vol.), HealthCom (Hornik et al., chap. 13, this vol.), and others described here, demonstrate that communication, like surgery, works sometimes and under some conditions.

Expectation Failures

Expectation failures are a category of failures that deserve a moment of attention when discussing efficacy. Expectations failures are programs that, unlike those reviewed here, appear to have been failures, but in fact may have been successes. One way of looking at the San Francisco AIDS case data, for example, is to reflect, as its recent critics have, that there still exists a 2% infection rate after many years of marketing programs. Critics argue that marketing programs have failed and must be replaced. Another way of looking at the same data is to say that in 1987 there were estimated to be 8,000 new infections of HIV per year in San Francisco and that by 1994, the number of new infections had dropped to 650 cases per year (Stryker et al., 1995). In a population of about 50,000 sexually active self-identified gay males, about half of whom carry the HIV virus, that reduction is likely to have been influenced at least in part by an epidemic burn out. But the reported changes in behavior that have accompanied the reduction in infection (i.e., increased condom use, fewer sexual partners, and less anal intercourse) suggest the remarkable success of grassroots marketing and communication, rather than the disappointing failure reported by Patton (1996) and others (Choi & Coates, 1994).

Similarly, critics of drug treatment programs regularly point out that close to half of all recovering addicts fail to maintain complete abstinence during the first year following treatment. They argue for public investment in drug control rather than drug prevention or treatment. But the reported failure rate of drug treatment programs is about the same failure rate as for diabetes treatment programs. There is no outcry to eliminate diabetes treatment because it fails to control diabetes. Clearly, definitions of success are affected by expectations.

What are the possible explanations for the failure these critics have identified? Are they correct and are their demands for, and concern about, changes in funding priorities useful or harmful? Does continued analysis of all failures provide helpful information to policymakers, or feed the growing sense that large-scale social interventions (communication, prevention, and treatment) are not working and alternatives are necessary? One response to the critics of alcohol programs, AIDS prevention, and drug abuse treatment is to suggest that these programs are not failures at all, but rather expectation failures—successes that have approached high levels of change, but because of false expectations are falsely defined as failures. The failure was in not understanding what was realistic, given the characteristics of each behavior, and what should constitute a worthwhile and reasonable expectation for success.

REPLICABILITY: DOES ONE SUCCESSFUL INTERVENTION WORK FOR OTHERS?

There is a key distinction to be made between two meanings of the word "others." Other can mean (a) other programs addressing the same behavior or (b) other behaviors. Among experienced communication professionals it is well recognized that there are important differences between behaviors that make it impossible to assume that a successful intervention to reduce teen smoking would necessarily be equally effective to reduce obesity. Unfortunately, this distinction is not well understood by policymakers looking for simple answers and magic bullets. Even among experienced professionals, the question is often raised as, "What can we learn from smoking that we can apply to obesity?" On the surface this is a perfectly logical question. But often, during debate, the question becomes a litmus test for the viability of the strategy itself. At a recent meeting of top communication experts, one expert voiced, "Nothing we have done in Africa to prevent AIDS has worked, we must have new strategies." Without questioning the conclusion, the group turned to open community debate as a viable alternative to purposeful interventions. This logic is a slippery slope and leads both policymakers and communication professionals to question whether a specific intervention works at all.

Replicability rests on two assumptions that draw heavily on a vaccine metaphor of prevention. First, there must be a belief that the intervention that led to change can be recreated with sufficient precision to replicate the effect. Second, there must be a belief that the conditions that the intervention addresses are common and relatively stable throughout the new system to which it is being applied. These conditions are rarely present in dealing with individual and community behavior.

This section proposes that, first, there are real differences among behaviors that many researchers have reported as significant. Second, there is value in searching for a set of systems that would allow characterization of behaviors by differences salient to their influence. But, third, there is not a robust system as yet. It is also suggested that replicability of interventions must be looked at in a different light than "does it work for everyone?" If behavioral differences are important, then one success cannot be expected to be replicated with the same efficacy across widely varying behaviors.

Behaviors differ in important ways that make some behaviors inherently more difficult to change than others, just like some diseases are more difficult to treat or prevent than others. Is this true? This section examines how marketing and social psychology have sought to characterize the differences among behaviors. In addition to differences among individual behaviors themselves, a number of other factors influence the replicability of an intervention. People also vary—some are more ready to change than others, some are more able to change than others. Timing causes important variations in the likelihood of successful replication. An intervention that worked well at one point can be rendered inadequate or just outdated by fast-moving events. Both Rock Hudson's and Magic Johnson's announcements of their HIV status fundamentally changed the way AIDS education needed to be done for thousands of Americans. The timing of programs, those occurring before versus those occurring after, may mean they need different standards of success.

In addition, there is an extensive literature on the "determinants" of behavior, which also suggests that even when the behavior itself is held constant, the determinants of behavior are affected by the same set of conditions already noted—significant and unpredictable variation due to differences among people, and changes in social, economic, and political conditions over time. Most people would agree, therefore, that there is a basis for believing that smoking cessation, domestic violence, and compliance with a hypertension treatment are behaviors significantly different in character. But what differences matter?

Even when looking at very narrow sets of behaviors in a single population, how long can we wait or how far can we go from the population and conditions the original intervention was designed to address? Where is the change ceiling for any given behavior? Because an immunization program achieves a 85% to 95% coverage rate does not mean that an HIV/AIDS testing program can achieve those same levels. The answers to these questions are critical to the ability to predict the replicability of interventions. If behaviors are different and if the determinants of behaviors vary from one setting to another, then replicability of programs cannot be understood as though it were a vaccine to be manufactured, even if there were the capacity to manufacture interventions the way vaccines are manufactured.

Currently, there is no standard way to talk about differences or similarities among behaviors other than to acknowledge in some general way that differences exist, leaving it open for critics to pick and choose their examples of comparative success or failure. Conversations that compare one program to another often focus on the unique elements of the one program and ignore what it has in common with programs excluded from analysis. What, for example, is the most salient aspect of the National High Blood Pressure Education Program: the fact that it was a concerted national effort with widespread exposure, the fact that it promoted a relatively simple and yet highly salient health behavior change (get your blood pressure checked and treated if needed), or both? Should it be compared with national smoking cessation programs that achieved similar levels of exposure, or with national immunization campaigns that promoted behaviors of more similar complexity?

How Behavioral Differences Have Been Characterized in the Literature

A number of models and approaches have been proposed for assessing, and thereby comparing, the characteristics of behaviors that make them different from other behaviors. Such a comparison is typically interested in differences that influence one or more of the following factors:

The Absolute Size of Change Reasonable to Expect (Did enough change occur to provide a health benefit?)

Comparative Change Achieved (Did we do better than a comparison group?)

The Speed of Change (How rapidly did change occur?)

The Durability of Change (How long did the change last?)

The Cost of Change (Is it worth the cost, affordable, and the cheapest alternative?)

Some recent models have suggested that behavioral differences are not as important as once thought. Stages of readiness to change, for example, have emerged as important in the past few years. Prochaska and DiClemente (1986) suggested that matching interventions with stages of change cuts through behavioral complexity among programs as diverse as smoking cessation, alcohol, and drug addiction. But there continues to be interest in how behavioral differences influence adoption and maintenance of behavior.

Ways to Group Behavior.   One of the most common means to cluster or group behaviors is by the health problem they address (smoking cessation, maternal childcare, HIV/AIDS, etc.). See Fig. 18.2 for a list of com-

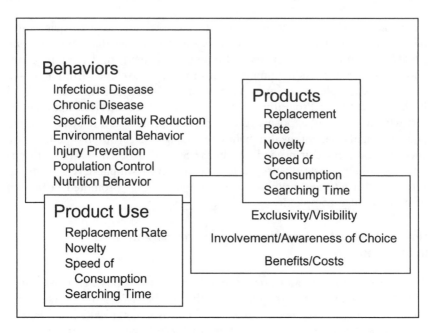

FIG. 18.2.   Common ways to group products/behavior.

mon groupings. This has practical value to the funding community, but it is less important to understanding differences that matter to adoption.

The commercial marketing literature is filled with factors and typologies of behaviors, using variables such as the visibility and exclusivity of a product, or the degree of consumer involvement and awareness of choice. Issues like the replacement rate of products, the degree of adjustment needed to adopt a new product, the speed of consumption of a product, and the searching time needed to find a product have all been widely discussed as dimensions important to both expectations for success and the selection of appropriate change mechanisms. These discussions have led to the creation of broad categories of products (Wilkie, 1994) that reflect differentiated marketing strategies for:

Convenience Products:	Bought frequently, used immediately.
Shopping products:	Wide assortment of choices available.
Specialty products:	High salience to the consumer.
Unsought products:	Impulse buying of familiar or novel items.

Subcategories, such as durable versus nondurable goods and over-the-counter versus prescription drugs, also reflect an effort to organize behaviors. These categories are attempts to be responsive to a company's need to better understand and organize its marketing procedures. Common wisdom has developed among marketers within industries and product categories to address these characterizations. Lovelock (1983) noted an important limitation to this intra-category expertise: "The majority of railroad managers, for instance, have spent their entire lives within the railroad industry—even within a single company. The net results of such narrow exposure is that it restricts a manager's ability to identify and learn from the experience of organizations facing parallel situations in other service industries" (p. 11).

A similar phenomenon is beginning to take shape in the arena of social communication and behavior change. Smoking cessation, family planning, child health, traffic safety, environmental protection and its many sub-arenas, plus nutrition, cancer prevention, and drug and alcohol abuse prevention, have developed groups of experienced professionals whose careers have focused primarily on specific behavioral domains. As new domains emerge (e.g., violence prevention), practitioners return to the domain they know best for models, with less reference to a broader understanding of behavioral influence. But which of the many behavior change communities offers the most relevant match for their interests, and how can a vocabulary be developed that enables a search among disparate domains for lessons and approaches?

Some analysts have tried to construct typologies or even matrices that organize behaviors by selected characteristics that offer prescriptive direction in matching interventions with behavioral types. Rangan, Karim, and Sandberg (1996) suggested an intriguing four-cell matrix with Cost (Low/High) on one axis and Benefits (Tangible personal/Intangible societal) on the other. They suggested that campaigns with low costs and high benefits need only address what they called "compliancy" issues, whereas programs with low tangible benefits and high costs must engage in "repositioning, leveraging and supply-side persuasion" (p. 47). They must, therefore, address structural as well as cognitive interventions.

There continues to be a set of practitioners who cross boundaries among communities. They tend to be theorists interested in the generic process of behavioral change (e.g., Fishbein, Bandura, Becker, Prochaska), or program directors who serve a wide variety of clients (e.g., the Academy for Educational Development, Novelli). Even among practitioners with multiple clients, however, the pressure is often to focus on the specifics of the client community's history rather than explore lessons from other communities.

Behavioral typologies, whether developed by commercial marketers or social communication professionals, have their limitations. To be effective, the categories should be mutually exclusive. Many typologists have run into problems with overlapping categories. Typologists also suffer from poor intercoder reliability. Experts disagree on which precise categories are most robust in predicating influence. Some of the categories are intended to be prescriptive, that is, once a behavior is classified into a particular box, the authors "prescribe" the kind of intervention needed to address that category. These prescriptions can easily become dogmatic "formulas" in the hands of less experienced program directors. It is interesting to note, for example, that even small changes in a single variable can produce different characterizations of behavior. By changing the categories in one typology from Tangible *Personal* Benefit to Tangible *Immediate* Benefit, smoking cessation can be reclassified from the personal to the delayed category. Because these categories are intended to be prescriptive, that is, they are designed to describe what interventions work by which cell the behavior is classified under, this variability in coding leaves much to be desired. As one marketing academic remarked, these categories are useful for teaching students the basics of marketing, but in actual fact, "marketing success comes from breaking these rules" (G. Day, personal communication, 1997).

Today many of the best interventions are theory based, targeting determinants of behavior that have been shown to vary over time and across individuals, making the problem of replicability even more complex to address. Determinants such as social norms, self-efficacy, and perceived consequences are being used now to select targets of opportunity for change. These determinants become de facto means of segmenting audiences—one segment may respond to social norms, whereas others are influenced more by their perceptions of consequences. Programs targeting one determinant should not be expected to influence segments not influenced by this determinant. The expectations for replicability by many politicians and program managers ignore the importance and expense of this targeting. They want to see large-scale change to justify public investment. This may be possible when a particular behavior is found to have a single dominant determinant, but if the population is highly segmented by determinants, single approaches should not be expected to produce large-scale change.

Checklists Instead of Typologies. Perhaps the best alternative to the formal typology is the *checklist*. Categories need not be mutually exclusive. Overlap is tolerable. Checklists can include up to 10 or 12 variables without becoming too cumbersome. Perhaps most important, a checklist more honestly reflects the state of present art—judgment is not displaced by tight prescriptive formulas. An early checklist developed by Rogers (1983) included variables, such as Compatibility, Flexibility, Reversibility, Relative Advantage, Complexity, Cost-Efficiency, and Risk. These characteristics can be used to compare different behaviors and predict the viability of a behavior change strategy. For example, in the case of seat belt use, "compatibility" would mean those individuals who can afford cars with seat belts, belong to a community of seat belt users, and both believe that safety is important and would be more likely to use seat belts than others. "Flexibility" refers more to the nature of the behavior than the nature of the user. Using a seat belt can be done in an airplane, a car, a van, and a variety of settings and therefore, according to Rogers' model, would be more likely to be adopted. Each characteristic is useful as a measure of the adoption rate of a particular behavior within a particular population. Similar checklists have been developed by behavioral psychologists (Smith, Pareja, Booth, & Touchette, 1985).

Checklists have problems too. Every distinction on the list does not provide guidance for intervention development. But checklists do help ensure that major distinctions between behaviors will surface. They help assess whether one successful intervention is applicable to the conditions of a very different behavior. Perhaps the behavior is not as different as it seems on the surface. For the purposes of this chapter, however, it may be enough to establish the problem and find an answer in a broader approach to the problem, an answer defined as a clinical care versus a vaccine model of intervention design, execution, and evaluation.

SUSTAINABILITY: WILL IT LAST FOREVER?

Now consider the final of the three success criteria, sustainability, while continuing to reflect as well on the issue of replicability. Both sustainability and replicability are related to the same false analogy. To address this issue, there are many analogies that might be helpful. How, for example, does Coca-Cola think of sustainability and the industry's use of marketing communication? Surely Coke has achieved maximum awareness of their product, so why do they continue to invest in advertising and promotion of such a well-known, admired, and successful product? Have their past programs been "sustainability failures"? Why, with their vast resources, have they failed to inoculate the American public with immunity to Pepsi Cola? The field of marketing, both commercial and social, offers a series of powerful analogies that can be drawn from to address the issue of program sustainability. This chapter will stay within the broad medical analogy already begun, and contrast a vaccine paradigm with a paradigm of clinical care for the chronic disease.

As illustrated in Fig. 18.3, a vaccine model of program development implies high efficacy, high stability, and low side effects of the intervention program, as well as requiring that the community receiving the intervention demonstrates stability over time, and a widespread homogeneous response.

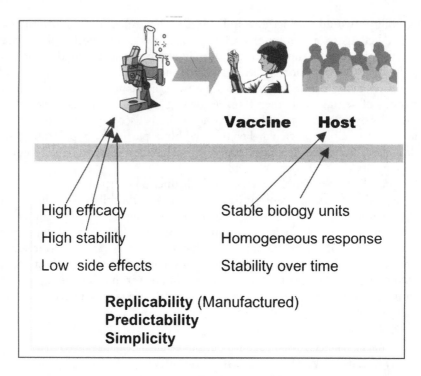

FIG. 18.3. The vaccine model.

The fundamental criteria for a successful "vaccine intervention" are that it is replicable, stable, predictable, and relatively simple. Rarely, if ever, do these conditions exist in human communities facing behavioral change.

A clinical care perspective (see Fig. 18.4), in contrast, addresses the variability between communities and within communities over time. It recognizes the unpredictability of external factors and it follows a circular pattern of execution from assessment to intervention, to adjustment of the intervention based on continual assessment. The goal is care, not immunity. A "care" perspective necessarily implies a different approach to the implementation of interventions. It looks for the interactions of ingredients rather than the contribution of individual elements. It addresses time as influencing the accumulation of effect, but also as shifting ground to which effective interventions must continually adjust.

Imagine for a moment a young, 24-year-old man. He tested positive for HIV 2 years ago. When he arrives at his primary care physician's office, he has a fever and a severe cough. His lab test shows that he is experiencing his first bout of pneumocistis pneumonia, one of the common opportunis-

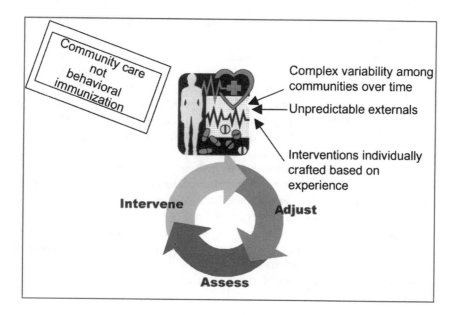

FIG. 18.4.   Clinical care model.

tic infections once associated with the transition from HIV to full blown AIDS. The physician is an experienced AIDS clinician and has seen this situation many times. He counsels the young man on his new status and prescribes three drugs. He explains that he has had good success with this combination in several patients recently, but he wants to monitor carefully the young man's response because this combination has produced some side effects in two other patients. The young man agrees, is put on a new regime of drugs, and is given advice about his eating and exercise habits.

Eight months later, the young man has another secondary infection. The physician prescribes another combination of drugs. This time the young man does not respond well and is hospitalized late one night. The physician runs more tests and changes the medication, believing that the interaction of two of the drugs has caused the negative response. One of the drugs has undergone clinical trials but the others have not. Again the young man responds unpredictably. He recovers from the serious infection, but experiences a severe skin rash. The rash is treated successfully with a sixth drug and within days the young man is back at work. But he enters a period of severe depression. He has lost his lifelong partner to AIDS and the patient begins to lose interest in his own care. He begins to drink alcohol and party until late into the night. Friends are unable to get through to him.

Six months later, the young man, on returning from a vacation in the Caribbean, comes down with another severe infection. The physician has seen a similar case recently in an older man. A new combination of three drugs, reported in the literature, worked effectively in other patients. At this point, the original young man's T cell count is down to 6; he has been losing weight consistently. He does not respond with the same speed as other patients. Three weeks later, the young man recovers.

The physician has kept careful records of this patient's response over the past 13 months, compares it to other patients, and finds some important similarities, but he also finds important differences as well. The young man has found a new long-term partner and reinitiates his original healthy regimen of diet, exercise, rest, and low stress. His clinical response to the combined medication becomes one more valuable piece of information in the practice of AIDS medicine.

The essential ingredients of this case are:

A patient

- who is neither exactly like every other patient, nor totally unique in his or her response to different clinical interventions. A patient whose response to treatment is not fully predictable but who benefits from the growing knowledge gained from previous patients.
- whose condition changes, both medically and psychologically, over time.
- who can decide whether or not to cooperate with his care regimen, but whose involvement in the treatment process significantly influences the efficacy of some treatments.

A Physician

- who is an experienced specialist, making complex judgments based on knowledge of scientific studies plus the empirical experience of his practice.

A Treatment Regimen

- not yet established as "Best Practices."
- composed of several drugs, some of which have undergone efficacy trials, others classified as experimental.
- that often combines several drugs to produce overall improvement in health status.

- that varies in efficacy from one patient to another and in the same patient over time.

A Monitoring System

- to determine how well the specific patient is responding to the treatment regimen.
- to determine if there are any side effects or unexpected drug interactions occurring in this patient.

Objectives

- Control disease consequence (pain, suffering, and cost of care) and reduce the likelihood of future infections.

A similar situation is emerging in helping both individuals and communities to develop effective programs for HIV/AIDS prevention. To illustrate how similar the two situations are, identical language is used, replacing treatment with community-based prevention vocabulary where appropriate:

A Community

- that is neither exactly like every other community, nor totally unique in its response to different prevention interventions. A community whose response to specific interventions is unpredictable, but it benefits from the growing knowledge gained in other communities.
- whose condition changes, both epidemiologically and sociopolitically over time.
- that can decide whether or not to participate in an intervention actively, but whose involvement in the intervention significantly influences the efficacy of some interventions.

A Prevention Program Management

- who are an experienced specialist team, making complex judgments based on knowledge of scientific studies plus empirical experience of past programs.

A Prevention Program

- not yet established as "Best Practices."
- composed of several classes of interventions (including interpersonal level interventions, i.e., counseling and testing), group-level interventions and community-wide interventions (mass media, advocacy, or

social marketing), some of which have undergone efficacy trials (counseling and testing), others of which are less studied but still widely practiced (public awareness campaigns on personal risk).

- that often combines several interventions to reduce risk on a large scale in a broad community, or to target a particularly difficult high risk behavior in a priority population that varies in efficacy from one community to another and in the same community over time.

A Monitoring System

- to determine how well specific elements of the community are responding to the intervention.
- to determine if there are any behavioral or political side effects or unexpected interactions between the various interventions (news, advocacy, media programs, counseling and testing promotions, etc.) going on at the same time.

Communities are not patients. And behavior is not disease. But interventionists too often act like virologists pursuing a quick-fix intervention vaccine, than they do like clinical physicians working with a patient as just one more source of help and support in a complex process influenced by time, unpredictable events, and the unique skills of both clinician and community. Note in Fig. 18.5 how the vaccine and clinical care models differ.

Parameter	Vaccine	Clinical Care
Process	Develop & deliver	Access, execute, adjust
Expectation	Permanent effect	Address immediate symptom
Timeframe	One-shot prevention	
Community	One of several types	Continuous care
Program manager	Administers intervention	Each is somewhat unique
Intervention		Participates with community
Externals	Replicable with precision	
		Replicable without precision
	Largely predictable	Largely unpredictable

FIG. 18.5. Assumptions in vaccine and clinical care models.

The process by which they are implemented differs greatly. The vaccine model supposes a "delivery" function, and the care model implies a more interactive approach. The expectation of the vaccine model is immunity, durable across long spans of time, whereas the care model assumes attention to changing symptomatic problems. The vaccine host is noted for its similarities to all other hosts, whereas in a care model it is differences among patients that matter most. The intervention in the vaccine model— a biological vaccine—is precisely replicable, able to be manufactured with great precision. Care, on the other hand, differs in its execution from one patient to another and is impossible to replicate with the same precision. Finally, external factors (temperature, humidity, availability of equipment) are important but much more predictable in a vaccine program, whereas in a care program externals (new infections, unexpected exposures, etc.) are much less predictable.

WHAT A COMMUNITY *CARE* MODEL LOOKS LIKE

Some of the programs reviewed here are examples of the kind of approach this chapter is advocating. They are long term. They are part of something much larger. They have been self-correcting over the years. And they continue today. The Philippines Immunization program (Zimicki et al., chap. 12, this vol.) is a good example. It was part of a much larger effort over more than 20 years to address infant mortality in developing countries. The larger program went through many stages and many names. This overall 20-year-plus effort is labeled the Child Survival Program (CSP).

CSP represents the kind of long-term partnership between medical research, communication science, and program development that can work. CSP made many mistakes over the years, but it carried within it the capacity to identify those mistakes, the courage to acknowledge and correct them, and the time and resources to make both problem identification and correction possible. CSP was never designed as a 20-year effort. Every 3 to 5 years another funding battle had to be fought to justify its continuation. But those battles were won and continue to be won today. CSP is an ongoing program, like the battle against smoking and the struggle against heart disease, from which lessons for a new generation of programs can be drawn.

In the 1950s, infant mortality in many developing countries of the world was 20 to 30 times higher than in most industrial countries. Five to seven million children were dying each year from diseases that no longer caused mortality in industrial countries. The biological causes were well known: diarrheal dehydration, respiratory infections, and complications from immunizable diseases. The structural/societal causes were also understood (although not as well as today): poverty and isolation leading to inadequate access to timely health care including vaccines commonly available in the West; poor nutritional status; repeated bouts of infection; and lack of clean water, sanitation, and safe food storage behaviors and systems. Most of these problems were fundamental problems of poverty and could not be easily addressed with existing resources. Investments in rural roads, massive urban sanitation systems, refrigeration, and electrification were considered impossible dreams by most of these people. But as a result of basic medical research in the 1950s and 1960s, it was believed that two of the biggest killers (diarrheal dehydration and immunizable diseases) could be effectively addressed without basic infrastructural changes in these societies. Millions of lives could be saved if two high priority medical programs could be put in place: universal early childhood immunization and oral rehydration therapy (ORT) of children with moderate to severe dehydration.

Characteristic 1. There was a big problem (infant mortality) and a possible practical solution (immunization and oral rehydration therapy).

Characteristic 2. There was an international consensus about the approach. The World Health Organization, UNICEF, and the Agency for International Development made child survival an international priority. This was a major accomplishment that took many years to achieve. But this consensus was fundamental to the ultimate success of this effort.

Characteristic 3. The medical interventions worked. That is, immunization when delivered properly did prevent disease. ORT, when used properly, did prevent death from dehydration. This is taken for granted now, but these interventions were themselves the result of extraordinary medical research to solve major dilemmas in delivering health care to isolated millions around the globe. An important lesson is worth noting here. Often there are no medical interventions as robust as these, nor problems as clearly defined.

Characteristic 4. A complex behavioral problem required changes in cultural norms, acquisition of complicated new skills by both health care providers and mothers, policy change, and infrastructural investment. These two, seemingly simple behaviors, immunization and oral rehydration therapy, had to be introduced across an enormous spectrum of cultural diversity, medical sophistication, and political resistance. It was recognized early, although not equally by all the players, that behavior change from traditional practices to these new practices was essential.

Characteristic 5.   A long-term, self-correcting process was based on continual reevaluation of changing behavioral information. The following are a few beliefs that changed over time as a result of continued monitoring:

Assumption: ORS was too complex to ask mothers to manage in the home. The key was to get mothers into health centers in time to treat dehydration.

Data: Two years of field trials comparing sugar and salt mixtures with prepackaged ORT salts showed that mothers forget the sugar–salt formulas more easily but could manage prepackaged formula well in the home. Similar results come in from other national programs. Parallel data shows that access to health centers for most mothers is inadequate.

Program change: Major new focus on ORT in the home.

Data: Mothers' attitudes are highly influenced by physicians' attitudes. Physicians believe ORT is second-class medicine for the poor.

Program change: Increase effort to "market" ORT to physicians. Involve private sector in commercialization to increase ORT's prestige and outreach.

Assumption: Immunization saves lives. ORT saves lives. Therefore, overall mortality will be reduced by the number of lives saved from immunizable disease and ORT.

Data: Immunizable diseases (particularly measles) and diarrheal dehydration are often the first cause of death in children, but many of those children will go on to die of respiratory infections and complications from malnutrition. Overall mortality is not reduced as a simple mathematical function of the effectiveness of these two interventions.

Program Change: Incorporate respiratory infections as a major new focus along with an emphasis on infant feeding, particularly breastfeeding.

Data: Behavioral observation of health care systems indicated that focusing on immunization and ORT had allowed overextended health care systems in developing countries to be more effective by concentrating resources on a few programs. With the inclusion of respiratory infections and nutritional interventions these systems could not respond with the same level of efficiency as they did with immunization and ORT. A systemic and policy level improvement was essential.

Program Change: Focus attention in monitoring wellness indicators of children. Introduce a way to look at child health with emphasized comprehensive disease monitoring of infants along with immunization, ORT, nutrition, and respiratory interventions.

Data: General development of several countries has improved considerably. Health systems have changed. Infant mortality is dropping, as

basic structures of development (water, sanitation, electricity) are becoming more available. Political urgency of infant mortality in many
countries is ebbing, but pockets of high mortality remain in some areas
of the countries.

Program Change: New emphasis is placed on cost-savings of these interventions to motivate continued policy support. Targeting of regions with
problems begins.

Characteristic 6. A program should be able to absorb this data,
make program changes, and continue to monitor the present situation for
additional changes needed. This is the key to a "clinical approach" to program development.

On the surface, this story may seem like one of simple human learning.
As things change, people adjust to the changes. But the key point is that
there existed an international program that has lasted for more than 30
years now addressing a single priority health issue. That program still has
some of the original designers working on the program and whereas thousands of new professionals have joined the effort over the years, there has
been a place for lessons to be learned, for programs to be reconsidered,
and for needed changes to be made. Those changes are the result of empirical evidence, not always case controlled trials, but often field information
from multiple sources reflecting changes in the patient's response to the international intervention. There were regular peer consultations, sometimes
in the form of international conferences, more often through the creation
of Technical Advisory Groups (TAGS), which reviewed the broad direction of programs at annual or semiannual meetings. Those meetings
seemed tiresome at the time, but today it is possible to see how that advice
shaped long-term development.

At every stage of this progression, program development was a partnership between social scientists sensitive to the cultural needs and societal
wants of the patient communities; of the local community patients themselves (physicians, politicians' families, and mothers); of medical professionals who were constantly refining the medical norms and procedures to
make them more "friendly" to communities; and to the funding agencies
who mustered the courage every 5 years or so to say, "There is no quick
fix, we are in this for the long-haul."

It is just as easy to imagine that after the first 5 or 6 years of funding,
say about 1985, victory had been declared. Funders demanding results
would have been told mortality was coming down. Immunization programs were taking hold, ORT had been proven a field success as well as a
laboratory success. It would have been easy to say, "Our job was to demonstrate the field effectiveness of immunization and ORT; we have done
that. Let's move on now." But the goal was not to introduce immunization

or ORT. It was to reduce infant mortality. That focus on a health benefit versus a health technology is critical to the success of a clinical versus a vaccine model.

In the vaccine trial of a new biological vaccine, the goal is to develop a specific technology. In the clinical management of chronic disease, the goal is to provide the patient with the best possible quality of life. This simple difference is fundamental to the successful organization of programs of complex public health communication. Whereas many have been able to work over time on a single large issue due to a combination of luck and tenacity, the continued domination of a vaccine model of change and its demands for case controlled evidence of narrowly defined success can be counterproductive.

New behavioral interventions must be tested. Case controlled studies of those interventions are invaluable to progress in social science just as they are in medical science. They cannot be replaced or deemphasized. But it must also be recognized that they are a part of any overall success. They are tools within a process of professional judgment that should occur during the implementation of long-term programs of change. Those programs must be able and willing to detect and respond to changes as they develop over time.

IMPLICATIONS

The Program Management Role

The community care model places a new set of demands on the project management team. In the vaccine model, the program management team is charged with the responsibility for implementing a fixed intervention, often designed at the outset of a project or based on a model implemented elsewhere. They are to make sure it is implemented as prescribed. In the community care model, the manager must have the capacity to consider a range of intervention strategies, and choose a subset among them—with the understanding that the appropriate subset will vary by segment of the population and over time. These are different skills and responsibilities, and demand that managers both have good knowledge of the broad armamentarium available to them, and have the ability to assess and monitor audience response and make use of that information in adjusting programs strategies.

Continual Program Research and Monitoring

The switch from a vaccine to a clinical/marketing model of program development and evaluation implies first that new models of research are needed to track and establish effects. Interventions are not designed to provide permanent immunity, so case controlled trials are less useful than processes of continual monitoring that reflect changes in both the external environment and the internal efficiency of interventions. Some models might include long-term tracking systems like the Health Message Testing Service operated by Porter and Novelli for many years in the 1980s.

Best Practices

Second, the switch from vaccine to clinical/marketing suggests an increased emphasis on best practices as a means to guide and control interventions. If there is no single vaccine, then there is certainly a set of best or better practices that should govern how an intervention is designed, monitored, and adapted to achieve maximum results. These practices need to include knowledge of proven interventions, assessment systems to determine community needs/wants, and guidelines for experimentation to get the right mix of intervention components (interpersonal and mediated communication, plus policy, service improvement, and structural change). A commitment to continuity of programming is also essential in order to address the simple reality that behavior and the determinants of behavior change. If it is accepted that time is a factor in change (things need time to work) but that over time things change, then an end must be put to this notion that behavior is like a microbe that can be eradicated forever by the correct treatment. The combined pressures of shifting political priorities and budget cuts cause program managers at all levels of the public health system to look for "solutions that last," so that funds can be redirected to new priorities or problems left unattended. This is natural, and to some degree necessary. But the costs of abandoning behavioral surveillance and maintenance must be recognized while shifting resources. And certainly it is necessary to stop believing these reallocations are justified because they have changed behavior and attention can now be shifted to the next behavior.

Continual Peer Consultation

Third, an increased emphasis on professional peer consultation rather than case controlled evaluation is needed to determine if programs are following best practices and to suggest novel ways to address new problems as they arise. Because so much of the practice of health communication and behavior change requires judgment as well as technique, greater use of peer review during the development of programs would be useful. The analysis of audience data is a critical point for peer review. This data is almost always inadequate. Program managers are often influenced by their prejudices in reviewing this data and outside peers can be tremendously helpful as part of an overall best practices approach. The key is organizing the peer review at a point in the process where it can make a difference, and not after a program is completed. Finally, a better understanding of how the differences between behaviors affect change is necessary. It has been suggested that these differences are important and they have been studied. But it was impossible to identify one single system that seems to work best. More work to refine and simplify the numerous models (some of which were reviewed earlier) that differentiate or categorize behaviors in meaningful ways would be useful. This work could yield tremendous benefits for the practice of health communication.

A shift from a vaccine to a clinical model provides different answers to three important questions:

Efficacy. Did communication work? To accomplish what, with what audience, as part of what broader program? If it did not work, then why not? Was it poorly done, did it address the wrong determinant, did the measurement instrument fail to detect the success, or did it in fact succeed, but too much was expected of it?

Replicability. Will it work for others? No, and it should not. It is designed to work for a specific subset of individuals in order to address a particular problem that is likely to change soon after it has been successfully addressed.

Sustainability. Will it last forever? No, nor should it. Behavior is constantly under pressure to change. There must be ways to monitor and address change, not sustainability.

Basic behavioral research is still badly needed. Vaccine models of proof are still vital to developing intervention elements and establishing the conditions under which they work best. But interventions themselves are multi-element, long-term, and must be adaptable to changing conditions. Though imperfect, the vaccine versus clinical care analogy stimulates a healthy discussion of how best to understand the programs being reviewed here and to explain some of the inconsistencies of effect across a broad spectrum of success and failure.

REFERENCES

Choi, K. H., & Coates, T. J. (1994). Prevention of HIV infection. *AIDS, 8*, 1371–1389.

Green, J. (1996, September 15). Just say no. *New York Times Magazine*, sect. 6.

Lovelock, C. H. (1983). Classifying services to gain strategic marketing insights. *Journal of Marketing, 47*(summer), 9–20.

Lynn, J. (1997). An 88-year-old facing the end of life. *Journal of the American Medical Association, 277*(20), 1633–1640.

Moskowitz, J. M. (1989). The primary prevention of alcohol problems: A critical review of the research literature. *Journal of Studies on Alcohol, 50*(1), 54–88.

Patton, C. (1996). *Fatal advice: How safe sex education went wrong.* Raleigh, NC: Duke University Press.

Prochaska, J. O., & DiClemente, C. C. (1986). Toward a comprehensive model of change. In W. R. Miller & N. Heather (Eds.), *Treating addictive behaviors* (pp. 3–27). New York: Plenum.

Rangan, V. K., Karim, S., & Sandberg, S. K. (1996). Do better at doing good. *Harvard Business Review*, May–June, pp. 42–54.

Rogers, E. M. (1983). *Diffusion of innovation.* New York: The Free Press.

Smith, W., Pareja, R., Booth, E. M., & Touchette, P. (1985). *Field note 3: Behavioral analysis applied to health communications.* HealthCom Communication for Child Survival, Field Notes.

Stryker, J., Coates, T. J., De Carlo, P., Haynes-Sanstad, K., Shriver, M., & Makadon, H. J. (1995). Prevention of HIV: Looking back, looking ahead. *Journal of the American Medical Association, 273*, 1143–1148.

Wilke, W. L. (1994). *Consumer behavior* (3rd ed.). New York: Wiley.

19

A META-ANALYSIS OF U.S. HEALTH CAMPAIGN EFFECTS ON BEHAVIOR: EMPHASIZE ENFORCEMENT, EXPOSURE, AND NEW INFORMATION, AND BEWARE THE SECULAR TREND

Leslie B. Snyder
Mark A. Hamilton
University of Connecticut

Case studies offer interesting but biased conclusions about the efficacy of health campaigns. The conclusions from case studies depend entirely on which cases the researcher chooses to examine. In contrast, meta-analysis allows researchers to assess the efficacy of health campaigns based on a population of studies. Conclusions drawn from meta-analysis using quantitative methods allow generalization to the population of campaigns.

Flay and Cook (1989) claimed that there is a strong need for meta-analysis to synthesize effects across campaign studies. They suggested that individual evaluations are frequently underpowered, lacking a sufficient number of respondents to find statistically significant campaign effects. This has led researchers to conclude falsely that campaigns have no effect. By combining a large number of studies, meta-analyses have sufficient power to detect a pattern of small effect sizes across studies. Similarly, the idiosyncrasies of any particular study in "treatment design, site uniqueness, respondent sampling, data collection, and so on" affect conclusions less when the study is one of many in a meta-analysis (Flay & Cook, 1989, p. 192). Furthermore, because campaigns use different communities and populations, the conclusions of the meta-analysis will have more generalizability than the results of a single evaluation.

This chapter uses meta-analysis to estimate the effect of media campaigns on behavior change. A prior meta-analysis of U.S. health behavior campaigns examined how the type of behavior addressed by the campaign affected its success, and found that campaigns promoting a new behavior were more successful than prevention or cessation campaigns (Snyder et al., in press). That study built on an earlier review of 28 studies of behavior change in mediated campaigns by Freimuth and Taylor (1995), which suggested that some campaigns can be very successful. The present study reviews the evidence for the average effects of campaigns and also examines whether message factors, exposure, secular trends, and campaign length influence the size of the effect of campaigns on behavior. Each factor is discussed in turn.

MESSAGE CHARACTERISTICS

When deciding on the direction of campaign messages, planners may choose from many approaches. Unfortunately, there is usually little information about campaign messages in published evaluations. There are, however, a few message characteristics that can be assessed, including whether the message contained enforcement messages, new information, service information, or role models advocating the target behavior.

Enforcement Messages

Beginning with Kelman (1958, 1961), researchers have distinguished social influence situations that attempt to *coerce* compliance from attempts to *persuade*. Messages about current or upcoming enforcement procedures for laws or rules, with the implicit threat of negative consequences such as arrests or fines, constitute a coercive appeal. The North Carolina seat belt campaign (Williams, Reinfurt, & Wells, 1996; chapter 5, this volume) was reported to be a successful campaign, perhaps partly because it combined enforcement with a media campaign. In that campaign, the media announced that police would be stopping people during a particular period of time at roadblocks to check for compliance with seat belt laws. Enforcement has long been recognized within environmental circles as a powerful agent of behavior change, alongside education (communication) and evaluation (McNamara, Kurth, & Hansen, 1981). Enforcement activities usually happen without public messages about the enforcement effort, but enforcement messages may be quite powerful. The first hypothesis is about the effect of enforcement messages on behavior change:

> H1: Campaigns with at least one message about upcoming or current enforcement of policies designed to promote a particular behavior will have a larger average campaign effect size than campaigns without enforcement messages.

New Information

Information about new health recommendations can spread quickly throughout a population. For example, the incidence of Reye's syndrome dropped precipitously during the initial upsurge in media coverage in 1982 of the recommendation to not give aspirin to young children (Soumerai, Ross-Degnan, & Kahn, 1992; chapter 15, this volume). By providing new reasons for people to change their behavior, new information can facilitate a sudden increase in behavior change. Sharing new information in a campaign message gives people a reason to change their behavior. Conversely, a campaign may restate old information, such as the harmful effects of smoking, or the importance of a mammogram to women above a certain age. Note that enforcement messages can be considered a special case of new information when the messages are about specific, upcoming checks on behavior. The second hypothesis predicts that when campaigns have new information to impart, they will be more successful than campaigns repackaging old or commonly known information:

> H2: Campaigns that contain at least one message with new information will have a larger average campaign effect size than campaigns without any new information.

Services

Messages may also differ with respect to whether they directly promote a health behavior or promote a service that promotes a health behavior. For the latter, the media supports services and interpersonal communication that occurs in face-to-face settings by advertising clinic services and by recruiting participants (Flora, Maibach, & Maccoby, 1989). Smoking campaigns have used both service promotion (promoting attendance at a stop-smoking clinic) and health behavior promotion (giving direct messages about how to quit). It is unclear which type of message would be more effective. Thus, the third hypothesis stated:

> H3: Campaigns using service-promotion messages have a different average campaign effect size from campaigns not using service-promotion messages.

Role Models

A recent approach to campaign messages entails using role models to share information. McAlister and Fernandez (chap. 17, this volume) calls this approach "behavioral journalism." The role model messages feature real members of the target audience who have changed their behavior. Media often include television news segments, newspaper feature stories, and flyers. The media are often supplemented by interpersonal communication through outreach or clinics. The present study tested whether campaigns known to use role model messages are more effective than campaigns not using role models:

> H4: Campaigns using role model messages will have a larger average campaign effect size than campaigns not using role models.

EXPOSURE

A potentially critical factor in the success of a campaign is the extent to which the audience is exposed to campaign messages. Hornik (Introduction, this volume) points out that weak exposure to the message may explain why some large-scale community campaigns (e.g., Project COMMIT and the Stanford Five City Study) had such small effects. If few people are exposed to the campaign, then it is unreasonable to expect a campaign to have a large impact. Exposure is a necessary, but not a sufficient, condition for change in the target population. Thus, it can be predicted that the more people exposed to campaign messages, the greater the impact of the campaign on behavior. So, another hypothesis is:

> H5: The greater the exposure to the campaign, the larger the campaign effect size.

CONTROL GROUP TREND

A pre- to post-test change in the control group in the direction the campaign is promoting can result in weak campaign effects. There are four potential explanations for why a positive trend in the control group may attenuate the effect of the campaign. First, the change in the control community could be caused by a national or "secular" trend towards change, such as a "fitness craze." The treatment effect would then test whether the campaign causes people to outperform a national trend. If a national trend were to absorb all the people capable of change at a particular point in time, then to demand performance beyond that of the national rate of change is unrealistic. Murray (1995) and Viswanath and Finnegan (chap. 16, this volume) offered the secular-trend as one explanation for the limited impact of the Minnesota Heart Health Project in the 1980s.

A second reason for change in the control group is the presence of a concurrent national message, such as national cereal ads touting oat bran. If the national campaign is very effective, then it will be difficult for a local campaign to have an additional effect (on top of the national communication) in the treatment community.

A third explanation for the control-group trend is that there is some noncampaign communication in the control community (as opposed to nationally) causing the change. For example, a nonprofit group not connected to the campaign may launch a new screening service in the control community with a spate of publicity. If this noncampaign communication exists only in the control community, then the evaluation design is really pitting two different communication approaches against each other. Null effects would indicate that both approaches were equally effective or ineffective, rather than that the campaign had no effect.

Finally, a positive control group trend could be caused by "leakage" of the campaign into the control community. In this case, the differential in exposure between the control and intervention communities measures the absence of leakage, and the differential in behavior measures the effect of the extra amount of communication in the intervention community.

A strong control-group trend, regardless of which of the four explanations prevails, would make it more difficult to obtain or detect a campaign effect. Thus, according to the sixth hypothesis:

H6: The greater the control-group trend, the smaller the campaign-effect size.

CAMPAIGN LENGTH

Another factor that may impact on campaign effectiveness is the length of the campaign. On the positive side, longer campaigns have a longer period of time in which to change people's behaviors. In addition, those people who are slower to change will have more time to make the change. On the negative side, longer campaigns allow more time for backsliding after an initial period of compliance. In addition, the fluidity of populations in a given community means that newcomers will have had less exposure to the message, and perhaps show less inclination to change. The prediction is that campaign effectiveness will be a curvilinear function of campaign length, such that short campaigns and long campaigns will not be as effective as mid-length campaigns. Stated as a hypothesis:

H7: Mid-length campaigns will have a larger average effect size than short or long campaigns.

In sum, the meta-analysis examines the impact of certain campaign characteristics on the effectiveness of media campaigns. Characteristics tested include messages containing enforcement, new information, service promotion, and role models; the extent of exposure to the campaign; control group trend; and length of campaign.

METHODS

Selection Criteria

Media campaigns were defined as organized outreach efforts using at least one form of community-wide mass media, such as radio, television, or widely distributed printed materials. Campaigns were included in the meta-analysis if the campaign evaluation was published in a journal or edited book, the evaluation design allowed for some form of quasi-experimental control of campaign exposure, and there was enough information in the evaluation to adequately assess the effect size of campaign exposure on behavior change. The meta-analysis was limited to U.S.-based campaigns to control for cultural, health, and media system differences; a later meta-analysis will deal with campaigns in other countries. Campaigns based only in workplaces or schools were excluded on the grounds that they did not use community-wide media.

The fact that only published evaluations of campaigns were included in the meta-analysis means there is the possibility of an upward bias in the estimation of effect size, because campaigns that are larger and produce interesting outcomes are more likely to be published. This potential bias is known as the *file drawer problem* in the meta-analysis literature. Yet, in nearly every domain studied thus far with meta-analysis, the magnitude of the file drawer problem has been found to be overstated (Hunter & Schmidt, 1990). Indeed, not all of the campaigns included in this meta-analysis reported statistically significant effects on behavior, so it is clear that the published literature does allow some unsuccessful programs to appear. In addition, the size of the campaigns in the published literature also varied widely from small community efforts to national campaigns, which suggests that campaign size is not a determining factor in publication.

The types of study designs included nonequivalent control group design, posttest only designs with control groups, one group pretest posttest design, a one-group design that post-facto partition the sample based on levels of exposure. Some of the over-time designs sampled a panel of people, and others drew a new cross-section. The effect of study design on campaign effect size is the subject of another meta-analysis (Snyder & Hamilton, 1999).

The meta-analysis included a wide variety of campaigns. The campaigns addressed all sorts of audiences: general populations of adults and youth, as well as ethnic-group-specific campaigns. Local, multiple city, and national campaigns were included. Many different types of behavior change objectives were represented, including sex, substance use, diet and physical activity, seeking appropriate health care, and use of seat belts. The media used and formats differed, from paid advertising to public service announcements to news. The complete list of campaigns is found in Table 19.1.

Search Procedure

The first step in a meta-analysis is to find all relevant studies. Four computerized databases (Psychlit, Soclit, Medline, and Eric), collections of case studies of media campaigns, and literature reviews were searched for publications in English. The database keywords "health," "campaign," and "communication" were supplemented with "education," "media," "mass media," "television," "posters," "billboards," "newspapers," "radio," and "intervention." Additional searches included "anti-drug," "smoking," "risk," "cancer," "AIDS," "seat belts," and "community." Several thousand abstracts and over 300 publications were examined.

The search located publications concerning 48 campaigns that met the selection criteria. In most cases, more than one publication was used to provide information about a campaign. For six campaigns, the outcome measure was physiological rather than behavioral; because a prior analysis (Snyder et al., in press) showed no difference in campaign effect size between studies using the two types of measures, the six campaigns with physiological measures were included in the analysis.

Of the rejected publications, 52% were reviews, did not test media effects, or only used media in schools or in the workplace rather than community-wide media. Another set did not report behavioral effects of the campaign, and focused instead on exposure, knowledge, or other outcomes (15%). Four percent of the articles were about campaigns for which there were no published evaluations to date. Another 4% would have qualified for inclusion, but the statistical reporting was incomplete.

Measures

The second step in meta-analysis is to code the studies. A team of advanced graduate students located and coded the study features; each study was thoroughly read and recoded by the first author. The effect sizes were coded by the two authors. The codes for each campaign are in Table 19.1.

Campaign Effect Size. The dependent variable was the effect of the media campaign intervention on behavior change. If a campaign evaluation reported on more than one behavior, then the campaign effects were averaged across behaviors. If there were several journal articles reporting on the same behavior in a campaign, then the campaign effect estimate was chosen that was the most fully specified statistically, represented the entire target population rather than a subset, and coincided with the end of media activities rather than long-term effects (see Snyder et al., in press).

The campaign effect size was computed for each campaign. The procedure was to locate the relevant statistic in the published evaluation reporting the campaign effect and, if it was not a correlation, convert it to one. The relevant statistic—such as an F-test, p-value, means, and SDs, or χ^2— was converted into a correlation using standard formulas (Rosenthal, 1994), and meta-analytic software (Hamilton, 1991; Hunter, 1993; Johnson, 1995). When posttest only control group designs or pre-post no control designs reported percentages instead of a statistic, d (a difference statistic) was calculated using Johnson's software, *D-Stat*, and then converted to r using the standard conversion (Hunter, 1993). When the campaign evaluation reported pretest and posttest percentages in both intervention and control communities ($k = 24$), the campaign effect size was computed by hand, because the current software packages cannot compute it. The following formula was used to compute d by hand:

$$d = \frac{(i_2 - i_1) - (c_2 - c_1)}{\sqrt{\frac{(i_1 + c_1)}{2} \cdot \left(1 - \frac{(i_1 + c_1)}{2}\right)}}$$

such that c represents the control community, i represents the intervention community, and the subscript specifies the pretest (1) or posttest (2). The formula states that the effect size d is equal to the change over time in the intervention community, minus the change over time in the control community, divided by the standard deviation of the average pretest score (J. E. Hunter, personal communication, September 27, 1997). The statistic d was then converted to r.

Enforcement Messages. Enforcement was a dichotomous variable measuring whether or not a campaign included an enforcement message as part of the campaign. Typically, enforcement messages inform people that there will be checks on their behavior and penalties if they do not comply. Enforcement was easy to code, because campaigns with enforcement messages prominently featured information about the enforcement aspects of the campaign. Only 4 of the 48 studied programs incorporated enforcement messages.

New Information. New information was coded based on whether or not a campaign included information that was new to the audience. New information included a new recommended behavior to solve a health problem, new services to make compliance easier (such as the opening of screening centers), and new threats to noncompliance (such as imminent enforcement). Twelve of the 48 programs included new messages. Of those, 3 were also enforcement messages.

Service Messages. The study coded whether or not a campaign message was about service promotion. Messages about service promotion included promotion of screenings (e.g., mammograms, pap smears, hypertension) and clinical treatment (e.g., control of hypertension, dentist visits). Seven of the studied campaigns incorporated service messages.

Role Model Messages. The last message characteristic coded was whether or not the campaign messages contained role models. Campaigns that identified themselves as using behavioral journalism or described the process of creating news stories based on real people who changed their behavior were coded as using role model messages. Four of the campaigns incorporated role model stories.

Reach. Although reach, frequency, and length of contact with the campaign may be important dimensions of exposure to a campaign, it was possible to code only reach, and even then many studies lacked a precise measure. The study coded reach based on the percentage of the audience that was exposed at least once to the media effort. The reported figures typically represent the percentage of people who recall being exposed to campaign materials or participating in campaign events. For studies that measured media reach apart from interpersonal communication reach, the figure for media reach alone was used. If studies measured media reach in the control communities, then the measure of reach used was reach in the intervention communities minus reach in the control communities. For studies with measures of reach in more than one community, the average rate of reach was used. In some cases ($n = 13$), only general descriptions of reach (e.g., weak, average, or high) were reported. To convert verbal description to numbers, studies reporting average reach were assigned 50% reach. Weak reach was assigned the midvalue in the bottom third of a 100% scale—halfway between 0% and 33%—17%. High reach was assigned the midvalue in the upper third of the scale—halfway between 66% and 100%—83%. Forty-one of the 48 campaigns had usable information about reach.

Control Group Trend. The control group trend in behavior change was coded from the difference between pretest and posttest measures of the percentage of people performing the target behavior in the control communities. This was only possible for studies that included control communities ($k = 21$, $n = 102,765$). If the campaign aimed at an increase in the behavior (i.e. seat belt use), then the pretest measure was subtracted from the posttest. If the campaign was designed to decrease the behavior (i.e. number of smokers), then the posttest measure was subtracted from the pretest. In both cases, the resulting percentage represents the amount gained toward the goal in the control group. Twenty-one campaigns provided information about control group trends.

Campaign Length. The length of the campaign was coded in years or fractions of years as reported.

RESULTS

The average media campaign effect on behavior was $M_r = .09$. (The notation indicates it is a mean of correlations.) It was calculated by averaging the 48 individual campaign effects, weighted by the number of cases used to provide each estimate. The total number of pooled cases in the sample was $N = 168,362$. The 95% confidence interval around the average media campaign effect was $M_r = .07$ to $.10$. The test of homogeneity revealed the set of campaigns was heterogeneous $SD_r = .06$, varying from a low campaign effect size of $.01$ to a high of $.41$. Sampling error explained 7% of the variance across campaigns, $\chi^2(47) = 655.74$ ($p < .001$). Given the wide range of effect sizes reported, and the fact that the differences were not explained by sampling error, it was appropriate to investigate the hypothesized moderators of effect size. (If the set of campaigns were homogeneous, then there would have been no statistical variation among campaign effects to explain.) Table 19.1 presents the list of campaigns, their attributes, and one key reference for each campaign. (The reference section includes all references with relevant information for each campaign.)

Table 19.2 presents the results for all of the hypotheses. It was predicted (H1) that campaigns with at least one message about enforcement of policies designed to promote a particular behavior would have a greater impact than campaigns without enforcement messages. Of all the variables tested, enforcement messages was the most powerful moderator of campaign effect size. The results for this hypothesis appear in the first two rows of Table 19.2. There were four campaigns ($k = 4$) that used enforcement messages. Note that because the seat belt enforcement campaigns had large sample sizes, 28% of individuals in the pooled sample were part of enforcement campaigns. They had a mean effect size of $M_r = .17$ with a standard deviation of $SD_r = .02$, based on a pooled sample (Tn) of $n = 46,771$ respondents. The enforcement campaigns were much more effective than campaigns that did not use enforcement messages, which had an

TABLE 19.1
Media Campaigns Used in the Analysis

Campaign	Cite	Behavior[a]	Campaign Effect Size	Sample Size	Reach	Message Variables[b]	Length (years)	Control Trend
A Su Salud	McAlister et al, 1992; Ramirez & McAlister, 1988	Smoking cessation	.20	175	.50	R	4	
AIDS Community Demonstration Project	Fishbein, Guenther-Grey, Johnson, et al., 1996	Condom use, vaginal sex, bleach use	.03	6,184	.43	R	2	
AIDS Prevention For Pediatric Life	Santelli, Celantro, Rozsenich, et al, 1995	Condom use	.05	1,509	.64		3	.05
America Responds to AIDS	Snyder, 1991	Risky sex	.01	163	.17		.17	
CA Tobacco Education Media Campaign	Popham, Potter, Hetrick, Muthen, Duerr, & Johnson, 1994	Smoking	.03	10,339	.47		1	
Cancer Control in a TX Barrio	McAlister, et al., 1995; McAlister, Ramirez, Amezcua, Pulley, Stern, & Mercado, 1992	Mammography screen, pap smear	.05	309	.42	N, R, S	1	
COMMIT	COMMIT Research Group, 1995a; 1995b; 1996; Corbett, Thompson, White, & Taylor, 1990–1991; Wallack & Sciandra, 1990–1991.	Quit smoking	.02	20,347	.17		4	
Community Trials Project: Underage Access Component	Grube, 1997	Alcohol sales to minors	.17	949	.17	N, E	1	.12

(Continued)

TABLE 19.1
(Continued)

Campaign	Cite	Behavior[a]	Campaign Effect Size	Sample Size	Reach	Message Variables[b]	Length (years)	Control Trend
Decreasing Binge Drinking at College	Haines and Spear, 1996	Binge drinking	.07	4,258	.50		4	.02
Drinking During Pregnancy	Kaskutas & Graves, 1994	Limiting drinking	.11	2,746	.83	S	2	
Farm Cancer Control Project	Gardiner, Mullan, Rosenman, Zhu, & Swanson, 1995	Mammography screening	.01	1,545	.33		1	.02
Five-A-Day for Better Health, CA	Foerster, Kizer, DiSogra, Bal, Krieg, & Bunch, 1995	Fruit and vegetable consumption	.01	2,002	.17		2	
Forsyth County Cervical Cancer Prevention	Dignan, Michielutte, Wells, & Bahnson, 1994	Pap smear	.04	1,830	.14	S	1.5	.02
Freedom from Smoking in St. Louis	Wheeler, 1988	Quit smoking	.18	429	.84		.14	
Friends Can Be Good Medicine	Hersey, Klibanoff, Lam, & Taylor, 1984	Supportive behavior	.09	340	.51		.08	
Headstrong	Rouzier & Alto, 1995	Bike helmets	.41	121		N	2	
Heart to Heart	Goodman, Wheeler, & Lee, 1995	Smoke, exercise, weight, cholesterol, blood pressure (PH)	.01	2,700	.17		4	-.03
Know When To Say No	Werch & Kersten, 1992; Werch, Kersten, & Young, 1992	Drinking	.12	314	.99	N	.17	
KY Rural High Blood Pressure Control	Kotchen, McKean, Jackson-Thayer, Moore, Straus, & Kotchen, 1986	Hypertension (PH)	.10	1,044	.13	S	5	.07

Media-based Mammography in San Diego	Mayer, Kossman, Miller, Crooks, Slymen, & Lee, 1993	Mammography screening	.05	506	.44	N, S	.5	
Minority Smoking Cessation In Chicago	Jason, Tate, Goodman, Buckenberger, & Gruder, 1988	Smoking cessation	.16	137	.31		.05	
MMHP, MN Adult Smoking Prevention	Jacobs, Luepker, Mittlemark, et. al., 1986; Lando, Pechacek, Pirie, et al., 1995; Luepker, Murray, Jacobs, et al., 1994	Smoking, physical activity	.05	7,400	.17		7	.05
MMHP, MN Youth Smoking Prevention	Perry, Klepp, & Sillers, 1989	Smoking prevention	.09	4,090	.50		5	−.21
MN Periodontal Awareness TV Campaign	Bakdash, McMillan, & Lange, 1984	Dental visits	.13	2,000	.70	S	.5	
MN/WI Adolescent Tobacco Use	Murray, Perry, Griffin, et al., 1992; Murray, Pirie, Leupker, & Pallonen, 1989; Murray, Prokhorov, & Harty, 1994	Smoking	.07	15,396	.17		5	.00
Mpowerment Project	Kegeles, Hays, & Coates, 1996	Unprotected anal sex	.12	188	.87		.75	−.01
Parents Magazine Intervention	Kishchuck, Laurendeau, Desjardin, & Perreault, 1995	Positive, negative interactions with kids	.02	307	.95	N	3	
Preventing Baby Bottle Tooth Decay	Bruerd, Kinney, & Bothwell, 1989	Tooth decay (PH)	.14	1,465	.45	N	3	
Programma Latino Para Dejar De Fumar	Marín, 1990; Marín, Pérez-Stable, Marín, & Hauck, 1994	Smoking	.06	5,701		R	1.5	

(Continued)

TABLE 19.1
(Continued)

Campaign	Cite	Behavior[a]	Campaign Effect Size	Sample Size	Reach	Message Variables[b]	Length (years)	Control Trend
Rural CVD Program in WV	Farquahar, Behnke, Detels, & Albright, 1997	Wellness score (PH)	.09	425			2	
Seat Belt Contest	Foss, 1989	Child seat belt use	.09	6,072	.59	N	.5	
Seat belt Use	Robertson, Kelley, O'Neill, wixom, Eiswirth, & Haddon, 1974	Seat belt use	.01	2,720	.17		.75	-.09
Seat belt Use in Elmira, NY	Williams, Lund, Preusser, & Blomberg, 1987	Seat belt use	.24	3,358		N, E	.06	-.05
Seat belt Use in Modesto, CA	Lund, Stuster, & Fleming, 1989	Seat belt use	.22	1,971		N, E	.15	-.06
Seat belts in VA	Roberts and Geller, 1994	Seat belt use	.16	40,493	.50	E	.6	-.01
Smoking Prevention in CA, Prop 99	Jenkins, McPhee, Le, Pham, Ha, & Stewart, 1997	Quit smoking, smoking	.04	5,125			2	-.01
Smoking Prevention In School	Flynn, Worden, Secker-Walker, Badger, Geller, & Costanza, 1992	Smoking	.10	2,540	.50		4	-.19
Smoking; Community Control Center, L.A.	Danaher, Berkanovic, & Gerber, 1984	Quit smoking attempts	.15	2,800	.37		.04	
Smoking; VA Hospital Clinic	Mogielnicki, Neslin, Dulac, Balstra, Gillie, & Corson, 1986	Smoking abstinence	.19	127	.61		.42	-.15

Study	Reference	Message						
Stanford 3 Community Study	Farquhar, Wood, Breitrose, et. al, 1977; Fortmann, Williams, Hulley, Haskell, & Farquhar, 1981; Meyer, Nash, McAlister, Maccoby, & Farquhar, 1980	Diet, weight, cholesterol, fat (PH)	.06	1,113	.50	N	2	.06
Stanford 5 Community Study	Fortmann, Winkleby, Flora, Haskell, & Taylor, 1990; Schooler, Chaffee, Flora, & Roser, 1998	Weight, cholesterol, blood pressure (PH), smoking, exercise	.01	3,458	.60		5	.11
Stop Smoking Clinic, NY	Dubren, 1977	Quit smoking	.11	293	.50		.08	
SuVida Su Salud	Saurez, Nickols, & Brady, 1993	Screenings: pap & mammograms	.10	376	.34	S	2	
Take A Bite Out of Crime	O'Keefe, 1985	Crime prevention	.10	1,049	.48		2	
Time to Quit in Buffalo	Cummings, Sciandra, & Markello, 1997	Smoking cessation	.16	321	.99		.02	
VT Drink Calculator Community Educ.	Worden, Flynn, Merrill, Waller, & Haugh, 1989	Blood alcohol (PH)	.08	487	.81	N	.5	
Weight-A-Thon	Wing & Epstein, 1982	Weight loss (PH)	.08	189	.50		.12	
Young Adolescent Smoking Behavior	Bauman, Brown, Bryan, Fisher, Padgett, & Sweeney, 1988; Bauman, La-Prelle, Brown, Koch, & Padgett, 1991; Bauman, Padgett, & Koch, 1991; Brown, Bauman & Padgett, 1990; La Prelle, Bauman, & Koch, 1992	Smoking	.03	951	.14		.6	.14

[a]Physiological measures are marked by (PH). [b]Message variables: N = New information, E = Enforcement, R = Role model messages and S = Services.

TABLE 19.2
Effect of Message Characteristics, Reach, Control Group Trend, and Length on Media Campaign Effect Size

	All Campaigns					Persuasive Campaigns				
Message Types	Avg. Effect Size (M_r)	SD_r	No. of Campaigns (k)	Pooled n	r	Avg. Effect Size (M_r)	SD_r	No. of Campaigns (k)	Pooled n	r
Enforcement messages										
Present	.17	.02	4	46,771	.82					
Absent	.05	.04	44	121,591						
New information messages										
Present	.14	.07	12	16,972	.30	.09	.04	9	10,694	.31
Absent	.08	.06	36	151,390		.05	.04	35	110,897	
Service message										
Present	.07	.05	7	7,610	−.06	.07	.05	7	7,610	.10
Absent	.09	.06	41	160,752		.05	.04	37	113,981	
Role model messages										
Present	.05	.02	4	12,369	−.17	.05	.03	4	12,369	−.05
Absent	.09	.06	44	155,993		.05	.04	40	109,222	
Reach										
Low ≤40%						.04	.03	13	59,274	.47
Average 41–54%						.05	.03	16	42,348	
High ≥55%						.08	.04	12	17,958	
Control trend										
Negative <−.02	.11	.09	7	17,506	−.21	.06	.04	5	12,177	−.48
None −.02–.02	.12	.05	7	68,835		.06	.02	6	28,342	
Positive >.02	.05	.04	7	16,424		.04	.02	6	15,475	
Campaign length										
Short ≤.5 year	.14	.08	16	16,893	−.50	.09	.06	14	11,564	−.04
Medium .6–1.5 years	.12	.06	9	64,716		.04	.02	7	23,274	
Long ≥2 years	.05	.03	23	86,753		.05	.04	23	86,753	

Note. The r column entries are the correlations between the characteristic and average campaign effect size.

average effect size of .05 (SD_r = .04, k = 44, and n = 121,591.). The correlation between enforcement messages and the campaign effect size was very large, r = .82.

Although three out of four of the enforcement campaigns involved seat belts, the observed effect does not appear to be an artifact of the topic. The three seat belt campaigns using enforcement were highly successful (M_r = .17, SD_r = .02; n = 45,822, k = 3), whereas two earlier seat belt campaigns prior to statewide seat belt laws and not using enforcement messages were not as successful (M_r = .07, SD_r = .03, n = 8792, k = 2). Also the sole nonseat belt campaign with enforcement messages (addressing alcohol sales to minors) was as successful as the seat belt campaigns with enforcement (M_r = .17, n = 949, k = 1). Finally, the impact of enforcement messages on campaign effect size (r = .82) was larger than the impact of seat belt as topic on campaign effect size (r = .74).

The study concluded that campaigns using enforcement messages, because they are based in part on coercion, represent a qualitatively different kind of campaign than one based solely on persuasion. Therefore, we analyzed the role of the remaining moderator variables both for all campaigns together and for the set of 44 persuasive campaigns separately. (There were not enough enforcement campaigns to conduct a separate analyses of those.) The results for the combined persuasive and enforcement campaigns are presented first.

Among the other message characteristics, only new information messages were positively correlated with campaign effect size for the combined persuasive and enforcement campaigns (Table 19.2). As predicted in H2, inclusion of a message that contained new information increased effect size (r = .30). The magnitude of the relationship held for the subset of persuasive campaigns (r = .31), indicating that new information about the behavior or service opportunities were as vital to campaign success as news about upcoming enforcement.

H3 predicted a difference between the service promotion and other campaigns, but it was negligible for combined enforcement and persuasive campaigns (r = −.06) and for persuasive campaigns alone (r = .10). The change in sign for services messages is due to the fact that none of the enforcement campaigns, which were highly successful, promoted services. When the enforcement campaigns were removed from the sample, the average effect size for campaigns with services messages was slightly greater than that for persuasion-only campaigns without services messages. The very small correlations indicate that the presence or absence of services messages is not critical to campaign effect sizes.

Contrary to expectations (H4), campaigns that included role model messages were not more effective than campaigns without role model messages; in fact, they had slightly less of an effect (r = −.17) when considering all campaigns, and a negligible effect among persuasive campaigns ($r = -.05$).

The fifth hypothesis predicted that the degree of reach was positively related to campaign effect size. Reach had a strong positive correlation with average effect size ($r = .47$, $k = 41$, $n = 119,580$). The correlation is representative of persuasive campaigns only, because no reach information was given in the reports of the enforcement campaigns. Table 19.2 presents the average effect sizes for reach when the unweighted sample is partitioned roughly into thirds. (The correlation reported is based on the continuous weighted variable.) Interestingly, plenty of campaigns had weak reach in the intervention communities—the mean reach rate was 36% ($SD = .20$, $k = 41$, $n = 119,580$). Among campaigns that reported an exact figure for reach, the mean reach rate was 42% ($SD = .20$, $k = 28$, $n = 66,758$). Note that for evaluation designs with a control group, reach represents the differential reach between control and intervention communities, and the mean reach rate was 30% ($SD = .18$) and the correlation between differential reach and average effect was a more moderate $r = .28$ ($n = 87,054$, $k = 26$). In the case of designs without control groups, the mean reach rate in the intervention communities alone was 52% ($SD = .16$) and the correlation between reach and average effect was $r = .79$ ($n = 32,526$, $k = 15$). Thus, despite the fact that it is harder to achieve a differential in exposure in the control group designs, the relationship between differential reach and campaign effect size was still substantial.

As predicted (H6), the effect of control group trend on campaign effect size was negative. This was true for both the total sample ($r = -.21$) and the persuasive campaigns ($r = -.48$). The control group trend varied from $-.21$ to $.14$, $M = -.01$, $SD = .06$. For illustrative purposes, Table 19.2 presents the average effect size for control trend categorized into three levels.

The effect of campaign length was not curvilinear, as was anticipated in H7. The short enforcement campaigns, some of which lasted only a month or two, were highly successful, along with some other campaigns that lasted about a year. For the total sample, the correlation between campaign length and campaign effect size was negative ($r = -.50$, $M = 2.3$ years, $SD = 1.9$ years). Table 19.2 contains estimates of effect sizes for campaigns up to six months long, those lasting two years or more, and those in-between, and illustrates that the relationship is more linear than curvilinear. By examining a graph, it was found that the cut-point in the trend seemed to be 1 year. Campaigns that lasted 1 year or less had a higher effect size ($M_r = .13$, $SD_r = .07$, $n = 74,078$, $k = 23$) than campaigns lasting more than 1 year ($M_r = .05$, $SD_r = .03$, $n = 94,284$, $k = 25$). Among persuasive campaigns, the effect of campaign length on campaign effect size was very small ($r = -.04$).

Effect of Other Predictors on Reach Among Persuasive Campaigns

Because the effect of reach was substantial, it was possible to see whether the message characteristics and some other variables had an indirect effect on campaign effect size by increasing reach to the campaign. Unfortunately, none of the enforcement campaigns measured reach, so it was impossible to measure the effect of enforcement messages on reach. The analysis of reach was therefore performed only using persuasive campaigns. The results indicate that reach was greater with persuasive campaigns that were shorter ($r = -.43$) and had new information messages ($r = .35$). There was a slight decrease in reach among persuasive campaigns with greater control group trends ($r = -.18$) and those using role model messages ($r = .14$).

DISCUSSION

A meta-analysis of 48 health behavior campaigns was conducted to estimate the average short-term effect that exposure to an intervention had on behavior change. In most of the studies, campaign exposure was manipulated within the context of a quasi-experimental design, comparing individuals within an intervention community that received a media campaign to individuals in a control community. Overall, there was an average short-term campaign effect size on behavior of $M_r = .09$, which roughly translates into 9% more people performing the behavior after the campaign than before. For persuasive campaigns—defined as those not using messages about the legal enforcement of the behavior—the average campaign effect size on behavior was $M_r = .05$. The average enforcement (coersion) message campaign effect size was $M_r = .17$. These figures should be helpful for campaign planners when setting specific behavioral goals, and for evaluators for comparative purposes and evaluation design decisions.

The average media campaign effect size was, reassuringly, similar to effect sizes found for family planning programs around the world ($M_r = .08$; Bauman, 1997), in-school smoking prevention interventions (5% change; Rooney & Murray, 1996), traditional in-school drug use prevention programs aimed at late elementary grades ($M_r = .06$ for Project Dare, and $M_r = .08$ for other programs; Ennett, Tobler, Ringwalt, & Flewelling, 1994). Clinic-based interventions may be more effective for the size audience they reach ($M_r = .27$; Mullen et al., 1997), although a study of clinic-based education for cardiac patients had an average effect sizes comparable to the media campaign effect sizes ($M_r = .08$, converted from the g-statistics in Table 7 and averaged; Mullen, Mains, & Velez, 1992). Building on a prior meta-analysis (Snyder et al., in press), the study compared the impact of a series of campaign characteristics on campaign effect sizes.

Message Characteristics

A much larger effect size was found for campaigns that included messages about enforcement than for persuasive campaigns without enforcement messages. Although there were only four enforcement campaigns, the fact that they involved two different topics (seat belt use and alcohol checks for minors) meant that the finding was not specific to a single topic. When there is an enforcement angle for a particular health topic, it would be worthwhile for campaign planners to create enforcement messages.

In the absence of an enforcement angle, it is valuable to emphasize messages containing information that is new to the audience. Analysis indicated that campaigns including messages with new information succeeded by contributing directly to campaign effects and by increasing the reach of the campaign.

Reach Effects

It was also confirmed that campaigns with greater reach—a higher percentage of people exposed to the campaign messages—have greater effects. Campaigns affecting smaller proportions of the target audiences often did not have adequate coverage, or they failed to have coverage greater than in nonintervention communities. The mediocre mean rates of reach in the intervention communities—averaging less than 40%—indicate that this is an area with much room for improvement in future campaigns.

Control Group Trends

It is difficult to outperform a rising trend in the control community. The control group trend may be due to a secular trend, such as was reportedly the case for the Minnesota Heart Project (Murray, 1995; Viswanath & Finnegan, chap. 16, this volume). Or, it may be due to a spillover of campaign information, other campaigns happening in the control community, or national campaigns. Given the importance of the control trend in dampening campaign effects, future research could attempt to tease out these potential explanations. When evaluators are concerned about the possibility of control group trends, it would be useful to employ multiple baselines (Cook & Shadish, 1994).

Campaign Length

Quite unexpectedly, it was found that campaigns lasting 1 year or less were more successful than those lasting longer, but the effect was largely due to the short enforcement campaigns having greater success rates.

Among persuasive campaigns, campaign length did not relate to campaign effect size, but was negatively related to reach. As operationalized in the study, this means that short persuasive campaigns were more effective at reaching a greater proportion of people in the intervention communities than long persuasive campaigns. Perhaps longer persuasive campaigns, in taking more time to reach the target audience, never rose to the same level of intensity as short campaigns. It is possible that longer campaigns may have achieved greater *frequency of contact* with the smaller subset of the audience they did reach. Unfortunately, it was not possible to code the frequency or intensity of the campaigns, so this cannot be tested. At present, however, it is recommended that large demonstration projects, which typically last for three to five years, attempt to reach larger numbers of people within intervention communities.

Limitations

There are some limitations with this approach to summarizing effects. It was assumed that the search for campaign evaluations was equally likely to locate successful and unsuccessful projects. If this is not true, then the studies may claim to describe the average effect of campaigns that reach public notice, rather than the average effect of all campaigns.

As noted earlier, it was decided to accept all cases with some form of control, but not limited to the strictest quasi-experimental designs. Many times, in meta-analysis, studies are rated by rigor and the results are presented for both the most rigorous and the full population of studies. In the current study, when examining the subset of studies with a pretest, posttest, control group design and a good (not self-selected) sample ($n = 106,964$), the correlations between campaign effect size and the moderator were similar to or slightly greater than those with the entire sample: enforcement ($r = .92$), new information ($r = .41$), role model messages ($r = -.28$), control group trend ($r = -.19$), and length ($r = -.57$). Reach appeared to have less of an effect ($r = .08$), whereas services messages appeared to become more negative ($r = -.21$). It is hard to know whether to give more weight to the results based on the rigorous subset, however, because less than half of the campaigns were included in the rigorous subset.

Another approach is to systematically examine the relationship between design and campaign effect size, which has been done elsewhere (Snyder & Hamilton, 1999), and then check for methodological confounds with campaign message characteristics. It is possible that some of the important design features (e.g., whether the sample was self-selected, the presence of a control group, and the presence of a pre-test) interact with some of the moderator variables identified in the current study. For example, it was reported earlier that studies with control groups had a smaller relationship between reach and campaign effect size than studies without control groups. In addition, studies with control groups were less likely to use new information but more likely to use enforcement messages in their campaigns. As the results of more studies become available, it will be possible to separate variance due to methodological features from variance due to campaign message features.

The mixing of projects with diverse audiences, behavioral objectives, and types and quality of communication interventions provides strength and generality to the claims, even though this complexity made it harder to be sure that moderator variables were not confounded with unmeasured characteristics of the campaigns. For example, campaign spending was impossible to code from the published record, but may covary with many of the measured characteristics and with campaign effect size. It would be very valuable for published evaluations to include spending information or cost-effectiveness data.

Another limitation of the present work is that only short-term effects were measured. Long-term effects logically should be less as people backslide into old behaviors, but the "rate of decay" that occurs over time is unknown. On the other hand, there may be some issues that show sleeper effects—greater effects after some time has passed. In the future, media campaigns need to be thought of as part of a long-term program to change a particular behavior or set of behaviors. The health communication field needs to learn how best to combine a series of modest impact campaigns for more sustainability. Finally, meta-analyses provide snapshots of relationships given the available studies at a particular point in time. As more campaign evaluations are published, there will be an opportunity to further refine the results presented here.

CONCLUSIONS

In conclusion, this analysis supports the claim that media campaigns can cause behavior change. As Flay and Cook (1989) speculated, the fact that many campaign evaluations find no effects is due to the small nature of campaign effects rather than null effects. The methodology of meta-analysis has also proved helpful in beginning to tease out which campaign factors are and are not related to campaign success. There was empirical support for two hypotheses that existed in the literature but were untested empirically—the difficulties of overcoming a control group trend and the importance of the extent of campaign reach in the intervention communities in producing effects. Future campaigns should have different expectations of success based on whether the campaign will use enforcement-linked messages or only persuasive messages, and whether there is new information to impart.

ACKNOWLEDGMENTS

Special thanks go to Vicki Freimuth for her help in locating some of the campaigns used in the study. Also, we thank Fran Fleming-Milici, Elizabeth Mitchell, James Kiwanuka-Tondo, and Dwayne Proctor for their assistance.

REFERENCES

*Bakdash, M. B., McMillan, D. G., & Lange, A. L. (1984). Minnesota periodontal awareness television campaign. *Northwest Dentistry, 63*(6), 12–17.

Bauman, K. E. (1997). The effectiveness of family planning programs evaluated with true experimental designs. *American Journal of Public Health, 87*, 666–669.

*Bauman, K. E., Brown, J. D., Bryan, E. S., Fisher, L. A., Padgett, C. A., & Sweeney, J. M. (1988). Three mass media campaigns to prevent adolescent cigarette smoking. *Preventive Medicine, 17*, 510–530.

*Bauman, K. E., LaPrelle, J., Brown, J. D., Koch, G. G., & Padgett, C. A. (1991). The influence of three mass media campaigns on variables related to adolescent cigarette smoking: Results of a field experiment. *American Journal of Public Health, 81*(5), 597–604.

*Bauman, K. E., Padgett, A., & Koch, G. G. (1989). A media-based campaign to encourage personal communication among adolescents about not smoking cigarettes: Participation, selection and consequences. *Health Education Research, 4*(1), 35–44.

*Brown, J. D., Bauman, K. E., & Padgett, C. A. (1990). A validity problem in measuring exposure to mass media campaigns. *Health Education Quarterly, 17*(3), 299–306.

*Bruerd, B., Kinney, M. B., & Bothwell, E. (1989). Preventing baby tooth decay in American Indian and Alaska Native communities: A model for planning. *Public Health Reports, 104*(6), 631–640.

*COMMIT Research Group. (1995a). Community intervention trial for smoking cessation (COMMIT): I. Cohort results from a four-year community intervention. *American Journal of Public Health, 85*(2), 183–191.

*COMMIT Research Group. (1995b). Community intervention trial for smoking cessation (COMMIT): II. Changes in adult cigarette smoking prevalence. *American Journal of Public Health, 85*, 193–200.

*COMMIT Research Group. (1996). Community intervention trial for smoking cessation (COMMIT): Summary of design and intervention. *Journal of the National Cancer Institute, 83*(22), 1620–1628.

Cook, T. D., & Shadish, W. R. (1994). Social experiments: Some developments over the past fifteen years. *Annual Review of Psychology, 45*, 545–580.

*Corbett, K., Thompson, B., White, N., & Taylor, M. (1990–1991). Process evaluation in the community intervention trial for smoking cessation (COMMIT). *International Quarterly of Community Health Education, 11*(3), 291–309.

*Cummings, M. K., Sciandra, R., & Markello, S. (1987). Impact of a newspaper mediated quit smoking program. *American Journal of Public Health, 77*(11), 1452–1453.

*Danaher, B. C., Berkanovic, E., & Gerber, B. (1984). Mass media based health behavior change: Televised smoking cessation program. *Addictive Behavior, 9*, 245–253.

*Dignan, M., Michielutte, R., Wells, H. B., & Bahnson, J. (1994). The Forsyth County Cervical Cancer Prevention Project–1. Cervical cancer screening for black women. *Health Education Research, 9*(4), 411–420.

*Dubren, R. (1977). Evaluation of a televised stop-smoking clinic. *Public Health Reports, 92*(1), 81–84.

Ennett, S. T., Tobler, N. S., Ringwalt, C. L., & Flewelling, R. L. (1994). How effective is drug abuse resistance education? A meta-analysis of project DARE outcome evaluations. *American Journal of Public Health, 84*(9), 1394–1401.

*Farquhar, J. W., Behnke, K. S., Detels, M. P., & Albright, C. L. (1997). Short- and long-term outcomes of a health promotion program in a small rural community. *American Journal of Health Promotion, 11*(6), 411–414.

*Farquhar, J. W., Wood, P. D., Breitrose, H., Haskell, W. L., Meyer, A. J., Maccoby, N., Alexander, J. K., Brown, B. W., McAlister, A. L., Nash, J. D., & Stern, M. P. (1977). Community education for cardiovascular health. *The Lancet,* 1192–1195.

*Fishbein, M., Guenther-Grey, C., Johnson, W. D., Wolitski, R. J., McAlister, A., Rietmeijer, C. A., & O'Reilly, K. (1996). Using a theory-based community intervention to reduce AIDS risk behaviors: The CDC's AIDS community demonstration projects. In S. Oskamp & S. C. Thompson (Eds.), *Understanding and preventing HIV risk behavior, safer sex and drug use* (pp. 177–206). Thousand Oaks, CA: Sage.

Flay, B. R., & Cook, T. D. (1989). Three models for summative evaluation of prevention campaigns with a mass media component. In R. E. Rice & C. K. Atkin (Eds.), *Public communication campaigns* (2nd ed., pp. 175–195). Newbury Park, CA: Sage.

Flora, J. A., Maibach, E. W., & Maccoby, N. (1989). The role of media across four levels of health promotion intervention. *Annual Review of Public Health, 10,* 181–201.

*Flynn, B. S., Worden, J. K., Secker-Walker, R. H., Badger, G. J., Geller, B. M., & Costanza, M. C. (1992). Prevention of cigarette smoking through mass media intervention and school programs. *American Journal of Public Health, 82*(6), 827–834.

*Foerster, S. B., Kizer, K. W., DiSogra, L. K., Bal, D. G., Krieg, B. F., & Bunch, K. L. (1995). California's "5 a Day-for better Health!" campaign: An innovative population-based effort to effect large-scale dietary change. *American Journal of Preventive Medicine, 11*(2), 124–131.

*Fortmann, S. P., Williams, P. T., Hulley, S. B., Haskell, W. L., & Farquhar, J. W. (1981). Effect of health education on dietary behavior: The Stanford Three Community study. *American Journal of Clinical Nutrition, 34,* 2030–2038.

*Fortmann, S. P., Winkleby, M. A., Flora, J. A., Haskell, W. L., & Taylor, C. B. (1990). Effects of long-term community health education on blood pressure and hypertension control: The Stanford five city project. *American Journal of Epidemiology, 132*(4), 629–646.

*Foss, R. D. (1989). Evaluation of a community-wide incentive program to promote safety restraint use. *American Journal of Public Health, 79*(3), 304–306.

Freimuth, V. S., & Taylor, M. (May, 1995). *Are mass mediated health campaigns effective? A review of the evidence.* Paper presented at the annual meeting of International Communication Association, Albuquerque, NM.

*Gardiner, J. C., Mullan, P. B., Rosenman, K. D., Zhu, Z., & Swanson, G. M. (1995). Mammography usage and knowledge about breast cancer in Michigan farm population before and after an educational intervention. *Journal of Cancer Education, 10*(3), 155–162.

*Goodman, R. M., Wheeler, F. C., & Lee, P. R. (1995). Evaluation of the Heart to Heart Project: Lessons from a community based chronic disease project. *American Journal of Health Promotion, 9*(6), 443–455.

*Grube, J. W. (1997). Preventing sales of alcohol to minors: Results from a community trial. *Addiction, 92*(2), S251–S260.

*Haines, M., & Spear, S. F. (1996). Changing the perception of the norm: A strategy to decrease binge drinking among college students. *Journal of American College Health, 45*(3), 134–140.

Hamilton, M. (1991). *Meta-Corr* [Computer software]. University of Connecticut.

*Hersey, J. C., Klibanoff, L. S., Lam, D. J., & Taylor, R. L. (1984). Promoting social support: The impact of California's "friends can be good medicine" campaign. *Health Education Quarterly, 11*(3), 293–311.

Hunter, J. E. (1993). *VGBARE* [Computer software]. Michigan State University.

Hunter, J. E., & Schmidt, F. L. (1990). *Methods of meta-analysis: Correcting error and bias in research findings.* Newbury Park, CA: Sage.

*Jacobs, D. R., Luepker, R. V., Mittlemark, M. B., Folsom, A. R., Pirie, P. L., Mascioli, S. R., Hannan, P. J. Pechacek, T. F., Bracht, N. S., Carlaw, R. W., Kline, F. G., & Blackburn, H. (1986). Community-wide prevention strategies: Evaluation design of the Minnesota heart health program. *Journal of Chronic Disease, 39*(10), 775–788.

*Jason, L. A., Tait, E., Goodman, D., Buckenberger, L., & Gruder, C. L. (1988). Effects of a televised smoking cessation intervention among low-income and minority smokers. *American Journal of Community Psychology, 16*(6), 863–876.

*Jenkins, C. N. H., McPhee, S. J., Le, A., Pham, G. Q., Ha, N. T., & Stewart, S. (1997). The effectiveness of a media-led intervention to reduce smoking among Vietnamese-American men. *American Journal of Public Health, 87*(6), 1031–1034.

Johnson, B. T. (1995). *DSTAT 1.11* [Computer software]. Hillsdale NJ: Lawrence Erlbaum Associates.

*Kaskutas, L. A., & Graves, K. (1994). Relationship between cumulative exposure to health messages and awareness and behavior-related drinking during pregnancy. *American Journal of Health Promotion, 9*(2), 115–124.

*Kegeles, S. M., Hays, R. B., & Coates, T. J. (1996). The Mpowerment project: A community-level prevention intervention for young gay men. *American Journal of Public Health, 86*(8), 1129–1136.

Kelman, H. C. (1958). Compliance, identification, and internalization: Three processes of attitude change. *Journal of Conflict Resolution, 2,* 51–60.

Kelman, H. C. (1961). Processes of opinion change. *Public Opinion Quarterly, 25,* 57–78.

*Kishchuk, N., Laurendeau, M., Desjardin, N., & Perreault, R. (1995). Parental support: Effects of a mass media intervention. *Canadian Journal of Public Health, 86*(2), 128–132.

*Kotchen, J. M., McKean, H. E., Jackson-Thayer, S., Moore, R. W., Straus, R., & Kotchen, T. A. (1986). Impact of a rural high blood pressure control program on hypertension control and cardiovascular disease mortality. *Journal of the American Medial Association, 255*(16), 2177–2182.

*Lando, H. A., Pechacek, T. F., Pirie, P. L., Murray, D. M., Mittlemark, M. B., Lichtenstein, E., Nothwehr, F., & Gray, C. (1995). Changes in adult cigarette smoking in the Minnesota heart health program. *American Journal of Public Health, 85*(2), 201–208.

*LaPrelle, J., Bauman, K. E., & Koch, G. G. (1992). High intercommunity variation in adolescent cigarette smoking in a 10-community field experiment. *Evaluation Review, 16*(2), 115–130.

*Luepker, R. V., Murray, D. M., Jacobs, D. R., Mittelmark, M. B., Bracht, N., Carlaw, R., Crow, R., Elmer, P., Finnegan, J., Folsom, A. R., Grimm, R., Hannan, P. J., Jeffrey, R., Landow, H., McGovern, P., Mullis, R., Perry, C. L., Pechacek, T., Pirie, P., Sprafka, J. M., Weisbrod, R., & Blackburn, H. (1994). Community education for cardiovascular disease prevention: Risk factor changes in the Minnesota heart health program. *American Journal of Public Health, 84*(9), 1383–1393.

*Lund, A. K., Stuster, J., & Fleming, A. (1989). Special publicity and enforcement of California's belt use laws: Making a secondary law work. *Journal of Criminal Justice, 17,* 329–341.

*Marín, B. V., Pérez-Stable, E. J., Marín, G., & Hauck, W. W. (1994). Effects of a community intervention to change smoking behavior among Hispanics. *American Journal of Preventive Medicine, 10*(6), 340–347.

*Marín, G. (1990). Changes in information as a function of a culturally appropriate smoking cessation community intervention for Hispanics. *American Journal of Community Psychology, 18*(6), 847–864.

*Mayer, J. A., Kossman, M. K., Miller, L. C., Crooks, C. E., Slymen, D. J., & Lee, Jr., C. D. (1993). Evaluation of a media-based mammography program. *American Journal of Preventive Medicine*, 8(1), 23–29.

*McAlister, A. L., Fernandez-Esquer, M. E., Ramirez, A. G., Trevino, F., Gallion, K. J., Villarreal, R., Pulley, L., Hu, S., Torres, I., & Qing, Z. (1995). Community level cancer control in a Texas barrio: Part II. Baseline and preliminary outcome. *Journal of the National Cancer Institute Monographs*, 18, 123–126.

*McAlister, A. L., Ramirez, A. G., Amezcua, C., Pulley, L., Stern, M. P., & Mercado, S. (1992). Smoking cessation in Texas–Mexico border communities: A quasi-experimental panel study. *American Journal of Health Promotion*, 6, 274–279.

McNamara, E. F., Kurth, T., & Hansen, D. (1981). Communication efforts to prevent wildfires. In R. E. Rice & W. J. Paisley (Eds.), *Public communication campaigns* (pp. 143–160). Beverly Hills, CA: Sage.

*Meyer, A. J., Nash, J. D., McAlister, A. L., Maccoby, N., & Farquhar, J. W. (1980). Skills training in a cardiovascular health education campaign. *Journal of Consulting and Clinical Psychology*, 48(2), 129–142.

*Mogielnicki, R. P., Neslin, S., Dulac, J., Balstra, D., Gillie, E., & Corson, J. (1986). Tailored media can enhance the success of smoking cessation clinics. *Journal of Behavioral Medicine*, 9(2), 141–161.

Mullen, P. D., Mains, D. A., & Velez, R. (1992). A meta-analysis of controlled trials of cardiac patient education. A meta-analysis of controlled trials of cardiac patient education. *Patient Education and Counseling*, 19, 143–162.

Mullen, P. D., Simons-Morton, D. G., Ramirez, G., Frankowski, F., Green, L. W., & Mains, D. A. (1997). A meta-analysis of trials evaluating patient education and counseling for three groups of preventive health behaviors. *Patient Education and Counceling*, 32, 157–173.

Murray, D. M. (1995). Designs and analysis of community trials: lessons from the Minnesota Heart Health Program. *American Journal of Epidemiology*, 142(6), 569–575.

*Murray, D. M., Perry, C. L., Griffin, G., Harty, K. C., Jacobs, D. R., Schmid, L., Daly, K., & Pallonen, U. (1992). Results from a statewide approach to adolescent tobacco use prevention. *Preventive Medicine*, 21, 449–472.

*Murray, D. M., Pirie, P., Luepker, R. V., & Pallonen, U. (1989). Five and six-year follow-up results from four seventh-grade smoking prevention strategies. *Journal of Behavioral Medicine*, 12(2), 207–218.

*Murray, D. M., Prokhorov, A. V., & Harty, K. C. (1994). Effects of a statewide antismoking campaign on mass media messages and smoking beliefs. *Preventive Medicine*, 23(1), 54–60.

*O'Keefe, G. J. (1985). "Taking a bite out of crime". The impact of a public information campaign. *Communication Research*, 12(2), 147–178.

*Perry, C. L., Klepp, K. I., & Sillers, C. (1989). Community-wide strategies for cardiovascular health: The Minnesota heart health program youth program. *Health Education Research*, 4(1), 87–101.

*Popham, W. J., Potter, L. D., Hetrick, M. A., Muthen, L. K., Duerr, J. M., & Johnson, M. D. (1994). Effectiveness of the California 1990–1991 tobacco education media campaign. *American Journal of Preventive Medicine*, 10(6), 319–326.

*Ramirez, A. G., & McAlister, A. L. (1988). Mass media campaigns-A su salud. *Preventive Medicine*, 17, 608–621.

*Roberts, D. S., & Geller, S. (1994). A statewide intervention to increase safety belt use: Adding to the impact of a belt use law. *American Journal of Health Promotion*, 8(3), 172–174.

*Robertson, L. S., Kelley, A. B., O'Neill, B., Wixom, C. W., Eiswirth, R. S., & Haddon, W. (1974). A controlled study of the effect of television messages on safety belt use. *American Journal of Public Health*, 64(11), 1071–1080.

Rooney, B. L., & Murray, D. M. (1996). A meta-analysis of smoking prevention programs after adjustment for errors in the unit of analysis. *Health Education Quarterly*, 23(11), 48–64.

Rosenthal, R. (1994). Parametric measures of effect size. In H. Cooper & L. V. Hedges (Eds.), *The handbook of research synthesis* (pp. 231–244). New York: Russell Sage Foundation.

*Rouzier, P., & Alto, W. A. (1995). Evolution of a successful community bicycle helmet campaign. *Journal of the American Board of Family Practice*, 8, 283–287.

*Santelli, J. S., Celantro, D. D., Rozsenich, C., Crump, A. D., Davis, M. V., Polacsek, M., Augustyn, M., Rolf, J., McAlister, A. L., & Burwell, L. (1995). Interim outcomes for a community-based program to prevent perinatal HIV transmission. *AIDS Education and Prevention*, 7(3), 210–220.

*Schooler, C., Chaffee, S. H., Flora, J. A., & Roser, C. (1998). Health campaign channels: Trade-offs among reach, specificity, and impact. *Human Communication Research*, 24(3), 410–432.

*Snyder, L. B. (1991). The impact of the surgeon general's understanding AIDS pamphlet in Connecticut. *Health Communication*, 3(1), 37–57.

Snyder, L. B., & Hamilton, M. A. (August, 1999). *When evaluation design affects results: Meta-analysis of evaluations of mediated health communication campaigns*. Paper presented at the annual conferences of the Association for Journalism and Mass Communication, New Orleans, LA.

Snyder, L. B., Hamilton, M. A., Mitchell, E. W., Kiwanuka-Tondo, J., Fleming-Milici, F., & Proctor, D. (in press). The effectiveness of mediated health communication campaigns: Meta-analysis of differences in adoption, prevention, and cessation behavior campaigns. In R. Carveth & J. Bryant (Eds.), *Meta-analysis of media effects*. Mahwah, NJ: Lawrence Erlbaum Associates.

Soumerai, S. B., Ross-Degnan, D., & Kahn, J. S. (1992). Effects of professional and media warnings about the association between aspirin use in children and Reye's syndrome. *Milbank Quarterly*, 70(1), 155–182.

*Suarez, L., Nichols, D. C., & Brady, C. A. (1993). Use of peer role models to increase pap smear and mammogram screening in Mexican-American and black women. *American Journal of Preventive Medicine*, 9(5), 290–296.

*Wallack, L., & Sciandra, R. (1990–1991). Media advocacy and public education in the community intervention trial to reduce health smoking (COMMIT). *International Quarterly of Community Health Education*, 11(3), 205–222.

*Werch, C. E., & Kersten, C. (1992). Effects of a community focused alcohol intervention employing an incentive contest and self-help materials. *Wellness Perspectives: Research, Theory, & Practice*, 8(4), 3–15.

*Werch, C. E., Kersten, C., & Young, M. (1992). Six-month follow-up of a community incentive and self-help alcohol intervention. *Journal of Health Education*, 23(6), 364–368.

*Wheeler, R. J. (1988). Effects of a community-wide smoking cessation program. *Social Science Medicine*, 27(12), 1387–1392.

*Williams, A. F., Lund, A. K., Preusser, D. F., & Blomberg, R. D. (1987). Results of a seat belt use law enforcement and publicity campaign in Elmira, New York. *Accident Analysis and Prevention*, 19(4), 243–249.

Williams, A. F., Reinfurt, D., & Wells, J. K. (1996). Increasing seat belt use in North Carolina. *Journal of Safety Research*, 27(1), 33–41.

*Wing, R. R., & Epstein, L. H. (1982). A community approach to weight control: The American Cancer Society Weight-a-thon. *Preventive Medicine*, 11, 245–250.

*Worden, J. K., Flynn, B. S., Merrill, D. G., Waller, J. A., & Haugh, L. D. (1989). Preventing alcohol-impaired driving through community self-regulation training. *American Journal of Public Health*, 79(3), 287–290.

*Publications used in the analysis

EPILOGUE:

EVALUATION DESIGN FOR PUBLIC HEALTH COMMUNICATION PROGRAMS

Robert C. Hornik
University of Pennsylvania

Large-scale public health communication programs create special problems in trying to make claims for effects. Some of those issues have been addressed by Flay and Cook (1989), and this chapter overlaps in part with their work. However, more than an additional decade of experience with evaluations of public health communication programs provides some new perspective. In addition, there are modified notions about the various mechanisms through which public health communication may affect behavior, some of which have been presented in the first chapter of this volume and are seen by example in the case studies. The role of summative evaluation is still the same, to understand whether a program has been implemented, whether its audience has been exposed to the messages as expected, whether there have been effects on intermediate process and distal (often behavioral) outcomes, and whether some members of the audience were more affected than others. In addition, an evaluation might try to elaborate the causal mechanism for achieving effects so future implementation would go better. The question is how best to meet those purposes.

This chapter draws from the cases presented in this volume and some other cases. They are used to illustrate how researchers have tried to evaluate such programs in practice, and to bring to the fore the design logic of their approaches. The question that underpins the entire chapter is whether or not it is possible to do useful evaluation that will reduce uncertainty about whether a program was successful, even if it is not possible to implement (or it does not make sense to implement) an "ideal" experimental design. This chapter discusses the logic of design in a context of often messy communication interventions.

A good evaluation of a public health communication program must simultaneously satisfy two criteria: First, it must respect the nature of how the program is expected to affect health behavior, and second, it must make it likely that attribution of effects to a program is not confounded by other explanations. These map closely onto the concepts of external and internal validity (Cook & Campbell, 1979). In many cases, satisfying both is a hard task. The tension between them is a constant theme of academic discussions of evaluation design (e.g., Boruch, 1997; Cronbach et al., 1980). There are many issues that loom here, but four have particular resonance for evaluation of mass media-based programs. They include use of controls; time periods of treatment, the appropriate lag before expecting effects and the magnitude of effects to be expected; matching the study population to the target population; and units of treatment and analysis.

THE USE OF CONTROLS

In some cases, the aspiration to unequivocal claims of effects (internal validity) has undermined the full expression of the public communication programs (e.g., Hornik, introduction, this vol.). In particular, classical experimental evaluation designs may constrain exposure. A desire to differentiate levels of exposure between control and experimental communities may lead program designers to reject some channels in fear that their reach extends to control areas. For example, the National High Blood Pressure Education Program worked through national professional organizations, network-sponsored public service announcements and news coverage, widely disseminated press releases, and other activities meant to affect the broad national climate about blood pressure (Roccella, chap. 4, this vol.). These channels were off-limits to the elegantly designed COMMIT trial, with its need to work only in the defined treatment cities and stay away from randomly chosen control cities (COMMIT, 1995).

Public health communication programs are often most successful when they are able to permeate the environment with their messages. Constraining the channels they can work with in order to accommodate control sites may reduce their potential effects even if they ease making valid inferences about effects. Incorporating control sites is particularly problematic in a context of (a) a need to evaluate the effects of programs or of changes in mass media coverage of an issue that are not mounted as research exercises; (b) a good deal of background exposure to messages whose effects have to be controlled away rather than investigated; (c) the possible need to depend on the national media machine to produce high levels of exposure to messages; and (d) the complex process, including changes in social policy, transformation of social norms, and responses of commercial marketing systems, which might underlie some effects but are not easily captured by geographically defined comparisons.

TIME PERIOD OF TREATMENT, THE APPROPRIATE LAG BEFORE EXPECTING EFFECTS, AND THE MAGNITUDE OF EFFECTS TO BE EXPECTED

Other desirable evaluation design elements may also constrain the ability to find effects. Many sponsors may want a quick understanding of whether the funds allocated to a program are well spent. But quick reads may be unfair reads. Programs often need some time to find their way: They have to get to know their audience, discover which channels produce exposure in a cost-effective way, and sort out which messages resonate with particular audience segments. Although good formative research speeds this process, projects often require trial and error and a recognition that they will constantly evolve. Definitive evaluation may need to await project maturity. Evaluations done prematurely may undervalue a project that will eventually learn to operate successfully. In the earliest phases of projects, monitoring exposure and changes in awareness and beliefs may be more appropriate.

Also, only some communication projects can expect quite rapid or large change in behavior. Their model of effect suggests that a substantial population is ready to be moved to action—people may already be well disposed to a behavior, and the communication program tells them how to take action. This may have been true, for example, for the childhood vaccination programs described in Zimicki et al. (chap. 12, this vol.) and the Reye's syndrome case study described by Soumerai et al. (chap. 15, this vol.). In those cases, an evaluation design may be able to find effects in months. However, for many important behaviors, the expected change associated with interventions may be slower. Their models of effect suggest that the population needs to move toward a new social norm about the appropriateness of a behavior, so communication programs may achieve change only slowly. For example, the extraordinary decline in smoking among adults has involved decreases from 1% to 2% per year over three decades, coincident with a broad change in the acceptability of smoking. An evaluation design would not help if it expected change after a short time, or if it included too few respondents to have the statistical power to detect minimal, but worthwhile, change.

MATCHING STUDY POPULATIONS AND TARGET AUDIENCES

There are two issues here: Some programs are targeted toward a particular audience and, if there are not enough of that audience in a study population, the effects can be undetected. Health communication programs also may not work equally well for all audiences. If evaluations are unable to focus their studies on the people most likely to be affected, then they risk missing effects.

An example of the first issue comes from some early evaluations of HIV/AIDS prevention campaigns. They found little evidence of effect when they looked for changes in condom use among all sexually active people. Most of the population were in (or were claiming to be in) long-term monogamous relationships and had no reason to adopt condom use. It was not until they began to focus their analyses on the population at higher risk (i.e., people with "casual" sexual partners) that they began to see the effects described in Wellings' analyses (chap. 8, this vol.).

Some examples of the second concern come from other cases in this volume. Siegel and Biener (chap. 7, this vol.) found effects of the Massachusetts antismoking campaign among younger but not among older adolescents; Worden and Flynn (chap. 1, this vol.) found bigger reductions in smoking initiation among girls than among boys, although this was consistent with their emphasis on girls in message development. Palmgreen and his colleagues (chap. 2, this vol.) found that only high sensation seekers are at risk of marijuana use, and they were the only ones affected by the antidrug advertising campaign.

Clearly, it is easier to match study population to target population when the target population is well-specified beforehand and the samples can be matched. Sometimes this cannot be done because it is not practical to screen for a particular characteristic, and then a post hoc focus on the subsample representing the target population will be needed. Estimates of the total sample size needed will have to be adjusted given the magnitude of the effects expected and the proportion of the sample who will come from the target population. If a sample of 500 people is required to have enough statistical power to make a claim of effect and the target population is only 25% of the total sample, then 2,000 people will be needed to provide that power. An alternative common situation is where theory does not define a priori which groups will be more or less susceptible to campaign effects, but there is a desire to test whether there are such interactions between group and campaign effects. Although post hoc fishing for any interactions that might be present is tempting and probably worthwhile, there is a substantial risk that important interactions will be missed because sample sizes for subgroups are inadequate. There is also some risk that interactions will appear, falsely, because enough tests for such interactions will produce some statistically significant effects, by chance, unless appropriate adjustments are made. Assuring appropriate subgroup sample sizes a priori, based on the specification of interactions to be examined, is less risky.

UNITS OF ANALYSIS AND TREATMENT

Finally, some communication programs have their effects through activating a social or institutional process of change. There may be diffusion of effects from individuals who are directly exposed to messages to others who only talk about the issues with those who are directly exposed. There may also be effects associated with elite exposure to messages, which results in changes in social policy at a local institutional level (e.g., smoking bans in buildings) or at a state or national level (e.g., drinking age restrictions). These social effects are not easily detected if the unit of analysis is the individual and evaluators focus on a comparison between those who are and are not exposed to messages. Indeed, if the social policy effects are shared at a regional or national level, even comparisons between cities with more or less exposure will be inadequate.

There is a real concern, then, that randomized experimental designs that are entirely appropriate when a well-defined treatment (e.g., a new surgical procedure or a new medication) is at issue may be misleading when applied to public health communication interventions, which are messy efforts. As Smith argues in chapter 18, at their best such interventions are constantly evolving, highly opportunistic in exploiting any channel available to reach the audience and reinforce a message. They affect individuals directly and indirectly through social norm and institutional changes. The most successful may operate in a national media environment where newspapers and televised news and talk shows and other media as well as professional channels are discussing the issue. Randomized experimental designs may simply not be feasible, or if enforced, may provide very clean answers to the wrong question. They will reveal how successful a constrained project has been.

ALTERNATIVES TO THE "IDEAL" EVALUATION DESIGN

This critique of ideal evaluation design and its focus on internal validity at the cost of external validity may have some legitimacy. But it founders if it has no alternative to offer. If randomized experimental designs are sometimes inappropriate or not feasible, then what is to be done? The need to evaluate programs remains, and the concerns about claims of success or failure based on weak inferential designs cannot be ignored. Are there legitimate alternative approaches to evaluating public health communication programs that meet both of the criteria set out previously: respect for the way public health communication affects behavior, and adequate consideration of threats to inferences of effects?

In part, the case studies in this volume are an answer to that question. In different ways, the authors maintained respect for the communication projects or processes they evaluated while still doing their best to make well-considered inferences about effects, wherever possible reducing concerns about alternative explanations for the observed results. However, it is useful to expand the implicit arguments of those cases and make their logic clearer. The next few pages systematically present alternative evaluation approaches reflecting the designs used in this volume along with some other cases.

These designs include after-only designs, pre–post designs, true and constructed cohort designs, interrupted time series designs, parallel time series designs with convincing narratives connecting exposure and outcome variables, comparison area or group designs, and as a complement to all of these, designs that allow the modeling of the process of influence. They are convincing insofar as they address the likely alternative hypotheses that would explain a particular result. A design that works well to show the effects of a vaccination campaign where simultaneous influences are less likely, may not work so well to evaluate an anti-HIV campaign in the context of multiple simultaneous interventions.

In general, these designs are stronger to the extent that they do one or more of the following:

- Incorporate measurement at multiple time points, particularly if there are multiple measurement points both before and after the initiation of an intervention.
- Make comparisons with unexposed populations, whether as natural control areas or unexposed individuals, if they are available.
- Establish that the model of effect of the program is consistent with the observed effects in terms of exposure, and on intermediate cognitive outcomes as well as on behavior.
- Triangulate evidence, showing effects through more than one analytic approach.
- Focus attention on the target population rather than on the broad population and/or analyze interactions recognizing that some groups will be more vulnerable than others.

It is possible to assess the strength of designs from two directions: How much better is it than having no evidence at all, or how much worse is it than the ideal? Sometimes evaluation is requested after the program is underway and/or when there is no opportunity to shape the intervention to make inferences easier. It is tempting to say that these can be impossible situations for evaluation, and they often are if the standard of success is a high level of certainty about inferences. However, if the goal is modest—to make a more informed judgment than would be possible without evidence—then it may be possible to proceed.

The After-Only Design

This review begins with a typical situation faced by an evaluator. The intervention has proceeded for some time, and there is an opportunity to do only a single "posttreatment" survey of the target audience. None of the case studies reported in this volume provide such an example, but it is common enough. Is there anything to be done that can be useful?

Assume that an anticigarette use intervention was directed toward 12- to 14-year-olds and it focused on reducing any smoking. It used television and radio spot advertising and centered its messages on the theme that cigarette smokers were being manipulated by the tobacco industry. Six months into the campaign, a survey of a representative sample of 12- to 14-year-olds was undertaken, which included measures of exposure to the advertising, beliefs about cigarette use and smoking cigarettes in the previous 30 days, as well as measures of demographic characteristics and other known predictors of cigarette use. An analysis of the survey data that answered each of the following questions affirmatively might permit an evaluator to move well away from the "better than no evidence at all" criterion:

1. Does much of the audience report a substantial level of exposure to the advertising? Assume the program intended their advertisements to be heard twice a week by the average child. Is this close to the level of recall reported?
2. Is recalled exposure negatively associated with use of cigarettes in the past 30 days?
3. Is that association robust, even when known predictors of cigarette use and/or exposure to media are controlled statistically?
4. Is there a dose–response association between exposure and cigarette use, such that there is a monotonically decreasing level of smoking with each increase in exposure?
5. Is there evidence that exposure affected smoking through its targeted beliefs:

(a) Is there a substantial negative relation between the belief that the tobacco industry is manipulating smokers and smoking?

(b) Is there a positive relation between exposure and the manipulation belief?

(c) Is the association between exposure and smoking reduced when the manipulation belief is controlled statistically—evidence that the targeted belief intervenes between exposure and outcome?

(d) Is this evidence for the manipulation belief as intervening between exposure and smoking not found when other, nontargeted beliefs are incorporated in these analyses instead of the manipulation belief (e.g., negative health consequences)?

If each of these results were consistent with expectations, then uncertainty about a claim of program effects would be reduced. A failure to confirm these expectations might lead to doubt about the program's efficacy. The use of the statistical controls accounts for some likely alternative hypotheses to explain the association between exposure and behavior. Finding a high level of exposure, a dose–response association between exposure and outcome, and showing that the effects flow through the targeted beliefs add to one's confidence about a claim of effect. They are consistent with a priori predictions, which makes evidence more telling. There would remain some concerns, of course.

On the one hand, two alternative hypotheses would threaten confidence in a claim of effects. The failure of the statistical controls to eliminate the exposure–outcome relation (Question 3) would reduce the concern about a spurious causal inference. There are increasingly sophisticated tools available for implementing statistical controls for such studies (e.g., Rosenbaum, 1995). However, there would still be a possibility that some unmeasured variable accounted for the observed association. Also, and perhaps a larger concern, there is a risk of reverse causal influence—those who are nonsmokers might be more likely to recall exposure to the messages that were consistent with their own behavior. That might lead to the observed association without the exposure having influenced the behavior.

On the other hand, failure to find all of these expected results might lead to an inappropriate inference of no effects. These expectations derive largely from an individual difference model of effects. They assume the program works because individuals see the advertisements, learn the specific messages addressed, and change their behavior. But, if the model of effects is different from this, then the evaluation approach can be misleading. If exposed individuals share what they learn with nonexposed individuals, then the correlation of exposure with beliefs and behavior can be small, despite real influence. If exposure to targeted belief messages generalizes to other anticigarette beliefs, then the evidence for the targeted belief as the prime intervening path may be problematic. Also, if behavior change by exposed individuals tends to influence the behavior of others, regardless of their direct exposure to messages, then the exposure–behavior association can be small. In general, if the model of effect does not match the analysis, then the survey analysis might fail to confirm the predicted results. Yet, the program might have been successful.

Thus, a posttreatment survey analysis contains risks, but that does not mean it cannot help. If the evaluators and their readers assess the likelihood of threats to inference of unmeasured variables and of reverse causation to be small, and are willing to stand by an individual difference model of effects, then this design provides worthwhile support to inference. If nothing else is possible, the after-only design can be informative. However, where it is possible to supplement the after-only design with additional evidence, certainly any evaluator will take that opportunity.

Pre–Post Designs

Sometimes a simple pre–post design, where a survey is undertaken before and after an intervention, can support strong inferences. This would happen under the unusual circumstance of a large change in behavior between two survey rounds and no credible alternative explanations for how that might have come about. For example, in Hornik et al. (chap. 13, this vol.), some of the claims of effect come, in part, from such comparisons. In one case, early initiation of breast-feeding among women giving birth in public hospitals and at home in Jordan went from about 42% to 67% over less than a 2-year period in the context of a broad promotion campaign. A search turned up no evidence for simultaneous substantial interventions that could account for such a large change in behavior. Spontaneous diffusion of the practice remained a possibility, but the fact that there was little change in behavior among women giving birth in private hospitals made this less likely (McDivitt, Zimicki, Hornik, & Abulaban, 1993).

The national European AIDS campaign evaluations presented by Wellings in chapter 8 mostly depend on before–after measurement, or on a before survey with several waves of after measurement. Although there is a possibility that sheer media coverage of the disease might have induced these changes in behavior, there is some reason to attribute influence to the campaigns as well. She noted that the magnitude of campaign effects in a country often varies with the size and straightforwardness of the national campaign, providing useful evidence of covariation between campaign exposure and outcomes, albeit at a very aggregated level.

Hill et al. (chap. 10, this vol.) used a similar three-wave design to show the effects of the SunSmart campaign in Melbourne, Australia. They showed a substantial decline in dangerous sun exposure and sunburn after the initiation of the campaign. They recognized that variation in such exposure could be an artifact of changes in the weather, particularly changes in ultraviolet radiation levels, so those and other potential confounders were measured and statistically controlled. In addition, to support the narrative attributing the behavioral effects to the SunSmart campaign, they were able to show that important beliefs relating to the risk of suntanning and the positive social and aesthetic value of suntans were changing in desirable directions.

In contrast to the post-only design, these types of comparisons do not depend on the assumption of an individual difference model for program effects because entire populations are to be compared before and after an intervention. Certainly, if an individual difference model can be assumed, then a combination of the pre–post and posttreatment survey analyses will provide more strength to inferences than either design alone. The sharpest concerns with these pre–post designs were alternative influences operating simultaneously with the program of interest or spontaneous diffusion of a behavior. Concerns about spontaneous diffusion of a behavior would be allayed if the postsurvey showed a substantial association between exposure and behavior after statistical controls. Also, one of the major concerns with the post-only analysis would be reduced. It is less likely that the observed association was the result of reverse causation, that is, that the behavior affected recalled exposure. In the context of a sharp before-to-after intervention change in behavior, an argument that exposure preceded behavior change becomes substantially stronger.

These designs can help, and are better than no evidence, but there are still concerns. Often there may be rival influences to explain a pattern of change, and they may not be easily ignored. For example, whereas initiation of breast-feeding in Jordan was not so likely to be affected by other substantial interventions, most HIV/AIDS interventions operated in a busy environment. In Ghana, for example, where McCombie and her colleagues (chap. 9, this vol.) evaluated a radio spot program, there were other planned interventions and unplanned natural media coverage of AIDS. They could not claim observed before–after changes to be the result of the intervention they studied without supplemental evidence. Also, if an individual difference model of effect cannot be assumed, analysis of the posttreatment survey is of less help. The presence or absence of individual-level associations of exposure and outcomes are then not informative.

An alternative approach—the one used by Zimicki et al. in chapter 12—exploits two cross-sectional surveys in yet another way. They found a substantial increase in timely vaccination in their target audience: The average child from 3 to 24 months old had 4.3 vaccinations before and 5.1 vaccinations after a substantial media campaign. They also knew that reported exposure to mediated vaccination messages was sharply up, from 31% who claimed to have heard or seen advertisements before the major campaign to 84% who said they had heard or seen them afterward. In addition, they knew that the logistic knowledge for immunization (when, where, and by what ages) was sharply up. They were then able to show that much of the association (about 75%) between time of measurement and vaccination level was accounted for by the mediating effects of logistic knowledge, and much of the association (about 65%) between time of measurement and logistic knowledge was accounted for by the mediating effects of exposure. They were able to show that all three variables were changing simultaneously, but also that it was the people who were exposed who were better informed about logistics, and the better informed people were more likely to obtain vaccinations. The before–after changes could be accounted for by processes associated with the model of effect of the campaign. These analyses make the before–after design more credible.

True and Constructed Cohort Studies

Causal inferences from simple cross-sectional associations in an after-only study are threatened by the effects of other unmeasured variables and by reverse causation. Another design solution to this problem is to undertake a cohort study. For example, Siegel and Biener (chap. 7, this vol.) examined the effects of the Massachusetts antismoking campaign with a two-survey cohort sample. The first survey wave measured exposure to antismoking messages, smoking behavior, and some background characteristics likely to be associated with smoking. The second wave measured smoking behavior 4 years later on the same sample. The authors showed that among 12- to 13-year-olds, those reporting higher exposure to messages at the first wave were half as likely as those reporting low exposure to have progressed to regular smoking over the next 4 years. Exposure was measured prior to smoking progression so reverse causal association was not a threat. Other likely background characteristics and any early smoking were measured at the first wave and could be statistically controlled.

The design shows that cohort subgroups with different exposures to television advertising not only varied in tobacco use at a postmeasurement wave, but also varied in their rates of progression to tobacco use. This evidence that exposure predicts progression is subjectively more convincing than the simple post-only correlation because the set of unmeasured variables that had accounted for the association of exposure and baseline smoking is effectively controlled. The remaining logical threat is that unmeasured variables may account for both early exposure to messages and subsequent progression to smoking. This threat—called the interaction of selection and maturation, or history, in Cook and Campbell's (1979) terminology—is a concern, but is perhaps a less sharp challenge than concern for the effects of unmeasured variables in a simple after-only analysis.

The cohort design is likely to be most convincing under the following circumstances:

1. The comparison groups are fairly similar in the outcome behavior at baseline once measured extraneous variables are controlled. This makes it less likely that unmeasured variables are affecting the behavior of concern.

2. The model of program effect assumes individual rather than socially shared effects. The analysis asks whether individuals with more and less exposure progress to the outcome behavior differently. If those with more direct exposure influence those with less exposure in their social networks, then the cohort design is likely to underestimate effects. This would not be true if the social networks themselves were the units of analysis, with social units with high and low exposure on average being compared for their progression to the behavior of interest.

3. The lag between exposure measurement and the period between the first and second waves of behavioral measurement is consistent with the likely timing of effects. If the effects of exposure occur very quickly but the second behavioral measure is long delayed, then the effects might have dissipated. Alternately, if the behavioral measure is taken too soon after the exposure, then some delayed effects will be lost.

4. The measure of exposure indicates not only very recent exposure to messages, but longer term exposure both before and after the point of measurement. It is likely that the effect of exposure to messages accumulates over time. Given the limits on the respondents' ability to recall, a good measure of exposure will focus on a specific and recent time period. "In the last month, about how often have you seen such antidrug ads on TV, or heard them on the radio?" However, that measure is de facto assumed to differentiate respondents on their exposure over a longer period. It is meant to capture the causally effective exposure accounting for behavioral progression over 1, 2, or, in the case of the Massachusetts evaluation, 4 years later. This is plausible only if the measure captures longer term exposure.

The true cohort design provides a good deal of uncertainty reduction under the right conditions. However, it can be quite difficult to maintain a cohort for two or more waves of data. A weaker alternative is to try to construct a cohort with two cross-sectional surveys of independent samples. It is possible to try to approximate the true cohort design through the use of proxy measures of exposure.

In Zambia, Yoder, Hornik, and Chirwa (1996) evaluated a 9-month anti-AIDS serial radio drama. They used two cross-sectional surveys of representative samples of adults from the target audience for the program. They found that more than 25% of the population were listeners to the serial, and there was an increase in safer sexual behavior over the period of the broadcasts. However, AIDS was a major topic in the media and there were other efforts operating to influence the same outcomes. They wanted additional evidence for the specific effects of the program. Ideally, they would have liked to compare those with more and less exposure to the program for their progression to safer behavior. This was not possible because there could be no measure of exposure in the before-intervention sample as it was selected independently of the after-intervention sample.

It was possible, however, to obtain a surrogate measure to differentiate those with higher and lower likelihood of exposure. They used a set of predictors of exposure in the after-survey, particularly radio ownership and listening. These predictors were available to before- and after-intervention survey respondents and were at stable levels for the population. Yoder and his colleagues compared sample members who had high and low access to the intervention and asked whether they were changing their behavior at different rates. They expected that access to exposure would matter more when the program had been on the air than when it had not. In this case, they found little evidence that those with high access were changing faster than those with low access and concluded that the program had been ineffective.

This constructed cohort study shares the assumptions of the true cohort study, but has the following additional requirements:

1. The set of predictors has to do quite a good job of accounting for exposure. The scaled measure based on those predictors is essentially a surrogate for exposure. If it is only a little related to exposure, it is like using an unreliable measure of exposure to study its influence. One would then expect that the observed association would be attenuated and the influence would be underestimated through this constructed cohort design.

2. Or, viewed from a complementary perspective, this approach will prove most useful when there is a true large influence of the intervention, so the effect will still show through despite the use of the surrogate measure of exposure.

3. Or, if the predictors are not powerful, or the expected effects of exposure are not large, a very large sample would be required to detect the effects through this surrogate approach.

Time Series Designs

Two types of time series designs are represented in this volume, and they can facilitate yet one more step toward confidence in inferences from evaluation designs. One form is the interrupted time series design where multiple estimates of some outcome precede and succeed some period of intervention, sometimes with treatment and control sites receiving interventions with different timing. Analyses focus on showing that the slope or intercept of the time series varies in expected ways with the presence or absence of the treatment. The other form is analogous but assumes that the intervention's intensity varies over time rather than being either present or absent. For example, level of exposure to some media programming varies over time, and analyses focus on the covariation between exposure measures and lagged outcome measures.

Interrupted Time Series Designs. Roccella (chap. 4, this vol.) evaluated the National High Blood Pressure Education Program based, in part, on the examination of time series data. He showed that a sharp change in annual rates of stroke-related death was coincident with the introduction of the program. The rate of decline was much slower over the period before the initiation of the program than in the period after its initiation. He also showed parallel changes in visits to physicians for blood pressure checks and in other expected outcomes. Although he did not provide the statistical tests of the shift in slope as did other authors, the changes are so sharp that there is little possibility they are due to chance. The more serious threat to inference is that other, simultaneous interventions account for the changes, although some likely hypotheses (i.e., changes in medications available, or in protocols for the treatment of stroke victims) have been investigated and do not account for the changes observed (see discussion in Hornik, introduction, this vol.). A similar use of descriptive time series is an important element of the arguments about the role of public attention to cardiovascular disease made by Viswanath and Finnegan (chap. 16, this vol.) and for the Soumerai et al. study (chap. 15, this vol.) of the effects of popular and professional media coverage of the link between aspirin and Reye's syndrome on the disappearance of the disease.

Pierce et al. (chap. 6, this vol.) analyzed the time series of changes in tobacco consumption in the context of the California Tobacco Control Program. They were able to address the concern about simultaneous other causes of the California decline somewhat more directly. They compared rates of decline in cigarette consumption before the initiation of the program, in its early phase, and in its late phase with comparable data for the United States as a whole. They could then make a compelling case that something unusual was happening in California, different from what was going on in California before the program, and different from what was going on in the rest of the country at the same time. These two comparisons clearly add to one's confidence in a claim that the program and its mass media component affected smoking.

Williams et al. (chap. 5, this vol.) used a formal interrupted times series to evaluate the effects on road injuries and fatalities of the "Click It or Ticket" pro-seat belt use campaign in North Carolina. They were able to show that drops in both of those outcomes occurred with the initiation of the campaign. Their inference of campaign effects is stronger because they could show that there was also high public awareness of the campaign, and a substantial increase in seat belt use comparing roadside observation data before and after initiation of the campaign. They had time series evidence for the effects of the campaign on the central outcome, and they had supplemental evidence to support the narrative that attributed the observed effects to the specific intervention.

Kincaid and his colleagues (chap. 11, this vol.) combined multiple waves of survey data with interrupted time series to demonstrate that an early television report and then two deliberate media promotion campaigns had sharp and immediate effects on demand for vasectomies in a Brazilian clinic. They were able to make their case even more convincingly because they showed that these behavioral effects match simultaneous changes in clients' reports about their sources of referral. Mass media sources were reported as the source in 70% of the cases, compared to a precampaign level of less than 20%.

Another formal use of interrupted time series comes from the field experimental study of the antidrug media interventions by Palmgreen and his colleagues (chap. 2, this vol.). They gathered monthly use data from small samples of adolescents from two cities over a 32-month period. They were able to show that two periods of intervention in one city and one period of subsequent intervention in the other were associated with statistically significant declines in the rate of initiation to drug use. Because they had a comparison city for the period of the first intervention, they were able to make the case that the observed decline in the treatment city was not an artifact of any national trend.

Continuously Varying Time Series Designs.   The other approach to time series analyses recognizes that the input variable can vary in magnitude over time rather than being described only as present or absent. This model is particularly appropriate when a treatment will vary in intensity over time and there is some continuously available measure of that intensity. The treatment may be a deliberate intervention that ebbs and flows over time or it may be the general media coverage of an issue. Fan (chap. 14, this vol.) presented a particular approach to analyzing media effects in this way. His "ideodynamic model" measures the nature of media coverage of a health issue (e.g., cocaine use) on a daily basis from an electronic database of media content. The shifts in that content are used to predict shifts in some outcome behavior, for example, cocaine use by high school seniors measured annually. The nonlinear models Fan fit to these data suggest that media coverage provides quite strong prediction of the outcome behavior at the aggregate level.

Field Experiments

The central argument of this chapter is that there are evaluation designs, other than formal field experiments, which can provide helpful information about the effectiveness of public health communication campaigns. Nonetheless, there are times when formal field experiments can be mounted in worthwhile ways, providing both strong inferences and an undistorted test of the effects of public health communication interventions.

There are two fundamental requirements for such a field experiment to work. First, it must be feasible to achieve a substantial difference in exposure to messages between treatment and control areas. This has two implications. On the one hand, the new messages must reach the treatment area in sufficient volume to expect to produce measurable differential effects. On the other hand, the background communication of parallel messages in the control area (e.g., from uncontrolled media coverage of a health issue) must be comparatively small.

Second, the model of effects for the communication program must match the nature of the experimental design. Three broad and complementary models of effect were presented in the introduction of this volume: an individual effects model, a social diffusion model, and an institutional diffusion model. Each may have different implications for the utility of field experiments. A model of effects focusing on individual learning would be consistent with field experiments, because that model presumes that individuals who are exposed to messages are the people who will be affected by them. Then comparison of individuals in the treatment and control areas would be meaningful. A social diffusion model can be consistent with a field experimental design as well. That model assumes that exposure does not affect only the individuals who are exposed but diffuses to their social networks. As long as the social networks are all within only the treatment or only the control area and the analysis focuses on comparisons between treatment and control populations rather than between exposed and unexposed populations, a field experiment will still be feasible.

The third model, the institutional diffusion model, may not be consistent with a field experiment. In this model, a health communication project works because it affects mass and elite opinion and generates new policy initiatives that affect the health behavior. If the relevant elite opinion is confined to the treatment area and policy initiatives are similarly restricted, then the field experiment may still be feasible. But local media and local elite opinion in one area may change only in the context of a regional or national public opinion environment. Elites in a single community may adopt new restrictions on restaurant smoking only in the context of a state (or nationwide) debate about the secondary effects of smoking. Then there may be no local institutional effects absent from such a supportive regional or national context, or even if there is independent local action, the media may well pick up news about such policy initiatives and diffuse it to other communities.

Other conditions decrease the likelihood that field experiments will detect institutional mechanisms of effect. Some influential policy initiatives are not under the control of local elites. If the communication program works through affecting state or national regulatory or legislative agencies, this often will not be detectable. A health communication program may work by affecting manufacturers' willingness to develop and distribute healthier products; the effects of that are unlikely to be restricted to a treatment area alone. Or a program may work by generating parallel messages through many channels and depend on national or regional organizations to get that to happen. For example, a program might encourage the American Academy of Pediatrics to endorse and diffuse messages about the value of supine sleeping position to avoid Sudden Infant Death Syndrome. It might encourage its membership to diffuse that message as a complement to public service announcements and stimulation of media coverage on national morning TV shows. Those effects will look the same in treatment and control areas.

There are three examples in this volume of such field experiments that do satisfy the needed conditions for field experiments, and provide good evidence for the effects of their interventions. The first is the Australian two-city design described by Pierce et al. (chap. 6, this vol.). It used a switching replicates design in which first Sydney received an antismoking campaign with Melbourne as the control, and then Melbourne received the campaign a year later. This worked quite well for the study reported here. Smoking prevalence declined in Sydney the first year while Melbourne did not change, but Melbourne showed a parallel decline in prevalence when the campaign was implemented there a year later.

The second field experiment, by Palmgreen et al. (chap. 2, this vol.), is also a two-city design. One Kentucky city received an antidrug advertising intervention, a second city served as a control, and then both cities received a second round of intervention. The measurement approach used a 32-month time series for each city, and the central analysis reported looks at each city as a separate case to see whether the initiation of the ad campaign produced a change in slope or intercept of the over-time regression line. However, subjectively, the availability of the control city for the first period of intervention, whose usage pattern remained stable while the treatment city's usage shifted, enhances the inferential power of the design.

Both of these two-city designs were useful, but the use of a single treatment and a single control site has to be seen as risky. The validity of the approach depends on the claim that the two cities were equivalent at the start, and, of even greater moment, that in the absence of the treatment they would have changed at the same rate. Whereas the "equivalent at the start" assumption can be tested, the "would have changed at the same rate" is, by definition, untestable. A subjective case can be made that the assumption is reasonable if the following conditions are met:

1. There is a pattern of similar rates of change before the initiation of the treatment.
2. There is a substantial (not only a statistically significant) difference in rates of change between the treatment and control areas.
3. Diligent journalism finds no other substantial events in either city that could account for the observed difference.

But there is no guarantee that these conditions will be met. A design that chooses the two-city path may find that the results at the end are less interpretable than had been hoped.

A closely linked issue is the problem of statistical analytic logic. The Australian study had no choice but to analyze differences using the individual survey respondents as the units of analysis. But the unit of assignment of treatment is clearly the city and not the individual. Then the appropriate unit of analysis should be the city, on the assumption that complex interactions within the city (the social and institutional processes described earlier) mean that each respondent in the treatment area is not independent of the other. Using individuals as units of analysis assumes they are independently sampled. Substantively, in using individual respondents as the units of analysis, the authors have to assume that the differences in rates of change achieved were not an artifact of something other than the treatment, shared within the treatment community and not found in the control community. This is essentially equivalent to the conditions already outlined.

One approach to dealing with two-city comparison studies is to make the case that the assumption of equivalence, absent the treatment, is credible. However, there are alternatives. One was used in the COMMIT (1995) trial seeking to reduce prevalence of heavy smoking. They chose 11 city pairs and randomly assigned one city in each pair to treatment or control. This gave them enough city pairs to do the analysis at the city level, and the idiosyncrasies of any one city would be only background noise for the analysis. It has been more common to solve this problem by increasing the number of cities studied and the number of time points of measurement. Using both the additional cities and the additional time points together gains enough statistical power to permit analysis at the city level.

Worden and Flynn (chap. 1, this vol.) took this approach, with two pairs of cities and six times of measurement. They show much lower rates of smoking initiation in the two communities with a school- and a media-based antitobacco program than in the two matched communities with a school program alone. A priori differences between the pairs of cities were small. They present analysis at the level of individual respondents, but then show that the effects hold even when analysis is done at the city level (with 6 measures at 4 cities, producing 24 units of analysis). They also show that treatment control city effects on smoking prevalence are matched by evidence for differences in targeted mediating attitudes (but not for non-targeted beliefs or behaviors), strengthening their claims of influence for the media campaign. The Palmgreen et al. study (chap. 2, this vol.) can be viewed not as a two-city design, but as a two-city, 32-measure design, an extension of the logic employed by Worden and Flynn. However, they did not analyze their data in this way, but instead used each city on its own.

Meta-Analyses

Interestingly, Flay and Cook (1989) raised the possibility of using one other technique for assessing the effects of public health communication programs: meta-analysis. Meta-analysis accumulates many different studies and looks for evidence that, on average, they were effective, or looks for characteristics of studies or interventions associated with success. They argued that this approach might, in a sense, cancel out the idiosyncratic problems of individual studies—too small samples, or a risk of chance differences in a two-city comparison, or particular confounder variables that might account for the difference between exposed and unexposed comparison populations. At the time, they did not reference any studies that actually undertook this approach, but Snyder and Hamilton have taken that task on, and some of their results are presented in chapter 19. They show that the average effect size across the 48 projects included is a small, but still notable .09; this varies sharply with a variety of population characteristics. Meta-analyses have these substantial advantages, and Snyder and Hamilton add to confidence that public health communication programs can have effects.

There are risks with this form of evidence as well. The technique averages together many different types of interventions addressing different behaviors for many populations. Thus, it can tell what is happening on average. But the average may be misleading. Some of the interventions are well done, and some not so well done. Some address hard behaviors to change and some address easier behaviors, and so on. A thoughtful meta-analysis that is able to characterize its studies on these dimensions can examine whether these differences matter (as do Snyder and Hamilton). But this can be done only if these and other important characteristics can be assessed. If the analysis cannot include relevant indicators, then there is a risk that the conclusion about the average will not apply in a particular new context. That is true if the average is positive, or if the average is not different from zero. Used judiciously, this approach can help clear away the underbrush and summarize a lot of information efficiently. However, the applicability of the research will still depend on how well the set of studies match the specific context considered.

CONCLUSIONS

There are many approaches to evaluating public health communication programs, all of them struggling to resolve the tension between making strong inferences and making sure that an intervention has gotten a fair test. This chapter presents many examples organized within six broad categories: after-only, pre–post, true and constructed cohorts, time series, field experimental, and meta-analytic designs. For each category there is a recognition of strengths and weakness associated with the design, and how it is researchers have tried to adjust for the weaknesses. There are some broad principles about what will make a design stronger.

First of all, a design needs to respect the model of effect of the program. This means the hypothesized model needs to be made explicit at the start. The model of effect includes considerations of how much exposure to messages will be achieved, who should be affected, and how fast the effects should occur and what magnitude they should be. The model must specify the mechanism(s) of effect: individual learning, social diffusion, and/or institutional diffusion. Designs appropriate to capture one model of effect may be inappropriate for another.

Second, there are some design elements likely to buy better inferences, all else being equal. These include having many measures over time, incorporating treatment comparison groups if they can be found, and supplementing evidence about outcomes with evidence that the campaign operated as it was supposed to (exposure at a high level associated with changes in beliefs, which are associated with changes in outcomes). Large samples are better than smaller samples not only because average effects will be easier to detect, but because they permit some examination of susceptibility to effects across subpopulations, and it is always a good guess that such interactions will be present.

Finally, designs are specific to a context. A pre–post design will be good enough if a strong case can be made that there are no rival events that could explain observed change in a behavior. This design may be relevant for a behavior that no one else is working on (SIDS and sleeping position in the Netherlands), but it would be uninformative for a behavior that many others are addressing (condom use in Ghana). Similarly, a program that only considers itself successful if it produces large and quick change in a behavior (immunization in the Philippines) will tolerate a "lesser" design than one that wishes to detect a small amount of change in an outcome (smoking prevalence among adults).

Some readers may be persuaded by each of the evaluations presented in this book. Others may be convinced by some of the evaluations and not by one or more of the others. Hopefully, they are convincing, at least, as a set of studies supporting the idea that public health communication can affect behavior.

Still, none can withstand a search for every possible flaw. There will always be some way to question the inferences made or the generality of the results to other contexts. That does not take away from the legitimacy of the evaluations. The fair question for them is whether they have gone reasonably down the path toward reducing uncertainty. A valuable study is one that can usefully inform the policy community about whether the intervention approach is worthy of support, without promising that there is no risk of a mistake. A study is valuable if future judgments about programs are better made taking this information into account than remaining ignorant of it. Studies are valuable if they respect the way that communication programs in real life are likely to affect behavior. On these criteria, these studies are of real value in showing that health communication can affect behavior.

REFERENCES

Boruch, R. F. (1997). *Randomized experiments for planning and evaluation: A practical guide.* Thousand Oaks, CA: Sage.

Community Intervention Trial for Smoking Cessation (COMMIT) (1995). I. Cohort results from a four year intervention. *American Journal of Public Health, 85,* 183–192.

Cook, T. D., & Campbell, D. T. (1979). *Quasi-experimentation: Design and analysis issues for field settings.* Boston: Houghton Mifflin.

Cronbach, L., Ambron, S., Dornbusch, S., Hess, R., Hornik, R., Phillips, D., Walker, D., & Weiner, S. (1980). *Toward reform of program evaluation.* San Francisco: Jossey-Bass.

Flay, B. R., & Cook, T. D. (1989). Three models of summative evaluation of prevention campaigns with a mass media component. In R. Rice & C. Atkin (Eds.), *Public communication campaigns* (2nd ed., pp. 175–196). Newbury Park, CA: Sage.

McDivitt, J. A., Zimicki, S., Hornik, R., & Abulaban, A. (1993). The impact of the Healthcom mass media campaign on timely initiation of breastfeeding in Jordan. *Studies in Family Planning, 24*(5), 295–309.

Rosenbaum, P. R. (1995). *Observational studies.* New York: Springer-Verlag.

Yoder, P. S., Hornik, R., & Chirwa, B. (1996). Evaluating the program effects of a radio drama about AIDS in Zambia. *Studies in Family Planning, 27*(4), 188–203.

Author Index

A

Aaro, L. E., 116, *129*
Abad, M., 227, 230, *248*
Abarbanel, R. M., 175, *177*
Abulaban, A., 220, 236, 247, 393, *405*
Adamchak, D. J., 220, *248*
Adams, E. H., 51, *56*
Aitchison, T., 164, *177*
Ajzen, I., 13, *17*, 24, *32*
Akers, R., 24, *32*
Albright, C. L., 370, *380*
Alcalay, R., 115, *128*
Aldrich, R. N., 57, 58, 59, 62, 65, 67, 68, *69*
Alexander, J. K., 4, *17*, 57, 60, 283, *286*, 290, 291, *310*, 371, *380*
Ali, M., 224, *247*
Alto, W. A., 368, *383*
Ama, E., 315, 321, 323, 324, *326*
Amaro, H., 321, *325*
Ambron, S., 386, *405*
Amezcua, C., 318, 320, *325*, *326*, 367, *382*
Amin, A., 59, 61, *70*
Andersen, A., 116, *129*
Anderson, C. M., 102, *114*
Anderson, R. M., 214, *216*

Anderson, R. T., 306, *309*
Anes, A., 135, *145*
Anonymous, 268, *286*
Aquilino, W. S., 42, *52*, *56*
Armitage, P., 169, *177*
Armstrong, B. K., 164, *177*
Armstrong, R. W., 86, *96*
Arnett, D. K., 306, *310*
Arrowsmith, J. B., 278, *286*
Arruda, J. M., 180, *194*
Assaf, A. R., 291, *309*
Atkin, C., 51, 53, 245, *248*
Atkinson, R., 281, *286*
Augustyn, M., 367, *383*

B

Bachman, G., 253, *264*
Backer, T., 51, *53*, 245, *246*
Backlund, E., 306, *309*
Badger, G. J., 24, 27, 29, *32*, 36, 51, *54*, 115, 116, *129*, *130*, 370, *380*
Baer, S. A., 37, *54*
Bahnson, J., 368, *379*
Bailey, C., 296, *309*
Bakdash, M. B., 369, *379*

407

Baker, C. D., 57, 70
Baker, E., 23, 32
Bal, D., 111, 113, 115, 130, 368, 380
Balbach, E. D., 98, 100, 101, 104, 113
Balraj, V., 198, 216
Balstra, D., 370, 382
Bandura, A., 13, 17, 24, 32, 315, 316, 317, 325
Baral, J., 267, 288
Barnea, Z., 36, 53
Barrett, M. J., 267, 268, 277, 283, 286, 287
Barros, F. C., 224, 231, 248
Barroso, C., 315, 321, 323, 324, 326
Battista, R. N., 57, 69
Bauman, K. E., 10, 17, 116, 128, 371, 375, 379, 381
Baume, C., 221, 246
Beck, E. J., 51, 53
Becker, L. B., 289, 309
Behnke, K. S., 370, 380
Belcher, D. W., 197, 198, 216
Bell, R. M., 23, 32
Beltzer, N., 135, 145
Beniger, J. R., 266, 284, 287
Bennett, S., 198, 216
Benoit, E., 179, 194
Bentler, P. M., 44, 54
Berry, C., 36, 55, 105, 111, 113, 118, 119, 126, 128, 129
Bertrand, J. T., 180, 193, 194
Bess, D. T., 269, 286
Best, J. A., 23, 32, 57, 70
Biener, L., 7, 18, 116, 117, 128, 130
Biritwum, R., 131, 145
Black, G. S., 51, 56
Blackburn, H., 6, 7, 18, 291, 292, 305, 306, 309, 310, 311, 369, 381
Blackburn, P., 179, 194
Blacklund, E., 306, 311
Blois, M. S., 175, 177
Blomberg, R. D., 86, 96, 370, 383
Blum, A., 115, 128
Blumer, H., 296, 309
Boldeman, C., 164, 177
Bongani, B., 233, 247
Booth, E. M., 343, 356
Borland, R., 9, 18, 164, 165, 167, 172, 174, 175, 177
Boruch, R. F., 386, 405
Bosk, C. L., 296, 301, 310
Bothwell, E., 369, 379

Botvin, E. M., 23, 32
Botvin, G. J., 23, 32
Bovbjerg, R., 88, 93, 96
Bracht, N., 1, 18, 291, 292, 305, 310, 311, 369, 381
Brady, C. A., 371, 383
Brannon, B. R., 116, 129
Bregman, D., 268, 277, 287
Breitrose, H., 4, 17, 57, 69, 283, 286, 371, 380
Brekke, M. L., 57, 69
Britton, C. F., 116, 129
Broadstock, M., 175, 177
Brookmeyer, R., 258, 263
Brorsson, B., 135, 140, 144, 145
Brown, A. K., 269, 286
Brown, B. W., Jr., 4, 17, 57, 69, 283, 286, 371, 380
Brown, C., 80, 83
Brown, J. D., 116, 128, 371, 379
Brown, K. S., 23, 32
Brown, R. D., 275, 288
Bruerd, B., 369, 379
Bryan, E. S., 371, 379
Buckenberger, L., 369, 381
Bunch, K. L., 368, 380
Burke, G. L., 6, 7, 18
Burke, N., 58, 59, 61, 69, 70, 115, 129
Burlington, D. B., 268, 277, 287
Burns, D. M., 115, 128
Burt, V., 80, 83
Burwell, L., 367, 383
Businski, K. L., 90, 96
Butz, W. P., 220, 247
Byass, P., 198, 216
BZgA, 135, 138, 145

C

Caldwell, T. W., 175, 177
Cameron, I. H., 164, 177
Campbell, B. J., 87, 90, 96
Campbell, D. T., 37, 38, 53, 59, 69, 386, 395, 405
Campbell, R. J., 267, 287
Carlaw, R., 1, 18, 291, 292, 305, 310, 311, 369, 381
Carleton, R. A., 291, 309
Carman, J. A., 86, 96
Carpenter, J. H., 24, 29, 32, 116, 130

Carpenter, T., 59, 61, *70*
Carter, C. A., 269, *286*
Cartwright, D., 289, *309*
Casper, M., 6, *17*
Caspi, A., 36, *53*
Cater, J. I., 224, *248*
Cattarello, A., 36, 52, *53*
Cavin, S. W., 105, *113*
Celantro, D. D., 367, *383*
Chaffee, S. H., 289, *309*, 371, *383*
Chakraborty, J., 224, 247, *248*
Chamberlain, A., 58, 59, 62, 65, *69*, *70*
Chapman, S., 58, *70*
Chassin, L., 126, *128*
Chayet, N., 273, 276, *286*
Cheadle, A., 26, *32*
Chen, M., 23, 24, 30, *33*
Chen, R. T., 214, *216*
Chikara, F., 220, *248*
Chilcote, S. D., 99, 112, *113*
Chirwa, B., 396, *405*
Choi, K. H., 336, *355*
Choi, W., 105, 111, *113*, 118, 119, 126,
    128, *129*, *130*
Chowdhury, S., 224, *247*
Cimons, M., 282, *286*
Citler, J. A., 80, *83*
Claeson, M., 220, *247*
Clayton, R. R., 36, 42, 52, *53*, *54*
Clemens, J. D., 224, *247*
Clements, C. J., 214, *216*
Cliff, J., 197, 198, *216*
Coate, D., 115, *129*
Coates, T. J., 336, *355*, *356*, 369, *381*
Cockburn, J., 175, *177*
Cody, R., 164, *177*
Cohen, C. S., 51, *53*
Cohen, J., 45, *53*
Cohen, P., 45, *53*
Cole, A., 198, *217*
Cole, P., 198, *217*
Coleman, P. L., 220, *247*
Collins, C., 306, *312*
Collins, L. M., 126, *128*
Colombo, S., 197, 198, *216*
Colon, S. E., 52, *53*
Coman, J. J., *95*
Connell, D. B., 58, *69*
Contreras, E., 231, 233, *247*
Convisser, J., 220, *247*, *248*

Cook, T. D., 37, 38, *53*, 59, *69*, 357,
    376, 378, *379*, *380*, 385, 386, 395,
    403, *405*
Corbett, K., 367, *379*
Corby, N. H., 322, *325*
Correa-Villasenor, A., 267, *287*
Corson, J., 370, *382*
Corty, E., 126, *128*
Corwin, M. J., 8, *19*
Costanza, M. C., 23, 24, 27, 29, 30, *32*,
    33, 115, *129*, 370, *380*
Couchey, S., 23, 24, 30, *33*
Cronbach, L., 386, *405*
Crooks, C. E., 369, *382*
Crow, R., 1, *18*, 291, 292, 305, *310*, *311*,
    369, *381*
Crump, A. D., 367, *383*
Cummings, M. K., 371, *379*
Cunningham, D. G., 51, *53*
Cutts, F. T., 197, 198, 214, *216*

D

Dab, W., 135, *145*
Daly, K., 116, *129*, 369, *382*
Danaher, B. C., 370, *379*
Da Vanzo, J., 220, *247*
Davis, C. E., 6, *17*
Davis, M. V., 367, *383*
Davis, S. K., 306, *309*
Davis-Hearn, M., 23, *33*
Dawson, N. E., 85, *96*
Day, G., 342, *355*
Dayrit, M., 227, 230, *248*
Dayton, D., 268, 277, *287*
De Carlo, P., 336, *356*
de Castro, B. M., 181, *194*
de Castro, M. P. P., 9, *18*, 181, *194*
de Castro Buffington, S., 9, *18*
Deeds, S. G., 174, *177*
DeFriese, G. H., 57, *69*
de Guzman, E., 227, 230, *248*
de Jesus, A., 198, *216*
de Jonge, G. A., 8, *17*
DeLeon, R., 14, *17*
Demers, D., 307, *311*
Demes, J., 88, 93, *96*
deMoor, C., 23, *32*
Dent, C., 116, *129*, *130*
Desjardin, N., 369, *381*

Detels, M. P., 370, *380*
Detsky, A. S., 116, *130*
de Vries, K., 8, *17*, 144, *145*
de Vroome, E., 8, *17*, 139, *145*
Diallo, S., 198, *216*
Dickson, D., 36, *53*
Dickson, N., 36, *53*
DiClemente, C. C., 13, *17*, 174, *178*, 315,
    316, 319, 320, *326*, 339, *356*
Diehr, P. H., 26, *32*
Dignan, M., 368, *379*
DiGusto, F., 59, 61, *70*
DiSogra, L. K., 368, *380*
DiTecco, 24, *32*
Dominguez, L. B., 267, *288*
Donegan, C., 51, *53*
Donohew, L., 36, 37, 51, 52, *53*, *54*, *55*
Donohue, G. A., 296, 298, 306, 307, *309*,
    311
Dorfman, L., 115, *129*
Dornbusch, S., 386, *405*
Dowdle, W. R., 268, 277, *287*
Drage, J. S., 268, 277, *287*
Dsilva, M. U., 37, *54*, *55*
Dubois-Arber, F., 8, *17*
Dubren, R., 371, *379*
Duerr, J. M., 115, 116, *130*, 367, *382*
Dulac, J., 370, *382*
Duncan, G., 306, *310*
Durbin, J., 88, *95*
Dusenbury, L., 23, *32*
Dussault, C., 86, *95*
Dwyer, T., 57, 58, 59, 61, 62, 65, 67, 68,
    69, *70*, 115, *129*

E

Easley, M. F., *95*
Easton, P. M., 224, *248*
Eckhardt, L., 23, *32*
Edwards, C., 23, *32*
Egger, G., 291, *309*
Eiswirth, R. S., 266, *288*, 370, *382*
Elder, J. P., 23, *32*
Elkamel, F., 220, *247*
Ellickson, P. L., 23, *32*
Elmer, P., 1, *18*, 291, 292, 305, *310*, 369,
    381
El-Rafie, M., 220, *247*
Emery, S. L., 36, *55*

Endreny, P., 265, *288*
Eng, E., 198, *216*
Engeland, A., 116, *129*
Engelberts, A. C., 8, *17*
Enguidanos, S. M., 322, *325*
Ennett, S. T., 375, *380*
Entman, R. M., 296, 301, *309*
Epstein, L. H., 371, *383*
Erickson, A., 7, *17*, 23, *32*, 115, *129*
Espinoza, R., 318, *325*
Evans, N., 105, 111, *113*, 118, 119, *130*
Everett, M., 37, *53*
Eysenck, H. J., 36, *54*

F

Faich, G. A., 278, *286*
Fairhurst, S. K., 13, *17*
Fairweather, W. R., 268, 277, *287*
Fallonen, U., 23, *33*
Fan, D. P., 252, 254, 255, 258, 260, 262,
    263
Farkas, A. J., 105, 111, *113*, 118, 119,
    126, *128*, *129*, *130*
Farquhar, J. W., 1, 2, 3, 4, 9, 11, *17*, *18*,
    36, 51, *53*, *54*, 57, 69, 283, *286*,
    290, 291, 292, 306, *309*, *310*, *311*,
    370, 371, *380*, *382*
Farrugia, H., 163, *177*
Faupel, C. E., 296, *309*
Fausto, A., 227, 230, *248*
Feinstein, A. R., 265, *286*
Feldman, H. A., 291, 292, *309*, *312*
Felix-Ortiz, M., 44, *55*
Ferencic, N., 231, 233, *247*
Fernandez-Esquer, M. E., 367, *382*
Ferraz, E., 180, *194*
Fidell, L. S., 45, *55*
Fikrig, S., 269, *286*
Filipp, L. C., 198, *216*
Finberg, L., 269, *286*
Finnegan, J., 1, *18*, 291, 292, 296, 299,
    300, 301, 304, 305, 306, *310*, *311*,
    312, 369, *381*
Fishbein, M., 13, *17*, 24, *32*, 143, *145*,
    305, *310*, 315, 321, 323, 324, *325*,
    326, 367, *380*
Fisher, L. A., 371, *379*
Fitzgerald, W., 291, *309*

Flay, B. R., 23, 24, *32*, 35, 51, *53*, *54*, 115, 116, 126, *129*, *130*, 266, 283, *286*, 357, 378, *380*, 385, 403, *405*
Fleming, A., 86, *96*, 370, *381*
Fleming-Milici, F., 358, 364, 376, *383*
Flewelling, R. L., 375, *380*
Flora, J. A., 1, 2, 3, 11, *17*, *18*, 36, 51, *53*, *54*, 291, 292, *309*, *310*, 359, 371, *380*, *383*
Flynn, B. S., 23, 24, 27, 29, 30, *32*, *33*, 36, 51, *54*, 115, 116, *129*, *130*, 370, 371, *380*, *383*
Foerster, S. B., 368, *380*
Folsom, A. R., 1, 6, 7, *18*, 291, 292, 305, *310*, 369, *381*
Foreit, K. G., 181, *194*
Fortmann, S. P., 1, 3, 4, 9, 11, *17*, *18*, 19, 36, 51, *53*, 291, 292, 306, *309*, *310*, 312, 371, *380*
Foss, R. D., 370, *380*
Fowler, F. J., Jr., 117, *128*
Fox, B. J., 98, 104, *113*
Franco Duarte, E. F., 181, *194*
Frank, E., 9, *18*, 306, *312*
Franklin, B. A., 220, *247*
Frankowski, F., 375, *382*
Frape, G., 58, *70*, 291, *309*
Freimuth, V., 51, *53*, 358, *380*
Freire, H. S., 183, *195*
Friede, A. M., 198, *216*
Fuchs, S. C., 224, 231, *248*
Fulginiti, V., 267, *286*
Fulker, D. W., 36, *54*

G

Galavotti, C., 51, *54*
Gallion, K. J., 51, *54*, 367, *382*
Gandy, O., 301, *310*
Gardiner, J. C., 368, *380*
Gareaballah, E. T., *216*
Garfield, B., 100, *113*
Gason, R., 175, *177*
Gearon, S. A., 220, *247*
Geller, B. M., 23, 24, 27, 29, 30, *32*, *33*, 36, 51, *54*, 115, *129*, 370, *380*
Geller, S., 370, *382*
Gerber, B., 370, *379*
Gibbs, A., 164, *177*
Gilbert, R., 57, *70*

Giles, G., 163, *177*
Gillie, E., 370, *382*
Gilpin, E. A., 36, *55*, 118, 119, 126, *128*, *129*, *130*
Gitlin, T., 289, *310*
Glantz, S. A., 36, *54*, 98, 100, 101, 104, *113*, 115, *129*
Glass, W., 220, *248*
Glezen, W. P., 269, *286*
Glik, D. C., 198, *216*
Glynn, T. J., 23, 25, *32*
Godkin, G., 164, *177*
Golbeck, A., 23, *32*
Goldman, A. I., 23, *33*
Goldman, L., 36, *54*, 115, *129*, 294, *310*
Goldman, N., 220, *247*
Goldman, P. A., 294, *310*
Goldsteen, K., 86, *96*
Goodman, D., 369, *381*
Goodman, R. M., 368, *380*
Gordon, A., 198, *216*
Grant, B. A., 85, *96*
Grant, N., 36, 37, *55*
Graves, K., 368, *381*
Gray, C., 369, *381*
Gray, N. J., 57, 67, 68, *69*
Green, J., 330, *355*
Green, L. W., 24, *32*, 174, *177*, 375, *382*
Griffin, G., 116, *129*, 296, *309*, 369, *382*
Griliches, Z., 48, *55*
Grimm, R., 291, 292, 305, *310*, 311, 369, *381*
Grossman, M., 115, *129*
Grube, J. W., 367, *380*
Gruder, C. L., 369, *381*
Guenther-Grey, C., 315, 321, 323, 324, 325, 326, 367, *380*
Gunn, W. J., 268, 277, 287, *288*
Guyer, B., 198, *216*

H

Ha, N. T., 370, *381*
Haba, F., 198, *216*
Habicht, J. P., 220, *247*
Haddon, W., Jr., 266, *288*, 370, *382*
Hafstad, A., 116, *129*
Haines, M., 368, *380*
Hall, L. J., 267, *287*

Hall, W. L., 86, *96*
Hall, W. N., 267, *288*
Halpin, T. J., 267, *287*
Hamilton, J. L., 115, *129*
Hamilton, M., 358, 362, 364, 376, 377, *380, 383*
Hanlon, P., 198, *216*
Hannam, C. D., 58, 59, 61, 69, 70, 115, *129*
Hannan, P. J., 291, 292, 296, 305, *310*, 312, 369, *381*
Hannan, P. R., 61, 62, 70, 299, 300, 301, *310*
Hanratty, S., 57, 67, 68, *69*
Hansen, D., 358, *382*
Hansen, W. B., 116, 126, *129, 130*
Harkin, A. M., 144, *145*
Harrington, H., 36, *53*
Harrington, N. G., 37, *55*
Harris, J. R. W., 51, *53*
Harty, K. C., 116, *129*, 369, *382*
Harvey, A. C., 88, *95*
Haskell, W. L., 1, 3, 4, 11, *17, 18*, 36, 51, *53, 57, 69*, 283, *286*, 291, *309*, 371, *380*
Hassouna, W. A., 220, *247*
Hauck, W. W., 369, *381*
Haugh, L. D., 371, *383*
Hawley, R. P., *95*
Hayes, R., 198, *216*
Haynes-Sanstad, K., 336, *356*
Hays, R. B., 369, *381*
Heath, G. W., 292, *311*
Hedeker, D., 116, *129*
Helm, D., 36, 37, *54, 55*
Helms, R. A., 269, *286*
Henderson, R. H., 214, *216*
Hennig, J., 36, *55*
Henrikus, D., 175, *177*
Hernandez, J. R., 227, 230, *248*
Hersey, J. C., 368, *380*
Hess, R., 386, *405*
Hetrick, M. A., 116, *130*, 367, *382*
Heymann, D. L., 131, *145*
Higgins, D., 315, 321, 323, 324, *326*
Higgins, M. A., 80, *83*
Hilgartner, S., 296, 301, *310*
Hill, D., 4, 9, *18*, 36, *55*, 57, 67, 68, *69*, 115, *130*, 164, 165, 167, 172, 174, 175, *177, 178*
Hindin, M. J., 220, *247, 248*
Hinds, M. D., 281, 285, *287*

Hirschhorn, N., 220, *247*
Hocheimer, J., 289, *309*
Hocking, B., 164, *177*
Hoffman, H. J., 8, *19*
Holland, R. R., 116, *130*
Holm, L. E., 164, *177*
Holtzbauer, F. J., 267, *287*
Holway, W. B., 255, 262, *263*
Horan, M. J., 80, *83*
Hornik, R., 12, *18*, 51, *54*, 220, 224, 227, 230, 231, 233, 236, 239, 242, 245, *247, 248*, 386, 393, 396, *405*
Horvath, P., 52, *54*
Hosmer, D. W., 119, 120, *129*
Houghland, J., 42, *54*
House, J., 306, *310*
Hovell, M., 23, *32*
Hoyle, R. H., 52, *53*
Hu, S., 367, *382*
Hu, T. W., 7, *18*, 36, *54*, 115, *129*
Huba, G. J., 36, 44, *54, 55*
Hughes, F. H., 256, *264*
Hughes, H. M., 289, *311*
Hulley, S. B., 4, *18*, 371, *380*
Hunink, M. G., 294, *310*
Hunt, M. K., 292, *311*
Hunter, J. E., 362, 364, *381*
Huntington, D., 220, 233, *247, 248*
Hurley, M., 144, *145*
Hurwitz, E. S., 267, 268, 277, 283, *286*, *287, 288*
Hyman, H. H., 289, *310*
Hymowitz, N., 256, *264*

I

Iribarren, C., 306, *310*
Islam, S., 193, *194*

J

Jackson-Thayer, S., 368, *381*
Jacobs, D. J., 61, 62, *70*
Jacobs, D. R., Jr., 1, 6, *18*, 116, *129*, 291, 292, 305, *310, 311*, 369, *381, 382*
Jansson, B., 164, *177*
Jason, L. A., 369, *381*
Jatulis, D., 1, 3, *19*, 306, *312*
Jeannin, A., 8, *17*

Jecque, A. V., 197, 198, *216*
Jeffrey, R., 291, 292, 305, *310, 311,* 369, *381*
Jeffries, D. J., 51, *53*
Jemmott, J. B., III, *326*
Jemmott, L. S., *326*
Jenkins, C. N. H., 370, *381*
Jessor, R., 24, *32*
Jessor, S., 24, *32*
John, T. J., 198, *216, 217*
Johnson, B. T., 364, *381*
Johnson, C. A., 116, 126, *129, 130*
Johnson, D., 23, *32*
Johnson, M., 111, *113,* 115, 116, *130,* 367, *382*
Johnson, N., 306, *309*
Johnson, T. P., 42, *54*
Johnson, W. D., 315, 321, 323, 324, *325,* 326, 367, *380*
Johnston, L., 253, *264*
Jonah, B. A., 85, *96*
Jones, E. F., 266, 284, *287*
Jones, R. R., 163, *177*

K

Kahn, E., 299, 300, 301, *310*
Kahn, J. S., 8, 16, *19,* 359, *383*
Kannel, W. B., 6, *18*
Kaplan, G. A., 306, *309*
Kaplan, R. M., 105, *113*
Karim, S., 341, *356*
Kaskutas, L. A., 368, *381*
Kaslow, R. A., 268, 277, *287*
Kay, L. S., 322, *325*
Kealey, S., 105, *113*
Keeler, T. E., 7, *18,* 36, *54,* 115, *129*
Kegeles, S. M., 369, *381*
Kelder, S., 23, *33,* 116, *129,* 292, *311,* 315, 321, 323, 324, *326*
Keller, J. B., 306, *311*
Kelley, A. B., 266, *288,* 370, *382*
Kelman, H. C., 358, *381*
Kennedy, D. L., 278, *286*
Kenny, C., 51, *53*
Kersten, C., 368, *383*
Kessler, R. C., 8, *19*
Kilpatrick, D. G., 36, *54*
Kim, Y. K., 220, *248*
Kim, Y. M., 220, *247, 248*

Kincaid, D. L., 9, *18,* 220, *247, 248*
Kinney, M. B., 369, *379*
Kiragu, K., 180, *194*
Kiriuki, J. W., 180, *194*
Kirkwood, B. R., 224, 231, *248*
Kishchuk, N., 369, *381*
Kiwanuku-Tondo, J., 358, 364, 376, *383*
Kizer, K. W., 368, *380*
Klein, B., 115, *130*
Klepp, K. I., 23, *33,* 116, *129,* 292, *311,* 369, *382*
Klibanoff, L. S., 368, *380*
Kline, F. G., 291, *310, 311,* 369, *381*
Knowles, J. C., 193, *194*
Ko, C. W., 8, *19*
Koch, G. G., 116, *128,* 371, *379, 381*
Koepke, C., 231, 233, *247*
Koepke, D., 23, *32*
Koepsell, T. D., 26, *32*
Kolata, G., 276, 277, *287*
Kols, A., 220, *247*
Konings, E., 8, *17*
Korhonen, H. J., 4, *18*
Kortbeek, S., 197, 198, *216*
Koskela, K., 4, *18,* 317, 318, *326*
Kossman, M. K., 369, *382*
Kostense, P. J., 8, *17*
Kotchen, J. M., 368, *381*
Kotchen, T. A., 368, *381*
Kotler, P., 220, 224, *247*
Kottke, T. E., 57, 61, 62, *69, 70,* 291, *311*
Kraft, P., 135, 144, *145*
Kraichy, P. P., 86, *96*
Kramer, M., 105, *113*
Krenn, S., 220, *247*
Kreuter, M. W., 174, *177*
Krieg, B. F., 368, *380*
Krohn, M., 24, *32*
Kronholm, W., 273, *287*
Ku, L., 8, *19,* 42, *55*
Kumah, O. M., 220, *247, 248*
Kunasol, P., 214, *216*
Kuritsky, J. N., 278, *286*
Kurth, T., 358, *382*
Kuseka, I., 220, *248*

L

Labarthe, D., 80, *83*
Lam, D. J., 368, *380*

Lamb, A., 85, 96
LaMontagne, J. R., 268, 277, 287
Lando, H., 291, 292, 305, 310, 369, 381
Landry, P. R., 86, 96
Lanese, R., 267, 287
Lange, A. L., 369, 379
Langley, J., 36, 53
Langmark, F., 116, 129
Lanza-Kaduce, L., 24, 32
LaPrelle, J., 116, 128, 371, 379, 381
Larcombe, I., 164, 178
Larson, A., 193, 194
Lasater, T. M., 291, 309
Lastovicka, J. L., 36, 54
Laurendeau, M., 369, 381
Lawton, K. B., 51, 56
Le, A., 370, 381
Lee, C., 164, 177, 369, 382
Lee, M. B., 227, 230, 248
Lee, P. R., 368, 380
Lemeshow, S., 119, 120, 129
Lenfant, C., 82, 83
Lettenmaier, C., 220, 247, 248
Levitz, M. D., 23, 32
Lewis-Beck, M. S., 45, 47, 48, 49, 54
Lewit, E. M., 115, 129
Lichtenstein, E., 369, 381
Liebkind, K., 324, 326
Lindberg, L. D., 42, 55
Linder, S. H., 180, 194
Lindsay, E. A., 57, 70
Lindsteadt, J. F., 220, 247
Ling, J., 220, 247
Liskin, L., 179, 194
Locke, R., 304, 310
Loevinsohn, B. P., 198, 216
Lombardi, C., 224, 231, 248
Lorch, E. P., 36, 37, 51, 53, 54, 55
Lordelo, E. R., 183, 195
Lovelock, C. H., 341, 355
Lowenthal, N., 198, 216
Loza, S., 220, 247
Luepker, R. V., 1, 18, 23, 30, 33, 291,
    292, 296, 305, 306, 310, 311, 312,
    369, 381, 382
Lund, A. K., 86, 90, 95, 96, 370, 381, 383
Lynn, J., 328, 355
Lynn, W., 220, 248

M

Macaskill, P., 4, 18, 36, 55, 115, 130
Maccoby, N., 1, 2, 3, 4, 11, 17, 18, 36,
    51, 53, 54, 57, 69, 283, 286, 290,
    291, 309, 310, 311, 317, 326, 359,
    371, 380, 382
Mack, T., 163, 178
MacKie, R. M., 163, 164, 176, 177
MacKinlay, S., 291, 309
Maibach, E. W., 51, 54, 359, 380
Mains, D. A., 375, 382
Makadon, H. J., 336, 356
Manduca, P. L., 85, 96
Mangnani, R. J., 193, 194
Manoff, R. K., 220, 247
Marcina, D., 86, 96
Marin, B. V., 369, 381
Marin, G., 369, 381
Markello, S., 371, 379
Marks, R., 9, 18
Martin, D. C., 26, 32
Martin de Castro, B., 9, 18
Mascioli, S., 291, 310, 369, 381
Mason, F. F., 58, 69
Masse, L. C., 36, 54
Mastrorocco, D. A., 181, 194
Matsebula, G., 233, 247
Mauss, A. L., 296, 310
Mayer, J. A., 369, 382
Mays, V. M., 326
Mbizvo, M. T., 220, 248
M'Boge, B. H., 198, 216
McAlister, A. L., 4, 17, 23, 33, 35, 51,
    54, 55, 57, 69, 116, 130, 283, 286,
    315, 317, 318, 319, 320, 321, 323,
    324, 325, 326, 367, 371, 380, 382,
    383
McCarthy, J. D., 308, 312
McCombs, M. E., 296, 310
Mccombs, M. E., 289, 309
McCullagh, P., 189, 195
McDivitt, J., 51, 54, 220, 221, 236, 247,
    393, 405
McDonough, P., 306, 310
McDowell, J., 221, 230, 236, 247
McGee, H., 267, 288
McGee, L., 52, 55
McGovern, P. G., 6, 7, 18, 291, 292, 305,
    306, 310, 369, 381
McGuigan, K., 23, 32

McGuire, C., 164, *177*
McGuire, W. J., 59, 63, *69*, 316, *326*
McKean, H. E., 368, *381*
McKenna, J. W., 7, *17*, 115, *129*
McLean, A. R., 214, *216*
McLeod, J. M., 289, *309*
McMillan, D. G., 369, *379*
McNamara, E. F., 358, *382*
McPhee, S. J., 370, *381*
McVey, D., 139, *146*
Ménard, C., 135, *145*
Mercado, S., 318, 320, *326*, 367, *382*
Merrill, D. G., 371, *383*
Merritt, A. P., 9, *18*
Merritt, R. K., 118, 119, *130*
Merson, M. H., 220, *247*
Mestel-Rauch, J., 126, *128*, *130*
Meyer, A. J., 4, *17*, 57, *69*, 283, *286*, 371, *380*, *382*
Meyer, R. C., 220, *247*
Michielutte, R., 368, *379*
Middlestadt, S. E., 143, *145*
Millar, W. J., 306, *310*
Miller, D. L., 51, *53*
Miller, L. C., 369, *382*
Miller, P., 220, *247*
Miller, T., 88, 93, *96*, 116, *129*
Mitchell, E. W., 358, 364, 376, *383*
Mitra, S. N., 193, *194*
Mittelmark, M. B., 1, *18*, 291, 292, 305, *310*, *311*, 369, *381*
Mittleman, M. A., 294, *310*
Mndzebele, A., 233, *247*
Moatti, J. P., 134, 135, *145*
Moffitt, T. E., 36, *53*
Mogielnicki, R. P., 370, *382*
Molgaard, C., 23, *32*
Molnar, L. J., 90, *96*
Monardi, F. M., 98, 104, *113*
Moore, R. W., 368, *381*
Morgan, G., 267, *288*
Morgan, W., 220, *247*
Morris, L., 180, 183, *194*, *195*
Morris, L. A., 278, 284, *287*
Morris, N., 231, 233, *247*
Mortimer, R. G., 86, *96*
Moskowitz, J. M., 329, 331, *356*
Moss, V., 51, *53*
Muir, C. S., 163, *178*
Mullan, P. B., 368, *380*
Mullen, P. D., 375, *382*

Mullis, R., 291, 292, 305, *310*, *311*, 369, *381*
Mumford, S. D., 181, *194*
Murphy, D. H., 269, *287*
Murphy, K. M., 115, *130*
Murray, D. M., 1, 10, *17*, *18*, 23, 25, 30, 33, 116, *129*, 291, 292, 305, *310*, *311*, *312*, 360, 369, 375, 376, *381*, *382*, *383*
Murry, J. P., Jr., 36, *54*
Muthen, L. K., 116, *130*, 367, *382*

N

Nagaty, A., 220, *247*
Naimoli, G., 198, *216*
Naimoli, J., 198, *216*
Nariman, H. N., 220, *248*
Nash, J. D., 4, *17*, 57, *69*, 283, *286*, 371, *380*, *382*
Nasser, S., 220, *247*
Neaton, J. D., 306, *311*
Nelder, J. A., 189, *195*
Nelkin, D., 265, *287*
Neslin, S., 370, *382*
Netter, P., 36, *55*
Newcomb, M. D., 44, 52, *54*, *55*
Nicholas, D. D., 197, 198, *216*
Nichols, D. C., 371, *383*
Nickerson, L., 9, *18*
Niemensivu, H., 317, 318, *326*
Nissinen, A., 4, *18*, 290, *311*
Nothwehr, F., 369, *381*
Novelli, W., 220, *248*
Noy, S., 164, 175, *177*

O

Ockene, J. K., 256, *264*
Ofori, J. K., 220, *247*
Ofosu-Amaah, S., 197, 198, *216*
Ojeda, G., 180, *195*
O'Keefe, G. J., 371, *382*
Olien, C. N., 296, 298, 306, 307, *309*, *311*
Olshavsky, R. W., 126, *128*
O'Malley, P., 253, *264*
O'Neill, B., 266, *288*, 370, *382*
Onoka, C., 180, *194*

O'Reilly, K., 315, 321, 323, 324, *325*, 326, 367, *380*
Orton, S., 144, *146*
Osterlind, A., 163, 164, *177*, *178*

P

Paalman, M., 8, *17*, 139, *145*
Paavola, M., 116, *130*
Paccaud, F., 8, *17*
Padgett, C. A., 116, *128*, 371, *379*
Pallonen, U., 116, *129*, 317, 326, 369, *382*
Palmgreen, P., 36, 37, 51, *53*, *54*, *55*
Pareja, R., 230, 231, 233, *247*, 343, *356*
Parker, K., 198, *216*
Parlato, M. B., 220, *248*
Parrott, R. L., 51, *54*
Partridge, K. B., 174, *177*
Pasick, R. J., 284, *287*
Patriarca, P. A., 214, *216*
Patton, C., 330, 336, *356*
Payne, C. D., 166, *178*
Pebley, A., 220, *247*
Pechacek, T., 291, 292, 305, *310*, *311*, 369, *381*
Pechmann, C., 115, 127, *129*
Pedersen, W., 36, *55*
Pereira, S. M., 198, *217*
Peres-Stable, E. J., 369, *381*
Perez, A. E., 193, *195*
Perreault, R., 369, *381*
Perrin, E. B., 26, *32*
Perry, C., 23, 25, *33*, 116, *129*, 291, 292, 305, *310*, *311*, 369, *381*, *382*
Peters, R., 315, 321, 323, 324, *326*
Pham, G. Q., 370, *381*
Phillips, D., 386, *405*
Pierce, J. P., 4, *18*, 36, *55*, 57, 58, 59, 61, 62, 65, 67, 68, *69*, *70*, 102, 105, 111, *113*, *114*, 115, 118, 119, 126, *128*, *129*, *130*
Pietinen, P., 4, *18*
Piha, T., 317, 318, *326*
Pinching, A. J., 51, *53*
Pineda, M. A., 180, *194*
Pinsky, P., 268, 277, *287*, *288*
Piotrow, P., 220, *247*, *248*
Pirie, P. L., 23, 24, 29, 30, *32*, *33*, 291, 292, 305, *310*, *311*, 369, *381*, *382*
Pleck, J. H., 8, *19*, 42, *55*

Polacsek, M., 367, *383*
Pollak, M., 135, *145*
Ponboon, K., 214, *216*
Popham, W. J., 115, 116, *130*, 367, *382*
Potter, L. D., 115, 116, *130*, 367, *382*
Presson, C. C., 126, *128*
Preuksaraj, S., 214, *216*
Preusser, D. F., 86, 90, *95*, *96*, 370, *383*
Prochaska, J. O., 13, *17*, 174, *178*, 315, 316, 319, 320, *326*, 339, *356*
Proctor, D., 358, 364, 376, *383*
Prokhorov, A. V., 116, *129*, 369, *382*
Psaty, B. M., 26, *32*
Pulley, L., 318, 320, *326*, 367, *382*
Puska, P., 4, *18*, 23, *33*, 57, *70*, 116, *130*, 290, 291, *311*, 317, 318, *326*
Putnam, G. L., 164, *178*

Q

Qing, Z., 367, *382*
Quesnel, P., 135, *145*
Quinn, V., 115, *130*
Quinnan, G. V., 268, 277, *287*

R

Radosevich, M., 24, *32*
Rahar, G., 36, *53*
Rahwan, G. L., 278, *288*
Rahwan, R. G., 278, *288*
Ramaboot, S., 214, *216*
Ramirez, A. G., 51, *54*, 318, 320, *325*, 326, 367, *382*
Ramirez, G., 375, *382*
Rangan, V. K., 341, *356*
Rao, M. R., 224, *247*
Rao, P., 48, *55*
Rassaby, J., 164, *178*
Ray, C. G., 267, *288*
Reese, S. D., 301, *311*
Reinfurt, D., 9, *19*, 86, 87, 90, *95*, *96*, 358, *383*
Reitmeijer, C. A., *325*
Reye, R. D. K., 267, *288*
Rice, J., 267, *287*
Rice, R., 52, *53*, 245, *248*
Richmond, R., 60, *70*
Rietmeijer, C. A., 367, *380*

Rimon, J. G., II, 220, *248*
Ringwalt, C. L., 375, *380*
Rise, J., 135, 144, *145*
Risi, J. B., Jr., 198, *216*
Riyad, S., 220, *247*
Roberts, D. S., 370, *382*
Robertson, L. S., 266, *288*, 370, *382*
Robinson, D. A., 214, *216*
Robinson, J. K., 164, *178*
Robinson, W. V., 277, 282, *288*
Roccella, E. J., 78, 80, 82, *83*
Rockhill, B., 9, *18*
Rodgman, E., 95, *96*
Rodriques, L. C., 198, *216*
Roed, I. S., 36, *55*
Rogers, E., 35, 51, 53, *55*, 239, 245, 246, 248, 289, *311*, 342, *356*
Rogers, M. F., 267, 283, *286*
Rogers, S., 42, *55*, 259, *264*
Rogus, M., 36, 37, *55*
Rolf, J., 367, *383*
Roman, A. M., 117, *128*
Romano, R. M., 7, *17*, 115, *129*
Romero, J., 230, *247*
Rood, D. H., 86, *96*
Rooney, B. L., 375, *383*
Rosbrook, B., 36, *55*, 105, 111, *113*
Rosenbaum, P. R., 392, *405*
Rosenman, K. D., 368, *380*
Rosenstock, I. M., 13, *18*, 51, *55*
Rosenthal, R., 364, *383*
Roser, C., 371, *383*
Ross-Degnan, D., 8, 16, *19*, 359, *383*
Rossi, J. S., 13, *17*
Rouzier, P., 368, *383*
Roy, C., 164, 165, 167, 172, 174, 175, *177*
Rozsenich, C., 367, *383*
Ruiter, D., 163, *177*
Russell, M. A. H., 57, *70*
Russell, S. H., 290, *311*
Rutenberg, N., 180, *194*
Rycroft, M. J., 176, *177*

S

Sagebiel, R. W., 175, *177*
Sakamoto, C. P. M., 183, *195*
Salariya, E. M., 224, *248*
Sallis, J. F., 23, *32*

Salmon, C., 245, *248*
Salonen, J. T., 4, *18*, 57, 61, 62, *70*, 291, 311
Sandberg, S. K., 341, *356*
Sandfort, T., 8, *17*, 139, *145*
Sankar, P., 233, *247*
Sanson-Fisher, R., 175, *177*
Santelli, J. S., 367, *383*
Santi, S., 23, *32*
Santiso, R., 180, *194*
Sarfaty, G., 59, 61, *70*
Schilling, R. F., 35, 51, *55*
Schlegel, R., 24, *32*
Schmid, L., 116, *129*, 369, *382*
Schmid, T. L., 292, *311*
Schmidt, F. L., 362, *381*
Schneider, L., 115, *130*
Schonberger, L. B., 267, 268, 277, 283, 286, 287, 288
Schooler, C., 292, *310*, 371, *383*
Schultz, R. H., 90, *96*
Sciandra, R., 367, 371, 379, *383*
Scott, R., 175, *177*
Secker-Walker, R. H., 23, 24, 27, 29, 30, 32, 33, 36, 51, *54*, 115, 116, *129*, 130, 370, *380*
Segel, B., 36, *55*
Serrand, C., 135, *145*
Shabecoff, P., 285, *288*
Shadish, W. R., 376, *379*
Shafer, J. L., 44, *55*
Shapiro, E., 108, *114*
Shaw, D. L., 296, *310*
Shaw, J., 59, 61, *70*
Sheatsley, P. B., 289, *310*
Shelley, J. M., 58, 59, 62, 65, *69*
Shelton, L. G., 23, 24, 30, *33*
Shepard, D. S., 214, *216*
Sherman, S. J., 126, *128*
Shoemaker, P. J., 301, *311*
Shriver, M., 336, *356*
Siddiqui, O., 116, *129*
Siegel, M., 7, *18*, 115, 116, *130*
Sigal, L. V., 301, *311*
Sillers, C., 369, *382*
Silva, P. A., 36, *53*
Silver, B., 163, *177*
Silverman, T., 220, *248*
Simon, N., 256, *264*
Simons-Morton, D. G., 375, *382*
Singarimbun, M., 198, *217*
Singer, E., 265, *288*

Singer, J. A., 57, *70*
Singer, J. L., 36, *55*
Skinner, W. F., 52, *53*
Slater, M. D., 51, *55*
Sleutjes, M., 8, *17*
Slymen, D. J., 369, *382*
Smith, A. D., 36, *54*
Smith, G. A., 85, *96*
Smith, G. D., 306, *311*
Smith, W., 231, 233, 247, 343, *356*
Snyder, J. D., 224, *248*
Snyder, L. B., 358, 362, 364, 367, 376, 377, *383*
Soares, A., 197, 198, *216*
Sobel, J. L., 35, *54*
Solomon, L. J., 23, 24, 30, *33*, 116, *130*
Sonenstein, F. L., 8, *19*, 42, *55*
Sopory, P., 51, *53*, 245, *246*
Sorlie, P., 306, *309*, *311*
Soumerai, S. B., 8, 16, *19*, 359, *383*
Spear, S. F., 368, *380*
Sprafka, J. M., 6, 7, *18*, 291, 292, 305, *310*, 369, *381*
Stam, A., 36, *54*
Stamler, J., 306, *311*
Stamler, R., 80, *83*, 306, *311*
Stanley, J. C., 38, *53*
Stanton, B. F., 224, *247*
Staples, M., 163, *177*
Starko, K. M., 267, *288*
Starr, S. A., 289, *311*
Steinhoff, M. C., 198, *217*
Stephenson, M. T., 37, *55*
Stern, M. P., 4, *17*, 283, *286*, 290, *311*, 318, 320, *326*, 367, 371, *380*, *382*
Stewart, J. R., 87, 90, *96*
Stewart, S., 370, *381*
Stone, B. J., 164, *178*
Stone, R., 198, *216*
Storey, J. D., 35, 51, *55*, 289, 307, *311*
Straus, R., 368, *381*
Stray-Pedersen, B., 116, *129*
Streatfield, K., 198, *217*
Streff, F. M., 90, *96*
Strogatz, D., 6, *17*
Stromberg, W. L., 267, *288*
Stryker, J., 336, *356*
Stuster, J., 86, *96*, 370, *381*
Stutts, J. C., 87, 90, *96*
Suarez, L., 371, *383*
Subramanyam, K., 197, *217*
Suchindrn, C. M., 10, *17*

Sung, H. Y., 7, *18*, 36, *54*, 115, *129*
Supple, A. J., 42, *56*
Sussman, S., 116, 126, *128*, *129*, *130*
Sutker, P. B., 36, *54*
Swanson, G. M., 368, *380*
Sweeney, J. M., 371, *379*

T

Tabachnick, B. G., 45, *55*
Tabije, T. L., 193, *195*
Tait, E., 369, *381*
Taylor, C. B., 1, 3, 11, *17*, *19*, 36, 51, *53*, 57, *70*, 291, 292, *309*, *310*, 371, *380*
Taylor, M., 358, 367, *379*, *380*
Taylor, R. L., 368, *380*
Taylor, W., 57, *70*
Tedeschi, G. J., 102, *114*
Teichman, M., 36, *53*
Terry, P., 51, *53*
Thompson, B., 367, *379*
Thomson, S. J., 23, *32*
Tichenor, P. J., 296, 298, 306, 307, *309*, *311*
Tielman, R. A., 8, *17*
Tobler, N. S., 375, *380*
Tolbert, W. G., 86, *96*
Torres, I., 367, *382*
Torres, M., 231, 233, *247*
Tortu, S., 23, *32*
Tosteson, A. N., 294, *310*
Touchette, P., 343, *356*
Trauner, D. A., 267, *288*
Tremblay, R. E., 36, *54*
Trevino, F., 367, *382*
Tsevat, J., 294, *310*
Tucker, M. A., 164, *178*
Tufte, E., 45, *55*
Tuomilehto, J., 4, *18*, 57, *70*, 290, *311*
Turner, C., 42, *55*, 259, *264*
Turner, R. R., 58, *69*
Tuttle, M. S., 175, *177*
Tyroler, H. A., 6, *17*

U

Underhill, G. S., 51, *53*
Unger, J. P., 198, 214, *217*

V

Valente, T. W., 220, 248
Van Amburg, G., 267, 288
Vartiainen, E., 4, 18, 23, 33, 116, 130, 290, 311
Vastagh, G. F., 277, 288
Vega, A., 180, 195
Velasquez, M. M., 13, 17
Velez, R., 375, 382
Velicer, W. F., 13, 17
Vernberg, D., 51, 56
Vernon, S. R., 180, 195
Verzosa, C. C., 227, 230, 248
Victora, C., 224, 231, 248
Villareal, R., 367, 382
Viswanath, K., 296, 299, 300, 301, 304, 306, 307, 310, 311, 312
Vito, D., 23, 32
Vogt, T. N., 256, 264

W

Wagenaar, A. C., 90, 96
Wagner, E. H., 26, 32
Wahed, M. A., 224, 248
Wake, F. R., 164, 178
Walden, K. P., 36, 52, 53
Waldman, R. J., 267, 288
Walker, D., 386, 405
Wallack, L., 35, 56, 115, 129, 130, 284, 287, 367, 383
Waller, J. A., 371, 383
Warner, K. E., 7, 19, 266, 288
Waterhouse, J., 163, 178
Waternaux, C., 198, 216
Webster, I., 60, 70
Weiner, S., 386, 405
Weinstein, M. C., 294, 310
Weisbrod, R., 291, 292, 305, 310, 369, 381
Wellings, K., 134, 139, 141, 144, 146
Wells, H. B., 368, 379
Wells, J., 9, 19, 86, 95, 96, 358, 383
Wentworth, D., 306, 311
Werch, C. E., 368, 383
Westoff, C. F., 266, 284, 287
Wheeler, F. C., 368, 380
Wheeler, R. J., 368, 383
Whelton, P., 80, 83
White, M. M., 36, 55

White, N., 367, 379
White, V., 9, 18, 57, 67, 68, 69, 164, 165, 167, 172, 174, 175, 177
Wiio, J., 317, 318, 326
Wilder, A. L., 51, 56
Wildey, M., 23, 32
Wilke, W. L., 340, 356
Wilkinson, D. W., 180, 194
Williams, A., 9, 19, 86, 90, 95, 96, 358, 370, 383
Williams, D., 306, 310, 312
Williams, K. N., 115, 129
Williams, L. W., 294, 310
Williams, P.T., 1, 3, 4, 11, 17, 18, 36, 51, 53, 291, 309, 371, 380
Willinger, M., 8, 19
Willms, D. G., 57, 70
Wilson, C., 57, 70
Wilson, D. M., 57, 70
Wilson, J. T., 275, 288
Wing, R. R., 371, 383
Wing, S., 6, 17
Winkleby, M. A., 1, 3, 9, 18, 19, 292, 306, 309, 310, 312, 371, 380
Winnard, K., 220, 248
Winsten, J. A., 280, 288
Wixom, C. W., 266, 288, 370, 382
Wodall, D. F., 267, 288
Wojtyniak, B., 224, 247
Wolf, P. A., 6, 18
Wolitski, R. J., 325, 367, 380
Wood, P. D., 1, 3, 4, 11, 17, 36, 51, 53, 57, 69, 283, 286, 290, 291, 309, 310, 371, 380
Woodruff, S. I., 23, 32
Worden, J. K., 23, 24, 27, 29, 30, 32, 33, 36, 51, 54, 115, 116, 129, 130, 370, 371, 380, 383
Wright, D. L., 42, 56
Wurapa, F. K., 197, 198, 216

X

Xu, B., 179, 195
Xue, S., 6, 7, 18

Y

Yamuah, M., 198, 216
Yangiasako, K. L., 164, 178

Yoder, P. S., 234, 243, 245, *248*, 396, *405*
Yong, C., 59, 61, *70*
Yound, R., 23, *32*
Young, M., 368, *383*
Yunus, M., 224, *248*

Z

Zald, M. N., 308, *312*

Zastowny, T. R., 51, *56*
Zhang, J., 179, *195*
Zheng, Z., 234, *248*
Zhu, S. H., 102, *114*
Zhu, Z., 368, *380*
Zimicki, S., 51, *54*, 220, 224, 227, 230, 236, *247*, *248*, 393, 403
Zimmerman, R. S., 51, *56*
Zinanga, A., 220, *248*
Zuckerman, M., 36, *52*, *54*, *56*

SUBJECT INDEX

A

Africa, 179–180
AIDS Community Demonstration Project
  behavioral journalism, 317, 321–323
  education programs, 317, 321–323
  effectiveness evaluation, 323
  peer modeling, 317, 321–323
AIDS prevention, Europe
  Austria
    condom usage, 138f
    effectiveness evaluation, 138f
    risk reduction strategy, 138f
  design
    cross-national comparison, 132, 133,
      142–143
    dose-controlled, 132
    experimental, 132
    knowledge/attitude/behavior (KAB)
      survey, 133, 143–145
    quasi-experimental, 132
  education programs, 133, 134, 136
  effectiveness evaluation
    AIDS awareness, 133–134
    AIDS susceptibility, 134
    Austria, 138f
    condom usage, 136–139, 141–142

France, 134, 135t, 136–138, 140–141
Germany, 135t, 137, 138f, 140–141
Ireland, 135t, 136, 137
Italy, 136
limitations, 131–133, 142–145
Netherlands, 7–8, 137, 138–139,
  140f, 142
Norway, 135t
risk reduction strategy, 136–142
sexual partner restriction, 136–139,
  140–141
Spain, 135t, 136
Sweden, 135t, 140f
transmission knowledge, 134–136
United Kingdom, 134, 135t, 136–139,
  141
Europe Against AIDS Programme, 133
France
  AIDS susceptibility, 134
  condom usage, 136, 137, 141
  effectiveness evaluation, 134, 135t,
    136–138, 140–141
  risk reduction strategy, 136, 137,
    138f, 140–141
  sexual partner restriction, 140–141
  transmission knowledge, 135t

AIDS prevention, Europe *(cont.)*
  Germany
    condom usage, 137, 138*f*, 141
    effectiveness evaluation, 135*t*, 137,
      138*f*, 140–141
    risk reduction strategy, 137, 138*f*,
      140–141
    sexual partner restriction, 140–141
    transmission knowledge, 135*t*
  Ireland
    condom usage, 136, 137
    effectiveness evaluation, 135*t*, 136, 137
    risk reduction strategy, 136, 137
    sexual partner restriction, 137
    transmission knowledge, 135*t*
  Italy
    condom usage, 136
    effectiveness evaluation, 136
    risk reduction strategy, 136
  measurement, 132–133
  media campaign, 133
  methodology, 132–133, 142–145
  Netherlands
    condom usage, 8, 137, 138–139
    effectiveness evaluation, 7–8, 137,
      138–139, 140*f*, 142
    nonpenetrative sex, 142
    risk reduction strategy, 137, 138–139,
      140*f*, 142
    sexual partner restriction, 137–139,
      140*f*
  Norway
    effectiveness evaluation, 135*t*
    transmission knowledge, 135*t*
  objectives, 132–133
  overview, 131
  results, 133–142
  sample, 133
  Spain
    effectiveness evaluation, 135*t*, 136
    needle sharing, 136
    risk reduction strategy, 136
    transmission knowledge, 135*t*, 136
  Sweden
    effectiveness evaluation, 135*t*, 140*f*
    risk reduction strategy, 140*f*
    transmission knowledge, 135*t*
  Switzerland
    condom usage, 8, 136–139, 141
    effectiveness evaluation, 7–8, 135*t*,
      136–139, 140*f*, 141

    risk reduction strategy, 136–139,
      140*f*, 141
    sexual partner restriction, 137–139,
      140*f*, 141
    Stop AIDS, 7–8, 137
    transmission knowledge, 135*t*
  United Kingdom
    AIDS susceptibility, 134
    condom usage, 136, 137, 138–139,
      141
    effectiveness evaluation, 134, 135*t*,
      136–139, 141
    risk reduction strategy, 136–139, 141
    sexual partner restriction, 137,
      138–139, 141
    transmission knowledge, 135*t*, 136
AIDS prevention, Ghana
  data analysis, 150
  design, 150
  education programs, 148, 160
  effectiveness evaluation
    AIDS communication, 155–156
    AIDS knowledge, 154–155
    AIDS susceptibility, 154
    attitudes, 154–156
    behavior, 156–159
    campaign awareness, 152–153,
      157–158
    campaign phrase recognition, 153–154
    condom knowledge, 155
    condom usage, 157–158
    knowledge, 152–156
    radio exposure, 153, 158
    sexual activity initiation, 156
    sexually transmitted disease (STD)
      impact, 158–159
    sexual partner restriction, 156–158
    television exposure, 152–153, 158
    transmission knowledge, 154–155
    urban vs. rural, 152–153
  media campaign, 147–148, 152–154,
    157–158
  methodology, 148–152
  overview, 147–148
  results, 152–159
  sample, 149–152
  summary, 159–160
AIDS prevention, persuasive information
  AIDS hotline calls, 260–261, 262
  HIV infection, 258–260, 262
American Cancer Society (ACS), 303

American Heart Association (AHA), 303, 304
American Legacy Foundation, 14
American Lung Association (ALA), 303
American Medical Association (AMA), 303
Americans for Nonsmokers Rights (ANR), 100
Aspirin industry, *see* Reye's syndrome
Australia, *see* Smoking prevention; Sunburn prevention (Australia)
Austria, AIDS prevention
  condom usage, 138*f*
  effectiveness evaluation, 138*f*
  risk reduction strategy, 138*f*

B

Back to Sleep (United States), 8
Behavioral journalism
  AIDS Community Demonstration Project
    education programs, 317, 321–323
    effectiveness evaluation, 323
    peer modeling, 317, 321–323
  community studies, 315, 317–324
  effectiveness evaluation, 323–325
    AIDS Community Demonstration Project, 323
    North Karelia Project (Finland), 318
    smoking prevention (Texas), 320–321
  North Karelia Project (Finland)
    cardiovascular disease prevention, 317–318
    effectiveness evaluation, 318
    group discussion format, 317–318
    media campaign, 317–318
    social modeling, 317–318
  overview, 315–317
  smoking prevention (Texas)
    documentary format, 317, 318–321
    effectiveness evaluation, 320–321
    media campaign, 317, 318–321
    social modeling, 319–320
  summary, 323–325
  theoretical basis of
    behavioral science theory, 315, 324–325
    fictional role modeling, 316, 317
    peer modeling, 316–317, 321–324
    social modeling, 315–317
    Stages of Change model, 316, 319

Behavioral science theory, 315, 324–325
Brazil, *see* Vasectomy promotion (Brazil)

C

California Smoker's Helpline, 102
California Tobacco Control Program
  adolescent smokers and
    effectiveness evaluation, 101, 112–113
    legislation, 101, 112–113
    media campaign, 101
    tobacco industry campaign, 101, 112–113
  California Tobacco Surveys (CTS), 102
  effectiveness evaluation
    adolescent smokers, 101, 112–113
    cigarette price reduction, 113
    evaluation contradiction, 7
    legislation and, 102, 112–113
    per capita consumption, 106–109, 110*f*, 111
    secondhand smoke, 101, 105–106, 107*f*, 111, 112–113
    smoking prevalence rates, 109–113
    tobacco industry campaign, 111–113
    tobacco industry portrayal, 100
  expenditures
    media campaign, 103, 104*t*, 111–112
    tobacco industry campaign, 103–105, 111–112
  funding, 97–98, 103
  legislation
    adolescent smokers, 101, 112–113
    Americans for Nonsmokers Rights (ANR), 100
    effectiveness evaluation, 102, 112–113
    secondhand smoke, 100, 101, 112–113
    Tobacco Education and Research Oversight Committee (TEROC), 98
    Tobacco Tax and Health Protection Act (1988), 97–98
  media campaign
    adolescent smokers, 101
    California Smoker's Helpline, 102
    cessation services, 101–102
    effectiveness evaluation, 100, 101, 105–113
    expenditures, 103, 104*t*, 111–112

California Tobacco Control Program *(cont.)*
  media campaign *(cont.)*
    funding, 98, 103
    inception proposals, 98
    litigation, 100, 101, 102, 112
    secondhand smoke, 100–101
    tobacco industry portrayal, 99–100
    tobacco industry veracity, 100
    vs. tobacco industry, 98–99, 100, 101, 102, 103–105, 111, 112
  news media coverage, 102
  objectives, 98
  overview, 97
  secondhand smoke and
    effectiveness evaluation, 101, 105–106, 107f, 111, 112–113
    legislation, 100, 101, 112–113
    media campaign, 100–101
  summary, 111–113
  target audiences, 98
  tobacco industry campaign
    adolescent smokers, 101, 112–113
    expenditures, 103–105, 111–112
    Joe Camel, 102
    litigation, 100, 101, 112
    price reduction, 113
    program effectiveness, 111–113
    program elimination, 98–99, 111, 112
    program portrayal of, 99–100
    veracity portrayal, 100
California Tobacco Surveys (CTS), 102
Centers for Disease Control (CDC)
  AIDS Community Demonstration Project, 317, 321–323
  Reye's syndrome, 267, 269–272, 276–277
Child Survival Program (HealthCom)
  clinical care model, 349–353
  data collection, 226–227
  Ecuador
    diarrhea project, 227, 231–233, 237–238, 244–245
    project description, 221, 222t
    vaccination project, 227, 228–229, 231
  education program
    communication strategy, 220–221, 225–226, 236–245
    effectiveness variation, 224–225, 236–245
    Health Belief Model, 221
    HealthCom project, 219–223, 225–226
    objectives, 221
    project description, 222–223t, 225–226

theoretical influence, 221, 224
    Theory of Reasoned Action, 221
  effectiveness evaluation
    behavior change opportunity, 236–239
    birth spacing project, 234, 235t
    breast-feeding project, 234, 235t, 236, 238–239
    diarrhea project, 231–234, 237–238, 243–245
    feeding supplementation project, 234, 235t
    message appropriateness, 243–245
    message exposure, 239–243
    vaccination project, 228–231, 245
    variation hypotheses, 224–225, 236–245
    vitamin A project, 234–236, 237
  implications, 245–246
  Indonesia (Central Java)
    diarrhea project, 227, 231–233
    project description, 221, 222t
    vitamin A project, 227–228, 234–236, 237
  Indonesia (West Java)
    diarrhea project, 227, 231–233
    project description, 221, 222t
  Jordan
    breast-feeding project, 228, 234, 235t, 236, 238–239
    feeding supplementation project, 228, 234, 235t
    project description, 221, 222t
  Lesotho
    diarrhea project, 227, 231–234
    project description, 221, 223t
    vaccination project, 227, 229
  measurement
    birth spacing project, 221, 225, 226, 228
    breast-feeding project, 221, 225, 228
    diarrhea project, 221, 225–226, 227
    feeding supplementation project, 221, 225, 228
    vaccination project, 221, 225, 226, 227
    vitamin A project, 221, 225, 227–228
  methodology, 225–228
  overview, 219–220
  Peru
    birth spacing project, 228, 234, 235t
    project description, 221, 223t
    vaccination project, 227, 228–230

Philippines (Manila)
project description, 221, 223t
vaccination project, 227, 228–229, 230
Philippines (national)
project description, 221, 223t
vaccination project, 227, 228–229,
230, 245
sample, 226–227
summary, 245–246
Swaziland
diarrhea project, 227, 231–233
project description, 221, 223t
Zaire
diarrhea project, 227, 231–233, 243
project description, 221, 223t
vaccination project, 227, 229
China, 179
Citizens for the Treatment of High Blood
Pressure, 75
Clinical care model, *see* Evaluation
development
Colombia, 180
Committee on the Care of Children (CCC),
273, 274–276
Community Intervention Trial for Smoking
Cessation (COMMIT), 3, 4–6, 10

D

Department of Health and Human Services
(DHHS), 14, 272–273

E

Ecuador
diarrhea project, 227, 231–233, 237–238,
244–245
project description, 221, 222t
vaccination project, 227, 228–229, 231
Europe, *see* AIDS prevention, Europe;
specific countries
Evaluation contradiction
community trials
cardiovascular disease prevention, 2–3,
4, 10–11
Community Intervention Trial for
Smoking Cessation (COMMIT), 3,
4–6, 10
education programs, 2–4, 9–11, 12–17

explanation of, 9–11, 12–13
marijuana study, 4
media campaign, 2–4, 10–11, 12–17
Minnesota Heart Health Program
(MHHP), 3, 4–6, 11
North Karelia Project (Finland), 3,
4–6
Pawtucket Heart Health Program
(Rhode Island), 3–6, 11
smoking prevention, 3, 4, 10
Stanford Five City Project (California),
2–6, 9, 10–11
Stanford Three City Project
(California), 4–6
education programs
community trials, 2–4, 9–11, 12–17
explanation of, 9–13
implications, 13–17
observational studies, 6–7, 8, 9–10,
11–17
explanation of
community trials, 9–11, 12–13
education programs, 9–13
evaluation design, 9–10, 15–17
media campaign, 10–13
observational studies, 9–10, 11–13
research design, 9–10, 15–17
implications
behavior vs. treatment, 13–17
education programs, 13–17
Health Belief Model, 13
individual effects model, 14–15
institutional diffusion model, 14–15
media campaign, 13–17
model development, 13, 14–15
prevention vs. cure, 13–14
Social Cognitive Theory, 13
social diffusion model, 14–15
Stages of Change model, 13
Theory of Reasoned Action, 13
media campaign
community trials, 2–4, 10–11, 12–17
explanation of, 10–13
implications, 13–17
observational studies, 6, 7–9, 11–17
observational studies
AIDS prevention, 7–8
Back to Sleep (United States), 8
California Tobacco Control Program, 7
children's health, 8–9
education programs, 6–7, 8, 9–10,
11–17

Evaluation contradiction *(cont.)*
  observational studies *(cont.)*
    explanation of, 9–10, 11–13
    hypertension, 6–7, 9–10, 11–12
    media campaign, 6, 7–9, 11–17
    National High Blood Pressure
      Education and Control Program
      (NHBPEP), 6–7, 9–10, 11–12
    Reye's syndrome, 8–9
    seat belt usage (North Carolina), 9
    smoking prevention, 7
    sunburn prevention (Australia), 9
    vaccination project (Philippines), 8
  overview, 1–2
Evaluation design
  after-only, 390, 391–393
  cross-national comparison, 132, 133,
    142–143
  dose-controlled, 132
  experimental, 132
  field experiments, 400–403
  guidelines, 390, 404–405
  ideal design
    alternatives to, 389–400
    analysis unit, 389
    controls, 386–387
    expectations, 387
    study/target population match,
      388–389
  interrupted time series
    characteristics, 390, 397–399
    cost-effectiveness analysis, 187, 188t,
      193–194
    marijuana study, 4, 36, 37–38, 42,
      46–50, 52
    sensation seeking targeting (SENTAR),
      36–37, 51–52
    vasectomy promotion (Brazil), 187,
      189–192, 193–194
  knowledge/attitude/behavior (KAB)
    survey, 133, 143–145
  overview, 385–386
  pre-post, 390, 393–395
  quasi-experimental, 132, 192–194
  summary, 404–405
  time series analysis
    continuously varying, 390, 397–398,
      399–400
    ideodynamic theory, 252–254
    structural time series models, 88
  true/constructed cohort, 390, 395–397
Evaluation design, meta-analysis

campaign effect size
  campaign length correlation, 374,
    376–378
  campaign reach correlation, 374, 375,
    376, 377–378
  control group trend correlation, 374,
    375, 376, 377–378
  effectiveness evaluation, 366–377
  enforcement message correlation, 366,
    373, 375, 377
  limitations, 377–378
  measurement, 363–364
  new information message correlation,
    373, 376, 377–378
  role model message correlation,
    373–374, 375, 377–378
campaign length
  campaign effect size correlation, 374,
    376–378
  characteristics, 361–362
  effectiveness evaluation, 367–372t,
    374, 376–377
  hypothesis of, 361
  measurement, 366
campaign reach
  campaign effect size correlation, 374,
    375, 376, 377–378
  effectiveness evaluation, 367–372t,
    374, 375, 376, 377
  measurement, 365
characteristics, 357–358, 361–362,
  403–405
control group trend
  campaign effect size correlation, 374,
    375, 376, 377–378
  characteristics, 360–361
  effectiveness evaluation, 367–372t,
    374, 375, 376, 377
  hypothesis of, 361
  measurement, 365–366
enforcement messages
  campaign effect size correlation, 366,
    373, 375, 377
  characteristics, 358
  effectiveness evaluation, 366–373,
    375, 376, 377
  hypothesis of, 358
  measurement, 364
exposure time
  characteristics, 360
  hypothesis of, 360
  reach measurement, 365

implications, 378
limitations, 377–378
methodology
    campaign selection criteria, 362–363
    campaign selection procedure, 363
    measurement, 363–366
new information messages
    campaign effect size correlation, 373,
      376, 377–378
    characteristics, 359
    effectiveness evaluation, 367–373, 375,
      376, 377
    hypothesis of, 359
    measurement, 364–365
overview, 357–358
results, 366–377
role model messages
    campaign effect size correlation,
      373–374, 375, 377–378
    characteristics, 359–360
    effectiveness evaluation, 367–374, 375,
      377
    hypothesis of, 360
    measurement, 365
service messages
    campaign effect size correlation, 373,
      377–378
    characteristics, 359
    effectiveness evaluation, 367–373, 377
    hypothesis of, 359
    measurement, 365
summary, 378
Evaluation development
clinical care model and
    assumptions, 348–349
    best practices, 354
    characteristics, 349–353
    Child Survival Program (HealthCom),
      349–353
    defined, 329
    efficacy, 355
    implications, 353–355
    peer consultation, 354–355
    program management, 353
    program monitoring, 353–354
    program research, 353–354
    replicability, 355
    sustainability, 344–349, 355
communication and
    behavior influence, 327–328
    best practices, 332–336, 354
    failure impact, 329–331

failure types, 331–333, 336–337
noncommunication influences, 328
public communication, 327
secular trends, 327
efficacy and
    best practices, 332–336, 354
    clinical care model, 355
    communication failures, 331–333,
      336–337
    defined, 330
    execution failure, 332
    expectation failure, 332, 336–337
    measurement failure, 332
    policy impact, 329–331
    strategy failure, 332
    surgery analogy, 331–333
    vaccine model, 343–344
overview, 327–329
policy impact
    efficacy, 329–331
    replicability, 330–331
    sustainability, 330–331
replicability and
    assumptions, 337
    behavioral checklists, 342–343
    behavioral determinants, 338–339
    behavioral differences, 337–339
    behavioral typologies, 339–342
    clinical care model, 355
    defined, 330
    policy impact, 330–331
    Stages of Change model, 339
    vaccine model, 337, 344
sustainability and
    AIDS intervention analogy, 344–348
    clinical care model, 344–349, 355
    defined, 330
    marketing analogy, 343
    policy impact, 330–331
    vaccine model, 343–344, 348–349
vaccine model and
    assumptions, 348–349
    best practices, 354
    defined, 328–329
    efficacy, 343–344
    implications, 353–355
    program management, 353
    program monitoring, 353–354
    program research, 353–354
    replicability, 337, 344
    sustainability, 343–344, 348–349

428

F

Federal Trade Commission (FTC), 275
Food and Drug Administration (FDA),
    269–278
France, AIDS prevention
  AIDS susceptibility, 134
  condom usage, 136, 137, 141
  effectiveness evaluation, 134, 135*t*,
      136–138, 140–141
  risk reduction strategy, 136, 137, 138*f*,
      140–141
  sexual partner restriction, 140–141
  transmission knowledge, 135*t*

G

Germany, AIDS prevention
  condom usage, 137, 138*f*, 141
  effectiveness evaluation, 135*t*, 137, 138*f*,
      140–141
  risk reduction strategy, 137, 138*f*, 140–141
  sexual partner restriction, 140–141
  transmission knowledge, 135*t*
Ghana, *see* AIDS prevention, Ghana
Guatemala, 180

H

Health Belief Model, 13, 221
HealthCom project, *see* Child Survival
    Program (HealthCom)
Health Research Group (HRG), 274–275

I

Ideodynamic theory, 252–255, 261–263
Immunization, *see* Child Survival Program
    (HealthCom); Vaccination project
    (Philippines)
India, 179
Individual effects model, 14–15
Indonesia
  Central Java
    diarrhea project, 227, 231–233
    project description, 221, 222*t*
    vitamin A project, 227–228, 234–236,
      237

West Java
  diarrhea project, 227, 231–233
  project description, 221, 222*t*
Institute of Medicine, 273
Institutional diffusion model, 14–15
International Society of Hypertension in
    Blacks, 75
Ireland, AIDS prevention
  condom usage, 136, 137
  effectiveness evaluation, 135*t*, 136, 137
  risk reduction strategy, 136, 137
  sexual partner restriction, 137
  transmission knowledge, 135*t*
Italy, AIDS prevention
  condom usage, 136
  effectiveness evaluation, 136
  risk reduction strategy, 136

J

Jordan
  breast-feeding project, 228, 234, 235*t*,
      236, 238–239
  feeding supplementation project, 228,
      234, 235*t*
  project description, 221, 222*t*

L

Legislation
  National Heart, Blood, Vessel, Lung and
      Blood Act (1972), 303
  seat belt usage (North Carolina), 86, 87,
      88–89, 94
  smoking prevention, 97–98, 102, 116
    secondhand smoke, 100, 101,
      112–113
  Tobacco Tax and Health Protection
      Act (1988), 97–98
Lesotho
  diarrhea project, 227, 231–234
  project description, 221, 223*t*
  vaccination project, 227, 229
Litigation
  California Tobacco Control Program
      media campaign, 100, 101, 102, 112
  tobacco industry campaign, 100, 101,
      112
Reye's syndrome

aspirin industry campaign, 272–273,
  275–277
consumer organizations, 274

M

Marijuana study, media campaign
  community trials, 4, 36, 38
  education programs, 35
  effectiveness evaluation, 46–51
    design, 35–36, 51–52
    guidelines, 37, 51–52
    limitations, 35–36
    time series analysis, 4, 36, 37–38, 42,
      46–50, 52
  implications, 51–52
  methodology
    data analysis, 44–45
    measurement, 44
    media campaign, 39–42
    public service announcements (PSAs),
      38–39
    recruitment, 42–43
    response rates, 43
    sample, 38, 43–44
    sampling procedures, 42–43
    study design, 37–38
  National Youth Anti-Drug Media
    Campaign (1999), 35, 42
  overview, 35–36
  results, 46–50
  sensation seeking targeting (SENTAR),
    36–37, 51–52
  sensation seeking trait, 36, 37
  sensation value messages, 36–37, 38–39,
    40t
  summary, 50–51
Massachusetts, see Smoking prevention
Minnesota Heart Health Program (MHHP)
  evaluation contradiction, 3, 4–6, 11
  secular trends impact, 290–293, 304–305,
    306–307

N

National Cholesterol Education Program
  (1985), 9, 303–304
National Heart, Blood, Vessel, Lung and
  Blood Act (1972), 303

National Heart, Lung and Blood Institute
  (NHLBI)
  cardiovascular disease prevention,
    290–293, 303–304
  high blood cholesterol, 303–304
  hypertension, 303
National High Blood Pressure Education
    and Control Program (NHBPEP)
  community collaboration, 75–76
  effectiveness evaluation
    awareness, 79–80
    control, 79–80
    evaluation contradiction, 6–7, 9–10,
      11–12
    knowledge, 78
    mortality rate, 80–83
    physician visitation, 78–79
    reduction, 80, 81f
    treatment, 79–80
  media campaign collaboration, 75–76,
    77f
  National High Blood Pressure Month,
    75–76
    High Blood Pressure Month Kits,
      75–76
  organizational collaboration, 75–76
  overview, 73–74
  target audiences, 74–75, 76f, 77f
National Institute of Allergy and Infectious
    Diseases, 272
National Youth Anti-Drug Media
    Campaign (1999), 14, 35, 42
Netherlands, AIDS prevention
  condom usage, 8, 137, 138–139
  effectiveness evaluation, 7–8, 137,
    138–139, 140f, 142
  nonpenetrative sex, 142
  risk reduction strategy, 137, 138–139,
    140f, 142
  sexual partner restriction, 137–139,
    140f
North Karelia Project (Finland)
  behavioral journalism and
    effectiveness evaluation, 318
    group discussion format, 317–318
    media campaign, 317–318
    social modeling, 317–318
  evaluation contradiction, 3, 4–6
  secular trends impact, 289–290, 291
Norway, AIDS prevention
  effectiveness evaluation, 135t
  transmission knowledge, 135t

O

Office of National Drug Control Policy, 14, 35, 42, 51–52

P

Pawtucket Heart Health Program (Rhode Island), 3–6, 11, 290–293
Peer consultation, 354–355
Peer modeling, 316–317, 321–324
Persuasive information
    controlled experiments, 251–252, 262, 263
    ideodynamic analysis
        AIDS hotline calls, 260–261, 262
        cocaine use, 255–261, 262
        effectiveness evaluation, 255–263
        ex-smoker recidivism, 256–258, 262
        HIV infection, 258–260, 262
    ideodynamic theory
        behavior prediction, 252–255, 261–263
        information assessment, 255, 263
    implications, 263
    overview, 251–252
    secular trends impact, 251–252
    summary, 261–263
    time series analysis
        ideodynamic theory, 252–254
        rationale for, 252
    uncontrolled experiments, 252, 262, 263
Peru
    birth spacing project, 228, 234, 235t
    project description, 221, 223t
    vaccination project, 227, 228–230
Philippines, see Vaccination project (Philippines)
PRO-PATER program, see Vasectomy promotion (Brazil)
Public Health Service (PHS), 268, 269, 273, 276–277, 278

R

Reye's syndrome
    aspirin industry campaign
        Aspirin Foundation of America, 273, 277

        aspirin warning labels, 268–269, 271t, 272, 273, 274–277
        Committee on the Care of Children (CCC), 273, 274–276
        education programs, 275–276, 277
        government action elimination, 273, 275–277
        litigation, 272–273, 275–277
        media campaign, 276, 277
        publications, 275, 276
    aspirin warning labels
        aspirin industry campaign, 268–269, 271t, 272, 273, 274–277
        effectiveness evaluation, 281–282
        government action, 269, 271t, 272, 273, 274–277, 281–282
        medical reports, 268–269
    consumer organizations
        aspirin warning labels, 274–275
        effectiveness evaluation, 278–279
        Health Research Group (HRG), 274–275
        litigation, 274
    consumer product warnings
        effectiveness evaluation, 265–266
        media campaign, 265–266
        publications, 265–266
        scare tactics, 265
    data collection, 279–280
    education programs
        aspirin industry campaign, 275–276, 277
        effectiveness evaluation, 278–279
        government action, 269, 272–277
        pharmacy reports, 269
    effectiveness evaluation, 8–9
        aspirin warning labels, 281–282
        consumer organizations, 278–279
        consumer product warnings, 265–266
        education programs, 278–279
        government action, 278–279, 280–283
        media campaign, 278–279, 280–283
        medical reports, 278–279, 280–281
    epidemiological studies
        Centers for Disease Control (CDC), 267, 269
        publications, 267–268
        Public Health Service (PHS), 268, 269, 273, 276–277, 278
        risk debate, 268
    government action

aspirin industry elimination, 273,
  275–277
aspirin warning labels, 269, 271*t*, 272,
  273, 274–277, 281–282
Centers for Disease Control (CDC),
  267, 269–272, 276–277
chronology of, 270–271*t*
congressional investigation, 272, 274,
  275
Department of Health and Human
  Services (DHHS), 272–273
education programs, 269, 272–277
effectiveness evaluation, 278–279,
  280–283
Federal Trade Commission (FTC), 275
Food and Drug Administration (FDA),
  269–278
House Committee on Energy and
  Commerce, 274, 275
House Committee on Natural
  Resources, Agriculture Research and
  the Environment, 272
Institute of Medicine, 273
media campaign, 272, 273, 274, 275
National Institute of Allergy and
  Infectious Diseases, 272
publications, 269, 272, 278
Public Health Service (PHS), 268, 269,
  273, 276–277, 278
risk debate, 269, 272–273
implications, 285
litigation
  aspirin industry campaign, 272–273,
    275–277
  consumer organizations, 274
media campaign
  aspirin industry campaign, 276, 277
  consumer product warnings, 265–266
  effectiveness evaluation, 278–279,
    280–283
  government action, 272, 273, 274, 275
medical reports
  aspirin warning labels, 268–269
  effectiveness evaluation, 278–279,
    280–281
  publications, 268–269
  risk debate, 269
methodology, 268
overview, 265–266
pharmacy reports
  education programs, 269
  publications, 269
publications
  aspirin industry campaign, 275, 276
  consumer product warnings, 265–266
  epidemiological studies, 267–268
  government action, 269, 272, 278
  medical reports, 268–269
  pharmacy reports, 269
risk debate, 268, 269, 272–273, 275–277
summary, 283–285
Role modeling
  behavioral journalism
    fictional, 316, 317
    social modeling, 315–317
  effectiveness evaluation, 359–360, 365,
    367–374, 375, 377–378

S

Seat belt usage (North Carolina)
  education programs
    Highway Safety Initiative (1993),
      86–87, 94–95
    pilot programs, 86–88
  effectiveness evaluation
    education programs, 9, 86–87, 88–95
    fatalities, 9, 91–93
    injuries, 9, 91–93, 94
    legislation enforcement, 88–89, 94, 95
    media campaign, 88–89
    medical expenditures, 91–93, 94
    program awareness, 93–94
    seat belt usage, 9, 86–87, 89–91, 94–95
  international contrast
    education programs, 85–86, 94
    legislation enforcement, 85–86, 94
    seat belt usage, 85–86, 94
  legislation enforcement, 86, 87, 88–89,
    94
  media campaign, 87, 88–89
  methodology
    education programs, 87
    fatalities, 88
    injuries, 88
    legislation enforcement, 87
    measurement, 87
    media campaign, 87
    medical expenditures, 88
    program awareness, 88
    sample, 87
    time series analysis, 88

Seat belt usage (North Carolina) *(cont.)*
  national contrast
    education programs, 86
    legislation enforcement, 85, 86
    seat belt usage, 85, 86
  overview, 85–87
  results, 88–94
  summary, 94–95
Secular trends
  evaluation development, 327
  persuasive information, 251–252
Secular trends, cardiovascular disease
    prevention
  community trials
    design reassessment, 290, 304–305
    history, 289–290, 303–304
    secular trends impact, 290–293,
      304–309
    subgroup differentials, 306
  high blood cholesterol
    media agenda impact, 301–304
    media campaign impact, 296, 299t,
      301–304, 306–307
    mortality impact, 293–295
    National Cholesterol Education
      Program (1985), 303–304
    secular trends impact, 293–295
  hypertension
    media agenda impact, 301–304
    media campaign impact, 296, 299t,
      301–304, 306–307
    mortality impact, 293–295
    National Heart, Blood, Vessel, Lung
      and Blood Act (1972), 303
    National High Blood Pressure
      Education Program (1992), 303
    secular trends impact, 293–295
  implications, 309
  media campaign
    agenda influences, 301–304
    design reassessment, 290
    education program impact, 301–304
    effectiveness evaluation, 295–300,
      301–304
    high blood cholesterol, 296, 299t,
      301–304, 306–307
    hypertension, 296, 299t, 301–304,
      306–307
    infrastructure impact, 300–301
    secular trends impact, 290, 292–293,
      295–304, 306–309

smoking, 296, 297–298t, 301–304,
  306–307
Minnesota Heart Health Program
  (MHHP)
  evaluation contradiction, 3, 4–6, 11,
    290–293
  secular trends impact, 290–293,
    304–305, 306–307
  mortality rates
    risk factor reduction, 293–295
    secular trends impact, 293–295
National Heart, Lung and Blood
  Institute (NHLBI), 290–293
  high blood cholesterol, 303–304
  hypertension, 303
North Coast (Australia), 291
North Karelia Project (Finland),
  289–290, 291
  evaluation contradiction, 3, 4–6
Pawtucket Heart Health Program
  (Rhode Island)
  evaluation contradiction, 3–6, 11,
    290–293
  secular trends impact, 290–293
smoking
  American Cancer Society (ACS), 303
  American Heart Association (AHA),
    303, 304
  American Lung Association (ALA),
    303
  American Medical Association (AMA),
    303
  media agenda impact, 301–304
  media campaign impact, 296,
    297–298t, 301–304, 306–307
  mortality impact, 293–295
  National Clearinghouse for Smoking
    and Health, 303
  secular trends impact, 293–295
Stanford Five City Project (California)
  evaluation contradiction, 2–6, 9,
    10–11, 290–293
  secular trends impact, 290–293
Stanford Three City Project (California),
  289–290, 291
  evaluation contradiction, 4–6
Smoking prevention, *see also* California
  Tobacco Control Program
  Australia media campaign
    community effectiveness, 64t
    community resources, 57, 61
    data analysis, 62–63

design, 58–59
effectiveness evaluation, 63–68
implications, 68
journalism resources, 59
measurement, 61–62
methodology, 58–63
news media resources, 59
newspaper resources, 59
objectives, 58
overview, 57–58
physician effectiveness, 63–64
physician resources, 57, 59–60
results, 63–67
sample, 61, 62
sampling procedures, 61
school resources, 58, 60–61
summary, 67–68
television awareness, 63, 64t
television effectiveness, 65–68
television resources, 57–58, 59, 60t
behavioral journalism and
documentary format, 317, 318–321
effectiveness evaluation, 320–321
media campaign, 317, 318–321
social modeling, 319–320
Community Intervention Trial for
Smoking Cessation (COMMIT), 3,
4–6, 10
evaluation contradiction
community trials, 3, 4, 10
implications, 14
observational studies, 7
Massachusetts media campaign
data analysis, 119–120
design, 116, 117
effectiveness evaluation, 7, 115–116,
120–127, 120–128
expenditures, 117
exposure effectiveness, 120–121, 122t,
123, 125–127
exposure measure, 116, 117, 118
funding, 116
implications, 127–128
legislation, 116
limitations, 127
measurement, 116, 117, 118–119
mediating variables, 119, 120, 123,
125t
methodology, 116–120
objectives, 117, 120
overview, 115–116

potential confounding variables,
118–120, 121–123, 124t
results, 120–123
sample, 117–118
smoking progression measure, 116,
117, 118
smoking progression rates, 121,
123–127
summary, 123, 125–127
vs. education programs, 116, 117,
118
media/school campaign contrast
alcohol consumption, 29
data analysis, 25–26
effectiveness evaluation, 23, 26–32
implications, 31–32
measurement, 25–26
media campaign design, 24–25, 30–31
mediating variables, 27–28
methodology, 23–26
objectives, 24, 25, 31
overview, 23
results, 26–29
sample, 23–24, 26–27, 30
school campaign design, 24, 25
school-media effectiveness, 23, 28–29,
31–32
school-only effectiveness, 23, 28–29
smokeless tobacco, 29
social learning theory, 24, 30
summary, 29–32
persuasive information, 256–258, 262
Social Cognitive Theory, 13
Social diffusion model, 14–15
Social modeling, 315–317
Spain, AIDS prevention
effectiveness evaluation, 135t, 136
needle sharing, 136
risk reduction strategy, 136
transmission knowledge, 135t, 136
Stages of Change model, 13, 316, 319,
339
Stanford Five City Project (California),
2–6, 9, 10–11, 290–293
Stanford Three City Project (California),
4–6, 289–290, 291
Sunburn prevention (Australia)
data analysis, 166–167
education programs
funding, 164, 165
SLIP! SLOP! SLAP!, 164
SunSmart, 164–165, 172, 174–176

Sunburn prevention (Australia) *(cont.)*
  effectiveness evaluation, 9
    attitudes, 167–169, 172, 174–176
    behaviors, 169–171, 172, 174–176
    sunburn trends, 171–176
  measurement, 164
  media campaign, 165
  melanoma rates, 163
  methodology, 165–167
  overview, 163–165
  results, 167–172
  summary, 172, 174–176
Swaziland
  diarrhea project, 227, 231–233
  project description, 221, 223*t*
Sweden, AIDS prevention
  effectiveness evaluation, 135*t*, 140*f*
  risk reduction strategy, 140*f*
  transmission knowledge, 135*t*
Switzerland, AIDS prevention
  condom usage, 8, 136–139, 141
  effectiveness evaluation, 7–8, 135*t*,
    136–139, 140*f*, 141
  risk reduction strategy, 136–139, 140*f*,
    141
  sexual partner restriction, 137–139, 140*f*,
    141
  Stop AIDS, 7–8, 137
  transmission knowledge, 135*t*

T

Theory of Reasoned Action, 13, 221
Tobacco Education and Research Oversight
  Committee (TEROC), 98
Tobacco industry, *see* California Tobacco
  Control Program
Tobacco Tax and Health Protection Act
  (1988), 97–98

U

United Kingdom, AIDS prevention
  AIDS susceptibility, 134
  condom usage, 136, 137, 138–139, 141
  effectiveness evaluation, 134, 135*t*,
    136–139, 141
  risk reduction strategy, 136–139, 141

sexual partner restriction, 137, 138–139,
  141
transmission knowledge, 135*t*, 136

V

Vaccination project (Philippines), *see also*
  Child Survival Program
  (HealthCom)
education programs, 199–200, 204–205
effectiveness evaluation, 8, 228–229,
    230, 245
  accessibility factor, 212
  age focus, 203–204, 213–214
  campaign knowledge, 208–211
  clinic personnel factor, 212–213
  education programs, 204–205
  knowledge, 204–211, 212–213
  measles focus, 205–206, 208,
    213–214
  place focus, 213–214
  time focus, 203, 206, 211–212,
    213–214
  urban focus, 213–215
  vaccination coverage, 203–204
  vaccination knowledge, 205–208, 209*t*
  vaccination supply factor, 212
implications, 215
media campaign
  age focus, 201
  communication strategy, 198,
    199–200, 214
  measles focus, 199, 200
  place focus, 199, 200
  time focus, 199, 200
  urban focus, 199
methodology
  health center study, 202
  measurement, 227
  surveys, 200–202
overview, 197–199, 221, 223*t*
summary, 213–215
Vaccine model, *see* Evaluation
  development
Vasectomy promotion (Brazil)
  context, 180–181
  education programs
    international contrast, 180
    PRO-PATER program, 181, 182, 183
  effectiveness evaluation

cost-effectiveness analysis, 187, 188*t*,
193–194
longitudinal analysis, 187, 189–192,
193–194
PRO-PATER clinic, 184–187
PRO-PATER program, 183–192
implications, 194
international contrast
Africa, 179–180
China, 179
Colombia, 180
education programs, 180
Guatemala, 180
India, 179
media campaign, 179–180
media campaign

Africa, 179–180
Colombia, 180
Guatemala, 180
international contrast, 179–180
PRO-PATER program, 181–183
methodology, 181–183
overview, 179–180
summary, 192–194

Z

Zaire
diarrhea project, 227, 231–233, 243
project description, 221, 223*t*
vaccination project, 227, 229